I0413758

Early Records

of the

First Reformed Church

of

Philadelphia

Volume 2, 1781-1800

F. Edward Wright

HERITAGE BOOKS
2019

HERITAGE BOOKS
AN IMPRINT OF HERITAGE BOOKS, INC.

Books, CDs, and more—Worldwide

For our listing of thousands of titles see our website
at
www.HeritageBooks.com

Published 2019 by
HERITAGE BOOKS, INC.
Publishing Division
5810 Ruatan Street
Berwyn Heights, Md. 20740

Originally pulished by
Family Line Publications
1994

On the cover is the First Reformed Church, erected in 1747.

All rights reserved. No part of this book may be reproduced or transmitted in any form or by any means, electronic or mechanical, including photocopying, recording or by any information storage and retrieval system without written permission from the author, except for the inclusion of brief quotations in a review.

International Standard Book Number
Paperbound: 978-1-58549-371-5

CONTENTS

Introduction v

Burials
Rev. Casper Weyberg (1781 - 1785) 1

Marriages
Rev. Casper Weyberg (1781 - 1785) 10

Baptisms
Rev. Casper Weyberg (1781 - 1789) 15

Marriages
Rev. Casper Weyberg (1786 - 1790) 73
Rev. Herman Winckhaus (1790 - 1793) 77
Rev. William Hendel (1793 - 1798) 79
Rev. Samuel Helffenstein (1799 - 1800) 84

Baptisms
Rev. Casper Weyberg (1789 - 1790) 85
Rev. Herman Winckhaus (1790 - 1793) 95
Rev. William Hendel (1793 - 1798) 122

Burials
Rev. Casper Weyberg (1786 - 1790) 123
Rev. Herman Winckhaus (1790 - 1793) 130
Rev. William Hendel (1794 - 1798) 141
Rev. Samuel Helffenstein (1799 - 1800) 153

Baptisms
Dr. William Hendel (1797 - 1798) 154
Rev. Samuel Helffenstein (1799-1804) 164

Index 187

Charles H. Glatfelter states that there was Lutheran and Reformed activity in Philadelphia long before 1740. Philip Boehm conducted services in the city soon after he assumed the duties of the ministry in 1725. George Michael Weiss organized a congregation before he returned to Europe in 1730.

A Union Church (Reformed and Lutheran) existed as early as 1734 in a rented building on Mulberry (or Arch) Street, between Fourth and Fifth Streets.

The Reformed began building a church of their own in 1745; Philip Boehm, their pastor at the time, laid the cornerstone. Michael Schlatter preached the first sermon in the new church on 6 December 1747. The patent for the graveyard lot on 14 December 1763 read to "the German reformed Calvinist Congregation of the Hexagon Church built by them in Sassafras [Race] Street." (See cover for sketch of the church.)

The records begin with Rev. Michael Schlatter who remained until 1755 despite his dismissal by the consistory in 1749. Schlatter refused to accept this action and preached in the Presbyterian church. In 1750 arbitrators in the dispute elected to have Schlatter return to the church. However, a split arose again in 1752 and for the next three years there were again two Reformed congregations in the city, Schlatter and Rev. Casper Rubel. Rev. William Stoy served from 1756 until 1758 when he was dismissed and Conrad Steiner followed in 1759, transferring from Frederick, Maryland. Steiner died in 1762 and shortly thereafter the congregation was able to get the services of Rev. Frederick Rothenbuehler from New York. The congregation soon became dissatisfied with Rothenbuehler and obtained Rev. Casper Weyberg, whose pastorate covered the period from 1763 until his death in 1790. It was during this period that the church has a significant growth. A larger church was completed in 1772 at the same location.

In looking at the table of contents one will see obvious gaps in the records with the absence of the names of some of the ministers who served during this period.

Pastors of the Reformed congregation included George Michael Weiss (1727-1730), Peter Miller (1730-1731), Bartholomew Rieger (1731-1734), Philip Boehm (1734-1746), Henry Goetschy (1735-1736, in competition with Boehm), Michael Schlatter (1746-1755), with interruptions), Conrad Steiner (1749-1751), Casper Rubel (1752-1755), William Stoy (1756-1758), William Kals (1758), Conrad Steiner (1759-1762), Frederick Rothenbuehler (1762-1763), Casper Weyberg (1763-1790), Herman Winckhaus (1790 - 1793), William Hendel, Sr. (1794-1798) and Samuel Helffenstein (1799-1831).

The records in this work were translated by William J. Hinke in 1939 from the original which was in four volumes covering the period, 1748 - 1831.

F. Edward Wright
Westminster, Maryland
1994

Most of the above information was taken from Charles H. Glatfelter, *Pastors and People: German Lutheran and Reformed Churches in the Pennsylvania Field, 1717-1793*, Volume I - Pastors and Congregations, published by The Pennsylvania German Society, 1980.

ABBREVIATIONS

b. - born
bur. - buried
bapt. - baptized
m. - married
mo(s). - month(s)
Spon. - Sponsor(s)
wk(s) - week(s)
yrs. - years

BURIALS BY REV. CASPER WEYBERG
1781 - 1785

Anna Veronica Gobler, age 66 yrs., 8 mos., 2 wks., 2 days, bur. Jan. 1, 1781.
Peter Edenborn, age 6 yrs., 6 mos., 11 days, bur. Jan. 8, 1781.
Benjamin Bertzen, age 40 yrs., bur. Feb. 2, 1780.
George Bachoffen, age 15 yrs., bur. Feb. 4, 1781.
Margaret Karsbach, age 78 yrs., 1 mo., bur. Feb. 6, 1781.
Elizabeth Veh, age 85 yrs., bur. Feb. 13, 1781.
Elizabeth Strup, age 10 mos., 2 wks., bur. Feb. 19, 1781.
Widow Schmaltz, age 62 yrs., bur. March 2, 1781.
Maria Werner, age 47 yrs., 3 mos., 2 wks., 4 days, bur. March 4, 1781.
Maria Sehler, age 46 yrs., bur. March 11, 1781.
Dorothy Krampf, age 6 yrs., bur. at Kensington on March 13, 1781.
Valentine Stillwagen, age 38 yrs., 1 mo., bur. March 27, 1781.
John Strup, age 55 yrs., 7 mos., bur. April 17, 1781.
Elizabeth Spangenberg, age 1 yr., 6 mos., bur. April 21, 1781.
Margaret Schuhlin, age 67 yrs., bur. April 23, 1781.
John Philip Glaser, age 50 yrs., bur. May 16, 1781.
Philip Jacob Bockemeyer, age 3 mos., 2 wks., 3 days, bur. May 17, 1781.
Jacob Jontzer, age 3 yrs., 4 mos., 17 days, bur. May 18, 1781.
Jacob Schreiber, age 1 yr., 8 mos., bur. May 24, 1781.
Anna Margaret Scheiw, age 8 mos., 2 days, bur. May 29, 1781.
George Theiss, age 1 yr., 6 mos., bur. June 1, 1781.
Anna Stillwagen, age 3 mos., bur. June 5, 1781.
Elizabeth Lapp, age 2 yrs., 6 mos., 2 wks., bur. June 10, 1781.
George Henritzy, age 10 yrs., 7 mos., 5 days, bur. June 25, 1781.
John Jacob Schaff, age 4 mos., bur. June 29, 1781.
Elizabeth Kres, age 2 yrs., 6 mos., 1 week, bur. June 30, 1781.
John Heiny, age 1 yr., 5 mos., 6 days, bur. July 9, 1781.
Henry Eschler, age 2 yrs., bur. July 17, 1781.
Elizabeth Magold, age 55 yrs., 11 mos., 17 days, bur. July 18, 1781.
Isaac Sumney, age 57 yrs., bur. July 19, 1781.
Wife of Peter Laub, Frankfurt, age 37 yrs., bur. July 20, 1781.
Anthony von der Schleis, age 5 mos., bur. July 23, 1781.
Jacob Coper, age 11 mos., 14 days, bur. Aug. 3, 1781.
Margaret Witman, age 24 yrs., 8 mos., 14 days, bur. Aug. 4, 1781.
George Bonner, age 1 yr., 4 mos., 2 wks., bur. Aug. 12, 1781.
Maria Elizabeth Kriescher, age 9 mos., 10 days, bur. Aug. 14, 1781.
Martin Gaul, age 1 yr., 3 mos., bur. Aug. 21, 1781.
Hannah Stricker, age 1 yr., 2 mos., 3 days, bur. Aug. 23, 1781.
George Liber, age 3 yrs., bur. Aug. 23, 1781.
Child of Casimir Dilwick, age 1 yr., bur. Aug. 26, 1781.
Maria Cliver, age 1 yr., 5 mos., bur. Aug. 27, 1781.
Matthias Abel, age 60 yrs., bur. Aug. 30, 1781.
Catherine Schreiner, age 10 yrs., 8 mos., bur. Sept. 3, 1781.
Magdalene Therry, age 2 yrs., 7 mos., 12 days, bur. Sept. 9, 1781.
Nicholas Baldewein, age 69 yrs., bur. Sept. 11, 1781.
Wife of George Fans, age 67 yrs., bur. Sept. 13, 1781.
Margaret Hahn, age 16 yrs., 6 mos., bur. Sept. 18, 1781.
Catherine Reinhardt, age 25 yrs., 7 mos., bur. Sept. 19, 1781.

Anna Maria Dies, age 2 yrs., 1 mo., bur. Sept. 22, 1781.
Hannah Gobler, age 6 mos., 2 wks., 1 day, bur. Oct. 10, 1781.
Jacob Madery, in Frankfurt, age 77 yrs., 10 days, bur. Oct. 11, 1781.
Anna Wardt, age 20 yrs., bur. Oct. 13, 1781.
Maria Gamber, age 78 yrs., 9 mos., 10 days, bur. Oct. 14, 1781.
Elizabeth Ritter, age 1 yr., 8 mos., 3 days, bur. Oct. 15, 1781.
Elizabeth Schmitt, age 66 yrs., bur. Oct. 28, 1781.
John Simon, age 12 yrs., bur. Oct. 28, 1781.
Daughter of Abraham Riblet, age 19 yrs., 6 mos., bur. Oct. 30, 1781.
Widow Kuhn, age 91 yrs., bur. Oct. 30, 1781.
Leonard Braun, age 2 yrs., 2 mos., bur. Nov. 2, 1781.
Daniel Krauer, age 2 yrs., bur. Nov. 7, 1781.
Elizabeth Bom, age 65 yrs., bur. Nov. 14, 1781.
Christine Jost, age 1 yr., 10 mos., 14 days, bur. Nov. 14, 1781.
Son of William Muntz, age 1 yr., 7 mos., 6 days, bur. Nov. 14, 1781.
John Froman, age 3 yrs., 2 mos., 12 days, bur. Nov. 20, 1781.
John Aug. Kirchhoff, age 1 yr., 22 days, bur. Nov. 26, 1781.
Henry Schmidt, Kensington, age 50 yrs., bur. Nov. 29, 1781.
Anna Christine Alberger, age 1 yr., bur. Dec. 6, 1781.
Henry Diehl, age 10 mos., bur. Dec. 16, 1781.
John Bom, age 7 mos., bur. Dec. 17, 1781.
Anna Catherine Zeisiger, age 43 yrs., bur. Dec. 22, 1781.
----, wife of Ulrich Jegly, age ----, bur. Dec. 28, 1781.
Ulrich Jegley, age 59 yrs., bur. Dec. 30, 1781.
Elizabeth Holtz, age 6 yrs., 9 mos., 2 wks., bur. Dec. 31, 1781.
Catherine Elizabeth Alberger, age 72 yrs., Jan. 2, 1782.
Charles Berckin, age 2 mos., 2 days, bur. Jan. 9, 1782.
Nancy Berry, age 2 mos., 3 wks., bur. Jan. 9, 1782.
Henrietta Werntz, age 1 yr., 8 mos., 10 days, bur. Jan. 15, 1782.
Widow Schuhl, age 80 yrs., bur. Jan. 20, 1782.
Anna McCormick, age 17 yrs., 9 mos., bur. Jan. --, 1782.
Elizabeth Henry, age 17 yrs., bur. Jan. 28, 1782.
Elizabeth Wilson, age 7 yrs., 10 mos., bur. Feb. 4, 1782.
----, wife of Lorentz Werntz, age 45 yrs., bur. Feb. 17, 1782.
John Jacob Becker, age 87 yrs., bur. March 1, 1782.
John Jegley, age 15 yrs., 6 mos., bur. March 3, 1782.
Jacob Werntz, age 4 yrs., 7 mos., bur. March 5, 1782.
Catherine Heins, age 2 yrs., 6 mos., 3 days, bur. March 11, 1782.
Christian van Erdten, age 61 yrs., bur. March 25, 1782.
Wendel Becker, age 49 yrs., 4 mos., bur. April 14, 1782.
Barbara Hauser, age 79 yrs., bur. April 23, 1782.
Maria Catherine Messemer, age 9 yrs., bur. April 24, 1782.
Maria Messemer, age 1 yr., 3 mos., bur. April 24, 1782.
Sarah Messemer, age 7 yrs., bur. April 27, 1782.
Widow Duerr, age 73 yrs., bur. April 28, 1782.
Widow of John Kreps, age 92 yrs., bur. May 7, 1782.
Wife of Martin Worn, age 69 yrs., 9 mos., 5 days, bur. May 13, 1782.
Sophia Birckenbeul, age 8 yrs., 7 mos., bur. May 14, 1782.
Elizabeth Schmit, age 77 yrs., bur. May 21, 1782.
Catherine Krebel, age 13 yrs., bur. May 31, 1782.
George Adam Pentler, age 12 yrs., 6 mos., 2 wks., bur. June 10,

1782.
William Fuhr, age 5 yrs., 4 mos., 2 wks., 2 days, bur. June 16, 1782.
Susanna Baerdt, age 74 yrs., 6 mos., bur. June 20, 1782.
Anna Maria Simon, age 1 yr., 1 mo., bur. June 23, 1782.
Maria Marg. Weil, age 10 mos., bur. June 28, 1782.
Gustavianna Frederica Graff, age 41 yrs., 7 mos., bur. July 1, 1782.
Oswald von der Hald, age 41 yrs., 9 mos., 3 days, bur. July 4, 1782.
John Reiffschneider, age 6 yrs., 3 mos., 3 wks., bur. July 8, 1782.
Catherine Schug, age 63 yrs., bur. July 10, 1782.
Frederick Allenbach, age 35 yrs., bur. July 12, 1782.
Hannah Kreider, age 1 yr., 7 mos., 2 wks., 5 days, bur. July 19, 1782.
Jacob Kuper, age 9 mos., bur. July 24, 1782.
Lucia Durant, age 60 yrs., 3 mos., bur. July 25, 1782.
Wm. Wendel Zerban, age 6 mos., bur. July 27, 1782.
Maria Stillwagen, age 66 yrs., 5 mos., bur. July 29, 1782.
Alexander William Miller, age 1 yr., 6 mos., bur. July 30, 1782.
Anna Mangold, age 1 yr., 3 mos., bur. July 30, 1782.
Anna Margaret Greiss, age 1 yr., 10 mos., 2 days, bur. Aug. 5, 1782.
Friederica Philippina Ritz, age 58 yrs., bur. Aug. 5, 1782.
Elizabeth Koch, age 1 yr., 10 mos., 5 days, bur. Aug. 8, 1782.
Margaret Gerritt, age 9 mos., 9 wks., 3 days, bur. Aug. 10, 1782.
Charlotte Schreiner, age 45 yrs., 11 mos., 17 days, bur. Aug. 11, 1782.
Joseph Stiel, age 19 mos., bur. Aug. 11, 1782.
Anna Margaret Schreiber, age 11 mos., 2 wks., 2 days, bur. Aug. 11, 1782.
Louise Stiel, age 35 yrs., bur. Aug. 15, 1782.
Jacob Eyler, age 1 yr., 6 mos., bur. Aug. 24, 1782.
Valentine Klages, age 1 yr., 8 mos., bur. Aug. 25, 1782.
William Kasselman, age 50 yrs., bur. Aug. 25, 1782.
Wife of Rotbert Burck, Kensington, age 27 yrs., bur. Sept. 4, 1782.
Mr. Lieber, drowned in Delaware, age ----, bur. Sept. 5, 1782.
Widow of Martin Boyer, age 62 yrs., bur. Sept. 5, 1782.
Frederick Froelig, age 2 yrs., 5 mos., bur. Sept. 6, 1782.
Jacob Klages, age 5 mos., 11 days, bur. Sept. 8, 1782.
Maria Pfeiffer, age 9 mos., 3 wks., bur. Sept. 9, 1782.
Simon Kuhley, age 10 mos., 9 days, bur. Sept. 9, 1782.
Catherine Birckenbeul, age 52 yrs., bur. Sept. 16, 1782.
Conrad Schmidt, Kensington, age 1 yr., bur. Sept. 22, 1782.
Anna Christine Motzfeld, age 73 yrs., 5 mos., 3 wks., bur. Sept. 24, 1782.
Sophia Fuchs, age 34 yrs., bur. Sept. 25, 1782.
John David Froelig, age 5 yrs., 3 mos., bur. Sept. 28, 1782.
Christopher Holtz, age 1 yr., 6 mos., bur. Sept. 30, 1782.
Arnold Kraemer, Kensington, age 65 yrs., 7 mos., bur. Oct. 17, 1782.
Wife of Jacob Handschuh, Kensington, age 47 yrs., bur. Oct. 18, 1782.
William Temper, age 73 yrs., bur. Oct. 18, 1782.
John Simon, age 9 mos., bur. Oct. 20, 1782.

John Kern, age 1 yr., 7 mos., 2 wks., bur. Oct. 27, 1782.
Susanna Boom, age 28 yrs., bur. Nov. 2, 1782.
John Schewer, age 63 yrs., 2 mos., bur. Nov. 4, 1782.
Samuel Fuss, age 17 yrs., 9 mos., 2 wks., bur. Nov. 5, 1782.
Elizabeth Reide, age 6 yrs., 6 mos., bur. Nov. 10, 1782.
Melchior Naeff, age 57 yrs., 10 mos., bur. Nov. 28, 1782.
George Johraus, age 1 yr., 7 mos., bur. Dec. 1, 1782.
John George Schuck, age 2 yrs., 10 mos. 2 wks., bur. Dec. 2, 1782.
John Jacob Schuck, age 6 yrs., 1 mo., bur. Dec. 3, 1782.
Henry Perry, age 28 yrs., 5 mos., 2 days, bur. Dec. 7, 1782.
Anna Barbara Schlottman, age 2 yrs., 2 mos., bur. Dec. 11, 1782.
John Fee, age 52 yrs., bur. Dec. 18, 1782.
John Philip Reis, age 42 yrs., 10 mos., bur. Dec. 20, 1782.
Maria Schneider, age 25 yrs., 6 mos., bur. Dec. 22, 1782.
Barbara Heiny, age 7 mos., 2 wks., 1 day, bur. Dec. 22, 1782.
George Umback, age 28 yrs., 7 mos., 14 days, bur. Dec. 22, 1782.
Philippina Moses, age 1 yr., 2 mos., bur. Dec. 23, 1782.
Child of John Weber, age 2 yr., 1 mo., 5 days, bur. Dec. 25, 1782.
Conrad Koehler, age 5 mos., bur. Dec. 27, 1782.
Elizabeth Bauer, age 1 yr., 1 mo., bur. Dec. 29, 1782.
Anna Margaret Justus, age 15 yrs., 9 mos., 3 days, bur. Jan. 7, 1783.
Anna Margaret Birckenbeil, age 1 yr., 6 mos., bur. Jan. 8, 1783.
Anna Esther Wiser, age 2 yrs., bur. Jan. 12, 1783.
Mary Magdalene Bamberger, age 1 yr., 5 mos., bur. Jan. 15, 1783.
Elizabeth Kuper, age 5 yrs., 9 mos., bur. Jan. 19, 1783.
John Gebhardt, age 2 mos., bur. Jan. 27, 1783.
Widow of Mr. Batz, age 67 yrs., bur. Feb. 2, 1783.
Catherine Boyer, age 4 mos., 6 days, bur. Feb. 6, 1783.
Peter Paris, age 56 yrs., bur. Feb. 9, 1783.
Wife of David Mueller, age 29 yrs., bur. Feb. 13, 1783.
William Clampfer, age 24 yrs., bur. Feb. 24, 1783.
Margaret Schnyder, Kensington, age 2 mos., 3 wks., bur. March 8, 1783.
Casper Klockener, age 24 yrs., bur. March 18, 1783.
Elizabeth Reyde, age 10 yrs., 2 mos., bur. March 21, 1783.
Son of David Jansson, age 6 yrs., bur. March 22, 1783.
Anna Elizabeth Werntz, age 88 yrs., bur. March 23, 1783.
Maria Albert, age 23 yrs., 11 mos., 3 days, bur. April 2, 1783.
Mr. Lorje, age 49 yrs., bur. April 2, 1783.
Margaret Schweighauser, age 56 yrs., 8 mos., bur. April 12, 1783.
Elizabeth Keehley, age 3 yrs., 2 mos., bur. April 12, 1783.
Daughter of Philip Ohler, age 4 yrs., 4 mos., bur. April 14, 1783.
Frederick Wm. zur Horst, age 4 yrs., 2 wks., 1 day, bur. April 16, 1783.
William McNehr, age 8 mos., 16 days, bur. April 20, 1783.
John Adam Mueller, age 45 yrs., 1 mo., 3 days, from Steinau in the district of Hanau, a musician of the Hesse-Hanau regiment, bur. April 21, 1783.
John Hahn, age 11 yrs., 2 mos., bur. April 26, 1783.
John Pistor, age 54 yrs., bur. April 28, 1783.
Susan Leonhard, age 1 yr., 2 mos., bur. May 4, 1783.
Daughter of Jacob Heimer, age 1 yr., 9 mos., 10 days, bur. May 11, 1783.
John Baerdt, age 1 yr., 5 mos., 5 days, bur. May 16, 1783.

Elizabeth Meyer, age 1 yr., 6 mos., bur. May 20, 1783.
Elizabeth von der Halt, age 68 yrs., bur. May 20, 1783.
John Philip Flick, age 52 yrs., bur. May 24, 1783.
Son of George Perkins, age 4 mos., bur. May 26, 1783.
Child of David Miller, age 4 mos., 10 days, bur. May 26, 1783.
Catherine Imdorff, age ----, bur. June 7, 1783.
Elizabeth Mercker, age 6 mos., bur. June 9, 1783.
Margaret Lehr, age 7 mos., 1 day, bur. June 14, 1783.
Maria Clara Merckle, age 4 mos., 2 wks., 4 days, bur. June 15,
    1783.
John Weber, age 7 yrs., 3 mos., 11 days, bur. June 23, 1783.
Margaret Knaus, age 11 mos., bur. June 23, 1783.
Elizabeth Stetzer and 1 yr., 8 mos., 10 days, bur. June 25, 1783.
Elizabeth Penther, age 77 yrs., bur. June 25, 1783.
John Peter Schreiber, age 5 mos., 6 days, bur. June 26, 1783.
Catherine Schmidt, age 1 yr., 6 mos., bur. July 8, 1783.
Jacob Fies, age 10 mos., 10 days, bur. July 8, 1783.
Wife of Peter Hahn, age 46 yrs., bur. July 10, 1783.
George Schneider, age 8 mos., bur. July 12, 1783.
Wife of Henry Maag, 55 yrs., bur. July 13, 1783.
Charles Ludwig Boehme, last pastor at Baltimore, age 40 yrs., bur.
    July 5, 1783.
Simon Schellenberger, age 55 yrs., bur. July 16, 1783.
Adam Bischoffberger, age 1 yr., 2 mos., bur. July 17, 1783.
Child of Ludwig Prahl, age 1 yr., 7 mos., 3 days, bur. July 24,
    1783.
Frederick Lange, age 2 yrs., bur. July 23, 1783.
Thomas Koch, age 27 yrs., bur. July 24, 1783.
Michael Blanckenhorn, age 40 yrs., bur. July 25, 1783.
Christian Scholler, age 1 yr., 1 mo., bur. July 26, 1783.
Elizabeth Dockney, age 1 yr., 2 mos., bur. July 26, 1783.
John Lewer, age 7 mos., 3 wks., 2 days, bur. July 26, 1783.
Philip Moser, age 56 yrs., bur. July 27, 1783.
Martin Warner, age 50 yrs., bur. July 31, 1783.
Anthony Scheppy, age 6 mos., bur. July 31, 1783.
Wife of Matthias Teuering, age 33 yrs., bur. Aug. 1, 1783.
Gottfried Munig, age 3 yrs., 3 wks., bur. Aug. 6, 1783.
Daughter of John Wever, age 1 yr., bur. Aug. 9, 1783.
Philip Otto, age 3 mos., 3 wks., bur. Aug. 9, 1783.
Matthew Krauer, age 1 yr., 6 mos., bur. Aug. 13, 1783.
Jacob Schwab, age 38 yrs., 9 mos., 7 days, bur. Aug. 14, 1783.
Philip Cascha, age 1 yr., 10 mos., bur. Aug. 17, 1783.
Henrietta Christine Heck, age 35 yrs., 8 mos., bur. Aug. 19, 1783.
George William Gucker, age 1 mo., 2 days, bur. Aug. 20, 1783.
Sarah Diehl, age 3 mos., bur. Aug. 27, 1783.
Jacob Diamond, age 27 yrs., 4 mos., bur. Sept. 3, 1783.
Andrew Jung, age 5 mos., bur. Sept. 5, 1783.
Son of Mr. Grauel, age 2 yrs., bur. Sept. 5, 1783.
John Jacob Schweighauser, age 65 yrs., bur. Sept. 8, 1783.
John Jacob Senn, age 50 yrs., bur. Sept. 13, 1783.
John Jacob Tauenheim, age 7 yrs., 2 mos., 5 days, bur. Sept. 17,
    1783.
Andrew Theis, age 44 yrs., 11 mos., bur. Sept. 17, 1783.
Anna Maria Eisenring, age 4 yrs., bur. Sept. 18, 1783.
Catherine Schuler, age 2 yrs., 2 mos., bur. Sept. 18, 1783.

Elizabeth Braunig, age 4 mos., 2 wks., bur. Sept. 20, 1783.
Jacob Huber, age 26 yrs., bur. Sept. 21, 1783.
Henry Peter, age 44, yrs., bur. Sept. 21, 1783.
Philip Worn, age 8 mos., bur. Sept. 22, 1783.
William Schuhler, age 22 yrs., bur. Sept. 27, 1783.
Phineas Palmer, age 20 yrs., bur. Sept. 26, 1783.
---- Bier, age 21 yrs., bur. Sept. 27, 1783.
Peter Neuschwanger, age 65 yrs., bur. Oct. 9, 1783.
Adam Leibinger, age 1 yr., bur. Oct. 12, 1783.
Matthias Stimmel, age 44 yrs., 4 mos., 12 days, bur. Oct. 17, 1783.
William Brand, age 9 yrs., 3 mos., bur. Oct. 23, 1783.
Peter Scherer, age 88 yrs., bur. Oct. 27, 1783.
George Schmidt, age 44 yrs., bur. Oct. 27, 1783.
William Kooper, age 5 wks., 4 days, bur. Dec. 2, 1783.
Christian William Schultz, age 2 yrs., bur. Dec. 7, 1783.
Catherine Peltz, age 31 yrs., 10 mos., bur. Dec. 16, 1783.
Philip Euler, age 49 yrs., bur. Dec. 17, 1783.
Barbara Matthias, age ----, bur. Dec. 19, 1783.
Son of Peter Merckel, age 2 yrs., 10 mos., 5 days, bur. Dec. --,
    1783.
Son of Christian Kouck, age 6 mos., 2 wks., bur. Dec. 19, 1783.
John Gilbert, age 7 mos., 5 days, bur. Jan. 7, 1784.
Richard Reichard, age 3 yrs., bur. Jan. 11, 1784.
Son of Jacob Bonner, age 4 mos., 6 days, bur. Jan. 13, 1784.
Margaret Sauder, age 3 yrs., 3 mos., bur. Feb. 1, 1784.
Son of Henry Derein, age 6 yrs., bur. Feb. 5, 1784.
Wife of Abraham Peter, age 46 yrs., 4 mos., 14 wks., bur. Feb. 9,
    1784.
Jacob Furer, age 69 yrs., 8 mos., 1 week, bur. Feb. 10, 1784.
Wife of Balthasar Richestein, age 27 yrs., bur. Feb. 11, 1784.
Wife of Jacob Rumel, age 25 yrs., 3 mos., bur. Feb. 13, 1784.
Henry Dominick, age 39 yrs., 5 mos., 10 days, bur. Feb. 15, 1784.
Son of Mr. Kinsley, age 1 yr., 4 mos., bur. Feb. 19, 1784.
Christian Kraft, age 72 yrs., bur. Feb. 20, 1784.
Maria Farmer, age 62 yrs., bur. Feb. 28, 1784.
Susanna Eschler, age 1 yr., 4 mos., 3 days, bur. Feb. 29, 1784.
Julianna Weith, age 36 yrs., bur. March 1, 1784.
Daniel Odenheimer, age 2 yrs., 2 mos., bur. March 2, 1784.
Wife of Henry Peter, age 36 yrs., 9 mos., bur. March 8, 1784.
John Henry Soest, age 31 yrs., 4 mos., bur. March 21, 1784.
John Miller, age 19 yrs., 6 mos., bur. April 3, 1784.
Christian Schnyder, age 88 yrs., bur. April 4, 1784.
Maria Ristein, age 18 wks., bur. April 12, 1784.
Daniel Heimer, age 34 yrs., bur. April 13, 1784.
Peter Schoeller, age 4 yrs., 3 wks., bur. April 14, 1784.
Albrecht Eschelmann, age 60 yrs., bur. April 27, 1784.
Charles Ludwig Spalter, age 2 yrs., 11 mos., bur. May 2, 1784.
Catherine Ruehl, Kensington, age 44 yrs., bur. May 2, 1784.
Maria Elizabeth Schuster, age 50 yrs., bur. May 3, 1784.
Michael Schnyder, age 46 yrs., 1 mo., bur. May 4, 1784.
Elizabeth Baechtley, age 7 mos., 8 days, bur. May 5, 1784.
Edward Oxley, age 44 yrs., bur. May 7, 1784.
Casimir Delwig, age 32 yrs., bur. May 17, 1784.
Catherine Souder, age 9 yrs., 7 mos., 14 days, bur. May 28, 1784.
Hannah Erringer, age 35 yrs., 1 mo., bur. May 31, 1784.

Wife of Martin Worn, age 58 yrs., bur. June 22, 1784.
Frederick Darner, age 1 yr., 8 mos., bur. June 24, 1784.
Daughter of Demands, age 1 yr., 2 mo., 7 days, bur. July 6, 1784.
Jacob Schneider, age 68 yrs., bur. July 8, 1784.
Jacob Enck, age 12 yrs., 10 mos., bur. July 11, 1784.
Child of Mr. Trautman, age 1 yr., 6 mos., 4 days, bur. July 14, 1784.
William Mixter, age 2 yrs., 2 mos., bur. July 13, 1784.
Maria Riedlinger, age 66 yrs., bur. July 21, 1784.
Wife of Peter Weil, age 37 yrs., 2 mos., bur. July 23, 1784.
Maria Barbara Penther, age 56 yrs., bur. July 23, 1784.
Maria Christine Nichols, age 1 yr., 4 mos., 6 days, bur. July 26, 1784.
Andrew Huck, age 69 yrs., bur. July 28, 1784.
Martha Muth, age 44 yrs., 11 mos., 4 days, bur. Aug. 2, 1784.
Jacob Weyel, age 5 mos., bur. Aug. 4, 1784.
Jacob Koch, age 9 mos., bur. Aug. 8, 1784.
Margaret Reis, age 65 yrs., 7 mos., 7 days, bur. Aug. 9, 1784.
Margaret Bamberger, age 1 yr., 3 mos., bur. Aug. 10, 1784.
William Stoll, age 5 yrs., 8 mos., bur. Aug. 10, 1784.
Wife of Dewald Diehl, age 75 yrs., bur. Aug. 12, 1784.
William Simon, age 1 yr., 3 mos., 11 days, bur. Aug. 13, 1784.
Rachel Bell, age 5 yrs., 10 mos., 2 wks., 2 days, bur. Aug. 14, 1784.
Adam Reifschneider, age 6 yrs., 1 mo., 6 days, bur. Aug. 15, 1784.
Maria Rumel, age 6 mos., 2 wks., bur. Aug. 17, 1784.
Philip Schumacher, age 1 yr., 8 mos., bur. Aug. 18, 1784.
Jacob Scheradin, age 3 yrs., 8 mos., bur. Aug. 20, 1784.
Rebecca Ehringer, age 1 yr., 2 mos., 2 wks., bur. Aug. 28, 1784.
Julianna Roesch, age 44 yrs., bur. Aug. 30, 1784.
Henry Schuck, age 11 mos., bur. Sept. 2, 1784.
Elizabeth Lukas, age 1 yr., 4 mos., bur. Sept. 6, 1784.
Daniel Dewald, age 19 yrs., bur. Sept. 6, 1784.
Peter Tischong, age 47 yrs., 1 week, 4 days, bur. Sept. 11, 1784.
Elizabeth Johraus, age 3 yrs., 4 mos., bur. Sept. 11, 1784.
Child of George Schulte, age ----, bur. Sept. 11, 1784.
Daughter of Jacob Finck, age 2 mos., bur. Sept. 15, 1784.
John Philip Ladamus, age 19 yrs., bur. Oct. 20, 1784.
Margaret Brown, age 9 mos., bur. Sept. 25, 1784.
Child of Philip Jung, age 10 mos., bur. Sept. 25, 1784.
George Hager, age 2 yrs., bur. Sept. 28, 1784.
Martin Schultes, age 2 yrs., 2 wks., bur. Sept. 30, 1784.
Jacob Binder, age 41 yrs., 5 mos., 2 days, bur. Oct. 4, 1784.
Margaret Schuh, age 1 yr., 7 mos., bur. Oct. 4, 1784.
Catherine Wetzler, age 55 yrs., bur. Oct. 7, 1784.
Catherine Gynre, age 80 yrs., 6 mos., bur. Oct. 7, 1784.
Peter Horn, age 35 yrs., bur. Oct. 8, 1784.
Maria Elizabeth Schoeller, age 38 yrs., 6 mos., bur. Oct. 9, 1784.
George Joraus, age 8 mos., bur. Oct. 11, 1784.
John George Heiny, age 10 mos., 4 days, bur. Oct. 12, 1784.
Maria Sarah Reinhard, age 53 yrs., bur. Oct. 20, 1784.
John Schmidt, age 4 yrs., 4 mos., 2 wks., 3 days, bur. Oct. 20, 1784.
Jacob Weinert, age 32 yrs., bur. Oct. 25, 1784.
Catherine Magdalene Miller, age 1 yr., 11 mos., 19 yrs., bur. Nov.

3, 1784.
Alexander Bartholome Gaillard, b. at Rolle, Switzerland, age 28 yrs., bur. Nov. 14, 1784.
Rudolph Bonner, age 76 yrs., 3 mos., bur. Nov. 16, 1784.
Son of Mr. Riegeler, age 6 wks., bur. Nov. 19, 1784.
Child of Daniel Kehr, age 3 mos., 3 wks., bur. Nov. 19, 1784.
Child of Mr Humberger, age 3 yrs., 2 mos., 3 days, bur. Nov. 19, 1784.
John Halberstadt, age 3 yrs., 1 mo., bur. Nov. 27, 1784.
John Chambers, age 21 yrs., 1 mo., bur. Nov. 28, 1784.
Christian Fans, age 7 mos., bur. Nov. 28, 1784.
Jacob Wollenschleger, age 50 yrs., 4 mos., 2 wks., bur. Nov. 30, 1784.
William Miller, age 33 yrs., 5 mos., bur. Dec. 8, 1784.
Maria Hager, age 5 yrs., bur. Dec. 8, 1784.
Gottfried Schuster, age 42 yrs., 6 mos., 2 wks., bur. Dec. 14, 1784.
Widow Berg, age 64 yrs., 8 mos., bur. Dec. 19, 1784.
John Mann, age 55 yrs., bur. Jan. 6, 1785.
Magdalene Froelig, age 5 yrs., 4 mos., 3 wks., 6 days, bur. Jan. --, 1785.
Anna Hess, age 11 mos., 7 wks., bur. Jan. 14, 1785.
Anna Maria Schreier, age 60 yrs., 1 mo., bur. Jan. 16, 1785.
Maria Elizabeth Stetzer, age 2 yrs., 3 days, bur. Jan. 25, 1785.
Anthony Lowden, age 3 yrs., 2 mos., bur. Jan. 28, 1785.
Catherine Lutz, Kensington, age 8 mos., 2 wks., bur. Feb. 2, 1785.
Matthias Hanson, age 1 yr., bur. Feb. 2, 1785.
Carl Hick, age 40 yrs., bur. Jan. 31, 1785.
John George Schultz, age 7 mos., bur. Jan. 31, 1785.
Elizabeth Dellwig, age 1 yr., 3 mos., bur. Feb. 3, 1785.
George Bonner, age 40 yrs., 4 mos., 13 days, bur. Feb. 6, 1785.
Susanna Koch, age 5 mos., 3 wks., bur. Feb. 6, 1785.
Ludwig Hoff, age 7 yrs., bur. Feb. 12, 1785.
Frederick Maus, age 11 mos., bur. March 9, 1785.
Wife of Robert Little, age 25 yrs., bur. March 13, 1785.
John Christian Froelig, age 46 yrs., 10 mos., bur. March 20, 1785.
Susanna Klockner, age 2 yrs., 6 mos., 2 wks., 5 days, bur. March 20, 1785.
Barbara Pampinior, age 44 yrs., bur. March 22, 1785.
Anna Margaret Reed, age 4 yrs., 2 wks., 2 days, bur. March 27, 1785.
John Eckert, age 76 yrs., 1 mo., bur. March 27, 1785.
Archibald Schneyder, age 4 mos., 3 wks., 3 days, bur. March 31, 1785.
Philip Schreiner, age 4 yrs., 6 mos., bur. April 22, 1785.
----, wife of Peter Emmel, age 40 yrs., bur. April 24, 1785.
Casper Schuster, Kensington, age 45 yrs., 3 mos., 1 day, bur. May 1, 1785.
Abraham Frioth, age 71 yrs., 6 mos., bur. May 25, 1785.
Elias Werth, from Ronsdorf, age 37 yrs., bur. June 17, 1785.
John Philip Tauenheim, age 20 yrs., bur. June 29, 1785.
Sarah Weissler, age 1 yr., 1 week, bur. July 3, 1785.
Child of Martin Stern, age 2 mos., bur. July 3, 1785.
Christine Schmidt, Kensington, age 3 mos., bur. July 7, 1785.
George Lettel (Little), age 1 yr., 1 mo., bur. July 11, 1785.

Catherine Walter, age 4 mos., bur. July 17, 1785.
Henry Christian Hohl, age 10 yrs., bur. July 22, 1785.
Elizabeth Oberman, age 1 yr., 4 mos., bur. July 26, 1785.
Philip Ulrich, age 67 yrs., bur. July 29, 1785.
John George Pfaff, age 3 yrs., 2 mos., 2 wks., bur. July 31, 1785.
Daniel Pantz, age 10 mos., 2 days, bur. July 29, 1785.
John Maag, age 33 yrs., 7 mos., 11 days, bur. Aug. 1, 1785.
Maria Loscher, age 13 mos., 7 days, bur. Aug. 3, 1785.
John Michael Schneider, age 4 yrs., bur. Aug. 7, 1785.
George Weed, age 9 mos., bur. Aug. 9, 1785.
Conrad Spangenberg, age 1 yr., 3 mos., bur. Aug. 9, 1785.
Samuel Klages, age 1 yr., 8 mos., bur. Aug. 11, 1785.
Sally Roth, age 8 mos., bur. Aug. 15, 1785.
Dewald Diehl, age 80 yrs., bur. Aug. 23, 1785.
Casper Moralt, age 67 yrs., bur. Aug. 23, 1785.
John Stillwagen, age 71 yrs., 10 mos., bur. Aug. 24, 1785.
Child of Mr. Spangenberg, age 10 mos., bur. Aug. 28, 1785.
Child of Mr. Kooper, age ----, bur. Sept. 2, 1785.
Fanny Habgood, age 1 yr., 6 mos., bur. Sept. 4, 1785.
Frederick Heimer, age 62 yrs., bur. Sept. 5, 1785.
Child of Jacob Schnyder, age 2 yrs., 2 mos., 11 days, bur. Sept. 9,
    1785.
John Becker, age 1 yr., 1 mo., bur. Sept. 12, 1785.
Elizabeth Huber, age 9 mos., 10 days, bur. Sept. 12, 1785.
Eva Franerina Bake, age 11 mos., bur. Sept. 13, 1785.
Anna Margaret Wilhelm, age ----, bur. Sept. 19, 1785.
Catherine Becker, age ----, bur. Sept. 20, 1785.
John Souder, age ----, bur. Sept. 25, 1785.
Eckhard Casander, age ----, bur. Sept. 26, 1785.
---- Muntz, age 1 yr., 1 mo., bur. Sept. --, 1785.
Wife of John Adam Hauser, age 45 yrs., 9 mos., bur. Sept. 29, 1785.
John George Grauel, age 1 yr., 10 mos., bur. Oct. 6, 1785.
Child of Jacob Heiner, age 1 yr., 7 mos., bur. Oct. 10, 1785.
Herriet Kirby, age 2 yrs., 7 mos., bur. Oct. 11, 1785.
Jacob Pund, age 44 yrs., 8 mos., bur. Oct. 12, 1785.
Anna Justina Lohrman, age 49 yrs., 9 mos., bur. Oct. 17, 1785.
Daughter of George Fies, age 1 yr., 4 mos., 5 days, bur. Oct. 20,
    1785.
William Sanders, age 1 yr., 3 mos., bur. Oct. 22, 1785.
Peter Reis, age 28 yrs., bur. Oct. 22, 1785.
Maria Elizabeth Naoks, age 35 yrs., bur. Oct. 23, 1785.
Jacob Bachoff, age 8 mos., 3 wks., bur. Oct. 23, 1785.
Susanna Ecky, age 1 yr., 1 mo., 2 wks., 5 days, bur. Oct. 23, 1785.
Anna Maria Beck, age 23 yrs., 9 mos., 3 wks., bur. Nov. 4, 1785.
Son of Charles Hunter, age 12 yrs., 6 mos., bur. Nov. 6, 1785.
Margaret Broun, age 1 yr., 2 mos., bur. Nov. 19, 1785.
Elizabeth Latsch, age 3 mos., bur. Nov. 19, 1785.
---- Thomas Lawersweil, age 35 yrs., 3 mos., bur. ----, 1785.
---- W. Doer, age 56 yrs., bur. ----, 1785.
(Christo)pher Keller, age 55 yrs., 10 mos., bur. ----, 1785.
Michael Fans, age 37 yrs., 10 mos., 11 days, bur. Nov. --, 1785.
Marcus Schmidt, age 21 yrs., bur. Nov. --, 1785.
George Schaaff, age 67 yrs., 6 mos., bur. Dec. 4, 1785.
Daughter of Pliges Stoffer, age 22 yrs., 3 mos., bur. Dec. 1, 1785.
Veronica Uttre, age 23 yrs., bur. Dec. 4, 1785.

Casper Souder, age 50 yrs., bur. Dec. 5, 1785.
Barbara Ord, age 45 yrs., bur. Dec. 9, 1785.
Elizabeth Gucker, age 52 yrs., bur. Dec. 18, 1785.
Child of Adam Stoll, age 20 mos., bur. Dec. 25, 1785.

MARRIAGES BY REV. CASPER WEYBERG
1781 - 1785

Philip Werth m. Dorothy Penther on Jan. 30, 1781.
Adam Lapp m. Catherine Jones on Feb. 2, 1781.
Charles Kerby m. Hannah Sellers on Feb. 2, 1781.
Griffith Owen m. Jane Hughes on Feb. 13, 1781.
Christian Earl m. Anne Harrison on Feb. 24, 1781.
John Leonhard m. Catherine Mickle on March 8, 1781.
Henry Ritter m. Anna Praupert on March 15, 1781.
Isaac Bedellion m. Magdalene Daun on March 16, 1781.
Daniel Shea m. Sarah Arenbold on March 29, 1781.
John McNachtane m. Cornelia Dorsius on March 29, 1781.
John Keyser m. Elizabeth Horning on April 8, 1781.
George Lesher m. Elizabeth Schmidt on April 19, 1781.
Jacob Schnyder m. Margaret Engle on April 25, 1781.
William Ogelbie m. Elizabeth Everman on April 30, 1781.
Isaac Jones m. Catherine Bedellion on May 10, 1781.
Christian Busch m. Elizabeth Senft on May 12, 1781.
John Brown m. Abia Whitmer on May 17, 1781.
David Turner m. Mary Day on June 2, 1781.
Conrad Steiger m. Sarah Cripps on June 4, 1781.
Patrick Grogan m. Catherine Southam on June 16, 1781.
Christian Kauck m. Maria Diemer on June 26, 1781.
Benjamin Loxley m. Mary Bryen on July 15, 1781.
Peter Leap m. Sarah Wills on Aug. 24, 1781.
John Gebhard m. Regina Warner on Sept. 9, 1781.
George Streeton m. Mary Ridge on Sept. 10, 1781.
Christian Glockener m. Catherine Lartsch on Oct. 30, 1781.
Henry Coldflesh m. Elizabeth Davis on Oct. 30, 1781.
Jacob Himpelman m. Elizabeth Burck on Nov. 8, 1781.
John Warner m. Sarah Toplift on Nov. 20, 1781.
George Degenhardt m. Wilhelma von Obstrand on Nov. 28, 1781.
Paul Sheridan m. Hannah Tedders on Dec. 16, 1781.
Jacob Wisseler m. Elizabeth Erl on Dec. 17, 1781.
Peter Laub m. Maria Leim on Dec. 18, 1781.
James Stats m. Rachel Klark on Dec. 22, 1781.
John Adam Steiner m. Elizabeth Foller on Jan. 15, 1782.
Henry William Guize m. Eva Gillman on Jan. 17, 1782.
Johannes John Latsch m. Margaret Kappel on Jan. 22, 1782.
Michael Worn m. Catherine Hafener on Jan. 31, 1782.
Christian Lawyer m. Maria Orlob on Feb. 21, 1782.
Jacob Woodward m. Mary Pepperley on March 12, 1782.
Johnston Beezley m. Maria Virgin on March 21, 1782.
William Mollohon m. Charlotte Moser on March 28, 1782.
Conrad Gerhard m. Elizabeth Jung on April 4, 1782.
Jacob Loscher m. Maria Fitler on April 11, 1782.
William Miller m. Susanna Hertzog on April 11, 1782.
Conrad Scholl m. Maria Kerch on April 11, 1782.
George Fiss m. Mary Steuerwald on April 14, 1782.

John Pello m. Anna Margaret Jentzer on April 16, 1782.
Martin Liest m. Elizabeth Gaul on April 16, 1782.
Lewis Price m. Margaret Miller on April 21, 1782.
James Trimble m. Clarissa Hastings on April 22, 1782.
John Niemand m. Maria Gunckel on May 9, 1782.
Jacob Schlemer m. Hannah Fuller on May 30, 1782.
Andrew Schuster m. Rosina Hey on June 3, 1782.
John Maag m. Elizabeth Goebler on June 13, 1782.
Martin Sigismund Zibolt m. Barbara Schober on June 16, 1782.
Henry Deuffinger m. Sarah Supper on June 20, 1782.
Martin Worn m. Catherine Jerger on June 20, 1782.
Nicholas Zessinger m. Margaret Henrietta Velbach on June 25, 1782.
Christian Alberger m. Catherine Hoover on June 30, 1782.
George Loscher m. Anna Lehman on July 4, 1782.
Conrad Rush m. Margaret Burchhardt on July 4, 1782.
Jacob Miley m. Margaret Keiler on July 16, 1782.
Lorentz Sandman m. Maria Kalbfleisch on July 25, 1782.
Thomas Hood m. Sarah Lambeth on July 31, 1782.
Henry Fenner m. Elizabeth von der Halt on Aug. 11, 1782.
Richard Gray m. Hannah Forster on Aug. 15, 1782.
Lorentz Werntz m. Margaret Orner on Aug. 20, 1782.
Peter Krim m. Elizabeth Kline on Aug. 22, 1782.
John Huhn m. Christine Mills on Aug. 29, 1782.
Adam Lehr m. Rebecca Schwartz on Sept. 12, 1782.
George Flauers m. Elizabeth Bonenacker on Oct. 4, 1782.
George Janus m. Margaret Faering on Nov. 1, 1782.
John George Gerster m. Anna Maria Burghart on Dec. 2, 1782.
Jacob Lutz m. Rosina Schlemmer on Dec. 5, 1782.
John Suter m. Catherine Colp on Dec. 19,
Jacob Latch m. Jane Rose on Dec. 24, 1782.
Peter Paris m. Fanny Fahns on Jan. 14, 1783.
Adam Wever m. Ketty Dielz on Feb. 11, 1783.
John Flachs m. Magdalene Schnyder on Feb. 11, 1783.
William Praupert m. Barbara Schneider on Feb. 18, 1783.
Conrad and Maria Genthemer m. on Feb. 22, 1783.
Johnston and Elizabeth Weierman m. on March 4, 1783.
Andrew Scholl m. Anna Catherine Bischoffberger on March 9, 1783.
Lorentz Foth m. Elizabeth Albert on March 13, 1783.
John Heimer m. Elizabeth Henrich on April 3, 1783.
John Reide m. Margaret Wisper on April 3, 1783.
Adam Roth m. Maria Asheuer on April 7, 1783.
John Steel m. Elizabeth Fritz on April 10, 1783.
Martin Runner m. Sophia Housman on April 13, 1783.
Jacob Bischoffberger m. Elizabeth Tschudy on April 29, 1783.
Henry Schmidt m. Martha Peterson on May 4, 1783.
Leonard Rothare m. Eleonore Gilyard on May 10, 1783.
Charles Ristein m. Hannah Gottschalck on May 23, 1783.
Daniel Klages m. Maria Rohrman on May 27, 1783.
Abraham Fox m. Dorothy Rhodt on May 27, 1783.
John Adams m. Catherine Oberdorff on May 29, 1783.
Zacharias Beckman m. Barbara Berckenbeil on June 3, 1783.
David Muller m. Anna Heidte on June 13, 1783.
Philip Frisseler m. Mary Stubert on June 13, 1783.
Michael Rummel m. Christine Dorffer on June 19, 1783.
John Milles m. Elizabeth Ernstdorff on June 19, 1783.

John Frederick Gaul m. Margaret Metzinger on June 24, 1783.
John Kempert m. Elizabeth Kempert on June 26, 1783.
Henry Rieseler m. Catherine Fauth on June 30, 1783.
Adam Cullman m. Susanna Neidlinger on June 30, 1783.
John Bingel m. Jacobina Warner on July 13, 1783.
Frederick Tschudy m. Elizabeth Schneck on July 18, 1783.
David Seltenreich m. Maria Laubach on Aug. 5, 1783.
Nicholas Schultz m. Catherine Schaaff on Aug. 8, 1783.
John Kreimes m. Anna Maria Elizabeth Gemeinbauers on Aug. 14, 1783.
Henry Oberman m. Gratia Donnel on Aug. 19, 1783.
Henry Stroud m. Catherine Meyers on Aug. 19, 1783.
Philip Rummel m. Rebecca Held on Sept. 25, 1783.
James Cunningham m. Catherine McCord on Sept. 9, 1783.
John Eberman m. Maria Henry on Sept. 28, 1783.
Adam May m. Catherine Diehl on Oct. 9, 1783.
Jacob Kreider m. Elizabeth Gramlich on Oct. 14, 1783.
Benjamin Tunis m. Mary Griffith on Oct. 15, 1783.
Francis William Troemner m. Chressely Brookman on Oct. 19, 1783.
George Bantz m. Isabella MecMollen on Oct. 23, 1783.
Jacob Schreiner m. Elizabeth Stillwagen on Nov. 2, 1783.
George Peddle m. Margaret Potts on Nov. 6, 1783.
Ludwig Hammer m. Catherine Bedford on Nov. 9, 1783.
Frederick Heimberger m. Margaret Stimmel on Dec. 1, 1783.
John George Streith m. Catherine Kuhl on Dec. 1, 1783.
Nicholas Eisenmenger m. Elizabeth Bowle on Dec. 4, 1783.
John Pollard m. Maria Duche on Dec. 19, 1783.
Daniel von der Schleis m. Philippina Halvilson on Jan. 5, 1784.
Charles Schakar m. Margaret Rudybach on Jan. 8, 1784.
Philip Schuck m. Sibylla Baselman on Jan. 14, 1784.
John Porter m. Catherine Ritter on Jan. 15, 1784.
Henry Maag m. Elizabeth Brown on Jan. 20, 1784.
Francis Joseph Uss m. Margaret Nick on Jan. 26, 1784.
John Hald auf der Heide m. Elizabeth Schlechter on Feb. 4, 1784.
Joseph Shambough m. Catherine Shepard on Feb. 10, 1784.
George Einwachter m. Elizabeth Keblehauser on Feb. 13, 1784.
Conrad Bachman m. Susanna Bridges on Feb. 15, 1784.
George Riehmer m. Sarah Broun on Feb. 19, 1784.
Philip Limeburner m. Mary Botz on Feb. 19, 1784.
Thomas Cave m. Catherine Meyer on Feb. 19, 1784.
John Ebert m. Elizabeth Button on Feb. 26, 1784.
William Fusselbach m. Margaret Diehl on Feb. 26, 1784.
John Wagoner m. Mary Baker on Feb. 29, 1784.
John Altberger m. Dorothy Scherreden on March 4, 1784.
Matthew Henssen m. Mary Meyer on March 22, 1784.
Fredeick Moyerley m. Catherine Bottom on March 23, 1784.
George Hess m. Anna Conver on April 1, 1784.
Michael Katz m. Margaret Keller on April 4, 1784.
Joseph Dawson m. Martha Schoen on April 4, 1784.
George Reif m. Rachel Pawling on April 7, 1784.
John Kalbfleisch m. Maria Lorentz on April 8, 1784.
John Zahner m. Barbara Kesen on April 12, 1784.
James Steel m. Kitty Boehme on April 15, 1784.
John Orefgen m. Elizabeth Schaeffer on April 22, 1784.
George Klein m. Elizabeth Andressen on April 27, 1784.
Abraham Schmidt m. Sophia Rhinhardt on May 2, 1784.

Benjamin Miller m. Hannah Stimmel on May 6, 1784.
John Walter m. Anna Rubsamen on May 16, 1784.
John Diedrich Berckenbeul m. Amalia Kremer on May 16, 1784.
William Peltz m. Maria Boehm on May 25, 1784.
Casper Graff m. Rebecca Lindley on May 31, 1784.
John Painter m. Mary Kline on June 3, 1784.
Peter Mensch m. Christine Muller on June 6, 1784.
Nicholas Wirick m. Catherine Grubb on June 6, 1784.
John Walker m. Margaret Friederich on June 8, 1784.
Philip Gasser m. Maria Dies on June 3, 1784.
Jacob Reitlinger m. Elizabeth Schwam on June 3, 1784.
John Froelig m. Marsey Thomas on June 10, 1784.
Conrad Kauwertz m. Anna Douglish on June 13, 1784.
Justus Flock m. Margaret Stuertz on June 22, 1784.
William Rudolph m. Mary Schmidt on June 24, 1784.
John George Ries m. Maria Klosbach on June 27, 1784.
Martin Gucker m. Catherine Souder on July 6, 1784.
Henry Schearer m. Elizabeth Davis on July 13, 1784.
George Hinckel m. Ruth Owen on Aug. 1, 1784.
Henry Hildebrand m. Anna Margaret Bamberger on Aug. 5, 1784.
Samuel Muschell m. Elizabeth Morgan on Aug. 5, 1784.
George Muller m. Mary Magdalene Wentzel on Aug. 8, 1784.
Robert Steward m. Sarah Staggart on Aug. 16, 1784.
George Birckenbeil m. Elizabeth Omenselter on Aug. 19, 1784.
Uriah Hughes m. Phoebe Rennard on Aug. 21, 1784.
John Jones m. Elizabeth Weithman on Sept. 2, 1784.
George Bloom m. Catherine Schaffery on Sept. 7, 1784.
Philip Loesch m. Margaret Fismeier on Sept. 17, 1784.
Joseph Smallwood m. Rebecca Jackson on Sept. 20, 1784.
Adam Fischer m. Elizabeth Gamber on Sept. 21, 1784.
Jacob Gucker m. Maria Heith on Sept. 22, 1784.
Frederick Kehlheffer m. Elizabeth Blum on Sept. 30, 1784.
Peter Fenner m. Catherine Schneider on Oct. 7, 1784.
Nicholas Rash m. Catherine Summers on Oct. 7, 1784.
Jacob Krantz m. Catherine Wilhelm on Oct. 14, 1784.
Martin Schuster m. Catherine Klein on Oct. 28, 1784.
Robert Johnson m. Mary Kroose on Oct. 28, 1784.
Nicholas Rummel m. Barbara Haller on Oct. 28, 1784.
George Bornhaus m. Elizabeth Zinck on Nov. 11, 1784.
Caleb Hughes m. Mary Haerth on Nov. 18, 1784.
Peter Bockius m. Hannah Lehman on Nov. 24, 1784.
John Casper Teilotz m. Anna Mary Loston on Nov. 26, 1784.
John Capp m. Catherine Schamberlaine on Nov. 30, 1784.
William Wever m. Margaret Price on Dec. 19, 1784.
John Kayser m. Pamelia Price on Dec. 23, 1784.
Michael Kremer m. Maria Miller on Dec. 23, 1784.
John McCluer m. Mary Steiger on Jan. 5, 1785.
Henry Wetzler m. Phoebe Miller on Jan. 12, 1785.
William Pidgeon m. Maria Broun on Jan. 13, 1785.
John Rudy m. Mary Crombie on Jan. 13, 1785.
John Cress m. Margaret Kintzler on Jan. 20, 1785.
Philip Haller m. Maria Threyer on Feb. 1, 1785.
Eilliam Reder m. Anna Maria Rummer on Feb. 8, 1785.
George Broun m. Maria Lubrian on Feb. 16, 1785.
Sirach Tschudi m. Barbara Scherer on Feb. 17, 1785.

14

Jacob Mueller m. Elizabeth Roos on Feb. 22, 1785.
John Folcker m. Elizabeth Penther on Feb. 23, 1785.
Manly Smallwood m. Elizabeth Fuller on Feb. 24, 1785.
Isac Smallwood m. Priscilla Stiles on Feb. 24, 1785.
Conrad Axs (Ochs) m. Margaret Ascher on March 1, 1785.
Jeremiah Vielmalter m. Catherine Thuye on March 2, 1785.
Charles Kitts m. Biddy Welch on March 3, 1785.
Martin Worn m. Hannah Powel on March 9, 1785.
Francis Curtis m. Anna Cope on March 13, 1785.
David Archer m. Mary Allin on March 15, 1785.
Daniel Niederhaus m. Elizabeth Reinhold on March 15, 1785.
Daniel Martin m. Elizabeth Wine on March 28, 1785.
John Herman Winckhaus m. Catherine Schnyder on March 31, 1785.
Leonard Schuster m. Sarah Point on March 31, 1785.
Daniel McCoy m. Elizabeth Kelly on April 6, 1785.
Jacob Frey m. Maria Delwich on April 7, 1785.
Benjamin Hancock m. Hannah Cross on April 11, 1785.
John Ginder m. Margaret Wack on April 14, 1785.
Christian Jacob m. Margaret Hess on April 24, 1785.
Peter Bockius m. Elizabeth Etter on April 24, 1785.
John Wester m. Margaret Schumacher on May 3, 1785.
George Engelhard m. Maria Schutz on May 6, 1785.
Anthony Weiss m. Elizabeth Hahn on May 7, 1785.
Anthony Muth m. Rebecca Neuman on May 10, 1785.
Nicholas Meyer m. Elizabeth Jouch on May 10, 1785.
Adam Boyer m. Rebecca Thomson on May 16, 1785.
Philip Maus m. Magdalene Anthony on May 19, 1785.
Jacob Erringer m. Magdalene Jaegli on May 24, 1785.
James Boutler m. Hannah Rees on May 28, 1785.
William Kahmer m. Elizabeth Fischer on June 2, 1785.
Robert Richerton m. Catherine Gamber on June 16, 1785.
John Jung m. Maria Griffith on June 21, 1785.
Conrad Rouw m. Maria Chamberlein on July 14, 1785.
George Barnet m. Sarah Fisher on July 18, 1785.
Casper Albert m. Nancy Connen on July 19, 1785.
Daniel Kuhn m. Nelly Coop on July 21, 1785.
James Cross m. Margaret Elizabeth Koch on July 24, 1785.
John Klap m. Maria Stucki on Aug. 11, 1785.
Philip Fritz m. Charlotte Deaberger on Aug. 11, 1785.
Jacob Haller m. Maria Ravans on Aug. 14, 1785.
John George Kehr m. Elizabeth Haas on Aug. 14, 1785.
John Henry Rumpf m. Elizabeth Grim on Aug. 16, 1785.
John Stricker m. Sarah Sellers on Aug. 18, 1785.
John Korterman m. Susanna Sutten on Sept. 17, 1785.
Frederick Miley m. Barbara Keiler on Sept. 25, 1785.
Peter Weiel m. Elizabeth Haubt on Sept. 27, 1785.
Henry Breda m. Anna Gilbert on Oct. 4, 1785.
George Herford m. Mary Bockius on Oct. 6, 1785.
Frederick Meyer m. Margaret Cax on Oct. 20, 1785.
Abraham Peter m. Barbara Binder on Oct. 25, 1785.
William Spade m. Sarah Kuemmel on Nov. 1, 1785.
Christian Kiegbert m. Magdalene Losch on Nov. 3, 1785.
Jonas Lewis m. Nancy Tschudy on Nov. 8, 1785.
John Wm. Stetzer m. Martha Edman on Nov. 14, 1785.
Michael Kaiser m. Catherine Hess on Nov. 16, 1785.

Daniel Arn m. Dorothy Streeper on Nov. 16, 1785.
William Rup m. Cath. Bergendaller on Nov. 28, 1785.
Michael Pfifer m. Catherine Bingeman on Nov. 30, 1785.
Frederick Dauber m. Elizabeth Edel on Dec. 6, 1785.
John Meibert m. Elizabeth Berner on Dec. 8, 1785.
Peter Emig m. Susanna Steuerwald on Dec. 15, 1785.
John Sproson m. Anna Brock on Dec. 17, 1785.
William Slide m. Maria Sullivan on Dec. 22, 1785.
John David Woelpper m. Hannah Stayger on Dec. 24, 1785.

BAPTISMS OF THE REV. CASPER WEYBERG
1781 - 1789
Hannah, daughter of Frederick Kreider and Veronica, b. Dec. 1,
1780, bapt. Jan. 1, 1781. Spon: John Wickhard and Hannah.
Ludwig, son of Robert Burck and Mary Catherine, b. Sept. 10, 1780,
bapt. Jan. 11, 1781. Spon: Parents.
Regina, daughter of Fabian Hammerle and Catherine, b. Jan. 1, 1781,
bapt. Jan. 21, 1781. Spon: Stephen Rigerler and Elizabeth.
Jacob, son of Jacob Eyler and Jane, b. Jan. 6, 1781, bapt. Jan. 21,
1781. Spon: David Rischong and Catherine.
George Christian, son of Christian Troutman and Elizabeth, b. Jan.
7, 1780, bapt. Jan. 21, 1781. Spon: George Fuckeroll and
Margaret Becklein.
Margaret, daughter of Casper Souder and Wilhelmina, b. Nov. 29,
1780, bapt. Jan. 21, 1781. Spon: Mr. Wegman and Margaret.
Bronner, son of Samuel Dorsten and Regina, b. Nov. 1, 1780, bapt.
Jan. 28, 1781. Spon: John George Bronner and Catherine Ketz.
Elizabeth, daughter of Frederick Bayer and Catherine, b. Jan. 12,
1781, bapt. Jan. 29, 1781. Spon: John Leibinger and Catherine.
William, son of William Oliver and Maria, b. Jan. 24, 1780, bapt.
Jan. 30, 1781. Spon: Parents.
John, son of John Jost Weyand and Magdalene, b. Jan. 10, 1781,
bapt. Feb. 4, 1781. Spon: John Weyand and Catherine Steiber.
Gottfried, son of John Souder and Catherine, b. Jan. 24, 1781,
bapt. Feb. 4, 1781. Spon: Casper Schoen and Margaret.
Philip Jacob, son of Philip Jacob Bockenmeyer and Maria, b. Jan.
29, 1781, bapt. Feb. 9, 1781. Spon: Michael Vaerner and Maria.
George, son of Charles Hicks and Hannah, b. Jan. 10, 1781, bapt.
Feb. 11, 1781. Spon: George Vogel and Maria.
Peter, son of Peter Tischong and Susa Louisa, b. Jan. 19, 1781,
bapt. Feb. 11, 1781. Spon: Christian Tischong and Elizabeth
Goebeler.
Catherine, daughter of Abraham Gloting and Juliana, b. ----, bapt.
Feb. 15, 1781. Spon: Parents.
Daniel, son of Henry Meyer and Eleonora, b. Feb. 10, 1781, bapt.
Feb. 18, 1781. Spon: Daniel Muller and Theresa Theis.
Elizabeth, daughter of John Bernard Simon and Christine, b. Jan.
23, 1781, bapt. Feb. 18, 1781. Spon: Walrab Simon and
Elizabeth.
Anna Elizabeth, daughter of Matthias Groff and Elizabeth, b. Aug.
5, 1780, bapt. Feb. 22, 1781. Spon: James Schmith and wife.
Peter, son of Ludwig Reineck and Mary Elizabeth, b. Feb. 14, 1781,
bapt. Feb. 25, 1781. Spon: Peter Nannetter and Anna Elizabeth.
John Daniel, son of Andrew Braderick and Maria, b. Jan. 4, 1781,

bapt. Feb. 25, 1781. Spon: John Daniel Greiner and Catherine.
John Philip, son of Christian Weyerich and Anna Catherine, b. Feb.
19, 1781, bapt. Feb. 25, 1781. Spon: Philip Wirth and Dorothea.
Regina, daughter of John Weber and Anna Maria, b. Feb. 7, 1781,
bapt. Feb. 25, 1781. Spon: Parents and Regina Weber.
Philip, son of John Fritz and Maria, b. Feb. 13, 1781, bapt. Feb.
25, 1781. Spon: Philip Fritz and Margaret.
John, son of Jacob Daubendistel and Barbara, b. Aug. 5, 1781, bapt.
Feb. 26, 1780. Spon: Casper Souder and Wilhelmina.
Henry, son of Nicholas Stimmel and Elizabeth, b. Feb. 7, 1781,
bapt. March 4, 1781. Spon: Henry Heyman and Catherine.
Henry, son of James Elliot and Sophia, b. Jan. 28, 1781, bapt.
March 4, 1781. Spon: Mr. Funck and wife.
Daniel, son of Daniel Carbon and Elizabeth, b. March 6, 1781, bapt.
March 11, 1781. Spon: ----.
Susanna, daughter of Jacob Schible and Elizabeth, b. Jan. 9, 1781,
bapt. March 11, 1781. Spon: Valentine Hoffman and Susanna.
Letitia, daughter of Philip Stimmel and Anna, b. Feb. 25, 1781,
bapt. March 11, 1781. Spon: Nicholas Stimmel and Elizabeth.
John Jacob, son of Peter Schaeff and Elizabeth, b. Feb. 24, 1781,
bapt. March 13, 1781. Spon: John Jacob Quandel and Elizabeth
Maria.
Bernard, son of David Stecker and Barbara Schly, b. Dec. 25, 1780,
bapt. March 13, 1781. Spon: Bernard Muth and Elizabeth.
William, son of William Dauns and Maria, b. Oct. 9, 1780, bapt.
March 16, 1781. Spon: Parents.
Anna, daughter of Valentine Stillwagen and Elizabeth, b. March 7,
1781, bapt. March 17, 1781. Spon: Parents.
Maria, daughter of Martin Wahl and Christine, b. Feb. 24, 1781,
bapt. March 18, 1781. Spon: Father and Jacob Stocky and wife.
Anthony, son of Anthony von der Schleiss and Elizabeth, b. Feb. 26,
1781, bapt. March 18, 1781. Spon: Jacob Prattler and Catherine.
John, son of John Kern and Maria Elizabeth, b. March 8, 1781, bapt.
March 18, 1781. Spon: John Lecheren and Maria Catherine.
Charlotte, daughter of Peter Walter and Charlotte, b. Dec. 9, 1780,
bapt. March 18, 1781. Spon: Parents.
William, son of Henry Huber and Maria, b. Dec. 7, 1780, bapt. March
18, 1781. Spon: Jacob Huber and Elizabeth.
Henry, son of John Diehl and Catherine, b. Feb. 11, 1781, bapt.
March 18, 1781. Spon: Parents.
Henry Moser, son of Jacob Bonner and Elizabeth, b. Dec. 31, 1781,
bapt. March 20, 1781. Spon: Philip Moser and Susanna.
Elizabeth, daughter of John Weber and Anna, b. March 20, 1781,
bapt. March 23, 1781. Spon: Peter Nannetter and Elizabeth.
Christian, son of Philip Gramlich and Elizabeth, b. March 9, 1781,
bapt. March 25, 1781. Spon: Christian Lutz and Carolina.
Nicholas, son of George Schultz and Susanna, b. March 10, 1781,
bapt. March 25, 1781. Spon: Nicholas Eisenmenger and Elizabeth
Pohl.
Christopher, son of Conrad Stoltz and Catherine, b. March 20, 1781,
bapt. April 1, 1781. Spon: Christopher Rauch and Rosina.
Anna Maria Magdalena, daughter of George Justus and Anna Margaret,
b. March 11, 1781, bapt. April 1, 1781. Spon: Parents.
Catherine, daughter of Christian Rossin and Catherine, b. March 16,
1781, bapt. April 1, 1781. Spon: Parents.

Elizabeth, daughter of Frederick Scholler and Christ., 13 mos. old, bapt. April 4, 1781. Spon: ----.

Christopher, son of David Schubert and Elizabeth, b. ----, bapt. April 4, 1781. Spon: Parents.

Christine, daughter of David Schubert and Elizabeth, b. ----, bapt. April 4, 1781. Spon: Parents.

Maria, daughter of David Schubert and Elizabeth, b. ----, bapt. April 4, 1781. Spon: Parents.

Elizabeth, daughter of David Schubert and Elizabeth, b. ----, bapt. April 4, 1781. Spon: Parents.

Frederick, son of John Reb and Catherine, b. ----, bapt. April 6, 1781. Spon: Mr. Lambach.

Magdalene, daughter of Daniel Hens and Catherine, b. March 6, 1781, bapt. April 8, 1781. Spon: Conrad Schmith and Anna Maria.

Sarah, daughter of Henry Wever and Anna, b. Nov. 18, 1780, bapt. April 8, 1781. Spon: Peter Dress and Maria.

Isaiah, son of Isaiah Eschelman and Sibylla, b. March 22, 1781, bapt. April 8, 1781. Spon: Parents.

Anna Margaret, daughter of Leonard Ried and Elizabeth, b. March 23, 1781, bapt. April 9, 1781. Spon: Parents.

John Peter, son of Daniel Penner and Catherine, b. March 29, 1781, bapt. April 9, 1781. Spon: Peter Ros and Sarah Elizabeth.

Jacob, son of Peter Merckle and Catherine, b. Feb. 21, 1781, bapt. April 13, 1781. Spon: Jacob Mueller and Barbara.

Frederick, son of Frederick Schneider and Barbara, b. April 14, 1781, bapt. April 14, 1781. Spon: Parents.

Hannah, daughter of Gottfried Goebler and Catherine, b. March 24, 1781, bapt. April 16. 1781. Spon: John Wucherer and Elizabeth.

George, son of George Schnyder and Catherine, b. Feb. 12, 1781, bapt. April 22, 1781. Spon: Parents.

Mary Magdalene, daughter of Jacob Bossart and Mary Magdalene, b. Dec. 28, 1780, bapt. April 23, 1781. Spon: Frederick Bayer and Catherine.

Elizabeth, daughter of Henry Diemel and Margaret, 4 wks. old, bapt. April 27. 1781. Spon: Parents.

Mary Magdalene, daughter of John Messemer and Maria Catherine, b. Feb. 3, 1781, bapt. May 3, 1781. Spon: Parents.

Henry, son of Jacob von der Schleis and Maria, b. April 26, 1781, bapt. May 6, 1781. Spon: Henry Haffener and Susan Barch.

Anna Barbara, daughter of Michael Kamper and Susanna, b. Feb. 8, 1781, bapt. May 9, 1781. Spon: John Wild and Anna Barbara.

Peter, son of Adam Durr and Catherine, b. April 23, 1781, bapt. May 13, 1781. Spon: Peter Weil and Catherine.

Maria Sophia, daughter of Henry Schmaltz and Margaret, b. April 16, 1781, bapt. May 13, 1781. Spon: Michael Schneider and Maria Sophia.

Sophia, daughter of Abraham Fuchs and Sophia, b. April 26, 1781, bapt. May 13, 1781. Spon: Parents.

John Christian, son of Christian Fans and Christine, b. Feb. 16, 1781, bapt. May 19, 1781. Spon: John Conrad Steiger and Catherine.

Anna, daughter of Frederick Mangold and Barbara, b. April 27, 1781, bapt. May 20, 1781. Spon: Henry Ries and Elizabeth.

John Jacob, son of Peter Souder and Margaret, b. March 17, 1781, bapt. May 27, 1781. Spon: Jacob Binder and Magdalene.

Samuel, son of John Peiffer and Jane, b. Jan. 26, 1781, bapt. June 1, 1781. Spon: Parents.

Joseph, son of Jacob Schifferer and Maria Juliana, b. March 10, 1781, bapt. June 2, 1781. Spon: Parents.

William, son of Jacob Steinmetz and Rachel, b. May 8, 1781, bapt. June 3, 1781. Spon: Parents.

Anna, daughter of John Meyer and Anna, b. March 23, 1781, bapt. June 3, 1781. Spon: David Gilman and Anna.

Anna Maria, daughter of Walrab Simon and Elizabeth, b. May 29, 1781, bapt. June 4, 1781. Spon: Parents.

Elizabeth, daughter of Henry Schmidt and Margaret, b. May 3, 1781, bapt. June 10, 1781. Spon: Jacob Schee and Elizabeth Langpater.

Maria Margaret, daughter of William Stoll and Christine Elizabeth, b. June 11, 1781, bapt. June 17, 1781. Spon: Michael Kitz and Maria Margaret.

Anna Margaret, daughter of William Clethen and Margaret, b. May 29, 1781, bapt. June 17, 1781. Spon: Parents.

Abraham, son of Isaac Stats and Demar, b. April 1, 1780, bapt. June 23, 1781. Spon: Albertus Schillach and Maria.

John, son of John Grauel and Sarah, b. June 5, 1781, bapt. June 24, 1781. Spon: John Scheiw and Christine.

John, son of John Bom and Susanna, b. May 11, 1781, bapt. June 24, 1781. Spon: John Gertner and Maria Eliz. Bom.

John Henry, son of David Muller and Christine, b. June 30, 1781, bapt. July 4, 1781. Spon: Henry Henritzy and Catherine.

Robert, son of Robert Morris and Elizabeth, b. June 28, 1781, bapt. July 7, 1781. Spon: Parents.

John Michael, son of Michael Grensdorffer and Anna Maria, b. March 19, 1781, bapt. July 8, 1781. Spon: John Geuler and Barbara Geuler.

Catherine, daughter of Jacob Enck and Catherine, b. June 15, 1781, bapt. July 8, 1781. Spon: Catherie Bossels.

Elizabeth, daughter of Adam Altberger and Elizabeth, b. July 4, 1781, bapt. July 13, 1781. Spon: Parents.

Jacob, son of Nicholas Kayser and Elizabeth, b. June 24, 1781, bapt. July 15, 1781. Spon: John Esch and Margaret.

William, son of Gottfried Bockius and Eva, b. June 27, 1781, bapt. July 15, 1781. Spon: Parents.

Martin, son of John Jost Leibinger and Catherine, b. July 7, 1781, bapt. July 19, 1781. Spon: Martin Peisch and Magdalene.

Catherine, daughter of Frederick Froelig and Catherine, b. July 16, 1781, bapt. July 20, 1781. Spon: Urban Friebel and Barbara.

John, son of Henry Denich and Maria, b. June 15, 1781, bapt. July 22, 1781. Spon: John Denich and Babara Denich.

Margaret, daughter of Conrad Becker and Maria, b. June 29, 1781, bapt. July 22, 1781. Spon: Parents.

John George, son of George Gerler and Elizabeth, b. July 9, 1781, bapt. July 22, 1781. Spon: Martin Burckhard and Maria Volbach.

Anna Margaret, daughter of John Birckenbeil and Margaret, b. June 31, 1781, bapt. July 23, 1781. Spon: John Schaub and Elizabeth.

John, son of Jacob Wever and Elizabeth, b. June 30, 1781, bapt. July 26, 1781. Spon: Parents.

George, son of Jacob Braunig and Margaret, b. June 26, 1781, bapt. July 27, 1781. Spon: Parents.

Maria Margaret, daughter of Daniel Rippette and Dorothea, b. May

22, 1781, bapt. July 27, 1781. Spon: Parents.
Samuel, son of Jacob Kinsey and Catherine, b. May 20, 1781, bapt.
July 28, 1781. Spon: Michael Rummel and Maria Wack.
John George, son of Thomas Koch and Elizabeth, 9 mos. old, bapt.
July 29, 1781. Spon: George Berckenbeil and Parents.
Maria Margaret, daughter of Adam Beck and Susanna, b. June 28,
1781, bapt. July 29, 1781. Spon: Frederick Meyer and Maria
Margaret.
John, son of Conrad Keller and Elizabeth, b. July 24, 1781, bapt.
Aug. 1, 1781. Spon: John Fruby and Elizabeth.
Elizabeth, daughter of Joseph Sockel and Susanna, b. May 31, 1781,
bapt. Aug. 19, 1781. Spon: Parents.
John, son of John Ecky and Lucretia, b. Aug. 16, 1781, bapt. Aug.
19, 1781. Spon: John Bigoney and Catherine.
Elizabeth, daughter of Peter Knell and Christine, b. Aug. 30, 1780,
bapt. Aug. 21, 1781. Spon: Parents.
Susanna, daughter of Kilian Rup and Catherine, b. Nov. 29, 1780,
bapt. Aug. 26, 1781. Spon: Michael Kamper and Susanna.
Daniel, son of Daniel Baechtle and Margaret, b. Aug. 13, 1781,
bapt. Aug. 26, 1781. Spon: Catherine Stern.
John Adam, son of Jacob Diamond and Elizabeth, b. Aug. 11, 1781,
bapt. Aug. 26, 1781. Spon: John Adam Rausch and Anna Maria.
Margaret, daughter of Matthias Fallies and Catherine, b. Aug. 13,
1781, bapt. Sept. 2, 1781. Spon: Charles Stoltz and Margaret.
Elizabeth, daughter of William Will and Anna, b. Aug. 17, 1781,
bapt. Sept. 2,1781. Spon: Parents and Eliz. Lawersweiler.
Anna Charlotte, daughter of Philip Will and Charlotte, b. Aug. 13,
1781, bapt. Sept. 4, 1781. Spon: Christian Schneider and Anna
Gottlieb.
John, son of John Kerschener and Catherine, b. July 27, 1781, bapt.
Sept. 4, 1781. Spon: Frederick Boyer and Catherine.
Anna Margaret, daughter of Peter Schreiber and Mary Magdalene, b.
Aug. 26, 1781, bapt. Sept. 9, 1781. Spon: George Lies and Anna
Margaret.
John Adam, son of John George Zahner and Catherine, b. Sept. 9,
1781, bapt. Sept. 16, 1781. Spon: John Adam Lehr and Maria
Lehr.
Maria Margaret, daughter of Peter Weyel and Catherine, b. Aug. 30,
1781, bapt. Sept. 16, 1781. Spon: Jacob Schwefel and Maria
Margaret.
Mary Magdalene, daughter of John Tauenheim and Mary Magdalene, 3
mos. old, bapt. Sept. 19, 1781. Spon: Parents and Maria Soreck.
Michael, son of Michael Vaerner and Maria, b. Sept. 9, 1781, bapt.
Sept. 23, 1781. Spon: Jacob Bockenmeyer and Catherine.
Christopher Abraham, son of William Busch and Elizabeth, b. Sept.
7, 1781, bapt. Sept. 23, 1781. Spon: Christopher Abraham
Ludwich and wife.
Henry, son of Henry Frick and Barbara, b. Sept. 8, 1781, bapt.
Sept. 30, 1781. Spon: Adam Schaeffer and Dorothea.
Sarah, daughter of Philip Wirth and Dorothea, b. Sept. 19, 1781,
bapt. Sept. 30, 1781. Spon: Gottfried Penther and Sarah Wirth.
Christine, daughter of Cyriacus Wagener and Elizabeth, b. Sept. 10,
1781, bapt. Sept. 30, 1781. Spon: Fred Wing and Christine.
John, son of William Fau and Barbara, 7 wks. old, bapt. Oct. 2,
1781. Spon: John Fau and Maria Elizabeth.

Elizabeth Catherine, daughter of George Wenzel and Joanna Charlotte, b. June 16, 1780, bapt. Sept. 7, 1781. Spon: Anthony Armbruster and Maria Elizabeth.

Anna Margaret, daughter of John Meyer and Rosina, b. Sept. 4, 1781, bapt. Sept. 7, 1781. Spon: Henry Peter Grimm and Anna Margr. Meyer.

Anna Esther, daughter of David Wisar and Maria, b. Aug. 27, 1781, bapt. Sept. 8, 1781. Spon: John Wucherer and mother of child.

Jacob, son of Charles Kuper and Maria, b. Sept. 30, 1781, bapt. Oct. 14, 1781. Spon: Parents.

Jacob, son of Jonas Plesch and Christine, b. Sept. 22, 1781, bapt. Oct. 14, 1781. Spon: ----.

Esther, daughter of Matthias Kuley and Hannah, b. Sept. 26, 1781, bapt. Oct. 23, 1781. Spon: Parents.

Jesse, son of Conrad Gilbert and Maria, b. Sept. 30, 1767, bapt. Oct. 24, 1781. Spon: Valentine Ulrich.

Anna, daughter of Conrad Gilbert and Maria, b. Dec. 11, 1770, bapt. Oct. 24, 1781. Spon: Anna Catherine Bischoffberger.

John Michael, son of Michael Schnyder and Sophia, b. Sept. 19, 1781, bapt. Oct. 28, 1781. Spon: Parents.

Elizabeth, daughter of Simon Schuchert and Barbara, b. Oct. 4, 1781, bapt. Oct. 28, 1781. Spon: Parents.

Nancy, daughter of Henry Berry and Rachel, b. Oct. 14, 1781, bapt. Oct. 28, 1781. Spon: Alexander Berry and China.

John, son of John Halberstadt and Catherine, b. Oct. 10, 1781, bapt. Oct. 30, 1781. Spon: Parents.

Simon, son of John Cooly and Catherine, b. Oct. 28, 1781, bapt. Nov. 4, 1781. Spon: Simon Schellenberger and Dorothea.

Anna, daughter of Herman Janston and wife, bapt. Nov. 4, 1781. Spon: William Will and Anna.

Anthony, son of Conrad Hinckel and Barbara, b. Nov. 4, 1781, bapt. Nov. 11, 1781. Spon: Anthony Unbereit and Louisa.

Frederick, son of Adam Lange and Catherine, b. Oct. 31, 1781, bapt. Nov. 11, 1781. Spon: Frederick Winter and wife.

Anna Maria, daughter of Nicholas Zessinger and Anna Catherine, b. Nov. 18, 1781, bapt. Nov. 22, 1781. Spon: Adam Lotz and Anna Maria.

John, son of Henry Lies and Maria Elizabeth, b. Nov. 14, 1781, bapt. Nov. 25, 1781. Spon: John Lehr and Catherine.

Hannah, daughter of Andrew Wever and Eva, b. Oct. 28, 1781, bapt. Nov. 25, 1781. Spon: John Wichhard and Anna.

Philip, son of Gabriel Cascha and Magdalene, b. Oct. 30, 1781, bapt. Nov. 25, 1781. Spon: Philip Alberger and Margr. Magdalene.

Maria Elizabeth, daughter of Anthony Liebeck and Elizabeth, b. Nov. 1, 1781, bapt. Nov. 26, 1781. Spon: Parents.

Maria, daughter of Henry Pfeiffer and Christine, b. Nov. 18, 1781, bapt. Nov. 27, 1781. Spon: Daniel Dres and Maria.

Bernard, son of John Felin and Anna Maria, b. Nov. 22, 1781, bapt. Dec. 3, 1781. Spon: Bernard Bruchholtz and Catherine.

Samuel, son of Christopher Madery and Elizabeth, b. Nov. 15, 1781, bapt. Dec. 9, 1781. Spon: Jacob Naeff and Anna.

Peter, son of Peter Becker and Mary Magdalene, 7 wks. old, bapt. Dec. 12, 1781. Spon: Parents and Elizabeth Brown.

John, son of Frederick Hein and Charlotte, 4 wks. 7 d. old, bapt.

Dec. 17, 1781. Spon: John Bronner and Catherine.
Jacob Weiny, son of Jacob Lawersweiler and Elizabeth, b. Nov. 5, 1781, bapt. Dec. 17, 1781. Spon: Parents.
Philippina Margaret, daughter of John Mueller and Maria, b. Oct. 20, 1781, bapt. Dec. 20, 1781. Spon: Peter Rose and Pale (Polly) Cup.
Samuel, son of John Fans and Margaret, b. April 19, 1781, bapt. Dec. 21, 1781. Spon: Parents.
Andrew, son of George Eisenring and Elizabeth, b. Dec. 7, 1781, bapt. Dec. 23, 1781. Spon: Andrew Lex and Maria.
John, son of Thomas Wind and Hannah, b. Nov. 20, 1781, bapt. Dec. 23, 1781. Spon: John Atkins and Eliza Zweifel.
John Peter, son of Valentine Brown and Regina, b. Dec. 16, 1781 bapt. Dec. 30, 1781. Spon: Peter Schreiber and Magdalene.
Matthew, son of Matthew Krehmer and Susanna, b. Dec. 18, 1781, bapt. Dec. 30, 1781. Spon: ----.
John Daniel, son of Daniel Kehr and Mary Magdalene, b. Dec. 16, 1781, bapt. Jan. 6, 1782. Spon: Parents.
John, son of Peter Bardt and Magdalene, b. Dec. 9, 1781, bapt. Jan. 6, 1782. Spon: John Christopher Assmus and Catherine.
Daniel, son of Philip Odenheimer and Catherine, b. Dec. 23, 1781, bapt. Jan. 6, 1782. Spon: Jacob Uttre and Mary Magdalene.
George, son of John Diehl and Catherine, b. Dec. 29, 1781, bapt. Jan. 13, 1782. Spon: George Mouckty and Elizabeth.
George, son of Henry Ries and Elizabeth, b. Dec. 7, 1781, bapt. Jan. 13, 1782. Spon: Gottfried Zeppernick and Parents.
Maria Elizabeth, daughter of John Stetzer and Margaret Elizabeth, b. Dec. 14, 1781, bapt. Jan. 13, 1782. Spon: Ludwig Hess and Catherine.
John George, son of Conrad Spangenberg and Elizabeth, b. Jan. 7, 1782, bapt. Jan. 20, 1782. Spon: John George Umbach and Elizabeth.
Elizabeth, daughter of Matthias Lamahr and Anna, b. Dec. 27, 1781, bapt. Jan. 20, 1782. Spon: Francis Jay and Elizabeth.
John, son of Thomas Fill and Catherine, b. Oct. 13, 1781, bapt. Jan. 28, 1782. Spon: Maria Albert.
Charles Lewis, son of John Baker and Elizabeth, b. Jan. 9, 1782, bapt. Jan. 29, 1782. Spon: Parents.
Elizabeth Catherine, daughter of John Schmidt and Margaret, b. Jan. 24, 1782, bapt. Jan. 30, 1782. Spon: John Beck and Catherine.
Charles, son of Casimir Dellwich and Maria, b. Jan. 20, 1782, bapt. Jan. 31, 1782. Spon: Charles Seitz and wife.
John, son of Peter Schnyder and Catherine, b. Jan. 29, 1782, bapt. Feb. 10, 1782. Spon: John Lorentz and Catherine.
Jacobus, son of Henry Roskes and Maria, b. Nov. 6, 1781, bapt. Feb. 11, 1782. Spon: Peter Roos and Sarah Elizabeth.
Maria Dorothea, daughter of Bernard Muth and Anna Elizabeth, b. Dec. 29, 1781, bapt. Feb. 12, 1782. Spon: Maria Dorothea Krampf.
William Wendel, son of Wendel Zerban and Catherine, b. Feb. 4, 1782, bapt. Feb. 14, 1782. Spon: Mrs. Becker and Parents.
Maria Veronica, daughter of John Fans and Catherine, b. Jan. 25, 1782, bapt. Feb. 18, 1782. Spon: George Cress and Veronica Fans.
John Jacob, son of John Jacob Koch and wife, b. Feb. 9, 1782, bapt.

Feb. 20, 1782. Spon: Parents.

Frederick, son of William Miller and Margaret, b. Jan. 19, 1782, bapt. Feb. 24, 1782. Spon: Frederick Wieng and Christine.

John, son of Christopher Penter and Catherine, b. Feb. 19, 1782, bapt. Feb. 26, 1782. Spon: Parents.

Peter, son of Christ. Penter and Catherine, 2 yrs., 8 mos. old, bapt. Feb. 26, 1782. Spon: Daniel Schutz and his mother.

Andrew, son of Jacob Weithman and Elizabeth, b. Jan. 20, 1782, bapt. March 3, 1782. Spon: Andrew Bartsch and Anna Maria.

Maria Catherine, daughter of Samuel Stern and Catherine, b. Feb. 21, 1782, bapt. March 3, 1782. Spon: Christopher Fot and Catherine.

Elizabeth, daughter of Adam Clampfer and Maria, b. Dec. 27, 1779, bapt. March 3, 1782. Spon: William Will and Anna Maria.

Sarah Goodwin, daughter of Adam Clampfer and Maria, b. Feb. 7, 1782, bapt. March 3, 1782. Spon: William Kerlin and Elizabeth Clampfer.

Anna, daughter of John Andrea and Maria, b. Feb. 26, 1782, bapt. March 6, 1782. Spon: Parents.

John, son of Bernard Simon and Christine, b. Feb. 4, 1782, bapt. March 10, 1782. Spon: Parents.

Mary Magdalene, daughter of Michael Rummel and Magdalene, b. Jan. 29, 1782, bapt. March 10, 1782. Spon: Nicholas Rumel and Maria Mason.

Susanna, daughter of Henry Strup and Susanna, b. Feb. 12, 1782, bapt. March 13,1782. Spon: Parents.

John William, son of Philip Zeller and Margaret, b. Feb. 28, 1782, bapt. March 14, 1782. Spon: Parents.

Daniel, son of Adam Stricker and Barbara, b. March 5, 1782, bapt. March 24, 1782. Spon: Daniel Sutter and Anna.

Susanna, daughter of Michael Lehnhard and Anna Catherine, b. Feb. 28, 1782, bapt. March 24, 1782. Spon: John Ried and Susanna.

Jacob Wever, son of Philip Maus and Veronica, b. Jan. 31, 1782, bapt. March 24, 1782. Spon: Parents.

Anna, daughter of Frederick Maus and Elizabeth, b. Nov. 29, 1781, bapt. March 24, 1782. Spon: Parents.

Benjamin, son of John Pus and Anna, b. Dec. 15, 1780, bapt. March 28, 1782. Spon: Jacob Keller and Elizabeth.

Anna Maria, daughter of George Helberger and Anna Maria, b. Nov. 16, 1781, bapt. March 29, 1782. Spon: Parents.

Ernst, son of Ernst Ziegeler and Catherine, b. Jan. 12, 1782, bapt. March 29, 1782. Spon: Parents.

Matthew, son of Ludwig Krauer and Margaret, b. March 1, 1782, bapt. March 30, 1782. Spon: Matthew Gilbert and Christine.

Anna Maria, daughter of Matthias Feiering and Anna Christine, 2 wks. old, bapt. April 1, 1782. Spon: Matthias Edel and Anna Maria Schmith.

John, son of Jacob Nannetter and Anna Catherine, b. March 29, 1782, bapt. April 4, 1782. Spon: Peter Nannetter and Elizabeth.

John, son of Gabriel Kehr and Mary Magdalene, b. March 15, 1782, bapt. April 7, 1782. Spon: John George Bastian and Maria.

Margaret Sarah, daughter of George Bensel and Christine Kern, 21 wks. old, bapt. April 8, 1782. Spon: Margaret Berckemeyer.

James, son of Robert Manle(y) and Catherine, b. April 5, 1782, bapt. April 16, 1782. Spon: Parents.

John Peter, son of George Lies and Anna Margaret, b. April 8, 1782, bapt. April 21, 1782. Spon: Peter Schreiber and Mary Magdalene.

Maria Margaret, daughter of Gabriel Gron and Catherine, b. March 11, 1782, bapt. April 21, 1782. Spon: Maria Margaret Gron.

Maria, daughter of Andrew Ries and Margaret, b. Feb. 21, 1782, bapt. April 21, 1782. Spon: Catherine Reinert.

Sarah, daughter of Jacob Weithman and Catharine, b. April 11, 1779, bapt. Apr 21, 1782. Spon: Parents and Elizabeth Schnyder.

Thomas, son of Jacob Weithman and Catharine, b. Dec. 16, 1781, bapt. April 21, 1782. Spon: Parents and Elizabeth Schnyder.

Jacob, son of John Klages and Rosina, b. March 26, ----, bapt. April 21, 1782. Spon: Parents.

Elizabeth, daughter of Fabian Hemerle and Catherine, b. April 12, 1782, bapt. May 5, 1782. Spon: Stephen Riegeler and Elizabeth.

Anna, daughter of Henry Ritter and Anna Maria, b. April 14, 1782, bapt. May 5, 1782. Spon: Parents.

John Conrad, son of Conrad Schmith and Anna Maria, b. Sept. 31, 1781, bapt. May 10, 1782. Spon: Parents.

George Washington, son of William Saunders and Maria, b. Aug. 24, 1781, bapt. May 12, 1782. Spon: Valentine Schmidt and Elizabeth Rup.

Anna Catherine, daughter of John Eckstein and Anna Catherine, b. May 3, 1782, bapt. May 12, 1782. Spon: John Eckstein and Anna Catherine.

Maria, daughter of John Kuhn and Catherine, b. Feb. 14, 1782, bapt. May 12, 1782. Spon: Peter Abraham and Magdalene.

Maria, daughter of Jacob Cliver and Maria, b. May 15, 1782, bapt. May 15, 1782. Spon: Conrad Ord and Catherine.

Frederick, son of Anthony Berckenbeul and Barbara, b. April 5, 1782, bapt. May 15, 1782. Spon: Frederick Tischong and Margaret.

John, son of Frederick Schneider and Barbara, b. April 27, 1782, bapt. May 17, 1782. Spon: Parents and Dinah Funck.

John, son of John Scheiwe and Christine, b. May 12, 1782, bapt. May 19, 1782. Spon: John Gunckel and Christine.

Elizabeth, daughter of William Haberstick and Maria, b. May 2, 1782, bapt. May 20, 1782. Spon: Parents.

John Andrew, son of George Mercker and Margaret, b. April 28, 1782, bapt. May 20, 1782. Spon: Parents.

Catherine, daughter of George Dies and Eva, b. Dec. 8, 1781, bapt. May 23, 1782. Spon: Henry Meyer and Catherine.

Salome, daughter of John Widerstein and Elizabeth, b. May 12, 1782, bapt. May 26, 1782. Spon: Parents.

George Henry, son of George Henry Schnyder and Elizabeth, b. May 17, 1782, bapt. June 9, 1782. Spon: Joseph Jarsky and Magdalene.

George, son of Lorentz Miller and Catherine, 3 yrs. old, bapt. June 9, 1782. Spon: Peter Pfeiffer and Maria and Geo. Heiberger.

John, son of Lorentz Miller and Catherine, 1 yr. old, bapt. June 9, 1782. Spon: Peter Pfeiffer and Maria and Geo. Heiberger.

Anna, daughter of Henry Fichter and Magdalene, 5 wks. old, bapt. June 16, 1782. Spon: David Gilbert and Anna.

Margaret, daughter of John Gerrith and Margaret, b. June 3, 1782, bapt. June 18, 1782. Spon: Adam Gerrith and Christine.

Maria, daughter of William Schmeile and Maria, b. Jan. 8, 1782, bapt. June 18, 1782. Spon: Adam Gerrith and Christine.

Joanna Sophia, daughter of David Rischong and Catherine, b. June 8, 1782, bapt. June 23, 1782. Spon: William Kahmer and Joanna Sophia Kopia.

Adam, son of Jacob Bischoffberger and Catherine, b. May 29, 1782, bapt. June 23, 1782. Spon: Adam Graff and Eva Catherine.

Catherine, daughter of Peter Hohl and Catherine, b. June 15, 1782, bapt. June 30, 1782. Spon: John Hohl and Catharine Bottem.

Maria, daughter of Henry Wever and Hannah, b. April 20, 1782, bapt. June 30, 1782. Spon: Parents.

Joseph, son of Henry Funck and Barbara, b. Aug. 20, 1781, bapt. June 30, 1782. Spon: Parents.

Maria, daughter of Joseph Haller and Susanna, b. June 3, 1781, bapt. June 30, 1782. Spon: Parents.

Maria Catherine, daughter of John George Schwartz and Barbara, b. June 29, 1782, bapt. July 7, 1782. Spon: John Andrew Messerschmidt and Catherine.

Jacob, son of Jacob Schielle and Elizabeth, b. June 21, 1782, bapt. July 7, 1782. Spon: Parents.

Maria Barbara, daughter of Christian Heinig and Maria Barbara, b. May 3, 1782, bapt. July 7, 1782. Spon: Henry Emig and Dorothea.

John, son of Franciscus Graff and Catherine, b. Aug. 5, 1782, bapt. July 8, 1782. Spon: ----.

Christian, son of Conrad Schoeller and Maria Elizabeth, b. June 25, 1782, bapt. July 13, 1782. Spon: Peter Jung and Magdalene.

Maria Catherine, daughter of Conrad Schoeller and Maria Elizabeth, b. June 25, 1782, bapt. July 13, 1782. Spon: Peter Jung and Magdalene.

John George, son of Jacob Finck and Maria Margaret, b. June 20, 1782, bapt. July 14 ,1782. Spon: John Geo. Mounty and Eva Margaret.

George, son of George Wirth and Salome, 11 yrs. old, bapt. July 14, 1782. Spon: George Hoffman and Rosina Fenemmen.

Elizabeth, daughter of John Braun and Abia, b. June 20, 1782, bapt. July 21, 1782. Spon: Jacob Diamont and Elizabeth.

Maria, daughter of Adam Brunner and Maria, b. July 19, 1782, bapt. July 28, 1782. Spon: John Charter and Maria.

Benjamin, son of Jacob Bayer and Elizabeth, 10 mos. old, bapt. July 31, 1782. Spon: Parents.

Catherine, daughter of Michael Gunckel and Catherine, b. July 24, 1782, bapt. July 31, 1782. Spon: Parents.

John, son of Christopher Huth and Elizabeth, 10 wks. old, bapt. Aug. 1, 1782. Spon: Parents.

Conrad, son of Abraham Koehler and Elizabeth, b. July 27, 1782, bapt. Aug. 4, 1782. Spon: Conrad Hester and Eleonora Catherine.

Maria Veronica, daughter of George Gilfert and Anna, b. July 9, 1782, bapt. Aug. 5, 1782. Spon: Parents and Maria Veronica Fans.

Benjamin, son of Joseph Gaetz and Maria, 1 yr. old, bapt. Aug. 10, 1782. Spon: John Heiss and Anna Margr. Sincer.

Christopher, son of George Degenhardt and Wilhelmina, b. July 29, 1782, bapt. Aug. 11, 1782. Spon: Christopher Jutte and Catherine.

Adam, son of William Lohman and Veronica, b. July 27, 1782, bapt. Aug. 1, 1782. Spon: Parents.

Christine, daughter of George Durr and Catherine, b. July 26, 1782, bapt. Aug. 18, 1782. Spon: John Geo. Seyferheld and Christ. Elizabeth.

Jacob, son of George Jentzer and Catherine, b. June 4, 1782, bapt. Aug. 18, 1782. Spon: Jacob Theis and Dorothea.

Ludwig, son of Joseph Bitting and Catherine, b. July 28, 1782 bapt. Aug. 18, 1782. Spon: Ludwig Bitting and Maria.

Henry, son of Michael Miltenberger and Elizabeth, b. Aug. 10, 1782, bapt. Aug. 25, 1782. Spon: Matthias Poth and Veronica.

William, son of John McNehr and Elizabeth, b. Aug. 2, 1782, bapt. Aug. 25, 1782. Spon: Parents.

Maria Elizabeth, daughter of John Kirchner and Magdalene, b. June 1, 1782, bapt. Aug. 29, 1782. Spon: Maria Barbara Othsnerni.

Elizabeth, daughter of Jacob Hempelman and Elizabeth, b. Aug. 15, 1782, bapt. Aug. 29, 1782. Spon: Philip Burck and Elizabeth.

Maria Christine, daughter of Jacob Latsch and Christine, b. Aug. 30, 1782, bapt. Aug. 30, 1782. Spon: Casper Klockner and Susanna.

Salome, daughter of Gottfried Gobeler and Catherine, b. Aug. 6, 1782, bapt. Sept. 3, 1782. Spon: Parents.

George, son of Samuel Russ and Christine, b. Dec. 4, 1780, bapt. Sept. 2, 1782. Spon: Henry Gilbert and Maria Strehley.

Susanna, daughter of Samuel Russ and Christine, b. July 31, 1782, bapt. Sept. 2, 1782. Spon: Michael Camper and Susanna.

Elizabeth, daughter of John Pister and Barbara, 8 mos. old, bapt. Sept. 3, 1782. Spon: Parents.

John George, son of John Pister and Rebecca, b. July 14, 1782, bapt. Sept. 3, 1782. Spon: Parents.

Adam, son of Christian Wigand and Elizabeth, b. Sept. 5, 1782, bapt. Sept. 7, 1782. Spon: Adam Wagener and Margaret.

Catherine, daughter of Gottfried Muennich and Veronica, b. Aug. 14, 1782, bapt. Sept. 8, 1782. Spon: Gabriel Gron and Catherine.

George, son of Wilrab Simon and Elizabeth, b. Aug. 7, 1782, bapt. Sept. 8, 1782. Spon: Parents.

George Henry, son of John Justus Roch and Susanna, b. Aug. 27, 1782, bapt. Sept. 10, 1782. Spon: George Dimpeler and Henry Dimpeler.

Joanna, daughter of Diederick Bayerle and Joanna, b. May 1, 1782, bapt. Sept. 12, 1782. Spon: Wilhelmina Nosser.

Sabina, daughter of George Klein and Eva Maria Folck, 7 wks. old, bapt. Sept. 13, 1782. Spon: Valentine Gaul and Sabina.

Maria Elizabeth, daughter of Martin Karsbach and Mary Magdalene, b. Aug. 18, 1782, bapt. Sept. 15, 1782. Spon: John Mirreth and Mary Magdalene.

Daniel, son of Valentine Gaul and Sabina, b. Aug. 26, 1782, bapt. Sept. 15, 1782. Spon: Daniel Berckemeyer and Margaret.

John Frederick, son of John Frederick Froelig and Catherine, b. Sept. 7, 1782, bapt. Sept. 15, 1782. Spon: Urbanus Friebele and Maria Barbara.

Jacob, son of George Fies an Dorothea, b. Sept. 8, 1782, bapt. Sept. 15, 1782. Spon: Jacob Schubbarth and Anna Steuerwald.

Margaret, daughter of Christian Hahn and Hannah, b. Aug. 29, 1782, bapt. Sept. 22, 1782. Spon: Parents and Elizabeth Hahn.

Margaret, daughter of Henry Knaus and Elizabeth, b. July 7, 1782, bapt. Sept. 22, 1782. Spon: Jacob von Ried and Margaret.

Susanna, daughter of John Williams and Maria, b. Sept. 7, 1782, bapt. Sept. 29, 1782. Spon: Andrew Oberdorff and Susan Schnyder.

Joseph, son of Adam Weiss and Elizabeth, 5 wks. old, bapt. Oct. 1, 1782. Spon: Parents.

Isaac, son of John Lauten and wife, 3 yrs. old, bapt. Oct. 1, 1782. Spon: Adam Weiss and Elizabeth.

John Jacob, son of John Jacob Keller and Elizabeth, b. Sept. 17, 1782, bapt. Oct. 6, 1782. Spon: John Lamsbach and Christine Himpel.

Christian August, son of Christian Aug. Kirchoff and Maria, b. Sept. 14, 1782, bapt. Oct. 6, 1782. Spon: Parents.

Sarah, daughter of John Jocum and Hannah, bapt. Jan. --, 1782, bapt. Oct. 6, 1782. Spon: Mother.

Susanna, daughter of John Stieffers and Catherine, b. May 1, 1781, bapt. Oct. 6, 1782. Spon: Parents.

Anna Margaret, daughter of Jacob Halter and Christine, b. Oct. 7, 1782, bapt. Oct. 12, 1782. Spon: Parents and Margaret Penther.

Martin, son of George Schultz and Susanna, b. Sept. 18, 1782, bapt. Oct. 13, 1782. Spon: Parents.

Sarah, daughter of William von Phul and Catherine, b. Sept. 15, 1782, bapt. Oct. 13, 1782. Spon: Parents.

George, son of William von Phul and Catherine, b. Nov. 3, 1776, bapt. Nov. 5, 1782. Spon: George Graff.

Catherine, daughter of William von Phul and Catherine, b. Oct. 6, 178, bapt. Oct. 11, 1782. Spon: Mrs. Graff.

William, son of William von Phul and Catherine, b. Aug. 12, 1780, bapt. Aug. 24, 1780. Spon: Parents.

Catherine, daughter of Frederick Boyer and Catherine, b. Sept. 30, 1782, bapt. Oct. 14, 1782. Spon: Catherine Schaaff.

Clara, daughter of John Wishart and Hannah, b. Sept. 26, 1782, bapt. Oct. 20, 1782. Spon: David Nies and Flora.

George, son of Michael Schnyder and Catherine, b. Oct. 7, 1782, bapt. Oct. 20, 1782. Spon: George Huber and Louisa.

Barbara, daughter of Isaiah Haselton and Sibylla, b. Oct. 2, 1782, bapt. Oct. 20, 1782. Spon: Michael Steinhauer and Barbara.

Albrecht, son of Albrecht Eschelman and Maria McPharrin, b. June 7, 1782, bapt. Oct. 20, 1782. Spon: Isaiah Haselton and Christine Jost.

Hannah, son of John son of Schmidt and Barbara, b. Aug. 30, 1782, bapt. Oct. 21, 1782. Spon: Parents.

Susanna, daughter of William Furrer and Susanna, b. April 29, 1781, bapt. Oct. 21, 1782. Spon: Conrad Schmidt and Anna Maria.

Michael, son of Michael Blanckenhan and Magdalene, b. Oct. 17, 1782, bapt. Oct. 27, 1782. Spon: Parents and Elizabeth Therry.

Adam, son of Paul Schlotman and Maria, b. Oct. 6, 1782, bapt. Nov. 3, 1782. Spon: Adam Login.

John Adam, son of John Jost Leibinger and Catherine, b. Oct. 23, 1782, bapt. Nov. 4, 1782. Spon: Parents.

George, son of John Lehr and Catherine, b. Oct. 20, 1782, bapt. Nov. 6, 1782. Spon: George Scheibeler and Margaret Berger.

Margaret, daughter of John Lehr and Catherine, b. Oct. 20, 1782, bapt. Nov. 6, 1782. Spon: George Scheibeler and Margaret Berger.

John Diehlman, son of John Diehlman Beck and Catherine, b. Oct. 16,

1782, bapt. Nov. 8, 1782. Spon: ----.
Elizabeth, daughter of Charles Cober and Maria, b. Nov. 8, 1782, bapt. Nov. 10, 1782. Spon: Parents and Eliz. Stillwagen.
John Christopher, son of William Muntz and Elizabeth, b. Sept. 19, 1782, bapt. Nov. 11, 1782. Spon: Parents.
Adam, son of George Hoffman and Anna Maria, b. Sept. 27, 1782, bapt. Oct. 15, 1782. Spon: Hannah Hill.
Jacob, son of John Michael Matzinger and Elizabeth, b. Oct. 23, 1782, bapt. Nov. 17, 1782. Spon: Jacob Rummel and Christine Albert.
William, son of Daniel Sutter and Anna Catherine, b. Oct. 26, 1782, bapt. Nov. 17, 1782. Spon: Parents.
Elizabeth, daughter of Peter Weyel and Catherine, b. Nov. 3, 1782, bapt. Nov. 17, 1782. Spon: Simon Moll and Elizabeth.
Catherine Elizabeth, daughter of Anthony von der Schleis and Elizabeth, b. Oct. 28, 1782, bapt. Nov. 17, 1782. Spon: Jacob Praetler and Catherine.
Susanna, daughter of Jacob Eschler and Susanna, b. Oct. 24, 1782, bapt. Nov. 17, 1782. Spon: Abraham Peter and Magdalene.
Esther, daughter of John Osman and Elizabeth, b. July 10, 1782, bapt. Nov. 17, 1782. Spon: Christopher Keller and Maria.
Christian, son of George Muller and Charlotte, 15 wks. old, bapt. Nov. 20, 1782. Spon: Christian Hoffman and Catherine Beck.
Elizabeth, daughter of Frederick Kreider and Veronica, b. Oct. 8, 1782, bapt. Nov. 24, 1782. Spon: George Flauer and Elizabeth.
John, son of John Adam Steiner and Elizabeth, b. Nov. 12, 1782, bapt. Nov. 24, 1782. Spon: John Eckstein and Anna Catherine.
Sarah, daughter of Peter Schmalwod and Catherine, b. Aug. 11, 1782, bapt. Nov. 26, 1782. Spon: Parents.
Anna Barbara, daughter of John Orefgen and Catherine Magdalene, b. Nov. 10, 1782, bapt. Dec. 1, 1782. Spon: Parents and Anna Haller.
Thomas, son of Philip Worn and Maria, b. Nov. 13, 1782, bapt. Dec. 1, 1782. Spon: Parents.
Daniel, son of Jacob Schneider and Hannah, b. Dec. 1, 1782, bapt. Dec. 8, 1782. Spon: Daniel Sutter and Anna Catherine.
Anna, daughter of Conrad Muenig and Eva Margaret, b. Nov. 22, 1782, bapt. Dec. 9, 1782. Spon: Parents.
Anna Maria, daughter of Henry Diemel and Margaret, b. Nov. 24, 1782, bapt. Dec. 12, 1782. Spon: Maria Schniff.
Elizabeth, daughter of Charles Jost and Christine, b. July 13, 1782, bapt. Dec. 11, 1782. Spon: Jacob Fries and Elizabeth.
William, son of John George Gerster and Margaret, 8 wks. old, bapt. Dec. 15, 1782. Spon: Valentine Hoffman and Catherine Heising.
Catherine Magdalene, daughter of John Henry Mueller and Anna, b. Nov. 15, 1782, bapt. Dec. 15, 1782. Spon: Frederick Froelig and Catherine.
George, son of Gottfried Hager and Anna Maria, b. Nov. 7, 1782, bapt. Dec. 15, 1782. Spon: George Reis and Maria Rambo.
Elizabeth, daughter of Andrew Mercker and Catherine, 8 d. old, bapt. Dec. 17, 1782. Spon: John Christopher Schultz and Eliz.
Anna Margaret, daughter of Peter Becker and Elizabeth, b. Dec. 9, 1782, bapt. Dec. 22, 1782. Spon: Philip Haffener and Anna Margaret.
Peter, son of Christopher Meinung and Margaret, b. Dec. 6, 1782,

bapt. Dec. 22, 1782. Spon: Peter Graff and Catherine.
Christian, son of Jacob Zing and Catherine, b. Nov. 11, 1782, bapt.
Dec. 25, 1782. Spon: Christian Jung and Caroline.
John Adam, son of Bernard Schwenck and Margaret, b. Nov. 22, 1782,
bapt. Dec. 25, 1782. Spon: John Adam Seifferth and wife.
John, son of Jacob Sehler and Amelia, b. Nov. 24, 1782, bapt. Dec.
26, 1782. Spon: John Sehler and Catherine.
Sophia, a servant child, Jacob Sehler had child bapt., 12 mos. old,
bapt. Dec. 26, 1782. Spon: John Sehler and Catherine.
John, son of Philip Bockius and Hannah, b. Nov. 26,1782, bapt. Dec.
29, 1782. Spon: John Bockius and Barbara.
Elizabeth, daughter of Jacob Steinmetz and Rachel, b. Dec. 15,
1782, bapt. Jan. 1, 1783. Spon: Elizabeth Stillwagen.
Catherine Magdalene, daughter of John Fritz and Mary Magdalene, b.
Dec. 12, 1782, bapt. Jan. 1, 1783. Spon: Parents.
Catherine Frederica, daughter of David Stetzer and Elizabeth, b.
Dec. 25, 1782, bapt. Jan. 3, 1783. Spon: Adam Wagener and
Catherine.
Anna, daughter of Philip Stimmel and Anna, b. Dec. 1, 1782, bapt.
Jan. 5, 1783. Spon: Nicholas Stimmel and Elizabeth.
Rebecca, daughter of John Froelig and Christine, b. Dec. 26, 1782,
bapt. Jan. 4, 1783. Spon: Parents.
Thomas, son of Aaron Collins and Hannah, 2 yrs., 8 mos. old, bapt.
Jan. 4, 1783. Spon: John Frolig and Christine.
Magdalene, daughter of Christian Fans and Christine, b. Oct. 15,
1782, bapt. Jan. 5, 1783. Spon: Parents.
Philip, son of Michael Worn and Catherine, b. Dec. 29, 1782, bapt.
Jan. 12, 1782. Spon: Philip Haffener and Catherine.
Rebecca, daughter of Andrew Mueller and Apollonia, b. Dec. 30,
1782, bapt. Jan. 19, 1783. Spon: Parents.
Maria, daughter of Henry Huber and Maria, b. Jan. 6, 1783, bapt.
Jan. 19, 1783. Spon: Parents.
Margaret, daughter of George Schnyder and Catherine, b. Dec. 20,
1782, bapt. Jan. 30, 1783. Spon: Margaret Bigle.
Margaret, daughter of John Weber and Anna, b. Aug. 2, 1781, bapt.
Feb. 2, 1783. Spon: George Weber and Margaret Weber.
William, son of Michael Steiber and Magdalene, b. Dec. 19, 1782,
bapt. Feb. 2, 1783. Spon: William Schmidt and Elizabeth Wispen.
John Peter, son of Peter Schreiber and Mary Magdalene, b. Jan. 19,
1783, bapt. Feb. 2, 1783. Spon: Jacob Schwefel and Anna
Margaret.
John Frederick, son of George Borcken and Catherine, b. Jan. 18,
1783, bapt. Feb. 9, 1783. Spon: John Frederick Laudenbach and
Christine Bracklin.
Maria Elizabeth, daughter of Henry Stetzer and Maria, b. Jan. 20,
1783, bapt. Feb. 16, 1783. Spon: John Stetzer and Maria
Elizabeth.
Sibylla, daughter of Charles Seitz and Charlotte, b. Jan. 30, 1783,
bapt. Feb. 20, 1783. Spon: Jacob Uttre and Maria.
John George, son of John Peter Schaeff and Elizabeth, b. Feb. 17,
1783, bapt. Feb. 21, 1783. Spon: John George Schaeff and Anna
Elizabeth.
Peter, son of Conrad Gerhard and Elizabeth, b. Feb. 14, 1783, bapt.
Feb. 23, 1783. Spon: Peter Nannetter and Anna Elizabeth.
John George, son of Matthias Krehmer and Susanna, 3 wks. old, bapt.

Feb. 23, 1783. Spon: John George Krehmer and Nancy.
John Jacob, son of John Latsch and Margaret, b. Dec. 24, 1782,
bapt. Feb. 23, 1783. Spon: Jacob Latsch and Christine.
Philip, son of Michael Schumacher and Elizabeth, 4 wks. old, bapt.
Feb. 23, 1783. Spon: Philip Pfankuchen and Magdalene.
Harriet, daughter of William Molchon and Charlotte, b. Jan. 14,
1783, bapt. Feb. 25, 1783. Spon: William Banks and Sarah.
Elizabeth, daughter of John Edris and Christine, b. Feb. 5, 1783,
bapt. Feb. 26, 1783. Spon: Parents.
Elizabeth, daughter of Jacob Gideon and Elizabeth, b. Feb. 6, 1783,
bapt. March 2, 1783. Spon: Casper Britton and Elizabeth
Kreider.
John Frederick, son of Henry Denig and Maria, 4 wks. old, bapt.
March 2, 1783. Spon: Frederick Heineman and Maria.
Elizabeth, daughter of Philip Wirth and Dorothea, b. Dec. 17, 1782,
bapt. March 2, 1783. Spon: William Will and Elizabeth.
Hannah Eleonore, daughter of Jacob Schlemmer and Hannah, b. Jan.
30, 1783, bapt. March 2, 1783. Spon: Conrad Schlemmer and
Hannah Eleonore.
John George, son of George Bachoff and Sarah, b. Nov. 29, 1782,
bapt. March 4, 1783. Spon: John Geo. Sturmfels and Anna
Margaret.
John Adam, son of Christian Lewyer and Maria, b. Dec. 2, 1782,
bapt. March 9, 1783. Spon: John Adam Lap and Anna Catharine.
Sarah, daughter of Peter Walter and Charlotte, b. Feb. 12, 1783,
bapt. March 9, 1783. Spon: Parents.
Maria, daughter of Jacon Hargesheimer and Maria, b. Aug. 31, 1782,
bapt. March 9, 1783. Spon: Parents.
Elizabeth, daughter of John Reifschnyder and Anna Maria, b. March
1, 1783, bapt. March 16, 1783. Spon: Philip Borg and Elizabeth.
Sarah, daughter of Christopher Wilpert and Margaret, b. Nov. 14,
1782, bapt. March 16, 1783. Spon: Sarah Fans.
Anne Elizabeth, daughter of Peter Tischong and Susanna, b. Feb. 23,
1783, bapt. March 16, 1783. Spon: Christian Tischong and
Elizabeth Kreider.
Henry, son of Henry Berry and Rachel, b. Jan. 27, 1783, bapt. March
16, 1783. Spon: Alexander Berry and Jane.
Anna Margaret, daughter of Jacob Schuh and Catherine, b. ----,
bapt. March 23, 1783. Spon: Christopher Meiniger and Anna
Margaret.
John George, son of John Sauder and Catherine, 2 wks. old, bapt.
March 23, 1783. Spon: John Grauel and Sarah.
John, son of Christian Heis and Janne (Jeane), b. Feb. 16, 1782,
bapt. March 23, 1783. Spon: John Prahl and Catherine.
Anna Maria, daughter of John Meile and Catherine, b. Feb. 21, 1783,
bapt. March 23, 1783. Spon: Parents and Barbara Keiler.
John, son of Peter Edenborn and Elizabeth, b. March 19, 1783, bapt.
March 30, 1783. Spon: John Grauel and Sarah.
Maria Christine, daughter of William Nickels and Joanna, b. March
19, 1783, bapt. March 30, 1783. Spon: ----.
Maria Elizabeth, daughter of Nicholas Zessinger and Margaret, b.
March 30, 1783, bapt. April 6, 1783. Spon: Ernst Vellbach and
Maria Elizabeth.
Anna Catherine, daughter of Peter Lorje and Christine, b. March 23,
1783, bapt. April 6, 1783. Spon: Christian Alberger and Anna

Sophia Fries.

Anna Catherine, daughter of Jacob Meyle and Elizabeth, 6 wks. old, bapt. April 13, 1783. Spon: Fred. Meyle and Maria Keiler.

Ludwig, son of John Heinig and Charlotte, b. March 5, 1783, bapt. April 14, 1783. Spon: Paul Casper Britton and Ludwig Kreider.

Catherine, daughter of John Jacob Schifferer and Juliana, b. Jan. 23, 1783, bapt. April 19, 1783. Spon: Anna Maria Gerber.

John Henry, son of John Conrad Scholle and Anna Maria, b. Jan. 28, 1783, bapt. April 19, 1783. Spon: John Henry Kirch.

Elizabeth, daughter of George Loescher and Anna, b. March 24, 1783, bapt. April 20, 1783. Spon: George Loscher and Elizabeth Lehman.

Anna Maria, daughter of Jacob Burghard and Margr. Humphreys, b. Jan. 17, 1783, bapt. April 21, 1783. Spon: George Zeissiger and Maria.

Elizabeth, daughter of Henry Schmaltz and Margaret, b. March 31, 1783, bapt. April 22, 1783. Spon: Parents.

Anna Maria, daughter of John Diehl and Catherine, b. March 7, 1783, bapt. April 21, 1783. Spon: Parents.

Maria Clara, daughter of Peter Merckel and Anna Catherine, b. Feb. 27, 1783, bapt. April 21, 1783. Spon: John Gunckel and Maria Clara.

Elizabeth, daughter of ---- Pfau and Barbara, b. March 31, 1783, bapt. April 27, 1783. Spon: John Pfau and Elizabeth.

Maria Barbara, daughter of John Schmidt and Margaret, b. April 20, 1783, bapt. April 27, 1783. Spon: Uranus Friebel and Maria Barbara.

John, son of Henry Meyer and Charlotte, b. March 28, 1783, bapt. April 27, 1783. Spon: John Becker.

John, son of Edward Garden and Susanna, 16 mos. old, bapt. May 9, 1783. Spon: Nicholas Rummel and Margaret Witzel.

Maria, daughter of Gottfried Bockius and Eva, b. April 17, 1783, bapt. May 11, 1783. Spon: John Gottschalck and Maria Steinfurth.

Mary Magdalene, daughter of Henry Funck and Barbara, b. Dec. 23, 1783, bapt. May 11, 1783. Spon: Parents.

John Jacob, son of John Weber and Anna Christine, b. May 5, 1783, bapt. May 13, 1783. Spon: John Mich. Kinseler and Anna Elizabeth.

John Conrad, son of Conrad Schmidt and and Anna Maria, b. Oct. 22, 1783, bapt. May 18, 1783. Spon: Christine Lotz.

Anna Maria, daughter of Christopher Penther and Catherine, b. Feb. 1, 1783, bapt. May 18, 1783. Spon: Conrad Schmidt and Anna Maria.

Andrew, son of Ludwig Jung and Caroline, b. April 4 1783, bapt. May 18, 1783. Spon: Andrew Piehler and Elizabeth.

Anna Margaret, daughter of Jacob Diamond and Elizabeth, b. April 29, 1783, bapt. May 18, 1783. Spon: John Adam Pausen and Anna Margaret.

Ludwig, son of Conrad Rosch and Margaret, b. April 17, 1783, bapt. May 18, 1783. Spon: Ludwig Farmer and Margaret.

Martha, daughter of Jacob Staats and Rachel, b. Oct. 9, 1782, bapt. May 18, 1783. Spon: Albertus Schillack and Maria.

Elizabeth, daughter of Charles Ristein and Hannah, b. April 1, 1783, bapt. May 23, 1783. Spon: Fred. Gottschalck and

Elizabeth.
Elizabeth, daughter of Jacob Braunig and Margaret, b. May 3, 1783, bapt. May 29, 1783. Spon: Parents.
Elizabeth, daughter of Nicholas Keyser and Elizabeth, 3 wks. old, bapt. June 1, 1783. Spon: John Esch and Margaret.
John Frederick, son of Henry Heineman and Charlotte, b. May 14, 1783, bapt. June 1, 1783. Spon: Fred. Heineman and Catherine.
William, son of Isaac Mixer and Elizabeth, b. May 15, 1782, bapt. June 5, 1783. Spon: William Haberstich and Maria.
Frederick Jacob, son of Henry Schrub and Eva, b. May 25, 1783, bapt. June 8, 1783. Spon: Frederick Jacob Rapp and Elizabeth.
George, son of Adam Lehr and Rebecca, b. May 26, 1783, bapt. June 8, 1783. Spon: Frederick Schwartz and Abigail.
John Peter, son of Nicholas Riebel and Salome, b. May 16, 1783, bapt. June 8, 1783. Spon: John Peter Grim and Elizabeth.
Catherine Louisa, daughter of Ludwig Nicke and Maria, b. May 19, 1783, bapt. June 8, 1783. Spon: Philip Weissman and Catherine.
Andrew, son of Jacob von der Schleis and Maria, b. April 25, 1783, bapt. June 9, 1783. Spon: Andrew Bartsch and Maria.
Catherine, daughter of John Ecky and Lucretia, b. June 1, 1783, bapt. June 9, 1783. Spon: Parents and Catherine Bigonne.
John William, son of Jacob Kinsley and Catherine, b. Oct. 7, 1782, bapt. June 11, 1783. Spon: Parents and Elizabeth Wack.
John Henry, son of Graft Weiand and Christine, 2 wks. old, bapt. June 15, 1783. Spon: Henry Penner and Margaret.
Elizabeth, daughter of Michael Kohler and Anna, b. May 24, 1783, bapt. June 15, 1783. Spon: Parents and Anna Maria Handschuh.
Henry, son of Peter Paris and Veronica, b. June 1, 1783, bapt. June 15, 1783. Spon: Henry Fans and Veronica.
Sabina, daughter of Casper Graff and Maria Chamberlein, 6 mos. old, bapt. June 17, 1783. Spon: Maria Chamberlein.
William, son of Bernard Simon and Christine, b. May 2, 1783, bapt. June 20, 1783. Spon: Parents.
John, son of David Gilbert and Anna, b. June 1, 1783, bapt. June 22, 1783. Spon: John Mayer and Barbara.
Catherine, daughter of Conrad Froman and Margaret, b. June 11, 1783, bapt. June 22, 1783. Spon: Jacob Nannetter and Catherine.
George, son of Christian Khuck and Maria, b. June 12, 1783, bapt. June 24, 1783. Spon: Franciscus Zinse and Maria Roth.
Christine, son of John Belo and Margaret, b. May 31, 1783, bapt. June 25, 1783. Spon: Andrew Lap and Christine.
Maria, daughter of Peter Auner and Margaret, b. June 2, 1783, bapt. June 30, 1783. Spon: Parents.
Margaret, daughter of Jacob Ehringer and Anna, b. June 12, 1783, bapt. June 30, 1783. Spon: Daniel Biegle and Margaret.
William, son of William Proupert and Barbara, 4 wks. old, bapt. June 30, 1783. Spon: William Schmidt and Magd. Schneider.
William, son of Jacob Enck and Catherine, b. June 14, 1783, bapt. June 30, 1783. Spon: Parents and Elizabeth Lohman.
Elizabeth, daughter of Jacob Euler and Joanna, b. May 25, 1783, bapt. June 31, 1783. Spon: Frederick Boyer and Catherine.
Sarah, daughter of Peter Diehl and Elizabeth, b. May 26, 1783, bapt. July 6, 1783. Spon: Henry Poth and Elizabeth.
John, son of William Haberstich and Maria, b. June 18, 1783, bapt. July 6, 1783. Spon: Parents.

Peter, son of Peter Kupper and Catherine, b. May 23, 1783, bapt. July 6, 1783. Spon: Andrew Boshard and Catherine.

Daniel, son of John Huhn and Christine, b. July 9, 1783, bapt. July 9, 1783. Spon: Parents.

John, son of John Huhn and Christine, b. July 9, 1783, bapt. July 9, 1783. Spon: Parents.

John George, son of John George Meyer and Sarah, b. May 24, 1783, bapt. July 9, 1783. Spon: Parents.

Henry Peter, son of Peter Grimm and Elizabeth, 2 wks. old, bapt. July 13, 1783. Spon: Peter Ros and Sarah.

George, son of Henry Fuhr and Elizabeth, b. June 13, 1783, bapt. July 13, 1783. Spon: George Sheible and Marg. Schumacher.

Anna, daughter of Frederick Mangold and Barbara, b. July 14, 1783, bapt. July 14, 1783. Spon: Elizabeth Ries.

Joseph, daughter of William Miller and Susanna, b. June 19, 1783, bapt. July 14, 1783. Spon: Parents.

Margaret, daughter of John Flachs and Magdalene, b. July 16, 1783, bapt. July 16, 1783. Spon: ----.

William, son of John Flachs and Magdalene, b. July 16, 1783, bapt. July 16, 1783. Spon: ----.

Elizabeth, daughter of Adam Doer and Catherine, b. July 23, 1783, bapt. Aug. 2, 1783. Spon: Conrad Rohrman and Elizabeth.

William, son of Henry Diefendorfer and Anna, b. Sept. 24, 1783, bapt. Aug. 3, 1783. Spon: ----.

Samuel, son of John Lofsberry and Elizabeth, b. July 9,1783, bapt. Aug. 4, 1783. Spon: Catherine Becker.

Rebecca, daughter of Benjamin Pepper and Elizabeth, b. Dec. 6, 1782, bapt. Aug. 4, 1783. Spon: John Lofsberry and Elizabeth.

George Christian, son of John George Zeisinger and Anna Maria, b. July 10, 1783, bapt. Aug. 10, 1783. Spon: Christian Hera and Charlotte.

Anna Maria, daughter of John Berckenbeil and Anna Margaret, b. July 21, 1783, bapt. Aug. 10, 1783. Spon: John Schaub and Elizabeth.

Anna Catherine, daughter of Adam Lange and Catherine, 4 yrs. old, bapt. Aug. 10, 1783. Spon: Peter Sander and Maria Catherine.

George William, son of Matthias Gucker and Magdalene, b. July 19, 1783, bapt. Aug. 10, 1783. Spon: William Moore and Susanna.

Sarah, daughter of John Jost Weiand and Magdalene, b. Feb. 25, 1783, bapt. Aug. 12, 1783. Spon: Alexander Greenwood and wife.

Jacob, son of Henry Pfeiffer and Christine, b. Aug. 8, 1783, bapt. Aug. 17, 1783. Spon: Ernst Häuser and wife.

William, son of William Clampfer and Catherine, b. Aug. 2, 1783, bapt. Aug. 17, 1783. Spon: William Will and Anna and Maria Clampfer.

Elizabeth, daughter of Christian Schneider and Maria Elizabeth, b. July 14, 1783, bapt. Aug. 18, 1783. Spon: Parents.

Daniel, son of John Marks and Margaret, b. Dec. 7, 1782, bapt. Aug. 26, 1783. Spon: Daniel Stoy and Eliz. Stoy.

Anna, daughter of Peter Story and Elizabeth, b. Sept. 7, 1782, bapt. Aug. 26, 1783. Spon: Parents and Catherine Janssen.

Anna Magdalene, daughter of Jacob Schnyder and Maria Elizabeth, b. June 28, 1783, bapt. Sept. 3, 1783. Spon: Henry Emig and Dorothea.

Edward, son of Jacob Meyer and Elizabeth, 2 wks. old, bapt. Sept. 5, 1783. Spon: Parents.

Thomas, son of Andrew Braderick and Maria, b. Aug. 24, 1783, bapt. Sept. 7, 1783. Spon: Parents.

Anna Maria, daughter of Jacob Greiss and Margaret, b. Aug. 30, 1783, bapt. Sept. 7, 1783. Spon: George Moore and Elizabeth Umbach.

Joanna Maria Sophia, daughter of John Pfister and Anna Maria, b. Sept. 5, 1783, bapt. Sept. 14, 1783. Spon: John Christoph Wilman and wife.

Catherine, daughter of George Heiberger and Maria, b. Aug. 10, 1783, bapt. Sept. 17. 1783. Spon: Parents.

David, son of John Pfeiffer and Jane, 9 mos. old, bapt. Sept. 17, 1783. Spon: Parents.

John, son of John Lamsbach and Christine, b. Sept. 5, 1783, bapt. Sept. 21, 1783. Spon: Christian Himbell and Maria Christine.

Anna Catherine, daughter of John Diehl and Catherine, b. Sept. 9, 1783, bapt. Sept. 21, 1783. Spon: George Mouty and wife.

Jacob, son of Jacob Schieble and Elizabeth, b. Sept. 4, 1783, bapt. Sept. 28, 1783. Spon: Parents.

Adam, son of Adam Stricker and Barbara, b. Sept. 16, 1783, bapt. Sept. 28, 1783. Spon: Parents and Elizabeth Stricker.

Henry, son of Wernig Meyer and Catherine, b. Sept. 20, 1783, bapt. Sept. 29, 1783. Spon: Magdalene Meyer.

Frederick, son of Cyriacus Wagener and Elizabeth, b. Sept. 15, 1783, bapt. Oct. 9, 1783. Spon: Frederick Wing and Christine.

John, son of John George Schwartz and Barbara, b. Oct. 8, 1783, bapt. Oct. 10, 1783. Spon: John Andrew Messerschmidt and Cath.

Elizabeth, daughter of Daniel Diehl and Maria, b. Sept. 29, 1783, bapt. Oct. 12, 1783. Spon: Peter Diehl and Susanna.

William, son of Jacob Loscher and Maria, b. Sept. 1, 1783, bapt. Oct. 12, 1783. Spon: George Loscher and Maria.

Elizabeth, daughter of Daniel Baechtle and Margaret, b. Sept. 25, 1783, bapt. Oct. 12, 1783. Spon: Lorentz Foth and Elizabeth.

Philip De Haas, son of William Craig and Henrietta, b. Oct. 2, 1783, bapt. Oct. 12, 1783. Spon: John Philip de Haas and Eleonore.

Elizabeth, daughter of John Daum and Maria, b. Sept. 29, 1783, bapt. Oct. 19, 1783. Spon: Fred. Greiner and Elizabeth.

William, son of Philip Pfeill and Susanna, b. Sept. 28, 1783, bapt. Oct. 19, 1783. Spon: Francis Wm. Trönner and Chressaly.

Elizabeth, daughter of David Faggot and Catherine, b. Aug. 5, 1783, bapt. Oct. 24, 1783. Spon: Parents.

Elizabeth, daughter of Casimir Dellwich and Maria, b. Oct. 15, 1783, bapt. Oct. 30, 1783. Spon: Parents.

Juliana, daughter of William Stoll and Christine, b. Oct. 21, 1783, bapt. Nov. 2, 1783. Spon: Wm. Dinges and Juliana Dinges.

Jacob, son of Thomas Koch and Elizabeth, b. Oct. 16, 1783, bapt. Nov. 2, 1783. Spon: Jacob Becker and Catherine Weis.

Solomon, son of John Halberstad and Catherine, b. Sept. 23, 1783, bapt. Nov. 3, 1783. Spon: Charles Jost and Christine.

John, son of Conrad Hinckel and Barbara, b. Oct. 31, 1783, bapt. Nov. 9, 1783. Spon: John Will and wife.

Christine Margaret, daughter of John George Stephan and Catherine Barbara, b. May 12, 1783, bapt. Nov. 9, 1783. Spon: John George Syserhelt and Christine Elizabeth.

Joseph, son of Griffith Riffert and Sarah, b. Dec. 22, 1779, bapt.

Nov. 14, 1783. Spon: Parents.

Robert, son of Griffith Riffert and Sarah, b. March 20, 1783, bapt. Nov. 14, 1783. Spon: Parents.

William, son of Charles Cooper and Maria, b. Oct. 21, 1783, bapt. Nov. 16, 1783. Spon: William Geiss and wife.

Elizabeth, daughter of Henry Lies and Maria Elizabeth, b. Nov. 11, 1783, bapt. Nov. 20, 1783. Spon: Parents.

Esther, daughter of Christopher Madery and Elizabeth, b. Oct. 29, 1783, bapt. Nov. 24, 1783. Spon: Parents and Esther Naeff.

John, son of John Adam Was and Elizabeth, 11 mos. old, bapt. Nov. 30, 1783. Spon: John Schnyder and Eva.

Maria, daughter of John Stetzer and Elizabeth, b. Oct. 25, 1783, bapt. Nov. 30, 1783. Spon: Philip Stimmel and Anna.

Margaret, daughter of George Bauer and Catherine Theyers, b. Nov. 4, 1783, bapt. Dec. 11, 1783. Spon: Margaret Theyers.

John George, son of John Grauel and Sarah, b. Dec. 1, 1783, bapt. Dec. 14, 1783. Spon: John George Sturmfels and Margaret.

John, son of John Bom and Margaret, b. Nov. 9, 1783, bapt. Dec. 14, 1783. Spon: John Krauskopf and Magdalene.

Nicholas, son of Peter Hahn and Catherine, 1 yr., 10 mos. old, bapt. Dec. 18, 1783. Spon: Parents.

John Peter, son of Daniel Hains and Catherine, 6 wks. old, bapt. Dec. 21, 1783. Spon: Peter Diehl and Elizabeth.

Samuel, son of Matthias Keely and Hannah, b. Oct. 9, 1783, bapt. Dec. 22, 1783. Spon: Parents.

Jacob Gideon, son of ----, 29 yrs. old, bapt. Dec. 23, 1783.

Henry, son of Isaac Wetstein and Anna Margaret, b. June 4, 1781, bapt. Dec. 26, 1783. Spon: Jacob Strumbeck and Anna Maria.

Sarah, daughter of Isaac Wetstein and Anna Maria, b. Nov. 24, 1783, bapt. Dec. 26, 1783. Spon: John Rudolph and Sarah.

Samuel, son of John Klages and Rosina, b. Dec. 9, 1783, bapt. Dec. 26, 1783. Spon: Andrew Bauer and Barbara.

John, son of John Adam Meyer and Hannah, b. Dec. 9, 1783, bapt. Dec. 26, 1783. Spon: John Feyl and Catherine.

Jacob, son of John Mesemer and Catherine, b. Nov. 26, 1783, bapt. Dec. 27, 1783. Spon: Parents.

John Jacob, son of Christian Weyerich and Anna Catherine, b. Dec. 28, 1783, bapt. Jan. 1, 1784. Spon: John Jacob Schmidt and Catherine.

John, son of Lorentz Foth and Elizabeth, b. Dec. 22, 1783, bapt. Jan. 1, 1784. Spon: Christoph Foth and Catherine.

Philip Rudolph, son of Jacob Bonner and Elizabeth, 3 mos. old, bapt. Jan. 2, 1784. Spon: Parents.

Maria, daughter of Balthasar Richtstein and Christine, b. Dec. 9, 1783, bapt. Jan. 4, 1784. Spon: Charles Richtstein and Maria Rosch.

Anna Catherine, daughter of Frederick Boyer and Catherine, b. Dec. 20, 1783, bapt. Jan. 5, 1784. Spon: Daniel Sutter and Anna Catherine.

David, son of Bernard Cappeler and Elizabeth, b. Oct. 24, 1783, bapt. Jan. 8, 1784. Spon: David Gilbert and wife.

Sarah, daughter of Henry Ritter and Anna, b. Dec. 11, 1783, bapt. Jan. 11, 1784. Spon: Parents.

John Michael, son of John Gebbert and Rachel, b. Dec. 15, 1783, bapt. Jan. 11, 1784. Spon: Michael Muny and Margaret.

Margaret, daughter of Valentine Brown and Regina, b. Jan. 4, 1784, bapt. Jan. 18, 1784. Spon: Thomas Heimberger and Margaret.
John, son of Wm. McSparren and Christine, b. Sept. 8, 1783, bapt. Jan. 25, 1784. Spon: George Meyer and Susanna.
Christian George, son of Jacob Jung and Sarah, b. Dec. 25, 1783, bapt. Jan. 26, 1784. Spon: Christian Jung and Caroline.
Catherine Susanna, daughter of Jacob Jung and Sarah, b. Dec. 25, 1783, bapt. Jan. 26, 1784. Spon: George Klockener and Cath. Mesemer.
Hannah, daughter of John Froelig and Christine, b. Jan. 18, 1784, bapt. Jan. 27, 1784. Spon: Parents.
Margaret, daughter of John McNehr and Elizabeth, b. Jan. 14, 1784, bapt. Jan. 28, 1784. Spon: Frederick Wichman and Margaret.
John, son of Christian Klockner and Catherine, b. Nov. 31, 1783, bapt. Feb. 1, 1784. Spon: John Latsch and Margaret.
Catherine, daughter of Jacob Grub and Catherine, b. Nov. 25, 1783, bapt. Feb. 1, 1784. Spon: Parents.
Thomas Charles, son of Bernard Lawersweiler and Abigail, b. May 6, 1783, bapt. Jan. 31, 1784. Spon: Thomas Lawersweiler and Maria.
John Peter, son of John Heimer and Catherine, b. Jan. 19, 1784, bapt. Feb. 1, 1784. Spon: John Peter Heimer and Maria Johnssen.
Veronica, daughter of Charles Gemberlein and Margaret, b. Jan. 11, 1784, bapt. Feb. 1, 1784. Spon: Parents.
Magdalene, daughter of Philip Jung and Elizabeth, 8 wks. old, bapt. Feb. 3, 1784. Spon: Parents.
Maria Esther, daughter of John Adams and Catherine, b. Jan. 7, 1784, bapt. Feb. 6, 1784. Spon: John Williams and Maria.
Jacob, son of Jacob Bischoffberger and Elizabeth, b. Feb. 1, 1784, bapt. Feb. 7, 1784. Spon: Parents and Barbara.
Elizabeth, daughter of John George Zahn and Ann Catherine, b. Jan. 31, 1784, bapt. Feb. 8, 1784. Spon: Adam Brimer and Maria.
Jacob, son of George Schultz and Susanna, b. Dec. 26, 1783, bapt. Feb. 8, 1784. Spon: Jacob Schnyder and Elizabeth.
Maria, daughter of Jacob Rummel and Christine, b. Feb. 8, 1784, bapt. Feb. 13, 1784. Spon: Grandmother.
Simon, son of Daniel Schittel and Elizabeth, b. Jan. 25, 1784, bapt. Feb. 15, 1784. Spon: Parents.
John George, son of Christian Heiny and Mary Barbara, b. Dec. 6, 1783, bapt. Feb. 15, 1784. Spon: George Schmidt and Elizabeth.
Margaret, daughter of William Miller and Margaret, b. Jan. 16, 1784, bapt. March 21, 1784. Spon: ----.
George, son of George Jonas and Elizabeth, b. Jan. 24, 1784, bapt. Feb. 15, 1784. Spon: George Mercker and Margaret.
Catherine Elizabeth, daughter of Jacob Lutz and Rosina, b. Jan. 18, 1784, bapt. Feb. 15, 1784. Spon: Conrad Schlemmer and Catherine.
Elizabeth, daughter of George Schnyder and Catherine, b. Jan. 5, 1784, bapt. Feb. 16, 1784. Spon: Elizabeth Beckly.
Catherine, daughter of John Steltz and Elizabeth, b. Feb. 1, 1784, bapt. Feb. 22, 1784. Spon: John Fritz and Catherine.
Michael, son of Andrew Weber and Eva, b. Jan. 26, 1784, bapt. Feb. 29, 1784. Spon: Michael Seidel and Catherine.
Maria, daughter of Henry Fenner and Elizabeth, b. Jan. 31, 1784, bapt. March 7, 1784. Spon: Felix Fenner and Maria.
Charles, son of Isaiah Eschelman and Sibylla, b. Feb. 10, 1784,

bapt. March 7, 1784. Spon: Charles Jost and Christine.
Catherine, daughter of Philip Odenheimer and Catherine, b. Feb. 17,
1784, bapt. March 7, 1784. Spon: Philip Hall and Catherine.
Matthias, son of Matthias Hensem and Marg. Meyer, b. Feb. 1, 1784,
bapt. March 8, 1784. Spon: Mother.
John, son of John Boyert and Hannah, b. Feb. 29, 1784, bapt. March
14, 1784. Spon: Christopher Meininger and Margaret.
Susanna, daughter of William Will and Elizabeth, b. Feb. 24, 1784,
bapt. March 15, 1784. Spon: Parents.
Elizabeth, daughter of John Becker and Elizabeth, b. Feb. 29, 1784,
bapt. March 16, 1784. Spon: Parents.
Anna Catherine, daughter of George Degenhardt and Wilhelmina, 3
wks. old, bapt. March 21, 1784. Spon: Parents.
Maria, daughter of Christian Rossy and Catherine, b. Feb. 15, 1784,
bapt. March 21, 1784. Spon: John Bot and Elizabeth.
Margaret, daughter of William Miller and Margaret, b. Jan. 16,
1784, bapt. March 21, 1784. Spon: Elias Frey and Margaret.
Thomas Lawersweiler, son of John Annis and Anna, b. Feb. 17, 1784,
bapt. March 22, 1784. Spon: Thomas Lawersweiler and Mary.
George Washington Jones, son of ----, b. Dec. 22, 1781, bapt. March
22, 1784. Spon: Joseph Erwin and Mary Lawersweiler.
Maria, daughter of John Gerrith and Margaret, b. March 5, 1784,
bapt. March 25, 1784. Spon: Adam Gerrith and Christine.
John Jacob, son of Peter Weiel and Catherine, b. Feb. 16, 1784,
bapt. March 28, 1784. Spon: Jacob Schwefel and Maria Margaret.
John George, son of Simon Schuckhard and Barbara, b. Feb. 9, 1784,
bapt. March 28, 1784. Spon: Parents.
Andrew, son of George Echenring and Elizabeth, b. March 15, 1784,
bapt. April 4, 1784. Spon: Andrew Lex and Anna Maria.
William, son of John Reude and Margaret, b. March 12, 1784, bapt.
April 4, 1784. Spon: William Schmidt and Elizabeth Wispen.
Sarah, daughter of Ludwig Bitting and Elizabeth, b. May 10, 1767,
bapt. April 4, 1784. Spon: Parents.
Conradt, son of Christian Fans and Christine, b. Feb. 3, 1784,
bapt. April 6, 1784. Spon: Conrad Steiger and Catherine.
Philippina, daughter of ---- Miller and wife, 15 yrs., 4 mos. old,
bapt. April 8, 1784. Spon: Thomas Heimberger and Anna Margaret.
David Israel, son of Ezechiel Schawe and Jemima, b. Jan. 21, 1777,
bapt. April 9, 1784. Spon: David Gilbert and Hannah.
John, son of Joseph Gwinn and Elizabeth, 16 yrs. old, bapt. April
9, 1784. Spon: Lorentz Schwab and Maria.
John George, son of John Wilky and Ann Barbara, b. Feb. 1, 1784,
bapt. April 11, 1784. Spon: John George Kurtz and Anna
Margaret.
Anna, daughter of Adam Hess and Elizabeth, b. Feb. 7, 1784, bapt.
April 12, 1784. Spon: Nicholas Hess and Wilhelmina.
Maria Clara, daughter of Peter Merckle and Catherine, b. March 8,
1784, bapt. April 12, 1784. Spon: John Gunckel and Maria Clara.
Hannah, daughter of David Wisar and Anna Maria, b. Oct. 29, 1783,
bapt. April 12, 1784. Spon: Henry Huber and Parents.
John, son of Michael Leonhard and Anna, b. March 13, 1784, bapt.
April 18, 1784. Spon: John Ried and Anna Susanna.
Frederick, son of Henricus Roskes and Maria, b. Feb. 25, 1784,
bapt. April 19, 1784. Spon: Parents.
John William, son of George Lies and Margaret, b. April 9, 1784,

bapt. April 25, 1784. Spon: Parents.

Anna Elizabeth, daughter of Henry Oberman and Gratia, b. March 25, 1784, bapt. April 25, 1784. Spon: Philip Kehr and Anna Elizabeth.

Anna Margaret, daughter of Gottfried Gobeler and Catherine, b. March 28, 1784, bapt. April 25, 1784. Spon: Frederick Tischong and Anna Margaret.

William, son of Henry Horn and Christine, b. Feb. 27, 1784, bapt. April 25, 1784. Spon: Christian Knies and Christine.

Frederick, son of Frederick Kreider and Veronica, b. April 15, 1784, bapt. May 2, 1784. Spon: Parents.

Christine, daughter of Jacob Haller and Christine, 6 wks. old, bapt. May 2, 1784. Spon: Peter Souder and Margaret.

Maria Elizabeth, daughter of Peter Klos and Catherine Elizabeth, b. Dec. 17, 1783, bapt. May 2, 1784. Spon: Peter Miller and Mary Elizabeth.

Anna Maria, daughter of George Schaker and Christine, b. March 26, 1784, bapt. May 2, 1784. Spon: Christian Brandel and Anna Maria.

John, son of Andrew Mercker and Catherine, b. May 3, 1784, bapt. May 3, 1784. Spon: John Schultz and wife.

Elizabeth, daughter of Jacob Schuhler and Elizabeth, b. April 10, 1784, bapt. May 4, 1784. Spon: Margaret Schnyder.

Catherine, daughter of Philip Gramlich and Elizabeth, b. April 14, 1784, bapt. May 9, 1784. Spon: Michael Baast and Catherine.

Conrad, son of Jacob Schlemmer and Hannah, b. May 2, 1784, bapt. May 9, 1784. Spon: Grandparents.

Joseph, son of Peter Immel and Elizabeth, b. March 13, 1784, bapt. May 9, 1784. Spon: Margaret Neaff.

Christine Susanna, daughter of John Fans and Anna Catherine, b. April 25, 1784, bapt. May 16, 1784. Spon: Andrew Dag and Christine.

Margaret, daughter of William Bell and Margaret, b. April 20, 1784, bapt. May 16, 1784. Spon: Mrs. Steinmetz.

Catherine, daughter of Michael Schneider and Sophia, b. April 16, 1783, bapt. May 20, 1784. Spon: Catherine Reis.

Anna Elizabeth, daughter of Adam Stoll ad Maria Elizabeth, 3 wks. old, bapt. May 23, 1784. Spon: John Martin and Anna Pfeiffer.

Isabella, daughter of Cornelius Beth and Maria Joanna, b. May 4, 1784, bapt. May 23, 1784. Spon: Rudolph Tillier, Abraham Soyer, Eliz. Helena Rionteau and Isabella Weiberg.

John, son of John Tauenheim and Mary Magdalene, b. March 20, 1784, bapt. May 26, 1784. Spon: Parents.

Joseph, son of Henry Scheible and Maria, b. Sept. 25, 1784, bapt. May 29, 1784. Spon: Maria Scheibele.

William, son of Herman Leck and Anna Margaret, b. Sept. 9, 1784, bapt. May 29, 1784. Spon: Parents.

Anna Maria, daughter of Rothar Leonhard and Eleonora, b. May 13, 1784, bapt. May 30, 1784. Spon: Conrad Verflas and Anna Maria.

Margaret, daughter of Adam Beck and Susanna, b. Dec. 19, 1783, bapt. June 6, 1784. Spon: Paul Schuster and Margaret.

Wilhelmina, daughter of William Kotten and Elizabeth, b. May 26, 1784, bapt. June 6, 1784. Spon: William Degenhart and Wilhelmina.

Sarah, daughter of Christopher Huth and Elizabeth, b. May 7, 1784, bapt. June 6, 1784. Spon: Parents.

Catherine, daughter of Christian Rucker and Dorothea, b. May 20, 1784, bapt. June 6, 1784. Spon: Martin Gucker and Catherine Sauder.

Maria, daughter of George Dies and Eva, b. Jan. 27, 1784, bapt. June 8, 1784. Spon: Philip Gasser and Maria.

Catherine, daughter of John Matzinger and Elizabeth, b. June 5, 1784, bapt. June 9, 1784. Spon: John Matzinger and Catherine.

Catherine, daughter of Nicholas Eisenmenger and Elizabeth, b. May 27, 1784, bapt. June 13, 1784. Spon: Adam Pohl and Catherine.

Conrad, son of Conrad Spangenberg and Elizabeth, b. May 24, 1784, bapt. June 13, 1784. Spon: Parents.

Frederick, son of Frederick Maus and Elizabeth, b. April 8, 1784, bapt. June 13, 1784. Spon: Parents.

Henry, son of John Lehr and Catherine, b. May 30, 1784, bapt. June 20, 1784. Spon: Henry Lies and Elizabeth.

Anna Maria, daughter of George Fies and Dorothea, b. June 14, 1784, bapt. June 26, 1784. Spon: Christian Fies and Anna Maria.

Maria Catherine, daughter of George Koch and Maria Catherine, b. June 23, 1784, bapt. June 27, 1784. Spon: George Pressler and Maria.

Elizabeth, daughter of George Koch and Maria Catherine, b. June 23, 1784, bapt. June 27, 1784. Spon: John Henry Schmidt and Elizabeth.

Elizabeth, daughter of John Birckenbeil and Barbara, 3 mos. old, bapt. July 4, 1784. Spon: Bernard Becker and Elizabeth.

Elizabeth, daughter of Adam May and Catherine, b. June 28, 1784, bapt. July 11, 1784. Spon: David Diehl and Elizabeth.

Elizabeth, daughter of Jacob Kinsely and Catherine, 17 wks. old, bapt. July 11, 1784. Spon: Henry Kinsely and Elizabeth Otto.

Elizabeth, daughter of Jacob Kreider and Elizabeth, b. June 28, 1784, bapt. July 18, 1784. Spon: Henry Gramlich and Elizabeth.

Maria, daughter of George Loescher and Anna, b. June 26, 1784, bapt. July 18, 1784. Spon: George Loscher and Maria.

Jacob, son of Frederick Mangold and Barbara, b. June 6, 1784, bapt. July 18, 1784. Spon: Henry Ries and Elizabeth.

Elizabeth, daughter of Jacob Boyer and Elizabeth, b. Sept. 26, 1783, bapt. July 20, 1784. Spon: Elias Boyer and Catherine Elizabeth.

John Philip, son of Michael Worn and Catherine, b. July 11, 1784, bapt. July 25, 1784. Spon: John Philip Haffener and Margaret.

Sarah Catherine, daughter of Samuel Stern and Margaret, b. July 10, 1784, bapt. July 25, 1784. Spon: Christopher Foth and Catherine.

Anna Elizabeth, daughter of Matthias Gucker and Magdalene, b. July 17, 1784, bapt. Aug. 1, 1784. Spon: George Wilhelm and Susanna Maria.

John, son of Graft Weyand and Christine, 2 wks. old, bapt. Aug. 12, 1784. Spon: Parents.

John Henry, son of John Jost Leibinger and Anna Catherine, b. July 30, 1784, bapt. Aug. 12, 1784. Spon: Parents.

Eva Margaret, daughter of Jacob Finck and Maria Margaet, b. July 19, 1784, bapt. Aug. 15, 1784. Spon: George Mounty and Eva Margaret.

William, son of Daniel Kehr and Mary Magdalene, b. July 27, 1784, bapt. Aug. 15, 1784. Spon: Parents.

Reichard, son of John Fordem and Maria, b. June 26, 1784, bapt. Aug. 16, 1784. Spon: Parents.

Frederick, son of Philip Rummel and Rebecca, b. Aug. 10, 1784, bapt. Aug. 21, 1784. Spon: Fred. Rothar.

John George, son of Matthias Lehmer and Anna, b. Aug. 10, 1784, bapt. Aug. 22, 1784. Spon: George Blum and Philippina.

Anna Maria, daughter of John Scheiwe and Christine, b. Aug. 7, 1784, bapt. Aug. 22, 1784. Spon: Andrew Materan and Anna Maria.

William, son of William Sanders and Maria, b. July 24, 1784, bapt. Aug. 25, 1784. Spon: William Miller and Elizabeth Rup.

Susanna, daughter of John Justus Koch and Susan, b. Aug. 18, 1784, bapt. Aug. 28, 1784. Spon: Grandparents.

Catherine, daughter of John Emmins and Elizabeth, b. Aug. 23, 1784, bapt. Aug. 28, 1784. Spon: Charles Wulpert and Catherine.

Dorothea, daughter of George Jentzer and Catherine, 6 wks. old, bapt. Aug. 29, 1784. Spon: Jacob Theis and Dorothea.

Anna Elizabeth, daughter of Martin Lantz and Juliana, b. April 16, 1777, bapt. Aug. 30, 1784. Spon: Jacob Rusch and Elizabeth.

Maria Margaret, daughter of Martin Lentz and Juliana, b. July 29, 1784, bapt. Aug. 30, 1784. Spon: Parents.

Paul Casper, son of Jacob Gideon and Elizabeth, b. Aug. 1, 1784, bapt. Aug. 30, 1784. Spon: Paul Casper Britton and Susanna.

Catherine, daughter of Zacharias Beckman and Barbara, b. Aug. 13, 1784, bapt. Sept. 5, 1784. Spon: David Gilbert and Catherine.

John, son of William Becker and Maria, b. Aug. 18, 1784, bapt. Sept. 5, 1784. Spon: John Sturtzebach and Maria Gerlach.

Sarah, daughter of Jacob Schreiner and Elizabeth, b. Aug. 31, 1784, bapt. Sept. 5, 1784. Spon: Parents.

Henry, son of William von Phul and Catherine, b. Aug. 14, 1784, bapt. Sept. 5, 1784. Spon: Parents.

Philip, son of John George Miller and Charlotte, b. Aug. 13, 1784, bapt. Sept. 5, 1784. Spon: Philip Rehbohl and wife.

John, son of George Lucas and Eva, 8 days old, bapt. Sept. 7, 1784. Spon: Anthony Frey and Barbara.

John, son of John Halt auf der Heide and Anna Elizabeth, b. Sept. 2, 1784, bapt. Sept. 10, 1784. Spon: Parents.

John Philip, son of William Darrch and Magdalene, b. Sept. 8, 1784, bapt. Sept. 13, 1784. Spon: John Kner and Anna.

Susanna, daughter of John Ecky and Lucretia, b. Sept. 5, 1784, bapt. Sept. 16, 1784. Spon: Parents and Elizabeth Becker.

Philip, son of Jacob Hempelman and Eliza, b. Sept. 4, 1784, bapt. Sept. 19, 1784. Spon: Philip Worck and Elizabeth.

Elizabeth, daughter of Franciscus Froemmer and Gretzelly, b. Aug. 24, 1784, bapt. Sept. 19, 1784. Spon: Elizabeth Froemmer.

John, son of John Williams and Maria, b. Aug. 29, 1784, bapt. Sept. 19, 1784. Spon: John Fiels and Susanna.

Margaret, daughter of Doctor Janus and wife, b. Nov. 1, 1783, Sept. 21, 1784. Spon: Parents.

John, son of John Kern and Elizabeth, b. Sept. 16, 1784, bapt. Sept. 22, 1784. Spon: Parents.

Maria, daughter of Jacob Braunig and Margaret, b. Aug. 13, 1784, bapt. Sept. 24, 1784. Spon: Parents.

John, son of Martin Wall and Christine, b. Aug. 14, 1784, bapt. Sept. 26, 1784. Spon: John Strub and Elizabeth Stocky.

Christian, daughter of Henry Heineman and Charlotte, b. Sept. 9, 1784, bapt. Sept. 26, 1784. Spon: Frederick Heineman and Catherine.

George, son of Martin Hatz and Amelia, b. Sept. 10, 1784, bapt. Sept. 26, 1784. Spon: George Schwartz and wife.

Elizabeth, daughter of Charles Seitz and Charlotte, b. Sept. 7, 1784, bapt. Sept. 26, 1784. Spon: George Fischer and Elizabeth.

Jacob, son of Christopher Busch and Elizabeth, b. Sept. 6, 1784, bapt. Sept. 27, 1784. Spon: Parents.

Joseph, son of Jacob Weithman and Catherine, b. Nov. 27, 1783, bapt. Sept. 28, 1784. Spon: Andrew Weithman and Veronica.

John, son of Frederick Kesselman and Susanna, b. June 21, 1784, bapt. Sept. 29, 1784. Spon: Parents.

Elizabeth, daughter of George Hoffman and Maria, b. Aug. 26, 1784, bapt. Sept. 30, 1784. Spon: Jacob Hill and Elizabeth Hill.

Margaret, daughter of John Brown and Abia, b. Sept. 9, 1784, bapt. Oct. 3, 1784. Spon: John Wacker and Margaret.

Elizabeth, daughter of Daniel Klages and Maria, b. Sept. 23, 1784, bapt. Oct. 3, 1784. Spon: Conrad Rohrman and Elizabeth.

Anna Sophia, daughter of Henry Cremer and Catherine, b. Sept. 19, 1784, bapt. Oct. 3, 1784. Spon: Parents.

Catherine, daughter of Michael Corewell and Dorothea, b. June 27, 1783, bapt. Oct. 5, 1784. Spon: Parents.

Catherine, daughter of John Fred. Gaul and Margaret, b. Sept. 11, 1784, bapt. Oct. 10, 1784. Spon: John Matzinger and Catherine.

Christine, daughter of Conrad Keller and Elizabeth, b. Sept. 21, 1784, bapt. Oct. 10, 1784. Spon: Parents.

Leonard, son of Christian Jung and Elizabeth, b. Oct. 10, 1784, bapt. Oct. 17, 1784. Spon: Leonard Zebold and Catherine.

Eva Francisca, daughter of Herman Bake and Caroline, b. Oct. 15, 1784, bapt. Oct. 20, 1784. Spon: Eva Christine Dentze and Francisca Havest de Fraras.

Peter, son of George Einwaechter and Elizabeth, b. Oct. 16, 1784, bapt. Oct. 24, 1784. Spon: Peter Oxemer and Barbara.

Christianna Catherine, daughter of Jacob Omensetter and Elizabeth, 14 mos. old, bapt. Oct. 23, 1784. Spon: Parents.

Elizabeth, daughter of Nicholas Birth and Catherine, 9 wks. old, bapt. Oct. 24, 1784. Spon: Peter Grim and Elizabeth.

Carl, son of Carl Schakar and Margaret, b. Oct. 17, 1784, bapt. Oct. 25, 1784. Spon: Parents.

Peter, son of Peter Hohl and Catherine, b. Oct. 27, 1784, bapt. Oct. 27, 1784. Spon: Parents.

Eckhard Casander, daughter of William Muntz and Elizabeth, b. Aug. 11, 1784, bapt. Oct. 28, 1784. Spon: Parents.

Anna Catherine, daughter of Christopher Meininger and Margaret, b. Oct. 18, 1784, bapt. Oct. 31, 1784. Spon: Jacob Bischoffberger and Anna Catherine.

Anna Maria, daughter of Ludwig Geivell and Anna, b. Sept. 28, 1783, bapt. Oct. 30, 1784. Spon: Simon Stelekom and Anna Maria.

Anna, daughter of Michael Kamper and Susanna, b. Nov. 30, 1782, bapt. Oct. 31, 1784. Spon: ----.

Michael, son of Michael Kamper and Susanna, b. Sept. 23, 1784, bapt. Oct. 31, 1784. Spon: ----.

Jacob, son of Peter Diehl and Elizabeth, b. Sept. 17, 1784, bapt. Oct. 31, 1784. Spon: Parents.

Charles, son of Samule Rosk and Christine, b. May 15, 1784, Oct. 31, 1784. Spon: John Hoffstaeller and Maria Kamper.
Sarah, daughter of Casper Griessem and Elizabeth, 3 wks. old, bapt. Nov. 2, 1784. Spon: Parents.
John George, son of Nicholas Schultz and Catherine, b. June 30, 1784, bapt. Nov. 5, 1784. Spon: George Schaaf and Maria.
Valentine, son of Valentine Gaul and Sabina, b. Oct. 20, 1784, bapt. Nov. 7, 1784. Spon: Parents.
William, son of Jaques Emanuel de Rogues and wife Charlotte Louise, b. Oct. 14, 1784, bapt. Nov. 8, 1784. Spon: William van der Locht and Solomon Kitt.
Mary Magdalene, daughter of Charles Cooper and Mary Magdalene, b. Oct. 24, 1784, bapt. Nov. 14, 1784. Spon: Parents.
Henry, son of William Bergheimer and Margaret, 10 wks. old, bapt. Nov. 20, 1784. Spon: Henry Schmith and Catherine.
John Adam, son of Martin Sigismund Zibolt and Barbara, b. Nov. 8, 1784, bapt. Nov. 21, 1784. Spon: Adam Striby and Dorothy Striby.
John, son of John George Meyer and Sarah, bapt. Oct. 16, 1784, bapt. Nov. 21, 1784. Spon: John Spalter and Elizabeth.
Isaac, son of Andrew Bergheimer and Elizabeth, b. Oct. 7, 1784, bapt. Nov. 24, 1784. Spon: Isaac le Febre and Magdalene.
George, son of Paul Schlotman and Maria, b. Nov. 7, 1784, bapt. Nov. 28, 1784. Spon: George Wack and Elizabeth.
Adam, son of Henry Frick and Barbara, b. Nov. 7, 1784, bapt. Nov. 28, 1784. Spon: Adam Schaeffer and Dorothea.
John, son of John Schuckhard and Maria, b. Nov. 15, 1784, bapt. Nov. 28, 1784. Spon: John Steinbach and Anna.
John, son of John Porter and Catherine, b. Nov. 14, 1784, bapt. Nov. 28, 1784. Spon: Parents.
Hannah, daughter of Jonathan Waide and Elizabeth, b. Nov. 6, 1784, bapt. Nov. 28, 1784. Spon: Hannah Rubsamen.
Sarah, daughter of Jacob Maag and Maria, b. Oct. 22, 1784, bapt. Nov. 28, 1784. Spon: Sarah Amstrong and grandparents.
Frances Elizabeth, daughter of Jacob Lawersweiler and Elizabeth, b. Nov. 24, 1784, bapt. Dec. 1, 1784. Spon: Parents.
Margaret, daughter of Christian Kauck and Maria, b. Nov. 3, 1784, bapt. Dec. 5, 1784. Spon: Nicholas Blum and Margaret Diemer.
Anna Margaret, daughter of Jacob Zinck and Catherine, 9 wks. old, bapt. Dec. 6, 1784. Spon: John Christopher Vetter and Anna Barbara.
Peter Henry, son of Matthew Fallies and Catherine, b. Nov. 24, 1784, bapt. Dec. 12, 1784. Spon: Henry Meyer and Catherine.
John, son of Morgan Ritch and Catherine, b. Nov. 2, 1784, bapt. Dec. 16, 1784. Spon: Martin Hohl and Mary Magdalene.
Elizabeth, daughter of Henry Huber and Maria, b. Dec. 1, 1784, bapt. Dec. 19, 1784. Spon: Parents.
Margaret, daughter of John Altberger and Dorothea, b. Nov. 28, 1784, bapt. Dec. 19, 1784. Spon: Philip Altberger and Margaret.
Maria, daughter of John Bam and Anna Maria, 3 wks. old, bapt. Dc. 19, 1784. Spon: Adam Bronner and Maria.
James, son of Daniel von der Schleis and Philippina, b. Oct. 10, 1784, bapt. Dec. 20, 1784. Spon: ----.
Abraham, son of Jacob Esler and wife, b. Dec. 19, 1784, bapt. Jan. 1, 1785. Spon: Abraham Peter and Anna Esler.

Anna Maria, daughter of Henry Denig and Anna Maria, 3 wks. old, bapt. Jan. 2, 1785. Spon: John Exley and Anna Maria.

Jacob, son of Frederick Froelig and Catherine, b. Dec. 11, 1784, bapt. Jan. 6, 1785. Spon: Parents.

Elizabeth, daughter of John Gamper and Elizabeth, b. Dec. 13, 1784, bapt. Jan. 9, 1785. Spon: John Hoffstaettel and Maria Gamper.

Burckhardt, son of John Geo. Pfaff and Anna, b. Jan. 29, 1780, bapt. Jan. 9, 1785. Spon: ----.

John George, son of John Geo. Pfaff and Anna, b. May 17, 1782, bapt. Jan. 9, 1785. Spon: ----.

John, son of John Geo. Pfaff and Anna, b. Dec. 20, 1784, bapt. Jan. 9, 1785. Spon: ----.

George, son of Jacob Bischoffberger and Elizabeth, b. Jan. 4, 1784, bapt. Jan. 9, 1785. Spon: George Hauser and wife.

Catherine, daughter of Martin Carsbach and Maria, b. Dec. 24, 1784, bapt. Jan. 9, 1785. Spon: Parents.

Catherine, daughter of Kilian Rup and Catherine, b. Oct. 16, 1783, bapt. Jan. 11, 1785. Spon: James Priesse and Magdalene.

Catherine, daughter of Philip Reinhold Pauli and Elizabeth, b. Dec. 25, 1784, bapt. Jan. 14, 1785. Spon: Melchior Steiner and Catherine Mosch.

John Peter, son of Conrad Bachman and Susanna, b. Jan. 9, 1784, bapt. Jan. 15, 1785. Spon: Parents.

John George, son of Carl William Conrath and Eliz. Catherine, b. Jan. 3, 1784, bapt. Jan. 16, 1785. Spon: John George Schaeff and wife.

Susanna, daughter of Peter Conver and Catherine, b. Jan. 2, 1784, Jan. 16, 1785. Spon: George Hess and Anna.

John Christian, son of Christian Weierich and Catherine, b. Jan. 19, 1785, bapt. Jan. 20, 1785. Spon: Parents.

Veronica, daughter of Peter Paris and Veronica, b. Nov. 18, 1784, bapt. Jan. 20, 1785. Spon: Gillome de Gallathan and Veronica Fans.

John, son of Anthony Lowdan and Elizabeth, b. Sept. 12, 1779, bapt. Jan. 22, 1785. Spon: ----.

Anthony, son of Anthony Lowdan and Elizabeth, b. Nov. 27, 1781, bapt. Jan. 22, 1785. Spon: ----.

Catherine, daughter of Carl Jost and Christine, b. Sept. 16, 1784, bapt. Jan. 27, 1785. Spon: John Halberstadt and Catherine.

Catherine Elizabeth, daughter of Philip Stimmel and Anna, b. Sept. 11, 1784, bapt. Jan. 28, 1785. Spon: Fred Heimberger and Maria.

Conrad, son of Peter Becker and Mary Magdalene, b. Dec. 26, 1784, bapt. Jan. 31, 1785. Spon: Parents.

Jacob, son of Philip Gasser and Anna, b. Dec. 14, 1784, bapt. Jan. 31, 1785. Spon: Jacob Hill and Anna Maria.

Thomas, son of Abraham Scherridan and Barbara, b. Jan. 19, 1785, bapt. Feb. 3, 1785. Spon: Parents.

Samuel, son of Frederick Steiner and Maria, b. Oct. 21, 1784, bapt. Feb. 11, 1785. Spon: Parents.

Matthias, son of John Riffit and Bright Weed, b. Sept. 10, 1784, bapt. Feb. 11, 1785. Spon: Nicholas Penther and Maria.

James, son of Francis Marshall and Margaret, b. Feb. 9, 1785, bapt. Feb. 11, 1785. Spon: Wm. Hoog and Nancy Correl.

Thomas, son of Jacob Sehler and Margaret, b. Dec. 13, 1784, bapt. Feb. 13, 1785. Spon: Thomas Hall and Hannah.

John, son of Conrad Muller and Margaret, b. Jan. 18, 1785, bapt.
Feb. 13, 1785. Spon: John Fulman and Maria Krauskopf.
Catherine, daughter of John Meily and Catherine, b. Dec. 26, 1784,
bapt. Feb. 13, 1785. Spon: Frederick Meily and Barbara Keuler.
Maria Margaret, daughter of Christian Lawyer and Maria, b. Jan. 10,
1785, bapt. Feb. 13, 1785. Spon: Philip Haller and Maria
Margaret.
John, son of Bernard Schwenck and Margaret, 7 wks. old, bapt. Feb.
20, 1785. Spon: John Durr and Susanna Eckel.
Michael, son of Wm. Haberstich and Maria, b. Feb. 3, 1785, bapt.
Feb. 26, 1785. Spon: Parents.
Anna, daughter of John Muller and Anna, b. Jan. 17,. 1785, bapt.
Feb. 26, 1785. Spon: Jacob Gallate and Sarah.
Elizabeth, daughter of Paul Couerty and Elizabeth, 3 wks. old,
bapt. Feb. 26, 1785. Spon: Christian Froelig and Elizabeth.
Fanny Bower, Magaret Schmidt had a mulatto child bapt. March 1,
1785. Spon: ----.
Michael, son of Michael Fans and Rebecca, b. Feb. 12, 1785, bapt.
March 2, 1785. Spon: Christian Fans and Christine.
Philip, son of Henry Jette and Catherine, b. Feb. 17, 1785, bapt.
March 6, 1785. Spon: Philip Witzel and Anna Margaret.
John George, son of Justus Flocke and Margaret, b. Feb. 9, 1785,
bapt. March 6, 1785. Spon: John Geo. Stats.
John Christian, son of Peter Dischong and Susanna, b. Feb. 15,
1785, bapt. March 6, 1785. Spon: Christian Dischong and Cath.
Keilman.
Philippina, daughter of John Christian Wagener and Magdalene, b.
Feb. 11, 1785, bapt. March 13, 1785. Spon: Parents.
Elizabeth, daughter of Peter Auner and Margaret, b. Dec. 28, 1784,
bapt. March 15, 1785. Spon: Elizabeth Gassner.
Anna, daughter of Daniel Sutter and Anna Catherine, b. Feb. 27,
1785, bapt. March 20, 1785. Spon: Parents.
Sally, daughter of Adam Rohd and Maria, b. Dec. 23, 1784, bapt.
March 20, 1785. Spon: Wm. Williams.
William, son of Nicholas Schreiner and Maria, b. Feb. 20, 1785,
bapt. March 20, 1785. Spon: Parents.
John, son of Richard Johnson and Maria, b. March 3, 1785, bapt.
March 23, 1785. Spon: Timotheus Keffener and Jane Green.
Thomas, son of Osman Captain and Elizabeth, b. June 16, 1784, bapt.
March 20, 1785. Spon: Christ. Keller and Elizabeth.
Christian Jacob, age 28 yrs.
Jemima Murray, age 19 yrs.
Magdalena Brown, age 21 yrs.
Jacob, son of Philip Wirth and Dorothea, b. Feb. 28, 1785, bapt.
March 25, 1785. Spon: Jacob Binder and Clara Wirth.
Maria, daughter of Henry Strub and Susanna, b. Jan. 14, 1785, bapt.
March 25, 1785. Spon: The Parents and Catharine Strub.
Christine Wilhelmina, daughter of Fred. Wm. Kuisman and Anna
Margaret, b. Feb. 18, 1785, bapt. March 27, 1785. Spon:
Frederick Wing and Christine Wilhelmina.
John, son of Jacob Reitlinger and Elizabeth, b. March 8, 1785,
bapt. March 27, 1785. Spon: The Parents.
George, son of William Nickels and Joanna, b. March 12, 1785, bapt.
March 28, 1785. Spon: George Weckerly and Catharine.
Mary Magdalene, daughter of David Rischong and Catherine, b. March

11, 1785, bapt. March 28, 1785. Spon: Conrad Haas and Mary Magdalene.

Catherine, daughter of Henry Stetzer and Maria, b. March 25, 1785, bapt. March 29, 1785. Spon: The Parents.

Elizabeth, daughter of Ludwig Wuest and Catherine, b. March 12, 1785, bapt. April 3, 1785. Spon: Henry Kinley and Elizabeth Lack.

Joseph, son of Charles Souder and Catherine, b. May 31, 1779, bapt. April 3, 1785, Spon: ----.

Eleonora, daughter of Charles Souder and Catherine, b. May 17, 1781, bapt. April 3, 1785. Spon: ----.

William, son of Charles Souder and Catherine, b. Feb. 17, 1783, bapt. April 3, 1785. Spon: ----.

Margaret, daughter of Charles Souder and Catherine, b. March 19, 1785, bapt. April 3, 1785. Spon: ----.

Sarah Anna, daughter of Charles Souder and Catherine, b. March 6, 1777, bapt. at Trenton, March 30, 1778. Spon: ----.

Catherine, daughter of Christian Wigand and Elizabeth, b. April 3, 1785, bapt. April 5, 1785, Spon: Adam Wagener and Catherine.

Catherine, daughter of Peter Walter and Charlotte, b. March 25, 1785, bapt. April 7, 1785. Spon: The Parents.

Elizabeth, daughter of William Peltz and Maria, b. March 21, 1785, bapt. April 10, 1785. Spon: Philip Boehm and Maria.

Henry, son of Christian Aug. Kirchoff and Mary Magdalene, b. March 12, 1785, bapt. April 10, 1785. Spon: Jacob Reitlinger.

Andrew, son of Jacob Weinert and Susanna, b. March 16, 1785, bapt. April 10, 1785. Spon: Andrew Lex and Maria.

Daniel, son of George Pantz and Isabella, b. Oct. 26, 1784, bapt. April 10, 1785. Spon: John Luro and Maria.

George, son of Peter Schnyder and Catherine, b. ----, 4 weeks old, bapt. April 10, 1785. Spon: George Hauser and Catherine.

George William, son of George Steinhauer and Elizabeth, b. Sept. 22, 1783, bapt. April 10, 1785. Spon: The Parents.

Thomas Hubsons, son of James Eliot and Sophia, b. May 8, 1782, bapt. April 14, 1785. Spon: Ebenezer Branham and Christine Funck.

Benjamin, son of James Eliot and Sophia, b. June 13, 1784, bapt. April 14, 1785. Spon: Ebenezer Branhma and Christine Funck.

Andrew, son of Conrad Rosch and Margaret, b. March 6, 1785, bapt. April 17, 1785. Spon: Andrew von Willer and Catherine.

Catherine, daughter of John George Freitag and Margaret Philippina, b. April 8, 1785, bapt. April 17, 1785. Spon: Catherine Otto.

Anna Maria, daughter of Jacob Reindahler and Elizabeth, b. Feb. 3, 1785, bapt. April 23, 1785. Spon: Anna Maria Reindahler.

Jacob, son of George Bachoff and Sarah, b. Jan. 30, 1785, bapt. April 23, 1785. Spon: The Parents.

Valentine, son of Christian Appel and Margaret, b. Oct. 24, 1773, bapt. April 24, 1785. Spon: Adolph Diehl and Catherine.

Sarah, daughter of Christian Appel and Margaret, b. Feb. 13, 1778, bapt. April 24, 1785. Spon: Jacob Facundus and Julianna.

Philip, son of Christian Appel and Margaret, b. Aug. 2, 1780, bapt. April 24, 1785. Spon: Adolph Diehl and Catherine.

Anna Maria, daughter of William Becker and Catherine, b. April 10, 1785, bapt. May 1, 1785. Spon: Henry Kienly and Maria Dinges.

John Charles, son of Jacob Nannetter and Catherine, b. March 8,

1785, bapt. May 3, 1785. Spon: The Parents.
Christiana Dorothea, daughter of Jacob Schultz and Charlotte, b. April 29, 1785, bapt. May 15, 1785. Spon: George Wiegman and Sophia.
Margaret, daughter of Nicholas Kayser and Elizabeth, b. April 1, 1785, bapt. May 15, 1785. Spon: Jacob Kitts and Margaret.
Elizabeth, daughter of Gottfried Munnig and Veronica, b. April 24, 1785, bapt. May 15, 1785. Spon: Frederick Brown and Elizabeth.
Anna Maria, daughter of George Schmidt and Elizabeth, b. Feb. 23, 1785, bapt. May 15, 1785. Spon: The Parents and Anna Schmidt.
Andrew, son of Jonas Plesh and Christine, b. March 8, 1785, bapt. May 16, 1785. Spon: Andrew Uhler and Regina.
----, Nicholas Penther brought a strange child to baptism, b. ----, bapt. May 16, 1785. Spon: ----.
Joseph, son of John Abel and Margaret, b. May 2, 1785, bapt. May 16, 1785. Spon: Peter Abel and Christine.
Maria, daughter of Henry Fiehman and Barbara, b. Feb. 18, 1785, bapt. May 16, 1785. Spon: The Parents.
Anna Maria, daughter of John Reiffschneider and Anna Maria, b. May 3, 1785, bapt. May 16, 1785. Spon: The Parents.
George Henry, son of George Berckin and Catherine, b. June 17, 1784, bapt. May 21, 1785. Spon: Henry Bletterman and Elizabeth.
John Henry, son of Christopher Schmidt and Ann Catherine, b. May 7, 1785, bapt. May 22, 1785. Spon: John Maag and Elizabeth.
William, son of William Miller and Susanna, b. May 10, 1785, bapt. May 23, 1785. Spon: Andrew Miller and wife.
Elizabeth, daughter of John Wilcky and Barbara, b. Jan. 29, 1785, bapt. May 29, 1785. Spon: The Parents.
Jacob, son of Fabian Hemerly and Catherine, b. May 8, 1785, bapt. May 29, 1785. Spon: Jacob Krieger and Eva Riegler.
John Michael, son of John Souder and Catherine, b. May 20, 1785, bapt. June 5, 1785. Spon: Casper Schoen and Margaret.
Christina, daughter of Andrew Mercker and Catherine, b. May 28, 1785, bapt. June 5, 1785. Spon: Sebastian Wulle and Christine Wulle.
Catherine, daughter of Samuel Muschel and Elizabeth, b. May 7, 1785, bapt. June 5, 1785. Spon: Conrad Hoff and Maria Sibylla.
Christine, daughter of Jacob Stribe and Christine, b. ----, bapt. June 10, 1785. Spon: Michael Muller and Christine.
Anna Elizabeth, daughter of Peter Becker and Elizabeth, b. May 22, 1785, bapt. June 12, 1785. Spon: Jacob Rumof and Elizabeth Grim.
Catherine, daughter of Philip Fries and Catherine, adopted the child, 3 mos., 2 wks. old, bapt. June 12, 1785.
Anna Margaret, daughter of Jacob Sehler and Anna Maria, b. May 18, 1785, bapt. June 12, 1785. Spon: George Kurtz and Anna Margaret.
George, son of George Blum and Catherine, b. June 1, 1785, bapt. June 12, 1785. Spon: The Parents.
Elizabeth, daughter of John George Schafe and Christine, b. June 10, 1785, bapt. June 19, 1785. Spon: Daniel Nord and Eliz. Umbach.
John William, son of John Wacker and Anna Margaret, b. June 9, 1785, bapt. June 26, 1785. Spon: John Wester and Margaret.
Rebecca, daughter of Adam Lehr and Rebecca, b. May 21, 1785, bapt.

June 26, 1785. Spon: The Parents and Grandparents.
Joseph, son of John Froelig and Christine, b. June 19, 1785, bapt.
June 26, 1785. Spon: The Parents.
Sarah, daughter of Jacob Miele and Margaret, b. May 15, 1785, bapt.
June 26, 1785. Spon: Fred. Korenter and Sarah Meile.
Christine, daughter of Conrad Schmidt and Anna Maria, b. April 6,
1785, bapt. June 28, 1785. Spon: Christine Lutz.
John, son of Adam Fischer and Elizabeth, b. April 9, 1785, bapt.
June 29, 1785. Spon: The Parents.
Maria, daughter of Conrad Gerhard and Elizabeth, b. June 25, 1785,
bapt. July 3, 1785. Spon: Gottfried Zeppernick and Maria.
Margaret, daughter of John Steltz and Elizabeth, b. June 26, 1785,
bapt. July 9, 1785. Spon: Margaret Oxley.
Maria, daughter of Henry Wurtzler and Philippina, b. May 30, 1785,
bapt. July 10, 1785. Spon: Maria Heimberger.
Catherine, daughter of Gottfried Hager and Anna Maria, b. June 5,
1785, bapt. July 10, 1785. Spon: The Parents.
George Henry, son of John Schmidt and Margaret, b. June 23, 1785,
bapt. July 11, 1785. Spon: Aug. Henry Pletterman and wife.
Susanna, daughter of Matthias Graff and Elizabeth, b. June 25,
1785, bapt. July 20, 1785. Spon: The Parents.
George, son of John Pfeiffer and Jane, b. March 11, 1785, bapt.
July 22, 1785. Spon: The Parents.
John Peter, son of Lorentz Miller and Catherine, 1 yr., 21 days
old, bapt. July 24, 1785. Spon: John Peter Pfeiffer and Anna
Maria.
John, son of Casper Soudern and Wilhelmina, b. June 26, 1785, bapt.
July 24, 1785. Spon: Jacob Wever and wife.
John Jacob, son of George Heiberger and Anna Maria, b. May 28,
1785, bapt. July 24, 1785. Spon: John Peter Pfeiffer and Anna
Maria.
William, son of George Hess and Anna, b. July 21, 1785, bapt. July
31, 1785. Spon: Peter Conver and Catherine.
Julianna, daughter of Jeremiah Vielmatter and Catherine, b. July 9,
1785, bapt. Aug. 3, 1785. Spon: Bernard Schomo and Julianna.
Elizabeth, daughter of John Spalter and Elizabeth, b. July 14,
1785, bapt. Aug. 7, 1785. Spon: Fred. Schaumenkessel and
Elizabeth Barbara.
John, son of Robert Johnson and Maria, b. June 7, 1785, bapt. Aug.
7, 1785. Spon: Rachel Rudy.
Elizabeth, daughter of Andrew Braderick and Maria, b. July 27,
1785, bapt. Aug. 14, 1785. Spon: The Parents.
Elizabeth, daughter of Joseph Sultzbach and Elizabeth, b. May 19,
1781, bapt. Aug. 14, 1785. Spon: Mrs. Schwartz.
Joseph, son of Joseph Sultzbach and Elizabeth, b. Aug. 30, 1784,
bapt. Aug. 14, 1785. Spon: Mrs. Schwartz.
Elizabeth, daughter of Christopher Wassem and Maria, b. Aug. 5,
1785, bapt. Aug. 15, 1785. Spon: The Parents.
Adam, son of Jacob Schible and Elizabeth, b. July 27, 1785, bapt.
Aug. 21, 1785. Spon: The Parents.
Anna Margaret, daughter of Nicholas Rummel and Anna Barbara, b.
Aug. 7, 1785, bapt. Aug. 21, 1785. Spon: Anna Barbara Haller.
A Child of William Darach and Maria, b. Aug. 13, 1785, bapt. Aug.
21, 1785. Spon: Philip Kehr and Anna Elizabeth.
Catherine Friderica, daughter of David Stetzer and Elizabeth, b. --

--, bapt. Aug. 21, 1785. Spon: Adam Wagener and Cath.
Friderica.
Elizabeth, daughter of David Stetzer and Elizabeth, b. July 25,
1785, bapt. Aug. 21, 1785. Spon: Christ. Weiand and Elizabeth.
Maria Elizabeth, daughter of Philip Losch and wife., b. Aug. 7,
1785, bapt. Aug. 21, 1785. Spon: Martin Sackman and Elizabeth.
John, son of Conrad Muenig and Eva Margaret, b. Aug. 18, 1785,
bapt. Aug. 21, 1785. Spon: The Parents.
Else, daughter of Jacob Greiss and Margaret, b. Aug. 13, 1785,
bapt. Aug. 21, 1785. Spon: The Parents.
John, son of John Kreimes and Elizabeth, b. Aug. 22, 1785, bapt.
Sept. 6, 1785. Spon: John Gemeinbauer and Catherine.
John, son of John Halt auf der Reide and Anna Elizabeth, b. Aug.
31, 1785, bapt. Sept. 7, 1785. Spon: John Schlechter and Anna
Elizabeth.
George, son of Michael Corewell and Anna Dorothea, b. ----, 6 yrs.,
bapt. Sept. 7, 1785. Spon: ----.
Joseph, son of Michael Corewell and Anna Dorothea, b. ----, 5 yrs.,
bapt. Sept. 7, 1785. Spon: ----.
John Adam, son of Michael Corewell and Anna Dorothea, b. May 7,
1785, bapt. Sept. 7, 1785. Spon: ----.
Catherine, daughter of Henry Becker and Gertrude, b. Sept. --,
1784, bapt. Sept. 8, 1785. Spon: ----.
Maria, daughter of Henry Becker and Gertrude, b. Jan. 4, 1779,
bapt. Sept. 8, 1785. Spon: ----.
William, son of Henry Becker and Gertrude, b. Oct. 20, 1781, bapt.
Sept. 8, 1785. Spon: ----.
Anna Catherine, daughter of Matthias Kremer and Susanna, b. Sept.
1, 1785, bapt. Sept. 9, 1785. Spon: The Parents.
John, son of Peter Shmallwood and Catherine, b. March 26, 1785,
bapt. Sept. 9, 1785. Spon: The Parents.
Maria, daughter of Michael Becker and Jana (Jenny), b. Aug. 10,
1785, bapt. Sept. 11, 1785. Spon: The Parents and Maria Becker.
Elizabeth, daughter of Cyriacus Wagener and Elizabeth, b. Aug. 23,
1785, bapt. Sept. 11, 1785. Spon: John Vogel and Elizabeth.
Elizabeth, daughter of John Latsch and Maria, b. Aug. 9, 1785,
bapt. Sept. 11, 1785. Spon: John Kappel and Elizabeth Kappel.
George, son of John Bom and Catherine, b. Aug. 16, 1785, bapt.
Sept. 11, 1785. Spon: The Parents.
Anna Maria, daughter of John Capp and Catherine, b. Aug. 28, 1785,
bapt. Sept. 11, 1785. Spon: Charles Chamberlein and Magdalene.
Susanna, daughter of Frederick Boyer and Catherine, b. Aug. 8,
1785, bapt. Sept. 11, 1785. Spon: John Heiler and Susanna.
Frederick, son of George Bornbhaus and Elizabeth, b. Aug. 27, 1785,
bapt. Sept. 11, 1785. Spon: Frederick Kreider and Veronica.
Joseph, son of Charles Ristein and Hannah, b. July 4, 1785, bapt.
Sept. 18, 1785. Spon: Balthasar Ristein and Catherine.
Maria, daughter of William Will and Anna Maria, b. Sept. 2, 1785,
bapt. Sept. 18, 1785. Spon: Adam Clampfer and Maria.
John, son of Adam Clampfer and Maria, b. Sept. 23, 1784, bapt.
Sept. 18, 1785. Spon: William Will and Maria Clampfer.
Maria, daughter of Caleb Hughes and Maria, b. Sept. 5, 1785, bapt.
Sept. 20, 1785. Spon: The Parents.
Henry, son of Nicolas Riebel and Salome, b. Sept. 26, 1785, bapt.
Sept. 26, 1785. Spon: Henry Emmerth and Maria.

Maria Elizabeth, daughter of John Lamsbach and Christine, b. Sept. 19, 1785, bapt. Oct. 2, 1785. Spon: George Rummel and Maria Elizabeth.

Elizabeth, daughter of Robert Pattison and Sarah, 4 wks. old, bapt. Oct. 3, 1785. Spon: Philip Wirth and Dorothea.

Peter, son of Philip Bockius and Hannah, b. Sept. 21, 1785, bapt. Oct. 9, 1785. Spon: The Parents.

Sarah, daughter of John Klages and Rosina, b. Sept. 19, 1785, bapt. Oct. 9, 1785. Spon: The Parents.

Mary Magdalene, daughter of Daniel Bachtle and Margaret, b. Sept. 22, 1785, bapt. Oct. 9, 1785. Spon: James Bell and Magdalene.

Charles Victor, son of William Muentz and wife, b. Sept. 14, 1785, bapt. Oct. 10, 1785. Spon: The Parents.

Frederick, son of John Schmidt and Barbara, b. Sept. 21, 1785, bapt. Oct. 13, 1785. Spon: Fred. Schmidt and Catherine. *NB. This child was bapt. on the 14th with the four other children. See below.*

Jacob, son of Jacob Enck and Catherine, b. Sept. 27, 1785, bapt. Oct. 13, 1785. Spon: The Parents.

Mary Magdalene, daughter of Jacob Schlemmer and Hannah, b. Oct. 3, 1785, bapt. Oct. 13, 1785. Spon: The Parents and Maria Klein.

Catherine, daughter of Frederick Schmidt and Catherine, b. May 17, 1777, bapt. Oct. 14, 1785. Spon: Eleonore Hirsch.

Elizabeth, daughter of Frederick Schmidt and Catherine, b. Oct. 15, 1779, bapt. Oct. 14, 1785. Spon: Eleonore Hirsch.

William, son of Frederick Schmidt and Catherine, b. Nov. 22, 1781, bapt. Oct. 14, 1785. Spon: Eleonore Hirsch.

Eleonore, daughter of Frederick Schmidt and Catherine, b. Jan. 8, 1785, bapt. Oct. 14, 1785. Spon: Eleonore Hirsch. *The oldest child, Christine, aged 9 yrs., was bapt. at Falckner Swamp.*

John Christopher, son of George Einwaechter and Elizabeth, b. Oct. 9, 1785, bapt. Oct. 16, 1785. Spon: John Anthony Frey and Barbara.

Sally, daughter of John Jones and Elizabeth, b. Sept. 23, 1785, bapt. Oct. 16, 1785. Spon: The Parents.

Susanna, daughter of Philip Feil and Susanna, b. Sept. 4, 1785, bapt. Oct. 18, 1785. Spon: The Parents.

Eleonora, daughter of Wendel Zerban and Catherine, b. Sept. 17, 1785, bapt. Oct. 23, 1785. Spon: Christine Becker.

John, son of Lorentz Ries and Elizabeth, b. Sept. 14, 1785, bapt. Oct. 23, 1785. Spon: The Parents.

Michael, son of Michael Steiber and Magdalene, 7 wks. old, bapt. Oct. 23, 1785. Spon: The Parents.

Christine Barbara, daughter of George Steffen and Catherine, 14 d. old, bapt. Oct. 24, 1785. Spon: George Seiberholt and Maria.

John Henry, son of John Schnyder and Agnes, b. Oct. 3, 1785, bapt. Oct. 23, 1785. Spon: Henry Emig and Dorothea.

Nicholas, son of John Penther and Maria, 4 wks. old, bapt. Oct. 30, 1785. Spon: Grandparents.

Henry, son of Henry Ritter and Anna, b. Oct. 9, 1785, bapt. Oct. 30, 1785. Spon: The Parents.

Susanna, daughter of Henry Lies and Anna Elizabeth, b. Oct. 22, 1785, bapt. Oct. 30, 1785. Spon: The Parents.

John, son of Philip Jung and Elizabeth, b. Sept. 9, 1785, bapt.
Nov. 1, 1785. Spon: The Parents.
Francis Reinhard, son of David Roehrman and Anna Margaret, 6 wks.
old, bapt. Nov. 6, 1785. Spon: Francis Reinhard Groninger and
Cath.
Maria Catherine, daughter of George Lies and Anna Margaret, b. Nov.
3, 1785, bapt. Nov. 13, 1785. Spon: Christopher Hansman and
Maria.
Anna, daughter of Frederick Schneider and Barbara, b. Oct. 31,
1785, bapt. Nov. 17, 1785. Spon: The Parents.
Henry, son of George Riegener and Sarah, b. Oct. 21, 1785, bapt.
Nov. 20, 1785. Spon: Henry Maag and Elizabeth.
Anna Catherine, daughter of Martin Gucker and Catherine, 14 d. old,
bapt. Nov. 20, 1785. Spon: John Seidel and Julianna.
John, son of George Neis and Veronica, 2 wks. old, bapt. Nov. 20,
1785. Spon: John Brenneisen and Cath. Heineman.
Magdalene Elizabeth, daughter of John Henry Pfeiffer and Christine,
b. Nov. 5, 1785, bapt. Nov. 20, 1785. Spon: Ernest Heuser and
Magdalene Elizabeth.
Catherine, daughter of George Schakar and Christine, b. Oct. 19,
1785, bapt. Nov. 21, 1785. Spon: Jacob Ochs and Barbara.
Elizabeth, daughter of Matthias Keely and Hannah, b. Oct. 4, 1785,
bapt. Nov. 24, 1785. Spon: The Parents.
Magdalene, daughter of John Jost Leonard and Catherine, b. Nov. 9,
1785, bapt. Nov. 27, 1785. Spon: Martin Weiland and Margaret.
Mary Magdalene, daughter of Charles Kern and Mary Magdalene, b.
Nov. 3, 1785, bapt. Nov. 27, 1785. Spon: Andrew Lex and Mary.
Mary Magdalene, daughter of John Orefgen and Elizabeth, b. Nov. 7,
1785, bapt. Nov. 27, 1785. Spon: Jacob Ries and Magdalene.
John George, son of Ned Green and Maria, b. Nov. 7, 1784, bapt.
Nov. 30, 1785. Spon: Catherine Ridge.
Robert, son of Edward Sutten and Catherine, b. Aug. 5, 1785, bapt.
Nov. 30, 1785. Spon: Catherine Winckler.
Sophia, daughter of Justus Sterdiger and Maria, b. Nov. 11, 1785,
bapt. Dec. 4, 1785. Spon: Philip Andreas and Sophia.
Susanna Louisa, daughter of Gottfried Boeler and Catherine, b. Nov.
18, 1785, bapt. Dec. 9, 1785. Spon: Christian Tischong and
Susanna.
Mary Magdalene, daughter of Peter Paris and Sarah, b. Aug. 6, 1785,
bapt. Dec. 11, 1785. Spon: Maria Becker.
George, son of William Wever and Margaret, 10 wks. old, bapt. Dec.
11, 1785. Spon: Fred. Schmidt and Margaret Wever.
Christopher, son of George Rothenbeck and Maria, 4 yrs. old, bapt.
Dec. 11, 1785. Spon: Mr. Wever.
Anna Maria, daughter of Henry Dephines and Sarah, b. Sept. 19,
1785, bapt. Dec. 14, 1785. Spon: Barbara Rieber.
John, son of John Miller and Elizabeth, b. Nov. 16, 1785, bapt.
Dec. 16, 1785. Spon: The Parents.
Daniel, son of William Fuselbach and Margaret, 6 wks. old, bapt.
Dec. 18, 1785. Spon: George Bronner and Dolly.
Anna, daughter of Ludwig Krauel and Margaret, b. Nov. 16, 1785,
bapt. Dec. 18, 1785. Spon: Michael Gilbert and Anna.
John Felix, son of Henry Fenner and Elizabeth, b. Nov. 25, 1785,
bapt. Dec. 18, 1785. Spon: Felix Tenner and Maria Eva.
John Philip, son of John Orefgen and Catherine, b. Nov. 18, 1785,

bapt. Dec. 20, 1785. Spon: The Parents.
Maria, daughter of Jacob Steinmetz and Rachel, b. Nov. 25, 1785, bapt. Dec. 25, 1785. Spon: Maria Schwob.
Elizabeth, daughter of John Huhn and Christine, b. Dec. 1, 1785, bapt. Dec. 25, 1785. Spon: William Ferley and Elizabeth.
Leonard, son of William Rosch and Maria, b. March 12, 1776, bapt. Dec. 26, 1785. Spon: ----.
Maria, daughter of William Rosch and Maria, b. March 12, 1778, bapt. Dec. 26, 1785. Spon: ----.
Anna, daughter of William Rosch and Maria, b. May 26, 1785, bapt. Dec. 26, 1785. Spon: ----.
Anna Margaret, daughter of John Weber and Anna Christine, b. Oct. 8, 1785, bapt. Dec. 26, 1785. Spon: Jacob Schmidt and Anna Margaret.
Edward, son of Matthias Hanssen and Maria, b. Aug. 30, 1785, bapt. Dec. 26, 1785. Spon: Jacob Weisser and Susanna.
John, son of Leonard Rothar and Nelly, b. Sept. 17, 1785, bapt. Dec. 26, 1785. Spon: Fred. Rothar and Eliz. Rothar.
Catherine Margaret, daughter of John Kutzrock and Priscilla, b. Dec. 16, 1785, bapt. Dec. 29, 1785. Spon: Mr. Nies and Margaret.
Susanna, daughter of Henry Scherer and Elizabeth, b. May 2, 1785, bapt. Jan. 1, 1786. Spon: ----.
Catherine, daughter of Henry Schmaltz and Margaret, b. Nov. 11, 1785, bapt. Jan. 1, 1786. Spon: Daniel Sutter and Anna Catherine.
Henry, son of George Ries and Maria, b. Dec. 4, 1785, bapt. Jan. 1, 1786. Spon: Henry Ries and Elizabeth.
Catherine Elizabeth, daughter of John Zahner and Barbara, 3 wks. old, bapt. Jan. 1, 1786. Spon: Michael Haag and Eliz. Stoudt.
John Philip, son of John Matzinger and Elizabeth, 4 wks. old, bapt. Jan. 1, 1786. Spon: Philip Witzel and Rebecca.
Maria Catherine, daughter of Adam May and Maria Catherine, b. Dec. 14, 1785, bapt. Jan. 1, 1786. Spon: The Parents.
George, son of George Schwartz and Barbara, b. Dec. 10, 1785, bapt. Jan. 1, 1786. Spon: The Parents.
Frederick, son of Martin Schuster and Catherine, b. Oct. 29, 1785, bapt. Jan. 6, 1786. Spon: The Parents.
Elizabeth, daughter of Leonard Sebold and Ann Catherine, 3 wks. old, bapt. Jan. 8, 1786. Spon: John Kreider and Elizabeth.
Christine, daughter of William Mueller and Margaret, b. Oct. 28, 1785, bapt. Jan. 8, 1786. Spon: Frederick Wing and Christine.
Leonard, son of Leonard Jundt and Sarah, b. Dec. 23, 1785, bapt. Jan. 8, 1786. Spon: The Parents.
Anna Maria, daughter of John Heimer and Elizabeth, 12 d. old, bapt. Jan. 8, 1786. Spon: John Conrad Gebhard and Anna Maria.
Maria, daughter of John Etris and Christine, b. Nov. 17, 1785, bapt. Jan. 8, 1786. Spon: The Parents.
John, son of Henry Hildebrand and Anna Margaret, b. Dec. 31, 1785, bapt. Jan. 15, 1786. Spon: Anna Margaret.
Christian, son of Fred. Gaul and Margaret, b. Dec. 4, 1785, bapt. Jan. 15, 1786. Spon: Christian Konig and Maria Hinckel.
John Jacob, son of Jacob Huth and Elizabeth, b. Dec. 23, 1785, bapt. Jan. 15, 1786. Spon: Jacob Ritter and Dorothea.
Catherine, daughter of Peter Edenborn and Elizabeth, b. Dec. 31,

1785, bapt. Jan. 19, 1786. Spon: The Parents.

Maria, daughter of George Loescher and Anna, b. Dec. 12, 1785, bapt. Jan. 22, 1786. Spon: George Loscher and Maria.

Elizabeth, daughter of Ludiwg Orth and Barbara, b. Nov. 19, 1784, bapt. Jan. 24, 1786. Spon: Charles Stoltz and Margaret.

Rosina, daughter of Nicholas Mack and Mary Magdalene, b. Jan. 10, 1786, bapt. Jan. 25, 1786. Spon: Christopher Rauch and Rosina.

Catherine, daughter of Henry Oberman and Gratia, b. Nov. 20, 1785, bapt. Jan. 29, 1786. Spon: Adam Mey and Catherine.

John, son of Adam Lange and Catherine, b. Jan. 16, 1786, bapt. Jan. 29, 1786. Spon: John Jouch.

Christine, daughter of Adam Beyer and Margaret, b. Jan. 1, 1786, bapt. Jan. 29, 1786. Spon: George Justus and Anne McAlroy.

John Andrew, son of George Joras and Elizabeth, b. Dec. 23, 1785, bapt. Jan. 29, 1786. Spon: Andrew Lex and Elizabeth.

Alice, daughter of Charles Kitts and Bridget, b. Jan. 4, 1786, bapt. Jan. 29, 1786. Spon: The Parents.

John, son of Henry Riegeler and Catherine, b. Dec. 25, 1785, bapt. Feb. 3, 1786. Spon: The Parents.

Conrad Adam, son of Adam Doerr and Catherine, b. Jan. 21, 1786, bapt. Feb. 4, 1786. Spon: Conrad Rohrman and Elizabeth.

John, son of Jacob Becker and Catherine, b. Nov. 1, 1785, bapt. Feb. 12, 1786. Spon: James Crass and Elizabeth.

John Peter, son of Jacob Halberstadt and Anna, b. Jan. 13, 1786, bapt. Feb. 15, 1786. Spon: John Halberstadt and Catherine.

Elizabeth, daughter of John Ginder and Margaret, b. Jan. 25, 1786, bapt. Feb. 19, 1786. Spon: George Wack and Elizabeth.

Michael, son of John Wickhert and Hannah, b. Feb. 5, 1786, bapt. Feb. 26, 1786. Spon: Michael Seidel and Cath. Spillenberg.

John, son of George Degenhart and Wilhelmina, b. Feb. 4, 1786, bapt. Feb. 26, 1786. Spon: John Kutzrock and Priscilla.

Frederick Meile, son of Frederick Meile and Barbara, b. Dec. 19, 1785, bapt. Feb. 26, 1786. Spon: The Parents.

Elizabeth, daughter of John Ecky and Lucretia, b. Feb. 14, 1786, bapt. Feb. 26, 1786. Spon: Cath. Bigonne.

Adam, son of Nicholas Eisenmenger and Elizabeth, b. Jan. 30, 1786, bapt. March 5, 1786. Spon: The Parents.

John, son of Balthasar Richtstein and Catherine, b. Dec. 26, 1785, bapt. March 4, 1786. Spon: Charles Richstein and Hannah.

Catherine, daughter of Michael Shumacher and Elizabeth, b. Jan. 4, 1786, bapt. March 5, 1786. Spon: Philip Pfannenkuchen and Catherine.

John Philip, son of Philip Zeller and Margaret, b. March 3, 1786, bapt. March 5, 1786. Spon: The Parents.

Susanna, daughter of Philip Wentz and Maria, b. Nov. 18, 1785, bapt. March 7, 1786. Spon: George Meyer and Susanna.

Maria, daughter of Adam Koehler and Gertrude, 4 wks. old, bapt. March 9, 1786. Spon: Stephen Gerlach and Maria.

Catherine, daughter of John Gerrith and Margaret, b. March 7, 1786, bapt. March 10, 1786. Spon: Adam Gerrith and Christine.

Catherine, daughter of William Proupert and Barbara, 4 wks. old, bapt. March 12, 1786. Spon: Jacob Buck and Cath. Proupert.

Jacob, son of John Lehr and Catherine, b. Feb. 19, 1786, bapt. March 12, 1786. Spon: John Schnyder and Catherine.

Samuel, son of Conrad Rauch and Maria, b. Feb. 12, 1786, bapt.

March 12, 1786. Spon: The Parents.
Peter, son of Wm. McSparren and Christine, b. Oct. 2, 1785, bapt. March 12, 1786. Spon: Peter Walter and The Parents.
Mary Magdalene, daughter of John Streith and Catherine, b. March 7, 1786, bapt. March 19, 1786. Spon: John Nicholas Willmer and Maria Dorothea.
Anna Catherine, daughter of William Kahmer and Elizabeth, b. March 17, 1785, bapt. March 22, 1786. Spon: Anna Fischer and Mr. Kahmer.
Maria, daughter of George Walter and Elizabeth, b. Feb. 28, 1786, bapt. March 26, 1786. Spon: Christopher Schmidt and Cath. Walter.
Christian, son of Christian Gilbert and Maria, b. March 24, 1786, bapt. March 27, 1786. Spon: The Parents.
John Conrad, son of John Conrad Hinckel and Barbara, b. March 23, 1786, bapt. April 2, 1786. Spon: The Parents.
Catherine, daughter of John Conterman and Susanna, b. March 22, 1786, bapt. April 2, 1786. Spon: Jacob Baumgart and Catherine.
John Felix, son of Peter Fenner and Catherine, b. March 14, 1786, bapt. April 2, 1786. Spon: Felix Fenner and Maria Eva.
Elizabeth, daughter of Christian Fans and Christine, b. Feb. 22, 1786, bapt. April 11, 1786. Spon: Jacob Hill and Elizabeth Hill.
John Jacob, son of Henry Denig and Maria, b. March 17, 1786, bapt. April 14, 1786. Spon: John Denig and Regina.
John George, son of John Weiand and Maria, b. Dec. 21, 1785, bapt. April 17, 1786. Spon: George Kress and Catherine.
Jacob, son of John King and Catherine, b. March 21, 1786, bapt. April 17, 1786. Spon: Jacob Ahner.
David, son of David Wisar and Maria, b. Jan. 31, 1786, bapt. April 17, 1786. Spon: The Parents.
Susanna, daughter of Jacob Jung and Sarah, b. Jan. 27, 1786, bapt. April 17, 1786. Spon: Casper Kloeckner and Susanna.
Christine, daughter of John Adam Stoll and Elizabeth, b. March 19, 1786, bapt. April 17, 1786, Spon: Theis Dinges and Christine Pfeiffer.
Margaret, daughter of John Henry Povert and Magdalene, b. April 16, 1786, bapt. April 23, 1786. Spon: John Durange and Margaret.
William, son of John Lefeber and Catherine, b. Feb. 16, 1786, bapt. April 23, 1786. Spon: William Weber and Elizabeth.
John Adam, son of John Fans and Catherine, b. Oct. 23, 1785, bapt. April 23, 1786. Spon: John Adam Striby and Sarah Fans.
Lydia, daughter of Charles Chamberlein and Maria, b. April 9, 1786, bapt. April 27, 1786. Spon: The Parents.
Conrad, son of Conrad Froman and Margaret, b. April 5, 1786, bapt. April 30, 1786. Spon: George Turner and Margaret.
Henry, son of Jacob Schreiner and Elizabeth, b. April 13, 1786, bapt. April 30, 1786. Spon: The Parents.
Joseph, son of Jacob Galladein and Sarah, 7 mos. old, bapt. May 8, 1786. Spon: Joseph Sens and Maria.
John Frederick, son of John Weisbach and Sophia, b. April 28, 1786, bapt. May 14, 1786. Spon: John Ricker and Cath. Coleman.
Peter, son of Peter Bockius and Elizabeth, b. April 23, 1786, bapt. May 14, 1786. Spon: The Parents and Catherine Etler.
Adam, son of John Justus Koch and Susanna, b. April 27, 1786, bapt.

May 21, 1786. Spon: Adam Dill and Catherine.
Maria, daughter of William von Phul and Catherine, b. May 17, 1786, bapt. May 25, 1786. Spon: Eva Krug.
Henry, son of Henry Funcke and Barbara, b. Nov. 30, 1786, bapt. May 25, 1786. Spon: Philip Reubold and Elizabeth.
Philip, son of Jacob Bonner and Elizabeth, b. May 26, 1786, bapt. May 26, 1786. Spon: Susanna Becker and Philippina Moser.
Michael, son of Michael Leonhard and Anna Catherine, b. April 22, 1786, bapt. May 28, 1786. Spon: Michael Wolff and Elizabeth Margaret.
Catherine, daughter of John Peter Schaeff and Elizabeth, b. May 3, 1786, bapt. June 2, 1786. Spon: George Schaeff and Elizabeth.
Ludwig, son of Christopher Schreiner and Elizabeth, b. May 18, 1786, bapt. June 3, 1786. Spon: The Parents.
Anna Maria, daughter of John George Krehmer and Anna, b. May 7, 1786, bapt. June 4, 1786. Spon: The Parents.
Sebastian, son of Andrew Mercker and Catherine, b. May 29, 1786, bapt. June 4, 1786. Spon: Sebastian Woolley and Christine.
Ludwig, son of Frederick Kreider and Veronica, b. May 3, 1786, bapt. June 3, 1786. Spon: Franciscus Froemmler and Christine.
William, son of Christopher Meininger and Anna Mary, b. May 20, 1786, bapt. June 4, 1786. Spon: William Henderson and Catherine.
Susanna, daughter of John Wiedbeck and Anna, 6 wks. old, bapt. June 4, 1786. Spon: The Parents.
William, son of Daniel Kayser and Regina, b. Jan. 17, 1786, bapt. June 4, 1786. Spon: William Moore and Susanna.
Francis Paul, son of David Marshall and Barbara, b. March 6, 1786, bapt. June 5, 1786. Spon: The Parents.
Christine, daughter of Isaiah Eschelman and Sibylla, b. [May 21]?, bapt. [June 11, 1786]?. Spon: Martin Wahl and Christine.
Maria, daughter of Isaiah Eschelman and Sibylla, b. May 21, 1786, bapt. [June 11, 1786]?. Spon: Engelbert Muntzer and Maria.
David, son of John Simon and Christine, b. April 13, 1786, bapt. June 12, 1786. Spon: The Parents.
Salome, son of John George Hoffman and Anna Maria, b. June 10, 1786, bapt. June 15, 1786. Spon: Jacob Hill and Elizabeth Hill.
Daniel, son of Zechariah Beckman and Barbara, b. May 27, 1786, bapt. June 18, 1786. Spon: Daniel Gilbert and Catherine.
Jacob, son of Jacob Riedlinger and Elizabeth, b. May 29, 1786, bapt. June 18, 1786. Spon: Jacob Bader and Maria Bader.
Jacob, son of Herman Leck and Margaret, 7 wks. old, bapt. June 18, 1786. Spon: The Parents.
John, son of John Klap and Maria, b. June 11, 1786, bapt. June 20, 1786. Spon: The Parents.
Susanna, daughter of Conrad Heney and Catherine, b. June 1, 1786, bapt. June 25, 1786. Spon: John Konterman and Susanna.
John Henry, son of George Fies and Dorothea, b. June 5, 1786, bapt. June 25, 1786. Spon: Henry Fies and Maria Steuerwald.
Susanna Miller, daughter of Joseph Hiller and Susanna, 4 yrs. old.
Nancy, daughter of Joseph Hiller and Susanna, 2 1/2 yrs.
John, son of Joseph Hiller and Susanna, 4 mos. old, bapt. ----.
Nancy Wheitman, daughter of ----, aged 20 yrs, bapt. June 27, 1786.
Maria Weithman, daughter of ----, aged 15 yrs., bapt. June 27, 1786.

John, son of Charles Kupper and Maria, b. June 29, 1786, bapt. June 30, 1786. Spon: The Parents.

Jacob, son of John Thiel and Catherine, b. June 1, 1786, bapt. July 2, 1786. Spon: The Parents.

James, son of James Creutz and Elizabeth, 10 wks. old, bapt. July 1, 1786. Spon: Nicholas Hess and Catherine Becker.

Elizabeth, daughter of George Bantz and Isabella, 4 wks. old, bapt. July 2, 1786. Spon: Philip Luro and Maria.

Henry, son of Philip Fritz and Charlotte, b. June 28, 1786, bapt. July 9, 1786. Spon: Henry Deaberger and Catherine Elizabeth.

Elizabeth, daughter of Captain Davis and Anna Mary Diehl, b. May 15, 1786, bapt. July 10, 1786. Spon: Elizabeth Dannecker.

Jacob, son of Andrew Ries and Margaret, b. June 6, 1786, bapt. July 12, 1786. Spon: John George Ries and Magdalene.

Christine, daughter of Jacob Lutz and Rosina, b. July 3, 1786, bapt. July 16, 1786. Spon: Sebastian Worle and Christine.

John, son of Daniel Klages and Maria, b. July 2, 1786, bapt. July 16, 1786. Spon: John Klages and Rosian.

Peter, son of Jacob Rumpf and Elizabeth, b. June 19, 1786, bapt. July 16, 1786. Spon: The Parents.

Henry, son of Henry Huber and Maria, b. May 31, 1786, bapt. July 18, 1786. Spon: The Parents.

Marianne, daughter of George Hinckel and Ruth, b. July 7, 1786, bapt. July 18, 1786. Spon: The Parents.

John Christopher, son of Jacob Sing and Catherine, b. June 3, 1786, bapt. July 20, 1786. Spon: Chrisotpher Vetter and Ann Barbara.

Anna, daughter of Philip Clumber and Susanna, b. July 14, 1785, bapt. July 20, 1786. Spon: The Parents and Maria Lora.

Rebecca and John, daughter and son of Philip Clumber and Susanna, b. July 16, 1786, bapt. July 20, 1786. Spon: The Parents and Maria Lora.

John George, son of George Brown and Maria, b. July 17, 1786, bapt. July 21, 1786. Spon: The Parents.

Maria, daughter of John Philips and Barbara, b. March 25, 1786, bapt. July 21, 1786. Spon: Catherine Stern.

Peter, son of Philip Haller and Maria, b. July 9, 1786, bapt. July 23, 1786. Spon: Peter Threyer and Barbara Haller.

William, son of Philip Worn and Maria, b. June 19, 1786, bapt. July 23, 1786. Spon: Philip Heyl and Maria Worn.

Catherine, daughter of George Schneider and Catherine, b. May 30, 1786, bapt. July 24, 1786. Spon: Catherine Reis.

William, son of John Riffet and wife, b. June 21, 1786, bapt. July 26, 1786. Spon: The Parents.

Anna Maria, daughter of William Stoll and Christine, b. July 16, 1786, bapt. July 30, 1786. Spon: Abrahm Hohman and Ann Mary Denis.

Philip, son of Henry Soest and Elizabeth, b. June 25, 1786, bapt. July 30, 1786. Spon: Philip Soest and Cath. Soest.

Joseph, son of Henry Schlatter and Anna Maria, b. May 27, 1783, bapt. July 30, 1786. Spon: John Jacob Dieder and Christine.

John Jacob, son of Henry Schlatter and Anna Maria, 8 mos. old, bapt. July 30, 1786. Spon: John Jacob Dieder and Christine.

Samuel and Elizabeth, son of Lorentz Roth and Elizabeth, b. Aug. 9, 1786, bapt. Aug. 11, 1786. Spon: The Parents.

Samuel, son of Jeremiah Weiser and Margaret, b. June 20, 1786, bapt. Aug. 13, 1786. Spon: John Rudolph and Sarah.

Anna Margaret, daughter of Peter Weiel and Elizabeth, b. July 21, 1786, bapt. Aug. 13, 1786. Spon: Jacob Schwefel and Maria Margaret.

Maria, daughter of Jacob Kampfer and Catherine, b. June 19, 1786, bapt. Aug. 14, 1786. Spon: Adam Schifferer and Barbara Strauss.

Conrad, son of John Lofsberry and Elizabeth, b. July 16, 1786, bapt. Aug. 15, 1786. Spon: Peter Becker and Mary Magdalene.

Hannah, daughter of John Furer and Anna Maria, b. April 21, 1786, bapt. Aug. 15, 1786. Spon: The Parents.

John, son of Peter Schug and Catherine, b. July 12, 1786, bapt. Aug. 20, 1786. Spon: -----.

Margaret, daughter of Conrad Keller and Elizabeth, 3 wks, 3 days old, bapt. Aug. 20, 1786. Spon: Henry Trubilly and Margaret.

Anna Margaret, daughter of Ludwig Reineck and Maria Elizabeth, b. Aug. 7, 1786, bapt. -----. Spon: The Parents.

Maria Elizabeth, daughter of Ludwig Reineck and Maria Elizabeth, b. Feb. 25, 1783, bapt. Aug. 20, 1786. Spon: The Parents.

John, son of George Zahner and Catherine, b. Aug. 15, 1786, bapt. Aug. 22, 1786. Spon: John Adam Logan and Maria.

Ludwig, son of Philip Pauli and Elizabeth, b. Aug. 10, 1786, bapt. Aug. 25, 1786. Spon: The Parents.

David, son of Henry Brede and Anna, b. July 20, 1786, bapt. Aug. 27, 1786. Spon: David Gilbert and Anna.

Henrietta, daughter of James Steel and Catherine, b. Aug. 28, 1786, bapt. Sept. 1, 1786. Spon: The Parents.

John, son of William Spaet and Sarah, b. Aug. 12, 1786, bapt. Sept. 3, 1786. Spon: The Parents.

Catherine, daughter of John Meibert and Elizabeth, b. July 14, 1786, bapt. Sept. 8, 1786. Spon: John Benner and Catherine.

George, son of Adam Roth and Maria, b. Aug. 18, 1786, bapt. Sept. 10, 1786. Spon: George Beumer and Maria Matthias.

Henry, son of Henry Horn and Christine, b. June 13, 1786, bapt. Sept. 10, 1786. Spon: The Parents.

Caroline Henrietta, daughter of Herman Bake and Caroline, b. Aug. 4, 1786, bapt. Sept. 10, 1786. Spon: The Parents.

Maria, daughter of John Becker and Elizabeth, b. Aug. 12, 1786, bapt. Sept. 10, 1786. Spon: The Parents.

Francis Clawsin, son of Philip Maus and Mary Magdalene, b. Aug. 17, 1786, bapt. Sept. 10, 1786. Spon: The Parents.

Margaret, daughter of Jacob Loscher and Margaret, b. July 28, 1786, bapt. Sept. 15, 1786. Spon: William Lehman and Margaret Fitler.

Margaret, daughter of John Wilcky and Barbara, b. May 18, 1786, bapt. Sept. 24, 1786. Spon: The Parents.

Elizabeth, daughter of Nicholas Schultz and Catherine, b. April 7, 1786, bapt. Sept. 20, 1786. Spon: -----.

Catherine, daughter of Jacob Heimer and Mercy, b. Aug. 31, 1786, bapt. Sept. 24, 1786. Spon: Catherine Heimer.

Samuel, son of Conrad Becker and Anna Maria, b. Aug. 22, 1786, bapt. Sept. 24, 1786. Spon: The Parents.

George, son of John Stricker and Sarah, b. Sept. 4, 1786, bapt. Sept. 24, 1786. Spon: The Parents.

Rebecca, daughter of Jacob Brown and Margaret, b. Aug. 28, 1786, bapt. Sept. 27, 1786. Spon: The Parents.

Robert, son of Robert Burch and Maria, b. Sept. 2, 1786, bapt.

Sept. 27, 1786. Spon: The Parents.
George, son of William Will and Maria, b. Aug. 12, 1786, bapt.
Sept. 28, 1786. Spon: The Parents.
Henry, son of John Wester and Margaret, b. Sept. 18, 1786, bapt.
Oct. 1, 1786, Spon: Henry Foer and Elizabeth.
Frederick, son of John Sehler and Susanna, b. Aug. 11, 1786, bapt.
Oct. 2, 1786. Spon: Frederick Cesh and Catherine.
Elizabeth, daughter of Samuel Stern and Catherine, b. Sept. 14,
1786, bapt. Oct. 4, 1786. Spon: The Parents.
John Samuel, son of Martin Zybold and Barbara, b. Sept. 17, 1786,
bapt. Oct. 8, 1786. Spon: The Parents.
Catherine, daughter of George Meyers and Sarah, b. Aug. 24, 1786,
bapt. Oct. 8, 1786. Spon: Christopher Jütte and Catherine.
Elizabeth, daughter of John Porter and Catherine, b. Sept. 24,
1786, bapt. Oct. 8, 1786. Spon: The Parents.
Abraham, son of Abraham Peter and Maria Barbara, b. Sept. 14, 1786,
bapt. Oct. 8, 1786. Spon: The Parents.
John, son of Michael Cunckel and Catherine, b. Aug. 19, 1786, bapt.
Oct. 15, 1786. Spon: The Parents.
John, son of John Latsch and wife, b. Oct. 10, 1786, bapt. Oct. 15,
1786. Spon: The Parents.
David, son of Lorentz Miller and Catherine, b. June 12, 1786, bapt.
Oct. 21, 1786. Spon: The Parents.
Maria, daughter of George Herford and Maria, b. Oct. 11, 1786,
bapt. Oct. 22, 1786. Spon: The Parents.
Maria, daughter of John Kern and Maria Elizabeth, b. Sept. 29,
1786, bapt. Oct. 22, 1786. Spon: John Kuhn and Maria Heffener.
Peter, son of William Stetzer and Martha, b. Aug. 11, 1786, bapt.
Oct. 22, 1786. Spon: Peter Bop and Elizabeth Foth.
William, son of Frederick Maus and Elizabeth, b. Sept. 18, 1786,
bapt. Oct. 22, 1786. Spon: William Troutwein and Maria.
John Conrad, son of Conrad Schmith and Anna Maria, b. Oct. 23,
1786, bapt. Oct. 27, 1786. Spon: Christine Lutz.
Nancy, daughter of William Haberstich and Maria, b. Oct. 8, 1786,
bapt. Oct. 29, 1786. Spon: The Parents.
Elizabeth, daughter of John Pott and Elizabeth, b. Oct. 25, 1786,
bapt. Nov. 6, 1786. Spon: The Parents.
Henry, son of Philip Gramlich and Elizabeth, b. Oct. 10, 1786,
bapt. Nov. 6, 1786. Spon: Henry Gramlich and Elizabeth.
Abraham, son of John Alburger and Dorothea, b. Oct. 17, 1786, bapt.
Nov. 6, 1786. Spon: Abraham Sherridan and Barbara.
John, son of John Brown and Abia, b. Sept. 7, 1786, bapt. Nov. 6,
1786. Spon: The Parents.
Margaret, daughter of Martin Haas and Jemima, b. Oct. 13, 1786,
bapt. Nov. 7, 1786. Spon: The Parents.
Maria Elizabeth, daughter of Jacob Halter and Eva Maria, b. Oct. 1,
1786, bapt. Nov. 9, 1786. Spon: The Parents.
Maria, daughter of Adam Hess and Elizabeth, b. Oct. 11, 1786, bapt.
Nov. 9, 1786. Spon: The Parents.
Anna Maria, daughter of Adam Bronner and Maria, b. Oct. 19, 1786,
bapt. Nov. 12, 1786. Spon: Henry Haffener and Maria.
John, son of Michael Heins and Maria, 4 wks. old, bapt. Nov. 12,
1786, Spon: Francis Hoffman and Margaret Penther.
Sarah, daughter of Martin Karsbach and Mary Magdalene, b. Oct. 13,
1786, bapt. Nov. 12, 1786. Spon: The Parents.

Eliz. Louisa, daughter of Jacob Caschah and Elizabeth, 2 yrs. old,
bapt. Nov. 16, 1786. Spon: Ludwig Faber and Eliz. Kreider.
Catherine, daughter of Daniel von der Schleis and Philippina, b.
Oct. 20, 1786, bapt. Nov. 19, 1786. Spon: Michael Seiffert and
Catherine.
William Joseph Fred., son of William Craig and Henrietta, b. Sept.
24, 1786, bapt. Nov. 19, 1786. Spon: John de Haas and Eleonora
Magd.
Philip Jacob, son of Adam Altberger and Elizabeth, b. Oct. 2, 1786,
bapt. Nov. 19, 1786. Spon: Philip Jacob Ohler and Catherine.
John Peter, son of Peter Pfeiffer and Maria Margaret, 5 wks. old,
bapt. Nov. 24, 1786. Spon: Peter Spengeler and Maria Emerig.
Magdalene, daughter of John Daum and Maria, 2 wks. old, bapt. Nov.
26, 1786. Spon: Sam Kloethy and Cath. Kloethy.
Michael, son of Adam Wever and wife, 1 yr. 4 mos. old, bapt. Nov.
30, 1786. Spon: The Parents.
Catherine, daughter of John Greenwood and Maria, 2 yrs 4 mos. old,
bapt. Dec. 1, 1786. Spon: The Parents.
Mary Magdalene, daughter of John Weller and Maria, b. Nov. 28,
1786, bapt. Dec. 3, 1786. Spon: Eberhard Langkof and Mary Magd.
Weller.
John Charles, son of Charles Schakar and Margaret, b. Oct. 13,
1786, bapt. Dec. 3, 1786. Spon: The Parents.
Elizabeth, daughter of John Steltz and Elizabeth, b. Nov. 16, 1786,
bapt. Dec. 10, 1786. Spon: The Parents.
Robert, son of John Williams and Maria, b. Dec. 3, 1786, bapt. Dec.
13, 1786. Spon: Robert Crass and wife.
John, son of Peter Reinhard and Sarah, b. Nov. 19, 1786, bapt. Dec.
17, 1786. Spon: Nicholas Eisenmenger and Sarah Reinhard.
John William, son of Peter Schreiber and wife, b. Nov. 29, 1786,
bapt. Dec. 17, 1786. Spon: Christopher Hensman and Maria
Barbara.
Catherine, daughter of Adam Wever and Catherine, b. Oct. 14, 1786,
bapt. Dec. 21, 1786. Spon: The Parents.
Robert, son of David Taggart and Catherine, b. May 28, 1784, bapt.
Dec. 21, 1786. Spon: The Parents.
David, son of Henry Wever and Hannah, b. Dec. 25, 1785, bapt. Dec.
21, 1786. Spon: The Parents.
Wilhelmina, daughter of Philip Odenheimer and Catherine, b. Nov.
30, 1786, bapt. Dec. 24, 1786. Spon: Jacob Uttre and Catherine.
Adam, son of Jonas Plesch and Christine, b. Nov. 27, 1786, bapt.
Dec. 24, 1786. Spon: Adam Doer and Catherine.
Christine, daughter of Matthias Krehmer and Susanna, b. Nov. 13,
1786, bapt. Dec. 24, 1786. Spon: The Parents and Christine
Bock.
Elizabeth, daughter of Werni Meyer and Catherine, b. Nov. 27, 1786,
bapt. Dec. 24, 1786. Spon: The Parents.
Gottfried, son of Jacob Baumgarth and Catherine, b. Dec. 18, 1786,
bapt. Dec. 31, 1786. Spon: Gottfried Munig and Veronica.
John, son of Jacob Meyer and Elizabeth, b. Nov. 19, 1786,bapt. Dec.
31, 1786. Spon: John Beck and Eva Maria.
Margaret, daughter of George Ozeas and Margaret, b. Dec. 11, 1786,
bapt. Dec. 31, 1786. Spon: Peter Ozeas and Margaret.
Charlotte, daughter of John Philip Rumel and Rebecca, b. Dec. 9,
1786, bapt. Dec. 31, 1786. Spon: Frederick Schreiner and

Charlotte Roden.

William, son of Christopher Schreiner and Elizabeth, b. Jan. 1, 1786, bapt. Jan. 4, 1787. Spon: Jacob Stucky and Margaret.

Sarah, daughter of Daniel Diehl and Maria, b. Dec. 17, 1786, bapt. Jan. 7, 1787. Spon: Jacob Diehl and Elizabeth Knies.

Rebecca, daughter of George Bachoff and Sarah, b. Oct. 22, 1786, bapt. Jan. 8, 1787. Spon: George Hoffman and Anna Maria.

Sophia, daughter of Philip Stimmel and Anna, b. July 24, 1786, bapt. Jan. 10, 1787. Spon: Christine Stimmel.

Jacobus, son of John Muller and Anna, b. Dec. 20, 1786, bapt. Jan. 14, 1787. Spon: Peter Mueller and Maria Montgomery.

Elizabeth, daughter of Henry Heineman and Charlotte, b. Dec. 27, 1786, bapt. Jan. 15, 1787. Spon: Jacob Schuhler and Elizabeth.

George, son of John Schutz and Maria, b. Dec. 31, 1786, bapt. Jan. 21, 1787. Spon: Barbara Schutz.

Jacob, son of William Pfeiffer and Margaret, b. Dec. 23, 1786, bapt. Jan. 21, 1787. Spon: The Parents.

Samuel, son of Daniel Sutter and Eva Catherine, b. Jan. 1, 1787, bapt. Jan. 21, 1787. Spon: The Parents.

Jacob, son of Jacob Himpelman and Elizabeth, b. Jan. 16, 1787, bapt. Jan. 28, 1787. Spon: Jacob Geyer and Margaret Borck.

Gottfried, son of Valentine Gaul and Sabina, b. Dec. 28, 1786, bapt. Jan. 28, 1787. Spon: Gottfried Muenig and Veronica.

William, son of Christian Heis and Sarah, b. Oct. 13, 1786, bapt. Jan. 28, 1787. Spon: The Parents.

Anna Margaret, daughter of Nicholas Mack and Magdalene, 6 wks old, bapt. Jan. 28, 1787. Spon: Sam Forter and Margaret.

Philip, son of Philip Schaeffer and Catherine, b. Jan. 20, 1787, bapt. Feb. 1, 1787. Spon: Philip Schaeffer.

Valentine, son of Peter Becker and Mary Magdalene, b. Jan. 9, 1787, bapt. Feb. 2, 1786. Spon: The Parents.

Sarah, daughter of Jacob Becker and Abia, b. Jan. 9, 1787, bapt. Feb. 2, 1787. Spon: John Loffberry and Elizabeth.

Jacob, son of Jacob Bischoffberger and Elizabeth, b. Jan. 22, 1787, bapt. Feb. 4, 1787. Spon: Jacob Jentzer and Barbara Tschudy.

Charlotte, daughter of Charles Seitz and Charlotte, b. Feb. 19, ----, bapt. Feb. 11, 1787. Spon: Charles Roush and John Roush.

George Ros, son of Frederick Froelig and Catherine, b. Jan. 16, 1787, bapt. Feb. 11, 1787. Spon: The Parents.

Sarah, daughter of John Osman and Elizabeth, b. Jan. 13, 1787, bapt. Feb. 12, 1787. Spon: John Stricker and Sarah.

Magdalene, daughter of Adam Weis and Elizabeth, b. Jan. 5, 1787, bapt. Feb. 16, 1787. Spon: The Parents.

Catherine, daughter of Conrad Bachman and Susanna, b. Feb. 7, 1787, bapt. Feb. 18, 1787. Spon: George Nies and Catherine.

Jacob, son of Michael Katz and Margaret, b. Jan. 19, 1787, bapt. Feb. 18, 1787. Spon: The Parents.

Elizabeth, daughter of Christopher Lughard and Elizabeth, b. Feb. 7, 1787, bapt. Feb. 18, 1787. Spon: Elizabeth Ritter.

Conrad, son of John Boom and Catherine, 4 wks, old, bapt. Feb. 18, 1787. Spon: Conrad Becker and Maria.

Catherine, daughter of John Braunig and Elizabeth, b. Jan. 7, 1787, bapt. Jan. 24, 1787. Spon: The Parents.

John, son of John Kurtzrock and Priscilla, b. Feb. 15, 1787, bapt. Feb. 25, 1787. Spon: John Bauer and Barbara.

Paul, son of Christian Rossin and Catherine, b. Feb. 5, 1787, bapt.
Feb. 25, 1787. Spon: The Parents.
Anna Barbara, daughter of George Dies and Eva, b. Oct. 16, 1786,
bapt. Feb. 25, 1787, Spon: Michael Kinsel and Barbara
Nagelschmidt.
Susanna, daughter of James Becke and Elizabeth, b. Dec. 16, 1786,
bapt. Feb. 28, 1787. Spon: Fred. Schenckel and Susanna.
John Bernard, son of George Gaul and Catherine, b. Feb. 12, 1787,
bapt. March 4, 1787. Spon: The Parents.
William, son of Peter Walter and Charlotte, b. Feb. 6, 1787, bapt.
March 4, 1787. Spon: The Parents.
Maria, daughter of William McSparren and Christine, b. Jan. 25,
1787, bapt. March 4, 1787. Spon: The Parents.
Conrad, son of Conrad Kraufferts and Anna, b. Feb. 23, 1787, bapt.
March 5, 1787. Spon: The Parents.
Anna Magdalene, daughter of John Leiberger and Anna Catherine, b.
Dec. 17, 1786, bapt. March 8, 1787. Spon: The Parents.
William, son of John Kelly and Elizabeth, 4 wks. old, bapt. March
8, 1787. Spon: William Ritter and Elizabeth.
Elizabeth, daughter of Henry Becker and Gertrude, b. Feb. 5, 1787,
bapt. March 11, 1787. Spon: John Scheive and Dina.
Anna Christine, daughter of William Rudolph and Magdalene, b. Feb.
19, 1787, bapt. March 11, 1787. Spon: Frederick Breunig and
Christine.
John, son of Jacob Kreider and Elizabeth, b. Feb. 17, 1787, bapt.
March 11, 1787. Spon: John Kreider and Elizabeth.
Jacob, son of Christian Aug. Krichoff and Mary Magdalene, b. Feb.
16, 1787, bapt. March 18, 1787. Spon: ----.
Elizabeth, daughter of Frederick Mangold and Barbara, b. Feb. 18,
1787, bapt. March 18, 1787. Spon: Henry Ries and Elizabeth.
Margaret, daughter of Jacob Becker and Elizabeth, b. Feb. 23, 1787,
bapt. March 18, 1787. Spon: Jacob Renck and Margaret.
John Henry, son of Cyriacus Wagner and Elizabeth, b. Jan. 28, 1787,
bapt. March 18, 1787. Spon: Henry Volck and Anna Catherine.
Hester, son of Caleb Hughes and Maria, b. March 4, 1787, bapt.
March 18, 1787. Spon: The Parents.
Samuel, son of Daniel Schittel and Elizabeth, b. Feb. 1, 1787,
bapt. March 26, 1787. Spon: William Roberts and Catherine.
Susanna, daughter of Jacob Esler and Susanna, b. Feb. 22, 1787,
bapt. March 26, 1787. Spon: The Parents.
Catherine, daughter of John Schuckard and Maria, b. March 7, 1787,
bapt. March 26, 1787. Spon: Charles Rauchbart and Anna Barbara.
Thomas, son of John Klages and Rosina, b. March 15, 1787, bapt.
March 27, 1787. Spon: Thomas Fischer and Elizabeth.
Henry, son of James Hoffman and Eva, b. March 12, 1787, bapt. April
1, 1787. Spon: Henry Heppler and Gertrude.
Catherine, daughter of William Nicholas and Hannah, b. April 1,
1787, bapt. April 1, 1787. Spon: John Baerdt and Catherine
Scherer.
Margaret, daughter of Simeon Mayland and Margaret, b. Jan. 27,
1781, bapt. April 3, 1787. Spon: Maria Oxley Gerin.
Samuel, son of Simeon Mayland and Margaret, b. Nov. 18, 1782, bapt.
April 3, 1787. Spon: Francisca McCannister.
Sarah, daughter of Simeon Mayland and Margaret, b. April 10, 1785,
bapt. April 3, 1787. Spon: Anna Thieleman.

William, son of Simeon Mayland and Margaret, b. Dec. 25, 1786, bapt. April 3, 1787. Spon: The Parents.
John Adam, son of Opethy Wilti and Anna Maria, b. Jan. 28, 1787, bapt. April 6, 1787. Spon: The Parents.
Elizabeth, daughter of George Schultz and Susanna, b. March 13, 1787, bapt. April 6, 1787. Spon: The Parents.
Magdalene, daughter of Bernard Schwenck and Margaret, b. Jan. 16, 1787, bapt. April 8, 1787. Spon: Magdalene Roberts.
Elizabeth, daughter of Christian Lawyer and Margaret, b. March 26, 1787, bapt. April 9, 1787. Spon: The Parents and Elizabeth Orlob.
Salome, son of John Hens and Elizabeth, b. Dec. 30, 1786, bapt. April 11, 1787. Spon: Catherine Kloh.
John, son of Christian Heny and Maria Barbara, b. April 10, 1787, bapt. April 14, 1787. Spon: John Haas and wife.
Daniel, son of Christopher Penther and Catherine, b. Dec. 25, 1785, bapt. April 14, 1787. Spon: The Parents.
Elizabeth, daughter of John Meile and Catherine, b. Feb. 22, 1787, bapt. April 15, 1787. Spon: Martin Keiger and Elizabeth Demuth.
Maria Catherine, daughter of George Schmnidt and Elizabeth, b. Feb. 3, 1787, bapt. April 16, 1787. Spon: John Fleitz and Elizabeth Schmidt.
George, son of Charles Joest and Christine, b. April 3, 1787, bapt. April 19, 1787. Spon: The Parents.
Philip, son of Nicholas Rummel and Barbara, b. April 6, 1787, bapt. April 22, 1787. Spon: Philip Haller and Maria.
Christine Margaret, daughter of George Eisenring and Elizabeth, b. March 27, 1787, bapt. April 22, 1787. Spon: Christine Margaret Sackman.
Anna Maria, daughter of Philip Gasser and Anna Maria, b. April 15, 1787, bapt. April 24, 1787. Spon: John Geo. Hoffman and Anna Maria.
George, son of Jacob Sehler and Maria, b. March 10, 1787, bapt. April 29, 1787. Spon: George Kurtz and Margaret.
Jacob, son of Nicholas Weyerich and Susanna, b. April 10, 1787, bapt. April 29, 1787. Spon: Jacob Diederich and Mrs. Meyer.
Andrew, son of Andrew Mercker and Catherine, b. April 27, 1787, bapt. May 2, 1787. Spon: Maria Nebel.
Henry and John George, sons of John George Pfaff and Anna, b. May 3, 1787, bapt. ----. Spon: The Parents.
Henry Peter, son of Jacob Wever and Elizabeth, b. April 11, 1787, bapt. May 5, 1787. Spon: The Parents.
Margaret, daughter of William Skinner and Elizabeth, b. April 11, 1787, bapt. May 6, 1787. Spon: The Parents.
Charlotte Elizabeth, daughter of George Zeisinger and Maria Margaret, b. March 24, 1787, bapt. May 13, 1787. Spon: Charlotte Louisa, Henry Loera and daughter Dorothea Elizabeth.
Jacob, son of Jacob Burckhardt and Margaret McMeeken, b. April 25, 1787, bapt. May 13, 1787. Spon: Daniel Weil and Eliz. Weil.
John Jacob, son of Jacob Burckhardt and Margaret McMeeken, b. April 25, 1784, bapt. May 13, 1787. Spon: Jacob Kaest and Susanna Renno.
Elizabeth, daughter of John Jameson and Elizabeth, b. April 17, 1787, bapt. May 13, 1787. Spon: John Broomsen and Elizabeth.
Catherine, daughter of John Scheive and Maria Christine, b. May 14,

1787, bapt. May 16, 1787. Spon: John Gunckel and Christine.
Thomas, son of Abraham Sheridan and Barbara, b. Jan. 20, 1785,
bapt. Jan. 30, 1785. Spon: The Parents.
Mary Magdalene, daughter of Jacob Jung and Sarah, b. March 18,
1787, bapt. May 17, 1787. Spon: George Haeffner and Mary
Magdalene.
Abraham, son of Abraham Sheridan and Barbara, b. April 16, 1787,
bapt. May 17, 1787. Spon: The Parents.
Catherine, daughter of John Farris and Magdalene, b. July 4, 1786,
bapt. May 17, 1787. Spon: Catherine Winckeler.
Anna Catherine, daughter of Francis Trimmer and Chresella, b. April
21, 1787, bapt. May 20, 1787. Spon: Nicholas Schultz, Anna
Catherine and William Brown.
Francis Casper Hasenclever, son of Jacob Schallus and Elizabeth, b.
June 8, 1781, bapt. May 20, 1787. Spon: The Parents.
Louisa, daughter of Jacob Schallus and Elizabeth, b. Sept. 15,
1783, bapt. May 20, 1787. Spon: The Parents.
Julianna, daughter of Jacob Schallus and Elizabeth, b. Oct. 17,
1785, bapt. May 20, 1787. Spon: The Parents.
Maria, daughter of Casparus Grissem and Elizabeth, b. July 30,
1786, bapt. May 21, 1787. Spon: The Parents.
Margaret, daughter of Thomas Schillingsworth and Rosina, 10 mos.
old, bapt. May 21, 1787. Spon: Margaret Lory.
Maria, daughter of Gottlieb Burg and Maria, b. Aug. 9, 1785, bapt.
May 21, 1787. Spon: ----.
John Conrad, son of Conrad Lies and Christine, b. April 2, 1787,
bapt. May 21, 1787. Spon: Grandparents.
Rebecca, daughter of Daniel Baechtle and Margaret, b. May 1, 1787,
bapt. May 24, 1787. Spon: The Parents.
Catherine, daughter of Henry Loehr and Elizabeth, b. April 24,
1787, bapt. May 27, 1787. Spon: Jacob Nannetter and Catherine.
Joseph, son of Carl Jacob Detz and Elizabeth, b. May 5, 1787, bapt.
May 27, 1787. Spon: The Parents.
John, son of Jacob Posser and Mary Magdalene, b. July 27, 1785,
bapt. May 27, 1787. Spon: Frederick Boyer and Catherine.
Christine, daughter of Frederick Boger and Susanna, b. April 29,
1787, bapt. May 27, 1787. Spon: Nicholas Juvenal and Susanna.
Maria Catherine, daughter of John Messemer and Maria Catherine, b.
March 1, 1787, bapt. May 28, 1787. Spon: The Parents.
George, son of Martin Mueller and Elizabeth, b. Jan. 22, 1787,
bapt. May 28, 1787. Spon: Janna Schacky and George Muller.
Jacob, son of Jacob Schlemmer and Hannah, b. May 18, 1787, bapt.
May 29, 1787. Spon: The Parents and Grandmother Cath.
Andrew, son of Gabriel Kern and Mary Magdalene, b. May 13, 1787,
bapt. June 3, 1787. Spon: Andrew Lex and Mary Magdalene.
George, son of Paul Sturmfels and Margaret, b. May 17, 1787, bapt.
June 3, 1787. Spon: George Sturmfels and Barbara Nushag.
Peter, son of Philip Loury and Susanna, b. April 22, 1787, bapt.
June 3, 1787. Spon: The Parents.
Christian, son of Frederick Jentzer and Jacobina, b. April 22,
1787, bapt. June 3, 1787. Spon: Christian Jentzer and Christine
Wing.
Margaret, daughter of John Ginder and Margaret, b. April 28, 1787,
bapt. June 10, 1787. Spon: George Wack and Elizabeth.
Ludwig, son of Philip Schreit and Elizabeth, b. Dec. 10, 1783,

bapt. June 10, 1787. Spon: The Parents.

Catherine, daughter of Henry Wetzler and Philipina, b. June 1, 1787, bapt. June 20, 1787. Spon: The Parents.

John Fried, son of John Fried Gauel and Margaret, b. April 2, 1787, bapt. June 24, 1787. Spon: The Parents.

John Fried, son of George Neiss and Veronica, b. June 8, 1787, bapt. June 25, 1787. Spon: Fried Heineman and Catherine.

Daniel Bergemeyer, son of William Himmelreich and Eva Barbara, b. Jan. 20, 1787, bapt. June 26, 1787. Spon: Philip Souder and Maria Klein.

Jacob, son of Joseph Funck and Maria, b. June 8, 1787, bapt. June 28, 1787. Spon: Jacob Fies and Anna.

Elizabeth, daughter of George Wm. Steinhauer and Elizabeth, b. June 12, 1787, bapt. July 1, 1787. Spon: The Parents.

John Michael, son of John Michael Rummel and Magdalene, b. May 21, 1787, bapt. July 1, 1787. Spon: Michael Matzinger and Elizabeth.

Eleonore, daughter of Samuel Rawle and Eleonora, 14 yrs. old, bapt. July 1, 1787. Spon: George Wm. Steinhauer and Elizabeth.

Elizabeth, daughter of Graft Weyand and Christine, b. June 28, 1787, bapt. July 5, 1787. Spon: The Parents.

Ludwig, son of Christian Rauck and Maria, b. June 20, 1787, bapt. July 7, 1787. Spon: Ludwig Diemer.

Elizabeth, daughter of Henry Sell and Maria, b. May 22, 1787, bapt. July 7, 1787. Spon: The Parents.

Martin, son of Henry Gate and Anna Catherine, b. June 19, 1787, bapt. July 8, 1787. Spon: Martin Wahl and Christine.

Elizabeth, daughter of Lorentz Ries and Elizabeth, b. April 27, 1787, bapt. July 8, 1787. Spon: The Parents.

Peter, son of Peter Diehl and Elizabeth, b. May 13, 1787, bapt. July 8, 1787. Spon: Alberti Schillack and Maria.

Catherine, daughter of Fabian Hemerlin and Catherine, b. June 19, 1787, bapt. July 8, 1787. Spon: Stephen Riegler and Elizabeth.

John, son of John Penther and Maria, b. April 26, 1787, bapt. July 10, 1787. Spon: The Parents.

William, son of Peter Auner and Margaret, b. April 22, 1787, bapt. July 11, 1787. Spon: The Parents.

Elizabeth, daughter of Jacob Finck and Maria Margaret, b. March 18, 1786, bapt. July 12, 1787. Spon: The Parents.

Maria, daughter of William Becker and Anna Maria, b. June 24, 1787, bapt. July 15, 1787. Spon: William Schmidt and Maria Gerlach.

Mary Magdalene, daughter of Philip Losch and Margaret, b. May 2, 1787, bapt. July 15, 1787. Spon: Christian Gilbert and Mary Magdalene.

Christine, daughter of Christopher Wassum and Maria, b. July 1, 1787, bapt. July 18, 1787. Spon: Jacob Karch and Christine Conradt.

Joseph, son of George Blum and Catherine, b. July 9, 1787, bapt. July 22, 1787. Spon: The Parents.

Joseph, son of John Kirschener and Catherine, 3 yrs. 7 mos. old, bapt. July 23, 1787, Spon: Jacob Brown and Catherine Souer.

Catherine, daughter of John Kirschener and Catherine, 4 mos. old, bapt. July 23, 1787. Spon: Jacob Brown and Catherine Souer.

Frederick David, son of George Schakar and Christine, b. July 17, 1787, bapt. July 24, 1787. Spon: Matthias Schakar and Anna

Maria Sophia Schakar.
Isabella, daughter of Matthias Gucker and Magdalene, b. July 13, 1787, bapt. July 24, 1787. Spon: Francis Becker and Isabella.
John Henry, son of John Kamper and Elizabeth, b. July 7, 1787, bapt. Jan. 29, 1787. Spon: Henry Kamper and Mary Magdalene.
Anna and Sarah, daughter of George Hesse and Anna, b. July 17, 1787, bapt. July 29, 1787. Spon: The Parents and Sarah Moore.
Joseph, son of Joseph Gressler and Susanna Stademan, b. July 23, 1787, bapt. July 29, 1787. Spon: ----.
John, son of Christian Hahn and Hannah, b. July 13, 1787, bapt. July 29, 1787. Spon: The Parents.
Jacob, son of Jacob Schneider and Anna, b. April 17, 1787, bapt. Aug. 1, 1787. Spon: Daniel Sutter and Anna Catherine.
Jacob, son of Frederick Weiler and Catherine, b. March 22, 1786, bapt. Aug. 6, 1787. Spon: Jacob Baumgardt and Anna Catherine.
Maria Margaret, daughter of Samuel Tarter and Margaret, b. Aug. 6, 1787, bapt. Aug. 6, 1787. Spon: Maria Helwig.
George, son of Peter Scherer and Anna Maria, b. March 21, 1787, bapt. Aug. 8, 1787. Spon: John Michael Baerdt and Catherine.
Elizabeth, daughter of Henry Ritter and Anna, b. July 22, 1787, bapt. Aug. 12, 1787. Spon: The Parents.
Michael, son of Nicholas Kaiser and Elizabeth, b. Feb. 21, 1787, bapt. Aug. 12, 1787. Spon: Michael Kitts and Margaret.
Sarah, daughter of Adam Wever and Catherine, b. July 1, 1787, bapt. Aug. 13, 1787. Spon: Cathies (?) Heuet and Cath. Hartman.
Christian, son of John Conterman and Susanna, b. Aug. 4, 1787, bapt. Aug. 19, 1787. Spon: Christian Schout.
Peter, son of George Peter and Anna Maria, b. Aug. 12, 1787, bapt. Aug. 19, 1787. Spon: John Peter Stoudt and Barbara.
Elizabeth, daughter of George Riegener and Sarah, b. July 31, 1787, bapt. Aug. 19, 1787. Spon: Elizabeth Maag.
Henry, son of Peter Emig and Susanna, b. Sept. 4, 1786, bapt. Aug. 23, 1787. Spon: The Parents.
Elizabeth,, daughter of Jacob Sehler and Margaret, b. May 15, 1787, bapt. July 26, 1787. Spon: John Sehler, Catherine, Thomas Gramlig and Anna Maria
Maria, daughter of Jacob Sehler and Margaret, b. May 15, 1787, bapt. July 26, 1787. Spon: John Sehler, Catherine, Thomas Gramlig and Anna Maria.
Margaret, daughter of John Kihn and Catherine, b. Aug. 20, ----, bapt. July 27, 1787. Spon: Jacob Orner and Sarah.
Anna Catherine, daughter of John Kreims and Elizabeth, b. Aug. 11, ----, bapt. July 31, 1787. Spon: John Wolfgang Gemeinbauer and Anna Maria.
John, son of John Gunckel and Margaret, b. Aug. 11, 1787, bapt. Sept. 2, 1787. Spon: Sophia Lampater.
Elizabeth, daughter of John Souder and Catherine, b. Aug. 19, 1787, bapt. Sept. 2, 1787. Spon: Jacob Kresman and Elizabeth.
Anna Elizabeth, daughter of James Aris and Catherine, b. ----, bapt. Sept. 3, 1787. Spon: Anna Eliz. Thresher.
Charles, son of George Loscher and Anna, b. Feb. 28, 1787, bapt. Sept. 4, 1787. Spon: The Parents.
Jacob, son of Jacob Striby and Christine, b. July 28, 1787, bapt. Sept. 9, 1787. Spon: Michael Mueller and Christine.
Andrew, son of Conrad Muller and Margaret, b. Aug. 28, 1787, bapt.

Sept. 10, 1787. Spon: Andrew Dag and Christine.
Elizabeth, daughter of George Baumer and Catherine, b. Sept. 5, 1787, bapt. Sept. 11, 1787. Spon: Elizabeth Herderling.
Margaret, daughter of Christian Kiepert and Anna Maria, b. Sept. 8, 1787, bapt. Sept. 13, 1787. Spon: Philip Losch and Margaret.
John, son of John Abel and Maria, b. Aug. 28, 1787, bapt. Sept. 16, 1787. Spon: Peter Abel and Christine.
Anna, daughter of Leonard Jundt and Sarah, b. Aug. 25, 1787, bapt. Sept. 23, 1787. Spon: Anna Junt.
John George, son of Isaac Mikzer and Elizabeth, b. Aug. 24, 1787, bapt. Sept. 16, 1787. Spon: The Parents.
Maria, daughter of William Peltz and Maria, b. Sept. 10, 1787, bapt. Sept. 25, 1787. Spon: The Parents.
Anna Margaret, daughter of John Berckenbeul and Barbara, b. May 9, 1787, bapt. Sept. 30, 1787. Spon: John Geo. Berckenbeul and Anna Margaret.
Mary Magdalene, daughter of John Bitting and Elizabeth, 18 mos. old, bapt. Sept. 30, 1788. Spon: Jeremiah Wasser and Margaret.
Elizabeth, daughter of Conrad Rush and Margaret, b. Aug. 30, 1787, bapt. Oct. 8, 1787. Spon: The Parents.
Catherine, daughter of Frederick Weiler and Catherine, b. Sept. 8, 1787, bapt. Oct. 9, 1787. Spon: Jacob Baumgarten and Catherine.
Elizabeth, daughter of Frederick Meile and Barbara, b. Oct. 12, 1787, bapt. Oct. 14, 1787. Spon: Christian Solcher and Elizabeth Reude.
Catherine, daughter of Jeremiah Vielmalter and Catherine, b. Oct. 1, 1787, bapt. Oct. 16, 1787. Spon: Nicholas Schultz and Caroline.
Henoch, son of John Froeling and Christine, b. Sept. 12, 1787, bapt. Oct. 19, 1787. Spon: The Parents.
Anthony, son of John Ecky and Lucretia, b. Oct. 10, 1787, bapt. Oct. 21, 1787. Spon: The Parents and Catherine Bigonne.
Elizabeth, daughter of George Bornhaus and Elizabeth, b. Oct. 1, 1787, bapt. Oct. 21, 1787. Spon: John Spalter and Elizabeth.
George, son of George Schroepel and Catherine, 5 mos. old, bapt. Oct. 25, 1787. Spon: Philip Haffener.
John Jacob, son of Jacob Wm. Friederich and Anna, b. Sept. 24, 1787, bapt. Oct. 28, 1787. Spon: Christopher Schmidt and Cath. Hoffman.
Maria Theresia, daughter of Matthias Fallies and Catherine, b. Oct. 7, 1787, bapt. Oct. 28, 1787. Spon: The Parents and Maria Rauch.
Charlotte Catherine, daughter of John Lamsbach and Christine, b. Oct. 13, 1787, bapt. Oct. 28, 1787. Spon: Christian Himpel and Charlotte Cath. Hagegatz.
Maria, daughter of Peter Paris and Veronica, b. Oct. 16, 1787, bapt. Nov. 6, 1787. Spon: Grandparents.
John, son of Lorentz Opman and Margaret, 7 wks. old, bapt. Nov. 6, 1787. Spon: The Parents.
William, son of William Bell and Margaret, b. Aug. 31, 1787, bapt. Nov. 11, 1787. Spon: The Parents and Margaret Steinmetz.
Elizabeth, daughter of Christopher Muller and Maria, 9 wks. old, bapt. Nov. 11, 1787. Spon: Fred. Tschudy and Elizabeth Schneider.
Morton Brealsford, son of Matthias Kaley and Hannah, b. Oct. 18,

1787, bapt. Nov. 17, 1787. Spon: Morton Breaslford and The Parents.

Maria, daughter of Philip Haller and Maria, b. Nov. 1, 1786, bapt. Nov. 22, 1787. Spon: Jacob Ries and Maria.

John, son of John Metzger and Helena, b. Nov. 11, 1787, bapt. Nov. 25, 1787. Spon: John Quast and Susanna.

Maria Catherine, daughter of Adam May and Catherine, b. Nov. 16, 1787, bapt. Nov. 25, 1787. Spon: Adam Wagener and Catherine.

Sarah, daughter of George Jentzer and Catherine, b. Sept. 15, 1787, bapt. Nov. 26, 1787. Spon: The Parents.

Elizabeth, daughter of John Sturtzebach and Margaret, b. Nov. 2, 1787, bapt. Dec. 2, 1787. Spon: Jacob Matthias and Elizabeth Lampeter.

Maria, daughter of Gottfried Gobeler and Anna Catherine, b. Oct. 27, 1787, bapt. Dec. 2, 1787. Spon: The Parents.

Joseph, son of John Pfeiffer and Jane, b. Sept. 17, 1787, bapt. Nov. 26, 1787. Spon: The Parents.

George, son of Adam Bagert and Margaret, b. Nov. 2, 1787, bapt. Nov. 25, 1787. Spon: George Justus and Meckle Ray.

Jacob, son of William Pfau and Barbara, 2 yrs. old, bapt. Dec. 6, 1787. Spon: William Pfau and Maria Elizabeth.

Jacob, son of William Pfau and Barbara, b. June 13, 1787, bapt. Dec. 6, 1787. Spon: The Parents.

Henry, son of Henry Krehmer and Catherine, b. Nov. 7, 1787, bapt. Dec. 9, 1787. Spon: The Parents.

John, son of William Sanders and Mary Margaret, b. March 12, 1787, bapt. Dec. 13, 1787. Spon: John Kamper and Elizabeth.

Samuel, son of William Orefgon and Susanna, b. Oct. 26, 1787, bapt. Dec. 19, 1787. Spon: The Parents.

Jacob, son of Peter Kupper and Catherine, b. Nov. 26, 1787, bapt. Dec. 24, 1787. Spon: Andrew Boshardt and Catherine.

John Henry, son of Casper Betzler and Elizabeth, b. June 9, 1787, bapt. Dec. 25, 1787. Spon: John Henry Beyer and Anna Margaret.

Anna Elizabeth, daughter of George Lies and Margaret, b. Dec. 15, 1787, bapt. Dec. 26, 1787. Spon: Christopher Hensman and Maria Schreiber.

Maria, daughter of Philip Wirth and Dorothea, b. July 5, 1787, bapt. Dec. 27, 1787. Spon: Maria Clara Wirth and Jacob Penther.

Henry, son of Henry Strup and Susanna, b. Nov. 6, 1787, bapt. Dec. 29, 1787. Spon: The Parents.

A Child of George Huffarth and Barbara, b. Dec. 19, 1787, bapt. Jan. 2, 1788. Spon: Francis Geis and Regina.

Sarah, daughter of John David Becker and Maria, b. Dec. 28, 1787, bapt. Jan. 10, 1788. Spon: John Stahl and Elizabeth.

John Ludwig, son of George Einwaechter and Elizabeth, b. Dec. 28, 1787, bapt. Jan. 13, 1788. Spon: Anthony Frey and Barbara Frey.

Rudolph, son of Adam Stricker and Barbara, b. Nov. 4, 1787, bapt. Jan. 13, 1788. Spon: The Parents.

John, son of Adam Lehr and Rebecca, b. Dec. 30, 1787, bapt. Jan. 14, 1788. Spon: The Parents.

Anna Maria, daughter of Thomas Hueter and Anna Catherine, b. Jan. 1, 1788, bapt. Jan. 18, 1788. Spon: Balthasar Taubstrich and Anna Maria Kochersberger.

Anna Maria, daughter of George Degener and Wilhelmina, 3 wks. old, bapt. Jan. 20, 1788. Spon: Frederick Frott and Catherine.

John Peter, son of Peter Fenner and Catherine, b. Jan. 6, 1788, bapt. Jan. 20, 1788. Spon: Peter Schneider and Catherine.
Anna Elizabeth, daughter of Francis Anthony Metzger and Hannah, b. Jan. 1, 1788, bapt. Jan. 20, 1788. Spon: William Will and Anna.
John Reinhard, son of William Ludwig Kahmer and Elizabeth, b. Jan. 11, 1788, bapt. Jan. 22, 1788. Spon: Reinhard Kahmer and Elizabeth Worck.
Maria Catherine, daughter of Peter Merckle and Anna Catherine, b. Jan. 25, 1786, bapt. Jan. 23, 1788. Spon: The Parents.
Maria Sarah, daughter of Peter Merckle and Anna Catherine, b. Sept. 4, 1787, bapt. Jan. 23 1788. Spon: Margaret Ulrich.
Frederick, son of Jacob Baumgardt and Catherine, b. Jan. 17, 1788, bapt. Jan. 24, 1788. Spon: Frederick Weiler and Catherine.
Dorothea, daughter of Chrisopher Schreiner and Elizabeth, b. Jan. 6, 1788, bapt. Jan. 26, 1788. Spon: Jacob Schreiner and Elizabeth.
Valentine, son of John Stillwagen and Margaret, b. Jan. --, 1788, bapt. Jan. 27, 1788. Spon: Jacob Schreiner and Elizabeth.
Martin, son of Martin Schuster and Catherine, b. Sept. 17, 1787, bapt. Jan. 31, 1788. Spon: John Klein and Hannah.
Anna Margaret, daughter of John George Birckenbeul and Elizabeth, b. Jan. 11, 1788, bapt. Feb. 2, 1788. Spon: John Schaub and Elizabeth.
John Henry, son of John Henry Fenner and Elizabeth, b. Nov. 19, 1787, bapt. Feb. 3, 1788. Spon: The Parents.
William, son of John Spaet and Philippina, b. Feb. 18, 1786, bapt. Feb. 7, 1788. Spon: John Peter Dietz and Anna Mary.
Daniel, son of John Grauel and Elizabeth, b. Jan. 27, 1788, bapt. Feb. 12, 1788. Spon: Daniel Grub.
Catherine, daughter of George Kins and Catherine, b. June 12, 1787, bapt. Feb. 14, 1788. Spon: Frederick Wentz.
Simon, son of David Roehrman and Anna Margaret, b. Dec. 28, 1787, bapt. Feb. 17, 1788. Spon: Simon Mertz and Elizabeth Mertz.
John George, son of John George Fies and Dorothea, b. Jan. 31, 1788, bapt. Feb. 24, 1788. Spon: The Parents.
Anna Elizabeth, daughter of John Jost Leonhardt and Catherine, b. Jan. 31, 1788, bapt. Feb. 24, 1788. Spon: John Neu and Anna Elizabeth.
Catherine, daughter of John Wever and Anna, b. Feb. 17, 1788, bapt. Feb. 24, 1788. Spon: John Brown and Catherine.
Jacob, son of John Schwartz and Barbara, b. Feb. 14, 1788, bapt. March 2, 1788. Spon: Jacob Keiser and Eva.
Veronica, daughter of John Stricker and Sarah, b. Feb. 7, 1788, bapt. March 2, 1788. Spon: The Parents.
George, son of William Haberstich and Maria, b. Feb. 7, 1788, bapt. March 2, 1788. Spon: The Parents.
George, son of John German and Elizabeth, 6 wks. old, bapt. March 9, 1788. Spon: The Parents.
Catherine, daughter of John Latsch and Catherine, b. Feb. 25, 1788, bapt. March 11, 1788. Spon: John Kappel and Catherine.
Catherine, daughter of Henry Diemer and Margaret, b. Nov. 28, 1784, bapt. March 15, 1788. Spon: John Bronner and Catherine.
Henry, son of Henry Diemer and Margaret, b. April 29, 1787, bapt. March 15, 1788. Spon: The Parents.
John, son of George Stephen and Catherine, b. Feb. 22, 1788, bapt.

March 16, 1788. Spon: John Hinckel and Maria.

William, son of Jacob Schreiner and Elizabeth, b. Feb. 22, 1788, bapt. March 16, 1788. Spon: The Parents.

Maria, daughter of Reinhard Kahmer and Elizabeth, b. March 13, 1788, bapt. March 23, 1788. Spon: The Parents and Maria Hotz.

Peter, son of Isaiah Eschelman and Sibylla, b. Feb. 9, 1788, bapt. March 23, 1788. Spon: The Parents.

Maria Margaret, daughter of John Wester and Maria Margaret, b. March 21, 1788, bapt. March 24, 1788. Spon: The Parents.

Magdalene, daughter of Peter Schmalwood and Catherine, 19 mos. old, bapt. March 24, 1788. Spon: The Parents.

John, son of Frederick Wm. Keessman and Anna Margaret, b. Sept. 20, 1787, bapt. March 24, 1788. Spon: John Kaiser and Anna Elizabeth.

John Frederick, son of Gottlieb Schlotterer and Elizabeth, b. Nov. 16, 1787, bapt. March 28, 1788. Spon: Frederick Heineman and Anna Catherine.

Catherine, daughter of Jacob Becker and Catherine, b. Feb. 24, 1788, bapt. March 30, 1788. Spon: The Parents.

Maria, daughter of John Gaul and Elizabeth, b. Feb. 27, 1788, bapt. March 30, 1788. Spon: Stephen Louden and Maria Lotz.

John, son of Christian Schaeffer and Margaret, b. Feb. 27, 1788, bapt. April 4, 1788. Spon: The Parents.

Elizabeth, daughter of Frederick Dickes and Catherine, b. Dec. 28, 1787, bapt. April 6, 1788. Spon: The Parents.

Julianna, daughter of Nicholas Schultz and Catherine, b. March 3, 1788, bapt. April 6, 1788. Spon: Anna Maria Schaaff.

Anna, daughter of John Etris and Christine, b. Feb. 25, 1788, bapt. April 6, 1788. Spon: The Parents.

Charles, son of Samuel Mussel and Elizabeth, b. Feb. 22, 1788, bapt. April 9, 1788. Spon: John Geo. Conrad Hoff and Maria Sibylla.

Catherine, daughter of Michael Hayns and Maria, 8 wks. old, bapt. April 10, 1788. Spon: Eva Hoffman.

Veronica Barbara, daughter of Gottfried Munig and Veronica, b. March 19, 1788, bapt. April 13, 1788. Spon: Frederick Brown and Elizabeth.

Susanna, daughter of Daniel Kayser and Regina, b. Jan. 30, 1788, bapt. April 13, 1788. Spon: William Moore and Susanna.

Samuel, son of Henry Oberman and Gratia, b. Feb. 13, 1788, bapt. April 13, 1788. Spon: Sam Daniel.

William, son of John Wiltfang and Anna, b. Jan. 16, 1788, bapt. April 13, 1788. Spon: Philip Simon and Maria Wiltfang.

Anna Margaret, daughter of John Henry Lies and Maria Elizabeth, b. March 31, 1788, bapt. April 13, 1788. Spon: John Haetterlein and Gertrude.

Elizabeth, daughter of Jacob Nannetter and Anna Catherine, b. Feb. 5, 1788, bapt. April 20, 1788. Spon: Henry Lies and Elizabeth.

John, son of Thomas Zeiner and Maria, b. Dec. 3, 1787, bapt. April 20, 1788. Spon: John Debus Becker and Maria.

Maria, daughter of George Ozeas and Maria, b. April 4, 1788, bapt. April 20, 1788. Spon: William Eckhardt and Maria.

Anna Catherine, daughter of Daniel Kasban and Maria Suess, b. Dec. 29, 1787, bapt. April 24, 1788. Spon: Daniel Sutter and Anna Catherine.

Veronica, daughter of Frederick Kreider and Veronica, b. March 25, 1788, bapt. April 27, 1788. Spon: George Bornhaus and Elizabeth.

Andrew, son of Jacob Schohwalter and Dorothea, b. Oct. 13, 1787, bapt. April 29, 1788. Spon: Philip Boehm and Anna Maria.

Casper, son of Christian Klockner and Catherine, b. March 28, 1788, bapt. April 30, 1788. Spon: Christine Latsch and Casper Klockner.

Isaac, son of John Lehr and Catherine, b. March 17, 1788, bapt. May 1, 1788. Spon: The Parents.

Christopher, son of Zacharias Beckman and Barbara, 5 wks. 3 d. old, bapt. May 1, 1788. Spon: Chrisotpher Jutte and Catherine.

Maria Magdalena, daughter of John Huhn and Christine, 14 d. old, bapt. May 11, 1788. Spon: Elizabeth Verle.

George, son of John Spalter and Elizabeth, b. April 26, 1788, bapt. May 11, 1788. Spon: George Bornhaus and Elizabeth.

John Christopher, son of Conrad Scholl and Anna, b. March 7, 1788, bapt. May 11, 1788. Spon: Christopher Gorden.

William, son of Jacob Meile and Margaret, b. March 21, 1788, bapt. May 12, 1788. Spon: William Reyde and Sarah Meile.

John, son of John Gerret and Margaret, b. April 19, 1788, bapt. May 12, 1788. Spon: The Parents.

Jacob, son of Christopher Meininger and Margaret, b. May 9, 1788, bapt. May 17, 1788. Spon: Jacob Durr and Christine.

George, son of George Miller and Catherine, b. Aug. 27, 1787, bapt. May 18, 1788. Spon: The Parents.

Jacob, son of Martin Gucker and Catherine, b. May 8, 1788, bapt. May 18, 1788. Spon: Jacob Gucker and Maria.

William, son of Christian Lawyer and Margaret, b. May 20, 1788, bapt. May 25, 1788. Spon: The Parents.

Sarah, daughter of Jacobus Staats and Rachel, b. Oct. 21, 1785, bapt. May 25, 1788. Spon: Albertus Schillack and Maria.

Peter, son of Jacobus Staats and Rachel, b. Sept. 9, 1786, bapt. May 25, 1788. Spon: Albertus Schillack and Maria.

Maria, daughter of Jacobus Staats and Rachel, b. Aug. 7, 1787, bapt. May 25, 1788. Spon: Albertus Schillack and Maria.

Viba (Phoebe?), daughter of Ezechial Scha and Jemima, b. Sept. 21, 1786, bapt. May 25, 1788. Spon: Albertus Schillack and Maria.

Catherine Elizabeth, daughter of John Heimer and Elizabeth, b. May 7, 1788, bapt. May 25, 1788. Spon: Henry Poth and Catherine Elizabeth.

Charles, son of Garret Hawes Staer and Susanna, b. April 11, 1788, bapt. May 25, 1788. Spon: Charles Chamberlein and Maria.

Margaret, daughter of John Praupert and Philippina, b. May 19, 1788, bapt. May 29, 1788. Spon: Henry Gassner and Margaret.

Barbara, daughter of John Hoffman and Maria, b. May 28, 1788, bapt. June 1, 1788. Spon: Barbara Lubrian.

Elizabeth, daughter of Conrad Froman and Margaret, b. May 1, 1788, bapt. June 1, 1788. Spon: The Parents.

Isaac, son of Christian Fans and Christine, b. Oct. 22, 1787, bapt. June 2, 1788. Spon: The Parents.

Maria, daughter of Conrad Lutz and Susanna, b. May 2, 1788, bapt. June 2, 1788. Spon: The Parents.

Jacob, son of Peter Weiel and Elizabeth, b. May 20, 1788, bapt. June 8, 1788. Spon: Jacob Schwefel and Maria Margaret.

Elizabeth, daughter of John Orefgen and Elizabeth, b. May 23, 1788, bapt. June 8, 1788. Spon: John Orefgen and Catherine.

Elizabeth, daughter of Christopher Huth and Elizabeth, b. April 20, 1786, bapt. June 9, 1788. Spon: The Parents.

Eva Wilhelmina, daughter of Francis Geisse and Regina, b. May 26, 1788, bapt. June 13, 1788. Spon: Henry Wm. Geisse and Eva.

William, son of Henry Epgert and Maria, b. Dec. 15, 1786, bapt. June 14, 1788. Spon: The Parents.

Anna, daughter of Henry Epgert and Maria, b. March 14, 1788, bapt. June 14, 1788. Spon: The Parents.

Maria, daughter of Matthias Lemair and Anna, b. May 12, 1788, bapt. June 16, 1788. Spon: George Blum and Philippina.

John, son of William Nichols and Joanna, b. June 6, 1788, bapt. June 22, 1788. Spon: John Lindeman and Margaret.

Samuel, son of John Simon and Christine, b. June 13, 1788, bapt. June 24, 1788. Spon: The Parents.

Elizabeth, daughter of Jacob Meyer and Elizabeth, b. June 3, 1788, bapt. June 29, 1788. Spon: The Parents.

John Philip, son of Peter Held and Elizabeth, b. June 7, 1788, bapt. June 29, 1788. Spon: Philip Petri and Elizabeth Margaret.

Sally, daughter of William Wever and Margaret, 6 wks. old, bapt. June 30, 1788. Spon: George Wever and Catherine.

Margaret, daughter of Peter Edenborn and Elizabeth, b. June 13, 1788, bapt. July 3, 1788. Spon: The Parents.

Maria Francis, daughter of Bernard Lawersweiler and Abigail, b. Oct. 3, 1785, bapt. July 6, 1788. Spon: The Mother.

Anna Catherine, daughter of Daniel Klages and Maria, b. June 12, 1788, bapt. July 6, 1788. Spon: Conrad Rohrman and Catherine Hains.

Daniel, son of Daniel Repart and Dorothea, b. June 9, 1788, bapt. July 9, 1788. Spon: The Parents.

Nicholas of Christopher Schreiner and Elizabeth, b. June 22, 1788, bapt. July 13, 1788. Spon: Nicholas Schreiner and Catherine Meng.

John, son of John Rifferth and Breide, 10 mos. old, bapt. Nov. 14, 1788. Spon: The Parents.

Elizabeth, daughter of John Leibinger and Catherine, b. June 26, 1788, bapt. July 16, 1788. Spon: The Parents.

John Peter, son of John Muth and Dolly, b. July 4, 1788, bapt. July 18, 1788. Spon: Peter Muth and Cath. Beudeman.

Peter, son of John Weigand and Magdalene, b. June 17, 1788, bapt. July 20, 1788. Spon: Peter Schmidt and wife.

Anna Maria, daughter of Leonard Ried and Elizabeth, b. ----, 5 yrs., bapt. July 21, 1788. Spon: The Parents.

Sarah, daughter of Leonard Ried and Elizabeth, b. ----, 3 yrs., bapt. July 21, 1788. Spon: The Parents.

John Leonard, son of Leonard Ried and Elizabeth, b. ----, 4 wks., bapt. July 21, 1788. Spon: The Parents.

Salome, son of John Hene and Elizabeth, b. March 8, 1788, bapt. July 25, 1788. Spon: Jacob Kloh and Catherine.

Joseph, son of Christian Heiss and Sarah, b. April 26, 1788, bapt. July 26, 1788. Spon: The Parents.

Martin, son of Martin Haas and Jemima, b. July 8, 1788, bapt. July 27, 1788. Spon: The Parents.

Andrew, son of Jacob Sing and Catherine, b. July 28, 1788, bapt.

July 28, 1788. Spon: John Simon and Catherine.
Eva Maria, daughter of Jacob Walter and Eva Maria, b. June 17, 1788, bapt. July 29, 1788. Spon: Maria Eliz. Revans.
John, son of John Stuber and Veronica, b. Sept. 30, 1787, bapt. Aug. 3, 1788. Spon: John Linn.
Catherine, daughter of Conrad Hinckel and Barbara, b. July 21, 1788, bapt. Aug. 6, 1788. Spon: Bernard Bruchholtz and Catherine.
Henry, son of William Becker and Catherine, b. July 6, 1788, bapt. Aug. 10, 1788. Spon: Henry Frick and Barbara.
John, son of John Reude and Margaret, b. June 28, 1788, bapt. Aug. 10, 1788. Spon: John Hertlein and Gertrude.
Thomas, son of John Porter and Catherine, b. July 24, 1788, bapt. Aug. 10, 1788. Spon: The Parents.
Jacob, son of Henry Theiss and Catherine, b. June 11, 1788, bapt. Aug. 10, 1788. Spon: Adam Lohit and Eliz. Lies.
Susanna, daughter of Jacob Bossert and Maria, 5 mos. 3 wks. old, bapt. Aug. 11, 1788. Spon: The Parents.
Elizabeth, daughter of Henry Riegeler and Catherine, b. April 25, 1788, bapt. Aug. 13, 1788. Spon: The Parents.
Anna, daughter of Jacob Sieble and Wilhelmina, b. Aug. 14, 1788, bapt. Aug. 14, 1788. Spon: Ludwig Hess and Wilhelmina.
Catherine, daughter of Jacob Halberstadt and Anna, b. Feb. 21, 1788, bapt. Aug. 14, 1788. Spon: The Parents.
William, son of John Halberstadt and Catherine, b. Aug. 4, 1788, bapt. Aug. 14, 1788. Spon: The Parents.
Sarah, daughter of Martin Wahl and Christine, b. Aug. 1, 1788, bapt. Aug. 17, 1788. Spon: Isaiah Eschelman and Sibylla.
Mary Magdalene, daughter of Peter Schreiber and Mary Magdalene, b. Aug. 10, 1788, bapt. Aug. 20, 1788. Spon: The Parents.
Anna, daughter of Philip Fritz and Charlotte, b. Aug. 4, 1788, bapt. Aug. 21, 1788. Spon: The Parents and Nancy Brown.
George, son of Peter Auel and Margaret, b. July 3, 1788, bapt. Aug. 21, 1788. Spon: The Parents.
William, son of Michael Keeler and Anna, b. Aug. 4, 1788, bapt. Aug. 24, 1788. Spon: William Kreider and Christ. Handschuh.
Peter, son of Jonas Blusch and Christine, b. July 31, 1788, bapt. Aug. 24, 1788. Spon: Peter Gabriel and Maria.
Anthony, son of Samuel Rosk and Christine, b. April 2, 1788, bapt. Aug. 26, 1788. Spon: George Fax and Peggi Consor.
Maria, daughter of Andrew Braderick and Maria, b. Aug. 18, 1788, bapt. Aug. 27, 1788. Spon: The Father.
Anna Maria, daughter of Justus Staeringer and Anna Maria, b. April 16, 1788, bapt. Aug. 31, 1788. Spon: The Parents.
Hannah, daughter of Jacob Greiss and Margaret, 3 mos. old, bapt. Aug. 31, 1788. Spon: Hannah Binder.
John, son of Henry Appel and Elizabeth, b. Aug. 31, 1788, bapt. Aug. 31, 1788. Spon: John Miebert and Anna Elizabeth.
William, son of Adam Doerr and Catherine, b. Aug. 21, 1788, bapt. Sept. 3, 1788. Spon: The Parents and Anna Schwartz.
Daniel, son of John George Koch and wife, b. June 16, 1788, bapt. Sept. 3, 1788. Spon: John George Koch and Anna Elizabeth.
Elizabeth, daughter of John Schutz and Maria, b. Aug. 29, 1788, bapt. Sept. 7, 1788. Spon: Peter Sonleder and Maria.
Frederick, son of Philip Wentz and Maria, b. July 14, 1788, bapt.

Sept. 9, 1788. Spon: The Parents and Christine Meyer.
Elizabeth, daughter of Ludw. Herman Jungst and Catherine, b. April 17, 1788, bapt. Sept. 7, 1788. Spon: Elizabeth and Henry Wm. Jungst.
Maria, daughter of William Pfeiffer and Margaret, b. Sept. 2, 1788, bapt. Sept. 14, 1788. Spon: The Parents.
Peter, son of Peter Schaeff and Elizabeth, b. Sept. 7, 1788, bapt. Sept. 15, 1788. Spon: The Parents.
Joseph, son of Joseph Hiller and Susanna, 7 mos. old, bapt. Sept. 15, 1788. Spon: The Parents.
Anna, daughter of John Jones and Elizabeth, 2 yrs. old, bapt. Sept. 15, 1788. Spon: The Parents.
Marianna, daughter of John Hopp and Nancy, b. Sept. 8, 1788, bapt. Sept. 19, 1788. Spon: Catherine Blum.
Catherine Friderica, daughter of Adam Roh and Maria, b. Sept. 5, 1788, bapt. Sept. 21, 1788. Spon: Adam Wagener and Cath. Friderica.
Henry, son of Henry Brede and Anna, b. Aug. 4, 1788, bapt. Sept. 28, 1788. Spon: The Parents.
Adam, son of John George Hoffman and Anna Maria, b. May 23, 1788, bapt. Sept. 29, 1788. Spon: The Parents.
John, son of Henry Diehl and Maria, b. Aug. 27, 1788, bapt. Sept. 29, 1788. Spon: Jost Eberth and Catherine.
Rebecca, daughter of Charles Jacob Kith and Margaret, b. Sept. 9, 1788, bapt. Oct. 5, 1788. Spon: Catherine Leonhard and Leonhard Prun.
Elizabeth, daughter of John Osman and Elizabeth, b. Aug. 21, 1788, bapt. Oct. 5, 1788. Spon: Christopher Keller and Anna Maria.
Mary Magdalene, daughter of John Steiner and Elizabeth, b. Oct. 2, 1788, bapt. Oct. 5, 1788. Spon: Adam Meyer and Magdalene.
Anna Maria, daughter of John Mercker and Elizabeth, b. Aug. 15, 1788, bapt. Oct. 9, 1788. Spon: Maria Margaret Mercker.
Elizabeth, daughter of Jacob Frey and Elizabeth Haveman, b. Oct. 5, 1788, bapt. Oct. 15, 1788. Spon: Catherine Forster.
Henrietta Maria, daughter of Wendel Zerban and Catherine, b. Sept. 19, 1788, bapt. Oct. 19, 1788. Spon: The Parents.
John, son of William Jonas and Elizabeth, b. Sept. 11, 1788, bapt. Oct. 19, 1788. Spon: The Parents.
Julianna, daughter of John Becker and Elizabeth, b. Sept. 20, 1788, bapt. Oct. 19, 1788. Spon: The Parents.
Catherine, daughter of John Klapp and Maria, b. Sept. 19, 1788, bapt. Oct. 11, 1788. Spon: The Parents and Miss Heller.
Frederick William, son of William Fuselbach and Margaret, b. Aug. 30, 1788, bapt. Oct. 26, 1788. Spon: Fred. William Neuman and Elizabeth.
Henrietta, daughter of William Will and Anna, b. Oct. 5, 1788, bapt. Nov. 2, 1788. Spon: Fred. Anthony Metzger and Hannah.
Anna Margaret, daughter of Jacob Burckhardt and Margaret, b. Oct. 4, 1788, bapt. Nov. 2, 1788. Spon: John Geo. Specht and Ann Marg. Specht.
Margaret, daughter of George Schneider and Catherine, b. Aug. 24, 1788, bapt. Nov. 13, 1788. Spon: Margaret Erb.
Maria, daughter of Jacob Diehl and Elizabeth, b. Oct. 10, 1788, bapt. Nov. 9, 1788. Spon: Charles Albrecht and Maria.
Maria, daughter of Jacob Lotz and Rosina, b. Oct. 19, 1788, bapt.

Nov. 16, 1788. Spon: Sebastian Wully and Eliz. Catherine.
William, son of William Becker and Anna Maria, b. Oct. 14, 1788, bapt. Nov. 16, 1788. Spon: Rudolph Hucky and Bessy.
William, son of Jacob Kreider and Elizabeth, b. Oct. 25, 1788, bapt. Nov. 16, 1788. Spon: William Kreider and Elizabeth.
John Valentine, son of George Joraus and Elizabeth, b. Oct. 18, 1788, bapt. Nov. 16, 1788. Spon: Valentine Krieg and Maria Eva.
John, son of John Worth and Maria, b. Nov. 7, 1788, bapt. Nov. 18, 1788. Spon: The Parents.
Daniel, son of Charles Kooper and Maria, b. Oct. 14, 1788, bapt. Nov. 16, 1788. Spon: The Parents.
Catherine, daughter of George Lorentz and Susanna, b. Sept. 23, 1788, bapt. Nov. --, 1788. Spon: The Parents.
Sarah, daughter of Jacob Enck and Catherine, b. Oct. 26, 1788, bapt. Nov. 23, 1788. Spon: The Parents.
Elizabeth Catherine, daughter of John Wiehler and Maria, b. Aug. 27, 1788, bapt. Nov. 23, 1788. Spon: John Bretter and Elizabeth.
Anna Catherine, daughter of Melchior Schaeffer and Anna Catherine, b. Oct. 25, 1788, bapt. Nov. 30, 1788. Spon: John Thiel and Anna Catherine.
Jacob, son of John Brown and Barbara, b. Nov. 10, 1788, bapt. Dec. 7, 1788. Spon: Grandparents.
Margaret Philippina, daughter of Henry Schmaltz and Margaret, b. Sept. 23, 1788, bapt. Dec. 14, 1788. Spon: George Freitag and Margaret Philippina.
Susanna, daughter of Peter Schuck and Catherine, b. Nov. 2, 1788, bapt. Dec. 14, 1788. Spon: Abraham Horn and Susanna.
Elizabeth, daughter of Conrad Keller and Elizabeth, b. Nov. 28, 1788, bapt. Dec. 14, 1788. Spon: Henry Solomon and Margaret Strubly.
Anna, daughter of Adam Weiss and Elizabeth, b. Sept. 14, 1788, bapt. Dec. 14, 1788. Spon: The Parents.
Maria, daughter of Edward Souter and Catherine, b. July 22, 1788, bapt. Dec. 21, 1788. Spon: Lydia Wernt.
Daniel, son of Casper Griffen and Elizabeth, b. Sept. 16, 1788, bapt. Dec. 21, 1788. Spon: ----.
Susanna, daughter of John Totham and Maria, b. Nov. 5, 1787, bapt. Dec. 21, 1788. Spon: The Parents.
Philip, son of Philip Odenheimer and wife, b. Dec. 23, 1788, bapt. Dec. 23, 1788. Spon: The Parents.
George, son of Fred. Jentzer and Christine, b. Dec. 6, 1788, bapt. Dec. 25, 1788. Spon: George Duerr and Veronica.
Peter, son of Gottlieb Zeil and Apollonia, b. Nov. 1, 1788, bapt. Dec. 25, 1788. Spon: Peter Heimer and Marlena Johannsson.
Jacob, son of Jacob Gideon and Rebecca, b. Nov. 28, 1788, bapt. Dec. 25, 1788. Spon: The Parents.
John, son of George Loscher and Anna, b. Nov. 10, 1788, bapt. Dec. 28, 1788. Spon: John Loscher and Barbara Loscher.
Anna Maria, daughter of Jacob Becker and Elizabeth, b. Dec. 4, 1788, bapt. Dec. 29, 1788. Spon: Conrad Becker and Anna Maria.
Matthew, son of Matthew Krehmer and Susanna, b. Dec. 18, 1788, bapt. Dec. 30, 1788. Spon: The Parents.
Anna Margaret, daughter of Jacob Halter and Christine, 9 wks. old, bapt. Jan. 1, 1789. Spon: Adam Was and Elizabeth.

Catherine, daughter of Daniel Ries and Anna Maria, b. Nov. 13, 1788, bapt. Jan. 1, 1789. Spon: John Beck and Catherine.
Maria Catherine, daughter of Peter Becker and Elizabeth, 7 mos. old, bapt. Jan. 4, 1789. Spon: Maria Catherine Flick.
Philip, son of William von Phul and Catherine, b. Dec. 17, 1788, bapt. Jan. 4, 1789. Spon: The Parents.
Sarah, daughter of Christian Ranck and Maria, b. Dec. 30, 1788, bapt. Jan. 4, 1789. Spon: Louis Diemer and Sarah Peffer Grub.
Barbara, daughter of William Praupert and Barbara, 4 wks. old, bapt. Jan. --, 1789. Spon: Jacob Rueber and Barbara.
Peter, son of Peter Paris and Veronica, b. Dec. 13, 1788, bapt. Jan. 14, 1789. Spon: The Parents.
Elizabeth, daughter of John George Krehmer and Anna, b. Dec. 1, 1788, bapt. Jan. 18, 1789. Spon: ----.
Henry, son of George Walter and wife, 3 mos. old, bapt. Jan. 18, 1789. Spon: Matthew Peth and Veronica.

MARRIAGES BY REV. CASPER WEYBERG
1786 - 1790

Peter Bockius m. Rosina Hess on Jan. 10, 1786.
Ludwig Orth m. Margaret Romer on Jan. 24, 1786.
John Bowen m. Maria Swoop on Jan. 26, 1786.
Lewis Farmer m. Elizabeth Fohr(er) on Feb. 2, 1786.
Jacob Baumgarth m. Catharine Weiler on Feb. 12, 1786.
William Fleck m. Maria Scheaf on Feb. 12, 1786.
Casper Petzler m. Elizabeth Boger on Feb. 17, 1786.
George Gaul m. Cathr. Mitschet on Feb. 19, 1786.
Christian Stahl m. Cathr. Morris on Feb. 22, 1786.
Henry Lehr m. Elizabeth Nannetter on March 2, 1786.
John Schutz m. Maria Eberhard on March 5, 1786.
John Land m. Phoebe Nobel on March 7, 1786.
Jacob Becker m. Elizabeth Mielefeld on March 9, 1786.
John Andrew Friederich m. Catharine Schaeff on March 9, 1786.
Richard Shaugh m. Elizabeth McGouen on March 9, 1786.
Martin Muller m. Elizabeth Sharky on March 26, 1786.
Mark Luty m. Margaret Schmitt on March 30, 1786.
Nicholas Hainy m. Rachel Wilson on April 6, 1786.
John Seiler m. Susanna Biel on April 6, 1786.
Andrew Starck m. Veronica Mercker on April 9, 1786.
Thomas Graff m. Hester Funck on April 17, 1786.
Henry Sell m. Mary Weith on April 18, 1786.
Christian Luchard m. Elizabeth Vergouderen on April 27, 1786.
George Mueller m. Anna Maria Korck on May 8, 1786.
Christian Alberger m. Susanna Meng on May 14, 1786.
James Aris m. Cathr. Threscher on May 14, 1786.
Lewis Hansal m. Mary Bond on May 16, 1786.
Joseph Funck m. Mary Schneider on May 30, 1786.
(John) Le Telier m. Sarah Withpain on June 2, 1786.
Christopher Schreiner m. Elizabeth Stucky on June 4, 1786.
Fred. Jentzer m. Jacobine Wengen on June 13, 1786.
Nicholas Weierich m. Susanna Diederich on June 15, 1786.
Jerem. Allioth m. Hannah Clear on June 22, 1786.
William Skinner m. Elizabeth Williams on June 22, 1786.
George Peter Stoud m. Ann Mary Lorah on June 29, 1786.

Peter Lory m. Jane Williams on July 23, 1786.
Samuel Armbruster (?) m. ---- on Aug. 13, 1786.
Gottfr. Ernst Schmid m. ---- on Aug. 20, 1786.
Melchior Schaeffer m. Catharine Schaeffer on Sept. 10, 1786.
John Theis Alhausen m. Anna Agitae Kinry on Sept. 12, 1786.
John Sturtzebach m. Margr. Conrad on Sept. 14, 1786.
John Bernard Knochel m. Anna Catharine Zacheri on Sept. 29, 1786.
Samuel Torter m. Margaret Helwig on Oct. 3, 1786.
David Bechtle m. Priscilla Hurff on Oct. 4, 1786.
Frederick Dellicker (Reformed Minister) m. Maria Juvenal on Oct.
    12, 1786.
John Christian Ziegeler m. Elizabeth Hess on Oct. 12, 1786.
Jacob Souder m. Margaret Konser on Oct. 26, 1786.
Christopher Muller m. Maria Becker on Oct. 26, 1786.
Garret Hughes m. Susanna Chamberlain on Nov. 18, 1786.
John Huber m. Veronica Frey on Dec. 10, 1786.
Reinhard Schmeltz m. Kitty Pfeiffer on Dec. 28, 1786.
John Grauel m. Elizabeth Grub on Dec. 19, 1786.
Lawrence Hoffman m. Maria Schling on Dec. 31, 1786.
Henry Jungst m. Anna Maria Haffener on Jan. 4, 1787.
Jacob Overstake m. Sarah Procter on Jan. 20, 1787.
Edward Healy m. Mary Matheas on Jan. 25, 1787.
George Weybel m. Charlotte Hoffman on Feb. 1, 1787.
George Hansell m. Maria Glentworth on Feb. 11, 1787.
Anthony Balde m. Christine Ohl on Feb. 13, 1787.
Adam Heiser m. Eva Wirth on Feb. 20, 1787.
John Schmidt m. Elizabeth Stoudt on Feb. 22, 1787.
Jacob Lehn m. Sarah Johnston on Feb. 22, 1787.
Jacob Orner m. Sarah Schmidt on Feb. 27, 1787.
Thomas Hueter m. Catharine Diek on March 4, 1787.
George Beumer m. Cathr. Scholl on March 6, 1787.
Jacob Whitman m. Margr. Steltz on March 8, 1787.
John Lentz m. Sarah Reinhard on March 8, 1787.
John Sattler m. Sarah Seibert on March 12, 1787.
John Martin m. Anna Matlack on March 14, 1787.
James Ditzer m. Abigail Worrall on March 21, 1787.
George Gerster m. Margr. Jung on March 22, 1787.
Jacob Meyer m. Margr. Gerster on March 27, 1787.
John Guwin m. Meine Richardson on March 27, 1787.
Francis Anthony Metzger m. Hannah Will on March 29, 1787.
John Fred. Dickes m. Catharine Herr on March 29, 1787.
John Haley m. Deborah Thomas on March 31, 1787.
John Reuter m. Maria Folck on April 10, 1787.
John Michael Baerdt m. Catharine Scherer on April 10, 1787.
John Shone m. Mary Skinner on April 16, 1787.
William Shlottery m. Catharine Wierman on April 17, 1787.
Jacob Diehl m. Elizabeth Knies on April 22, 1787.
John Abraham Gauel m. Elizabeth Lotz on May 1, 1787.
John Wiltfang m. Anna Conrad on May 2, 1787.
John Dinges m. Catharine Wilky on May 2, 1787.
John Boutscher m. Rachel Bener on May 5, 1787.
Francis Geiss m. Regina Schussler on May 10, 1787.
Alexander Weber m. Catharine Zeuner on May 20, 1787.
George Lauris m. Polly Cox on May 24, 1787.
Peter Rifferth m. Maria Fries on May 28, 1787.

John Minck m. Christine Senderik on June 18, 1787.
George Hetton m. Frances Gilmore on June 19, 1787.
Samuel Green m. Mary White on June 28, 1787.
Jacob Erwin m. Cathr. Cloedy on July 19, 1787.
Henry Ciprian m. Elizabeth Scherer on July 24, 1787.
Edward Graham m. Margaret Steuerwald on Aug. 23, 1787.
Peter Helt m. Ann Elizabeth Petri on Sept. 2, 1787.
John Philip Petry m. Elizabeth Helt on Sept. 2, 1787.
Henry Appel m. Anna Elizabeth Danecker on Sept. 6, 1787.
James Leonhard m. Mary McClain on Sept. 8, 1787.
Henry Tepes m. Maria Huber on Sept. 23, 1787.
Jacob Penther m. Sarah Patissen on Sept. 26, 1787.
Jacob Coffin m. Caty Jerkis on Sept. 27, 1787.
Jacob Zible m. Wilhelmina Hess on Sept. 30, 1787.
Adam Alberger m. Mary Colloday on Oct. 4, 1787.
Jacob Bischoffberger m. Susanna Mueller on Oct. 17, 1787.
William Jones m. Elizabeth Frioth on Oct. 28, 1787.
Henry Schmidt m. Sarah Bachman on Oct. 28, 1787.
Conrad Scherer m. Maria Cathr. Leokerom on Nov. 1, 1787.
Abraham Willet m. Rachel Hertzog on Nov. 4, 1787.
William Maag m. Elizabeth Schumacher on Nov. 11, 1787.
Henry Diehl m. Maria Eberth on Nov. 22, 1787.
Jacob Schmidt m. Maria Penther on Nov. 29, 1787.
William Schmidt m. Maria Reide on Dec. 6, 1787.
Frederick Haas m. Elizabeth Friederich on Dec. 27, 1787.
Christian Schaeffer m. Anna Margaret Huck on Jan. 1, 1788.
Henry Wever m. Margaret Breding on Jan. 1, 1788.
John Pope m. Margr. Peters on Jan. 24, 1788.
John Philip Volckrath m. Anna Maria Schmitt on Jan. 29, 1788.
William Conrad m. Eva Kochenberger on Feb. 13, 1788.
Jacob Hill m. Elizabeth Bachoffen on March 9, 1788.
Michael Grub m. Betsy Devick on March 13, 1788.
Christian Giebert m. Marl. Lafarty on March 18, 1788.
Gerhard Bischhoven m. Elizabeth Jamissen on March 25, 1788.
Alexander Square m. Diana Foster on March 30, 1788.
Isaac Bedellion m. Ursula Rohe on April 1, 1788.
Conrad Scherer m. Dorothea Bayer on April 1, 1788.
Melchior Meng m. Elizabeth Lehman on April 5, 1788.
Samuel Walker m. Catharine Huhn on April 8, 1788.
John Ludwig Taber m. Catharine Riffert on April 10, 1788.
Jacob Broun m. Maria Fling on April 29, 1788.
Jacob Edenborn m. Maria Schreiber on May 1, 1788.
John Bergman m. Elizabeth Buddy on May 4, 1788.
Martin Souerman m. Rosina Peters on May 8, 1788.
Christopher Kinsle m. Susanna Gilbert on May 25, 1788.
Daniiel Whiles m. Rebecca Pepper on June 1, 1788.
Philip Frederick Mischodt m. Maria Clara Denn on June 5, 1788.
Joseph Shafley m. Catharine Praupert on June 5, 1788.
Bartholomeus Beaumies m. Maria Frances Lombard on June 6, 1788.
George Lampater m. Maria Gerstener on June 9, 1788.
Jacob Jentzer m. Barbara Tschudy on June 10, 1788.
Daniel Kreider m. Marl. Williams on June 22, 1788.
Jacob Hains m. Eva Miller on June 24, 1788.
John Miller m. Hannah Willet on July 10, 1788.
Frederick Gaul m. Clara Walten on July 27, 1788.

Peter Jung m. Rebecca Werntz on Aug. 21, 1788.
Nicholas Penther m. Marg. Schwab on Aug. 21, 1788.
John Cortis m. Elizabeth von der Halt on Sept. 4, 1788.
Christian Groh m. Sally Dennis on Sept. 30, 1788.
Peter Forest m. Ann Bonnet on Sept. 30, 1788.
John Graft m. Elizabeth Kart on Oct. 5, 1788.
Andrew Broderick m. Clara Reble on Oct. 12, 1788.
William Reude m. Sarah Meile on Oct. 16, 1788.
Claudius Antonius Betier m. Sarah Bartram on Nov. 29, 1788.
Jacobus Tethers m. Cathr. Neu on Dec. 9, 1788.
Anthony Redissen m. Elizabeth Neu on Dec. 9, 1788.
George Duerr m. Veronica Jentzer on Dec. 25, 1788.
Stephen Gerlach m. Maria Espay on Dec. 25, 1788.
Nathaniel Davids m. Ann Thomas on Jan. 13, 1789.
John Linck m. Elizabeth Rasber on Jan. 30, 1789.
Philip Peltz m. Rebecca Broun on Feb. 3, 1789.
James Geary m. Dinah Cerral on Feb. 26, 1789.
George Beltz m. Cathr. Zahner on March 5, 1789.
John George Becker m. Sophia Milefeld on March 10, 1789.
Joseph Dougherty m. Mary Long on March 25, 1789.
James Middleton m. Margr. Coffin on April 2, 1789.
William Kreider m. Mary Schreiner on April 5, 1789.
George Westenberger m. Elizabeth Lair on April 7, 1789.
Philip Mieser m. Maria Diehl on April 14, 1789.
Henry Tiss m. Cathr. Schmidt on April 19, 1789.
George Schet m. Maria Schubart on April 23, 1789.
John Dawn m. Mary Kartrieth on May 12, 1789.
Francis Lynn m. Margr. Clarck on May 15, 1789.
Peter Immel m. Ann Maria Philip on May 25, 1789.
Stephen Green m. Cathr. Henry on May 28, 1789.
John Jacob Belsterling m. Mary Magdalene Bolleck on June 9, 1789.
John Christopher Gotter m. Christina Zimmerman on June 11, 1789.
Conrad Pfaffhausen m. Maria Christine Crames on June 26, 1789.
John Philip Reis m. Elizabeth Hill on July 5, 1789.
John Michael Jobst m. Catharine Kep on July 26, 1789.
Daniel Walter m. Maria Schuf on July 26, 1789.
Gerard Huhn m. Anna Maria Gerbach on Aug. 4, 1789.
Conrad Weiel m. Elizabeth Keyser on Aug. 11, 1789.
Jacob Schreiner m. Elizabeth Stillwagen on Aug. 29, 1789.
Melchior Steiner m. Susanna ---- on Sept. 4, 1789.
Adam Seibert m. Anna Cloyer on Sept. 15, 1789.
Philip Alburger m. Dorothy Betsch on Sept. 15, 1789.
Jacob Wentz m. Susanna Biesle on Sept. 22, 1789.
Michael Weitener m. Susanna Huhn on Sept. 22, 1789.
William Schmidt m. Cathr. Jouch on Nov. 15, 1789.
Joseph Wright m. Sarah van der Voordt on Dec. 5, 1789.
John Meyer m. Cathr. Schmidt on Jan. 1, 1790.
William Prethast m. Maria Klein on Jan. 1, 1790.
Conrad Becker m. Ann Maria Sorg on Jan. 21, 1790.
Joseph Bennet m. Cathr. Becker on Feb. 2, 1790.
Edward Bush m. Barbara Eakele on Feb. 4, 1790.
Thomas Ried m. Mary Handschuh on Feb. 9, 1790.
John Ewald Ellenberger m. Julia Dinges on March 4, 1790.
Jacob Siegmund m. Cathr. Hoffman on March 30, 1790.
Henry Weisbrod m. Maria Tauen Reimer on April 8, 1790.

Christopher Rarah m. Jan Curry on April 15, 1790.
John Marers m. Bebs Bayer on April 17, 1790.
Ludwig Frescher m. Christine Peiffer on April 17, 1790.
John Rummel m. Marl. Becker on April 17, 1790.
Cornelius Henckel m. Maria Lotz on May 3, 1790.
John Schreiner m. Elizabeth Dannecker on May 25, 1790.
Andrew Meyer m. Cathr. Strupt on May 27, 1790.
Paul Bauer m. Polly Roun on June 1, 1790.
Christopher Meyer m. Elizabeth Ferringer on June 2, 1790.
Charles Istwick m. Mary Taylor on June 12, 1790.
John Kuhn m. Elizabeth Kehr on July 18, 1790.
Peter Nannetter m. Magd. Baerth on July 25, 1790.

MARRIAGES BY REV. HERMAN WINCKHAUS
1790 - 1793
John Behrns m. Sophia Rosenbusch on Oct. 12, 1790.
Henry Bretz m. Eva Espy on Oct. 31, 1790.
George Schreier m. Elizabeth Schlaechter on Nov. 10, 1790.
Ludwig Schill m. Barbara Bauer on Nov. 11, 1790.
John Lauri m. Maria Barbara Wiltfang on Nov. 18, 1790.
Thomas Watson m. Maria Gross on Nov. 23, 1790.
Adam Widerstein m. Dorothy Mueller on Dec. 2, 1790.
Jeremiah Barrel m. Maria Clinton on Dec. 8, 1790.
Matthias Dishong m. Elizabeth Mogy on Dec. 21, 1790.
John Kohl m. Elizabeth Kuhly on Jan. 13, 1791.
William Whitman m. Maria Stoltz on Jan. 23, 1791.
Peter Schreiber m. Sarah Bating on Feb. 17, 1791.
John Rubert m. Dorothy Rauh on March 8, 1791.
Jacob Horning m. Nancy North on March 24, 1791.
John Hofstaedler m. Mary Magdalene Gamber on April 7, 1791.
Michael Reader m. Sarah Bard on April 19, 1791.
John Gerreth m. Catharine Goebler on April 26, 1791.
William Wolffkuehl m. Elizabeth Weingaertner on April 28, 1791.
John Leish m. Maria Blum on May 5, 1791.
Christian George Geissel m. Hannah Christine Jett on May 9, 1791.
Philip Baron m. Helena Schopp on May 22, 1791.
Christian Kuck m. Margaret Maria Carlsen on May 27, 1791.
Jacob Kappes m. Catharine Traut on July 3, 1791.
John George Mill m. Anna Dannecker on July 10, 1791.
Martin Rothhaar m. Anna Maria Weissman on July 17, 1791.
Abraham Ziegler m. Elizabeth Stamm on July 21, 1791.
Jacob Sorck m. Elizabeth Nohw of Nohw on Aug. --, 1791.
Anthony Deusing m. Elizabeth Graf on Aug. --, 1791.
John Drangenstein m. Maria Schlatter on Sept. --, 1791.
Thomas Walpert m. Margaret Meyer on Sept. --, 1791.
Christopher Mueller m. Susanna Statelman on Sept. --, 1791.
John George Rieger m. Anna Maria Johnson on Sept. 25, 1791.
Henry Trimper m. Elizabeth Weaver on Dec. 17, 1791.
Christian Kreider m. Anna Elizabeth Pigler on Dec. 18, 1791.
Henry Plenn m. Catharine Cart on Dec. 24, 1791.
John Jobst m. Charlotte Aufforth on Dec. 25, 1791.
John Schnyder m. Elizabeth Mayer on Dec. 25, 1791.
Peter Huth m. Barbara Kriger, from Montgomery Co., on Jan. 10,
1792.

Jacob Muench m. Barbara Etris on Jan. 29, 1792.
Lorentz Schuessler m. Clara Jenser on Feb. 27, 1792.
Jacob Gerhardt m. Magdalene Mueller on April 3, 1792.
Peter Jost m. Elizabeth Zigler on April 3, 1792.
John Dowel m. Barbara Eschman on April 19, 1792.
Jacob Berey m. Maria Protzman m. April 22, 1792.
George Roebsamen m. Maria Hoeffly on May 15, 1792.
Henry Schmaltz m. Elizabeth Spatz on May 17, 1792.
Henry Leck m. Maria Schnell on May 5, 1792.
Christian Hiebel m. Anna Margaret Deuss on May 8, 1792.
Christian Jacob m. Barbara Rheily on May 8, 1792.
John Schneider m. Catharine Heher on June 24, 1792.
John Tuttel m. Elizabeth Mayer on July 22, 1792.
Joseph Gally m. Catharine Dorffer on July 25, 1792.
Gottlieb Marsh m. Johanna Christine Henrietta Hecht on Aug. 4, 1792.
George Weiser m. Susanna Doeringer on Aug. 5, 1792.

The following persons who had come from Europe were married before they set out for the Genesee country:
Joachim Lorentz m. Anna Catharine Jentz on Aug. 7, 1792.
Daniel Frederick Feifferth m. Maria Eliz. Michaelsen on Aug. 7, 1792.
John Gottlieb Wichor m. Mary Magdalene Gelers on Aug. 7, 1792.

William Dietz m. Margaret Bolebacher on Aug. 23, 1792.
Arent Braun m. Catharine Zerbehn on Sept. 8, 1792.
John Keller m. Mary Magdalene Pfeifer on Sept. 16, 1792.
Daniel Zeller m. Elizabeth Schwob on Sept. 20, 1792.
William Euler m. Anna Gertrude Rupert on Sept. 21, 1792.
Daniel Peltz m. Susanna Gruninger on Sept. 27, 1792.
Valentine Ulrich m. Elizabeth Weiss on Sept. 27, 1792.
Benjamin Davis m. Jemimah Roberts on Nov. 4, 1792.
Wendel Zerban m. Philippina Zerban on Nov. 4, 1792.
John Dithmar m. Rebecca Riester on Dec. 2, 1792.
George Schwartz m. Maria Burth on Nov. 29, 1792.
Daniel Boehm m. Catharine Peltz on Dec. 2, 1792.
Jacob Boog m. Anna Schneider on Dec. 9, 1792.
Frederick Rieser m. Maria Reyli on Dec. 18, 1792.
Henry Sehnn m. Susanna Heehr on Dec. 14, 1792.
Conrad Pfaffhausen m. Catharine Loescher (widow) on Jan. 17, 1793.
Paul Kochard m. Maria Elizabeth Young on Jan. 27, 1793.
Henry Wattles m. Sarah Mey on Jan. 25, 1793.
William Cornelius m. Margaret Diess on Jan. 31, 1793.
Jacob Faans m. Phoebe Tomblenson on Feb. 7, 1793.
John Hanlon m. Catharine Heller on Feb. 16, 1793.
Isaac Hough m. Elizabeth Eberth on Feb. 16, 1793.
John Becker m. Barbara Nilforth on March 10, 1793.
Michael Kinsinger m. Elizabeth Potey on March 17, 1793.
George Heineman m. Maria Klein on March 17, 1793.
Daniel von der Schleuss m. Catharine Schuck on March 19, 1793.
Christian Reinhardt m. Christine Scheller on March 23, 1793.
Jacob Stoll m. Jenny Creucker on April 1, 1793.
Jonathan Miller m. Catharine Peffer on April 19, 1793.

John Hange m. Susanna Reinholdt on April 24, 1793.
John Preh m. Catharine Weid on May 23, 1793.
George Doerffer m. Rachel Rubsamen on June 29, 1793.
Martin Haas m. Anna Kehr on July 14, 1793.
Reinhardt Scholl m. Maria Rupp on July 13, 1793.
John Freier m. Eva Trollinger on Sept. 8, 1793.
Diederich Buth m. Susanna Krafft on Sept. 14, 1793.
Albion Cox m. Maria Anna Harmstadt on Sept. 19, 1793.

(Reverend H. Winckhaus died on Oct. 3, 1793.)

MARRIAGES BY REV. WILLIAM HENDEL
1793 - 1798

George Degenhart m. Elizabeth List on Nov. 16, 1793.
Daniel Bergmayer m. Christine Gaul on Feb. 25, 1794.
John Lehmann m. Elizabeth Blattberger on March 6, 1794.
John Sinsfeld m. Sarah Nicholson on March 8, 1794.
Jean Baptiste Cerisier, French officer, m. Ursula Lapostolait on
    March 11, 1794.
Noah Davis m. Catharine Lies on March 26, 1794.
George William Steinhauer m. Catharine Sackreuter on March 28,
    1794.
Sebastian Salade m. Mary Magdalene Ohmensetter on March 30, 1794.
Jonathan Dewees m. Rebecca Johnson on April 2, 1794.
Andrew Roth m. Margaret Fuchs on April 13, 1794.
Jean Descamps m. Sarah Pluncket on April 15, 1794.
Daniel Miller m. Magdalene Henrich on April 22, 1794.
George Abel m. Dorothea Koch on April 29, 1794.
Philip Mitmann m. Rebecca Hertzog on April 30, 1794.
Adam Lotz m. Margaret Schaberer on May 23, 1794.
Jacob Eckstein m. Elizabeth Kert on June 5, 1794.
Charles Rotzell m. Mary White on June 16, 1794.
Ricloff Edridge m. Catharine Reischel on June 19, 1794.
George Picard m. Catharine Martzle on June 29, 1794.
George Hahns m. Maria Schaffer on June 29, 1794.
Jacob Brauer m. Maria Festinger on July 17, 1794.
Frederick Boss m. Wilhelmina Weber on July 19, 1794.
Jacob Gros m. Rosina Valentin on July 24, 1794.
Moses Williams m. Sophia Auffahrt on Aug. 10, 1794.
Andrew von Weiler m. Elizabeth Owens on Aug. 19, 1794.
Philip Ehringer m. Magdalene Feltzner on Aug. 21, 1794.
Henry Bender m. Magdalene Becker on Aug. 24, 1794.
John Reil m. Elizabeth Becker on Aug. 28, 1794.
William Stoltz m. Christine Gut on Sept. 18, 1794.
Christopher Schreiner m. Elizabeth Baxter on Sept. 28, 1794.
John Dettenweiler m. Margaret Diehl on Oct. 7, 1794.
William Schneider m. Margaret Behrt on Oct. 12, 1794.
Jacob Mitschet Kert m. Elizabeth Kammer on Oct. 19, 1794.
George Mill m. Catharine Hoff on Oct. 26, 1794.
Abraham Dix m. Catharine Stattler on Nov. 11, 1794.
Conrad Ruppel m. Catharine Herman on Nov. 19, 1794.
Nicholas Knauf m. Maria Mason on Nov. 23, 1794.
Joseph Rickets m. Elizabeth Schallus on Nov. 28, 1794.

John Montgomery m. Elizabeth Dorr on Dec. 7, 1794.
Peter Martin Hess m. Veronica Reis on Dec. 7, 1794.
Henry Braun m. Christine Pfeiffer on Dec. 26, 1794.
Hugh McCully m. Willy Nottenius on Dec. 31, 1794.
Francis Ries m. Sarah Neefis on Jan. 4, 1795.
Christian Benedict m. Juliana Wurges on Jan. 8, 1795.
Daniel Sutter, Senior, m. Susanna Muller on Jan. 31, 1795.
John Falbier m. Anna Stickjes on Feb. 5, 1795.
Ludwig Thomas m. Esther Pauks on Feb. 17, 1795.
Carl Schaffer m. Elizabeth Strohmann, Montg. Co., on March 4, 1795.
Jacob Allburger m. Margaret Gassman on April 5, 1795.
Philip Rossel m. Catharine Hein on April 15, 1795.
John Philip Mayer m. Wilhelmina Steiner on April 16, 1795.
Henry Lang m. Catharine Blecker on April 18, 1795.
George Keller m. Margaret Pfeiffer on April 19, 1795.
James More m. Eleonore Fehbrit on May 21, 1795.
Andrew Hansen m. Anna Maria Sieberick on June 14, 1795.
George West m. Catharine Beiert on June 16, 1795.
David Hall m. Elizabeth Black on July 16, 1795.
David Gilbert m. Maria Schwartz on July 19, 1795.
Samuel Duffs m. Mary Hancock on July 31, 1795.
James McCauley m. Elizabeth Kruse on Aug. 20, 1795.
Henry Seibert m. Dorothea Muth on Aug. 24, 1795.
Frederick Wolf m. Barbara Beck on Sept. 6, 1795.
George Pfaff m. Catharine Pfaffhauser on Sept. 9, 1795.
John Born m. Elizabeth Freund on Oct. 15, 1795.
Adam Schmid m. Catharine Pieter on Oct. 18, 1795.
John Metzger m. Christine Krumbach on Oct. 29, 1795.
William Ashton m. Susanna Munich on Nov. 1, 1795.
John Clunn m. Susanna Keiler on Nov. 4, 1795.
George Schmid m. Elizabeth Simpson on Nov. 5, 1795.
Benage Brown m. Sarah Britton on Nov. 5, 1795.
Frederick Schinckel m. Salome Hall on Dec. 3, 1795.
John Buchhammer m. Elizabeth Heissler on Dec. 22, 1795.
Henry Seiler m. Maria Wundert on Jan. 3, 1796.
Christopher Claudy m. Maria Valentin on Jan. 9, 1796.
George Dorffer m. Susanna Rubsam on Jan. 14, 1796.
Jacob Riehle m. Hannah Weber on Jan. 21, 1796.
Jacob Reus m. Petronella Flicker on Jan. 26, 1796.
John Marshall m. Mary Griffin on Jan. 31, 1796.
John Clarckson m. Elizabeth Stezenbach on Feb. 4, 1796.
Adam Heller m. Sarah Cowan on Feb. 4, 1796.
John Tuston m. Catharine Schweick on Feb. 7, 1796.
William Chyasy m. Catharine Spengler on Feb. 7, 1796.
Simon Moll m. Maria Wilt on Feb. 23, 1796.
Matthias Heineberg m. Maria Hackedy on March 8, 1796.
Frederick Nordiock m. Sarah Galle on March 10, 1796.
Philip Miller m. Susanna Sinck on March 13, 1796.
John Laury m. Dorothy Gassman on March 15, 1796.
Carl Zollner m. Elizabeth Rohr on March 22, 1796.
John Traut m. Catharine Scherer on March 24, 1796.
James Lane of Bedford m. Hannah Rittenhouse of Philadelphia
    County, on March 24, 1796.
James Seeright m. Mary Hanley on March 31, 1796.

Richard Hemer m. Christine Fischer on April 2, 1796.
Jacob Gucker m. Mary Horton on April 7, 1796.
Peter Backer m. Comfort Higgins on April 21, 1796.
Albertus Schnack m. Elizabeth Reybold on April 24, 1796.
Joseph Juncker m. Maria Schutz on May 1, 1796.
John Foring m. Catharine Knorr on May 1, 1796.
Valentine Ulrich m. Elizabeth Bischoffsberger on May 5, 1796.
William Lane m. Susanna van Sciver on May 17, 1796.
Henry Schell m. Anna Fax on May 17, 1796.
Jacob Tag m. Catherine Diehl on May 19, 1796.
Samuel Dupuy m. Anna Musch on May 24, 1796.
George Lambert m. Catharine Haas on May 26, 1796.
John Baer m. Elizabeth Conrad on May 29, 1796.
John Bachofen m. Maria Hoffmann on July 9, 1796.
Sebastian Fischer m. Elizabeth Dincker on July 13, 1796.
George Trump m. Christine Bischoffberger on Aug. 1, 1796.
Christian Schaffer m. Jemima Stanton on Aug. 13, 1796.
George Janey m. Elizabeth Becker on Aug. 14, 1796.
John Keiler m. Sarah Douglas on Sept. 6, 1796.
George Schad m. A. Maria Weber, from Montgomery Co., on Sept. 19, 1796.
Peter Angel Stottenwork m. Ann Doman on Sept. 24, 1796.
Philip Jacob Gamber m. Christine Ross on Oct. 6, 1796.
Job Creaghead m. Mary Harford on Oct. 6, 1796.
Aart van Veen m. Maria Becker on Oct. 11, 1796.
David Wissauer m. Barbara Schaup on Oct. 11, 1796.
Henry Kauffman m. Catharine Kort, from Chester Co., on Oct. 11, 1796.
Matthew Gebler m. Anna Scholl on Oct. 13, 1796.
John George Tauer m. A. Maria Hansen on Oct. 20, 1796.
John Conrad m. Hannah Williams on Oct. 30, 1796.
Jacob Ebel m. Margaret Engel on Oct. 30, 1796.
Simon Sorg m. Christine Handschuh on Oct. 31, 1796.
Jacob Hausler m. Catharine Hut, from Montgomery Co., on Nov. 3, 1796.
James German m. Victory Maillard on Nov. 7, 1796.
Nicholas Knauf m. Margaret Bart on Nov. 11, 1796.
Conrad Beck m. Susanna Fraly on Nov. 13, 1796.
Samuel Park m. Maria Lock on Nov. 14, 1796.
Hugh Quigley m. Christine Neu on Nov. 14, 1796.
Goerge Lutz m. Hannah Diehm, from Montgomery Co., on Nov. 15, 1796.
Francis Latour m. Margaret Smith on Nov. 17, 1796.
John Ohman m. Eva Trippel on Nov. 27, 1796.
Jacob Miller m. Sarah Daubendistel on Dec. 3, 1796.
Henry Fischer m. Maria Faut on Dec. 8, 1796.
Martin Dubs m. Sarah Jones on Dec. 8, 1796.
Philip Odenheimer m. Barbara Schreiber on Dec. 25, 1796.
John Rudolph Stamm m. Maria Kuhn on Dec. 31, 1796.
Jacob Fahns m. Catharine Klein on Jan. 2, 1797.
Pierre Savoy m. Esther Essler on Jan. 3, 1797.
John Pfau m. M. Magdalene Baumgart on Jan. 5, 1797.
John Messemer m. Maria Reinhard on Jan. 8, 1797.
Anthony Barton m. Charity Cook on Jan. 17, 1797.
Valentine Schweitzer m. Polly Armstrong on Jan. 26, 1797.

Henry Schneider m. Elizabeth Stubert on Feb. 12, 1797.
Daniel Stellwagen m. Maria Fischer on Feb. 16, 1797.
Christian Flowers m. Catharine Daubert on Feb. 20, 1797.
Sebastian Hoffmann m. Elizabeth Hentz on Feb. 23, 1797.
Peter Slesman m. Jeane Ryan on Feb. 27, 1797.
John Kelly m. Catharine Faber on Feb. 28, 1797.
Philip Gros m. Christina Kraus on March 16, 1797.
Jacob Jung m. Magdalene Zahn on March 21, 1797.
Frederick Zahn m. Susanna Cowan on March 21, 1797.
George Sauerheber m. Philippina Wentz on March 23, 1797.
John Spangenberger m. Charlotte Krafft on April 3, 1797.
Charles Stewart m. Sally Pearson on April 6, 1797.
George Karstens m. Johanna Catharine Sporn on April 8, 1797.
George Juncker m. Maria Kornstock on April 9, 1797.
Henry Nehs m. Elizabeth Nehs from Montgomery Co. on April 18,
    1797.
Ulrich Weckerle m. Elizabeth Diehl on April 20, 1797.
Abraham Eberhard m. Margaret More on April 20, 1797.
John Leck m. Catharine Tessle on April 25, 1797.
Michael Freytag m. Christine Gerrit on April 30, 1797.
Herman Sander m. Margaret Marks on June 5, 1797.
Abraham Klein m. Maria Ottinger on June 10, 1797.
John Melcher m. Catharine Mauger on June 11, 1797.
Martin Waters m. Maria Hensel on June 11, 1797.
Christian Benner m. Elizabeth Weller on June 13, 1797.
Peter Eschman m. Helena ---- on June 29, 1797.
John Carl Preis m. Maria Fohringer on July 1, 1797.
John Ryan m. Mary Byram on July 1, 1797.
Philip Laury m. Margaret Meistersheim on July 6, 1797.
Joseph Muntzer m. Elizabeth Fischbach on July 27, 1797.
Peter Schneider m. Susanna Lyons on Aug. 2, 1797.
Paul Randon m. Aimé Blondel Heron on Aug. 5, 1797.
Frederick Weber m. Fredericka Gunther on Aug. 10, 1797.
Stephen Bouden m. Rachel Finck on Aug. 10, 1797.
Peter Held m. Maria Schneider on Aug. 17, 1797.
Henry Ernst m. Henrietta Simons on Aug. 20, 1797.
John Krafft Weber m. Christine Keller on Aug. 29, 1797.
David Danneberg m. Eva Reimer on Aug. 30, 1797.
Henry Benson m. Elizabeth Wissauer on Oct. 2, 1797.
William Woodman m. Catharine Miller on Oct. 2, 1797.
Weygand Miller m. Hannah Beltz on Oct. 10, 1797.
Jacob Kucher from Northampton Co. m. Maria Magdalene Veit from
    the City on Oct. 26, 1797.
Francis Connelly m. Philippina Knaus on Oct. 26, 1797.
John Gummy m. Maria Molitor on Oct. 26, 1797.
Joseph Robinson m. Elizabeth Doerr on Oct. 27, 1797.
John Michaelis m. Maria Schaaf on Nov. 8, 1797.
Peter Thomas m. Elizabeth Widerstein on Nov. 9, 1797.
Thomas Lorentz Huttemann m. Barbara Bender on Nov. 11, 1797.
John Engel m. Catharine Richstein on Nov. 14, 1797.
Jacob, alias Joachim, Kopp m. Johanna Maria Krafft on Nov. 21,
    1797.
Daniel Zahner m. Harietta Walton on Nov. 23, 1797.
Peter Wallauer m. Margaret Walton on Nov. 23, 1797.
John Pitt, Junior m. Mary Sharp on Nov. 30, 1797.

John Held m. Margaret Wentz on Dec. 7, 1797.
George Beck m. Lydia Fullerton on Dec. 7, 1797.
William ---- m. Esther Braun on Dec. 10, 1797.
John ---- of North Carolina m. Johanna Stewart on Dec. 10, 1797.
Stephen Fetteral m. Catharine Ruault on Dec. 14, 1797.
John Gamber m. Anna Maria Euler on Jan. 2, 1798.
Charles Dougherty m. Fanny Lee on Jan. 21, 1798.
John Rubel m. Carolina Mariann Schlagmueller on Jan. 22, 1798.
Bernard Nay m. Agnes Monschehr on Jan. 25, 1798.
Isaac Comeley m. Maria Getter from Montgomery Co. on Feb. 1, 1798.
David Givin m. Elizabeth Grimes on Feb. 1, 1798.
John Lyons m. Jane Fynn on Feb. 4, 1798.
Samuel Schaaf m. Catharine Koch on Feb. 6, 1798.
Jacob Hill m. Elizabeth Dixon on Feb. 11, 1798.
Leonard Rothhaar m. Elizabeth Busch on Feb. 22, 1798.
Peter Muller m. Elizabeth Sanders on Feb. 22, 1798.
Godfrey Mercker m. Maria Schmid on Feb. 22, 1798.
William Bock m. Maria Diehl on Feb. 28, 1798.
Alexander Johnson m. Elizabeth Doerr on March 4, 1798.
John Kubler m. Esther Stauffer on March 6, 1798.
John Frederick Warnouer m. Catharine Diehl on March 25, 1798.
George Schneider m. Christine Kitts on April 3, 1798.
Jacob Sinck m. Anna Catharine Ohler on April 10, 1798.
John Kastenbach m. Christine Sinck on April 11, 1798.
John Dietrich m. Maria Doernberger on April 12, 1798.
Joseph Good m. Christine Carrigan on April 18, 1798.
Christopher Schreiner m. Susanna Rhoads on April 19, 1798.
James Tate m. Catharine Gunther on April 23, 1798.
Daniel Wilkeson m. Nancy Curren on April 25, 1798.
George Schaed m. Elizabeth Becker on April 26, 1798.
John Gleim m. Fanny Rudy on May 13, 1798.
Francis ---- m. Margaret Merckel on May 14, 1798.
Samuel Perrot m. Mary Jefferys on May 18, 1798.
Jacob Koerber m. Catharine Heist on May 22, 1798.
Peter Rudolph m. Elizabeth Riehm on May 23, 1798.
Addis Hays m. Catharine Lamberter on May 27, 1798.
George Baumer m. Susanna Urweiler on May 28, 1798.
George Peterman m. Catharine Monsers on May 31, 1798.
Andrew Tauschemer m. M. Christine Hartneck on June 3, 1798.
Anthony Hauer m. Margaret Koster on June 7, 1798.
Andrew Sprohl m. Hannah Mayer on June 10, 1798.
Philip Kramer m. Catharine Kraemer on June 11, 1798.
Jacob Zeller m. Elizabeth Worn on June 21, 1798.
George Schmid m. Jeane Pfeiffer on June 26, 1798.
William Muller m. Rosina Linck on July 8, 1798.
Philip Mueller m. Sarah Lehmann on July 19, 1798.
Conrad Weigand m. Elizabeth Blocher on July 29, 1798.
Bernard Neiler m. Catharine Ernst on Aug. 5, 1798.
John Henry Schmid m. Catharine Tauenheim on Aug. 16, 1798.
Elias Toy m. Elizabeth Wallis from Jersey on Aug. 13, 1798.
Richard Lindsay m. Esther Fisher (crossed out) on Aug. 19, 1798.
Moses Wadlow m. Jane Wright on Aug. 19, 1798.
(Rev. Wm. Hendel died of yellow fever on Sept. 29, 1798.)

MARRIAGES BY REV. SAMUEL HELFFENSTEIN
1799 - 1800
Philip Alberger m. Dolly Snyder on March 6, 1799.
Peter Blais m. Barbara Sherrer on March 7, 1799.
Joseph Huber m. Anna Maria Tise on March 15, 1799.
John Gardner m. Maria Christine ---- on March 13, 1799.
James White m. Margaret Smith on March 17, 1799.
David Fisher m. ---- Smith on March 21, 1799.
John Harry Blum m. Ann Gertrude ---- on March 21, 1799.
Samuel Fenner m. Sarah Worl on April 4, 1799.
Fred. Grave m. Cath. Mum on April 5, 1799.
Christman Lono m. Eleonora Miedermott on April 7, 1799.
William Ehrman m. Elizabeth Hoff on April 15, 1799.
Christopher Ottinger m. Elizabeth Bringhurst on April 18, 1799.
John Backius m. Hannah Downing on April --, 1799.
Casper Zollinger m. Cath. Barn on May 5, 1799.
John Gunderman m. Elizabeth Truber on May 9, 1799.
John Watson m. Polly Lyon on May 23, 1799.
William Hill m. Caty Wagner on May 29, 1799.
Jacob Berckelbach m. Philippina Hein on June 8, 1799.
Henry Sommers m. Elizabeth Sinniff on June 9, 1799.
Christian Franck m. Margaret Holl on June 12, 1799.
Conrad Keller m. Elizabeth Jund on June 12, 1799.
Charles Meder m.Nancy Davis on June 24, 1799.
Jacob Hell m. Catharine Benser on July 4, 1799.
Christian Bobschel m. Elizabeth Alberry on July --, 1799.
Matthew Watson m. Rachel Grosman on July 17, 1799.
John Dickel m. J. Wilheme Smith on July 20, 1799.
John Smith m. Anna Mack on July 21, 1799.
Ernst Snider m. Maria Mohr on July 29, 1799.
Cornelius Kruse m. Molly Race on Aug. 1, 1799.
Valentine Bert m. Margaret Bencil on Aug. 1, 1799.
Philip Bockius m. Maria Desny on Aug. 4, 1799.
John Geo. Walter m. Hannah Lenon on Aug. 8, 1799.
Jno. Bockius m. Hannah ---- on Aug. --, 1799.
Richard Hickham m. Hannah Buckingham on Dec. 11, 1799.
Nicholas Mayer m. Catharine Walker on Oct. 27, 1800.
Abraham Rosenberger m. Mary Morris on Oct. --, 1800.
John Albach m. Maria Rosenberger, Montgomery Co., on Oct. --,
    1800.
John Banks m. Cath. Willow on Oct. 28, 1800.
Henry Shumacher m. Cath. Stremel on Nov. 6, 1800.
John Geo. Walter m. Hannah Leonard on Aug. 4, 1800.
Fred. Troll m. Maria Duvall on Dec. 24, 1800.
Gerhard Dutill m. A. Cath. Hess on Dec. 23, 1800.
William Caul m. Frederica Foebel on Jan. 14, 1801.
John Lutts m. ---- Rusk on Jan. 18, 1801.
Matthew Cooper m. Dolly Merkel on Jan. 22, 1801.
Geo. Spannenberg m. Mary Bigg on Jan. 30, 1801.
Wm. Hibbs m. Mary Breeding on Feb. 1, 1801.
Peter Rumbo m. Mary Grubb on Feb. 1, 1801.
Zacharias Levill m. Mary Woods on Feb. 10, 1801.
Geo. Vanderslice m. Melia Smith on Feb. 23, 1801.
Geo. Rechern m. Cath. Moore on Feb. 26, 1801.
John Huber m. Susanna Dauberman on Feb. --, 1801.

Fred. Adam m. Cath. Hail on Feb. 27, 1801.
Francis Alentrue m. Lydia Lee on March 15, 1801.
John Chamberlain m. Elizabeth Sellers on April 10, 1801.
John Wiser m. Sally Piper on April 12, 1801.
Christian Hartman m. Elizabeth Jost on April 12, 1801.
John Geo. Panekuchen m. Elizabeth Bare on April 13, 1801.
Jacob Salder m. Catharine Snider on April 14, 1801.
Augustus Reichel m. Elizabeth Jerymey on April 14, 1801.
John Geo. Jung m. Susan Markle on April 23, 1801.
Jacob Jones m. Marg. Lowery on May 10, 1801.
John Wille m. Susanna Hahn on May 14, 1801.
Enoch Koller m. Maria Bitting on May 14, 1801.

BAPTISMS BY REV. CASPER WEYBERG
1789 - 1790

Joseph Henry, son of Daniel Von der Schleiss and Phoebe, b. Dec.
4, 1788, bapt. Jan. 18, 1789. Spon: Godfrey Hameler and
Barbara.
Margaret, daughter of Valentine Gaul and Sabina, b. Dec. 25,
1788, bapt. Jan. 18, 1789. Spon: Samuel Berge Megert and
Margaret.
Charles John, son of Daniel Sutter and Anna Catharine, b. Dec.
31, 1788, bapt. Jan. 18, 1789. Spon: The Parents.
Anna Margaret, daughter of Jacob Rumpf and Elizabeth, b. Dec. 15,
1788, bapt. Jan. 18, 1789. Spon: Ludwich Diemer and Anna
Marg. Diemer, his sister.
Anna Maria, daughter of Fred Gul (Gaul) and Clara, b. Jan. 5,
1789, bapt. Jan. 18, 1789. Spon: Martin Gaul and Anna Maria.
John William, son of William Stoll and Christine, b. Jan. 17,
1789, bapt. Jan. 25, 1789. Spon: The Parents.
John George, son of John George Schmidt and Elizabeth, b. Jan. 6,
1789, bapt. Feb. 1, 1789. Spon: The Parents and Maria Fehn.
John Jacob, son of Frederick Froelig and Catharine, b. Jan. 2,
1789, bapt. Feb. 1, 1789. Spon: The Parents.
Elizabeth, daughter of Henry Jungst and Maria, b. Jan. 17, 1789,
bapt. Feb. 1, 1789. Spon: The Parents and Anna Eliz. Jungst.
Maria Catharine, daughter of Lawrence Toth and Elizabeth, b. Nov.
25, 1788, bapt. Feb. 4, 1789. Spon: Daniel Biegle and
Catharine Stern.
Frederick, son of John Kurtzrock and Priscilla, b. Jan. 7, 1789,
bapt. Feb. 8, 1789. Spon: Fred Boyer and Catharine.
Frederick, son of David Wisar and Anne Maria, b. Dec. 18, 1788,
bapt. Feb. 8, 1789. Spon: The Parents.
William, son of Jacob Braning and Maria, b. Sept. 20, 1788, bapt.
Feb. 7, 1789. Spon: The Parents.
Sophia Maria, daughter of John Stillwagen and Margaret, b. Jan.
16, 1789, bapt. Feb. 8, 1789. Spon: Henry Sixkel and Sophia.
William Henry, son of John Fred. Gaul and Margaret, 2 weeks old,
bapt. Feb. 8, 1789. Spon: Eliz. Liest.
Sarah, daughter of John Diehl and Catharine, b. Dec. 26, 1788,
bapt. Feb. 8, 1789. Spon: John Bedder and Elizabeth.
George, son of Jacob Hannebach and Maria Susanna, b. Aug. 1,
1788, bapt. Feb. 11, 1789. Spon: The Parents.
Ruth, daughter of William M'Starren and Christine, b. Jan. 17,

1790 (?), bapt. May 3, ----. Spon: The Parents.

Elizabeth, daughter of Jacob Schneider and Elizabeth, b. Jan. 4,
1789, bapt. Jan. 25, 1789. Spon: The Parents.

Philip, son of Adam Schifferer and Dorothy, b. Jan. 17, 1789,
bapt. Feb. 1, 1789. Spon: The Parents and Maria Barb.
Strauch.

Jacob, son of Jacob Hill and Elizabeth, b. Feb. 10, 1789, bapt.
March 1, 1789. Spon: The Grandparents.

Anna Maria, daughter of Jacob Hill and Elizabeth, b. Feb. 10,
1789, bapt. March 1, 1789. Spon: Anna Maria Hoffman and
Husband.

Philip, son of Philip Gramlich and Elizabeth, b. Feb. 3, 1789,
bapt. March 2, 1789. Spon: The Parents.

Maria, daughter of George Fleeck and Sarah, b. Oct. 23, 1787,
bapt. March 5, 1789. Spon: The Parents.

Joseph, son of John Muller and Anna, b. Feb. 3, 1789, bapt. March
8, 1789. Spon: Jacob Galladin and Sarah.

John Michael, son of Joseph Funck and Maria, b. Feb. 16, 1789,
bapt. March 12, 1789. Spon: The Parents and Sophia Schnyder.

Sarah, daughter of Jeremiah Weisser and Margaret, b. Jan. 8,
1789, bapt. March 15, 1789. Spon: George Riegener and Sarah.

William, son of Charles Schakahr and Margaret, b. Jan. 11, 1789,
bapt. March 15, 1789. Spon: William Dender and Barbara.

Henry, son of Nicholas Weyerich and Susanna, b. Jan. 18, 1789,
bapt. March 15, 1789. Spon: Henry Haffener and Anna Maria.

Elizabeth, daughter of Philip Stimmel and Hannah, b. Dec. 23,
1788, bapt. March 18, 1789. Spon: The Parents.

Elizabeth, daughter of John Boom and Catharine, 5 weeks old,
bapt. March 21, 1789. Spon: Peter Diehl and Elizabeth.

Jacob, son of Peter Walter and Margaret, 12 weeks old, bapt.
March 21, 1789. Spon: Susanna Krauskopf.

Anna Magdalene, daughter of John Michael Matzener and Elizabeth,
b. Feb. 8, 1789, bapt. March 21, 1789. Spon: Jacob Bronner
and Magdalene Rummel.

Philip, son of Henry Ham and Christine, b. Jan. 20, 1789, bapt.
March 22, 1789. Spon: Philip Sommerkamp and Hannah Knies.

Simon, son of Simon Schuchhard and Barbara, b. Jan. 16, 1789,
bapt. March 22, 1789. Spon: The Parents.

Catharine, daughter of Jacob Edenborn and Maria, b. Feb. 25,
1789, bapt. March 22, 1789. Spon: The Parents.

Peter Nella (Petronella), son of Christopher Wesem and Maria, b.
March 15, 1789, bapt. March 29, 1789. Spon: George Stuart and
Peter Nella (Petronella).

Maria Anna, daughter of Christian Alberger and Susanna, b. Jan.
31, 1789, bapt. March 29, 1789. Spon: The Parents.

Christine, daughter of Henry Pfeiffer and Christine, b. March 18,
1789, bapt. April 5, 1789. Spon: The Mother and Ernest
Hauser.

Francis Rowles, son of Geo. William Steinhauer and Elizabeth,
b. ----, bapt. April 6, 1789. Spon: The Father.

Charles William, son of Christopher Schreiner and Elizabeth, b.
March 19, 1789, bapt. April 10, 1789. Spon: William Lehman
and wife.

George William, son of John Kehm and Maria Elizabeth, b. March
30, 1789, bapt. April 12, 1789. Spon: John Buhn (?) and wife,

Father Kehrn.

John, son of Conrad Gerhard and Elizabeth, b. Feb. 4, 1789, bapt. April 12, 1789. Spon: The Parents.

Anna Maria, daughter of Jacob Schmidt and Anna Maria, b. Feb. 4, 1789, bapt. April 13, 1789. Spon: ----.

Rosina, daughter of George Blum and Catharine, b. April 11, 1789, bapt. April 14, 1789. Spon: The Parents.

William, son of Philip Losch and Margaret, b. March 20, 1789, bapt. April 17, 1789. Spon: William Stein and Maria.

Catharine, daughter of George Lampater and Maria, 4 weeks old, bapt. April 18, 1789. Spon: Sophia Lampater.

John Philip, son of Henry Heineman and Charlotta, b. Dec. 14, 1788, bapt. April 18, 1789. Spon: R. Kalkbrenner and Maria.

John, son of Henry Funck and Barbara, b. Feb. 15, 1788, bapt. April 22, 1789. Spon: The Parents.

Peter, son of Peter Becker and Mary Magdalene, b. March 21, 1789, bapt. April 23, 1789. Spon: ----.

William, son of Jacob Reutlinger and Elizabeth, b. March 23, 1789, bapt. April 26, 1789. Spon: John Lauder and Elizabeth.

John George, son of Martin Zibold and Barbara, b. March 15, 1789, bapt. April 26, 1789. Spon: The Parents.

Sarah Elizabeth, daughter of Jacob Seiler and Mary Magdalene, b. Jan. 14, 1789, bapt. April 29, 1789. Spon: George Kurtz and Sarah Elizabeth Muntzer.

Jacob, son of Bernard Meyer and Catharine, b. April 15, 1789, bapt. May 3, 1789. Spon: Jacob Meyer and Elizabeth.

John George, son of John Buetting and Elizabeth, 8 mos., 14 days old, bapt. May 3, 1789. Spon: George Riegener and Sarah.

William, son of John Klages and Rosina, b. April 3, 1789, bapt. May 3, 1789. Spon: The Parents.

Louisa, daughter of Ludwig Faber and Catharine, b. April 7, 1789, bapt. May 10, 1789. Spon: Casper Britton and Louisa.

Christopher Hansman, son of George Lies and Margaret, b. April 14, 1789, bapt. May 10, 1789. Spon: Christ. Hansman and Barbara.

John, son of Jacob Heiberger and Elizabeth, 6 weeks old, bapt. May 10, 1789. Spon: John Weissman and Susan Weissman.

Maria, daughter of Henry Hoffstaetler and Margaret, b. Dec. 14, 1788, bapt. May 10, 1789. Spon: Christian Omen and Nancy.

Elizabeth, daughter of Abraham Scheridan and Anna Barbara, b. April 20, 1789, bapt. May 10, 1789. Spon: The Parents.

John Fred, son of Fred Boyer and Catharine, b. April 20, 1789, bapt. May 10, 1789. Spon: Fried. Froelig and Catharine.

Rebecca, daughter of Philip Riffert and Ursula, b. April 24, 1789, bapt. May 24, 1789. Spon: The Parents.

Maria, daughter of Nicholas Mack and Magdalene, b. May 20, 1789, bapt. May 24, 1789. Spon: Rudolph Spielhoffer and Maria.

Mary Magdalene, daughter of Peter Schneider and Catharine, b. April 9, 1789, bapt. May 31, 1789. Spon: Henry Emmerth and Mary Magdalene.

Margaret, daughter of Stephen Coates and Catharine, b. Sept. 26, 1788, bapt. May 31, 1789. Spon: George Fleek and Margaret.

Maria, daughter of Daniel Kreider and Margaret, b. May 12, 1789, bapt. May 31, 1789. Spon: William Kreider and Maria.

Margaret, daughter of Lawrence Fans and Magdalene, b. March 31,

1789, bapt. June 3, 1789. Spon: The Parents.
William, son of John Feris and Maria, 7 mos. old, bapt. June 4,
1789. Spon: Edward Zotten and Catharine.
Anna Catharine, daughter of Gottlieb Schlatter and Elizabeth, b.
April 9, 1789, bapt. June 4, 1789. Spon: Fred Heineman and
Anna Catharine.
Mary Magdalene, daughter of Jacob Kinsely and Catharine, b. Dec.
31, 1785, bapt. June 4, 1789. Spon: The Parents.
Sarah, daughter of Jacob Kinsely and Catharine, b. Dec. 9, 1787,
bapt. June 4, 1789. Spon: The Parents.
Susanna, daughter of Jacob Kinsely and Catharine, b. April 8,
1789, bapt. June 4, 1789. Spon: The Parents.
Sophia, daughter of William Stepfen and Mary Elizabeth, b. Feb.
1, 1789, bapt. June 6, 1789. Spon: Henry Giohl and Sophia.
John, son of John Kihn and Catharine, b. May 17, 1789, bapt. June
7, 1789. Spon: The Parents.
John, son of Jacob Orner and Sarah, b. March 28, 1789, bapt. June
7, 1789. Spon: John Kihn and Catharine.
Sarah, daughter of Adam May and Catharine, b. May 30, 1789, bapt.
June 14, 1789. Spon: Adam Gilhauer and Sarah.
Elizabeth, daughter of Anthony Balte and Christine, b. June 10,
1789, bapt. June 18, 1789. Spon: Elizabeth Ohle.
Elizabeth, daughter of John Fichter and Catharine, b. May 4,
1781, bapt. June 18, 1789. Spon: Elizabeth Ohl.
William, son of William Skinner and Elizabeth, b. May 20, 1789,
bapt. June 21, 1789. Spon: Jacob Strembeck and Maria.
Henry, son of Herman Leck and Margaret, b. April 3, 1789, bapt.
June 28, 1789. Spon: Henry Dewald and Ann Margaret.
Catharine, daughter of George Herford and Maria, b. June 7, 1789,
bapt. June 30, 1789. Spon: The Parents.
James, son of Christian Gilbert and Magdalene, b. June 28, 1789,
bapt. July 4, 1789. Spon: James Rafferty.
John, son of John Alberger and Dorothy, b. June 2, 1789, bapt.
July 5, 1789. Spon: The Parents and Sophia Fries.
Maria, daughter of Frederick Mangold and Barbara, b. May 18,
1789, bapt. July 5, 1789. Spon: Henry Ries and Elizabeth.
Susanna, daughter of William Spaet and Sarah, b. May 14, 1788,
bapt. July 6, 1789. Spon: The Parents.
Sarah, daughter of Adam Bronnert and Maria, b. June 10, 1789,
bapt. July 7, 1789. Spon: The Parents.
William, son of William Reyde and Sarah, b. July 7, 1789, bapt.
July 8, 1789. Spon: William Reyde and wife.
Lydia, daughter of William Fleck and Maria, b. Aug. 29, 1788,
bapt. July 11, 1789. Spon: The Parents and Maria Schaaff.
Elizabeth, daughter of Conrad Bachman and Susanna, b. July 7,
1789, bapt. July 12, 1789. Spon: Henry Ries and Elizabeth.
James, son of John Meiber and Ann Elizabeth, b. June 2, 1789,
bapt. July 12, 1789. Spon: James Nock and wife.
Catharine, daughter of Nicholas Kayser and Elizabeth, b. July 9,
1789, bapt. July 16, 1789. Spon: Christian Tischong and
Catharine Esch.
Christopher, daughter of John Mast and Anna, b. June 20, 1785,
bapt. July 24, 1789. Spon: The Parents.
Maria, daughter of John Mast and Anna, b. May 27, 1789, bapt.
July 24, 1789. Spon: The Parents.

Elizabeth, daughter of Matthew Birckenbeil and Maria, b. June 21, 1789, bapt. July 26, 1789. Spon: The Parents.

Anna Catharine, daughter of Adam Stricker and Barbara, b. April 17, 1789, bapt. July 26, 1789. Spon: Daniel Sutter and Anna Catharine.

Maria Catharine, daughter of Paul Sturmfels and Anna Margaret, b. July 20, 1789, bapt. Aug. 2, 1789. Spon: Charles William Nushag and Maria Catharine.

James, son of Henry Scherer and Margaret, b. March 11, 1787, bapt. Aug. 2, 1789. Spon: John Kimp and Nancy Perry.

Elizabeth, daughter of James Schmit and Janne, b. Nov. 14, 1788, bapt. Aug. 2, 1789. Spon: Henry Scherer and Elizabeth.

William, son of Henry Scherer and Elizabeth, 3 weeks old, bapt. Aug. 2, 1789. Spon: John Kimp and Nancy Perry.

Maria, daughter of Fred Theis and Elizabeth, b. July 16, 1789, bapt. Aug. 9, 1789. Spon: Philip Gatter and Anna Maria.

Joseph, son of Daniel Keiser and Regina, b. July 18, 1789, bapt. Aug. 9, 1789. Spon: The Parents.

Maria, daughter of Jacob Jentzer and Barbara, b. July 21, 1789, bapt. Aug. 16, 1789. Spon: The Parents.

James, son of James Miller and Barbara, b. June 13, 1789, bapt. Aug. 16, 1789. Spon: The Parents.

Maria, daughter of John Geo. Zahner and Catharine, b. March 30, 1789, bapt. Aug. 16, 1789. Spon: John Diehl and Catharine.

John, son of Henry Dewald and Margaret, b. July 28, 1789, bapt. Aug. 23, 1789. Spon: John Stein and Magdalene.

Charlotte, daughter of Adam Lewer and Maria, b. July 18, 1789, bapt. Aug. 23, 1789. Spon: George Lex and Charles Herman.

Adam, son of Anthony von der Schleis and Elizabeth, 4 yrs. old, bapt. ----. Spon: ----.

Samuel, son of Anthony von der Schleis and Elizabeth, 18 mos. old, bapt. Aug. 24, 1789. Spon: ----.

Wm. Ludwig, son of Wm. Ludwig Kahmer and Elizabeth, b. Aug. 10, 1789, bapt. Aug. 26, 1789. Spon: Elisabeth Reinhard.

William, son of Philip Haller and Maria, b. Aug. 15, 1789, bapt. Aug. 29, 1789. Spon: The Parents.

Anna Catharine, daughter of Henry Joette and Ann Catharine, b. Aug. 12, 1789, bapt. Aug. 30, 1789. Spon: Martin Wahl and Christine.

Julianna, daughter of John Meile and Catharine, b. June 18, 1789, bapt. Aug. 30, 1789. Spon: The Parents and Catharine Stucky.

George, son of George Beumer and Catharine, b. Aug. 5, 1789, bapt. Sept. 1, 1789. Spon: The Parents.

Anna Catharine, daughter of Henry Toer and Elizabeth, b. Aug. 3, 1789, bapt. Sept. 6, 1789. Spon: John Moyer and Ann Schmitt.

Nicholas, son of Nicholas Penther and Maria, b. Aug. 10, 1789, bapt. Sept. 6, 1789. Spon: The Parents.

Ann Rosina, daughter of Andrew Bradeneck and Clara, b. Aug. 15, 1789, bapt. Sept. 6, 1789. Spon: Magdalene Jeremias.

George, son of Michael Katz and Margaret, b. July 1, 1789, bapt. Sept. 6, 1789. Spon: George Stoud.

Catharine, daughter of George Riegener and Sarah, b. Aug. 24, 1789, bapt. Sept. 9, 1789. Spon: Catharine Riegener.

Susanna, daughter of Peter Walter and Charlotte, b. Aug. 29, 1789, bapt. Sept. 10, 1789. Spon: The Parents.

Elizabeth, daughter of Joseph Schmidt and Barbara, b. Aug. 3,
1789, bapt. Sept. 13, 1789. Spon: Michael Fleming and
Elizabeth Schmidt.
John William, son of Gottfried Gobeler and Catharine, b. Aug. 13,
1789, bapt. Sept. 13, 1789. Spon: John Wucherer and
Elizabeth.
John Adam, son of Adam Gaul and Elizabeth, b. Aug. 4, 1789, bapt.
Sept. 13, 1789. Spon: Adam Lotz and Maria.
John Nicholas, son of Adam Hesse and Elizabeth, b. Sept. 13,
1789, bapt. Sept. 17, 1789. Spon: Nicholas Hess and
Wilhelmina.
Anna Julianna, daughter of John Steltz and Elizabeth, b. Aug. 23,
1789, bapt. Sept. 17, 1789. Spon: The Parents.
Conrad, son of George Pfaff and Anna, b. Aug. 15, 1789, bapt.
Sept. 20, 1789. Spon: John Conrad Haas and wife.
Mary Magdalene, daughter of John Messemer and Maria Catharine, b.
May 5, 1789, bapt. Sept. 22, 1789. Spon: The Parents.
Jacob, son of Jacob Baumgartner and Catharine, b. Sept. 3, 1789,
bapt. Sept. 24, 1789. Spon: The Parents.
Anna Maria, daughter of John Peter Schaff and Elizabeth, b. Sept.
14, 1789. bapt. Sept. 26, 1789. Spon: Henry Schuck and Anna
Maria.
John Peter, son of John Fred. Dickes and Catharine, b. July 16,
1789, bapt. Sept. 27, 1789. Spon: John Peter Dickes and
Chris. Kantzer.
William, son of Christopher Huth and Elizabeth, b. Dec. 11, 1788,
bapt. Sept. 27, 1789. Spon: -----.
Catharine, daughter of Thomas Hueter and Catharine, b. Aug. 29,
1789, bapt. Sept. 27, 1789. Spon: Martin Kochersberger and
Rosina.
George, son of George Peter Stoud and Anna Maria, b. Sept. 12,
1789, bapt. Sept. 27, 1789. Spon: George Hoffman and Ann
Maria.
Anna Maria Frederica, daughter of John Herman Reisner and
Catharine, b. March 27, 1789, bapt. Oct. 2, 1789. Spon: Anna
Maria Zeller (?).
John, son of John Scheh and Philippina, 1 yr. old, bapt. Oct. --,
1789. Spon: Valentine Schneider and Rosina.
John Christ Ludwig, son of Charles Ludwig Baumgarten and Mary
Magd., b. Aug. 6, 1789, bapt. Sept. 4, 1789. Spon: John
Christian Franck, Christian Denne and Christopher Ludwig.
Anna Margaret, daughter of Henry Wm. Zimmerman and Elizabeth, b.
July 4, 1789, bapt. Sept. 4, 1789. Spon: Philip Haeffener and
Anna Margaret.
John, son of George Fish and Dorothy, b. July 22, 1789, bapt. ---
-. Spon: The Parents.
Lydia, daughter of Gerard Jus and Susanna, b. Aug. 23, 1789,
bapt. -----. Spon: The Parents.
Catharine, daughter of Hendericus Roskes and Maria, b. Aug. 28,
1789, bapt. Oct. 24, 1789. Spon: The Parents.
Anna Dorothy, daughter of William Schmidt and Margaret, b. Sept.
29, 1789, bapt. Oct. 25, 1789. Spon: Jacob Theiss and Anna
Dorothy.
Salome, daughter of John Ungar and Elizabeth, b. ----, bapt. Oct.
27, 1789. Spon: John Bouman and Salome.

Thomasina Maria, daughter of Samuel Stern and Catharine, b. Sept.
3, 1789, bapt. Oct. 28, 1789. Spon: Samuel Weyberg and Maria
Neveling.
Johanna Solomome, daughter of Samuel Stern and Catharine, b.
Sept. 3, 1789, bapt. Oct. 28, 1789. Spon: John Weyberg and
Solomomeh.
Charles, son of Peter Hohl and Catharine, b. Oct. 30, 1789, bapt.
Nov. 1, 1789. Spon: Charles Stoltz and Margaret.
John Peter, son of Peter Tenner and Catharine, b. Oct. 14, 1789,
bapt. Nov. 1, 1789. Spon: Peter Dick and Susanna Schnyder.
John Peter, son of John Peter Held and Elizabeth, b. Nov. 2,
1789, bapt. Nov. 8, 1789. Spon: John Philip Petri and
Elizabeth.
Anna Elizabeth, daughter of George Hess and Anna, b. Oct. 28,
1789, bapt. Nov. 8, 1789. Spon: The Parents.
Adam, son of John Gerrith and Margaret, b. Nov. 8, 1789, bapt.
Nov. 8, 1789. Spon: The Parents.
Edward, son of Edward Corton and Susanna, b. Sept. 18, 1789,
bapt. Nov. 14, 1789. Spon: The Parents.
Maria, daughter of Jacob Reckstein and Catharine, b. Nov. 1,
1789, bapt. Nov. 15, 1789. Spon: The Parents.
Sarah, daughter of Wm. Kesman and wife (husband absent), b. Oct.
7, 1789, bapt. Nov. 16, 1789. Spon: George Ehrlich and Sarah.
John, son of John Simon and Elizabeth, b. Feb. 5, 1789, bapt.
Nov. 17, 1789. Spon: James Lapiti.
Maria, daughter of John Surzebach and Margaret, b. Oct. 14, 1789,
bapt. Nov. 22, 1789. Spon: Mich. Krehmer and Maria.
Philip, son of Philip Alberger and Susanna, 4 weeks old, bapt.
Nov. 22, 1789. Spon: The Parents.
John, son of Philip Peltz and Rebecca, b. Nov. 21, 1789, bapt.
Nov. 23, 1789. Spon: The Grandparents.
Rebecca, daughter of Christian Fans and Christine, b. Oct. 5,
1789, bapt. Nov. 24, 1789. Spon: Rebecca Fanz (?).
Peter, son of Philip Gasser and Anna Maria, b. Oct. 11, 1789,
bapt. Nov. 24, 1789. Spon: Peter Gasser.
Peggy, daughter of Christopher Schmidt and Maria, 2 weeks old,
bapt. Nov. 29, 1789. Spon: George Zenck and Barbara.
Elizabeth, daughter of John Kreimes and Elizabeth, b. Nov. 9,
1789, bapt. Dec. 2, 1789. Spon: The Parents.
Ann Margaret, daughter of Opidien Wind (?) and Ann Maria, 5 mos.
old, bapt. Dec. 6, 1789. Spon: Ann Margaret Linnen and
Schick.
Hannah, daughter of William Miller and Maria, b. Sept. 19, 1789,
bapt. Dec. 6, 1789. Spon: Catharine Eiland.
Catharine, daughter of John Sing and Elizabeth, b. Dec. 7, 1789,
bapt. Dec. 9, 1789. Spon: The Grandparents.
James, son of George Kins and Catharine, b. Oct. 2, 1789, bapt.
Dec. 13, 1789. Spon: James Metz and Philippina.
Charlotte, daughter of Henry Schmidt and Elizabeth, b. ----,
bapt. Dec. 13, 1789. Spon: Christian Brown and Charlotte
Kindern.
Christine Margaret, daughter of Henry Schmidt and Elizabeth, b. -
---, bapt. Dec. 13, 1789. Spon: Christian E. Shard and
Christine Krohn.
Sarah, daughter of Jacob Eshler and Susanna, b. Nov. 13, 1789,

bapt. Dec. 13, 1789. Spon: The Parents.
Magdalene, daughter of Henry Tenner and Elizabeth, b. Nov. 19,
1789, bapt. Dec. 14, 1789. Spon: Andrew Muller's wife.
George, son of George Schaed and Maria, b. Nov. 19, 1789, bapt.
Dec. 14, 1789. Spon: The Parents.
Conrad, son of Christian Haer and Anna Ursula, b. Dec. 6, 1789,
bapt. Dec. 14, 1789. Spon: Conrad Keller and Elizabeth.
Elizabeth, daughter of Adam Boyer and Margaret, b. Sept. 20,
1789, bapt. Dec. 14, 1789. Spon: Conrad Keller.
Susan, daughter of Philip Alberger and Dorothea, b. Nov. 20,
1789, bapt. Dec. 20, 1789. Spon: Margaret Alberger.
George, son of George Bornhaus and Elizabeth, b. Dec. 24, 1789,
bapt. Dec. 26, 1789. Spon: ----.
Christian, son of George Bornhaus and Elizabeth, b. Dec. 25,
1789, bapt. Dec. 26, 1789. Spon: ----.
Frederick, son of Conrad Spangenberg and Barbara, b. Sept. 28,
1789, bapt. Jan. 3, 1790. Spon: Frederick Taxes and wife.
John, son of John Schaeffer and Susanna, b. Nov. 7, 1789, bapt.
Jan. 3, 1790. Spon: The Parents.
Susan, daughter of John Wagner and Elizabeth, b. Nov. 12, 1789,
bapt. Jan. 3, 1790. Spon: The Parents.
Jemimah, daughter of James Stats and Rachel b. March 30, 1789,
bapt. Jan. 3, 1790. Spon: Albert Schillack and Maria.
William, son of John Jones and Elizabeth, b. Sept. 16, 1789,
bapt. Jan. 3, 1790. Spon: James Heini and Peggy Pratler.
John Jacob, son of John Stuber and Veronica, b. June 25, 1789,
bapt. Jan. 10, 1790. Spon: John von der Lind.
William, son of Francis Metzger and Anna, b. Dec. 19, 1789, bapt.
Jan. 10, 1790. Spon: William Will and the Parents.
Philip Frederick, son of Ph. Fred. Bischot and Maria, b. Dec. 29,
1789, bapt. Jan. 10, 1790. Spon: The Parents.
John Ludwig, son of Jacob Ziebble and Wilhelmina, b. Nov. 15,
1789, bapt. Jan. 11, 1790. Spon: Ludwig Hess and Anna
Juliana.
Henry, son of Adam Lange and Catharine, 6 weeks old, bapt. Jan.
17, 1790. Spon: Henry Scharp and Maria Eva.
Anna Margaret, daughter of Lawrence Opman and Anna Mary, 6 weeks
old, bapt. Jan. 17, 1790. Spon: Martin Broun and Margaret
Schling.
John Henry, son of George Weindel and Charlotte, b. Jan. 9, 1790,
bapt. Jan. 17, 1790. Spon: John Henry Miller.
Maria Magdalene, daughter of Morgan Ritsch and Catharine, b. Nov.
3, 1789, bapt. Jan. 24, 1790. Spon: Martin Hohl and Mary
Magdalene.
Catharine, daughter of William Becker and Ann Maria, b. Dec. 7,
1789, bapt. Jan. 24, 1790. Spon: The Parents.
Henry Lies, son of Henry Lies and Maria Elizabeth, b. Jan. 10,
1790, bapt. Jan. 24, 1790. Spon: Henry Pheisser and
Christine.
Anna Dorothea, daughter of George Broun and Maria, b. Jan. 6,
1790, bapt. Jan. 24, 1790. Spon: Lawrence Lapp and Ann
Dorothea.
Maria, daughter of John Justus Koch and Susanna, b. Dec. 17,
1789, bapt. Jan. 24, 1790. Spon: John Hatkins and Maria.
John Adam, son of Samuel Neidlinger and Susanna, b. Jan. 28,

1790, bapt. Feb. 7, 1790. Spon: Adam Coleman and Susanna.
William, son of Henry Frick and Barbara, b. Jan. 4, 1790, bapt.
Feb. 14, 1790. Spon: William Becker and Catharine.
John Paul, son of Casper Betzler and Elizabeth, 2 mos. old, bapt.
Feb. 19, 1790. Spon: John Paul and Agnes.
----, child of James Bell and ----, b. ----, bapt. ----. Spon: -
----.
John Conrad, son of Melchior Steiner and wife, b. ----, bapt.
Feb. 22, 1790. Spon: Casper Weyberg and Salome.
Sarah, daughter of Leonard Jund and Sarah, b. Jan. 1, 1790, bapt.
Feb. 28, 1790. Spon: The Parents.
Maria Barbara, daughter of John Huhn and Christine, b. Feb. 18,
1790, bapt. Feb. 28, 1790. Spon: William Terle and Elizabeth
Terle.
Peter, son of John Gunckel and Margaret, b. Jan. 29, 1790,
bapt. ----. Spon: Peter Laury and Jane.
John, son of Peter Weiel and Elizabeth, b. Feb. 8, 1790, bapt.
March 7, 1790. Spon: The Parents.
Elizabeth, daughter of Henry Fish and Catharine, b. Dec. 25,
1789, bapt. March 7, 1790. Spon: Peter Schmidt and Elizabeth.
Samuel, son of George Becker and Sophia, b. Feb. 14, 1790, bapt.
March 16, 1790. Spon: The Parents.
John Peter, son of John Jacob Hallem and Maria, b. Feb. 29, 1790,
bapt. March 21, 1790. Spon: Conrad Axt and Maria.
Eleonora, daughter of John Stein and Gratia, b. March 14, 1790,
bapt. March 22, 1790. Spon: David Harder and Maria.
Sarah, daughter of Jacob Bischoffberger and Elizabeth, b. Dec.
23, 1790 (?), bapt. March 27, 1790. Spon: The Parents.
John Conrad, son of George Degenhard and Wilhelmina, b. March 10,
1790, bapt. March 28, 1790. Spon: Conrad Water and Elizabeth.
Ann Margaret, daughter of Henry Jungst and Ann Maria, b. Feb. 13,
1790, bapt. April 4, 1790. Spon: Philip Haffener and Ann
Margaret.
Catharine Barbara, daughter of John Spalter and Elizabeth, b.
March 26, 1790, bapt. April 4, 1793. Spon: Geo. Fred.
Schaumenkessel and Eliz. Barbara.
David Jouman, son of Peter Auner and Margaret, b. Feb. 18, 1790,
bapt. April 8, 1790. Spon: The Parents.
Elizabeth, daughter of Jacob Schlemmer and Anna, b. Feb. 13,
1790, bapt. April 11, 1790. Spon: The Parents.
John Frederick, son of Zacharias Beckman and Barbara, b. March
18, 1790, bapt. April 11, 1790. Spon: John Fred. Tischong and
Margaret.
James, son of James Stiel and Catharine, b. March 19, 1790, bapt.
April 11, 1790. Spon: Susan Moser.
Maria Christianna, daughter of Jacob Belsterling and Mary
Magdalene, b. April 13, 1790 (?), bapt. April 11, 1790. Spon:
Conrad Seipert and Maria.
John, son of Louis Diemer and Hannah, b. Feb. 21, 1790, bapt.
April 11, 1790. Spon: Christian Kauck and Maria.
Anna Maria, daughter of Stocker Hahl and Catharine, b. Feb. 1,
1790, bapt. April 11, 1790. Spon: Christ. Kouck and Maria.
Rachel, daughter of Jacob Steinmetz and Rachel, b. Feb. 19, 1790,
bapt. (May) 8, 1790. Spon: ----.
Elizabeth, daughter of Bernard Schwenck and Margaret, 4 mos., 8

days old, bapt. (May) 9, 1790. Spon: Henry Dollman and
Elizabeth Doerrn.
Elizabeth, daughter of George Lorentz and Susanna, 4 mos. old,
bapt. May --, 1790. Spon: ----.
George, son of Daniel Biegle and Margaret, b. Jan. 17, 1790,
bapt. May 17, 1790. Spon: The Parents.
George, son of George Eisenring and Elizabeth, b. April 14, 1790,
bapt. May 17, 1790. Spon: ----.
Salome, daughter of John Abel and Maria, b. May 1, 1790, bapt.
May 18, 1790. Spon: George Abel and Maria Seiffert.
William, son of William Wever and Elizabeth, b. April 16, 1790,
bapt. May 18, 1790. Spon: John George Weaver and Ann
Catharine.
Joseph, son of George Schwartz and Barbara, b. April 18, 1790,
bapt. May 18, 1790. Spon: Jacob Reiser and Eva.
Anna Margaret, daughter of John Stoll and Elizabeth, 2 yrs. old,
bapt. May 18, 1790. Spon: Ann Margaret Diemer.
John Christian, son of Martin ---- and Catharine, 4 weeks old,
bapt. ----. Spon: Christian Gucker and Dorothy.
Sarah, daughter of Jacob Eckoff and Maria, b. Sept. 15, 1783,
bapt. May --, 1790. Spon: Peter Merckel and Ann Catharine,
Margaret Ulrich.
John David, son of Jacob Eckoff and Maria, b. Nov. 19, 1785,
bapt. May --, 1790. Spon: Peter Merckel and Ann Catharine,
Margaret Ulrich.
Anna Margaret, daughter of Jacob Eckoff and Maria, b. March 9,
1788, bapt. May --, 1790. Spon: Peter Merckel and Ann
Catharine, Margaret Ulrich.
Jacob, son of Jacob Maurer (son of Rudolph Maurer, one of
founders of Frankford Reformed Church) and Esther Lebler, b.
Feb. 4, 1790, bapt. May --, 1790. Spon: The Parents.
Jane, daughter of Martin Miller and Elizabeth, b. Feb. 11, 1790,
bapt. May --, 1790. Spon: The Parents.
Maria, daughter of John Lehr and Catharine, b. Nov. 25, 1789,
bapt. May --, 1790. Spon: John Schneider and Margaret.
Elizabeth, daughter of George Ozeas and Maria, b. April 29, 1790,
bapt. May --, 1790. Spon: The Parents.
Anna Margaret, daughter of Henry Juengst and Margaret, b. Feb.
13, 1790, bapt. ----. Spon: Philip Haffener and Margaret.
Catharine Barbara, daughter of John Spalter and Elizabeth, b.
March 26, 1790, bapt. ----. Spon: Geo. Schaumenkessel and
Elizabeth.
Henry, son of Henry Thiel and Maria, b. April 15, 1790, bapt.
(June) 13, 1790. Spon: The Parents.
John George, son of Fred Meile and Barbara, b. March 10, 1790,
bapt. (June) 13, 1790. Spon: Maria Greenstat.
Maria, daughter of Frederick Steiner and Maria, b. Nov. 20, 1789,
bapt. June 14, 1790. Spon: The Parents.
Catharine, daughter of Henry Becker and Gertrude, b. Nov. 16,
1789, bapt. June 14, 1790. Spon: The Parents.
John, son of John Brown and Barbara, b. April 26, 1790, bapt.
June 20, 1790. Spon: ----.
Elizabeth, daughter of John Reudy and Margaret, b. June 8, 1790,
bapt. ----. Spon: Elizabeth Wiston.
Catharine, daughter of John Reudy and Margaret, b. June 8, 1790,

bapt. ----. Spon: John Herlein and Catharine.
John Casper, son of John Karpp and Catharine, b. June 8, 1790,
bapt. Aug. 4, 1790. Spon: Casper Geyer and Elizabeth.
----, child of Jonas Frisch and Christine, b. May 17, 1790, bapt.
Aug. 3, 1790. Spon: Michael Eckert and the Parents.
Anna Margaret, daughter of John Souder and Catharine, b. June 17,
1790, bapt. July 1, 1790. Spon: Casper Schoen and Anna
Margaret.
Adam, son of David Rohrman and Anna Margaret, b. April 25, 1790,
bapt. July 18, 1790. Spon: Adam May and Catharine.
William, son of Peter Dies and Elizabeth, 5 weeks old, bapt. July
18, 1790. Spon: ----.
Sarah, daughter of Conrad Froman and Margaret, b. ---- 17, 1790,
bapt. July 18, 1790. Spon: John Kuhn and Elizabeth.
George, son of John Penther and Maria, 6 weeks old, bapt. July
22, 1790. Spon: Anna Marg. Fornes.
Nicholas, son of Nicholas Keyser and Elizabeth, b. June 9, 1790,
bapt. July 25, 1790. Spon: Michael Kitts and Margaret.
Maria Barbara, daughter of Jacob Meile and Margaret, b. March 19,
1790, bapt. July 25, 1790. Spon: P. Grensteffer and Maria.
Frances Heap Maus, ---- of ---- Maus and wife, b. June 22, 1790,
bapt. July 29, 1790. Spon: ----.
Gottfried (Godfrey), son of Ludwig Reincke and wife, 1 week old,
bapt. Aug. 1, 1790. Spon: Gottfried Munig and Veronica.
Adam, son of Adam Reis and Elizabeth, b. July 28, 1790, bapt.
Aug. 5, 1790. Spon: The Parents.
Anna Maria, daughter of John Fordheim and Anna Maria, b. July 8,
1790, bapt. Aug. 8, 1790. Spon: The Parents.
Maria, daughter of Martin Schuster and Catharine, b. Dec. --,
1789, bapt. ----. Spon: Thomas Deussen.

(Rev. Weyberg died on Aug. 21, 1790 in Philadelphia.)

BAPTISMS BY REV. HERMAN WINCKHAUS
August 22, 1790 - Sept. 1793
Margaret, daughter of Jacob Becker and Catharine, b. June 1,
1790, bapt. Aug. 7, 1790. Spon: The Parents.
Adam, son of Henry Mayer and Hannah, b. July 20, 1790, bapt. Aug.
16, 1790. Spon: The Parents.
John Peter Weyand, son of John Jost Weyand and Maria, b. July 16,
1788, bapt. ----, 1790. Spon: ----.
Anna, daughter of Martin Ebersbach and Anna Maria, b. Feb. 1,
1789, bapt. Aug. 9, 1790. Spon: The Parents.
John, son of John Heimer and Elizabeth, b. Aug. 10, 1790, bapt.
Aug. 22, 1790. Spon: Peter Klein and Maria.
Elizabeth, daughter of Francis Geiss and Regina, b. July 28,
1790, bapt. Aug. 23, 1790. Spon: Lewis Farmeret and
Elizabeth.
Elizabeth, daughter of John Loveburry and Elizabeth Becker, b.
Aug. 11, 1790, bapt. Sept. 5, 1790. Spon: Catharine Bennet.
Catharine, daughter of Leonard Rueb and wife, b. Sept. 7, 1790,
bapt. Sept. 9, 1790. Spon: The Parents.
Charles, son of Charles Seitz and Charlotte, b. July 29, 1790,

bapt. Sept. 5, 1790. Spon: The Parents.
Elizabeth, daughter of Jacob Meyer and Elizabeth, b. June 13,
1790, bapt. Sept. 7, 1790. Spon: The Parents.
Maria Eva, daughter of Gabriel Kern and Mary Magdalene, b. Aug.
9, 1790, bapt. Sept. 18, 1790. Spon: George Bastian and Maria
Eva.
Rebecca, daughter of Matthew Lammert and Anna, b. Sept. 18, 1790,
bapt. Sept. 18, 1790. Spon: George Bloom and Philippina.
Susanna, daughter of Henry Moser and Susanna, b. May 12, 1789,
bapt. Sept. 18, 1790. Spon: The Mother.
Graff, son of William van Phul and Catharine, b. Sept. 1, 1790,
bapt. Sept. 26, 1790. Spon: The Parents.
William, son of Jacob Schreiner, Jr. and wife, b. Sept. 14, 1790,
bapt. Sept. 25, 1790. Spon: Jacob Schreiner and wife.
Rebecca, daughter of Jacob Schreiner, Sr. and wife, b. Aug. 26,
1790, bapt. Sept. 26, 1790. Spon: The Parents.
Maria, daughter of Henry Ritter and wife, b. Aug. 10, 1790, bapt.
Sept. 26, 1790. Spon: The Parents.
Albertus, son of Ezekiel Shaw and Jemimah, b. Sept. 29, 1782,
bapt. Oct. 8, 1790. Spon: Albertus Schillack.
Daniel, son of Adam Keiser and Maria, b. July 9, 1790, bapt. Oct.
10, 1790. Spon: Daniel Kaiser and Regina.
Anna Margaret, daughter of Jacob Cinch and Catharine, b. Sept. 2,
1790, bapt. Oct. 15, 1790. Spon: Christopher Vetter and Anna
Barbara.
John Lawrence, son of Daniel Walter and Anna Maria, b. Aug. 8,
1790, bapt. Oct. 17, 1790. Spon: John Carl Lenninschid and
Anna Margaret.
John Jacob, son of Jacob Lutz and Elizabeth Catharine, b. Sept.
28, 1790, bapt. Oct. 17, 1790. Spon: Sebastian Wolfinger and
Elizabeth Catharine.
John Michael, son of Christian Stahl and Catharine, b. July 21,
1790, bapt. Oct. 17, 1790. Spon: Michael Schloesman and
Philippina.
Elizabeth, daughter of John Clarman (?) and wife, b. Sept. 11,
1790, bapt. Oct. 17, 1790. Spon: The Parents.
Isaac, son of Anthony van der Schleuss and Elizabeth, b. Sept.
30, 1790, bapt. Oct. 21, 1790. Spon: The Parents.
Anna, daughter of Martin Haas and Jemimah, b. Oct. 6, 1790, bapt.
Oct. 24, 1790. Spon: The Parents.
Isaac, son of William Johns and Elizabeth, b. Sept. 27, 1790,
bapt. Oct. 24, 1790. Spon: The Parents.
John Peter, son of Peter Schuck and Catharine, b. Sept. 26, 1790,
bapt. Oct. 24, 1790. Spon: Philip Mieser and Maria.
Peter, son of John Philip Reis and Elizabeth, b. Oct. 1, 1790,
bapt. Oct. 24, 1790. Spon: The Parents.
Sarah, daughter of Jacob Hill, Jr. and Elizabeth, b. Sept. 8,
1790, bapt. Oct. 24, 1790. Spon: Jacob Hill, Sr. and Salome
Backoffen.
Margaret, daughter of George Hoffman and Maria, b. Sept. 20,
1790, bapt. Oct. 24, 1790. Spon: Jacob Binder and Maria.
John, son of John Wildfang and Anna, b. Feb. 3, 1790, bapt. Oct.
31, 1790. Spon: The Parents.
John Peter, son of Henry Lehr and Elizabeth, b. Sept. 30, 1790,
bapt. Oct. 31, 1790. Spon: John Peter Nannetter and

Magdalene.

William, son of John Porter and Catharine, b. Oct. 13, 1790, bapt. Nov. 3, 1790. Spon: The Parents.

Anna Maria, daughter of Christopher Luckhart and Elizabeth, b. Nov. 3, 1790, bapt. Nov. 7, 1790. Spon: The Parents.

Elizabeth, daughter of Philip Fritz and Elizabeth, b. Sept. 22, 1790, bapt. Nov. 7, 1790. Spon: The Parents.

Elizabeth, daughter of Henry Berly and Maria, b. Feb. 5, 1790, bapt. Nov. 7, 1790. Spon: The Father and Anna Catharine Meng.

Anna Catharine, daughter of Christopher Schreiner and Elizabeth, b. Oct. 16, 1790, bapt. Nov. 7, 1790. Spon: The Parents.

Jacob, son of Jacob Schmidt and Anna Maria, b. Oct. 23, 1790, bapt. Nov. 8, 1790. Spon: The Parents.

Thomas England, son of William Kommer and Elizabeth, b. Oct. 24, 1790, bapt. Nov. 14, 1790. Spon: The Father and his Mother, Maria.

Samuel, son of Christian Hautzel and Margaret, b. Oct. 28, 1790, bapt. Nov. 21, 1790. Spon: Peter Nannetter and Magdalene.

John Peter, son of Christian Hautzel and Margaret, b. Nov. 14, 1790, bapt. Nov. 21, 1790. Spon: Peter Nennetter and Magdalene.

Anna, daughter of John Geo. Birckenbeil and Anna Margaret, b. Nov. 6, 1790, bapt. Nov. 26, 1790. Spon: John Schaup and Anna Elizabeth.

Catharine, daughter of Reinhard Komer and Elizabeth, b. Nov. 12, 1790, bapt. Nov. 28, 1790. Spon: The Father and Catharine Hutz.

Jacob, son of Jacob Heiberger and Elizabeth, b. Nov. 13, 1790, bapt. Dec. 5, 1790. Spon: The Parents.

Carolus, daughter of John Osman and Elizabeth, b. Sept. 11, 1790, bapt. Dec. 6, 1790. Spon: Charles Korbi and wife.

Daniel, son of John Estrisch and Christine, b. Nov. 26, 1790, bapt. Dec. 19, 1790. Spon: The Parents.

Maria Elizabeth, daughter of John Krafft Weiand and Christine, b. Dec. 11, 1790, bapt. Dec. 23, 1790. Spon: The Parents.

Jacob, son of Conrad Scholle and Anna, b. Aug. 21, 1790, bapt. Dec. 24, 1790. Spon: J. George Freitag and Margaret Philippina.

Jacob, son of Valentine Gaertner and Mary Magdalene, b. Dec. 11, 1790, bapt. Dec. 26, 1790. Spon: The Father and Elizabeth Eberhardt.

Maria Elizabeth, daughter of Jacob Eckstein and Catharine, b. Dec. 1, 1790, bapt. Dec. 26, 1790. Spon: The Parents.

Maria Elizabeth, daughter of Jacob Meyer and Margaret, b. Nov. 22, 1790, bapt. Dec. 26, 1790. Spon: Frederick Kaester and Elizabeth.

Anna Maria, daughter of William Fuselbach and Margaret, b. Dec. 29, 1789, bapt. Dec. 26, 1790. Spon: John Conrad Fehrglass and Anna Maria.

Peter, son of Jacob Becker and Elizabeth, b. Dec. 4, 1790, bapt. Dec. 30, 1790. Spon: The Parents.

George, son of Philip Hasselbach and Maria, b. Nov. 9, 1790, bapt. Dec. 30, 1790. Spon: The Parents.

Samuel, son of Daniel Klages and Maria, b. Dec. 31, 1790, bapt. Jan. 8, 1791. Spon: Samuel Mauss and Maria.

Stephanus, son of Jacob Nannetter and Anna Catharine, b. Nov. 28, 1790, bapt. Jan. 9, 1791. Spon: Stephen Pyeron and wife Sarah Riet.

Julianna, daughter of Philip Haller and Maria, b. Dec. 17, 1790, bapt. Jan. 9, 1791. Spon: Bernard Schemo and Juliana.

Anna Maria, daughter of John Contreman and Susanna, b. Dec. 17, 1790, bapt. Jan. 9, 1791. Spon: The Parents.

Eva, daughter of John Mueller and Anna Maria, b. Aug. 25, 1789, bapt. Jan. 9, 1791. Spon: John Contreman and Susanna.

Joseph, son of Valentine Clemens and Catharine, b. Jan. 8, 1789, bapt. Jan. 9, 1791. Spon: Thomas McCharti and Abigail.

Jesse, son of Christian Heist and Sarah, b. July 10, 1790, bapt. Jan. 11, 1791. Spon: Peter Stricker and Elizabeth.

George, son of John Lotsch and Margaret, b. Jan. 1, 1791, bapt. Jan. 15, 1791. Spon: The Parents.

William, son of William Fleck and Maria, b. May 21, 1790, bapt. Jan. 16, 1791. Spon: The Parents.

Michael, son of Jacob Diehl and Elizabeth, b. Jan. 8, 1791, bapt. Jan. 23, 1791. Spon: The Parents.

Mary Magdalene, daughter of Martin Carspach and Mary Magdalene, b. Jan. 22, 1791, bapt. Jan. 23, 1791. Spon: Mary Magdalene Merreth.

Elizabeth, daughter of John Cinck and Elizabeth, b. Jan. 7, 1791, bapt. Jan. 24, 1791. Spon: John Rasber and Eva Krebs.

Maria Christine, daughter of Jacob Ecrob and Anna Maria, b. Oct. 24, 1790, bapt. Jan. 28, 1791. Spon: Peter Merckel and Christine Schneyder.

John William, son of John Keiser and Elizabeth, b. Jan. 20, 1791, bapt. Jan. 30, 1791. Spon: John Wm. Hoffstat and Elizabeth Catharine.

Louisa, daughter of Adam Koehler and Catharine, b. Oct. 27, 1790, bapt. Jan. 30, 1790. Spon: Louisa Hekedy.

Sarah, daughter of Adam Schifferer and Dorothy, b. Jan. 22, 1791, bapt. Jan. 30, 1791. Spon: The Parents.

Regula, daughter of Thomas Rieth and Maria, b. Aug. 27, 1790, bapt. Feb. 3, 1791. Spon: Elizabeth Rudi.

Jacob, son of Michael Kollier and Anna, b. Oct. 21, 1790, bapt. Feb. 3, 1791. Spon: The Parents.

John, son of Joseph Bennet and Catharine, b. Dec. 26, 1790, bapt. Feb. 3, 1791. Spon: The Parents.

Carl, son of Peter Helt and Elizabeth, b. Jan. 28, 1791, bapt. Feb. 6, 1791. Spon: The Parents.

John Henry, son of Ludwig Faber and Catharine, b. Jan. 19, 1791, bapt. Feb. 6, 1791. Spon: Henry Goebeler.

Henry, son of Nicholas Schultz and Catharine, b. Jan. 5, 1791, bapt. Feb. 13, 1791. Spon: Henry Goebel.

Lydia, daughter of Matthew Seiler and Anna, b. Dec. 10, 1790, bapt. Feb. 13, 1791. Spon: Jacob Schoch and Margaret.

Emmanuel, son of David Wisor and Anna Maria, b. July 30, 1790, bapt. Feb. 13, 1791. Spon: The Parents.

John Gabriel, son of George Schultz and wife, b. Jan. 26, 1791, bapt. Feb. 17, 1791. Spon: John Gabriel Fahl and Catharine Jung.

Elizabeth, daughter of Christian Gibhert and wife, b. Aug. 31, 1790, bapt. Jan. 17, 1791. Spon: The Father and Elizabeth

Erhart.

Magdalene, daughter of Frederick Jenser and Jacobina, b. Jan. 9, 1790, bapt. Feb. 20, 1791. Spon: John Wieney and Magdalene.

John, son of Matthew Birckenbeil and Maria, b. Dec. 17, 1790, bapt. Feb. 20, 1791. Spon: The Parents.

John, son of John Elfferig and Elizabeth, b. Feb. 19, 1791, bapt. Feb. 20, 1791. Spon: The Parents.

Maria Catharine, daughter of David Marschal and Maria Barbara, b. March 28, 1790, bapt. Feb. 24, 1791. Spon: The Parents.

William, son of William Schneider and Prudence, b. Jan. 3, 1791, bapt. Feb. 28, 1791. Spon: The Parents.

Jacob, son of George Schet and Maria, b. Dec. 10, 1790, bapt. March 3, 1791. Spon: The Parents.

Susanna, daughter of William Spath and Sarah, b. Nov. 10, 1789, bapt. March 3, 1791. Spon: The Parents.

Catharine Christine, daughter of Frederick Schederer and Catharine, b. Aug. 12, 1790, bapt. March 3, 1791. Spon: The Parents.

John George, son of John Mercker and Elizabeth, b. March 10, 1790, bapt. March 5, 1791. Spon: The Parents.

William, son of Christian Alberger and Susanna, b. Feb. 4, 1791, bapt. March 6, 1791. Spon: The Parents.

George, son of George Rummel and Magdalene, b. Feb. 7, 1791, bapt. March 6, 1791. Spon: Jacob Rummel and Cath. Koehle.

Maria, daughter of John Jost Weiand and Magdalene, b. Jan. 9, 1791, bapt. March 6, 1791. Spon: Maria Kress and The Father.

Anna Maria, daughter of Conrad Becker and Anna Maria, b. Jan. 16, 1791, bapt. March 9, 1791. Spon: Valentine Ferry and Anna Maria.

John Carl, son of John Clinneck and Catharine, b. Dec. 27, 1790, bapt. March 9, 1791. Spon: Peter Becker and Mary Magdalene.

Conrad, son of Conrad Keller and Elizabeth, b. Feb. 14, 1791, bapt. March 13, 1791. Spon: Herman Schneider and Margaret Salome.

John, son of Christopher Wassem and Maria, b. March 4, 1790, bapt. March 20, 1791. Spon: John Conrad and Anna Marg. Wenzel.

William, son of John Meyer and Maria, b. July 24, 1790, bapt. March 20, 1791. Spon: The Parents.

Sophia, daughter of George Lambach and Anna Maria, b. Jan. 14, 1790, bapt. March 20, 1791. Spon: Sophia Lambach.

Joseph Herman, son of Frederick Mauss and Elizabeth, b. May 26, 1790, bapt. March 20, 1791. Spon: The Father and Catharine Mencher.

John George, son of John Mayer and Catharine, b. Feb. 26, 1791, bapt. March 24, 1791. Spon: Philip Mayer and Philippina Steiner.

John Philip, son of Jacob Edebohrn and Magdalene, b. Feb. 20, 1791, bapt. March 24, 1791. Spon: The Parents.

Catharine, daughter of George Bornhaus and Elizabeth, b. Feb. 23, 1791, bapt. March 27, 1791. Spon: The Parents.

William, son of John Jauch and Eva, b. March 4, 1791, bapt. March 27, 1791. Spon: William Lohman and Veronica.

Susanna, daughter of Carl Jacob Goetz and Brigitta, b. Feb. 17, 1791, bapt. March 27, 1791. Spon: Richard Wacker and Susanna.

Matthew, son of Matthew Wallis and Catharine, b. March 21, 1791, bapt. March 28, 1791. Spon: The Parents.

Sarah, daughter of Frederick Dickes and Catharine, b. Jan. 19, 1791, bapt. April 5, 1791. Spon: The Father and Frederica Hehring.

Sarah, daughter of George Riegner and Sarah, b. March 17, 1790, bapt. April 4, 1791. Spon: The Parents.

Mary Magdalene, daughter of John Gamber and Elizabeth, b. July 27, 1790, bapt. April 7, 1791. Spon: John Henry Gamber and Mary Magdalene.

Catharine, daughter of Ludwig Jung and Catharine, b. March 28, 1790, bapt. April 8, 1791. Spon: Catharine Jung.

Jacob, son of George Strohhauer and Margaret, b. March 9, 1791, bapt. April 10, 1791. Spon: The Parents.

John, son of John Alberger and Dorothy, b. March 8, 1791, bapt. April 10, 1791. Spon: John Alberger and Elizabeth Alberger.

Daniel, son of Frederick Tiess and Elizabeth, b. Jan. 15, 1791, bapt. April 10, 1791. Spon: The Parents.

Anna, daughter of Casper Milhaus and Catharine, b. March 23, 1791, bapt. April 10, 1791. Spon: Henry Koch and Anna.

John Adam, son of Jacob Burckhardt and Margaret, b. Oct. 23, 1790, bapt. April 10, 1791. Spon: John Adam West and Elizabeth.

Thomas, son of Frederick Froelich and wife, b. ----, bapt. April 10, 1791. Spon: ----.

Abraham, son of Abraham Sheridan and Barbara, b. March 29, 1791, bapt. April 11, 1791. Spon: The Parents.

Elizabeth, daughter of Joseph Dihmer and Dulcine, b. Feb. 19, 1791, bapt. April 19, 1791. Spon: The Parents.

Joseph, son of Joseph Dihmer and Dulcine, b. Sept. 8, 1789, bapt. April 19, 1791. Spon: The Parents.

John, son of Joseph Dihmer and Dulcine, b. Jan. 12, 1788, bapt. April 19, 1791. Spon: The Parents.

Jacob, son of Jacob Zebly and Wilhelmina, b. March 15, 1791, bapt. April 19, 1791. Spon: The Parents.

Anna, daughter of Joachim Richard and Elizabeth, b. Dec. 26, 1790, bapt. April 23, 1791. Spon: Jacob Schaeffer and Juliana.

Jacob, son of Jacob Kress and Margaret, b. Feb. 12, 1791, bapt. April 24, 1791. Spon: The Father and Elizabeth Klein.

Maria Elizabeth, daughter of John Van Dilje and Elizabeth, b. Sept. 22, 1790, bapt. April 25, 1791. Spon: Jacob Elsterly and Mary Magdalene.

John, son of John Henry Weissbrod and Maria, b. Feb. 14, 1791, bapt. April 25, 1791. Spon: John Tauenheim and Mary Magdalene.

John, son of Peter Deal and Elizabeth, b. March 3, 1791, bapt. April 25, 1791. Spon: John Ecki and Lucretia.

William Henry, son of William Pfau and Barbara, b. Aug. 15, 1789, bapt. April 25, 1791. Spon: The Mother.

Elizabeth, daughter of John Kremess and Elizabeth, b. Feb. 7, 1791, bapt. April 26, 1791. Spon: The Parents.

Maria, daughter of Henry Heineman and Charlotte, b. Jan. 8, 1791, bapt. April 27, 1791. Spon: Philip Kalckbrenner and Maria.

Carl, son of John Klages and Rosina, b. April 12, 1791, bapt. May

1, 1791. Spon: Thomas Fischer and Elizabeth.
Andrew, son of Herman Heck and Anna Margaret, b. Jan. 9, 1791,
bapt. May 1, 1791. Spon: The Parents.
Anna, daughter of Henry Suther and Anna, b. March 17, 1791, bapt.
May 1, 1791. Spon: Eva Andreas.
Jacob, son of Nicholas Juvenal and Susanna, b. April 20, 1791,
bapt. May 2, 1791. Spon: Jacob Braun and Maria.
Maria, daughter of Francis Tremmer and Christine, b. Jan. 28,
1791, bapt. May 3, 1791. Spon: Maria Tremmer.
Susanna, daughter of Francis Tremmer and Christine, b. Sept. 23,
1788, bapt. May 3, 1791. Spon: Philip Pfeihl and Susanna.
Veronica, daughter of Valentine Gaul and Sabina, b. April 15,
1791, bapt. May 8, 1791. Spon: Gottfried Minich and Veronica.
John, son of Henry Strup and Susanna, b. March 22, 1791, bapt.
May 9, 1791. Spon: ----.
Anna Catharine, daughter of John George Jung and Anna Maria, b.
April 6, 1790, bapt. May 10, 1791. Spon: The Parents.
John George, son of John George Schacka and Christine, b. Feb. 7,
1791, bapt. May 11, 1791. Spon: John George Escher and
Elizabeth Brandel.
Maria Martha, daughter of Nicholas Painter and Mary Magdalene, b.
April 1, 1791, bapt. May 15, 1791. Spon: Margaret Schwab.
John Adam, son of John Bott and Elizabeth, b. Nov. 28, 1790,
bapt. May 18, 1791. Spon: The Parents.
Catharine, daughter of Jacob Breuning and Margaret, b. Sept. 24,
1790, bapt. May 19, 1791. Spon: The Parents.
John George, son of William Schmidt and Margaret, b. April 28,
1791, bapt. May 22, 1791. Spon: George Eckert and Margaret.
Abigail, daughter of Daniel van der Schleuss and Phoebe, b. March
27, 1790, bapt. May 22, 1791. Spon: Joseph Braun and Abigail
Barr.
Catharine, daughter of John Braubet and Philippina, b. May 16,
1791, bapt. May 22, 1791. Spon: John Just Schneider and
Catharine.
Maria, daughter of John Braubet and Philippina, b. May 16, 1791,
bapt. May 22, 1791. Spon: John Just Schneider and Catharine.
Reinhardt, son of William Skinner and wife, b. April 24, 1791,
bapt. May 22, 1791. Spon: Reinhardt Schmoltz and Catharine.
John, son of John Benn and Leona, b. Aug. 13, 1790, bapt. May 22,
1791. Spon: ----.
Maria, daughter of Anthony Baldi and Christine, b. May 4, 1791,
bapt. May 22, 1791. Spon: Daniel Frismuth and the Mother.
Carl, son of John Stellwagen and Margaret, b. May 2, 1791, bapt.
May 22, 1791. Spon: Jacob Schreiner and Elizabeth.
Sigmund Frederick, son of Frederick Gaul and Dorothy, b. May 22,
1791, bapt. May 24, 1791. Spon: The Parents.
Philip, son of Robert Scherer and Elizabeth, b. Sept. 20, 1789,
bapt. May 25, 1791. Spon: Maria Perjeh.
John, son of John George Kurtz and Margaret, b. Jan. 17, 1791,
bapt. May 26, 1791. Spon: Jacob Seiler and Anna Maria.
Maria, daughter of John Klapp and Maria, b. May 13, 1791, bapt.
May 26, 1791. Spon: John Fischer and Catharine Schmidt.
Daniel, son of Michael Hains and Maria, b. April 4, 1791, bapt.
June 5, 1791. Spon: Daniel Hains and Catharine.
Maria Elizabeth, daughter of John Zahner and Barbara, b. April

31, 1791, bapt. June 5, 1791. Spon: The Father and Elizabeth Dreehs.

Anna Maria, daughter of Jacob Enck and Catharine, b. April 20, 1791, bapt. June 5, 1791. Spon: Gottfried Goebeler and wife.

Margaret, daughter of John Frederick Gaul and Margaret, b. Nov. 13, 1791 (?), bapt. June 10, 1791. Spon: The Father and Catharine Koch.

Elizabeth, daughter of George Schmidt and Elizabeth, b. June 1, 1791, bapt. June 13, 1791. Spon: Lawrence Forth and Elizabeth.

Daniel, son of John Froelich and Christine, b. March 10, 1791, bapt. June 14, 1791. Spon: The Parents.

William, son of William Hetzer and Margaret, b. Aug. 28, 1790, bapt. June 16, 1791. Spon: The Parents.

Susanna, daughter of John Stently and Anna Maria, b. May 26, 1791, bapt. June 19, 1791. Spon: John Reinhard and Catharine Gerlach.

Philip, son of Philip Peltz and Rebecca, b. June 1, 1791, bapt. June 19, 1791. Spon: The Parents.

Jacob, son of John Groskop and Margaret, b. Sept. 30, 1790, bapt. June 21, 1791. Spon: The Parents.

Peter, son of John Bump and Catharine, b. Nov. 1, 1790, bapt. June 24, 1791. Spon: The Parents.

Maria, daughter of Philip Pheil and Susanna, b. March 3, 1791, bapt. June 29, 1791. Spon: Philip Roth and Maria.

Philip, son of Philip Pheil and Susanna, b. Sept. 7, 1788, bapt. June 29, 1791. Spon: Philip Roth and Maria.

Carl, son of Adam Hess and Elizabeth, b. April 28, 1791, bapt. June 28, 1791. Spon: The Parents

Frederick, son of Frederick Schmidt and Catharine, b. Jan. 28, 1787, bapt. July 2, 1791. Spon: The Parents.

David, son of Frederick Schmidt and Catharine, b. March 12, 1789, bapt. July 2, 1791. Spon: The Parents.

Anna Catharine, daughter of Valentine Schmidt and Hannah, b. Oct. 30, 1790, bapt. July 2, 1791. Spon: Frederick Schmidt and Anna Catharine.

John, son of John Fehrer and Maria, b. Dec. 10, 1790, bapt. July 3, 1791. Spon: The Mother.

Anna Barbara, daughter of Martin Zipolt and Barbara, b. June 24, 1791, bapt. July 3, 1791. Spon: The Parents.

John Adam, son of John Adam Holl and Elizabeth, b. April 5, 1791, bapt. July 6, 1791. Spon: ----.

Maria, daughter of Jacob Finck and Maria Margaret, b. May 24, 1791, bapt. July 7, 1791. Spon: The Parents.

Samuel, son of William Reide and Sarah, b. June 20, 1791, bapt. July 9, 1791. Spon: The Parents.

Elizabeth, daughter of Henry Wm. Zimmerman and Elizabeth, b. July 8, 1791, bapt. July 15, 1791. Spon: Philip Haffner and Anna Margaret.

Apollonia, daughter of George Brunner and Catharine, b. July 7, 1791, bapt. July 15, 1791. Spon: The Parents.

Elizabeth, daughter of David Jenkins and Elizabeth, 2 yrs., 1 mo. old, bapt. June 16, 1791. Spon: The Parents.

Maria, daughter of David Jenkins and Elizabeth, 11 mos., 1 week old, bapt. June 16, 1791. Spon: The Parents.

Anna, daughter of Frederick Mangold and Barbara, b. May 31, 1791, bapt. July 17, 1791. Spon: The Parents.

Anna Catharine, daughter of George Jenser and Catharine, b. May 18, 1790, bapt. July 18, 1791. Spon: The Parents.

George Peter, son of George Braun and Elizabeth, b. July 7, 1791, bapt. July 20, 1791. Spon: The Parents.

Maria, daughter of Jacob Mercker and Christine, b. July 4, 1791, bapt. July 24, 1791. Spon: Jacob Heneisen and Maria.

Maria, daughter of Nicholas Himmel and Elizabeth, b. Feb. 27, 1787, bapt. July 28, 1791. Spon: The Parents.

Albrecht, son of Nicholas Himmel and Elizabeth, b. July 3, 1791, bapt. July 28, 1791. Spon: The Parents.

John, son of John Mueller and Anna, b. Jan. 27, 1791, bapt. July 31, 1791. Spon: John Menche and Anna.

John, son of John Becker, alderman, and Elizabeth, b. June --, 1791, bapt. July 31, 1791. Spon: The Parents.

John George, son of George Lies and Anna Margaret, b. July 9, 1791, bapt. Aug. 1, 1791. Spon: Christopher Hansman and Maria Barbara.

George, son of William Becker and Anna Maria, b. July 25, 1791, bapt. Aug. 4, 1791. Spon: The Parents.

John Henry, son of Jacob Henry Rumpf and Anna Elizabeth, b. July 31, 1791, bapt. Aug. 6, 1791. Spon: The Parents.

Barbara, daughter of John Vogel and Dorothy, b. Dec. 20, 1790, bapt. Aug. 7, 1791. Spon: Catharine Morrison.

Magdalene, daughter of John George Kraemer and Anna, b. June 13, 1791, bapt. Aug. 7, 1791. Spon: The Parents.

Carl, son of George Heder (?) and Susanna, b. May 18, 1791, bapt. Aug. 7, 1791. Spon: The Parents.

Sarah, daughter of David Redicker and Catharine, b. Feb. 23, 1791, bapt. Aug. 7, 1791. Spon: Dorothy Vogel.

Sarah, daughter of Peter Huner and Margaret, b. July 8, 1791, bapt. Aug. 7, 1791. Spon: The Father and Sarah Jumen.

Rosina, daughter of George Michael Kamper and Susanna, b. Sept. 20, 1787, bapt. Aug. 8, 1791. Spon: The Parents.

Peter, son of Jacob Bosserth and Maria, b. July 29, 1791, bapt. Aug. 15, 1791. Spon: The Parents.

Margaret, daughter of Philip Lesch and Margaret, b. July 31, 1791, bapt. Aug. 21, 1791. Spon: Carl Holtz and Margaret.

Rebecca, daughter of Jacob Eshler and Susanna, b. Aug. 2, 1791, bapt. Aug. 21, 1791. Spon: The Parents.

Frederick, son of Frederick Weihler and Catharine, b. June 11, 1791, bapt. Aug. 27, 1791. Spon: The Parents.

Jacob, son of Jacob Kreider and Elizabeth, b. Aug. 13, 1791, bapt. Aug. 28, 1791. Spon: The Parents.

Maria, daughter of George Langenbach and Elizabeth, b. June 8, 1791, bapt. Aug. 28, 1791. Spon: John Godfrey Meyer and Maria.

George, son of Casper Farner and Maria, b. July 31, 1791, bapt. Aug. 28, 1791. Spon: The Parents.

Margaret, daughter of Conrad Bachman and Susanna, b. Aug. 9, 1791, bapt. Aug. 28, 1791. Spon: George Weili and Charlotte.

John George, son of John Christian Franck and Anna Elizabeth, b. Aug. 20, 1791, bapt. Aug. 29, 1791. Spon: John Hange and Geo. Mengel, Susanna Reinholdt.

Eleonora, daughter of John Lauri and Maria, b. June 16, 1791,
  bapt. Sept. 4, 1791. Spon: ----.
John, son of Michael Worm and Catharine, 4 mos. old, bapt. Sept.
  8, 1791. Spon: Philip Haffner and Anna Margaret.
Elizabeth, daughter of William Wever and Margaret, b. Aug. 15,
  1791, bapt. Sept. 11, 1791. Spon: Nicholas Kemp and Elizabeth
  Wever.
John, son of Jacob Jensohr and Barbara, b. Sept. 7, 1791, bapt.
  Sept. 12, 1791. Spon: The Parents.
Frederick, son of Adam Gaul and Elizabeth, b. Sept. 9, 1791,
  bapt. Sept. 12, 1791. Spon: Frederick Heims and Sarah.
Ludwig, son of Jeremiah Vielmalter and Catharine, b. Aug. 18,
  1791, bapt. Sept. 13, 1791. Spon: The Parents.
Christine, daughter of Jacob Hoff and Catharine, b. Aug. 25,
  1791, bapt. Sept. 18, 1791. Spon: The Parents.
George Frederick, son of Conrad Spangenberger and Barbara, b.
  July 17, 1791, bapt. Sept. 18, 1791. Spon: The Parents.
Maria, daughter of John Stricker and Sarah, b. Aug. 22, 1791,
  bapt. Sept. 18, 1791. Spon: The Parents.
Joseph William, son of Daniel Sutter and Anna Catharine, b. Aug.
  23, 1791, bapt. Sept. 18, 1791. Spon: The Parents.
John, son of Joseph Funck and Maria, b. Sept. 9, 1791, bapt.
  Sept. 18, 1791. Spon: The Parents.
Anna Maria, daughter of John Philip Alberger and Dorothy, b. Aug.
  14, 1791, bapt. Sept. 18, 1791. Spon: Philip Klever and
  Maria.
George, son of George Hinckel and Barbara, b. Aug. 19, 1791,
  bapt. Sept. 19, 1791. Spon: The Parents.
Joseph, son of Peter Peres and Fanny, b. Aug. 20, 1791, bapt.
  Sept. 19, 1791. Spon: The Parents.
Anna Maria, daughter of Daniel Diehl and Maria, b. Aug. 28, 1791,
  bapt. Sept. 22, 1791. Spon: The Father and Catharine Hepple.
John, son of George Neiss and Veronica, b. Sept. 9, 1791, bapt.
  Sept. 25, 1791. Spon: The Parents.
Hannah, daughter of Peter Fenner and Catharine, b. Sept. 18,
  1791, bapt. Sept. 25, 1791. Spon: Jacob Back and Hannah
  Schneider.
Abraham, son of Abraham Wild and wife Sophia Freund, b. Oct. 28,
  1786, bapt. Sept. 26, 1791. Spon: ----.
Barbara, daughter of Jacob Fried and Elizabeth, b. Dec. 17, 1790,
  bapt. Oct. 2, 1791. Spon: Conrad Spangenberger and Barbara.
Anna Elizabeth, daughter of Adam Roth and Maria, b. Sept. 13,
  1791, bapt. Oct. 2, 1791. Spon: Henry Mueller and Anna
  Elizabeth.
Samuel, son of Henry Fiss and Catharine, b. Aug. 31, 1791, bapt.
  Oct. 2, 1791. Spon: The Parents.
Mary Magdalene, daughter of George Loescher and Elizabeth, b.
  July 30, 1791, bapt. Oct. 2, 1791. Spon: The Parents.
Sarah, daughter of Paul Sturmfeldt and Margaret, b. Sept. 20,
  1791, bapt. Oct. 2, 1791. Spon: Charles William Nusag and
  Maria Catharine.
Anna, daughter of Henry Kinsly and Maria, b. Nov. 22, 1786, bapt.
  Oct. 5, 1791. Spon: The Parents.
Rudolph, son of Henry Kinsly and Maria, b. May 18, 1790, bapt.
  Oct. 5, 1791. Spon: The Parents.

Maria, daughter of Henry Kinsly and Maria, b. Sept. 22, 1791, bapt. Oct. 5, 1791. Spon: The Parents.

Sarah, daughter of Matthew Laemehr and Anna, b. Sept. 14, 1790, bapt. Oct. 5, 1791. Spon: The Parents.

Catharine, daughter of Philip Enck and Elizabeth, b. Sept. 12, 1791, bapt. Oct. 16, 1791. Spon: Gottfried Goebeler and Catharine.

John George, son of Henry Lies and Elizabeth, b. Oct. 3, 1791, bapt. Oct. 16, 1791. Spon: George Eckert and Margaret.

Mary Magdalene, daughter of Christian Fuchs and Dorothy, b. Sept. 27, 1791, bapt. Oct. 16, 1791. Spon: The Parents.

Christine, daughter of Zacharias Bachman and Barbara, b. Sept. 30, 1791, bapt. Oct. 20, 1791. Spon: George Geissel and Christine Geissel.

John, son of Philip Klumberger and Catharine, b. Oct. 13, 1791, bapt. Oct. 21, 1791. Spon: The Parents.

Francis, ---- of Matthias Kuehly and Hannah, b. April 11, 1791, bapt. Oct. 22, 1791. Spon: The Parents.

John, son of Henry Bretz and Eva, b. Oct. 2, 1791, bapt. Oct. 23, 1791. Spon: John Bretz and wife Eva.

John Carl, son of John Daniel Carban and Maria Elizabeth, b. Oct. 12, 1791, bapt. Oct. 25, 1791. Spon: Daniel Sutter and Anna Clara Gaul.

Elizabeth, daughter of Lawrence Fahns and Magdalene, b. May 29, 1791, bapt. Oct. 29, 1791. Spon: The Parents.

Elizabeth, daughter of John Wester and Anna Margaret, b. Sept. 22, 1791, bapt. Oct. 29, 1791. Spon: Henry Fuhr and Elizabeth.

Catharine, daughter of Martin Mueller and Elizabeth, b. Aug. 2, 1791, bapt. Oct. 30, 1791. Spon: Michael Mueller and Catharine.

Hannah, daughter of John Spaeth and Philippina, b. Oct. 18, 1790, bapt. Oct. 31, 1791. Spon: Henry Goeger and Barbara.

David, son of Edward Lewis and Polly, b. Sept. 19, 1791, bapt. Nov. 1, 1791. Spon: The Parents.

Sarah, daughter of William von Phost and Regina Obischue, from Hesse Cassel, b. Oct. 6, 1791, bapt. Nov. 4, 1791. Spon: The Mother.

Mary Magdalene, daughter of Joseph Schmidt and Maria Barbara, b. Oct. 25, 1971, bapt. Nov. 6, 1791. Spon: Christian Schuetz and Mary Magdalene.

Catharine, daughter of Nicholas Teppenborth and Catharine, b. Oct. 9, 1791, bapt. Nov. 13, 1791. Spon: Casper Stribel and Catharine.

John, son of Christian Kauck and Maria, b. Oct. 16, 1791, bapt. Nov. 13, 1791. Spon: The Parents.

Louisa, daughter of Simon Schuchart and Anna Barbara, b. Oct. 15, 1791, bapt. Nov. 13, 1791. Spon: The Parents.

Hannah Barbara, daughter of Richard Fiston and Hannah, b. Sept. 17, 1790, bapt. Nov. 17, 1791. Spon: Hannah Barbara Vetter and John Vetter.

Catharine, daughter of Jacob Hahlter and Eva Maria, b. Oct. 27, 1791, bapt. Nov. 19, 1791. Spon: The Parents..

Magdalene, daughter of Jacob Schneider and Elizabeth, b. Oct. 30, 1791, bapt. Nov. 20, 1791. Spon: The Parents.

Anna Catharine, daughter of George Hess and Anna Catharine, b.
Nov. 10, 1791, bapt. Nov. 20, 1791. Spon: The Parents.
John, son of Christian Lawyer and Polly, b. Oct. 12, 1791, bapt.
Nov. 27, 1791. Spon: John Haalman and Margaret.
Elizabeth, daughter of John Koehl and Elizabeth, b. Oct. 21,
1791, bapt. Nov. 27, 1791. Spon: Peter Schoeff and Elizabeth.
Adam, son of Michael Katz and Margaret, b. Oct. 10, 1791, bapt.
Nov. 27, 1791. Spon: The Parents.
Anna Maria, daughter of George Beumer and Catharine, b. Sept. 27,
1791, bapt. Nov. 27, 1791. Spon: Joseph Lehm and Anna Maria.
Jacob, son of Philip Fred. Mischot and Maria Clara, b. Nov. 8,
1791, bapt. Nov. 27, 1791. Spon: Jacob Graff and Anna Sabina.
Catharine Elizabeth, daughter of Michael Bamberger and wife, b.
Nov. 1, 1791, bapt. Nov. 28, 1791. Spon: John Dietz and
Catharine Elizabeth.
Susanna, daughter of John Lehr and Catharine, b. Nov. 7, 1791,
bapt. Dec. 1, 1791. Spon: John Schneider and Margaret.
Anthony, son of Anthony Kaercher and wife, b. Sept. 26, 1791,
bapt. Dec. 4, 1791. Spon: ----.
Marianna, daughter of Samuel Karcher and wife, b. Aug. 10, 1791,
bapt. Dec. 4, 1791. Spon: ----.
John George, son of William Braubert and Hannah, b. Nov. 16,
1791, bapt. Dec. 11, 1791. Spon: John Geo. Schneider and
Catharine.
Anna Margaret, daughter of Henry Jetter and Anna Catharine, b.
Nov. 22, 1791, bapt. Dec. 11, 1791. Spon: Philip Witzell and
Anna Margaret.
Joseph, son of Adam Lehr and Rebecca, b. Nov. 30, 1791, bapt.
Dec. 11, 1791. Spon: The Parents.
John Jacob, son of William Rudolph and Magdalene, b. Dec. 2,
1791, bapt. Dec. 18, 1791. Spon: Jacob Schmidt and Magdalene.
John Henry, son of John Henry Freund and Maria, b. Dec. 4, 1791,
bapt. Dec. 22, 1791. Spon: The Parents.
Frederick, son of Matthias Dischong and Elizabeth, b. Nov. 28,
1791, bapt. Dec. 24, 1791. Spon: Frederick Dischong and wife.
Anna Catharine, daughter of Conrad Abel and Margaret, b. Dec. 6,
1791, bapt. Dec. 25, 1791. Spon: Andrew Diehl and Anna
Catharine.
Anna Maria, daughter of John George Becker and Sophia, b. Dec. 2,
1791, bapt. Dec. 29, 1791. Spon: The Parents.
Jacob, son of Frederick Kuck and Maria, b. Dec. 28, 1791, bapt.
Dec. 29, 1791. Spon: Jacob Koch and Barbara.
Anna Catharine, daughter of Daniel Hartung and Elizabeth, b. Nov.
29, 1791, bapt. Jan. 1, 1792. Spon: The Parents.
John, son of Henry Pfau and Maria, b. Dec. 9, 1791. bapt. Jan. 2,
1792. Spon: John Pfau and Maria Elizabeth.
Henry, son of Jacob Belsterling and Mary Magdalene, b. Dec. 26,
1791, bapt. Jan. 4, 1792. Spon: Henry Reegerstein and Maria
Christine Seibert.
Adam, son of Jacob Schlimmer and Hannah, b. Dec. 8, 1791, bapt.
Jan. 8, 1792. Spon: Adam Lockin and Maria.
Anna Catharine, daughter of John Herman Winckhaus and Catharine,
b. Dec. 19, 1791. bapt. Jan. 8, 1792. Spon: William van Phul
and Anna Catharine.
Anna, daughter of Philip Grammel and Elizabeth, b. Dec. 12, 1791,

bapt. Jan. 10, 1792. Spon: Conrad Leichbrandt and Hannah.
Elizabeth, daughter of Henry Fenner and Elizabeth, b. Dec. 18,
1791, bapt. Jan. 15, 1792. Spon: The Father and Elizabeth
Fenner.
Sophia, daughter of John Finck and Rachel, b. Dec. 22, 1791.
bapt. Jan. 15, 1792. Spon: The Parents.
Carl, son of Carl Schacka and Margaret, b. Dec. 12, 1791, bapt.
Jan. 15, 1792. Spon: Thomas Griffi and Elizabeth.
Maria, daughter of Peter Hohl and Catharine, b. Jan. 15, 1792,
bapt. Jan. 22, 1792. Spon: Philip Kalckbrenner and Maria.
John Jacob, son of George Adam Jahraus and Elizabeth, b. Jan. 4,
1792, bapt. Jan. 22, 1792. Spon: John Jacob Deiss and
Dorothy.
Susanna, daughter of Philip Lauer and Susanna, b. Dec. 25, 1791,
bapt. Jan. 22, 1792. Spon: The Parents.
Adam, son of Adam Becker and Elizabeth, b. Aug. 20, 1789, bapt.
Jan. 24, 1792. Spon: Adam Stricker and Barbara.
John, son of Matthew Kraemer and Susanna, b. Dec. 25, 1791, bapt.
Jan. 24, 1792. Spon: The Parents.
Anna Catharine, daughter of John Grauel and Elizabeth, b. Jan.
11, 1792, bapt. Jan. 29, 1792. Spon: The Parents.
John, son of John Ruppert and Dorothy, b. Jan. 4, 1792, bapt.
Jan. 29, 1792. Spon: Bernard Rauh and Catharine Brentz.
John, son of Jacob Krug and Catharine, b. Dec. 9, 1791, bapt.
Jan. 29, 1792. Spon: John Graul and Elizabeth.
William Conrad, son of Conrad Wheeler and Elizabeth, b. Jan. 19,
1792, bapt. Feb. 5, 1792. Spon: The Parents.
Elizabeth, daughter of Daniel McDonnel and Anna, b. Aug. 11,
1791, bapt. Feb. 5, 1792. Spon: Daniel Wheil and Elizabeth
Wheil.
Samuel, son of Francis Hoffman and Margaret, b. Jan. 28, 1792,
bapt. Feb. 5, 1792. Spon: The Parents.
Mary Magdalene, daughter of Nicholas Mack and Mary Magdalene, b.
Sept. 23, 1791, bapt. Feb. 5, 1792. Spon: Adam Neess and
Magdalene Scherer.
Catharine, daughter of Henry Beerly and Maria, b. Nov. 12, 1792
(?), bapt. Feb. 6, 1792. Spon: The Parents.
Jacob, son of Daniel Klages and Maria, b. Jan. 27, 1792, bapt.
Feb. 12, 1792. Spon: Jacob Schreiner and Elizabeth.
Anna Catharine, daughter of Francis Geiss and Regina, b. Feb. 2,
1792, bapt. Feb. 20, 1792. Spon: Nicholas Klein from
Flowertown and Anna Eva.
Jacob, son of Jacob Loescher and Maria, b. Dec. 17, 1792, bapt.
Feb. 22, 1792. Spon: The Parents.
Carl, son of William Haberstick and Maria, b. Feb. 5, 1792, bapt.
Feb. 26, 1792. Spon: Carl Deschler and Anna Rausch.
Regina Elizabeth, daughter of James Ingerth and Elizabeth, b.
Feb. 13, 1792 (8 mos., 10 days after the death of the father),
bapt. Feb. 26, 1792. Spon: Jacob Schuler and Elizabeth.
Susanna, daughter of Henry Denig and Maria, b. Oct. 8, 1791,
bapt. Feb. 28, 1792. Spon: Lawrence Schirsler and Clara.
Elizabeth, daughter of John Metzger and Helena, b. Jan. 16, 1792,
bapt. Feb. 29, 1792. Spon: The Parents.
Mary Magdalene, daughter of George Jenser and Catharine, b. Dec.
16, 1791, bapt. Feb. 29, 1792. Spon: Peter Klein and Maria.

John George, son of John George Zahner and Catharine, b. Feb. 21, 1792, bapt. March 2, 1792. Spon: John George Moor and Margaret.

John George, son of Peter Wivel and Elizabeth, b. Feb. 15, 1792, bapt. March 11, 1792. Spon: George Daun and Sarah.

Gabriel, son of Gabriel Kern and Mary Magdalene, b. Feb. 15, 1792, bapt. March 11, 1792. Spon: The Parents.

Sarah, daughter of John Meichly and Catharine, b. Dec. 14, 1791, bapt. March 11, 1792. Spon: The Parents.

Elizabeth, daughter of John Lampspach and Anna Christine, b. March 1, 1792, bapt. March 15, 1792. Spon: Philip Sauerman and Elizabeth.

Joseph, son of Jacob Schreiner and Elizabeth, b. Feb. 24, 1792, bapt. March 18, 1792. Spon: Jacob Schreiner and Elizabeth.

Rebecca, daughter of Adam Bayard and Rebecca, b. March 4, 1792, bapt. March 20, 1792. Spon: Conrad Keller and Elizabeth.

John Philip, son of Christian Heibel (?) and Anna Margaret, b. Oct. 23, 1791, bapt. April 1, 1792. Spon: Philip Haffner and Anna Margaret. (Christian Heibel is really the father of the above child.)

George, son of John Kuehn and Catharine, b. Jan. 24, 1792, bapt. April 1, 1792. Spon: George Graul and Rosina.

Elizabeth, daughter of Gottlieb Schlotter and Elizabeth, b. Dec. 28, 1791, bapt. April 5, 1792. Spon: Philip Jung and Elizabeth.

Anna Barbara, daughter of George Pfaff and Anna, b. Sept. 16, 1791, bapt. April 8, 1792. Spon: Conrad Hauss and Anna Barbara.

John, son of Martin Kucher and Catharine, b. March 13, 1792, bapt. April 8, 1792. Spon: Christian Kucker and Dorothy.

John, son of Henry Hohrn and Christine, b. Dec. 27, 1791, bapt. April 8, 1792. Spon: The Parents.

Margaret, daughter of George Bohrnhaus and Elizabeth, b. March 21, 1792, bapt. April 9, 1792. Spon: The Parents.

Maria, daughter of John Bernard Simon and Christine, b. June 1, 1791, bapt. April 9, 1792. Spon: Conrad Keller and Elizabeth.

John Michael, son of Bernard Meyer and Catharine, b. March 15, 1792, bapt. April 15, 1792. Spon: Geo. Michael Mueller and Anna Catharine Mackel.

John, son of William Holl and Christine, b. April 9, 1792, bapt. April 16, 1792. Spon: The Parents.

Elizabeth, daughter of John Adam Gummer and Susanna, b. Jan. 2, 1792, bapt. April 17, 1792. Spon: The Parents.

Sarah, daughter of Leonard Roothar and Eleonora, b. April 2, 1792, bapt. April 22, 1792. Spon: Conrad Forklar and Anna Maria.

Christian, son of Matthew Birckenbeil and Maria, b. March 29, 1792, bapt. April 29, 1792. Spon: The Parents.

Jacob, son of Jacob Sigman and Carolina, b. March 27, 1792, bapt. April 29, 1792. Spon: John Schneider and Margaret.

George Peter, son of John Leibinger and Catharine, b. March 15, 1791, bapt. April 29, 1792. Spon: John George Braun and Maria.

Elizabeth, daughter of Ludwig Dihmer and Hannah, b. Jan. 25,

1792, bapt. April 30, 1792. Spon: The Parents.
Catharine, daughter of William Fusselbach and Margaret, b. Dec. 10, 1791, bapt. May 2, 1792. Spon: John Diehl and wife.
Catharine, daughter of John Bott and Elizabeth, b. March 23, 1792, bapt. May 6, 1792. Spon: George Herford and Maria.
Harriet, daughter of Jacob Shallus and Elizabeth, b. Nov. 25, 1787, bapt. May 6, 1792. Spon: The Parents.
Henrietta, daughter of Jacob Shallus and Elizabeth, b. Dec. 31, 1789, bapt. May 6, 1792. Spon: The Parents.
Wm. August, son of Jacob Shallus and Elizabeth, b. Feb. 11, 1792, bapt. May 6, 1792. Spon: The Parents.
Ludwig Henry, son of John Jost Wever and Anna Catharine, b. April 26, 1792, bapt. May 13, 1792. Spon: John Henry Juengst and Maria Elizabeth.
Margaret, daughter of Jacob Frei and Elizabeth, b. Oct. 5, 1790, bapt. May 14, 1792. Spon: Leonard Notz and Margaret.
George, son of Jacob Frei and Elizabeth, b. April 27, 1792, bapt. May 14, 1792. Spon: Conrad Seibert and Maria Christine.
Susanna, daughter of Samuel Neitlinger and Elizabeth, b. ----, bapt. May 21, 1792. Spon: Adam Koohlman and Susanna.
Michael, son of John Stozelbach and Margaret, b. April 23, 1792, bapt. May 27, 1792. Spon: The Parents.
Maria, daughter of John Schaeffer and Susanna, b. April 11, 1792, bapt. May 27, 1792. Spon: The Parents.
Maria, daughter of George Smith and Margaret, b. June 9, 1786, bapt. May 27, 1792. Spon: The Parents.
Elizabeth, daughter of George Smith and Margaret, b. March 27, 1789, bapt. May 27, 1792. Spon: The Parents.
Margaret, daughter of George Smith and Margaret, b. May 16, 1792, bapt. May 27, 1792. Spon: The Parents.
John, son of Daniel Schuettel and Elizabeth, b. July 23, 1791, bapt. May 28, 1792. Spon: The Parents.
Henry, son of Philip Jacob Speth and Anna Maria, b. May 12, 1792, bapt. May 28, 1792. Spon: ----.
Thomas, son of Isaac Nafty and Cunigunda, b. Dec. 16, 1791, bapt. May 28, 1792. Spon: The Parents.
Elizabeth, daughter of John Jauch and Eva, b. May 24, 1792, bapt. May 31, 1792. Spon: Nicholas Meyer and Elizabeth.
Abraham, son of Jacob Stats and Rachel, b. Dec. 19, 1790, bapt. June 3, 1792. Spon: Albertus Schillack and Maria.
John Henry, son of John George Mill and Anna, b. May 20, 1792, bapt. June 3, 1792. Spon: Henry Appel and Elizabeth.
Anna Maria, daughter of Adam Helm and Anna Gertrude, b. May 23, 1792, bapt. June 3, 1792. Spon: Matthew Noelsel and Anna Maria.
Maria, daughter of John Pomp and Catharine, b. March 31, 1792, bapt. June 10, 1792. Spon: John Vulman and Maria.
Maria, daughter of Peter Tues and Elizabeth, b. Dec. 14, 1791, bapt. June 10, 1792. Spon: John Becker and Maria.
Anna Maria Catharine, daughter of Henry Wever and Margaret, b. May 29, 1792, bapt. June 10, 1792. Spon: Christopher Gurtler and Anna Maria, and Catharine Hauser.
George, son of John Diehl and Catharine, b. May 11, 1792, bapt. June 10, 1792. Spon: The Parents.
Michael, son of Michael Lenhardt and Anna Catharine, b. May 23,

1792, bapt. June 10, 1792. Spon: The Parents.

Sarah, daughter of Martin Roothaar and Anna Maria, b. May 14, 1792, bapt. June 15, 1792. Spon: The Parents.

Johannetta, daughter of David Weissman and Sarah, b. March 20, 1780, bapt. June 15, 1792. Spon: Martin Rothhaar and Anna Maria.

Henry, son of Henry Appel and Elizabeth, b. June 4, 1792, bapt. June 17, 1792. Spon: The Parents.

William, son of Adam Leber and Mary Magdalene, b. May 8, 1792, bapt. June 17, 1792. Spon: William Geier and Susanna.

Anna Susanna, daughter of Adam Leber and Mary Magdalene, b. May 8, 1792, bapt. June 17, 1792. Spon: William Geier and Susanna.

John Leonard, son of George Peter Staut and Anna Maria, b. Feb. 27, 1792, bapt. June 17, 1792. Spon: John Leonard Fichter and Helena Catharine.

Magdalene, daughter of Christian Gilbert and Martha, b. June 6, 1792, bapt. June 20, 1792. Spon: The Parents.

John, son of Conrad Turner and Catharine Orphy, b. June 19, 1792, bapt. June 27, 1792. Spon: John Orphy and wife.

Anna Maria, daughter of John Johns and Elizabeth, b. Oct. 28, 1791, bapt. June 27, 1792. Spon: Martin Rothhaar and Anna Maria.

John Dilman, son of George Beck and Catharine, b. June 9, 1792, bapt. July 1, 1792. Spon: The Parents.

Gabriel, son of John Crum and Anna, b. May 29, 1792, bapt. July 1, 1792. Spon: The Parents.

John George, son of John Michael Maxinger and Elizabeth, b. June 7, 1792, bapt. July 1, 1792. Spon: John George Rummel and Magdalene.

Anna Catharine, daughter of Frederick Gaul and Dorothy, b. June 23, 1792, bapt. July 1, 1792. Spon: The Parents.

John, son of John Zeller and Maria, b. Dec. 28, 1790, bapt. July 1, 1792. Spon: The Parents.

Maria, daughter of John Zeller and Maria, b. April 2, 1792, bapt. July 1, 1792. Spon: The Parents.

Elizabeth, daughter of John Huber and Veronica, b. Aug. 25, 1790, bapt. July 3, 1792. Spon: John Huber and Elizabeth.

John, son of George Scheit and Maria, b. May 20, 1792, bapt. July 4, 1792. Spon: The Parents and Margaret Kessler.

Susanna Elizabeth, daughter of Stephen Pfifs (Reputed) and Susanna Krafft, b. Dec. 4, 1791, bapt. July 5, 1792. Spon: -- --.

Anna Magdalene, daughter of John Fred Fuchs and Maria, b. Dec. 18, 1791, bapt. July 15, 1792. Spon: John Schlacter and Anna Magdalene.

Carl, son of John Philip Fritz and Charlotte, b. Jan. 31, 1792, bapt. July 17, 1792. Spon: The Parents.

John, son of Christian Kucker and Maria Dorothy, b. June 2, 1792, bapt. July 22, 1792. Spon: John Gerret and Catharine.

Andrew Christian, son of Henry Volck and Catharine, b. July 3, 1792, bapt. July 22, 1792. Spon: Andrew Christian Mercker and Anna Maria.

Jacob Frederick, son of John George Huff and Margaret Philippine, b. June 16, 1792, bapt. July 22, 1792. Spon: Jacob Fred.

Sauber and Catharine.

John, son of George Ozias and Maria, b. June 25, 1792, bapt. July 22, 1792. Spon: The Parents.

Jacob, son of Frederick Steiner and Maria, b. April 27, 1792, bapt. July 23, 1792. Spon: The Parents.

Anna, daughter of Philip Gasser and Maria, b. July 13, 1792, bapt. July 25, 1792. Spon: Henry Pooth and Dorothy.

Samuel, son of Henry Schmidt and Catharine, b. June 2, 1792, bapt. July 29, 1792. Spon: The Parents.

Joseph, son of John Weiand and wife Magdalene, b. July 27, 1792, bapt. July 29, 1792. Spon: The Parents.

Margaret, daughter of Matthias Seiler and wife Ammi, b. July 2, 1792, bapt. July 29, 1792. Spon: The Parents.

Nancy, daughter of Conrad Kessler and Charlotte, b. June 15, 1792, bapt. July 29, 1792. Spon: The Parents.

Maria, daughter of Zander Forth and Maria, b. June 6, 1792, bapt. July 29, 1792. Spon: The Parents.

Christopher, son of Daniel Beckly and Margaret, b. April 1, 1792, bapt. July 29, 1792. Spon: The Parents.

Catharine, daughter of Edward Sethen and Catharine, b. Feb. 12, 1791, bapt. July 26, 1792. Spon: Jacob Winckler and the Mother, Catharine Winckler.

Regina, daughter of Daniel Kaiser and Hannah, b. Aug. 18, 1792 (?), bapt. July 27, 1792. Spon: Daniel Kaiser and Regina.

Andrew, son of Adam Kaiser and Maria, b. July 13, 1792, bapt. July 27, 1792. Spon: Andrew Weisnohr and Rosina.

John William, son of William Braun and Apollonia, b. June 27, 1791, bapt. Aug. 2, 1792. Spon: John Andrew Cressel and Elizabeth Classen.

Anna Maria, daughter of John Rein and Catharine, b. July 25, 1792, bapt. Aug. 5, 1792. Spon: Maria Stanly and the Father.

Sophia, daughter of John Kunckel and Margaret, b. July 28, 1792, bapt. Aug. 5, 1792. Spon: Sophia Lombrandt, the Grandmother.

David, son of George Wilson and Hannah, b. June 26, 1792, bapt. Aug. 5, 1792. Spon: Justus Stoerger and Anna Maria.

George, son of John Lych and Maria, b. Aug. 11, 1792, bapt. Aug. 11, 1792. Spon: George Blum and Philippina.

Esther, daughter of Jacob Maurer and Esther, b. March 22, 1792, bapt. Aug. 11, 1792. Spon: Esther Zoeble, the Grandmother.

Jacob, son of Rudolph Zoeble and Rachel, b. June 2, 1792, bapt. Aug. 11, 1792. Spon: Jacob Zoeble and Esther.

Elizabeth, daughter of Henry Mayer and Margaret, b. April 30, 1792, bapt. Aug. 11, 1792. Spon: Gottfried Loehr and Cath. Hirschhorn.

Nancy, daughter of ---- Thomson and Nelly, b. Nov. 10, 1788, bapt. Aug. 15, 1792. Spon: Peter Steinheiser and Christine.

John, son of Frederick Schmidt and Catharine, b. July 22, 1792, bapt. Aug. 19, 1792. Spon: ----.

Jacob Francis, son of John Oth and Elizabeth, b. July 8, 1792, bapt. Aug. 19, 1792. Spon: Jacob Beck and Elizabeth.

Adam, son of Henry Prete and Anna, b. Nov. 1, 1791, bapt. Aug. 19, 1792. Spon: The Parents.

Magdalene, daughter of John Capp and Catharine, b. July 30, 1792, bapt. Aug. 19, 1792. Spon: The Parents.

Maria, daughter of John Parish and Catharine, b. Oct. 15, 1789,

bapt. Aug. 20, 1792. Spon: The Parents.
John George, son of George Meyer and Sarah, b. Nov. 25, 1788,
bapt. Aug. 21, 1792. Spon: The Parents.
Philippina, daughter of George Meyer and Sarah, b. Oct. 10, 1791,
bapt. Aug. 21, 1792. Spon: The Parents.
Leonard, son of Henry Scherer and Elizabeth, b. Sept. 22, 1791,
bapt. Aug. 22, 1792. Spon: James Gibson and Margaret Tyl.
John, son of Valentine Gaertner and Mary Magdalene, b. Aug. 12,
1792, bapt. Aug. 26, 1792. Spon: The Parents.
Elizabeth, daughter of Robert Mordoch and Maria Christine, b.
July 22, 1792, bapt. Aug. 26, 1792. Spon: The Parents.
Anna Rosina, daughter of Frederick Scheivelin and Anna, b. Dec.
11, 1791, bapt. Aug. 31, 1792. Spon: The Parents.
Anna Christina, daughter of George Degenhardt and Wilhelmina, b.
Aug. 17, 1792, bapt. Sept. 2, 1792. Spon: George Geissel and
Anna Christina.
John, son of Adam Brunner and Maria, b. July 25, 1792, bapt.
Sept. 2, 1792. Spon: John Muller and Anna.
Susanna, daughter of Elias MacNorten and Maria, b. Feb. 9, 1792,
bapt. Sept. 3, 1792. Spon: John Kaiser and Catharine Meili.
John Henry, son of John Kaiser and Elizabeth, b. Sept. 2, 1792,
bapt. Sept. 9, 1792. Spon: John Henry Dallman and Margaret.
Eva, daughter of George Schwartz and Barbara, b. Aug. 26, 1792,
bapt. Sept. 3, 1792. Spon: Jacob Reyser and Eva.
Maria, daughter of John Steinmetz and Priscilla, b. Aug. 20,
1792, bapt. Sept. 9, 1792. Spon: The Parents.
John George, son of Peter Ross and Sophia, b. Aug. 16, 1792,
bapt. Sept. 9, 1792. Spon: Peter Ross, Grandfather, and
Sarah, Grandmother.
John, son of David Fahns and Elizabeth, b. Aug. 23, 1792, bapt.
Sept. 16, 1792. Spon: The Parents.
John, son of Christian Heiss and Sarah, b. June 27, 1792, bapt.
Sept. 16, 1792. Spon: The Parents.
Jacob, son of Jacob Becker and Catharine, b. Aug. 2, 1792, bapt.
Sept. 18, 1792. Spon: The Parents.
William, son of Christian Kirchhof and Maria, b. Sept. 15, 1792,
bapt. Sept. 19, 1792. Spon: Thomas Wind and Hannah.
Margaret, daughter of Jacob Lutz and Rosina, b. Sept. 1, 1792,
bapt. Sept. 20, 1792. Spon: Peter Armbrister and Magdalene
Helm.
John, son of John Huhn and Christine, b. Sept. 7, 1792, bapt.
Sept. 23, 1792. Spon: The Parents.
Henry, son of Leonardt Riedt and Elizabeth, b. June 28, 1792,
bapt. Sept. 23, 1792. Spon: John Fritz and Catharine.
Elizabeth, daughter of Reinhardt Kahmer and Elizabeth, b. Sept.
3, 1792, bapt. Sept. 23, 1792. Spon: The Father and
Grandmother, Elizabeth Kahmer.
John, son of Charles Dominick and Maria, b. Sept. 1, 1792, bapt.
Sept. 23, 1792. Spon: The Parents.
Elizabeth, daughter of John Buetting and Elizabeth, b. April 2,
1791, bapt. Sept. 28, 1792. Spon: Elizabeth Moog.
Anna, daughter of George Riegner and Sarah, b. Sept. 9, 1792,
bapt. Sept. 28, 1792. Spon: The Father and Anna Seidel.
Catharine, daughter of John Drangenstein and Magdalene, b. Sept.
13, 1792, bapt. Sept. 30, 1792. Spon: Christian Vetter and

Catharine.
Anthony, son of Frederick Kreider and Veronica, b. Aug. 24, 1792, bapt. Sept. 30, 1792. Spon: The Parents.
Anna Martha Catharine, daughter of William Conrad and Eva, b. Sept. 12, 1792, bapt. Sept. 30, 1792. Spon: Andrew Diehl and Anna Martha Catharine.
Henry, son of Adam Stuber and Maria, b. Aug. 12, 1792, bapt. Sept. 30, 1792. Spon: Henry Kurtz and Rosina.
William, son of Philip Peltz and Rebecca, b. Sept. 7, 1792, bapt. Oct. 1, 1792. Spon: The Parents.
David, son of Peter Foluk and Maria, b. Sept. 14, 1792, bapt. Oct. 2, 1792. Spon: David Franck and Hannah Abt.
Sarah, daughter of Christian Faans and Catharine, b. Aug. 24, 1792, bapt. Oct. 4, 1792. Spon: The Parents.
Samuel Henry, son of Philip Worn and Maria, b. Aug. 1, 1791, bapt. Oct. 8, 1792. Spon: Henry Mercker and Maria Worn, the Mother.
Michael, son of Henry Wuertzler and Philippina, b. Sept. 22, 1792, bapt. Oct. 14, 1792. Spon: Michael Schloessman and Philippina.
John William, son of John Schreiner and Anna Maria, b. June 18, 1792, bapt. Oct. 14, 1792. Spon: Elizabeth Pop.
Elizabeth, daughter of William von Phul and Catharine, b. Oct. 2, 1792, bapt. Oct. 14, 1792. Spon: John Becker and Elizabeth.
Thomas, son of William Wind and Maria, b. Sept. 2, 1792, bapt. Oct. 21, 1792. Spon: Thomas Wind and Margaret Pop.
Anna Maria, daughter of John Dowdel and Barbara, b. Sept. 8, 1792, bapt. Oct. 21, 1792. Spon: Maria Meilich.
Sarah, daughter of Bernard Schwenck and Margaret, b. July 28, 1792, bapt. Oct. 21, 1792. Spon: The Parents.
John, son of William Fleck and Margaret, b. Aug. 11, 1792, bapt. Oct. 21, 1792. Spon: John Reiger and Maria Huth.
Henry, son of Henry Rosker and Maria, b. Aug. 23, 1792, bapt. Oct. 24, 1792. Spon: The Parents.
John, son of John Mercker and Elizabeth, b. Jan. 7, 1792, bapt. Oct. 24, 1792. Spon: The Parents.
Thomas, son of Peter Odenheimer and Veronica, b. April 26, 1792, bapt. Oct. 28, 1792. Spon: The Parents.
Henry, son of George Lescher and Anna, b. July 15, 1790, bapt. Oct. 29, 1792. Spon: The Parents.
Anna, daughter of George Lescher and Anna, b. Aug. 22, 1792, bapt. Oct. 29, 1792. Spon: The Parents.
Esther, daughter of ---- Cryscom and Catharine, b. Oct. 26, 1792, bapt. Nov. 3, 1792. Spon: William Kreider and Maria.
John William, son of William Stuart and Elizabeth, b. Oct. 6, 1792, bapt. Nov. 4, 1792. Spon: John Zahner and Barbara.
Philip, son of Joseph Bennet and Catharine, b. Sept. 18, 1792, bapt. Nov. 4, 1792. Spon: John Loefler and Elizabeth.
Jonathan, son of Michael Gunckel and Catharine, b. Oct. 8, 1792, bapt. Nov. 5, 1792. Spon: The Parents.
John George, son of John George Einwaechter and Elizabeth, b. Dec. 20, 1789, bapt. Nov. --, 1792. Spon: The Parents.
John William, son of John George Einwaechter and Elizabeth, b. Sept. 6, 1792, bapt. Nov. --, 1792. Spon: The Parents.
John, son of John Reider and Margaret, b. Oct. 16, 1792, bapt.

Nov. 18, 1792. Spon: The Parents.
Jacob, son of John George Rummel and Magdalene, b. Oct. 2, 1792,
bapt. Nov. 18, 1792. Spon: Jacob Rummel and Elizabeth
Metzinger.
Catharine, daughter of Peter Fenner and Catharine, b. Nov. 9,
1792, bapt. Nov. 25, 1792. Spon: Felix Fenner and Maria Eva.
Philip, son of Philip Asselbach and Margaret, b. Nov. 27, 1792,
bapt. Nov. 29, 1792. Spon: The Parents.
George, son of Matthias Kucker and Magdalene, b. Nov. 12, 1792,
bapt. Dec. 2, 1792. Spon: Frederick Hascher and Philippina.
Maria, daughter of George Bantz and Elizabeth, b. Feb. 25, 1792,
bapt. Dec. 2, 1792. Spon: The Parents.
Maria Eva, daughter of John Ludwig Faber and Catharine, b. Nov.
11, 1792, bapt. Dec. 2, 1792. Spon: Joseph Fetschut and Maria
Eva.
George, son of Christopher Schreiner and Elizabeth, b. Nov. 8,
1792, bapt. Dec. 2, 1792. Spon: The Parents.
Rachel, daughter of Jacob Stats and Rachel, b. Dec. --, 1792,
bapt. Dec. 8, 1792. Spon: Albertus Schillack and Maria. (At
the same time the mother of this child was baptized. See next
entry.)
Rachel, daughter of Joseph Clerck and Elizabeth, b. April 24,
1758, bapt. Dec. 8, 1792. Spon: ----.
Henry, son of Henry Lehr and Elizabeth, b. Nov. 8, 1792, bapt.
Dec. 9, 1792. Spon: The Parents.
Philip, son of Henry Dewald and Margaret, b. Nov. 6, 1792, bapt.
Dec. 9, 1792. Spon: Philip Witzer and Margaret.
Catharine, daughter of Conrad Spangenberg and Barbara, b. Sept.
5, 1792, bapt. Dec. 13, 1792. Spon: Frederick Taxes and
Catharine.
Anna, daughter of Henry Appel and Maria, b. Nov. 9, 1792, bapt.
Dec. 16, 1792. Spon: The Parents.
John, son of Frederick Meilich and Barbara, b. Oct. 28, 1792,
bapt. Dec. 16, 1792. Spon: John Meilich and Catharine.
John, son of Martin Dubs and Elizabeth, b. Dec. 3, 1792, bapt.
Dec. 16, 1792. Spon: The Parents.
Henry, son of Henry Overman and Gratia, b. Oct. 3, 1792, bapt.
Dec. 16, 1792. Spon: John Mather Umbrister and Maria.
Sarah, daughter of John Peter Penther and Maria, b. Dec. 7, 1792,
bapt. Dec. 19, 1792. Spon: Jacob Zillender and Wilhelmina.
John George, son of Jacob Kinsely and Catharine, b. Nov. 24,
1792, bapt. Dec. 19, 1792. Spon: The Parents.
John George, son of John George Jung and Magdalene, b. Dec. 6,
1792, bapt. Dec. 20, 1792. Spon: John George Geisel and
Christine.
Elizabeth Louisa, daughter of John Souder and Catharine, b. Nov.
27, 1792, bapt. Dec. 25, 1792. Spon: Philip Laysle and
Elizabeth Louise.
Adam, son of Herman Leck and Anna Margaret, b. Nov. 9, 1792,
bapt. Dec. 25, 1792. Spon: Adam Schlatter and Maria
Catharine.
John George, son of Conrad Scholl and Anna, b. June 18, 1792,
bapt. Dec. 25, 1792. Spon: John Michael Freitag.
William, son of Lewis Young and Catharine, b. Dec. 5, 1792, bapt.

Dec. 26, 1792. Spon: Henry Wm. Young and Maria.
Conrad, son of Frederick Foster and Catharine, b. Dec. 16, 1792,
   bapt. Dec. 30, 1792. Spon: Conrad ----.
Juliana, daughter of Matthew Schuetz and Barbara, b. Sept. 6,
   1792, bapt. Dec. 30, 1792. Spon: Philip Forster and Johanna
   Catharine.
William, son of Christopher Waasem and Maria, b. Dec. 20, 1792,
   bapt. Jan. 6, 1793. Spon: John Wm. Hutteman and Alitta.
George, son of John Abel and Maria, b. Dec. 9, 1792, bapt. Jan.
   6, 1793. Spon: Peter Abel and Christine.
Joseph, son of James Patton and Elizabeth, b. Oct. 12, 1792,
   bapt. Jan. 6, 1793. Spon: The Parents.
Sarah, daughter of Lawrence Riess and Elizabeth, b. Nov. 21,
   1789, bapt. Jan. 6, 1793. Spon: The Grandparents and Father,
   and Elizabeth Riess.
Lawrence Ford, son of Lawrence Riess and Elizabeth, b. Jan. 4,
   1793, bapt. Jan. 6, 1793. Spon: The Grandparents and Father,
   and Elizabeth Riess.
Stephen, son of John Heimer and Elizabeth, b. Jan. 4, 1793. bapt.
   Jan. 9, 1793. Spon: Stephen Grey and Catharine.
Eva Elizabeth, daughter of Gottfried Soyer and Apollonia, b. Oct.
   16, 1791, bapt. Jan. 9, 1792 (?). Spon: Elizabeth Heymer.
Elizabeth, daughter of William Brauhart and Barbara, b. Dec. 22,
   1792, bapt. Jan. 10, 1793. Spon: The Parents.
Sophia Catharine, daughter of John Peter Schlauch and Eva
   Elizabeth, b. Dec. 14, 1792, bapt. Jan. 13, 1793. Spon: Henry
   Seckel and Sophia Catharine.
Maria, daughter of John Opman and Maria, b. Dec. 1, 1792, bapt.
   Jan. 13, 1793. Spon: The Parents.
William, son of Jacob Eckstein and Catharine, b. Dec. 19, 1792,
   bapt. Jan. 13, 1793. Spon: The Father and his sister
   Margaret.
Regula, daughter of Michael Coller and Anna, b. Nov. 4, 1792,
   bapt. Jan. 13, 1793. Spon: Elizabeth Dihna.
Carl, son of Christopher Hezenbach and Eliasi(sic), b. Oct. 13,
   1792, bapt. Jan. 20, 1793. Spon: The Parents.
Maria, daughter of Carl Moser and Margaret, b. Nov. 25, 1792,
   bapt. Dec. 27, 1793. Spon: Samuel Moser and Cornelia Moser.
Michael, son of John Lutsch and Margaret, b. Jan. 24, 1793, bapt.
   Jan. 30, 1793. Spon: Michael Flemming and Philippina Eliz.
   Moor.
John Peter, son of John Peter Schreiber and Sarah, b. Jan. 30,
   1793, bapt. Feb. 3, 1793. Spon: The Parents.
Maria Anna, daughter of John Stellwagen and Margaret, b. Jan. 13,
   1793, bapt. Feb. 3, 1793. Spon: John Beving and Maria.
Anna, daughter of Christopher Kinsi and Susanna, b. Jan. 19,
   1792, bapt. Feb. 4, 1793. Spon: David Gilbert and Anna.
Elizabeth, daughter of John Meibert and Anna Elizabeth, b. Jan.
   27, 1793, bapt. Feb. 10, 1793. Spon: John Benner and
   Catharine.
George, son of Jacob Baumgarten and Catharine, b. Jan. 29, 1793,
   bapt. Feb. 13, 1793. Spon: The Parents.
George, son of Jacob Mercker and Christine, b. Jan. 11, 1793,
   bapt. Feb. 14, 1793. Spon: George Mercker and Mother Margaret
   Mercker.

William, son of Henry Ritter and Anna, b. Jan. 22, 1793, bapt.
Feb. 17, 1793. Spon: The Parents.
Joseph, son of George Blum and Catharine, b. Feb. 3, 1793, bapt.
Feb. 18, 1793. Spon: The Parents.
Maria, daughter of George Strohauer and Margaret, b. Feb. 11,
1793, bapt. March 3, 1793. Spon: The Parents.
John George, son of John Schneider and Elizabeth, b. Feb. 4,
1793, bapt. March 3, 1793. Spon: John George Mayer and
Susanna.
John, son of Frederick Diess and Elizabeth, b. Feb. 4, 1793,
bapt. March 3, 1793. Spon: John Gottlieb Steinbrecher and
Maria Cath.
Henry, son of Jacob Muller and Barbara, b. Sept. 10, 1792, bapt.
March 3, 1793. Spon: The Parents.
Philip Jacob, son of John Gampfer and Elizabeth, b. Nov. 10,
1792, bapt. March 4, 1793. Spon: Philip Jacob Gampfer and
Catharine Bicker.
Sarah, daughter of Nicholas Kaiser and Elizabeth, b. Jan. 25,
1793, bapt. March 10, 1792. Spon: Michael Kitz and Margaret.
Samuel, son of Valentine Clemens and Elizabeth, b. Feb. 23, 1793,
bapt. March 10, 1793. Spon: John Haugh and wife.
Dorothy, daughter of David Rohrman and Anna Margaret, b. Jan. 8,
1793, bapt. March 10, 1793. Spon: Peter Roth and Dorothy.
Catharine, daughter of John Leonhard and Catharine, b. Jan. 19,
1793, bapt. March 17, 1793. Spon: Henry Getter and Catharine.
Regina, daughter of Philip Haller and Maria, b. Feb. 24, 1793,
bapt. March 17, 1793. Spon: Leonard Hocker and Regina.
John Henry, son of John Henry Schmaltz and Elizabeth, b. Feb. 17,
1793, bapt. March 17, 1793. Spon: John Henry Ginder and
Margaret.
Rosina Philippina Eliz., daughter of Wendel Zerbur and
Philippina, b. Dec. 27, 1792, bapt. March 22, 1793. Spon: The
Parents.
Samuel, son of Jacob Meili and Margaret, b. Jan. 8, 1793, bapt.
March 23, 1793. Spon: The Parents.
Elizabeth, daughter of Adam Lang and Catharine, b. Feb. 1, 1793,
bapt. March 23, 1793. Spon: Benedict Schneider and wife.
George, son of George Braun and Elizabeth, b. Feb. 23, 1793,
bapt. March 23, 1793. Spon: The Parents.
Anna Maria, daughter of James Johnson and Margaret, b. Nov. 29,
1792, bapt. March 25, 1793. Spon: ----.
Juliana, daughter of Adam Schieffer and Sarah, b. March 23, 1790,
bapt. March 31, 1793. Spon: Jacob Schieffer and Juliana.
Hannah, daughter of Adam Schieffer and Sarah, b. May 14, 1791,
bapt. March 31, 1793. Spon: Jacob Schieffer and Juliana.
Henry, son of Joachim Richardt and Elizabeth, b. Dec. 8, 1792,
bapt. March 31, 1793. Spon: The Parents.
William, son of Adam Wever and Catharine, b. Aug. 1, 1792, bapt.
March 30, 1793. Spon: The Parents.
Samuel, son of Adam Wever and Catharine, b. Aug. 7, 1789, bapt.
March 30, 1793. Spon: The Parents.
Elizabeth, daughter of John Schneider and Maria, b. March 15,
1793, bapt. March 31, 1793. Spon: Eberhard ---- and
Elizabeth.
Elizabeth, daughter of John Wildfang and Elizabeth, b. Sept. 7,

1792, bapt. March 31, 1793. Spon: Elizabeth Wiltfang.
Jacob, son of Jacob Stoll and Jenny, b. Sept. 24, 1792, bapt.
April 31, 1794. Spon: The Parents.
Anna, daughter of John Hebenstreit and Anna Elizabeth, b. Jan.
14, 1792, bapt. April 1, 1793. Spon: John Wever and Anna.
John, son of Jacob Hill and Elizabeth, b. Jan. 26, 1793, bapt.
April 1, 1793. Spon: John Reiss and Elizabeth.
Peter, son of John Jenny and Maria, b. Feb. 28, 1793, bapt. April
1, 1793. Spon: Peter Becker and Mary Magdalene.
Samuel, son of Conead Becker and Anna Maria, b. March 8, 1793,
bapt. April 1, 1793. Spon: Valentine Sorg and Anna Maria.
Susanna, daughter of John Fordhen and Anna Maria, b. March 18,
1793, bapt. April 1, 1793. Spon: The Parents.
Anna Maria Christine, daughter of Anthony Deusing and Elizabeth,
b. Dec. 17, 1792, bapt. April 8, 1793. Spon: John Philip
Munger and Anna Maria Christine.
Catharine, daughter of Adam Deist and Christine, b. Feb. 13,
1787, bapt. April 15, 1793. Spon: John George Young and Anna
Maria.
Barbara, daughter of Adam Deist and Christine, b. Jan. 16, 1789,
bapt. April 15, 1793. Spon: John George Young and Anna Maria.
John George, son of Adam Deist and Christine, b. April 4, 1793,
bapt. April 15, 1793. Spon: John George Young and Anna Maria.
Henry, son of Jacob Schler and Anna Maria, b. Jan. 18, 1793,
bapt. April 25, 1793. Spon: George Kurtz and Margaret.
David, son of Daniel Kaiser and Regina, b. March 31, 1793, bapt.
April 28, 1793. Spon: Andrew Weinemar and Regina.
John, son of William Euler and Anna Gertrude, b. April 29, 1793,
bapt. May 5, 1793. Spon: John Schlauch.
Peter, son of Henry Pfeiffer and Christine, b. April 16, 1793,
bapt. May 5, 1793. Spon: The mother and Maria Lorentz.
Elizabeth Charlotte, daughter of William Schmidt and Margaret, b.
April 3, 1793, bapt. May 5, 1793. Spon: William Schmidt and
wife.
Maria Catharine, daughter of John van Dilge and Elizabeth, b.
Nov. 22, 1792, bapt. May 5, 1793. Spon: Jacob Pelsterling and
Mary Magdalene.
Philip, son of Philip Alberger and Dorothy, b. April 9, 1793,
bapt. May 8, 1793. Spon: The Parents.
Adam, son of Jeremiah Vielwalter and Catharine, b. April 2, 1793,
bapt. May 10, 1793. Spon: Adam Duey and the Mother.
Catharine, daughter of George Weiss and Susanna, b. April 21,
1793, bapt. May 12, 1793. Spon: Jeremiah Weiss and Margaret.
Daniel Jacob, son of Philip Kinsel and Margaret, b. April 24,
1792, bapt. May 12, 1793. Spon: Daniel Sutter and Anna Cath.
Ohler.
Henry, son of John Jeckly and Anna Maria, b. May 1, 1793, bapt.
May 12, 1793. Spon: The Parents.
Salome, daughter of Elizabeth Widerstein and ---- Phoenix
(reputed father), b. March 13, 1793, bapt. May 13, 1793.
Spon: The Mother.
Jesse, son of Adam Weiss and Elizabeth, b. Feb. 12, 1793, bapt.
May 14, 1792. Spon: The Parents.
Edward, son of Gerard Huys and Susanna, b. Dec. 15, 1792, bapt.
May 19, 1793. Spon: The Parents.

Elizabeth, daughter of Anthony Baldi and Christine, b. April 15,
1793, bapt. May 19, 1793. Spon: The Parents.
Catharine, daughter of Frederick Dickes and Catharine, b. Nov.
29, 1792, bapt. May 20, 1793. Spon: The Parents.
John, son of Martin Krampf and Catharine, b. March 12, 1793,
bapt. May 22, 1793. Spon: The Grandmother.
John, son of John Reiss and Elizabeth, b. April 12, 1793, bapt.
May 22, 1793. Spon: Anna Maria Hill, Grandmother.
Maria, daughter of William Haberstick and Maria, b. May 6, 1793,
bapt. May 26, 1793. Spon: The Parents.
Lawrence, son of George Eisenring and Elizabeth, b. April 26,
1793, bapt. May 28, 1793. Spon: The Parents.
Elizabeth, daughter of John George Sahner and Anna Catharine, b.
May 20, 1793, bapt. May 28, 1793. Spon: George Moor and
Rebecca.
Nancy, daughter of John Frietz and Sarah, b. May 5, 1793, bapt.
June 2, 1793. Spon: David Riegel and Nacy MacPhy.
Andrew, son of John Loveberry and Elizabeth, b. March 25, 1793,
bapt. June 4, 1793. Spon: Jacob Winckler and Elizabeth.
John, son of William Skinner and Elizabeth, b. May 24, 1793,
bapt. June 6, 1793. Spon: John Walter and Rachel Keppert.
Maria, daughter of Jacob Behler and Margaret, b. May 4, 1793,
bapt. June 6, 1793. Spon: The Parents.
George Jacob, son of Philip Wentz and Maria, b. Dec. 24, 1792,
bapt. June 15, 1793. Spon: George Denzel and Catharine Meyer.
Maria, daughter of Joseph Gally and Catharine, b. June 2, 1793,
bapt. June 16, 1792. Spon: Christian Gally and Maria Albert,
Grandmother.
Peter, son of Casper Henrich and Elizabeth, b. May 29, 1793,
bapt. June 18, 1793. Spon: Adam Widderstein and Sophia.
Elizabeth, daughter of William Kreider and Maria, b. May 26,
1793, bapt. June 16, 1793. Spon: Jacob Schreiner and
Elizabeth.
John, son of William Reinhardt and Elizabeth, b. May 16, 1793,
bapt. June 16, 1792. Spon: The Parents.
William, son of Thomas MacSherry and Catharine, b. May 14, 1791,
bapt. June 18, 1793. Spon: The Parents.
Jacob, son of Jacob Orner and Sarah, b. Feb. 26, 1792, bapt. June
22, 1793. Spon: The Father and Maria Orner.
Maria, daughter of George Lambach and Maria, b. Jan. 15, 1793,
bapt. June 23, 1793. Spon: The Parents.
John, son of Henry Trimper and Elizabeth, b. May 2, 1793, bapt.
June 23, 1793. Spon: The Parents.
Anna Margaret, daughter of Godfrid Minich and Veronica, b. May
13, 1793, bapt. June 24, 1793. Spon: The Parents.
Susanna, daughter of Christian Schoen and Margaret, b. Dec. 31,
1785, bapt. June 28, 1793. Spon: The Mother.
George, son of Jacob Becker and Elizabeth, b. June 8, 1793, bapt.
June 30, 1793. Spon: The Parents.
Anna Maria, daughter of Jacob Meyer and Elizabeth, b. June 2,
1793, bapt. June 30, 1793. Spon: Jacob Gerner and Anna Maria
Lesky.
John, son of Jacob Minich and Barbara, b. June 5, 1793, bapt.
June 30, 1793. Spon: John Etris and Christine.
Anna Maria, daughter of John Staud and Anna Maria, b. May 22,

1793, bapt. July 1, 1793. Spon: The Parents.
Catharine, daughter of John Krauser and Maria, b. Nov. 5, 1792, bapt. July 5, 1793. Spon: The Parents.
William Henry, son of Francis Anthony Metzger and Hannah, b. June 1, 1793, bapt. July 6, 1793. Spon: William Will and wife.
John, son of Adam Stoll and Elizabeth, b. May 22, 1793, bapt. July 7, 1793. Spon: The Parents.
Catharine, daughter of Joseph Georg and Anna Barbara, b. Feb. 27, 1788, bapt. July 7, 1793. Spon: The Parents.
Veronica, daughter of Joseph Georg and Anna Barbara, b. Nov. 5, 1790, bapt. July 7, 1792. Spon: The Parents.
Maria, daughter of Jacob Edeborn and Maria, b. June 9, 1793, bapt. July 7, 1793. Spon: The Parents.
Elizabeth, daughter of Ludwig List and Catharine, b. July 2, 1793, bapt. July 14, 1792. Spon: Elizabeth Warner.
Catharine, daughter of John Dinges and Catharine, b. Jan. 16, 1791, bapt. July 13, 1793. Spon: Jacob Schmidt and Susanna Lutz.
John Jacob, son of John Dinges and Catharine, b. June 25, 1793, bapt. July 13, 1792. Spon: Jacob Schmidt and Susanna Lutz.
Catharine, daughter of Michael Rummel and Maria, b. Feb. 9, 1792, bapt. July 14, 1793. Spon: John Contreman and the Mother.
John Adam, son of Casper Grissum and Elizabeth, b. Jan. 1, 1790, bapt. July 15, 1793. Spon: The Parents.
Emilia Margaret, daughter of Philip Enck and Elizabeth, b. July 12, 1793, bapt. July 21, 1793. Spon: Frederick Dischong and Margaret.
Philippina, daughter of Frederick Jenser and Jacobina, b. June 30, 1793, bapt. July 21, 1793. Spon: The Father and Philippina Wing.
William, son of John Freund and Maria, b. July 3, 1793, bapt. July 21, 1793. Spon: The Parents.
George, son of John Steel and Maria, b. June 31, 1793, bapt. July 21, 1793. Spon: The Parents.
Carl, son of Jacob Diehl and Elizabeth, b. July 3, 1793, bapt. July 21, 1793. Spon: Carl Albrecht and Maria.
Jacob, son of Frederick Gaul and Dorothea, b. July 6, 1793, bapt. July 21, 1793. Spon: Jacob Almindeyer (?) and Catharine.
Philip, son of Philip Rasper and Elizabeth, b. June 28, 1793, bapt. July 21, 1793. Spon: Philip Mueller and Elizabeth Warner.
Susanna, daughter of Martin Carspach and Maria, b. June --, 1793, bapt. July 21, 1793. Spon: The Parents.
William, son of William Hickeribodem and Elizabeth, b. July --, 1793, bapt. July 21, 1793. Spon: The Parents.
Catharine, daughter of John Angel and Anna Maria, b. Aug. 25, 1787, bapt. July 21, 1793. Spon: The Parents.
Valentine, son of John Angel and Anna Maria, b. Feb. 12, 1793, bapt. July 21, 1793. Spon: The Parents.
Elizabeth, daughter of John French and Catharine, b. Dec. 18, 1792, bapt. July 22, 1793. Spon: The Parents.
Elizabeth, daughter of Nicholas Weirich and Susanna, b. July 9, 1793, bapt. July 22, 1793. Spon: The Parents.
Elizabeth, daughter of William Becker and Anna Maria, b. July 18, 1793, bapt. July 23, 1793. Spon: The Parents.

William, son of William Becker and Anna Maria, b. July 18, 1793,
bapt. July 23, 1793. Spon: The Parents.
Sarah, daughter of George Becker and Sophia, b. July 7, 1793,
bapt. July 28, 1792. Spon: The Parents.
Herman, son of Conrad Keller and Elizabeth, b. July 10, 1793,
bapt. July 28, 1793. Spon: Herman Schneider and Salome.
James, son of Joseph Wood and Margaret, b. July 2, 1793, bapt.
July 28, 1793. Spon: James Stewart and Barbara Walter.
John George, son of John Henry Appel and Elizabeth, b. July 14,
1793, bapt. July 28, 1793. Spon: John George Mill and Anna.
Wilhelmina, daughter of Nicholas Hess, Jr. and Elizabeth, b. Feb.
2, 1788, bapt. July 28, 1793. Spon: The Parents.
Rachel, daughter of Nicholas Hess, Jr. and Elizabeth, b. July 26,
1790, bapt. July 28, 1793. Spon: The Parents.
Nicholas, son of Nicholas Hess, Jr. and Elizabeth, b. July 6,
1793, bapt. July 28, 1793. Spon: The Parents.
David, son of David Marschall and Maria Barbara, b. June 27,
1792, bapt. Aug. 2, 1793. Spon: The Parents.
Anna Maria, daughter of Henry Huber and Magdalene, b. July 6,
1793, bapt. Aug. 4, 1793. Spon: The Parents.
Ludwig, son of Ludwig Orth and Anna Margaret, b. Feb. 25, 1791,
bapt. Aug. 4, 1793. Spon: The Parents.
Anna Maria, daughter of Michael Haens and Margaret, b. Dec. 18,
1792, bapt. Aug. 4, 1793. Spon: Henry Keppler and Gertrude.
Anna Maria, daughter of Henry Bretz and Eva, b. July 7, 1793,
bapt. Aug. 7, 1793. Spon: The Parents.
Catharine, daughter of Daniel Fiess and Catharine, b. May 2,
1793, bapt. Aug. 11, 1793. Spon: The Parents.
Jacob, son of George Fiess and Dorothy, b. Nov. 13, 1792, bapt.
Aug. 11, 1793. Spon: The Parents.
Salome, daughter of Daniel Fiess and Catharine, b. May 8, 1791,
bapt. ----, 1791 by an English preacher. Spon: ----.
(Recorded here by request.)
Christian, son of Henry Wm. Zimmerman and Elizabeth, b. Aug. 4,
1793, bapt. Aug. 11, 1793. Spon: Christian Hiebel and Anna
Margaret.
Anna Maria, daughter of John Klion and Susanna Keiler, b. Aug.
26, 1792, bapt. Aug. 11, 1793. Spon: The Grandmother.
Anna Dorothea, daughter of Peter Oemig and Susanna, b. June 2,
1792, bapt. Aug. 12, 1793. Spon: George Fiess and Anna
Dorothea.
Catharine, daughter of Adam Burgeth and Apollonia, b. June 28,
1793, bapt. Aug. 13, 1793. Spon: Andrew Kressel and Sophia.
John, son of John Zahner and Barbara, b. July 26, 1793, bapt.
Aug. 15, 1793. Spon: The Parents.
Hannah, daughter of John Clawyes and Rosina, b. July 26, 1793,
bapt. Aug. 15, 1793. Spon: The Parents.
George, son of Jacob Caest and Barbara, b. Aug. 6, 1793, bapt.
Aug. 18, 1793. Spon: The Parents.
Elizabeth, daughter of Jacob Hahrdt and Catharine Collins, b.
Oct. 1, 1792, bapt. Aug. 22, 1793. Spon: Jacob Heneisen and
Maria.
Peter, son of John Asberger and Dorothea, b. July 17, 1793, bapt.
Aug. 23, 1793. Spon: Philip Alberger and Margaret.
Sophia, daughter of Ludwig Scheller and Barbara, b. Aug. 9, 1793,

bapt. Aug. 23, 1793. Spon: The Parents.
Elizabeth, daughter of Carl Geiger and Dorothea, b. June 18, 1793, bapt. Aug. 25, 1793. Spon: The Father and his sister Eliz. Geiger.
Isaac, son of Jacob Eschler and Susanna, b. July 31, 1793 (?), bapt. Aug. 25, 1793. Spon: The Parents.
Maria Elizabeth, daughter of John Fred. Gaul and Margaret, b. Jan. 15, 1792, bapt. Sept. 1, 1793. Spon: Simon Webb and Elizabeth List.
Elizabeth, daughter of Jacob Brunner and Elizabeth, b. June 21, 1793, bapt. Sept. 1, 1793. Spon: The Parents.
Anna Maria, daughter of John Graul and Elizabeth, b. Aug. 17, 1793, bapt. Sept. 8, 1793. Spon: The Parents.
George, son of Matthias Graebel and Margaret, b. Aug. 12, 1793, bapt. Sept. 9, 1793. Spon: Andrew Berenstecher and Margaret Esslin.
George, son of George Schoen and Maria, b. Aug. 31, 1793, bapt. Sept. 9, 1793. Spon: The Parents.
Elizabeth, daughter of Jacob Jenser and Barbara, b. June 12, 1793, bapt. Sept. 10, 1793. Spon: Elizabeth Bischob.
William, son of Daniel Boehm and Catharine, b. Aug. 11, 1793, bapt. Sept. 10, 1793. Spon: The Parents.
Elizabeth, daughter of Peter Schoeff and Elizabeth, b. Sept. 2, 1793, bapt. Sept. 11, 1793. Spon: John Meibert and Elizabeth.
Maria, daughter of Paul Sturmfels and Margaret, b. Sept. 6, 1793, bapt. Sept. 13, 1793. Spon: Carl William Nusag and Mother of the child.
Anna Maria, daughter of Daniel Simon and Catharine, b. Aug. 20, 1793, bapt. Sept. 15, 1793. Spon: Cath. Marg. Kreibel, Grandmother.
Benjamin Farmer, son of Frederick Froelich and Catharine, b. Aug. 10, 1793, bapt. Sept. 16, 1793. Spon: The Parents.
Joseph Whister, son of Frederick Froelich and Catharine, b. Aug. 10, 1793, bapt. Sept. 16, 1793. Spon: The Parents.
John, son of William McClatschie and Anna, b. Dec. 22, 1778, bapt. by former minister Neveling at Amweil, NJ. Spon: ----.
Alexander, son of William McClatschie and Anna, b. May 27, 1781, bapt. by former minister Neveling at Amweil, NJ. Spon: ----.
Susanna, daughter of William McClatschie and Anna, b. Dec. 4, 1785, bapt. Sept. 16, 1793. Spon: ----.
Andrew, son of William McClatschie and Anna, b. July 9, 1788, bapt. Sept. 16, 1793. Spon: ----.
Maria, daughter of William McClatschie and Anna, b. Jan. 8, 1791, bapt. Sept. 16, 1793. Spon: ----.
Carl, son of William Watson and Elizabeth, b. June 2, 1793, bapt. Sept. 18, 1793. Spon: Nicholas Dorr and Catharine.
Susanna, daughter of John Diehl and Mary Magdalene, b. Sept. 21, 1793, bapt. Sept. 23, 1793. Spon: Peter Diehl and Susanna.
Elizabeth, daughter of John Ferres and Magdalene, 6 weeks old, bapt. Sept. 23, 1793. Spon: The Mother.
Philip, son of Christopher Schmidt and Maria, b. Aug. 15, 1793, bapt. Sept. 23, 1793. Spon: Philip Gasser and Maria.
William, son of Nicholas Stadt (Staadt) and Barbara, b. Sept. 17, 1790, bapt. Sept. 25, 1793. Spon: The Parents.
Esther, daughter of Nicholas Stadt (Staadt) and Barbara, b. Aug.

14, 1793, bapt. Sept. 25, 1793. Spon: The Parents.

(Rev. Winckhaus died of yellow fever in Philadelphia on Oct. 7, 1793.)

John George, son of John Hange and Susanna, b. Dec. 4, 1793, bapt. Dec. 25, 1793. Spon: John George Seiber and Anna Eva Jungeling.

John, son of John Drangenstein and Maria, b. Nov. 14, 1793, bapt. Dec. 26, 1793. Spon: John Schlatter and Anna Magdalene.

Michael, son of Jacob Siegmund and Catharine, b. Sept. 27, 1793, bapt. Oct. 18, 1793. Spon: The Parents.

Sarah, daughter of John Miller and Sarah, b. Oct. 5, 1793, bapt. Oct. 20, 1793. Spon: George Dietz and Sarah Montgomery.

Anna Maria, daughter of Adam Roth and Maria, b. Oct. 15, 1793, bapt. Oct. 20, 1793. Spon: The Parents.

Adam, son of Adam May and Catharine, b. Oct. 10, 1793, bapt. Nov. 3, 1793. Spon: Adam Wagner and Catharine.

Elizabeth, daughter of John Garret and Catharine, b. Oct. 31, 1793, bapt. Nov. 7, 1793. Spon: Matthias Dischong and Elizabeth.

Sarah, daughter of George Walter and Elizabeth, b. April 1, 1793, bapt. Nov. 20, 1793. Spon: Christopher Schmidt and Sarah.

Elizabeth, daughter of Christian Hautzel and Margaret, b. Oct. 28, 1793, bapt. Nov. 24, 1793. Spon: Peter Nonnetter and Magdalene.

Jacob, son of Henry Pfau and Maria, b. Oct. 22, 1793, bapt. Dec. 1, 1793. Spon: The Mother.

BAPTISMS BY REV. WILLIAM HENDEL
1793 - 1798

Margaret, daughter of Philip Gramlich and Elizabeth, b. Sept. 4, 1793, bapt. Sept. 29, 1793. Spon: The Parents.

John George, son of George Pfaff and Anna, b. Sept. 13, 1793, bapt. Oct. 7, 1793. Spon: The Father.

Catharine, daughter of Nicholas Bender and Maria, b. July 28, 1793, bapt. Oct. 27, 1793. Spon: Robert Hall and Catharine Schwab.

William, son of Matthew Birckenbeil and Maria, b. Oct. 26, 1793, bapt. Nov. 10, 1793. Spon: The Parents.

William, son of William Weber and Margaret, b. Sept. 30, 1793, bapt. Nov. 10, 1793. Spon: Christian Henry Denckle.

Jonas, son of Jonas Plusch and Christine, b. Feb. 4, 1792, bapt. Nov. 24, 1793. Spon: The Parents.

Maria Elizabeth, daughter of John Duttil and Anna Elizabeth, b. Aug. 10, 1793, bapt. Dec. 8, 1793. Spon: The Parents.

Margaret, daughter of Jacob Schneider and Elizabeth, b. Dec. 30, 1793, bapt. Jan. 19, 1794. Spon: The Parents.

Catharine, daughter of John Sinck and Catharine, b. Oct. 5, 1793, bapt. Nov. 21, 1793. Spon: George Glockner and Catharine Raster.

Catharine, daughter of Henry Fiss and Catharine, b. Sept. 30, 1793, bapt. Dec. 1, 1793. Spon: ----.

Magdalene, daughter of Daniel Zeller and Elizabeth, b. Sept. 25,

1793, bapt. Dec. 8, 1793. Spon: Maria Schwob.
Elizabeth, daughter of George Seitz and Charlotte, b. Sept. 16,
1793, bapt. Dec. 8, 1793. Spon: George Weckerle and
Elizabeth.
Joseph Frederick, son of Daniel Weil and Rebecca, b. Nov. 17,
1793, bapt. Dec. 8, 1793. Spon: Frederick Boos.
John Jacob, son of Jacob Schirmer and Hannah, b. Aug. 6, 1793,
bapt. Dec. 8, 1793. Spon: Jacob Burckert and Margaret.
Elizabeth, daughter of Daniel Hartung and Elizabeth, b. Sept. 11,
1793, bapt. Dec. 12, 1793. Spon: The Parents.
George, son of George Kraemer and Anna, b. Nov. 12, 1793, bapt.
Dec. 22, 1793. Spon: ----.
Margaret, daughter of Jacob Belsterling and Mary Magdalene, b.
Nov. 14, 1793, bapt. Dec. 11, 1793. Spon: Jacob Schweffel and
Elizabeth.
John George, son of Adam Gaul and Elizabeth, b. July 4, 1793,
bapt. Oct. 4, 1793. Spon: George Botz and Maria.

Magdalene, daughter of Henry Lies and Elizabeth, b. Oct. 18,
1793, bapt. Oct. 22, 1793. Spon: The Parents.
Michael, son of Jacob Siegmund and Catharine, b. Sept. 7, 1793,
bapt. Sept. 21, 1793. Spon: The Parents.
Matthew, son of Jacob Slemmer and Hannah, b. Oct. 29, 1793, bapt.
----. Spon: The Parents.

(The baptisms of Hendel from 1794-1798 seem to be missing.)

BURIALS BY REV. CASPER WEYBERG
1786 - 1790
William Becker, age 68 yrs., 3 mos., 1 week, bur. May 11, 1786.
Nicholas Ribbel, age 33 yrs., bur. May 21, 1786.
John Michael Douder, age 1 yr., bur. May 23, 1786.
Ann Maria Oreffgen, age 6 mos., bur. May 23, 1786.
Simon Schittel, age 2 yrs., 4 mos., bur. May 26, 1786.
Fred. Maus (father of Mrs. Stoy), age 79 yrs., 5 mos., bur. May
30, 1786.
Sarah Wetzstein, age 2 yrs., bur. May 30, 1786.
John Philip de Haas (General), age 52 yrs., 3 mos., bur. June 4,
1786.
Susanna Schinckel, age 13 yrs., 3 mos., bur. June 9, 1786.
Henry Pollman, age 10 yrs., 5 mos., bur. June 15, 1786.
William Witner, age 1 yr., 8 mos., 2 wks., bur. June 18, 1786.
Adam Frick, age 1 yr., 6 mos., bur. June 24, 1786.
Maria Gilbert, age 48 yrs., 4 mos., bur. June 30, 1786.
Sarah Grauel, age 32 yrs., bur. July 3, 1786.
----, child of Daniel Sutter, age 1 yr., 4 mos., bur. July 3,
1786.
Mary Magdalene Bechtle, age 9 mos., bur. July 4, 1786.
Mary Eliz. Cross, age 34 yrs., 5 mos., bur. July 8, 1786.
William Muentz, age 42 yrs., bur. July 12, 1786.
Mary Magdalene Kern, age 9 mos., bur. July 14, 1786.
Philip Schifferer, age 3 yrs., 2 mos., bur. July 17, 1786.
Thomas McNair, age 8 mos., bur. July 23, 1786.

Sam Steiner, age 1 yr., 9 mos., bur. July 30, 1786.
----, child of Fred Scheller, age 7 mos., bur. Aug. 1, 1786.
Catharine Gucker, age 10 mos., bur. Aug. 1, 1786.
Dorothy Helmig, age 62 yrs., bur. Aug. 4, 1786.
Peter McSporren, age 9 mos., bur. Aug. 6, 1786.
Catharine Mosell, age 15 mos., bur. Aug. 7, 1786.
Catharine Gerrith, age 5 mos., bur. Aug. 7, 1786.
Magdalene Lefevere, age 9 yrs., 4 mos., bur. Aug. 8, 1786.
John Wohl, age 1 yr., bur. Aug. 8, 1786.
Maria Wurtzler, age 1 yr., 2 mos., bur. Aug. 10, 1786.
Maria Elizabeth Ebberth, age 11 yrs., 5 mos., bur. Aug. 12, 1786.
Magdalene, daughter of Leonard Kinsig, age 9 mos., bur. Aug. 15, 1786.
Adam Orlob, age 31 yrs., bur. Aug. 20, 1786.
----, child of Mr. Kersman, age 1 yr., bur. Aug. 20, 1786.
Elizabeth Jost, age 78 yrs., bur. Aug. 24, 1786.
John Jansson, age 1 yr., 6 mos., bur. Aug. 26, 1786.
----, child of Mr. Creutz, age 4 mos., bur. Aug. 31, 1786.
John Schweitzer, age 23 yrs., 5 mos., 2 wks., bur. Sept. 3, 1786.
Dorothy Wirth, age 1 yr., 7 mos., 4 wks., bur. Sept. 6, 1786.
----, daughter of Peter Held, age 9 mos., bur. Sept. 7, 1786.
Maria Loscher, age 9 mos., bur. Sept. 9, 1786.
Anna Catharine Meininger, age 2 yrs., bur. Sept. 12, 1786.
----, daughter of Mr. Leferber, age 4 yrs., 1 mo., 2 wks., bur. Sept. 12, 1786.
John Muenig, age 1 yr., 1 mo., 2 wks., bur. Sept. 15, 1786.
Catharine Kurtzrock, age 3 yrs., 9 mos., bur. Sept. 21, 1786.
William Friederich, age 67 yrs., 3 mos., bur. Sept. 26, 1786.
John Tauenheim, age 2 yrs., 5 mos., bur. Sept. 26, 1786.
John Gebhard, age 3 yrs., bur. Sept. 27, 1786.
William Kayser, age 9 mos., bur. Oct. 2, 1786.
Elizabeth Patterson, age 1 yr., 1 mo., bur. Oct. 2, 1786.
Peter Holl, age 2 yrs., 2 wks., bur. Oct. 10, 1786.
Anthony Ecki, age 89 yrs., bur. Oct. 12, 1786.
William Meininger, age 6 mos., bur. Oct. 12, 1786.
Child of Mr. Flocker, age 1 yr., 1 mo., bur. Oct. 12, 1786.
Peter Nannetter, age 4 yrs., 6 mos., 2 wks., bur. Oct. 13, 1786.
Child of Jacob Schlemer, age 2 yrs., bur. Oct. 15, 1786.
John McSparren, age 3 yrs., bur. Oct. 18, 1786.
John Hill, age ----, bur. Oct. 22, 1786.
Child of Philip Losch, age 14 mos., 2 wks., bur. Oct. 23, 1786.
Catharine Konterman, age 7 mos., bur. Oct. 25, 1786.
Elizabeth Froelig, age 44 yrs., bur. Oct. 24, 1786.
John Adam Gerich, age 66 yrs., 9 mos., bur. Oct. 25, 1786.
Henry Hinckel, age 2 yrs., 6 mos., bur. Oct. 29, 1786.
Daniel Hinckel, age 2 yrs., 6 mos., bur. Oct. 30, 1786.
Elizabeth Keely, age 1 yr., 1 mo., bur. Nov. 7, 1786.
Henry Wester, age 7 mos., bur. Nov. 8, 1786.
Anna Margaret Zinck, age 2 yrs., 3 mos., bur. Nov. 12, 1786.
Conrad Schlemmer, age 67 yrs., 10 mos., bur. Nov. 14, 1786.
Wife of John Meyer, age 43 yrs., bur. Nov. 18, 1786.
Wife of Peter Reinhardt, age 21 yrs., 3 mos., bur. Nov. 26, 1786.
Christian Biegle, age 73 yrs., bur. Nov. 26, 1786.
Michael Wever, age 1 yr., 4 mos., bur. Dec. 1, 1786.
Henry Deubener, age 35 yrs., 8 mos., 5 wks., bur. Dec. 16, 1786.

Catharine Ecky, age 3 yrs., 6 mos., 5 wks., bur. Dec. 22, 1786.
Child of George Miller, age 4 yrs., 4 mos., bur. Dec. 23, 1786.
Child of John Streit, age 10 mos., 3 wks., bur. Dec. 28, 1786.
Margaret Werntz, age 31 yrs., 9 mos., 3 wks., bur. Dec. 29, 1786.
Elizabeth Ecky, age 10 mos., 2 wks., bur. Dec. 31, 1786.
Margaret Orner, age 59 yrs., bur. Jan. 3, 1787.
John Miller, age 64 yrs., 2 mos., bur. Jan. 6, 1787.
Henry Maag, age 64 yrs., 6 mos., bur. Jan. 12, 1787.
Valentine Brown, age 44 yrs., 6 mos., bur. Jan. 16, 1787.
Fred. Schwartz, age 56 yrs., bur. Jan. 17, 1787.
Philip Jaette, age 1 yr., 11 mos., bur. Jan. 28, 1787.
Maria Schreiner, age 44 yrs., 5 mos., bur. Feb. 6, 1787.
John George Benther, age 26 yrs., bur. Feb. 8, 1787.
Elizabeth Huber, age 57 yrs., 6 mos., 6 wks., bur. Feb. 19, 1787.
Nicholas Benther, age 63 yrs., 8 mos., bur. Jan. 21, 1787.
Maria Catharine Walter, age 7 yrs., 4 mos., 9 wks., bur. Jan. 28, 1787.
Catharine Peltz, age 70 yrs., bur. March 1, 1787.
John Jacob Deis, age 32 yrs., bur. April 1, 1787.
Esther van Deren, age 27 yrs., 5 mos., bur. April 11, 1787.
Elizabeth Tippert, age 19 yrs., bur. April 16, 1787.
Daniel Penther, Kensington, age 1 yr., 4 mos., bur. April 16, 1787.
Conrad Mast, Kensington, age 62 yrs., bur. April 16, 1787.
---- Batow, age ----, bur. April 20, 1787.
Anna Maria Stoll, age 9 mos., bur. April 22, 1787.
Salome Hains Kingsy, age 4 mos., bur. April 27, 1787.
Anna Catharine Bischoffberger, age 44 yrs., 1 mo., bur. April 29, 1787.
Carl Joest, age 45 yrs., bur. May 2, 1787.
Anna Catharine Mercker, age 28 yrs., bur. May 5, 1787.
Jacob Froman, age 1 yr., 1 mo., bur. May 9, 1787.
Eliz. Margaret Meiland, age 32 yrs., bur. May 17, 1787.
Maria Becker, age 6 yrs., 4 mos., bur. May 21, 1787.
Adam Hoffman, age 4 yrs., 8 mos., bur. May 26, 1787.
Elizabeth von Weht, age 4 yrs., 3 mos., bur. June 2, 1787.
Peter Becker, age 6 yrs., 8 mos., bur. June 25, 1787.
Margaret Diemer, age 53 yrs., 4 mos., bur. June 30, 1787.
Jacob Hembelman, age 39 yrs., 9 mos., bur. June 30, 1787.
Philip Will, age 34 yrs., bur. July 3, 1787.
Fabian Hemerlin, age 42 yrs., bur. July 7, 1787.
Sophia Stimel, age 1 yr., bur. July 9, 1787.
Jacob Hempelman, age 6 mos., bur. July 11, 1787.
Christine Krehmer, age 8 mos., bur. July 12, 1787.
Christine Guth, age 10 mos., bur. July 16, 1787.
Conrad Schmidt, age 8 mos., 3 wks., bur. July 17, 1787.
John William Schreiber, age 7 mos., 3 wks., bur. July 17, 1787.
Jacob Enck, age 1 yr., 9 mos., 3 wks., bur. July 19, 1787.
William Walter, age 5 mos., 2 wks., bur. July 23, 1787.
Philip Jacob Altberger, age 9 mos., 3 wks., bur. July 24, 1787.
Elizabeth Finck, age 1 yr., 4 mos., 1 week, bur. July 26, 1787.
Elizabeth Schultz, age 1 yr., 3 mos., 3 wks., bur. July 29, 1787.
John Felix Tehner, age 1 yr., 8 mos., bur. July 31, 1787.
Wife of Spangenberg, age 34 yrs., 4 mos., bur. Aug. 1, 1787.
Charles Parcker, age 1 yr., 8 mos., 3 wks., bur. Aug. 2, 1787.

Peggy Wackeren, age 67 yrs., 2 wks., bur. Aug. 2, 1787.
John Diehl, age 2 yrs., 6 wks., bur. Aug. 5, 1787.
Michael Leonhard, age 1 yr., 3 mos., 2 wks., bur. Aug. 6, 1787.
Abigail Lehr, age 4 yrs., 2 mos., 2 wks., bur. Aug. 7, 1787.
Child of Jacob Halter, age 10 mos., bur. Aug. 7, 1787.
Jacob Weiler, age 1 yr., 4 mos., bur. Aug. 7, 1787.
Nicholas Cordier, age 34 yrs., bur. Aug. 14, 1787.
William Meyland, age 8 mos., bur. Aug. 14, 1787.
John Reinhard, age 8 mos., bur. Aug. 26, 1787.
William Schreiner, age 8 mos., bur. Aug. 27, 1787.
Wife of Herman Bakes, age 26 yrs., bur. Aug. 28, 1787.
Frederick Sehler, age 1 yr., 3 wks., bur. Aug. 28, 1787.
George Strieker, age 1 yr., bur. Aug. 28, 1787.
Martha Martin, age 7 yrs., 4 mos., bur. Sept. 4, 1787.
Anna Magd. Leibinger, age 8 mos., 3 wks., bur. Sept. 7, 1787.
John Fans, Kensington, age 9 yrs., 9 mos., 2 wks., bur. Sept. 7, 1787.
Magdalene Hauser, age 75 yrs., 2 mos., 3 wks., bur. Sept. 11, 1787.
Wife of Mr. Saffran, age 35 yrs., 5 mos., bur. Sept. 10, 1787.
Wife of Christian Kieper, age 23 yrs., bur. Sept. 15, 1787.
John Fordland, age 1 yr., 5 mos., 3 wks., bur. Sept. 25, 1787.
Christopher Schubert, age 39 yrs., bur. Sept. 26, 1787.
Elizabeth Layer, age 6 mos., bur. Sept. 30, 1787.
John Jacob Losch, age 67 yrs., bur. Oct. 6, 1787.
Daughter of John Finck, age 1 yr., 6 mos., 2 wks., bur. Oct. 7, 1787.
Anna Kahmer, age 1 yr., 6 mos., 3 wks., bur. Oct. 12, 1787.
Wife of Lawrence Walter, age 57 yrs., 3 mos., bur. Oct. 13, 1787.
Anna Maria Walk, age 25 yrs., bur. Oct. 13, 1787.
Maria Frey, age 38 yrs., bur. Oct. 16, 1787.
Catharine Joest, age 3 yrs., 1 mo., bur. Oct. 21, 1787.
Daughter of Mr. Eschman, age 7 yrs., bur. Nov. 3, 1787.
Margaret Kiebert, age 2 mos., bur. Nov. 7, 1787.
William Miller, age 30 yrs., bur. Nov. 11, 1787.
Edward McKay, age 32 yrs., bur. Nov. 12, 1787.
Maria Reimer, age 76 yrs., bur. Nov. 17, 1787.
Peter Haller, age 1 yr., 4 mos., bur. Nov. 22, 1787.
Wife of Barnabas Kay, age ----, bur. Nov. 27, 1787.
George Schaeff, age 55 yrs., bur. Dec. 1, 1787.
William Pfau, age 2 yrs., 9 mos., bur. Dec. 24, 1787.
Peter Henry Fallies, age 3 yrs., 1 mo., bur. Dec. 26, 1787.
Maria Wirth, age 6 mos., bur. Dec. 30, 1787.
Child of George Schmidt, age 11 mos., bur. Jan. 4, 1788.
Catharine Gaeff, age 25 yrs., bur. Jan. 6, 1788.
Anna Catharine Eckstein, age 60 yrs., bur. Jan. 22, 1788.
Elizabeth Could, age 60 yrs., bur. Jan. 21, 1788.
Barbara Meyer, age 70 yrs., bur. Jan. 25, 1788.
Gottfried Gaul, age 1 yr., 1 mo., bur. Jan. 27, 1788.
Cath. Barbara Springer, age 45 yrs., 3 mos., bur. Feb. 4, 1788.
Maria Paris, age 4 mos., 1 week, bur. Feb. 13, 1788.
Barbara Maag, age 68 yrs., bur. Feb. 14, 1788.
Maria Marckel, age 60 yrs., 8 mos., bur. March 3, 1788.
Jacob Koch, age 27 yrs., bur. March 7, 1788.
George Bachoff, age 55 yrs., 10 mos., bur. March 20, 1788.

Maria Shmalwood, age 1 yr., 7 mos., 2 wks., bur. March 26, 1788.
John Schuck, age 1 yr., 9 mos., 1 week, bur. March 18, 1788.
Jacob Weitman, age 34 yrs., 1 mo., bur. April 22, 1788.
George Muller, age 1 yr., 3 mos., bur. March 27, 1788.
Charles Muschel, age 9 wks., bur. April 28, 1788.
Jacob Frolig, age 3 yrs., 4 mos., 5 wks., bur. April 29, 1788.
Anna Elizabeth Metzger, age 4 mos., bur. May 4, 1788.
Sam Graff, age 52 yrs., 9 mos., bur. May 2, 1788.
Ludwig Karcher, age 8 mos., 1 week, bur. May 15, 1788.
Sarah Scherer, age 8 yrs., 4 mos., bur. May 22, 1788.
Philip Rummel, age 1 yr., 1 mos., 2 wks., bur. May 25, 1788.
Elizabeth Weisert, age 54 yrs., bur. May 28, 1788.
Jacob Janus, age 4 mos., 6 wks., bur. June 4, 1788.
Nicholas Rosch, age 48 yrs., bur. June 19, 1788.
Peter Seffereng, age 41 yrs., 5 mos., 10 wks., bur. July 6, 1788.
Joseph Blume, age 1 yr., 3 wks., bur. July 13, 1788.
John George Fies, age 5 mos., 2 wks., bur. July 16, 1788.
Esther Hughes, age 1 yr., 4 mos., 2 wks., bur. July 24, 1788.
John George Sturmfels, age 1 yr., 2 mos., 1 week, bur. July 24, 1788.
Joseph Gressler, age 1 yr., bur. July 24, 1788.
Margaret Miltenberger, age 65 yrs., 10 mos., 1 week, bur. July 27, 1788.
George Seffran, age 15 yrs., 5 mos., 2 wks., bur. July 30, 1788.
Susanna Kayser, age 6 mos., bur. July 31, 1788.
Susanna Keiser, age 6 mos., bur. July 31, 1788.
Sally Foever, age 10 wks., bur. July 31, 1788.
Charles Heewer, age 3 mos., 2 wks., bur. Aug. 1, 1788.
Lawrence Werntz, age 52 yrs., 2 mos., bur. Aug. 2, 1788.
Henry Quast, age 9 yrs., 5 mos., 1 week, bur. Aug. 3, 1788.
John Raesman, age 10 mos., 3 wks., bur. Aug. 6, 1788.
Daniel Arn, age 34 yrs., 4 mos., 2 wks., bur. Aug. 10, 1788.
John William Hahn, age 19 yrs., 8 mos., bur. Aug. 13, 1788.
Anna Elizabeth Lies, age 8 mos., bur. Aug. 17, 1788.
John Gerrith, age 4 mos., bur. Aug. 17, 1788.
Rudolph Stricker, age 9 mos., 2 wks., bur. Aug. 24, 1788.
Maria Bamberger, age 33 yrs., 5 mos., bur. Aug. 24, 1788.
Frederick Dauber, age 65 yrs., bur. Aug. 24, 1788.
Martin Jaete, age 1 yr., 2 mos., bur. Aug. 25, 1788.
Wife of Mr. Braderck, age 34 yrs., bur. Aug. 26, 1788.
Rebecca Jung, age 23 yrs., 6 mos., bur. Aug. 30, 1788.
Children of George Koch, ages ----, bur. Aug. 30, 1788.
Jacob Helwig, age 64 yrs., bur. Aug. 31, 1788.
Anna Hess, age 1 yr., 1 mo., 2 wks., bur. Sept. 1, 1788.
Maria Sophia Schmaltz, age 7 yrs., 4 mos., 2 wks., bur. Sept. 4, 1788.
Jeremiah Thiel, age 5 mos., bur. Sept. 4, 1788.
George Roth, age 2 yrs., 1 mo., bur. Sept. 5, 1788.
Anna Elizabeth Meyer, age 20 yrs., 4 mos., bur. Sept. 5, 1788.
Abraham Sheridan, age 1 yr., 4 mos., 3 wks., bur. Sept. 9, 1788.
Child of Jonas Bleshe, age 1 yr., 9 mos., 1 week, bur. Sept. 9, 1788.
Eva Goetz, age 8 yrs., 8 mos., bur. Oct. 14, 1788.
John Stuber, age 1 yr., 1 mo., bur. Oct. 26, 1788.
Nicholas Schreiner, age 4 mos., bur. Oct. 27, 1788.

Elizabeth Boehm, age 10 yrs., 7 mos., bur. Oct. 30, 1788.
Joseph Pfeiffer, age 1 yr., 2 mos., bur. Nov. 3, 1788.
John Adam Altberger, age 21 yrs., 6 mos., 26 wks., bur. Nov. 6, 1788.
Christine Boyer, age 18 mos., 2 wks., bur. Nov. 14, 1788.
Henry Miller, age 16 yrs., 6 mos., bur. Nov. 14, 1788.
Christian Gloeckner, age 39 yrs., bur. Dec. 12, 1788.
Sarah Penther, age 29 yrs., 2 mos., 1 week, bur. Dec. 17, 1788.
Susan Fordham, age 6 wks., bur. Dec. 27, 1788.
Mrs. Descheler, age 60 eyars 10 mos., bur. Dec. 28, 1788.
Michael Fans, age 3 yrs., 10 mos., 2 wks., bur. Dec. 31, 1788.
Robert Scherer, age 56 yrs., 2 mos., 5 wks., bur. Feb. 14, 1789.
Martin Worn, age 70 yrs., bur. Feb. 18, 1789.
Maria Sehler, age 1 yr., 11 mos., bur. Feb. 19, 1789.
Anna Cath. Remel, age 61 yrs., bur. March 3, 1789.
Jost Eberth, age 64 yrs., bur. March 13, 1789.
Gottlieb Anthony, age 53 yrs., bur. March 16, 1789.
Philip Odenheimer, age 3 mos., bur. March 18, 1789.
John Schaeffer, age 22 yrs., 3 mos., bur. March 21, 1789.
Adam Diamond, age 7 yrs., 7 mos., bur. March 23, 1789.
Elizabeth Steinhauer, age 46 yrs., 6 mos., bur. April 1, 1789.
William Schreiner, age 1 yr., 1 mo., 2 wks., bur. April 7, 1789.
John Wagener, age 11 mos., 1 week, bur. April 19, 1789.
Magdalene Daum, age 2 yrs., 6 mos., 2 wks., bur. April 22, 1789.
Mary Magdalene Funck, age 6 yrs., 4 mos., bur. April 22, 1789.
Maria Schoeller, age 11 mos., 9 wks., bur. May 3, 1789.
George Auner, age 10 mos., 9 wks., bur. May 13, 1789.
Son of John Diehl, age 17 yrs., bur. May 24, 1789.
Child of Peter Weiel, age 1 yr., bur. June 6, 1789.
John Dielman Beck, age 55 yrs., bur. June 14, 1789.
Jacob McNair, age 1 yr., bur. June 14, 1789.
John George Krehmer, age 6 yrs., 5 mos., bur. June 16, 1789.
Sam Seiffert, age 60 yrs., bur. June 21, 1789.
Fred Kurtzrock, age 6 mos., bur. July 4, 1789.
Maria Keller, age 61 yrs., bur. July 8, 1789.
Child of William Spaet, age 1 yr., 2 mos., bur. July 8, 1789.
Child of William Becker, age 9 mos., bur. July 12, 1789.
Lydia Fleck, age 10 mos., 2 wks., bur. July 12, 1789.
Wife of Mr. MacNair, age 31 yrs., bur. July 12, 1789.
Jacob Stucki, age 70 yrs., bur. July 12, 1789.
John Herberg, age 72 yrs., bur. July 13, 1789.
Juliana Roemer, age 2 yrs., 9 mos., 2 wks., bur. July 28, 1789.
Magdalene Huhn, age 1 yr., 5 mos., bur. July 29, 1789.
Catharine Wieler, age 11 mos., bur. July 31, 1789.
Thomas Thetzer, age 18 mos., bur. Aug. 16, 1789.
Wife of Jonathan von Weh, age 37 yrs., bur. Aug. 20, 1789.
Elizabeth Rosch, age 2 yrs., bur. Aug. 21, 1789.
Salome Hains, age 1 yr., 6 mos., bur. Aug. 22, 1789.
Child of Mr. Held, age 1 yr., 2 mos., bur. Aug. 23, 1789.
John Michael Gucker, age 9 yrs., bur. Aug. 23, 1789.
Anna Maria Steinmetz, age 75 yrs., bur. Aug. 31, 1789.
Child of Adam Bronner, age 3 mos., bur. Sept. 6, 1789.
Jacob Kupper, age 1 yr., 10 mos., 3 wks., bur. Sept. 8, 1789.
John Fred. Schlotterer, age 1 yr., 9 mos., 3 wks., bur. Sept. 8, 1789.

Anna Weis, age 1 yr., bur. Sept. 13, 1789.
Catharine Finck, age 1 yr., 5 mos., 2 wks., bur. Sept. 15, 1789.
Margaret Weber, age 3 yrs., 11 mos., 2 wks., bur. Sept. 22, 1789.
George Schlottman, age 4 yrs., bur. Sept. 22, 1789.
Peter Williams, age 57 yrs., 4 mos., 3 wks., bur. Oct. 14, 1789.
John Schneider, age 23 yrs., 6 mos., 3 wks., bur. Oct. 18, 1789.
Maria Kaersbach, age 9 yrs., 3 mos., 2 wks., bur. Oct. 18,, 1789.
Jes. Eschelman, age 34 yrs., bur. Oct. 23, 1789.
John Eschelman, age 21 mos., bur. Oct. 23, 1789.
Martin Wahl, age 34 yrs., bur. Nov. 6, 1789.
Maria Catharine Wolf, age 57 yrs., bur. Nov. --, 1789.
John Degenhardt, age 3 yrs., bur. Nov. --, 1789.
Peter Williams, bur. 57 yrs., bur. Nov. --, 1789.
Christian Jouch, age 59 yrs., 7 mos., 2 wks., bur. Nov. 10, 1789.
Christopher Huth, age 1 yr., bur. Nov. 11, 1789.
Wife of John Gerrit, age 40 yrs., bur. Nov. 11, 1789.
Mr. Kern, age ---, bur. Nov. 13, 1789.
Elizabeth Hahnengrad, age 84 yrs., bur. Nov. 13, 1789.
John Schuetz, age 84 yrs., 4 mos., 3 wks., bur. Nov. 16, 1789.
Catharine Stimel, age 76 yrs., bur. Dec. 2, 1789.
Martin Schuster, age 49 yrs., bur. Dec. 29, 1789.
Ottilia H. Heny, age 37 yrs., 6 mos., bur. Dec. 29, 1789.
Child of Reinhard Kamer, age 4 mos., 3 wks., bur. Dec. 31, 1789.
Wife of Valentine Ulrich, age 73 yrs., 6 mos., bur. Jan. 1, 1790.
Ernest Heuser, age 71 yrs., bur. Dec. 10, 1789.
Sam Oberman, age 2 yrs., bur. Jan. 17, 1790.
Child of Reinhard Kahmer, age 1 yr., 10 mos., 5 wks., bur. Jan.
    22, 1790.
Wife of Mr. Nannetter, age 58 yrs., bur. Jan. 22, 1790.
Wife of Mr. Kiessy, age 49 yrs., 9 mos., bur. Jan. 24, 1790.
William Peiffer, age 40 yrs., bur. Jan. 31, 1790.
Mr. Schwob, age 41 yrs., bur. Feb. 10, 1790.
Anna Maria Worn, age 7 mos., bur. Feb. 11, 1790.
Peter Kern, age ----, bur. Feb. 15, 1790.
Daughter of John Leibinger, age 1 yr., 7 mos., bur. Feb. 17,
    1790.
John Bolin, age 2 yrs., 2 mos., bur. March 2, 1790.
Wife of Mr. Zerban, age 41 yrs., bur. March 9, 1790.
John Philip Lambach, age 58 yrs., 6 mos., bur. March 3, 1790.
Child of Mr. Peiffer, age 1 yr., 6 mos., bur. March 14, 1790.
Jacob Ren, age 66 yrs., bur. April 11, 1790.
John Schaeffer, age 41 yrs., 10 mos., bur. April 12, 1790.
Charles Gotz, age 2 mos., 1 week, bur. April --, 1790.
Son of Philip Peltz, age 7 mos., bur. April 19, 1790.
George Riese, age 8 yrs., 6 mos., 3 wks., bur. May 31, 1790.
Christian Forth, age 67 yrs., 11 mos., 1 week, bur. June 12,
    1790.
Child of Jost Weber, age 1 yr., 6 mos., bur. June 13, 1790.
Daughter of Mr. Morray, age 26 yrs., 8 mos., bur. June 14, 1790.
Child of Heineman, age ----, bur. July 2, 1790.
Child of Jonas Plesche, age 1 yr., 11 mos., bur. July 6, 1790.
Isaac Matchio, age 41 yrs., bur. July 8, 1790.
Child of Mr. Fiss, age 1 yr., bur. July --, 1790.
Elizabeth Heimer, age 2 yars 2 wks., bur. July 25, 1790.
Child of Mrs. Kessman, age 10 mos., bur. Aug. 2, 1790.

Conrad Hen, age 6 mos., bur. Aug. 3, 1790.
Child of Heutlinger, age ----, bur. Aug. 4, 1790.
Henrietta Will, age 1 yr., 10 mos., 8 wks., bur. Aug. 5, 1790.
George Kornhaus, age 7 mos., bur. Aug. 8, 1790.
Child of Peter Auler, age 6 mos., bur. Aug. 9, 1790.
Charles, son of Charles Schake, age 3 yrs., 10 mos., 2 wks., bur.
    Sept. 4, 1790.
Elizabeth, daughter of Bernard Muth, age 11 yrs., 4 mos., bur.
    Sept. 5, 1790.
John Ozeas, age 25 yrs., 1 week, bur. Sept. 19, 1790.
Maria Margaret Schmaltz, age 43 yrs., 4 mos., bur. Sept. 19,
    1790.
Valentine, son of Valentine Gaul, age 5 yrs., 11 mos., bur. Sept.
    19, 1790.

BURIALS BY REV. HERMAN WINCKHAUS
1790 - 1793

Master Philip Boehm (John Philip Boehm), youngest son of Rev.
    John Philip Boehm, age ----, bur. Sept. 17, 1790.
Widow of John Zeller, age 75 yrs., bur. Oct. 1, 1790.
Elizabeth, daughter of Michael Bamberger, age 1 yr., 11 mos.,
    bur. Oct. 4, 1790.
Margaret Dinges, wife of ----, age 36 yrs., bur. Oct. 1, 1790.
Maria Meeter, wife of George Meeter, age 62 yrs., 10 mos., 2
    wks., bur. Oct. 11, 1790.
Anna Wetzler, wife of Adam Wezler, age 24 yrs., 8 mos., bur. Oct.
    12, 1790.
Christopher Hansman Lees, son of George Lees, age 1 yr., 5 mos.,
    1 week, bur. Oct. 21, 1790.
Jacob Schneider, age 37 yrs., 10 mos., bur. Oct. 21, 1790.
Rachel Steinmetz, daughter of Jacob Steinmetz, age 8 mos., bur.
    Oct. 21, 1790.
Elizabeth, daughter of Matthew Berckenbeil, age 1 yr., 4 mos.,
    bur. Oct. 22, 1790.
John Ludwig, son of Geo. Einwachter, age 2 yrs., 9 mos., bur.
    Oct. 24, 1790.
Maria Steinmetz, daughter of Jacob, age 4 yrs., 11 mos., bur.
    Oct. 31, 1790.
Catharine, daughter of Melchior Schaeffer, age 2 yrs., 7 days,
    bur. Nov. 2, 1790.
Maria, daughter of Lawrence Forth, age 1 yr., 11 mos., 4 days,
    bur. Nov. 2, 1790.
Rev. Michael Schlatter, age 74 yrs., 3 mos., 17 days, bur. on our
    cemetery on Nov. 4, 1790.
Elizabeth, daughter of Jacob Schmidt, age 1 yr., 8 mos., 2 days,
    bur. Nov. 8, 1790.
Widow Magdalene Gaul, age 75 yrs., bur. Nov. 8, 1790.
Elizabeth, wife of Francis Schae, age 65 yrs., bur. Nov. 12,
    1790.
John Wm., son of Gottfried Göbler, age 1 yr., 3 mos., 2 days,
    bur. Nov. 17, 1790.
Frederick, son of Zacharias Bickman, age 8 mos., 2 wks., bur.
    Nov. 19, 1790.
Godfrey, son of Ludwig Reineck, age 3 mos., 3 wks., bur. Nov. 21,

1790.
Maria Diehl, daughter of Daniel Diehl, age 1 yr., 8 mos., 4 days, bur. Nov. 22, 1790.
Francois Reti Piere, Frenchman, age 34 yrs., 5 mos., bur. Nov. 22, 1790.
Valentine Lesch, age 37 yrs., bur. Dec. 1, 1790.
Elizabeth, daughter of Henry Riegel, age 2 yrs., 7 mos., 4 days, bur. Dec. 1, 1790.
Sarah, daughter of John Miller, age 5 yrs., 10 mos., 12 days, bur. Dec. 1, 1790.
Peter Dickes, son of John Frederick, age 1 yr., 4 mos., bur. Dec. 12, 1790.
John Bosch, age 18 yrs., 3 mos., bur. Dec. 15, 1790.
William, son of Charles Schaka, age 1 yr., 11 mos., 6 days, bur. Dec. 17, 1790.
Barbara, wife of Adam Brittel, age 30 yrs., bur. Dec. 23, 1790.
John Michael, son of Christian Stahl, age 5 mos., 1 day, bur. Dec. 23, 1790.
Maria, wife of George Hoffman, age 36 yrs., 10 mos., bur. Jan. 2, 1791.
Jenny Pfeiffer, wife of John, age 40 yrs., bur. Jan. 6, 1791.
Catharine, daughter of Leonard Rueb, age 4 mos., bur. Jan. 9, 1791.
Jacob, son of John Kiehn, age 4 yrs., 9 mos., 3 wks., bur. Jan. 16, 1791.
Anna Maria Wood, widow, age 53 yrs., 9 mos., bur. Jan. 19, 1791.
Anna Cath; wife of Peter Merckel, age 30 yrs., 2 mos., 25 days, bur. Jan. 27, 1791.
Daniel, son of Charles Cooper, age 2 yrs., 3 mos., 8 days, bur. Feb. 3, 1791.
Mary Magdalene, wife of Mr. Drangenstein, age 38 yrs., 10 mos., bur. Feb. 17, 1791.
Conrad Froman, age 56 yrs., 10 mos., 10 wks., bur. Feb. 18, 1791.
Peter Grauel, age 52 yrs., 2 mos., bur. Feb. 25, 1791.
Anna Seitz, wife of Adam Seitz, age 23 yrs., 3 mos., bur. Feb. 27, 1791.
Anna Margaret, daughter of Henry Lies, age 2 yrs., 11 mos., bur. Feb. 27, 1791.
Catharine, daughter of Peter Walter, age 5 mos., bur. Feb. 27, 1791.
Rebecca, wife of John Kreider, age 59 yrs., 7 mos., bur. March 7, 1791.
----, daughter of Peter Emmel, age 6 mos., 3 wks., bur. March 8, 1791.
Frederick, son of Conrad Spangenberg, age 1 yr., 5 mos., 8 days, bur. March 9, 1791.
Charlotte, daughter of Jacob Frei, age 2 yrs., 5 days, bur. March 9, 1791.
Elizabeth, wife of Philip Schreit, age 47 yrs., 4 mos., 11 days, bur. March 10, 1791.
John, son of Lawrence Opman, age 3 yrs., 5 mos., 2 wks., bur. March 13, 1791.
Susanna, daughter of William Spaeth, age 1 yr., 4 mos., 1 day, bur. March 13, 1791.
Anna Ursula Bunner, widow, age 76 yrs., 11 mos., 2 wks., bur.

March 15, 1791.
Elizabeth, daughter of Philip Stimmel, age 3 yrs., 2 mos., 2 wks., bur. March 16, 1791.
Carl, son of William Nickler, age 5 mos., 3 wks., bur. March 17, 1791.
Johanna, wife of John Klein, age 24 yrs., 8 mos., 9 days, bur. March 19, 1791.
Casper Gloeckner, age 77 yrs., 10 mos., 8 days, bur. March 20, 1791.
Maria Crouss, widow, age 39 yrs., bur. March 23, 1791.
Catharine, wife of Stephen Cooth, age 28 yrs., 4 mos., 19 days, bur. March 25, 1791.
John Wever, age 45 yrs., bur. April 12, 1791.
Philip Jacob Ohler, age 44 yrs., 5 mos., 8 wks., bur. April 18, 1791.
Anna Catharine, daughter of John Meili, age 6 yrs., 3 mos., 3 wks., bur. April 19, 1791.
Anna Maria, daughter of John Meili, age 8 yrs., 2 mos., bur. April 19, 1791.
Elizabeth, daughter of Joseph Dihmer, age 3 mos., 2 days, bur. April 24, 1791.
Michael Kummel, age 32 yrs., 8 mos., 2 wks., bur. April 26, 1791.
Carl, son of Peter Hohl, age 1 yr., 6 mos., bur. April 28, 1791.
William Henrich, son of Wm. Pfau, age 1 yr., 8 mos., 12 days, bur. April 29, 1791.
Elizabeth Hinckel, widow, age 80 yrs., bur. April 30, 1791.
Maria, daughter of the late Martin Schuster, age 1 yr., 4 mos., bur. May 5, 1791.
Hannah, daughter of John Heineman, age 3 yrs., 10 mos., bur. May 11, 1791.
Barbara, daughter of John Huhn, age 1 yr., 2 mos., 3 wks., bur. May 11, 1791.
Hannah Christine, daughter of John Lensbach, age 1 yr., 5 mos., 5 days, bur. May 11, 1791.
John Adam, son of John Bott, age 5 mos., 3 wks., bur. May 20, 1791.
Sarah, daughter of Conrad Schiller, age 1 yr., 2 mos., 4 days, bur. May 21, 1791.
Magdalene, daughter of Leonard Rueb, age 7 yrs., 8 mos., 3 wks., bur. May 22, 1791.
Frederick, son of the late Martin Schuster, age 5 yrs., 6 mos., 3 wks., bur. May 25, 1791.
Philip, son of Robert Scherer, age 1 yr., 8 mos., 2 wks., bur. June 5, 1791.
Sarah, daughter of Ludwig Wagner, age 7 yrs., 7 mos., 2 wks., bur. June 5, 1791.
Lydia, daughter of Matthias Seiler, age 6 mos., bur. June 7, 1791.
Jacob, son of Jacob Schlimer, age 4 yrs., 3 wks., bur. June 9, 1791.
Rhoda, wife of Henry Bolender, age 28 yrs., 8 mos., bur. June 10, 1791.
Elizabeth Dorr, age 91 yrs., 5 mos., bur. June 11, 1791.
George, son of George Schmidt, age 2 yrs., 6 mos., 8 days, bur. June 14, 1791.

Daniel, son of John Frolich, age 3 mos., 4 days, bur. June 16, 1791.
Sophia, daughter of Justus Stoerger, age 5 yrs., 7 mos., 5 days, bur. June 16, 1791.
William, son of the late Anthony Lauth, age 4 yrs., 4 mos., 7 days, bur. June 17, 1791.
Elizabeth, daughter of Abraham Sheridan, age 2 yrs., 3 mos., bur. June 18, 1791.
Conrad, son of John Degenhardt, age 1 yr., 4 mos., 4 days, bur. June 20, 1791.
Anna Maria, daughter of Justus Storger, age 3 yrs., 2 mos., 5 days, bur. June 21, 1791.
Elizabeth, daughter of the late John Eckert, age 23 yrs., 4 mos., bur. June 22, 1791.
John, son of John Heimer, age 11 mos., 3 days, bur. July 2, 1791.
Elizabeth, daughter of John Branby, age 2 yrs., 11 mos., bur. July 5, 1791.
Christian Stahl, age 49 yrs., bur. July 12, 1791.
William MacClatschi, age 38 yrs., bur. July 14.
Catharine, daughter of Wm. Becker, age 1 yr., 7 mos., 6 days, bur. July 14, 1791.
Simon, son of Simon Schuckardt, age 2 yrs., 6 mos., 3 days, bur. July 20, 1791.
George Mether, age 65 yrs., bur. July 27, 1791.
Elizabeth, daughter of Francis Geise, age 1 yr., bur. July 27, 1791.
Elizabeth Schmidt, age 24 yrs., bur. July 30, 1791.
Jesse, son of Christian Hess, age 1 yr., 3 mos., bur. July 30, 1791.
Magdalene, daughter of Peter Ottenheimer, age 5 yrs., 1 mo., 1 day, bur. July 31, 1791.
John, son of John Stricker, age 1 yr., 9 mos., 2 wks., bur. July 31, 1791.
Margaret, daughter of George Hofman, age 10 mos., 9 days, bur. July 31, 1791.
Sarah, daughter of George Ruegner, age 4 mos., 2 wks., bur. Aug. 2, 1791.
Catharine Rup, widow, age 51 yrs., 4 mos., 4 days, bur. Aug. 3, 1791.
Catharine, daughter of George Bornhaus, age 5 mos., 12 days, bur. Aug. 5, 1791.
Susanna, daughter of Ludwig Faber, age 2 yrs., 5 mos., bur. Aug. 6, 1791.
Magdalene, daughter of Peter Daubert, age 19 yrs., 1 mo., 4 days, bur. Aug. 8, 1791.
Magdalene Somini, widow, age 68 yrs., 6 mos., bur. Aug. 10, 1791.
Magdalene, daughter of John Weiand, age 7 mos., 9 wks., bur. Aug. 11, 1791.
----, daughter of Bernard Haens, age 9 yrs., 7 mos., bur. Aug. 14, 1791.
Lawrence, son of Daniel Walter, age 1 yr., 8 days, bur. Aug. 16, 1791.
Peter, son of Christian Hautzel, age 1 yr., 3 mos., 3 days, bur. Aug. 18, 1791.
John, son of John Weber, age 1 yr., 2 mos., 2 wks., bur. Aug. 18,

1791.
Margaret, daughter of Adam Stoll, age 3 yrs., 3 mos., bur. Aug. 23, 1791.
John, son of Peter Walter, age 10 mos., 2 wks., bur. Aug. 27, 1791.
Margaret, daughter of Justus Storger, age 10 mos., 7 days, bur. Aug. 31, 1791.
Frederick, son of Rev. Winckhaus, age 1 yr., 7 mos., 11 days, bur. Sept. 9, 1791.
Ruth, daughter of Mr. MacSpurnaer, age 1 yr., 7 mos., 4 days, bur. Sept. 14, 1791.
Philippine Frederica, daughter of Ludwig Baumgarten, age 8 yrs., 2 mos., bur. Sept. 17, 1791.
Frederick, son of Frederick Weiler, age 2 mos., 5 days, bur. Sept. 17, 1791.
Apollonia, daughter of Henry Fenner, age 1 yr., 10 mos., 1 day, bur. Sept. 21, 1791.
Samuel, son of Conrad Becker, age 5 yrs., 1 mo., bur. Sept. 22, 1791.
Sarah, daughter of Leonard Roothaar, age 1 yr., 8 mos., 2 wks., bur. Sept. 23, 1791.
Susanna, wife of Frederick Schingel, age 59 yrs., 4 days, bur. Sept. 26, 1791.
John Diel, age 53 yrs., 6 mos., bur. Oct. 2, 1791.
George Justus, age 64 yrs., 11 mos., bur. Oct. 23, 1791.
John Jacob Bratler, age 50 yrs., 2 mos., 2 wks., bur. Oct. 20, 1791.
Joseph, son of Jacob Hoffman, age 1 yr., 1 week, bur. Oct. 23, 1791.
John, son of Casper Simon, age 1 yr., 10 days, bur. Oct. 23, 1791.
Anna, wife of George Justus, age 30 yrs., 11 mos., bur. Oct. 24, 1791.
Francis, son of Matthias Kuehly, age 6 mos., 11 days, bur. Oct. 24, 1791.
Elizabeth, daughter of George Kraemer, age 2 yrs., 10 mos., 1 day, bur. Oct. 24, 1791.
Elizabeth, daughter of Anthony Baldi, age 2 yrs., 4 mos., 2 wks., bur. Oct. 28, 1791.
Barbara, wife of Urban Friebeli, age 60 yrs., 6 mos., 11 days, bur. Oct. 28, 1791.
Henry, son of John Spaeth, age 1 yr., 2 mos., bur. Nov. 2, 1791.
Susanna Maus, widow, age 75 yrs., 9 mos., 2 days, bur. Nov. 4, 1791.
Catharine, daughter of John Waacker, age 4 yrs., 2 mos., 10 days, bur. Nov. 6, 1791.
Peter Schuck, age 39 yrs., 9 mos., 8 days, bur. Nov. 8, 1791.
Maria Whitmore, age 72 yrs., bur. Nov. 14, 1791.
Elizabeth, daughter of John Greim, age 9 mos., 11 days, bur. Nov. 20, 1791.
John Peltz, age 77 yrs., 5 mos., 2 wks., bur. Nov. 21, 1791.
John Peter, son of the late Peter Schuck, age 1 yr., 2 mos., bur. Nov. 24, 1791.
William, son of Widow Wm. Miller, age 6 yrs., 6 mos., 2 wks., bur. Nov. 26, 1791.

Ludwig Dies, Kensington, age 75 yrs., 8 mos., bur. Nov. 27, 1791.
Conrad, son of Michael Bamberger, age 6 yrs., 11 mos., bur. Nov.
28, 1791.
John Jacob, son of the late Nich. Gathier, age 3 yrs., 7 mos., 3
wks., bur. Dec. 1, 1791.
Jacob, son of Michael Katz, age 4 yrs., 10 mos., 2 wks., bur.
Dec. 9, 1791.
Christine, daughter of Henry Pfeiffer, age 2 yrs., 9 mos., 1
week, bur. Dec. 27, 1791.
Catharine, daughter of John Klap, age 3 yrs., 3 mos., 3 wks.,
bur. Jan. 9, 1792.
John, son of John Finck, age 1 yr., 9 mos., 3 wks., bur. Jan. 11,
1792.
Barbara Luprian, widow, age 67 yrs., 8 mos., bur. Jan. 12, 1792.
John George, son of Wm. Brauhart, age 2 mos., 5 days, bur. Jan.
23, 1792.
John Rennoh, age 22 yrs., 6 mos., 3 wks., bur. Jan. 29, 1792.
Susanna Tuttel, age 52 yrs., 2 mos., bur. Jan. 20, 1792.
Anna Catharine, daughter of John Grauel, age 6 days, bur. Jan.
29, 1792.
Julia, daughter of Jacob Schallus, age 6 yrs., 4 mos., 17 days,
bur. March 4, 1792.
John George, son of John Geo. Zahner, age 11 days, bur. March 4,
1792.
Annanias, son of Daniel Vial, age 11 yrs., 6 mos., 5 days, bur.
March 8, 1792.
George, son of George Hinckel, age 7 wks., bur. March 8, 1792.
Anthony Birckenbeil, age 52 yrs., 8 mos., bur. March 8, 1792.
Elizabeth, wife of Peter Stey, age 50 yrs., bur. April 8, 1792.
John Romp, age 30 yrs., 2 mos., 12 days, bur. April 11, 1792.
Ludwig, son of Jeremiah Vielmalter, age 7 mos., 2 wks., bur.
April 26, 1792.
Catharine, daughter of Henry Dewalt, age 7 yrs., 5 mos., 2 wks.,
bur. May 13, 1792.
Anna, daughter of Henry Kinsley, age 3 yrs., 6 mos., 2 wks., bur.
June 12, 1792.
Hannah, daughter of Philip Gramly, age 6 mos., 5 days, bur. June
19, 1792.
Mary Magdalene Wolff, age 29 yrs., 3 mos., 9 days, bur. June 20,
1792.
Anna Maria Contreman, age 1 yr., 6 mos., 6 days, bur. June 24,
1792.
Anna Catharine, wife of Fred. Heiss, age 41 yrs., 7 mos., bur.
June 24, 1792.
Daniel, son of John Etris, age 1 yr., 7 mos., bur. June 26, 1792.
Maria Eliz., wife of Christopher Schreiner, age 25 yrs., 3 mos.,
bur. June 27, 1792.
Christine, daughter of John Schneyder, age 2 yrs., 2 wks., bur.
July 5, 1792.
Michael, son of Henry Wever, age 3 yrs., 3 mos., 9 days, bur.
July 17, 1792.
Maria, daughter of Philip Wirth, age 3 yrs., 2 mos., 3 wks., bur.
July 22, 1792.
Jacob Hill, age 63 yrs., 2 mos., 3 days, bur. July 26, 1792.
Anna Elizabeth Becker, single, age 49 yrs., 6 mos., 8 days, bur.

July 26, 1792.

Peter, son of Philip Casser, age 2 yrs., 10 mos., 3 days, bur. Aug. 5, 1792.

Anna Barbara Rup, widow, age 81 yrs., 1 mo., 2 wks., bur. Aug. 11, 1792.

Hannah, daughter of John Schmidt, age 9 yrs., 11 mos., 3 wks., bur. Aug. 13, 1792.

William, son of Wm. Stoezer, age 1 yr., 11 mos., 2 wks., bur. Aug. 17, 1792.

John Justus Coock, age 35 yrs., bur. Aug. 17, 1792.

Adam, son of Adam Stein, age 7 mos., 1 day, bur. Aug. 20, 1792.

Susanna, daughter of Jacob Goetz, age 1 yr., 6 mos., 1 day, bur. Aug. 21, 1792.

Nancy, daughter of the late William Thomson, age 1 yr., 9 mos., 2 days, bur. Aug. 23, 1792.

Elizabeth, daughter of Henry Zimmerman, age 1 yr., 1 mo., 5 days, bur. Aug. 29, 1792.

Henry, son of John Ludwig Faber, age 1 yr., 7 mos., 1 week, bur. Aug. 30, 1792.

Mary Magdalene, daughter of the late Christ. Huth, age 2 yrs., 1 week, bur. Sept. 2, 1792.

Maria, daughter of John Braubert, age 1 yr., 3 mos., 3 wks., bur. Sept. 8, 1792.

Susanna, daughter of Elias MacNorthen, 7 mos., bur. Sept. 9, 1792.

Margaret, daughter of Peter Walter, age 10 mos., 3 wks., bur. Sept. 9, 1792.

Carl, son of Carl Schacka, age 9 mos., bur. Sept. 13, 1792.

Maria Cath, daughter of Henry Rosker, age 3 yrs., 2 mos., bur. Sept. 15, 1792.

Johanna Cath, daughter of Jacob Zimmerman, age 14 yrs., 8 mos., bur. Sept. 15, 1792.

John Adam, son of Jacob Burckhard, age 1 yr., 10 mos., 14 days, bur. Sept. 16, 1792.

John, son of Jacob Jenser, age 1 yr., 9 days, bur. Sept. 19, 1792.

Casper Geyer, Germantown, age 67 yrs., 8 mos., bur. Sept. 19, 1792.

Clara, wife of John Fred. Mischott, age 38 yrs., bur. Sept. 20, 1792.

Sarah, daughter of Peter Auner, age 1 yr., 2 mos., 16 days, bur. Sept. 20, 1792.

Christine Seivert, age 54 yrs., Sept. 27, 1792.

Elizabeth, daughter of John Jonas, age 2 yrs., 2 wks., bur. Sept. 28, 1792.

Henry, son of Henry Frieck, age 11 yrs., 1 mo., 3 wks., bur. Sept. 28, 1792.

Catharine, daughter of Jacob Meyle, age 9 yrs., 6 mos., 2 wks., bur. Oct. 1, 1792.

John Geo., son of John Mayer, age 1 yr., 7 mos., 5 days, bur. Oct. 2, 1792.

Jacob, son of Frederick Mischott, age 10 mos., 3 wks., bur. Oct. 3, 1792.

George Haeger, a stranger, age 28 yrs., bur. Oct. 3, 1792.

Joseph, son of George Fleck, age ----, bur. Oct. 4, 1792.

Maria Marg., daughter of Nicholas Painter, age 1 yr., 6 mos., 2 days, bur. Oct. 4, 1792.
Anna Maria, daughter of George Becker, age 10 mos., 2 days, bur. Oct. 5, 1792.
Theodore Boom, a stranger from Rotterdam, age ----, bur. Oct. 8, 1792.
Cath. Barbara, daughter of John Spalter, age 2 yrs., 6 mos., 2 wks., bur. Oct. 10, 1792.
Anna Philippina, wife of Geo. Blum, age 65 yrs., 6 mos., bur. Oct. 16, 1792.
Maria, daughter of Philip Pheil, age 1 yr., 7 mos., 2 wks., bur. Oct. 18, 1792.
Patty, daughter of Joseph Edward, age 1 yr., 7 mos., 2 wks., bur. Oct. 26, 1792.
Frederick, son of Conrad Spangenberg, age 1 yr., 3 mos., bur. Oct. 16, 1792.
Jacob Wethman, age 38 yrs., 9 mos., 4 days, bur. Oct. 29, 1792.
Anna Brigitta, wife of Carl Goetz, age 28 yrs., bur. Oct. 29, 1792.
Elizabeth Magd., wife of Jacob Ehringer, age 54 yrs., bur. Nov. 4, 1792.
John, son of John Miller, age 1 yr., 4 mos., 7 days, bur. Nov. 5, 1792.
Maria, daughter of Jacob Jenser, age 1 yr., 4 mos., 7 days, bur. Nov. 8, 1792.
Maria Christine, wife of Conrad Pfaffhausen, age 34 yrs., bur. Dec. 4, 1792.
Maria, daughter of George Bantz, age 9 mos., 8 days, bur. Dec. 6, 1792.
Jemimah, wife of Martin Haas, age 27 yrs., 11 days, bur. Dec. 21, 1792.
Jacob Schermer, age 61 yrs., 5 mos., bur. Dec. 23, 1792.
Matthias Fallier, age 43 yrs., 2 mos., bur. Dec. 25, 1792.
Philippina, wife of Daniel von der Schleuss, age 30 yrs., 4 wks., bur. Dec. 28, 1792.
John Graebel, age 74 yrs., bur. Dec. 31, 1792.
Elizabeth, wife of Lawrence Ries, age 31 yrs., 11 mos., bur. Jan. 6, 1793.
Elizabeth, wife of Christopher Ziegler, age 37 yrs., 9 mos., 7 days, bur. Jan. 21, 1793.
Philip Werntz, age 59 yrs., 11 mos., bur. Jan. 22, 1793.
Paul Buchert, age 55 yrs., bur. Jan. 23, 1793.
Reinhardt Kahmer, age 26 yrs., 3 mos., 18 days, bur. Jan. 24, 1793.
Henry Martin or Martin Henrich, age 34 yrs., 3 mos., 11 days, bur. Jan. 25, 1793.
---- Kaiser, widow, age 85 yrs., bur. Jan. 30, 1793.
Abba Catharine, wife of Daniel Suther, age 44 yrs., 3 mos., 4 days, bur. Feb. 5, 1793.
Mary Magdalene, daughter of John Capp, age 6 mos., 7 days, bur. Feb. 8, 1793.
Maria, daughter of John Schaeffer, age 10 mos., 14 days, bur. Feb. 17, 1793.
Frederick Scheller, age 39 yrs., 6 mos., bur. Feb. 26, 1793.
Christine, daughter of the late Godfrey Schursler, age 11 yrs.,

11 mos., 9 days, bur. Feb. 28, 1793.

Catharine, widow of John Anderson, age 59 yrs., bur. March 1, 1793.

Maria, daughter of the late Daniel Schuster, age 26 yrs., 1 mo., 5 wks., bur. March 5, 1793.

Daniel North, age 42 yrs., 3 mos., 11 days, bur. March 7, 1793.

Elizabeth, wife of John Doersten, age 50 yrs., bur. March 24, 1793.

Sarah, wife of Jacob Young, age 34 yrs., 7 mos., bur. March --, 1793.

Christine, daughter of Zacharias Beckman, age 1 yr., 6 mos., 8 days, bur. April 9, 1793.

William, son of Adam Weber, age 1 yr., 5 mos., bur. April 10, 1793.

Thomas, son of Peter Odenheimer, age 11 mos., 3 wks., bur. April 24, 1793.

Philip, son of Philip Peltz, age 1 yr., 10 mos., bur. April 28, 1793.

John, son of George Hess, age 7 mos., 6 days, bur. April 28, 1793.

Jacob, son of Henry Teiss, age 4 yrs., 8 mos., bur. April 24, 1793.

Emmanuel Bob, age 60 yrs., bur. May 9, 1793.

Christine Jost, widow, age 45 yrs., 3 mos., bur. May 15, 1793.

John, son of Joseph Funck, age 1 yr., 8 mos., 12 days, bur. May 23, 1793.

Magdalene Rummel, widow, age 67 yrs., 11 mos., bur. June 6, 1793.

Michael Sickman, age 79 yrs., 6 mos., bur. June 7, 1793.

----, daughter of Nicholas Staad, age 7 yrs., 6 mos., 3 days, bur. June 7, 1793.

John George, son of John Schneider, age 4 mos., 9 days, bur. June 13, 1793.

Frederick, son of Fred. Kielhoffer, age 3 yrs., 5 mos., 7 days, bur. June 22, 1793.

John, son of Christopher Wassem, age 2 yrs., 3 mos., 5 days, bur. June 23, 1793.

Margaret, daughter of George Bornhaus, age 1 yr., 3 mos., 5 days, bur. June 27, 1793.

William, son of Christopher Wassem, age 6 mos., 13 days, bur. July 4, 1793.

Margaret, wife of Peter Auner, age 34 yrs., 1 mo., 10 days, bur. July 11, 1793.

Hannah, daughter of Casper Grissum, age 8 mos., 2 days, bur. July 13, 1793.

Wm. David, son of Peter Volk, age 10 mos., 6 days, bur. July 13, 1793.

David, son of Daniel Kaiser, age 3 mos., 2 wks., bur. July 18, 1793.

Lawrence, son of Lawrence Riess, age 6 mos., 2 wks., bur. July 22, 1793.

Elizabeth Lauten, widow, age 43 yrs., 6 mos., bur. July 25, 1793.

Anna, daughter of George Loescher, age 11 mos., 5 days, bur. July 28, 1793.

Elizabeth, daughter of John Meyer, age 11 mos., 2 days, bur. July 28, 1793.

John, son of Bernard Meyer, age 1 yr., 4 mos., 1 week, bur. July 28, 1793.
Anna Christine Rick, widow, age 87 yrs., bur. July 28, 1793.
Sophia, daughter of John Kunckel, age 1 yr., bur. July 29, 1793.
David Fackert, age 34 yrs., 9 mos., bur. July 31, 1793.
David, son of the late Matthew Falliere, age 2 yrs., 4 mos., 11 days, bur. Aug. 2, 1793.
Susanna Kramp, single, age 27 yrs., 7 mos., 8 days, bur. Aug. 8, 1793.
John Peter, son of Adam Waas, age 16 yrs., 9 mos., 6 days, bur. Aug. 9, 1793.
Maria Elizabeth, wife of Jacob Hill, age 28 yrs., 4 mos., 2 days, bur. Aug. 13, 1793.
Matthias Schakor, age 39 yrs., 4 mos., 2 days, bur. Aug. 16, 1793.
George, son of Jacob Mercker, age 7 mos., 4 days, bur. Aug. 16, 1793.
Fanny Johnson, widow, age 74 yrs., 5 mos., bur. Aug. 19, 1793.
Conrad Schmidt, Kensington, age 55 yrs., 3 mos., 7 days, bur. Aug. 20, 1793.
John Felix Fenner, age 67 yrs., 9 mos., 2 wks., bur. Aug. 21, 1793.
John William Hertzog, age 79 yrs., 2 mos., 3 wks., bur. Aug. 25, 1793.
John Christian, son of Carl Ludw. Baumgarten, age 4 yrs., 2 wks., bur. Aug. 25, 1793.
John Peter Buttner, Kensington, age 37 yrs., 1 mo., 2 wks., bur. Aug. 26, 1793.
Matthias Saehler, age 66 yrs., bur. Aug. 26, 1793.
John Lamsbach, age 38 yrs., bur. Aug. 28, 1793.
Conrad Fehrclass, age 40 yrs., bur. Aug. 28, 1793.
John Schreiber, age 59 yrs., bur. Aug. 29, 1793.
Samuel Merian, from Switzerland, age 55 yrs., bur. Aug. 30, 1793.
Anna Cath., daughter of John Muller, age 2 yrs., 9 mos., 2 wks., bur. Aug. 30, 1793.
Henry Scherer, age ----, bur. Aug. 31, 1793.
Anna Catharine, daughter of Rev. John Herman Winckhaus, age 1 yr., 8 mos., 2 wks., bur. Sept. 2, 1793.
John Pfeiffer, age 20 yrs., bur. Sept. 4, 1793.
Jacob Essler, age 38 yrs., 9 mos., bur. Sept. 4, 1793.
John, son of John Reudi, age 11 mos., bur. Sept. 5, 1793.
Sarah, daughter of George Becker, age 2 mos., bur. Sept. 5, 1793.
Magdalene Kledie, age 30 yrs., bur. Sept. 6, 1793.
Philip Hassenbach, age 35 yrs., 11 mos., 2 wks., bur. Sept. 6, 1793.
Catharine, wife of Jacob Erwin, age 20 yrs., bur. Sept. 7, 1793.
William, son of Peter Cooper, age 22 yrs., 6 mos., bur. Sept. 8, 1793.
John MacKnair, age 39 yrs., bur. Sept. 8, 1793.
Philip Enck, age 25 yrs., 3 mos., 5 wks., bur. Sept. 9, 1793.
Nicholas Stimmel, age ----, bur. Sept. 10, 1793.
Philip Clumberger, age ----, bur. Sept. 10, 1793.
John Henry Wuertzler, age 33 yrs., 5 mos., 11 days, bur. Sept. 12, 1793.
Susanna, daughter of John Daum, age 17 yrs., bur. Sept. 13, 1793.

Jacob Schreiner, Sr., age 57 yrs., 1 mo., 2 wks., bur. Sept. 13, 1793.
Elizabeth, daughter of Jacob Fleck, age 9 yrs., 5 mos., 2 wks., bur. Sept. 13, 1793.
Barbara, wife of Henry Schneider, age 53 yrs., 3 mos., bur. Sept. 14, 1793.
Henry, son of Jacob Enck, age ---, bur. Sept. 14, 1793.
Elizabeth Weil, age ----, bur. Sept. 15, 1793.
Jacob Weirich, age 75 yrs., bur. Sept. 16, 1793.
Peter Enck, age ----, bur. Sept. 16, 1793.
Christopher Berger, age ----, bur. Sept. 16, 1793.
Joseph Keiser, age ----, bur. Sept. 16, 1793.
John Diehl, age 19 yrs., 6 mos., 9 days, bur. Sept. 16, 1793.
Anna Maria, daughter of David Wisauer, age 17 yrs., 4 mos., 4 days, bur. Sept. 17, 1793.
John Jenny, age ----, bur. Sept. 17, 1793.
Frederick Schneider, age ----, bur. Sept. 17, 1793.
George Bantz, age ----, bur. Sept. 17, 1793.
Jacob Enck, age ----, bur. Sept. 17, 1793.
John Baldi, age 29 yrs., 3 mos., 1 week, bur. Sept. 17, 1793.
Margaret, wife of John H. Guenther, age ----, bur. Sept. 18, 1793.
John Stellwagen, age ----, bur. Sept. 18, 1793.
Paul Leck, age 14 yrs., 10 mos., bur. Sept. 18, 1793.
William Hickeribadem, age ----, bur. Sept. 18, 1793.
George Neiss, age ----, bur. Sept. 18, 1793.
John Adam Schaeffer, age 47 yrs., 8 mos., 3 wks., bur. Sept. 19, 1793.
William Hauzel, age ----, bur. Sept. 19, 1793.
Christian Alberger, age 27 yrs., 11 mos., 3 wks., bur. Sept. 19, 1793.
Catharine Beck, age ----, bur. Sept. 19, 1793.
William Stein, age ----, bur. Sept. 19, 1793.
John, son of Jacob Heiberger, age 5 yrs., bur. Sept. 20, 1793.
Jacob Berck, age ----, bur. Sept. 20, 1793.
Maria Johnston, age ---, bur. Sept. 21, 1793.
Elizabeth Sehler, age ----, bur. Sept. 22, 1793.
John Gaertner, age ----, bur. Sept. 22, 1793.
Anna, wife of John George Pfaff, age ----, bur. Sept. 22, 1793.
Christian Kreider, age ----, bur. Sept. 22, 1793.
Adolph Gaul, age ----, bur. Sept. 22, 1793.
George Koch, age ----, bur. Sept. 22, 1793.
Mary Magdalene Diehl, age ----, bur. Sept. 23, 1793.
Adam Wever, age ----, bur. Sept. 23, 1793.
Elizabeth, wife of Adam Waass, age ----, bur. Sept. 23, 1793.
Catharine, daughter of Henry Wuertzler, age ---, bur. Sept. 23, 1793.
John Frietz, age ----, bur. Sept. 23, 1793.
John Abel, age 32 yrs., 8 mos., bur. Sept. 24, 1793.
Henry Schneider, age ---, bur. Sept. 23, 1793.
Casper Silvius, age ----, bur. Sept. 23, 1793.
John, son of Adam Helm, age ----, bur. Sept. 24, 1793.
Christine Odenheimer, age ----, bur. Sept. 24, 1793.
Maria Schaff, age ----, bur. Sept. 24, 1793.
Peter Engel, age ----, bur. Sept. 25, 1793.

Susanna, daughter of Anna McClatschie, age 7 yrs., 9 mos., 3
    wks., bur. Sept. 25, 1793.
Andrew, son of Widow McClatschie, age 5 yrs., 2 mos., 2 wks.,
    bur. Sept. 25, 1793.
Son of Jacob Fleck, age 5 yrs., 2 mos., 2 wks., bur. Sept. 25,
    1793.
Nancy Waith, age ----, bur. Sept. 25, 1793.
Sophia, wife of Bernard Schaeffer, age ----, bur. Sept. 26, 1793.
Christopher Schreiner, age ----, bur. Sept. 26, 1793.
Catharine, wife of Philip Odenheimer, age ---, bur. Sept. 26,
    1793.
George Bornhaus, age ----, bur. Sept. 26, 1793.
Lora Weber, age ----, bur. Sept. 26, 1793.
Child of Jacob Fleeck, age 3 mos., 4 days, bur. Sept. 27, 1793.
(This is the last burial by Rev. Winckhaus. He died himself of
    yellow fever on Oct. 7, 1793.)
John Wetterstein, age ----, bur. Sept. 27, 1793.
Christina Weyl, age ----, bur. Sept. 27, 1793.
Wife of Ludwig Demut, age ----, bur. Sept. 27, 1793.
Elizabeth Rausch, age ----, bur. Sept. 27, 1793.
John Foltz, age ----, bur. Sept. 27, 1793.
Mr. Rummel, age ----, bur. Sept. 28, 1793.
Child of Jacob Fleck, age ----, bur. Sept. 28, 1793.
Child of Mrs. Kletsche, age ----, bur. Sept. 28, 1793.
Maria Hinckel, age ----, bur. Sept. 28, 1793.
Child of Jacob Fleck, age ----, bur. Sept. 28, 1793.
Elizabeth Schreiner, age ----, bur. Sept. 29, 1793.
Lawrence Schwop, age ----, bur. Sept. 29, 1793.
John Allberger, age ----, bur. Sept. 29, 1793.
(The loss of members during the epidemic was as follows: Aug. -
    17; Sept. - 92; Oct. - 143.)

BURIALS BY REV. WILLIAM HENDEL
1794 - 1798
Abraham Peter, age 62 yrs., 2 mos., bur. Feb. 21, 1794.
Elizabeth Miller, age 4 mos., 28 days, bur. Feb. 27, 1794.
Anna Maria Bortz, age 7 mos., 20 days, bur. Feb. 28, 1794.
Christopher Bockle, age 1 yr., 11 mos., bur. March 2, 1794.
Joseph Funck, age 4 mos., less 5 days, bur. March 8, 1794.
George Freytag, age 73 yrs., 2 mos., 24 days, bur. March 9, 1794.
William Schuttel, age 4 yrs., 8 mos., 6 days, bur. March 11,
    1794.
Anna Kleopha Ruebsam, age 56 yrs., 8 mos., 15 days, bur. March
    14, 1794.
John Hans, was burnt, age 1 yr., 6 mos., 17 days, bur. March 14,
    1794.
Jacob Glas, age 74 yrs., bur. March 16, 1794.
John Schuttel, age 1 yr., 7 mos., 25 days, bur. March 21, 1794.
John Kauck, age 2 yrs., 5 mos., 18 days, bur. April 3, 1794.
Frederick Conrad, age 69 yrs., 10 mos., 10 days, bur. April 4,
    1794.
Elizabeth Charlotte Schmid, age 1 yr., bur. April 4, 1794.
Joseph Frederick Weil, age 4 mos., 29 days, bur. April 15, 1794.
Henry Hans, age 2 yrs., 2 mos., 5 days, bur. April 17, 1794.

Nicholas Hess, age 66 yrs., 10 mos., 10 days, bur. April 30, 1794.
Catharine Krieger, age 42 yrs., bur. May 7, 1794.
Bernard Schawes, age 39 yrs., 9 mos., less 6 days, bur. May 17, 1794.
Jacob Mayer, age 5 yrs., 1 mo., 5 days, bur. May 18, 1794.
Child of Jacob Mercker, age ----, bur. May 18, 1794.
---- Rausch, widow, age 88 yrs., bur. May 20, 1794.
Child of Adam Brunner, age 1 yr., 10 mos., less 5 days, bur. May 21, 1794.
Maria Ley, age 42 yrs., 2 mos., bur. May 29, 1794.
Sarah Schwenck, age 1 yr., 10 mos., 2 days, bur. May 31, 1794.
Regina Bornhaus, age 5 mos., 3 days, bur. June 3, 1794.
Jacob Zeple, age 3 yrs., 6 days, bur. June 9, 1794.
Sarah Bay, age 8 mos., 1 day, bur. June 9, 1794.
Helena Metzger, age 40 yrs., 1 mo., 27 days, bur. June 10, 1794.
Margaret Immel, age 2 yrs., 2 mos., 12 days, bur. June 13, 1794.
Anna Mill, age 33 yrs., 8 mos., 7 days, bur. June 18, 1794.
Elizabeth Catharine Urlob, age 72 yrs., 2 mos., bur. June 20, 1794.
Anna Catharine Friedrich, age 72 yrs., 3 mos., 7 days, bur. June 21, 1794.
Martin Haass, age 5 yrs., 10 mos., 2 days, bur. June 22, 1794.
Hannah Klages, age 11 mos., bur. June 23, 1794.
Joseph Heller, age 6 yrs., 5 mos., 5 days, bur. June 26, 1794.
Elizabeth Zeyher, age 2 yrs., 10 mos., 12 days, bur. July 10, 1794.
Elizabeth Karschbach, fell off the roof, 11 yrs., 10 mos., 23 days, bur. July 13, 1794.
Elizabeth Schof, age 10 mos., 10 days, bur. July 13, 1794.
Matthias Field, drowned in river, age 5 yrs., 8 mos., 2 days, bur. July 14, 1794.
Frederick Thiel, age 2 mos., 14 days, bur. July 16, 1794.
William Schmid, age 11 mos., 5 days, bur. July 20, 1794.
Catharine Schmid, age 5 mos., 21 days, bur. July 22, 1794.
Nicholas Stimmel, age 11 mos., 18 days, bur. July 25, 1794.
Susanna Karschbach, age 1 yr., 1 mo., 1 day, bur. July 27, 1794.
George Uller, age 6 mos., 27 days, bur. July 28, 1794.
Peter Jeanil, age 1 yr., 5 mos., 1 day, bur. July 29, 1794.
John Gartner, age 2 yrs., less ----, bur. Aug. 3, 1794.
Susanna Regina Haller, age 1 yr., 5 mos., 10 days, bur. Aug. 4, 1794.
Philippina Jenser, age 1 yr., 1 mo., 5 days, bur. Aug. 4, 1794.
Elizabeth Harmer, age 33 yrs., bur. Aug. 4, 1794.
Child of Bernard Haehn, age ----, bur. Aug. 5, 1794.
John Fleck, age 1 yr., 7 mos., 20 days, bur. Aug. 6, 1794.
Peter Alberger, age 1 yr., 2 days, bur. Aug. 7, 1794.
Mary Magdalene Millen, age 1 yr., 8 days, bur. Oct. 15, 1794.
Anna Maria Cath. Weber, age 2 yrs., 4 mos., 17 days, bur. Oct. 16, 1794.
Maria Balde, age 3 yrs., 5 mos., 11 days, bur. Oct. 17, 1794.
Catharine Baumer, age 31 yrs., 12 days, bur. Oct. 21, 1794.
Henry Rub, age 2 yrs., 3 mos., 23 days, bur. Oct. 22, 1794.
Ludwig Zeple, age 4 yrs., 11 mos., 10 days, bur. Oct. 26, 1794.
John Huber, age 33 yrs., bur. Oct. 28, 1794.

John Stanley, age 42 yrs., bur. Oct. 29, 1794.
Margaret Schmid, age 2 yrs., 9 mos., 6 days, bur. Oct. 29, 1794.
Maria Suter, age 34 yrs., 10 mos., 11 days, bur. Nov. 2, 1794.
Catharine Rummel, age 2 yrs., 9 mos., 14 days, bur. Nov. 2, 1794.
Margaret Lesch, age 3 yrs., 3 mos., 6 days, bur. Nov. 7, 1794.
Elizabeth Mercker, age 2 mos., 13 days, bur. Nov. 11, 1794.
Reinhard Kahmer, age 71 yrs., 19 days, bur. Nov. 12, 1794.
Charlotte Weiberg, age 18 yrs., 11 mos., 15 days, bur. Nov. 13,
1794.
Anna Maria Meile, age 1 yr., 2 mos., bur. Nov. 17, 1794.
Henry Wester, age 2 mos., 2 days, bur. Nov. 18, 1794.
John Henry Belsterling, age 2 yrs., 10 mos., 23 days, bur. Nov.
19, 1794.
Salome Karger, age 1 yr., 11 mos., 9 days, bur. Nov. 19, 1794.
John George Fleck, age 71 yrs., bur. Nov. 22, 1794.
A. Margaret Mayer, age 1 mo., 24 days, bur. Nov. 26, 1794.
Carl Holtzberger, age 55 mos., bur. Dec. 15, 1794.
Anna Maria Begle, age 21 yrs., 5 mos., less 1 day, bur. Dec. 15,
1794.
Elizabeth Mayer, age 2 yrs., 7 mos., 17 days, bur. Dec. 18, 1794.
Andrew Kuper, age 14 yrs., 5 mos., 13 days, bur. Dec. 20, 1794.
Elizabeth Corby, age 11 mos., 1 day, bur. Dec. 23, 1794.
Anna Maria Datz, age 71 yrs., 11 mos., less 2 days, bur. Dec. 24,
1794.
Anna Maria May, age 2 mos., 18 days, bur. Dec. 27, 1794.
Jacob Weiny, age 77 yrs., 11 mos., 12 days, bur. Jan. 1, 1795.
Elizabeth Nord, age 37 yrs., 3 mos., 15 days, bur. Jan. 4, 1795.
Eleonora Kuhn, age 2 yrs., 5 mos., 26 days, bur. Jan. 11, 1795.
Magdalene Hoffman, age 40 yrs., bur. Jan. 15, 1795.
Benjamin Farmer Fraehly, age 1 yr., 5 mos., 7 days, bur. Jan. 18,
1795.
Peter Kuper, age 56 yrs., 7 mos., 13 days, bur. Jan. 28, 1795.
Sophia Schell, age 1 yr., 6 mos., 6 days, bur. Feb. 16, 1795.
Maria Margaret Metzger, age 19 yrs., 3 mos., 12 days, bur. Jan.
18, 1795.
Paul Hammerich, age 74 yrs., 8 mos., 11 days, bur. Jan. 22, 1795.
George Jenser, age 37 yrs., 10 mos., bur. Jan. 24, 1795.
---- McDougal, widow, age 67 yrs., bur. March 2, 1795.
---- Wagenhorst, widow, age 76 yrs., 22 days, bur. March 5, 1795.
---- Asch, widow, age 66 yrs., 24 days, bur. March 6, 1795.
Maria Layer, age 35 yrs., 7 mos., 9 days, bur. March 8, 1795.
John Jacob Heimer, age 47 yrs., 21 days, bur. March 10, 1795.
Anna Maria Pfeiffer, age 64 yrs., 1 mo., 24 days, bur. March 13,
1795.
Margaret Stetzenbach, age 8 mos., 10 days, bur. March 14, 1795.
Maria Birckenbeil, age 26 yrs., 2 mos., 18 days, bur. March 15,
1795.
Jacob Schweffel, age 60 yrs., 6 mos., 24 days, bur. March 18,
1795.
Agnes Buchert, age 64 yrs., 10 mos., 3 days, bur. March 18, 1795.
Maria Stucki, age 59 yrs., 5 mos., 9 days, bur. March 22, 1795.
Elizabeth Metzger, age 3 yrs., 2 mos., 4 days, bur. March 22,
1795.
Ferdinand Rosset, age 36 yrs., bur. March 31, 1795.
Catharine McChildon, age 1 yr., 4 mos., 4 days, bur. April 12,

1795.
John Ludwig Faber, age 44 yrs., 10 mos., 7 days, bur. April 19, 1795.
Margaret Ecker, age 7 mos., 5 days, bur. April 23, 1795.
Salome Ecker, age 2 yrs., 1 mo., 9 days, bur. April 27, 1795.
George Justus, age 36 eyars 11 mos., 10 days, bur. April 28, 1795.
Catharine Klages, age 83 yrs., 7 mos., bur. May 5, 1795.
Jacob Reidle, age 45 yrs., 3 mos., 20 days, bur. May 5, 1795.
Elizabeth Ford, age 5 yrs., 1 mo., 13 days, bur. May 9, 1795.
Catharine Weiler, age 6 yrs., 8 mos., 3 days, bur. May 11, 1795.
Magdalene Wagner, age 23 yrs., bur. May 19, 1795.
Henry Pfeiffer, age 44 yrs., 3 mos., 26 days, bur. May 24, 1795.
Thomas Elliot, age 13 yrs., 25 days, bur. June 3, 1795.
A. Sophia Kraemer, age 10 yrs., 8 mos., 16 days, bur. June 5, 1795.
Susanna Breese, age 9 mos., 22 days, bur. June 8, 1795.
Elizabeth Schlotter, age 3 yrs., 5 mos., 9 days, bur. June 10, 1795.
Maria Ozeas, age 54 yrs., 3 mos., 6 days, bur. June 11, 1795.
Daniel Miller, age 38 yrs., 9 mos., 27 days, bur. June 12, 1795.
William Edwards, age 3 yrs., 7 mos., 5 days, bur. June 21, 1795.
Samuel Edwards, age 6 yrs., 1 mo., less 1 day, bur. June 26, 1795.
John Alburger, age 4 yrs., 3 mos., 24 days, bur. June 27, 1795.
Catharine Klemmer, age 81 yrs., 4 mos., bur. June 30, 1795.
Carl Friedrich, age 1 yr., 2 mos., 6 days, bur. July 2, 1795.
Maria Zollinger, age 1 yr., 1 mo., 25 days, bur. July 3, 1795.
Hannah Schlotter, age 2 mos., 10 days, bur. July 5, 1795.
Child of Jacob Schibele, age 2 yrs., 11 mos., less 2 days, bur. July 5, 1795.
Rebecca Birckenbeil, age 4 mos., 15 days, bur. July 7, 1795.
Samuel Karpium (?), age 7 mos., 1 day, bur. July 9, 1795.
Francis Geisse, age 49 yrs., 2 mos., 27 days, bur. July 11, 1795.
Maria Reide, age 1 yr., 20 days, bur. July 11, 1795.
Samuel Spaeth, age 1 yr., 3 mos., 13 days, bur. July 11, 1795.
George Bachmann, age 1 yr., 1 mo., 16 days, bur. July 11, 1795.
John Hickinbottom, age 12 yrs., 4 mos., 13 days, bur. July 12, 1795.
Lousia Karcher, age 1 yr., 7 mos., less 3 days, bur. July 14, 1795.
Henry Peter Weber, age 8 yrs., 3 mos., 3 days, bur. July 15, 1795.
George Lamsbach, age 1 yr., 4 mos., 13 days, bur. July 15, 1795.
Elizabeth Schreiner, age 47 yrs., 3 mos., bur. July 16, 1795.
Henry Rothhaar, age 7 mos., 19 days, bur. July 20, 1795.
Hannah Ehringer, age 10 mos., 6 days, bur. July 20, 1795.
Elizabeth Buser, age 1 yr., 9 mos., 12 days, bur. July 20, 1795.
Simon Muenich, age 17 yrs., 1 mo., 5 days, bur. July 22, 1795.
Christine Fuchs, age 1 yr., 5 mos., 9 days, bur. July 22, 1795.
Maria Kreutz, age 65 yrs., bur. July 28, 1795.
Catharine Fiss, age 1 yr., 9 mos., 27 days, bur. July 28, 1795.
Adam Gorker, age 50 yrs., 11 mos., 27 days, bur. July 30, 1795.
Samuel Haus, age 8 mos., 17 days, bur. July 31, 1795.
John Clunn, age 5 mos., 21 days, bur. July 31, 1795.

Maria Stucky, age 1 yr., 1 mo., 2 days, bur. Aug. 1, 1795.
Child of Catharine Asch, age 3 yrs., bur. Aug. 2, 1795.
Henry Rothhaar, age 7 mos., 18 days, bur. Aug. 3, 1795.
Barbara Beckmann, age 33 yrs., bur. Aug. 5, 1795.
John Dickes, age 10 mos., 25 days, bur. Aug. 6, 1795.
Maria Collins, age 4 mos., 23 days, bur. Aug. 8, 1795.
Elizabeth Hoffmann, age 11 mos., less 4 days, bur. Aug. 10, 1795.
Eva Miller, age 4 yrs., 2 mos., 19 days, bur. Aug. 12, 1795.
Child of Anna Langstraak, age 10 mos., 12 days, bur. Aug. 12, 1795.
Rachel Gartner, age 1 yr., 3 mos., 12 days, bur. Aug. 12, 1795.
Eleonora Paine, age 1 yr., 7 mos., 26 days, bur. Aug. 12, 1795.
A. Elizabeth Breh, age 4 mos., 1 day, bur. Aug. 14, 1795.
John Huhn, age 2 yrs., 11 mos., 7 days, bur. Aug. 15, 1795.
Maria Braun, age 5 mos., 5 days, bur. Aug. 17, 1795.
John Peter Rogers, age 10 mos., 17 days, bur. Aug. 18, 1795.
George Kilhofer, age 2 yrs., 6 mos., 5 days, bur. Aug. 18, 1795.
A. Maria Hacker, age 48 yrs., 7 mos., 25 days, bur. Aug. 19, 1795.
Barbara Hammerich, age 75 yrs., 2 mos., 11 days, bur. Aug. 20, 1795.
William Wiand, age 10 mos., 28 days, bur. Aug. 20, 1795.
Anthony Wagner, age 8 mos., 19 days, bur. Aug. 23, 1795.
Mary Magdalene Braun, age 63 yrs., 4 mos., 24 days, bur. Aug. 25, 1795.
Mary Magdalene Mayer, age 10 mos., 23 days, bur. Aug. 25, 1795.
Margaret Elizabeth Ebel, age 7 mos., 28 days, bur. Aug. 25, 1795.
John Stanley, age 85 yrs., 4 mos., 2 days, bur. Aug. 27, 1795.
Wife of Frederick Schock, age 25 yrs., 9 mos., 9 days, bur. Aug. 27, 1795.
Jacob Behlert, age 1 yr., 4 mos., less 3 days, bur. Aug. 27, 1795.
Elizabeth Louisa, age 11 mos., 26 days, bur. Aug. 28, 1795.
Thomas Wiand, age 2 yrs., 11 mos., 26 days, bur. Aug. 28, 1795.
George Miller, age 3 yrs., 6 mos., 7 days, bur. Aug. 30, 1795.
Salome Schmid, age 1 yr., 9 days, bur. Aug. 31, 1795.
John Daubel, age 6 mos., 15 days, bur. Aug. 31, 1795.
Maria Kreider, age 1 yr., 2 mos., 19 days, bur. Sept. 3, 1795.
Sarah Jones, age 1 yr., 9 mos., 7 days, bur. Sept. 3, 1795.
John George Jenser, age 1 yr., 7 days, bur. Sept. 4, 1795.
Magdalene Lutz, age 7 yrs., 4 mos., 3 days, bur. Sept. 6, 1795.
Samuel Eisenmenger, age 5 mos., 24 days, bur. Sept. 8, 1795.
Sarha Wohlfahrt, age 5 mos., 20 days, bur. Sept. 9, 1795.
Frederick Schmid, age 9 yrs., 11 mos., 21 days, bur. Sept. 12, 1795.
John Dorr, age 36 yrs., 4 mos., bur. Sept. 12, 1795.
Elizabeth Kayser, age 11 mos., 5 days, bur. Sept. 13, 1795.
John Bonner, age 52 yrs., bur. Sept. 17, 1795.
Elizabeth Ryan, age 1 yr., 4 mos., 6 days, bur. Sept. 19, 1795.
M. Magdalene Leber, age 35 yrs., 11 mos., bur. Sept. 21, 1795.
Maria Euler, age ----, bur. Sept. 22, 1795.
John Kron, age 24 yrs., 4 mos., less 3 days, bur. Sept. 27, 1795.
Andrew Kayser, age 3 yrs., 2 mos., 14 days, bur. Sept. 28, 1795.
A. Maria Trum, age 28 yrs., 4 mos., 19 days, bur. Sept. 30, 1795.
Griseli Trimmler, age 31 yrs., 1 mo., 12 days, bur. Oct. 1, 1795.

Maria Williams, age 33 yrs., 9 mos., 28 days, bur. Oct. 2, 1795.
Maria Peres, age 1 yr., 6 days, bur. Oct. 2, 1795.
Christian Wiegand, age 40 yrs., 10 mos., 9 days, bur. Oct. 3, 1795.
Maria Hohl, age 64 yrs., 5 mos., 9 days, bur. Oct. 4, 1795.
William Rudolph, age 1 yr., 5 mos., 17 days, bur. Oct. 4, 1795.
Dorothy Alburger, age 32 yrs., bur. Oct. 7, 1795.
Elizabeth Gucker, age 1 yr., 8 mos., 2 days, bur. Oct. 10, 1795.
Edward ----, age 1 yr., 9 mos., bur. Oct. 8, 1795.
Peter Warner, age 25 yrs., 12 days, bur. Oct. 16, 1795.
A. Maria Weil, age 8 mos., 6 days, bur. Oct. 18, 1795.
Pouilhan Gerbon, from St. Domingo, age 60 yrs., bur. Oct. 20, 1795.
Elizabeth Dups, age 28 yrs., 2 mos., 18 days, bur. Oct. 23, 1795.
Philp Schmid, age 2 yrs., 2 mos., 9 days, bur. Oct. 25, 1795.
Charlotte Tripolet, age 24 yrs., 5 mos., 9 days, bur. Oct. 25, 1795.
Barbara Wolf, age 80 yrs., 5 mos., 6 days, bur. Oct. 26, 1795.
Child of Margaret Kuhl, age 7 mos., 14 days, bur. Nov. 2, 1795.
Margaret Maenchen, age 69 yrs., bur. Nov. 3, 1795.
Judith Beloni, age 79 yrs., bur. Nov. 7, 1795.
Catharine Klober, age 22 yrs., bur. Nov. 11, 1795.
Magdalene Rummel, age 1 yr., 1 mo., 15 days, bur. Nov. 14, 1795.
Magdalene Hartmann, age 47 yrs., bur. Nov. 18, 1795.
Jacob Moog, age 47 yrs., 8 mos., 5 days, bur. Nov. 22, 1795.
Charlotte Leber, age 6 yrs., 4 mos., 8 days, bur. Nov. 26, 1795.
Maria Cornelius, age 5 mos., 23 days, bur. Dec. 2, 1795.
Child of William Adair, age 1 yr., 10 mos., 23 days, bur. Dec. 6, 1795.
Susanna Reis, age 54 yrs., bur. Dec. 7, 1795.
Christopher Scheibele, age 39 yrs., 6 mos., less 1 day, bur. Dec. 11, 1795.
George Hasselbach, age 5 yrs., 6 days, bur. Dec. 17, 1795.
Elizabeth Wright, age 6 mos., less 1 day, bur. Dec. 24, 1795.
John Kron, age 1 yr., 9 mos., 2 days, bur. Dec. 25, 1795.
Sophia Magdalena Leber, age 1 yr., 3 mos., 1 day, bur. Jan. 1, 1796.
Nocholas Herd, age 47 yrs., bur. Jan. 3, 1796.
Elizabeth Edenborn, age 19 yrs., 8 mos., 22 days, bur. Jan. 10, 1796.
Philippina Hof, age 8 yrs., 5 mos., 25 days, bur. Jan. 10, 1796.
George Henry Sassemanshausen, age 5 yrs., 3 mos., 3 days, bur. Jan. 14, 1796.
Margaret Jones, age 2 yrs., 3 mos., 11 days, bur. Jan. 14, 1796.
Margaret Stucky, age 24 yrs., 5 mos., 7 days, bur. Jan. 23, 1796.
Elizabeth Steel, age 62 yrs., bur. Jan. 24, 1796.
Rachel Kabler, age 3 yrs., 3 mos., 7 days, bur. Jan. 25, 1796.
Thomas West, age 2 yrs., 5 mos., 16 days, bur. Jan. 28, 1796.
John West, age 2 mos., 10 days, bur. Jan. 28, 1796.
Henry Jeckle, age 32 yrs., bur. Jan. 29, 1796.
George German, age 1 yr., 6 mos., 12 days, bur. Jan. 29, 1796.
Wilhelmina Spaet, age 33 yrs., 10 days, bur. Feb. 3, 1796.
Peter Lesch, age 73 yrs., bur. Feb. 9, 1796.
Christine Mill, age 37 yrs., 7 mos., 16 days, bur. Feb. 10, 1796.
Catharine von der Schleus, age 40 yrs., 2 mos., 5 days, bur. Feb.

18, 1796.
Jacob Franck, age 2 mos., 3 days, bur. Feb. 18, 1796.
John Henry Freund, age 50 yrs., 5 mos., less 1 day, bur. Feb. 21,
1796.
Mary Magdalene Becker, age 48 yrs., 6 mos., 11 days, bur. March
1, 1796.
Maria Knauf, age 20 yrs., bur. March 7, 1796.
Maria Schlack, age 56 yrs., 2 mos., 13 days, bur. March 10, 1796.
Peter McCosh, age 1 yr., less 8 days, bur. March 10, 1796.
Child of George Schuck, age 2 mos., 11 days, bur. March 16, 1796.
Maria Funck, age 26 yrs., 11 mos., 16 days, bur. March 27, 1796.
Margaret Staut, age 61 yrs., bur. March 29, 1796.
Bernard Gecke, age 34 yrs., bur. March 30, 1796.
Sarah Schmaltz, age 1 yr., 11 mos., 15 days, bur. April 10, 1796.
Jacob Schallus, age 45 yrs., 7 mos., 22 days, bur. April 20,
1796.
Michael Ganiter, age 62 yrs., 8 mos., 9 days, bur. April 24,
1796.
Peter Pfeiffer, age 17 yrs., 11 mos., 9 days, bur. April 25,
1796.
Catharine Klages, age 9 mos., 23 days, bur. April 26, 1796.
Francis Kiely, age 7 mos., 16 days, bur. April 28, 1796.
John Pfeiffer, age 47 yrs., 6 mos., bur. May 2, 1796.
Elizabeth Hoff, age 6 yrs., 4 mos., 6 days, bur. May 4, 1796.
George Hoff, age 6 yrs., 26 days, bur. May 7, 1796.
John Messemer, age 62 yrs., 5 mos., less 1 day, bur. May 16,
1796.
Godfried Munch, age 50 yrs., 3 mos., 25 days, bur. May 19, 1796.
Peter Frederick Defort, age 1 yr., 4 mos., 22 days, bur. May 20,
1796.
A French child, age 1 yr., 2 mos., bur. May 28, 1796.
Frederick Jenser, age 44 yrs., bur. May 29, 1796.
Jacob Bossert, age 45 yrs., 7 mos., bur. June 4, 1796.
John Matthew von Hoff, age 1 yr., 6 mos., less 3 days, bur. June
12, 1796.
John Schneider, age 57 yrs., bur. June 16, 1796.
Abraham Engelmann, age 1 yr., 6 mos., less 5 days, bur. June 17,
1796.
Elizabeth Braun, age 8 mos., 10 days, bur. June 18, 1796.
Peter Hohl, age 1 yr., 3 mos., 18 days, bur. June 25, 1796.
Joseph Harrer, age 1 yr., 1 mo., 18 days, bur. June 26, 1796.
Henrietta Huguen, age 6 yrs., 2 mos., less 3 days, bur. June 27,
1796.
Child of Walker, age 1 yr., 5 mos., 5 days, bur. June 27, 1796.
Catharine Wester, age 3 mos., 1 day, bur. June 29, 1796.
Henry Pfau, age 1 yr., 1 mo., 23 days, bur. July 1, 1796.
John Adam Roth, age 41 yrs., 6 mos., 6 days, bur. July 3, 1796.
Elizabeth Miller, age 8 mos., 11 days, bur. July 6, 1796.
William Schreiner, age 2 mos., 13 days, bur. July 10, 1796.
A. Maria Klampfer, age 92 yrs., bur. July 12, 1796.
Henrietta May, age 7 mos., 22 days, bur. July 12, 1796.
Jane Steinmetz, age 29 yrs., 2 mos., 17 days, bur. July 14, 1796.
Sarah Christine Galle, age 1 yr., 5 mos., bur. July 15, 1796.
John Ludwig Schell, age 1 yr., 24 days, bur. July 17, 1796.
Maria Pfeiffer, age 7 mos., 25 days, bur. July 21, 1796.

Margaret Jahns, age 1 yr., 2 mos., 13 days, bur. July 25, 1796.
Child of Mr. Price, age 2 mos., bur. July 27, 1796.
George Meyer, age 1 yr., 3 mos., 20 days, bur. July 28, 1796.
Margaret Sigmund, age 10 mos., 23 days, bur. July 29, 1796.
Elizabeth Theiss, age 6 mos., 24 days, bur. July 29, 1796.
Samuel Karcher, age 9 mos., 24 days, bur. Aug. 2, 1796.
Child of Maria Thiel, age 1 yr., 2 mos., 26 days, bur. Aug. 6, 1796.
Maria Finck, age 5 yrs., 2 mos., 12 days, bur. Aug. 6, 1796.
Child of James Sheppard, age 3 yrs., bur. Aug. 7, 1796.
Maria Edenborn, age 8 yrs., 1 mo., 24 days, bur. Aug. 7, 1796.
Child of Maria Schmid, age 9 mos., bur. Aug. 7, 1796.
Rebecca Weil, age 1 yr., 6 mos., 3 days, bur. Aug. 12, 1796.
Wife of Bernard Rothhaar, age 41 yrs., 7 mos., 12 days, bur. Aug. 13, 1796.
Peter Ozeas, age 1 yr., 8 mos., 8 days, bur. Aug. 13, 1796.
A. Margaret Munch, age 3 yrs., 3 mos., less 1 day, bur. Aug. 13, 1796.
Carl Ludwig Baumgarten, age 53 yrs., 3 mos., 6 days, bur. Aug. 14, 1796.
Nicholas Heckman, age 47 yrs., 4 mos., bur. Aug. 15, 1796.
Elizabeth Nunnemacher, age 7 mos., 19 days, bur. Aug. 17, 1796.
John Light, age 10 mos., 23 days, bur. Aug. 19, 1796.
George Pfeiffer, age 1 yr., 5 mos., 19 days, bur. Aug. 20, 1796.
Child of Godfried Bockius, age 1 yr., 6 mos., 6 days, bur. Aug. 22, 1796.
Child of Michael Esch, age 10 mos., 11 days, bur. Aug. 26, 1796.
Frederick Scheible, age 8 mos., 14 days, bur. Aug. 28, 1796.
Elizabeth Davis, age 12 yrs., bur. Aug. 29, 1796.
Frederick Rummel, age 12 yrs., 21 days, bur. Sept. 3, 1796.
George Eisenring, age 6 yrs., 4 mos., 19 days, bur. Sept. 4, 1796.
---- Wester, widow, age 76 yrs., bur. Sept. 6, 1796.
Anna van Sant, age 25 yrs., bur. Sept. 12, 1796.
Henry Senn, age 11 mos., 9 days, bur. Sept. 16, 1796.
Margaret Kros, age 67 yrs., 6 mos., 7 days, bur. Sept. 18, 1796.
Elizabeth Stubert, age 5 yrs., 1 mo., bur. Sept. 19, 1796.
M. Christine Jahraus, age 26 yrs., 9 mos., 27 days, bur. Sept. 19, 1796.
Maria Schmid, age 38 yrs., bur. Sept. 25, 1796.
Michael Worn, age 43 yrs., bur. Sept. 30, 1796.
Peter Fuchs, age 3 mos., less 3 days, bur. Oct. 2, 1796.
Paul Samson, age 39 yrs., 1 day, bur. Oct. 2, 1796.
Maria Pomp, age 4 yrs., 6 mos., 7 days, bur. Oct. 9, 1796.
John Rambo ('s-?), age 10 mos., 4 days, bur. Oct. 9, 1796.
George Schad, age 33 yrs., bur. Oct. 17, 1796.
Rudolph Zoble, age 10 mos., bur. Oct. 18, 1796.
George Michael Gamber, age 2 yrs., 2 mos., 21 yrs., bur. Oct. 19, 1796.
A. Maria Meile, age 2 yrs., 1 mo., 7 days, bur. Oct. 19, 1796.
John Hoffman, drowned in the river, age 7 yrs., 9 mos., 23 days, bur. Oct. 19, 1796.
David Weidmann, age 5 mos., 9 days, bur. Oct. 20, 1796.
Catharine Reed, age 31 yrs., 10 mos., 21 days, bur. Oct. 21, 1796.

John Zobke, age 3 yrs., 3 mos., less 2 days, bur. Oct. 21, 1796.
John Bom, age 41 yrs., 4 mos., bur. Nov. 2, 1796.
Thomas Wind, age 23 yrs., 6 mos., 22 days, bur. Nov. 3, 1796.
Jacob Handschuh, age 86 yrs., 24 days, bur. Nov. 5, 1796.
Maria Gros, age 13 yrs., 2 mos., 7 days, bur. Nov. 7, 1796.
John Faust, age 1 yr., 11 mos., bur. Nov. 7, 1796.
John George Hangen, age 2 yrs., 11 mos., 5 days, bur. Nov. 11, 1796.
John Benner, age 65 yrs., 14 days, bur. Nov. 28, 1796.
George Loscher, age 9 mos., 14 days, bur. Nov. 28, 1796.
John Meibert, age 1 yr., 10 mos., 26 days, bur. Dec. 1, 1796.
Maria Weidman, age 4 yrs., 1 mo., 16 days, bur. Dec. 3, 1796.
Margaret ----, age 36 yrs., 1 mo., 6 days, bur. Dec. 3, 1796.
Anna Schlopfer, age 85 yrs., 11 mos., 12 days, bur. Dec. 8, 1796.
John Sauter, age 51 yrs., 10 mos., 25 days, bur. Dec. 18, 1796.
Maria Wirtz, age 32 yrs., 8 mos., 13 days, bur. Dec. 20, 1796.
Jonathan Plusch, age 45 yrs., 7 mos., 16 days, bur. Dec. 24, 1796.
Catharine Gilbert, age 40 yrs., bur. Jan. 3, 1797.
Nicholas Hess, age 32 yrs., 4 mos., 22 days, bur. Jan. 15, 1797.
Sarah Weidman, age 7 yrs., less 3 days, bur. Jan. 15, 1797.
Henry Geyer, age 1 yr., 8 mos., 8 days, bur. Jan. 17, 1797.
Maria Jones, age 39 yrs., less 5 days, bur. Jan. 29, 1797.
John Munch, age 3 yrs., 8 mos., less 2 days, bur. Feb. 5, 1797.
John Loesch, age 6 mos., less 1 day, bur. Feb. 13, 1797.
John Steinmetz, age 8 mos., 15 days, bur. Feb. 16, 1797.
Catharine Langkopf, age 54 yrs., 10 mos., bur. Feb. 21, 1797.
John Pfau, fell from a horse, age 73 yrs., bur. Feb. 21, 1797.
John George Degenhart, age 5 mos., 5 days, bur. Feb. 28, 1797.
Susanna Laury, age 31 yrs., 11 mos., 1 day, bur. March 12, 1797.
A. Maria Freund, age 38 yrs., 9 mos., 17 days, bur. March 15, 1797.
Maria Jauch, age 68 yrs., bur. March 19, 1797.
Samuel Moser, age 22 yrs., 2 mos., 26 days, bur. March 27, 1797.
Maria Peres, age 8 mos., 12 days, bur. March 31, 1797.
Matthias Rost, drowned in the river, age 24 yrs., 11 mos., 7 days, bur. April 6, 1797.
Henry Best, age 45 yrs., bur. April 8, 1797.
Frederick Baumgart, age 9 yrs., 2 mos., 24 days, bur. April 11, 1797.
Leonard Ried, age 45 yrs., bur. April 11, 1797.
Frederick Mast, age 27 yrs., 2 mos., bur. April 12, 1797.
Margaret Kelker, age 10 yrs., 9 mos., less 3 days, bur. April 25, 1797.
Conrad Gerhard, age 46 yrs., 6 mos., bur. April 30, 1797.
Elizabeth Bom, age 1 yr., 3 mos., bur. May 7, 1797.
John Schucker, age 57 yrs., bur. May 15, 1797.
Lawrence Oberman, age 32 yrs., 7 mos., 15 days, bur. May 18, 1797.
Esther Stath, age 3 yrs., 9 mos., bur. May 18, 1797.
Daniel Weil, age 30 yrs., 8 mos., 14 days, bur. May 23, 1797.
George Mercker, age 23 yrs., 2 mos., 22 days, bur. May 24, 1797.
John Peter Braun, age 1 yr., 6 mos., 1 day, bur. June 16, 1797.
Elsie Gros, age 11 yrs., 10 mos., 14 days, bur. June 28, 1797.
William Husselbach, age 36 yrs., 3 mos., bur. July 6, 1797.

Anna Schwartz, age 53 yrs., bur. July 8, 1797.
Bernard Kast, age 1 yr., bur. July 9, 1797.
Catharine Beck, age 25 yrs., 9 mos., 19 days, bur. July 14, 1797.
Margaret Schoen, age 68 yrs., 2 mos., bur. July 16, 1797.
Jacob Schneider, age 1 yr., 4 mos., 26 days, bur. July 17, 1797.
Sarah Hill, age 6 yrs., 10 mos., 10 days, bur. July 18, 1797.
Martha Miller, age 6 mos., 8 days, bur. July 18, 1797.
Sibylla Seitz, age 14 yrs., 5 mos., 19 days, bur. July 20, 1797.
Elizabeth Ried, age 1 yr., 1 mo., 8 days, bur. July 22, 1797.
John Ulrich Weckerle, age 58 yrs., 9 mos., 26 days, bur. July 23, 1797.
Lawrence Otto, age 24 yrs., 1 mo., 25 days, bur. July 23, 1797.
Bernard Eckstein, age 10 mos., 10 days, bur. July 25, 1797.
Margaret Whittaker, age 10 mos., 22 days, bur. July 28, 1797.
Catharine Schmid, age 5 yrs., 12 days, bur. July 30, 1797.
George Brennerman, age 1 yr., 4 mos., 26 days, bur. July 30, 1797.
Margaret Lutz, age 4 yrs., 11 mos., 1 day, bur. Aug. 3, 1797.
John Jost Appel, age 8 mos., 23 days, bur. Aug. 3, 1797.
Marianne Karcher, age 58 yrs., 11 mos., 1 day, bur. Aug. 4, 1797.
Samuel Walker, age 3 yrs., 4 mos., 17 days, bur. Aug. 5, 1797.
Catharine Zahner, age 1 yr., 7 mos., 5 days, bur. Aug. 6, 1797.
Isaac Kullenberg, age 43 yrs., 11 mos., less 1 day, bur. Aug. 11, 1797.
Anna van Cleve, age 28 yrs., bur. Aug. 12, 1797.
John Nicholas Getter, age 1 yr., 2 mos., less 4 days, bur. Aug. 12, 1797.
Gottfried Joad Gobler, age 2 mos., 20 days, bur. Aug. 14, 1797.
Anna Stricker, age 3 yrs., 6 mos., bur. Aug. 15, 1797.
Margaret Edwards, age 1 yr., 8 mos., less 2 days, bur. Aug. 18, 1797.
Jacob Volck, age 11 mos., 3 days, bur. Aug. 19, 1797.
John Volck, age 23 yrs., less 2 days, bur. Aug. 19, 1797.
Catharine Sinck, age 51 yrs., bur. Aug. 21, 1797.
Rebecca Preis, age 64 yrs., bur. Aug. 23, 1797.
Susanna Heller, age 7 mos., 22 days, bur. Aug. 24, 1797.
Philip Rummel, age 1 yr., 7 mos., 16 days, bur. Aug. 27, 1797.
Sarah Husselbach, age 1 yr., 6 mos., 2 days, bur. Aug. 28, 1797.
Sarah Reinhard, age 2 yrs., 10 mos., less 1 day, bur. Aug. 29, 1797.
William Reindy, age 4 mos., 3 days, bur. Aug. 30, 1797.
A woman, age ---, bur. Sept. 3, 1797.
George Freytag, age 19 yrs., 10 mos., 23 days, bur. Sept. 7, 1797.
Ludwig List, age 39 yrs., 2 mos., 8 days, bur. Sept. 9, 1797.
Robert Maxfield, age 55 yrs., bur. Sept. 9, 1797.
Hannah Faut, age 28 yrs., bur. Sept. 9, 1797.
Susanna Diehl, age 19 yrs., bur. Sept. 11, 1797.
Andrew Kramer, age ----, bur. Sept. 11, 1797.
Margaret Wagner, age 67 yrs., 4 mos., bur. Sept. 14, 1797.
Daniel Walther, age ----, bur. Sept. 14, 1797.
Dorothea Fiss, age 44 yrs., bur. Sept. 17, 1797.
Child of John Becker, age 1 yr., 3 mos., bur. Sept. 19, 1797.
---- Wiand, widow, age 55 yrs., bur. Sept. 21, 1797.
Maria Schermer, age 1 yr., 9 mos., less 3 days, bur. Sept. 21,

1797.
Nicholas Knauf, age 40 yrs., bur. Sept. 24, 1797.
Child of John Wagner, age 1 mo., 4 days, bur. Sept. 25, 1797.
John Kinsinger, age 2 yrs., 4 mos., 15 days, bur. Sept. 29, 1797.
Child of Henry Thielmann, age 1 yr., 3 mos., less 2 days, bur.
   Sept. 30, 1797.
Michael Hentz, age 10 mos., bur. Sept. 30, 1797.
Margaret Knauf, age ----, bur. Sept. 30, 1797.
Christine Murdock, age 46 yrs., bur. Oct. 2, 1797.
David Marshall, age 43 yrs., bur. Oct. 6, 1797.
James Murdock, age 40 yrs., bur. Oct. 8, 1797.
Louisa Lesch, age 72 yrs., bur. Oct. 9, 1797.
Catharine Kintzinger, age 3 yrs., 9 mos., 22 days, bur. Oct. 10,
   1797.
Martha Schmid, age 63 yrs., 10 mos., 9 days, bur. Oct. 10, 1797.
Maria Christine Balde, age 27 yrs., 8 mos., 10 days, bur. Oct.
   13, 1797.
Maria Thiel, age 2 yrs., 3 mos., 14 days, bur. Oct. 15, 1797.
Catharine Gartner, age 2 yrs., 4 mos., 17 days, bur. Oct. 18,
   1797.
Elizabeth Balde, age 4 yrs., 6 mos., 7 days, bur. Oct. 23, 1797.
William Christie, age 28 yrs., bur. Oct. 26, 1797.
John Stubert, age 67 yrs., bur. Oct. 27, 1797.
John von der Schleiss, age 3 mos., 13 days, bur. Oct. 29, 1797.
Magdalene Stumb, age 1 yr., 16 days, bur. Oct. 31, 1797.
Sophia Frey, age 1 yr., bur. Nov. 5, 1797.
John Dominick, age 5 yrs., 2 mos., 10 days, bur. Nov. 12, 1797.
Rebecca Wind, age 10 mos., 11 days, bur. Nov. 12, 1797.
Christian Gally, age 66 yrs., 7 mos., 16 days, bur. Nov. 19,
   1797.
----, child of Captain Osmann, age 4 yrs., bur. Nov. 22, 1797.
John Walker, age 1 yr., 3 mos., 13 days, bur. Dec. 19, 1797.
Catharine List, age 35 yrs., 6 mos., bur. Dec. 22, 1797.
John Huhn, age 5 mos., less 1 day, bur. Dec. 26, 1797.
Hannah Lamply, age 23 yrs., 6 mos., 16 days, bur. Dec. 28, 1797.
Elizabeth Gebler, age 21 yrs., 8 mos., 28 days, bur. Dec. 31,
   1797.
Elizabeth Leck, age 1 yr., 1 mo., 6 days, bur. Jan. 4, 1798.
Margaret Sigmund, age 72 yrs., bur. Jan. 5, 1798.
Adam Mayer, age 57 yrs., 2 mos., 3 days, bur. Jan. 9, 1798.
Jacob Bonner, age 47 yrs., 2 mos., 9 days, bur. Jan. 30, 1798.
Catharine Mueller, age 71 yrs., 9 mos., bur. Feb. 1, 1798.
Johanna Stoll, age 29 yrs., 3 mos., 4 days, bur. Feb. 12, 1798.
William Will, age 55 yrs., 7 mos., 17 days, bur. Feb. 12, 1798.
Jacob Wittmann, age 51 yrs., 4 mos., 8 days, bur. Feb. 20, 1798.
George Schmid, age 37 yrs., 11 mos., 19 days, bur. Feb. 25, 1798.
Martin Kramp, age 1 yr., 1 mo., 13 days, bur. March 6, 1798.
John Bender, age 36 yrs., 5 mos., 4 days, bur. March 16, 1798.
--- von Erden, widow, age 79 yrs., bur. March 17, 1798.
Catharine Muth, age 78 yrs., bur. Sept. 26, 1798.
Conrad Stoltz, age 60 yrs., 3 mos., 19 days, bur. Sept. 28, 1798.
Alexander Greenwood, age 65 yrs., bur. April 1, 1798.
Margaret Traub, age 1 yr., 3 mos., bur. April 1, 1798.
---- Gortjus, widow, age 70 yrs., bur. April 3, 1798.
Carl Keller, age 1 yr., 9 mos., 6 days, bur. April 6, 1798.

M. Magdalene Rasber, age 2 yrs., 6 mos., less 3 days, bur. April 7, 1798.
Maria Festinger, age 68 yrs., 11 mos., 9 days, bur. April 11, 1798.
George Degenhard, age 39 yrs., bur. April 22, 1798.
William Felton, age 13 yrs., 5 mos., 6 days, bur. April 23, 1798.
John Eimel, age 1 yr., 9 mos., less 2 days, bur. May 10, 1798.
Maria Obermann, age 5 yrs., 5 mos., 10 days, bur. May 11, 1798.
John Christian Jung, age 4 mos., 12 days, bur. May 17, 1798.
A. Maria Simon, age 4 yrs., 9 mos., 1 day, bur. May 22, 1798.
---- Lescher, widow, age 78 yrs., 2 mos., 15 days, bur. May 29, 1798.
John George Blum, age 69 yrs., 2 mos., 14 days, bur. June 6, 1798.
Joseph Muller, age 9 yrs., 4 mos., 6 days, bur. June 10, 1798.
Elizabeth Zollinger, age 44 yrs., 2 mos., bur. June 13, 1798.
Margaret Willer, age 24 yrs., 1 mo., 11 days, bur. June 13, 1798.
Sarah Miller, age 4 yrs., 8 mos., 10 days, bur. June 15, 1798.
M. Susanna Muller, age 9 mos., less 3 days, bur. June 18, 1798.
Ludwig Reinecke, age 45 yrs., 10 mos., 4 days, bur. June 19, 1798.
Henry Jones Dubs, age 10 mos., less 4 days, bur. June 26, 1798.
John Reichert, age 1 yr., 7 mos., 18 days, bur. June 26, 1798.
Henrietta Braun, age 1 mo., 23 days, bur. June 29, 1798.
John Michael Spangenberg, age 4 mos., 27 days, bur. July 1, 1798.
M. Juliana Jung, age 74 yrs., 5 mos., 1 day, bur. July 1, 1798.
Anna Howe, age 6 mos., 18 days, bur. July 3, 1798.
George Strohhauer, age 32 yrs., 6 mos., 18 days, bur. July 7, 1798.
Michael Hahns, age 1 yr., 3 mos., less 1 day, bur. July 20, 1798.
George Simon, age 1 yr., 3 mos., 14 days, bur. July 20, 1798.
Elizabeth Ried, age 11 mos., 11 days, bur. July 22, 1798.
Catharine Muller, age 6 yrs., 11 mos., 21 days, bur. July 24, 1798.
John Frederick Preuss, age 6 mos., 17 days, bur. July 24, 1798.
Elizabeth Learight, age 9 mos., 6 days, bur. July 25, 1798.
Henry Allburger, age 1 yr., 3 mos., 4 days, bur. July 25, 1798.
Catharine Schaffer, age 1 yr., 5 mos., 13 days, bur. July 26, 1798.
Christian Sinck, killed by a fall from a wagon, age 15 yrs., 8 mos., 17 days, bur. July 29, 1798.
Elizabeth Hartmann, age 54 yrs., 1 mo., 4 days, bur. July 29, 1798.
Catharine Jorden, age 21 yrs., 4 mos., 24 days, bur. July 30, 1798.
Frederick A. Schneider, age 7 mos., 25 days, bur. Aug. 1, 1798.
Sarah Newton, age 11 mos., 5 days, bur. Aug. 2, 1798.
Elizabeth Dewald, age 17 yrs., 4 mos., 6 days, bur. Aug. 6, 1798.
M. Magdalene Leonhard, age 10 mos., 4 days, bur. Aug. 9, 1798.
Elizabeth Cronetfield, age 1 yr., less 6 days, bur. Aug. 10, 1798.
John Aesch, age ----, bur. Aug. 11, 1798.
Thomas Wind, age 1 yr., 8 mos., 3 days, bur. Aug. 15, 1798.
A. Margaret Jones, age 1 yr., 7 mos., less 1 day, bur. Aug. 15, 1798.

Susanna Graul, age 1 yr., 1 mo., 24 days, bur. Aug. 18, 1798.
Rachel Dorffer, age 1 yr., 3 mos., 14 days, bur. Aug. 19, 1798.
Samuel Kreiter, age 8 mos., less 3 days, bur. Aug. 19, 1798.
---- Hoffman, age ----, bur. Aug. 20, 1798.
Wife of Michael Schmid, age ----, bur. Aug. 21, 1798.
Conrad Scherer, age 63 yrs., 10 mos., 11 days, bur. Aug. 22, 1798.
Conrad Munch, age 68 yrs., 5 mos., less 3 days, bur. Aug. 24, 1798.
----, age 85 yrs., bur. Aug. 25, 1798.
Thomas West, age ----, bur. Aug. 26, 1798.
--- Etris, age 18 yrs., bur. Aug. 26, 1798.
Sarah Stricker, age ----, bur. Aug. 28, 1798.
---- Schlemmer, widow, age ----, bur. Aug. 28, 1798.
Elizabeth Loyd, age 1 yr., 6 mos., 19 days, bur. Aug. 29, 1798.
Magdalene Flick, age ----, bur. Aug. 29, 1798.
Susanna Follwell, age 1 yr., 5 mos., 10 days, bur. Aug. 30, 1798.
William Skinner, age ----, bur. Aug. 30, 1798.
(Rev. John William Hendel died of yellow fever on Sept. 29, 1798.)

BURIALS BY REV. SAMUEL HELFFENSTEIN
1799 - 1800

John Bodt, age 34 yrs., 5 mos., bur. March 6, 1799.
Henry Frick, age 48 yrs., 2 mos., 4 days, bur. March 5, 1799.
Elizabeth Reed, age 48 yrs., bur. March 21, 1799.
Anna Maria Dashimer, age 23 yrs., 3 mos., 2 days, bur. April 16, 1799.
Anna Magdalene Schaffner, age 63 yrs., 5 mos., bur. April 22, 1799.
---- (Mrs.) Boem, age 65 yrs., bur. May 4, 1799.
Hannah Deal, age 76 yrs., bur. May 5, 1799.
George Zahner, age 48 yrs., 2 mos., 3 days, bur. May 21, 1799.
Anna Volck, age 7 mos., 2 days, bur. June 7, 1799.
J. Christian Fuhr, age 54 yrs., 8 mos., 3 days, bur. June 10, 1799.
Elizabeth Spies, age 38 yrs., 6 mos., bur. June 24, 1799.
John Henry Waskan, age 25 yrs., 4 mos., bur. July 5, 1799.
Barbara Volweiler, age 72 yrs., 9 mos., 9 days, bur. July 7, 1799.
Valentine Leyer, age 92 yrs., 6 mos., 2 days, bur. July 10, 1799.
Child of Jacob Fan, age 9 mos., 15 days, bur. July 25, 1799.
Wm. Castmer, age 7 mos., 3 days, bur. July 29, 1799.
Fredeica Ulrick, age 40 yrs., 5 mos., bur. Aug. 1, 1799.
Anna M. Menn, age 46 yrs., 17 days, bur. Aug. 3, 1799.
Maria Backoven, age 1 yr., 4 mos., bur. Aug. 3, 1799.
Adam Lutz, age 68 yrs., 2 mos., 2 days, bur. Aug. 10, 1799.
Child of Jacob Holliday, age 2 yrs., 9 mos., bur. Aug. 10, 1799.
Child of John Snider, age 2 yrs., 9 mos., 3 days, bur. Aug. 13, 1799.
Child of George Faunce, age 1 yr., 8 mos., 5 days, bur. Aug. 26, 1799.
Child of Wm. Raul, age 8 mos., 3 days, bur. Aug. 27, 1799.
Jenny Williams, age 27 yrs., 2 mos., 10 days, bur. Sept. 25,

1799.
Anna Maria Dahlman, age 1 yr., 3 mos., 25 days, bur. Sept. --,
  1799.
John Pistor, age 59 yrs., bur. Sept. 25, 1799.
David Guldi, age 5 yrs., 6 mos., 27 days, bur. Sept. 25, 1799.
Paul Britton, died of stroke, age 77 yrs., 2 mos., bur. Nov. 7,
  1799.
John Fraily, age 52 yrs., 2 mos., bur. Sept. 29, 1800.
Child of John Osmon, age 2 yrs., bur. Oct. 2, 1800.
Child of Ludwig Hirt, age 11 mos., bur. Oct. 2, 1800.
Anna Mar. Jork, age 53 yrs., 4 mos., bur. Oct. 4, 1800.
Child of Peter Walter, age 1 yr., 12 mos., bur. Oct. 18, 1800.
John Weiberg, age 28 yrs., 4 mos., bur. June 1, 1801.
Elijah Raus, age 63 yrs., bur. June 13, 1801.
Cath. Bradler, age 67 yrs., bur. June 15, 1801.
Eliz. Steemel, age 40 yrs., bur. June 1, 1801.
Maria Welsh, age 1 yr., 2 days, bur. June 20, 1801.
Christ. Reiff, age 69 yrs., 1 mo., 4 days, bur. June 22, 1801.
David Sauers, age 4 yrs., 1 mo., 12 days, bur. June 23, 1801.
Albertus Pharlock, age 70 yrs., 9 mos., 13 days, bur. Feb. 1,
  1801.
Anna Muralt, age 67 yrs., 27 days, bur. Feb. 23, 1801.
Child of Mr. Porkenpine, age 2 mos., 2 days, bur. Feb. 25, 1801.
Child of John Blyeler, age 10 mos., 10 days, bur. March 10, 1801.
---- Mackentier, widow, age 22 yrs., 5 mos., bur. March 10, 1801.
Child of David Bloyd, age 1 yr., 7 mos., bur. March 11, 1801.
Child of John Wacker, age 3 yrs., 2 mos., 20 days, bur. March 14,
  1801.
Wm. Rebsel, age 79 yrs., 1 mo., bur. March 15, 1801.
Elizabeth Elfey, age 13 yrs., bur. March 20, 1801.
Child of Mr. Wacker, age 3 yrs., 2 mos., bur. ----.
Wife of Heltzheimer, age 33 yrs., 4 mos., bur. ----.
Eliz. Yeager, age 25 yrs., 11 mos., 2 days, bur. March 27, 1801.

BAPTISMS BY DR. WILLIAM HENDEL
1797 - 1798
Andrew, son of Adam Bayer and Rebecca, b. June 18, 1797, bapt.
  July 22, 1797. Spon: Andrew Levy and Magdalene.
Anna, daughter of John Frantz and Catharine, b. May 6, 1797,
  bapt. July 27, 1797. Spon: The mother.
John, son of George von der Schleis and Elizabeth, b. July 14,
  1797, bapt. July 27, 1797. Spon: Anthony von der Schleis and
  Elizabeth.
Jacob, son of John Hoffman and Catharine, b. Feb. 5, 1797, bapt.
  July 30, 1797. Spon: Parents.
Elizabeth, daughter of Henry Wagner and Catharine, b. July 6,
  1797, bapt. July 30, 1797. Spon: Parents.
Hannah, daughter of Benjamin Paul and Susanna, b. Jan. 13, 1796,
  bapt. July 30, 1797. Spon: Philip Weber and Hannah.
Samuel, son of Samuel Walker and Catharine, b. March 17, 1794,
  bapt. Aug. 1, 1797. Spon: Christine Huhn, grandmother.
John, son of Samuel Walker and Catharine, b. Sept. 5, 1796, bapt.
  Aug. 1, 1797. Spon: The mother.
John George, son of Henry Strupp and Susanna, b. June 27, 1797,

bapt. Aug. 11, 1797. Spon: The father.
Jacobina Wilhelmina, daughter of Abraham Friederis and
Wilhelmina, b. July 2, 1797, bapt. Aug. 12, 1797. Spon: Jean
Boussier and Sarah Rabel.
Elizabeth, daughter of Gottfried Mayer and Elizabeth, b. July 21,
1797, bapt. Aug. 13, 1797. Spon: George Langenbach and
Elizabeth.
Carl, son of Peter Umrichhaus and Maria, b. Nov. 19, 1796, bapt.
Aug. 14, 1797. Spon: Parents.
Sarah, daughter of William Fusselbach and Margaret, b. Feb. 26,
1796, bapt. Aug. 14, 1797. Spon: ------.
John Frederick, son of Casper Hollenbrand and A. Elizabeth Weber,
b. March 23, 1797, bapt. Aug. 14, 1797. Spon: Margaret
Eichbach.
Carl, son of Carl Geyer and Maria, b. July 1, 1797, bapt. Aug.
20, 1797. Spon: Parents.
Anna, daughter of Forbes Newton and Elizabeth, b. June 18, 1797,
bapt. Aug. 20, 1797. Spon: The mother.
M. Margaret, daughter of Henry Trimber and Elizabeth, b. July 24,
1797, bapt. Aug. 20, 1797. Spon: Parents.
Elizabeth, daughter of Jacob Bretz and Eva, b. July 17, 1797,
bapt. Aug. 20, 1797. Spon: Parents for Elizabeth Bortz.
Elizabeth, daughter of John Ried and Elizabeth, b. Aug. 10, 1797,
bapt. Aug. 21, 1797. Spon: Parents.
Frederick, son of Frederick Scheiblin and Anna, b. July 9, 1797,
bapt. Aug. 21, 1797. Spon: Parents.
Thomas, son of Jacob Zeiner and Elizabeth, b. Aug. 20, 1797,
bapt. Aug. 21, 1797. Spon: The father and Maria Zimmerman.
Catharine, daughter of George Mill and Margaret, b. Aug. 12,
1797, bapt. Aug. 25, 1797. Spon: Catharine Doerr.
Samuel, son of Casper Henrich and Elizabeth, b. Aug. 15, 1797,
bapt. Aug. 27, 1797. Spon: Parents.
Ludwig, son of Adam Stoll and Elizabeth, b. July 26, 1797, bapt.
Aug. 27, 1797. Spon: Ludwig Froscher and Christine.
John, son of Jacob Lescher and Maria, b. July 29, 1797, bapt.
Aug. 29, 1797. Spon: Parents.
John, son of John Newman and A. Margaret, b. ---- 1793, bapt.
Aug. 31, 1797. Spon: Henry Volck and A. Catharine.
Peter, son of Peter Koch and Elizabeth, b. Aug. 24, 1797, bapt.
Aug. 31, 1797. Spon: Regina Otto.
William, son of John Lehman and Elizabeth, b. Aug. 14, 1797,
bapt. Sept. 3, 1797. Spon: William Nickels and Hannah.
Elizabeth, daughter of Jacob Ebel and Margaret, b. Aug. 7, 1797,
bapt. Sept. 3, 1797. Spon: John Christian and Elizabeth Ried.
Martha, daughter of William Johnson and Catharine, b. Aug. 15,
1797, bapt. Sept. 4, 1797. Spon: Parents.
Maria, daughter of Henry Lisch and Elizabeth, b. March 17, 1797,
bapt. Sept. 4, 1797. Spon: Parents.
Elizabeth, daughter of Daniel Schittel and Elizabeth, b. April 5,
1797, bapt. Sept. 6, 1797. Spon: Adam Ford and the mother.
Christopher, son of Nicholas Ries and M. Dunsula, b. Sept. 15,
1797, bapt. Oct. ---- 1797. Spon: J. M-------- (torn).
A. Maria, daughter of Adam May and Catharine, b. Oct. 8, 1797,
bapt. Oct. ---- 1797. Spon: Parents.
William, son of Anthony Weis and Elizabeth, b. Sept. 19, 1797,

bapt. Oct. 1797. Spon: William von Phul and A. Catharine.
Joseph, son of Joseph West and Maria, b. Oct. 11, 1793, bapt.
Oct. ---- 1797. Spon: Susanna Weit.
John, son of Frederick Dickes and Catharine, b. Sept. 10, 1797,
bapt. Oct. ---- 1797. Spon: John Pfau and M. Elizabeth.
Maria, daughter of Peter Peres and Veronica, b. Sept. 25, 1797,
bapt. Oct. ---- 1797. Spon: Henry Fahns and Veronica.
William, son of Edward Rigg and Charlotte, b. Sept. 1, 1797,
bapt. Oct. 9, 1797. Spon: Elizabeth Rabanus, grandmother.
Jacob, son of Thos. Shillingford and Rosina, b. Dec. 9, 1793,
bapt. Oct. 9, 1797. Spon: The mother.
Sarah, daughter of Jacob Halter and Maria, b. Aug. 25, 1797,
bapt. Oct. 9, 1797. Spon: Rosina Shillingsford.
Jacob, son of Lawrence Hill and Susanna, b. July 4, 1797, bapt.
Oct. 9, 1797. Spon: The mother.
Elizabeth, daughter of Jacob Hoffmann and Eva, b. Oct. 12, 1797,
bapt. Oct. ---- 1797. Spon: Veronica Poht.
Robert, son of Robert King and Dorothy Schneider, b. Oct. 14,
1797, bapt. Oct. ---- 1797. Spon: -----
William, son of William Wiand and Maria Christine, b. Sept. 22,
1797, bapt. Oct. 30, 1797. Spon: Parents.
A. Maria, daughter of Frederick Meile and Barbara, b. Sept. 11,
1797, bapt. Nov. 2, 1797. Spon: A. Maria Grunstatt.
Catharine Elizabeth, daughter of George Braun and Elizabeth, b.
Oct. 28, 1797, bapt. Nov. 1, 1797. Spon: M. Catharine Reyer.
Margaret, daughter of Robert Murdock and M. Christine, b. Oct.
12, 1797, bapt. Nov. 3, 1797. Spon: The mother.
Alexander, son of Alexander Crawford and Elizabeth, b. Oct. 19,
1797, bapt. Nov. 9, 1797. Spon: George Bell and Catharine
Lamber.
A. Margaret, daughter of George Mayer and Sarah, b. Oct. 1, 1797,
bapt. Nov. 9, 1797. Spon: Conrad Dittman and Gertrude.
Sophia Magdalene, daughter of Adam Becker and M. Magdalene, b.
Sept. 30, 1797, bapt. Dec. 2, 1797. Spon: John Adam Rehbein
and Sophia M. Marty.
Barbara Elizabeth, daughter of J. George Einwachter and
Elizabeth, b. Oct. 18, 1797, bapt. Dec. ---- 1797. Spon: The
mother.
Margaret, daughter of George Becker and Sophia, b. Oct. 27, 1797,
bapt. Nov. ---- 1797. Spon: Jacob Ru---- and Margaret (torn).
Jacob, son of John Ostheim and Johanna, b. Nov. 7, 1797, bapt.
Nov. ---- 1797. Spon: Jacob Huhn.
Elizabeth, daughter of Henry Jeckle and Anna, b. Nov. 14, 1797,
bapt. Nov. ---- 1797. Spon: George Weis and Elizabeth Ederis.
Sarah, daughter of William Reichard and Elizabeth, b. Oct. 29,
1797, bapt. Nov. 24, 1797. Spon: Parents.
Elizabeth, daughter of Matthew Dischong and Elisabeth, b. Nov.
17, 1797, bapt. Nov. 24, 1797. Spon: Parents.
Carl, son of Henry Strub and Susanna, b. Oct. 25, 1797, bapt.
Nov. 25, 1797. Spon: Parents.
Thomas, son of John Porter and Catharine, b. Oct. 25, 1797, bapt.
Nov. 26, 1797. Spon: Parents.
Henry, son of John Porter and Catharine, b. Jan. 26, 1793, bapt.
Feb. 15, 1793. Spon: Parents.
John Casper, son of John Ludwig Faber and Catharine, b. Oct. 31,

1797, bapt. Nov. 30, 1797. Spon: John Casper and Louisa
Bruch(?).
A. Margaret, daughter of Herman Leck and A. Margaret, b. Nov. 8,
1797, bapt. Nov. 30, 1797. Spon: Jacob Schesterstein(?) and
A. Margaret.
Margaret, daughter of Ludwig Diemer and Hannah, b. June 7, 1797,
bapt. Nov. 30, 1797. Spon: Parents.
Elizabeth, daughter of Martin Guckes and Catharine, b. Feb. 7,
1797, bapt. Nov. 30, 1797. Spon: John Bernard May and
Elizabeth Walther.
Elizabeth, daughter of Philip Justus and Elizabeth, b. Nov. 8,
1797, bapt. Nov. 30, 1797. Spon: Parents.
Adam, son of Adam Bayer and Rebecca, b. Oct. 18, 1797, bapt. Nov.
30, 1797. Spon: Adam Bayer, the father.
Margaret, daughter of Henry Schmid and Elizabeth, b. Nov. 19,
1797, bapt. Dec. 7, 1797. Spon: John Aescher and Margaret.
John, son of Joseph Woods and Margaret, b. Nov. 2, 1797, bapt.
Dec. 7, 1797. Spon: John Ryan and Catharine.
John, son of Lawrence Herman and Maria, b. Oct. 26, 1797, bapt.
Dec. 7, 1797. Spon: The mother.
A. Maria, daughter of George Wilson and Hannah, b. Aug. 18, 1797,
bapt. Dec. 8, 1797. Spon: Justus Stoo---- and Maria.
Magdalene, daughter of John George Rummel and Magdalene, b. Sept.
29, 1797, bapt. Dec. 11, 1797. Spon: Parents.
Elizabeth, daughter of Nicholas Juvenal and Susanna, b. Dec. 3,
1797, bapt. Dec. ---- 1797. Spon: The father and -----.
Peter, son of John Froh (?) and Catharine, b. Nov. 4, 1797, bapt.
Nov. 11, 1797. Spon: Peter Weidner and Catharine.
Henry William, son of Jonathan Miller and Catharine, b. Sept. 23,
1797, bapt. Nov. 12, 1797. Spon: Parents.
George, son of John Becker and Barbara, b. Oct. 15, 1797, bapt.
Nov. 18, 1797. Spon: Parents.
Maria, daughter of Michael Esch and Sarah, b. Oct. 15, 1797,
bapt. Nov. 19, 1797. Spon: Parents.
A. Maria, daughter of Philip Ehringer and Magdalene, b. Oct. 21,
1797, bapt. Nov. 19, 1797. Spon: Parents.
Elizabeth, daughter of Matthew Benner and Sarah, b. Sept. 15,
1797, bapt. Nov. 22, 1797. Spon: Elizabeth Ockel.
Joshua, son of Christopher Schmid and Maria, b. Nov. 19, 1797,
bapt. Nov. 20, 1797. Spon: Joshua Schmid.
Simon Peter, son of Jacob Diel and Elizabeth, b. Nov. 1, 1797,
bapt. Dec. 3, 1797. Spon: Parents.
John George, son of Matthias Nelson and A. Maria, b. Nov. 19,
1797, bapt. Nov. 26, 1797. Spon: John George and Margaret
Miller.
Elizabeth, daughter of Peter Dickes and Elizabeth, b. Sept. 22,
1797, bapt. Dec. 10, 1797. Spon: Parents.
Sarah Anna, daughter of John Mckelroy and Catharine, b. Oct.
8, 1797, bapt. Dec. 10, 1797. Spon: Christopher Henrich and
Anna.
Elizabeth, daughter of Henry Appel and Elizabeth, b. Nov. 27,
1797, bapt. Dec. 10, 1797. Spon: David Dreichsler and
Margaret.
Elizabeth, daughter of Nicholas Macks and M. Magdalene, b. Oct.
6, 1797, bapt. Dec. ---- 1797. Spon: Thomas West and

Elizabeth.

Frederick, son of Sebastian Sallede and M. Magdalene, b. Dec. 1, 1797, bapt. ------. Spon: Parents.

Joseph, son of John Schneider and M. Magdalene, b. Dec. 9, 1797, bapt. ------. Spon: Parents.

Bernard, son of Frederick Thies and Elizabeth, b. Nov. 23, 1797, bapt. ------. Spon: Bernard Kauffman and Margaret.

David, son of Casper Weideman and Maria, b. Oct. 4, 1797, bapt. - -----. Spon: Henry Sauer and Barbara Berger.

Margaret Weber nee Breeding of ----, b. March 23, 1769, bapt. Dec. 24, 1797. Spon: ----.

John, son of Gerhard Huhn and Maria, b. July 26, 1797, bapt. Dec. 25, 1797. Spon: Daniel Huhn and Christiana.

Maximilian, son of John Litsch and Maria, b. Nov. 30, 1797, bapt. Dec. 25, 1797. Spon: Susanna Moser.

Frederick August, son of Jacob Schneider and Agnes, b. Dec. 7, 1797, bapt. Dec. 28, 1797. Spon: Frederick August and Margaret Bach.

John George, son of Peter Schreiber and Sarah, b. Dec. 12, 1797, bapt. Dec. 28, 1797. Spon: Parents.

John, son of Jacob Hoffman and Anna, b. Dec. 24, 1797, bapt. Dec. 31, 1797. Spon: John Meisner and A. Maria.

John, son of Henry Green and Catharine, b. Sept. 12, 1797, bapt. Dec. 31, 1797. Spon: John Weber and Anna.

Magdalene, daughter of Jacob Weyand and Salome, b. Jan. 3, 1797, bapt. Jan. 1, 1798. Spon: George Dibleret(?) and Magdalene.

Andrew, son of John Kelly and Catharine, b. Nov. 11, 1797, bapt. Jan. 1, 1798. Spon: Andrew Nelson and Lucy.

Peter, son of John Immel and Maria, b. Dec. 28, 1797, bapt. Jan. 2, 1798. Spon: Parents.

Elizabeth, daughter of John Hopp and Margaret Bollbach, b. Jan. 4, 1798, bapt. Jan. 4, 1798. Spon: Elizabeth ---.

George, son of Michael Haehns and Magdalene, b. Oct. 15, 1797, bapt. Jan. 7, 1798. Spon: George Jung and Maria.

Charlotte, daughter of Henry Schmid and Elizabeth, b. Dec. 23, 1797, bapt. Jan. 11, 1798. Spon: John ------ and Charlotte.

Amelia, daughter of George Ozeas and Maria, b. Dec. 22, 1797, bapt. Jan. 12, 1798. Spon: Parents.

John Christian, son of Christopher Jung and Maria, b. Jan. 4, 1798, bapt. Jan. 14, 1798. Spon: Christian ------and Magdalene.

Henry and Jacob (twins), sons of Werner Defort and M. Magdalene, b. Nov. 13, 1797, bapt. Jan. 14, 1798. Spon: Frederick Erckes(?) and Parents.

M. Catharine, daughter of Jacob Schlemmer and Hannah, b. Dec. 18, 1797, bapt. Jan. 15, 1798. Spon: George Lutz and Maria.

Rachel, daughter of Henry Roskes and M., b. Jan. 2, 1798, bapt. Jan. 15, 1798. Spon: Parents.

William, son of Jacob Reineck and A. Maria, b. Jan. 7, 1798, bapt. Jan. 17, 1798. Spon: Parents.

George, son of Nicholas Weyrich and Susanna, b. May 7, 1797, bapt. Jan. 18, 1798. Spon: George Mayer and Susanna.

Anna, daughter of James Cameron and Elizabeth, b. Jan. 8, 1798, bapt. Jan. 21, 1798. Spon: Henry Coxe and Ann Wiley.

David, son of John Leher and Catharine, b. Jan. 15, 1798, bapt.

Jan. 22, 1798. Spon: John Schneider and Margaret.
William, son of Jacob Kemp and Maria, b. Jan. 12, 1798, bapt.
Jan. 28, 1798. Spon: Adam Dorr and Catharine.
M. Margaret, daughter of John Walker and A. Margaret, b. Dec. 23,
1797, bapt. Jan. 28, 1798. Spon: John Wester and M. Margaret.
A. Maria, daughter of Adam Buser and Margaret, b. Dec. 21, 1797,
bapt. Feb. 1, 1798. Spon: A. Maria Velten.
Elizabeth, daughter of William Skinner and Elizabeth, b. Jan. 6,
1798, bapt. Feb. 4, 1798. Spon: Parents.
M. Catharine, daughter of George Sauerhoffer and Philippina, b.
January 11, 1798, bapt. Feb. 4, 1798. Spon: Jacob
Sauerhoffer and Catharine.
Joseph, son of John Huhn and Christine, b. Dec. 10, 1797, bapt.
Feb. 4, 1798. Spon: Parents.
Peter Laury, son of Samuel Karcher and Susanna, b. Jan. 1, 1798,
bapt. Feb. 4, 1798. Spon: Peter Laury and Johanna.
Norris Philip, son of Samuel Karcher and Susanna, b. Jan. 1,
1798, bapt. Feb. 4, 1798. Spon: Philip Helffenstein.
Johanna Maria, daughter of John Michael and Johanna Maria, b.
Jan. 23, 1798, bapt. Feb. 6, 1798. Spon: Parents.
Samuel, son of Frederick Kreider and Veronica, b. Dec. 21, 1797,
bapt. Feb. 11, 1798. Spon: Parents.
Sophia, daughter of John Schneider and Elizabeth, b. Feb. 25,
1797, bapt. Feb. 17, 1798. Spon: Parents.
M. Magdalene, daughter of John Schuteis and Margaret, b. Feb. 7,
1798, bapt. Feb. 18, 1798. Spon: Daniel Muller and M.
Magdalene.
Mariann, daughter of Jacob Alburger and Margaret, b. Jan. 26,
1798, bapt. Feb. 18, 1798. Spon: Philip Allburger and M.
Gassman.
William, son of John Braupert and Philippina, b. Feb. 7, 1798,
bapt. Feb. 18, 1798. Spon: Parents.
Henry, son of Jacob Hahns and Catharine, b. Jan. 31, 1798, bapt.
Feb. 19, 1798. Spon: Henry Hahns and Veronica.
A. Elizabeth, daughter of Jost Menes and Maria, b. Feb. 13, 1798,
bapt. Feb. 22, 1798. Spon: Ludwig Schneider and Elizabeth.
A. Catharine, daughter of Frederick Balt and A. Christine, b.
Feb. 10, 1798, bapt. Feb. 22, 1798. Spon: Henry Bald and A.
Catharine.
Rebecca, daughter of Philip Peltz and Rebecca, b. Feb. 21, 1798,
bapt. Feb. 24, 1798. Spon: Parents.
Solomon, son of Jacob Vollback and Christine, b. Feb. 20, 1798,
bapt. Feb. 25, 1798. Spon: Parents.
Sarah, daughter of George Juncker and Maria, b. Jan. 27, 1798,
bapt. Feb. 26, 1798. Spon: Bernard Kaufman and Margaret.
George, son of Henry Lange and A. Catharine, b. Feb. 16, 1798,
bapt. March 4, 1798. Spon: George Nic. Hausel and Hannah.
Maria, daughter of Jacob Sigmund and Catharine, b. Jan. 26, 1798,
bapt. March 5, 1798. Spon: Henry Dipperling and Margaret.
John, son of Joseph Schmid and Barbara, b. Feb. 26, 1798, bapt.
March 6, 1798. Spon: Matthias Poht and Veronica.
Henry, son of Henry Schneider and Elizabeth, b. Dec. 12, 1797,
bapt. March 11, 1798. Spon: Parents.
Catharine, daughter of Jacob Belsterling and M. Magdalene, b.
Feb. 7, 1798, bapt. March 11, 1798. Spon: Carl Hesel and

Catharine.
John Henry, son of John Klapp and Maria, b. Feb. 13, 1798, bapt.
March 13, 1798. Spon: Parents.
Joseph, son of Jacob Kreider and Elizabeth, b. Feb. 2, 1798,
bapt. March 15, 1798. Spon: Parents.
Margaret, daughter of John Simpson and Susanna, b. Feb. 1, 1797,
bapt. March 15, 1798. Spon: John Davison and the mother.
Rebecca, daughter of Joseph Bennet and Catharine, b. Nov. 21,
1797, bapt. March 16, 1798. Spon: The mother
Henry, son of John Reide and Margaret, b. Feb. 24, 1798, bapt.
March 18, 1798. Spon: Henry Emert and Magdalene.
Margaret, daughter of Henry Schell and Hannah, b. Feb. 27, 1798,
bapt. March 18, 1798. Spon: Parents.
Henry, son of Frederick Schmid and Margaret, b. Feb. 18, 1798,
bapt. March 18, 1798. Spon: Parents.
Elizabeth, daughter of George Brunner and Catharine, b. Jan. 30,
1798, bapt. March 18, 1798. Spon: Parents.
John, son of William Reinhard and Christine, b. Jan. 5, 1798,
bapt. Jan. 25, 1798. Spon: Parents.
Michael, son of Michael Keller and Hannah, b. Nov. 12, 1797,
bapt. March 26, 1798. Spon: The mother
Salome, daughter of Philip Gasser and Maria, b. March 15, 1798,
bapt. March 26, 1798. Spon: The father and Maria Sorg.
John Frederick, son of Carl Preis and Maria, b. Jan. 6, 1798,
bapt. March 26, 1798. Spon: John Fred. Dickes and Catharine.
Elizabeth, daughter of Carl Preis and Maria, b. Jan. 6, 1798,
bapt. March 26, 1798. Spon: Parents.
William, son of Abraham Hunoltz and Catharine, b. Jan. 9, 1798,
bapt. March 30, 1798. Spon: Philippina Hein and Anna Procter.
Maria, daughter of Frederick Zahn and Susanna, b. March 23, 1798,
bapt. March 31, 1798. Spon: John Dietrich and Maria
Derenberger.
Samuel, son of Jacob Eckstein and Elizabeth, b. March 7, 1798,
bapt. April 1, 1798. Spon: Parents.
Magdalene, daughter of John Stumpf and Magdalene, b. Jan. 15,
1798, bapt. April 1, 1798. Spon: Parents.
Catharine, daughter of John Messner and Maria, b. Jan. 3, 1798,
bapt. April 1, 1798. Spon: Parents.
Catharine Elizabeth, daughter of John Jost Bald and A. Maria, b.
Aug. 18, 1797, bapt. April 5, 1798. Spon: Parents.
Cordilla Volck of ----, b. Jan. 27, 1774, bapt. April 6, 1798.
Spon: ----
Magdalene, daughter of John Beck and Catharine, b. March 14,
1798, bapt. April 8, 1798. Spon: Herman Beck and A. Margaret.
Maria, daughter of Martin Muller and Elizabeth, b. Sept. 15,
1797, bapt. April 9, 1798. Spon: Parents.
Catharine, daughter of John Ryan and Catharine, b. March 7, 1798,
bapt. April 11, 1798. Spon: Parents.
Jacob Rust, son of Frederick Haster and Elizabeth, b. Feb. 18,
1798, bapt. April 15, 1798. Spon: The father and Christine
Hautz.
Maria, daughter of Matthew Birckenbeil and Catharine, b. March
12, 1798, bapt. April 15, 1798. Spon: Parents.
Elizabeth, daughter of Philip Alburger, Jr. and Dorothy, b. March
21, 1798, bapt. April 15, 1798. Spon: John Alburger and Maria

Kleber.
Maria, daughter of J. Conrad Steinmetz and Anna, b. Dec. 3, 1797, bapt. April 15, 1798. Spon: John Fischer and A. Maria.
Elizabeth, daughter of Abraham Ohlwein and Rebecca, b. Oct. 17, 1793, bapt. April 16, 1798. Spon: Conrad Scherer and Mary Magdalene.
Anthony Wayne, son of Abraham Ohlwein and Rebecca, b. Aug. 30, 1797, bapt. April 16, 1798. Spon: Conrad Scherer and Mary Magdalene.
John, son of George Eisenring and M. Elizabeth, b. March 22, 1798, bapt. April 19, 1798. Spon: Parents.
Catharine, daughter of Frederick Weber and Frederica, b. April 1, 1798, bapt. April 19, 1798. Spon: John Jost Weber and Catharine.
A. Maria, daughter of Conrad Becker, Jr. and Susanna, b. March 23, 1798, bapt. April 19, 1798. Spon: Frederick Fraly and A. Maria Becker.
Jacob, son of John Schreiner and A. Maria, b. Feb. 22, 1797, bapt. April 19, 1798. Spon: Christopher Schreiner and Susanna.
Amelia, daughter of Adam May and Catharine, b. March 5, 1798, bapt. April 22, 1798. Spon: Parents.
Elizabeth, daughter of Joseph Vogel and Johanna Maria, b. April 1, 1798, bapt. April 24, 1798. Spon: The mother.
Christiana, daughter of Frederick Novick and Sarah, b. April 20, 1798, bapt. May 2, 1798. Spon: The father and Margaret Gally, grandmother.
Jacob, son of Jacob Gucker, Jr. and Magdalene, b. April 4, 1798, bapt. May 4, 1798. Spon: Jacob Gucker and Magdalene.
William, son of Christian Hans and Sophia, b. April 25, 1798, bapt. May 6, 1798. Spon: Henry Kress and Maria.
Elizabeth, daughter of Conrad Weil and Elizabeth, b. April 6, 1798, bapt. May 6, 1798. Spon: Nicholas Rothenwalder and Elizabeth.
George William, son of John Becker, Jr. and Catharine, b. April 4, 1798, bapt. May 6, 1798. Spon: Geo. William Gebel.
Catharine, daughter of Valentine Gaertner and M. Magdalene, b. April 24, 1798, bapt. May 7, 1798. Spon: Anthony Zahner and Catharine.
Casper, son of William Reide and Sarah, b. April 25, 1798, bapt. May 10, 1798. Spon: Parents.
Margaret, daughter of Joseph Wood and Margaret, b. Oct. 10, 1797, bapt. May 13, 1798. Spon: George Alexander and Margaret Stetzebach, grandmother.
Rachel, daughter of Martin Haas and Anna, b. April 23, 1798, bapt. May 14, 1798. Spon: Parents.
Elizabeth, daughter of John Stricker and Sarah, b. April 28, 1798, bapt. May 20, 1798. Spon: Parents.
Anna, daughter of John Osman and Elizabeth, b. Feb. 15, 1797, bapt. May 20, 1798. Spon: Parents.
William, son of John Miller and Margaret, b. Nov. 1, 1795, baptized May 23, 1798. Spon: Elizabeth Frasher and the father.
Henrietta, daughter of John Miller and Margaret, b. Oct. 30, 1797, bapt. May 23, 1798. Spon: Magdalene Langkopf.

William, son of Adam Gaul and Elizabeth, b. Feb. 17, 1798, bapt.
May 27, 1798. Spon: Elizabeth Degenfeld.
Joseph, son of Jacob M. Kaert and Elizabeth, b. May 6, 1798,
bapt. May 27, 1798. Spon: Bernard Kaert and Catharine.
Maria, daughter of Frederick Jordan and Catharine, b. May 6,
1798, bapt. May 28, 1798. Spon: Frederick Becker and Maria.
Anna Maria, daughter of Joseph Cloud and A. Maria Hessheisen, b.
June 24, 1797, bapt. June 3, 1798. Spon: Jacob Henrigel and
Maria Dietz.
A. Maria, daughter of Richard Teston and Hannah, b. May 10, 1798,
bapt. June 3, 1798. Spon: Jacob Sinck and Catharine.
Catharine, daughter of Philip Ohler and Catharine, b. May 18,
1798, bapt. June 3, 1798. Spon: Jacob Sinck and Catharine.
John, son of John Jost Weber and A. Catharina, b. May 27, 1798,
bapt. June 7, 1798. Spon: Parents.
Maria, daughter of Joseph Kubler and Rachel, b. April 29, 1798,
bapt. June 10, 1798. Spon: Parents.
Henrietta, daughter of Peter Braun and Catharine, b. May 5, 1798,
bapt. June 10, 1798. Spon: John Braun and Margaret Grob.
Jacob, son of Adam Mayer and Hannah, b. June 2, 1798, bapt. June
10, 1798. Spon: Parents.
Elizabeth, daughter of Andrew Sprohl and Hannah, b. June 6, 1798,
bapt. June 10, 1798. Spon: Parents.
Joseph, son of Jacob Egoff and Maria, b. July 27, 1797, bapt.
June 15, 1798. Spon: Frederick Hailer and A. Christine.
John, son of John Stetzenbach and Margaret, b. May 15, 1798,
bapt. June 16, 1798. Spon: Parents.
Peter, son of Henry Jetter and Catharine, b. June 9, 1798, bapt.
June 24, 1798. Spon: Peter Schaaff and M. Eva.
John Phillip, son of John Jones and Elizabeth, b. April 5, 1798,
bapt. June 24, 1798. Spon: John Philip Kaltwasser and
Elizabeth.
Michael, son of John Spangenberg and Charlotte, b. Feb. 3, 1798,
bapt. June 25, 1798. Spon: Parents.
Eleonora, daughter of Patrick Smith and Elizabeth, b. May 31,
1798, bapt. June 27, 1798. Spon: Parents.
John Ludwig, son of Ludwig Klotz and Elizabeth Gertrude, b. June
24, 1798, bapt. June 30, 1798. Spon: The father.
Anna, daughter of Samuel Howe and Margaret, b. Dec. 14, 1797,
bapt. July 2, 1798. Spon: Elizabeth Stuber.
Henry, son of Henry Franck and A. Maria, b. June 13, 1798,
baptized July 3, 1798. Spon: Parents.
Adeline, daughter of Alexander Tardy and Catharine, born
December 2, 1797, bapt. July 3, 1798. Spon: John Jousse
and A. Catharine Elliot.
William, son of Peter Peres and Veronica, b. June 15, 1798, bapt.
July 5, 1798. Spon: Henry Hahns and Veronica.
Benjamin, son of John Schermayer and Catharine, b. March 25,
1798, bapt. July 7, 1798. Spon: John Schmidt and M.
Magdalene.
Dorothy, daughter of Jacob Maurer and Catharine, b. April 5,
1798, bapt. July 8, 1798. Spon: Dorothy Diemer.
Maria, daughter of John Fred. Gaul and M. Margaret, b. Aug. 18,
1797, bapt. July 8, 1798. Spon: Parents.
John, son of John Rasber and Eva, b. May 23, 1798, bapt. July 8,

1798. Spon: John Nagel and Magd. Eliza.

Christian, son of Christian Bauman and Catharine, b. Dec. 27, 1797, bapt. July 13, 1797. Spon: Catharine Rubel.

John, son of Adam Helm and Gertrude, b. July 2, 1798, bapt. July 15, 1798. Spon: John Mayer and Christine.

William, son of Adam Weis and Elizabeth, b. July 1, 1797, bapt. July 15, 1798. Spon: Parents.

Elizabeth, daughter of Philip Justus and Elizabeth, b. April 3, 1798, bapt. July 15, 1798. Spon: Parents.

Elizabeth, daughter of Jacob Tauberman and Susanna, b. June 28, 1798, bapt. July 22, 1798. Spon: Elizabeth Hempelman.

George Lucas, son of Philip Mayer and Wilhelmina, b. May 16, 1798, bapt. July 22, 1798. Spon: James Lucas and Margaret Schmid.

A. Maria, daughter of Frederick Foster and Catharine, b. June 23, 1798, bapt. July 22, 1798. Spon: Parents.

Henry, son of Henry Abka (?) and Sarah, b. June 21, 1798, bapt. July 22, 1798. Spon: Parents.

Peter May, son of Peter Thomas and Elizabeth, b. March 2, 1798, bapt. July 22, 1798. Spon: ------ May and Maria Wiederstein.

Sarah, daughter of George Newton and Margaret, b. Aug. 29, 1797, bapt. July 28, 1798. Spon: William Schneider and Catharine.

William, son of John Reuss and Elizabeth, b. June 26, 1798, bapt. July 29, 1798. Spon: William Bender and Maria.

William, son of Charles Nelson and Elizabeth, b. July 17, 1798, bapt. July 29, 1798. Spon: William Hanna and Catharine Wilbank.

Martha, daughter of Michael Kintzinger and Martha, b. March 19, 1798, bapt. July 31, 1798. Spon: Parents.

Maria, daughter of Henry Kinsle and Maria, b. June 1, 1798, bapt. Aug. 2, 1798. Spon: Parents.

John Hill, son of John Fordheim and A. Maria, b. Feb. 14, 1798, bapt. Aug. 7, 1798. Spon: The mother.

Louisa Elizabeth, daughter of John Rudolph Stamm and Maria, b. April 28, 1798, bapt. Aug. 8, 1798. Spon: Parents.

George Ludwig, son of George Kuhn and Margaret, b. April 20, 1798, bapt. Aug. 8, 1798. Spon: Parents.

John Carl, son of Henry Hupfeld and Charlotte, b. March 22, 1798, bapt. Aug. 9, 1798. Spon: John Carl Hupfeld.

John Jost, son of Krafft Schneider and M. Elizabeth, b. Nov. 6, 1787, bapt. Nov. 12, 1787. Spon: John Jost Dickel, Catharine Fischer and M. Gertrude Schmid.

John Frederick, son of Krafft Schneider and M. Elizabeth, b. September 29, 1796, bapt. Oct. 9, 1796. Spon: John Fred. Henrich, Catharine Bald and Johanna Bandes.

A. Maria, daughter of Krafft Schneider and M. Elizabeth, b. Aug. 2, 1798, bapt. Aug. 12, 1798. Spon: Henry Bald, Maria Becker and A. M. Spetzroler.

Jacob, son of George Madery and Anna, b. Dec. 23, 1797, bapt. Aug. 13, 1798. Spon: Parents.

Eliza, daughter of John Porter and Catharine, b. Aug. 5, 1798, bapt. Aug. 14, 1798. Spon: Parents.

Alitha Jacoba, daughter of Thomas Hutterman and Barbara, b. Aug. 4, 1798, bapt. Aug. 28, 1798. Spon: William Hutter and Alitha Jacoba.

Anna, daughter of Henry Thielman and Anna, wife, b. Aug. 11,
1798, bapt. Aug. 30, 1798. Spon: Anna Welt
Regina, daughter of Stephen Bouden and Regina, b. July 28, 1798,
bapt. Sept. 2, 1798. Spon: The mother.
M. Magdalene, daughter of William Pfau and Barbara, b. Dec. 6,
1797, bapt. Sept. 6, 1798. Spon: M. Magdalene Pfau.
George, son of William Archibald and Catharine, b. Oct. 26, 1791,
bapt. Sept. 9, 1798. Spon: Parents.
Sarah, daughter of William Archibald and Catharine, b. Sept. 16,
1793, bapt. Sept. 9, 1798. Spon: Parents.
William, son of William Archibald and Catharine, b. Aug. 27,
1796, bapt. Sept. 9, 1798. Spon: Parents.
Elizabeth, daughter of Jacob Schermer and Hannah, b. Aug. 12,
1798, bapt. Sept. 9, 1798. Spon: Geo. Schoch and Elizabeth.
Joshua, son of John Gunckel and Margaret, b. Aug. 5, 1798, bapt.
Sept. 12, 1798. Spon: Joshua Lambert and Elizabeth.

*Dr. Hendel died Sept. 29, 1798. The next baptisms are by an
unknown hand.*
Susanna Catharine, daughter of Joseph Gally and Anna Catharine,
b. Nov. 24, 1798, bapt. Dec. 9, 1798. Spon: George Durhor and
Maria Albert.
Christine Margaret, daughter of Joseph Gally and Anna Catharine,
b. Nov. 24, 1798, bapt. Dec. 9, 1798. Spon: John Henrich and
Christine.

BAPTISMS BY REV. SAMUEL HELFFENSTEIN
1799 - 1804
Charles, son of Christian Rauch and wife, b. Dec. 23, 1798.
Susanna, daughter of George Hess and wife Anna Cath., b. Nov. 1,
1798, bapt. March 7, 1799. Spon: Parents.
Louise Cameron Duval, daughter of Seraphim Duval and wife, b.
Nov. 9, 1798, bapt. March --, 1799. Spon: Parents.
Elizabeth, daughter of William Reinhard and Elizabeth, b. March
1, 1798, bapt. March --, 1799. Spon: Parents.
Margaret, daughter of Henry Fou and Maria, b. Feb. 3, 1798, bapt.
March --, 1799. Spon: Parents.
Jacob, son of Jacob Muller and Salome, b. Dec. 14, 1798, bapt.
March --, 1799. Spon: Parents.
Margaret, daughter of Martin Rothar and Maria, b. Jan. 17, 1799,
bapt. March --, 1799. Spon: Parents.
Christian Frederick, son of John Friend and Catharine, b. Feb.
10, 1799, bapt. March --, 1799. Spon: Parents.
Peter, son of Peter Hess adn Maria Veronica, b. Feb. 5, 1799,
bapt. March --, 1799. Spon: ----.
Peter, son of Wm. Hess and Kisiah, b. Aug. 18, 1798, bapt.
March --, 1799. Spon: ----.
Samuel, son of Gottlieb Stutere and Elizabeth, b. Dec. 10, 1798,
bapt. March --, 1799. Spon: ----.
Catharine, daughter of Thomas West and Elizabeth, b. Jan. 26,
1799, bapt. March --, 1799. Spon: ----.
Maria, daughter of Philip Miller and Sarah, b. Jan. 31, 1799,
bapt. March --, 1799. Spon: Martin ------ and Susanna.

John George, son of Philip Lowery and Rebecca, b. Dec. 3, 1798,
  bapt. March --, 1799. Spon: Immanuel ----- and Re --.
Charles Stewart, son of John Fineton and Elizabeth, b. Oct. 9,
  1792, bapt. March 17, 1799. Spon: ----.
Elizabeth, daughter of Bernard May and Agnes, b. Jan. 4, 1799,
  bapt. March 17, 1799. Spon: Henry Wisenbach and Elizabeth.
Sarah, daughter of Conrad Wigand and A. M. Elizabeth, b. Jan. 23,
  1799, bapt. March 17, 1799. Spon: Parents.
John Peter, son of Peter Ashman and Magdalene, b. Sept. 13, 1798,
  bapt. April 4, 1799. Spon: Simon ------ and Maria.
Elizabeth, daughter of John Miller and Margaret, b. Nov. 21,
  1798, bapt. April 4, 1799. Spon: Parents.
Samuel, son of Herman Ley and Anna Margaret, b. Dec. 10, 1798,
  bapt. April --, 1799. Spon: Parents.
Anna Magdalene, daughter of John Frankenstein and wife, b. Nov.
  2, 1798, bapt. April 5, 1799. Spon: John Stat---- and wife.
John, son of John Bernet and wife, b. Aug. 14, 1798, bapt. April
  5, 1799. Spon: Parents.
Gottfried (Godfrey), son of Ludwig Jung and Catharine, b. March
  15, 1799, bapt. April 5, 1799. Spon: Parents.
John Michael, son of John Keyser and wife, b. March 7, 1798,
  bapt. April --, 1799. Spon: John Michael and Elizabeth.
Sarah, daughter of John Snyder and wife, b. Feb. 17, 1799, bapt.
  April --, 1799. Spon: Parents.
George, son of Maria Strohouer, b. Feb. 15, 1799, bapt. April --,
  1799. Spon: Maria Strohouer and John Philips.
William, son of Geo. Wilson and wife, b. Feb. 1, 1799, bapt.
  April 7, 1799. Spon: Justus Berger and Maria Adam.
William, son of Jacob Heiberger and Elizabeth, b. Dec. 6, 1798,
  bapt. April 7, 1799. Spon: J. Peterson and Susanna.
Jacob, son of Jacob Ford and Catharine, b. Feb. 21, 1799, bapt.
  April 7, 1799. Spon: Lena Belsterman.
John Adam, son of Maria Campher, b. Oct. 4, 1798, bapt. April 7,
  1799. Spon: Adam Logan and Maria.
Jacob, son of George Durster and wife, b. Oct. 26, 1798, bapt.
  April 8, 1799. Spon: Jacob Rubsam.
Anna Maria and Elizabeth, daughters of Jacob Berkinhaus and
  Susanna, b. July 25, 1798, bapt. April 8, 1799. Spon:
  Parents.
Tester, son of Wendel Witeman and Susanna, b. July 5, 1791, bapt.
  ------. Spon: Parents.
Hendel, son of Wendel Witeman and Susanna, b. Jan. 7, 1798,
  baptized April 10, 1799. Spon: ----.
Peter, son of Wendel Witeman and Susanna, b. Sept. 25, 1793,
  bapt. ----. Spon: ----.
M. Barbara, daughter of Fred. Meyly and M. Barbara, b. Oct. 14,
  1798, bapt. April 14, 1799. Spon: Parents.
Johanna Sophia, daughter of John Peter Hess and wife, b. Jan. 5,
  1799, bapt. ------ 1799. Spon: Maria ----.
Sarah, daughter of Maria Smith, b. Sept. 15, 1798, bapt. April --
  , 1799. Spon: Philip Justus and Elizabeth.
Elizabeth, daughter of Jacob Smith and wife, b. Sept. 18, 1798,
  bapt. April 14, 1799. Spon: Daniel Hain and Elizabeth Smith.
Sarah, daughter of Michael Hains and wife, b. Feb. 1, 1799, bapt.
  April 14, 1799. Spon: George Wilkins and Sarah Mark.

Maria, daughter of ------ Gardner and wife, b. March 12, 1799,
bapt. April 14, 1799. Spon: Parents.
Wm. Jones, son of Martin Dubs and Sarah, b. Feb. 7, 1799, bapt.
April 14, 1799. Spon: Parents.
George, son of Geo. Vonder Slize and Elizabeth, b. Nov. 15, 1798,
bapt. April 15, 1799. Spon: Parents.
Daniel, son of Daniel Vonder Slize and Margaret, b. Feb. 10,
1799, bapt. April 15, 1799. Spon: Parents.
Anna Louisa, daughter of Nicholas Juvenal and Susanna, b. Nov.
28, 1798, bapt. April 15, 1799. Spon: Parents.
Carl, son of Christian Rauch and wf,. b. Jan. 24, 1799, bapt.
April 20, 1799. Spon: Parents.
Maria, daughter of Jacob Gardner and wife, b. March 12, 1799,
bapt. April 20, 1799. Spon: Parents.
Godfrey, son of ------ Folwell and wife, b. March 31, 1799, bapt.
April 20, 1799. Spon: Godfrey ------ and Eliz. Robert.
Anna Maria, daughter of John Bakofen and Maria, b. March 10,
1798, bapt. April 24, 1799. Spon: Anna M. ------.
Michael, son of Jacob Fahn and Elizabeth, b. Oct. 7, 1798, bapt.
April 24, 1799. Spon: Rebecca Fahn.
Daniel, son of Jacob Hill and wife, b. Dec. 10, 1798, bapt. April
24, 1799. Spon: Parents.
Charlotte, daughter of James Dade and Catharine, b. March 11,
1799, bapt. April 26, 1799. Spon: Sam Ginder and Charlotte.
William, son of Jacob Zeller and wife, b. April 9, 1799, bapt.
April 28, 1799. Spon: Parents.
Sophia, daughter of James Hunt and Anna Maria, b. Dec. 16, 1798,
bapt. April 28, 1799. Spon: Parents.
John Theobald, son of John Weber and Margaret, b. April 2, 1799,
bapt. April 28, 1799. Spon: Henry Theobald and Margaret.
Susanna, daughter of Fred. Schreiner and Elizabeth, b. Feb. 11,
1799, bapt. May 11, 1799. Spon: Parents.
Franklin, son of Jacob Jebly and Miliana, b. Oct. 18, 1798, bapt.
May 12, 1799. Spon: John L. Hess and Catharine.
Sarah, daughter of Henry Alberger and Sarah, b. Feb. 27, 1799,
bapt. May 12, 1799. Spon: Margaret Alberger.
Henry, son of Henry Dentsch and wife, b. Aug. 4, 1798, bapt. May
13, 1799. Spon: Parents.
Abraham, son of Albert Winthebel and wife, b. Oct. 28, 1798,
bapt. May 13, 1799. Spon: Parents.
Carl, son of Geo. Wilson and Maria, b. April 15, 1799, bapt. ----
--. Spon: Conrad Keller and M. Wolfurt.
Peter, son of P. Vitalis and Catharine, b. Jan. 12, 1796, bapt. -
-----. Spon: Conrad Keller
Elizabeth, daughter of P. Vitalis and Catharine, b. Dec. 2, 1798,
bapt. ------ 1799. Spon: Conrad Keller.
George, son of Henry Branson and Elizabeth, b. July 19, 1798,
bapt. ------ 1799. Spon: P. Wehaher and Elizabeth.
Elizabeth, daughter of Jacob Merker and wife, b. March 6, 1799,
bapt. June --, 1799. Spon: Parents.
Catharine, daughter of John Weineman and Barbara, b. March 6,
1790, bapt. June --, 1799. Spon: J. Merker and wife.
Henry, son of Christian Jung and Maria, b. April 24, 1799, bapt.
June --, 1799. Spon: Henry Rickels and Cath. Dorothy.
Elizabeth, daughter of Bernard Shrunk and Eloisa, b. April 24,

1799, bapt. June 3, 1799. Spon: James Baker and Elizabeth
Lewis.
Anna Catharine, daughter of Jacob Seller and Maria, b. Jan. 19,
1799, bapt. June 3, 1799. Spon: Fred. Ash and Catharine.
Patty, daughter of David Jones and wife, b. Feb. 22, 1796, bapt.
June 3, 1799. Spon: M. Kiths and wife.
Margaret, daughter of David Jones and wife, b. Nov. 18, 1798,
bapt. June 3, 1799. Spon: ----.
Catharine, daughter of Ludwig Wenkle and Elizabeth, b. July 15,
1798, bapt. June 3, 1799. Spon: Parents.
Elizabeth, daughter of J. Wenkle and A. Maria, b. April 2, 1799,
bapt. June --, 1799. Spon: Parents.
Maria, daughter of M. Kortz and Margaret, b. April 9, 1799, bapt.
June 4, 1799. Spon: Parents.
William, son of Henry Hains and Phoebe, b. April 25, 1799, bapt.
June 5, 1799. Spon: Parents.
Jacob, son of John Francis and wife, b. Oct. 9, 1798, bapt. June
6, 1799. Spon: Parents.
Eliza, daughter of Fred Seiffer and Eliza, b. Nov. 28, 1798,
bapt. Dec. 18, 1798. Spon: Parents.
Joseph, son of Geo. Lescher and Anna, b. Dec. 22, 1798, bapt.
June 16, 1799. Spon: Parents.
George, son of Henry Appel and wife, b. May 27, 1799, bapt. June
16, 1799. Spon: Parents.
George, son of George Smith and Elizabeth, b. Dec. 18, 1798,
bapt. ------. Spon: P. Smith ------.
A. Margaret, daughter of C. Reed and Elizabeth, b. Oct. 28, 1798,
bapt. ------. Spon: Parents.
Catharine, daughter of J. Abel and Margaret, b. May 6, 1799,
bapt. June 16, 1799. Spon: Parents.
A. Maria, daughter of Barbara Rosch, b. May 12, 1799, bapt. June
26, 1799. Spon: ----.
Elizabeth, daughter of G. Sorg and Barbara, b. June 5, 1799,
baptized June 26, 1799. Spon: Parents.
Daniel, son of Peter Pot and Maria, b. Jan. 22, 1799, bapt. June
26, 1799. Spon: Daniel Lewis and Elizabeth.
John, son of Geo. Schubert and wife, b. April 25, 1799, bapt.
June 26, 1799. Spon: ----.
Elizabeth, daughter of Geo. Fluck and wife, b. April 30, 1798,
bapt. June 26, 1799. Spon: Parents.
Hatty, daughter of Luy (Louis) Robinson and Maria, b. April 5,
1799, bapt. June 26, 1799. Spon: Parents.
Jacob, son of John Sneider and wife, b. Jan. 12, 1799, bapt. July
4, 1799. Spon: J. Haet and Elizabeth Schuler.
George, son of Sam Gerwirt and wife, b. June 20, 1799, bapt. July
4, 1799. Spon: Geo. Hess and M. Kress.
John, son of James Muckelray and Detty Arethe, b. June 21, 1799,
bapt. July 8, 1799. Spon: ----.
Francis, son of Francis Hoffman and Margaret, b. May 21, 1799,
bapt. July 21, 1799. Spon: Parents.
Simon, son of P. Schuchart and Barbara, b. Sept. 11, 1798, bapt.
July 21, 1799. Spon: Parents.
Joseph, son of Henry Meyers and Margaret, b. March 3, 1799, bapt.
July 22, 1799. Spon: Parents.
John Balsar, son of Henry Ernst and wife, b. June 26, 1799, bapt.

July 29, 1799. Spon: Henrietta Maria ------.
Anna Eva, daughter of Jacob Rein and Anna, b. May 30, 1799, bapt.
Aug. 4, 1799. Spon: Parents.
Anna Maria, daughter of Daniel Schittel and Elizabeth, b. July 9,
1799, bapt. Aug. 6, 1799. Spon: Parents.
Nancy, daughter of Daniel Klages and Polly, b. June 1, 1799,
bapt. Aug. 7, 1799. Spon: Parents.
Christian Bernard, son of Franciscus Faust and Elizabeth Bell, b.
June 4, 1799, bapt. Aug. 7, 1799. Spon: Parents.
Catharine, daughter of Geo. Martery and Anna, b. June 23, 1796,
bapt. Aug. 9, 1799. Spon: Parents.
John, son of Abraham Frederic and Wilhelmina, b. March 14, 1799,
bapt. Aug. 10, 1799. Spon: John Boskis and M. Cath.
Jacob, son of Jacob Schuster and Mary, b. July 28, 1799, bapt.
Aug. 12, 1799. Spon: ----.
Nancy, daughter of John Becker and Sophia, b. Aug. 1, 1799, bapt.
Aug. 14, 1799. Spon: Parents.
William, son of John Stumpf and Magdalene, b. March 1, 1799,
bapt. Aug. 14, 1799. Spon: ----.
Andrew, son of William Conrad and wife Eva, b. March 29, 1799,
bapt. Aug. 15, 1799. Spon: Andrew Deal.
Jacob, son of Jacob Schuster and Mary, b. July 28, 1799, bapt.
Aug. 12, 1799. Spon: ----.
William, son of Wm. Snyder and Magdalene, b. Jan. 8, 1797, bapt.
Aug. 25, 1799. Spon: Magdalene Nanneker.
William, son of Henry Leer and Elizabeth, b. Aug. 5, 1799, bapt.
Aug. 25, 1799. Spon: Jacob Naneker and Elizabeth Leer.
Henry, son of Geo. Hains and Maria, b. April 9, 1799, bapt. Aug.
25, 1799. Spon: Parents.
Elizabeth, daughter of Jacob Rustein and Maria Eliza, b. Aug.
19, 1799, bapt. Aug. 26, 1799. Spon: Parents.
John, son of Andrew Zees and Mary, b. Aug. 15, 1799, bapt. Aug.
26, 1799. Spon: John Mecky and the mother.
Sarah, daughter of John Porkepine and Hetty, b. July 15, 1799,
bapt. Nov. 1, 1799. Spon: The mother.
Catharine, daughter of Philip Hinkle and Catharine, b. May 27,
1799, bapt. Nov. 10, 1799. Spon: ----.
Philippa, daughter of John Baltist and Wedje, b. July 4, 1797,
bapt. Nov. 10, 1799. Spon: ----.
Sarah, daughter of John Schaffer and Susanna, b. Sept. 9, 1799,
bapt. Nov. 10, 1799. Spon: Peter Rebalt and Anna.
Margaret, daughter of Ludwig Snider and Christine, b. Sept. 7,
1799, bapt. Nov. 10, 1799. Spon: ----.
Maria, daughter of Wm. Probert and Hannah, b. Sept. 29, 1799,
bapt. Nov. 10, 1799. Spon: Daniel Butret and Catharine.
Dorothy, daughter of John Huhn and Christine, b. Oct. 23, 1799,
bapt. Nov. 10, 1799. Spon: P. Wirth and Dorothy.
Henry, son of H. Lewis and Elizabeth, b. Aug. 14, 1799, bapt.
Nov. 10, 1799. Spon: Henry Lewis and M. Karcker.
Joseph, son of Jacob Eckstein and Elizabeth, b. Oct. 11, 1799,
bapt. Nov. 10, 1799. Spon: ----.
Catharine, daughter of H. Smith and Catharine, b. June 30, 1799,
bapt. Nov. 16, 1799. Spon: ----.
George, son of Philip Stoud and Margaret, b. Sept. 15, 1799,
bapt. Nov. 18, 1799. Spon: ----.

Sarah, daughter of Edward Pick and Charlotte, b. Sept. 30, 1799,
bapt. Nov. 19, 1799. Spon: ----.
John Daniel, son of Sebastian Hoffman and Elizabeth, b. Aug. 5,
1799, bapt. Nov. 21, 1799. Spon: ----.
John, son of John Huwar and Susanna Edenborn, b. Oct. 13, 1799,
bapt. Nov. 24, 1799. Spon: J. Taupe and Dorothy.
Catharine, daughter of John Carl and Elizabeth, b. Oct. 17, 1799,
bapt. Nov. 24, 1799. Spon: John Lindeman and Catharine.
John, son of Jacob Sigmund and Catharine, b. Sept. 16, 1799,
bapt. Nov. 25, 1799. Spon: ----.
George, son of J. Baker and Catharine, b. Sept. 24, 1799, bapt.
Nov. 26, 1799. Spon: ----.
Sarah, daughter of J. Dennis and Catharine, b. July 15, 1799,
bapt. Nov. 26, 1799. Spon: ----.
Barbara, daughter of G. Henvecter and Elizabeth, b. Oct. 22,
1799, bapt. Nov. 28, 1799. Spon: Barbara Breyen.
Peter Barras, son of Adam Baker and Elizabeth, b. Jan. 11, 1796,
bapt. Dec. 1, 1799. Spon: Parents.
Peter, son of Peter Braun and Catharine, b. Aug. 16, 1799, bapt.
Dec. 4, 1799. Spon: ----.
George, son of Adam Alberger and Elizabeth, b. Nov. 16, 1799,
bapt. Dec. 23, 1799. Spon: Geo. Esterle and wife.
Henry, son of Samuel Sailer and Mary, b. Oct. 9, 1799, bapt. Dec.
23, 1799. Spon: Henry Taylor and Mary.
Sarah, daughter of James Lukes and Margaret, b. Oct. 23, 1799,
bapt. Dec. 23, 1799. Spon: J. Jonson and Susan Cure.
Conrad, son of Francis Plumer and Gertrude, b. Dec. 8, 1799,
bapt. Dec. 13, 1799. Spon: ----.
Conrad, son of Dennis Roodt and A. Margaret, b. Nov. 5, 1799,
bapt. Dec. 14, 1799. Spon: Cath. Titman.
John Henry, son of Henry Frey and Barbara, b. Oct. 31, 1799,
bapt. Dec. 14, 1799. Spon: ----.
Elizabeth, daughter of Geo. Runner and Maria, b. Aug. 30, 1799,
bapt. Dec. 14, 1799. Spon: ----.
Maria, daughter of Wm. Zomster and Catharine, b. Dec. 30, 1798,
bapt. Dec. 14, 1799. Spon: ----.
George, son of William Fer and wife, b. Sept. 10, 1799, bapt.
Dec. 14, 1799. Spon: ----.
Mar. Anna, daughter of John Weaver and Catharine, b. Dec. 17,
1799, bapt. Dec. 17, 1799. Spon: Andrew Lob and Elizabeth.
George, son of Fred. Fies and Elizabeth, b. Nov. 11, 1799, bapt.
Dec. 22, 1799. Spon: G. Esherich and Marg.
Maria, daughter of Jacob Fisher and Susanna, b. Aug. 2, 1798,
bapt. Dec. 25, 1799. Spon: ----.
Sarah, daughter of Jacob Fisher and Susanna, b. Oct. 29, 1799,
bapt. Dec. 25, 1799. Spon: ----.
Frederick, son of Charles Dominick and Maria, b. March 4, 1797,
bapt. Dec. 25, 1799. Spon: ----.
John, son of Charles Dominick and Maria, b. Sept. 25, 1799, bapt.
Dec. 25, 1799. Spon: ----.
Robert, son of George Fleck and Sarah, b. Dec. 25, 1799, bapt.
Dec. 25, 1799. Spon: ----.
Catharine, daughter of P. Dicks and Catharine, b. Oct. 30, 1799,
bapt. Dec. 26, 1799. Spon: ----.
J. Bernard, son of B. Swenck and Elizabeth Johnson, b. Aug. 10,

1799, bapt. Dec. 27, 1799. Spon: ----.
Elizabeth, daughter of Michael ------ and Sarah, b. Nov. 15,
1799, bapt. Dec. 28, 1799. Spon: ----.
Christine, daughter of John Hutter and Susan, b. Sept. 25, 1799,
bapt. Dec. 28, 1799. Spon: ----.
Esther, daughter of John Fux and Margaret, b. July 10, 1799,
bapt. Dec. 28, 1799. Spon: ----.
Catharine, daughter of Jacob Nanecker and Catharine, b. Oct. 4,
1799, bapt. Dec. 28, 1799. Spon: John Brey and Catharine.
Maria, daughter of Jacob Finck and Margaret, b. Dec. 11, 1799,
bapt. Dec. 29, 1799. Spon: ----.
Conrad, son of P. Conrad Baker and Susanna, b. Dec. 19, 1799,
bapt. Jan. 8, 1800. Spon: Fred. Frayley and Catharine.
John Ludwig, son of J. Wm. Smith and Christine, b. Nov. 10, 1799,
bapt. Jan. 11, 1800. Spon: Ludwig Kester and A. Maria.
Philip Henry, son of Jacob Prest and Eva, b. Dec. 21, 1799, bapt.
Jan. 11, 1800. Spon: Philip Prest and Krants Nuch.
William, son of Henry Tremper and Elizabeth, b. Dec. 24, 1799,
bapt. Jan. 11, 1800. Spon: Parents.
Maria, daughter of Jacob Lesher and Maria, b. Nov. 8, 1799,
baptized Jan. 12, 1800. Spon: Parents.
Sarah, daughter of P. Fonderbeck and Elizabeth, b. Aug. 4, 1791,
bapt. Jan. 20, 1800. Spon: Parents.
Elizabeth, daughter of John Deal and Elizabeth, b. Dec. 23, 1799,
bapt. Jan. 20, 1800. Spon: Parents.
Anna Maria, daughter of George Schreiner and Anna Maria, b. Jan.
3, 1800, bapt. Jan. 21, 1800. Spon: Parents.
Peter, son of Daniel Deal and A. Maria, b. June 7, 1799, bapt.
Jan. 21, 1800. Spon: Andrew Steiner and Catharine.
Milcah, son of Wm. Wallas and Margaret, b. Dec. 15, 1799, bapt.
Jan. 21, 1800. Spon: Mary Peiler(?).
Conrad, son of Conrad Baker and Maria, b. Sept. 25, 1799, bapt.
Jan. 21, 1800. Spon: Maria ?.
Adam, son of John Fordem and A. Maria, b. Oct. 8, 1799, bapt.
Jan. 21, 1800. Spon: Parents.
William, son of Wm. Corn and Margaret, b. Dec. 18, 1799, bapt.
Jan. 21, 1800. Spon: Parents.
Maria, daughter of P. Peltz and Rebecca, b. June 5, 1799, bapt.
Jan. 22, 1800. Spon: Parents.
John Jacob, son of John Belgestimel and Mar. Catharine, b. Jan.
15, 1800, bapt. Jan. 23, 1800. Spon: J. Ristein and J.
Stimel.
Wilemin, son of John Gardner and M. Christine, b. Dec. 8, 1799,
bapt. Jan. 24, 1800. Spon: J. Restein and Wilm. Phile.
Peter, son of Christopher Smith and Maria, b. Dec. 17, 1799,
bapt. Jan. 24, 1800. Spon: Parents.
Murger, son of Henry Painter and Magdalene, b. Dec. 29, 1799,
bapt. Jan. 24, 1800. Spon: Mary Painter.
Elizabeth, daughter of John Becker and Barbara, b. Dec. 26, 1799,
bapt. Jan. 25, 1800. Spon: J. Baker and Elizabeth.
Maria, daughter of George Suneber and Philippina, b. Dec. 28,
1799, bapt. Jan. --, 1800. Spon: Michael Hag and Christine.
John, son of John Witeman and Maria, b. Aug. 25, 1798, bapt. Jan.
--, 1800. Spon: John Man.
Charles, son of John Witeman and Maria, b. Oct. 24, 1799, bapt.

Jan. --, 1800. Spon: John Man.
Jacob, son of Jacob Man and Elizabeth, b. Oct. 13, 1799, bapt.
Jan. --, 1800. Spon: John Man.
John, son of David Witeman and Nancy, b. Dec. 29, 1798, bapt.
Jan. --, 1800. Spon: M. Woodlein and Maria.
Rebecca, daughter of David Witeman and Nancy, b. Dec. 29, 1798,
bapt. Jan. --, 1800. Spon: M. Woodlein and Maria.
Catharine, daughter of Philip Alberger and Dolly, b. Jan. 3,
1799, bapt. Jan. 25, 1800. Spon: P. Alberger and Margaret.
Molly, daughter of Jacob Shimer and Elizabeth, b. Jan. 1, 1800,
bapt. Jan. 25, 1800. Spon: Parents.
John, son of Jacob Deal and Edith, b. Jan. 12, 1800, bapt. Jan.
25, 1800. Spon: Parents.
M. Theresa, daughter of Jacob Oeller and Leah, b. Dec. 29, 1799,
bapt. Jan. 31, 1800. Spon: Francis Zens and Anna.
Anna Maria, daughter of Jacob Karr and Elizabeth, b. Jan. 26,
1800, bapt. Jan. 31, 1800. Spon: Catharine Hertz.
Jost, son of Ludwig Henk and Anna Maria, b. Jan. 9, 1800, bapt.
Feb. 1, 1800. Spon: Jos. Hennel and A. M. Bald.
Sophia, daughter of Fred Baldin and Christine, b. Jan. 17, 1800,
bapt. Feb. 1, 1800. Spon: Sophia Baldin.
Geo. Conrad, son of Henry Sheller and Susanna, b. Jan. 3, 1800,
bapt. Feb. 2, 1800. Spon: Geo. Haffner and M. Magdalene.
Catharine, daughter of Henry Wagener and Catharine, b. Feb. 5,
1800, bapt. Feb. --, 1800. Spon: Parents.
John, son of John Leniman and Elizabeth, b. June 8, 1799, bapt.
Feb. 20, 1800. Spon: Parents.
Anna, daughter of James Mill and Sarah, b. Nov. 2, 1799, bapt.
Feb. 20, 1800. Spon: Parents.
John, son of John Hauch and Mary, b. Oct. 10, 1799, bapt. Feb.
20, 1800. Spon: Parents.
Elizabeth, daughter of Philip Geisin and Elizabeth, b. June 11,
1799, bapt. Feb. 25, 1800. Spon: Parents.
Elizabeth, daughter of Martin Kramp and Catharine, b. Feb. 4,
1800, bapt. Feb. 23, 1800. Spon: J. Rice and Elizabeth.
Laury Peter, daughter of Samuel Karcher and Susanna, b. Jan. 16,
1799, bapt. Feb. 23, 1800. Spon: P. Laury and Jean.
Murger, son of John Lodge and Mary, b. Jan. 31, 1800, bapt. March
3, 1800. Spon: Parents.
Charlotte Elizabeth, daughter of Carl Huppefield and Sarah, b.
Dec. 25, 1799, bapt. March 7, 1800. Spon: C. Holler and
Charles Huppfield.
Catharine, daughter of Adam Boser and Rebecca, b. Dec. 30, 1799,
bapt. March 16, 1800. Spon: J. Casner and Catharine.
Catharine, daughter of John Conterman and Elizabeth, b. Feb. 23,
1800, bapt. March 23, 1800. Spon: Parents.
Susanna, daughter of Jacob Slemer and Hannah, b. March 9, 1800,
bapt. March 23, 1800. Spon: Parents.
Child of Conrad Baker and Susanna, b. Dec. 8, 1799, bapt. Dec. 9,
1799. Spon: Fred Fraily and Catharine.
John Ludwig, son of John Wm. Smith and Christine, b. Nov. 10,
1799, bapt. Dec. 8, 1799. Spon: L. Kerter and A. Mary.
Anna M., daughter of Fred. Weaver and Frederica, b. Feb. 23,
1800, bapt. March 23, 1800. Spon: Sebastian Detrich and A. M.
Gener.

John, son of John Snider and M. Margr., b. March 2, 1800, bapt.
March 23, 1800. Spon: Parents.
William, son of Wm. Reinhart and Elizabeth, b. Feb. 9, 1800,
bapt. March 23, 1800. Spon: Parents.
Rebecca, daughter of Geo. Fanse and Susanna, b. Oct. 13, 1799,
bapt. March 24, 1800. Spon: Parents.
Regina, daughter of George Junker and Maria, b. Oct. 22, 1799,
bapt. March 26, 1800. Spon: Regina Genns.
Elizabeth, daughter of Jacob Rosset and Elizabeth, b. Oct. 10,
1796, bapt. March 30, 1800. Spon: ----.
Maria, daughter of Jacob Rosset and Elizabeth, b. Feb. 18, 1799,
bapt. March 30, 1800. Spon: ----.
Jacob, son of Samuel Hower and Margaret, b. Jan. 4, 1800, bapt.
March 30, 1800. Spon: Parents.
Elizabeth, daughter of Elst. Hugart and Margaret, b. ------,
bapt. March 30, 1800. Spon: Parents.
Maria, daughter of Adam Stein and Catharine, b. Feb. 28, 1800,
bapt. April 1, 1800. Spon: ----.
Carl, son of James Hunt and Polly, b. March 28, 1800, bapt. April
3, 1800. Spon: John Asm--- and Catharine.
A. Margaret, daughter of George Mill and Margaret, b. March 9,
1800, bapt. April 6, 1800. Spon: Carl Gentel and Anna
Margaret.
Catharine Eliza., daughter of Jacob Henn and Catharine, b. March
19, 1800, bapt. April 6, 1800. Spon: Engelbert Neadn(er--)
and M. Huffner.
Fanny, daughter of Jacob Fonse and Elizabeth, b. April 1, 1800,
bapt. April 12, 1800. Spon: Rebecca Fonse.
Elizabeth, daughter of John Backoven and Anna Maria, b. March 27,
1800, bapt. April 12, 1800. Spon: A. Mar (--- torn).
Joseph, son of John Lake and Catharine, b. Feb. 15, 1800, bapt.
April 13, 1800. Spon: Parents.
Martin, son of Philip Lesh and Margaret, b. Nov. 27, 1799, bapt.
April 13, 1800. Spon: M. Gates and wife Margaret.
A. Maria, daughter of P. Waltuwer and Margaret, b. March 14,
1799, bapt. April 13, 1800. Spon: C. Goff and A. M------.
Leonard, son of Leonard Rothshull and Elizabeth, b. March 16,
1800, bapt. April 14, 1800. Spon: M. Kr---- and Catharine.
Matthias, son of Wm. Smith and Margaret, b. March 8, 1800, bapt.
April 17, 1800. Spon: Parents.
William, son of Wm. Reyde and Sarah, b. Feb. 12, 1800, bapt.
April 17, 1800. Spon: ----.
Elizabeth, daughter of Adam Hains and Catharine, b. March 10,
1800, bapt. April 18, 1800. Spon: Adam Hains and Sophina.
William, son of Michael Witeman and Susanna, b. March 30, 1800,
bapt. April 23, 1800. Spon: ----.
John, son of John Graul and Elizabeth, b. March 27, 1800, bapt.
April 24, 1800. Spon: ----.
Frederick, son of Jacob Danzibech and Anna Maria, b. March 12,
1800, bapt. April 27, 1800. Spon: ----.
Margaret and Elizabeth (twins), daughters of Matth. Berkenber and
Catharine, b. Jan. 11, 1799, bapt. April --, 1800. Spon: John
Jund and Maria.
John Philip, son of J.P. Berlebach and Catharine, b. April 4,
1800, bapt. May 4, 1800. Spon: Philip Felker.

Anna Mary, daughter of John Brey and Catharine, b. April 10,
1800, bapt. May 4, 1800. Spon: Anna Marg. Weidner.
Maria, daughter of Robert Adams and Maria, b. March 24, 1800,
bapt. May --, 1800. Spon: Fred. Haas and Elizabeth.
M. Louisa, daughter of George Dechel and Hannah, b. April 16,
1800, bapt. May --, 1800. Spon: Andrew Guldin and M. Louisa.
Catharine, daughter of John Geo. Gramer and Anna, b. April 6,
1800, bapt. May --, 1800. Spon: John Ludwig Kurtz.
Elizabeth, daughter of John Ludwig Klotz and Elizabeth Gertrude,
b. April 14, 1800, bapt. May --, 1800. Spon: ----
William, son of William Ehrman and Elizabeth, b. April --, 1800,
bapt. ------. Spon: ----.
Rebecca, daughter of Henry Fehman and Anna, b. March --, 1800,
bapt. ------ 1800. Spon: ----.
Catharine, daughter of Nicholas Mack and M. Magdalene, b. April
27, 1800, bapt. May 18, 1800. Spon: Cath. Kurris and Christ.
Huckes.
William, son of Adam May and Catharine, b. March 28, 1800, bapt.
May 21, 1800. Spon: Parents.
John, son of Peter Bluis and Barbara, b. Dec. 25, 1799, bapt. May
22, 1800. Spon: Parents.
William, son of Philip Lowery and Rebecca, b. April 18, 1800,
bapt. May 23, 1800. Spon: ----.
William, son of John Lehr and Catharine, b. May 6, 1800, bapt.
May 26, 1800. Spon: John Snider and Rebecca.
Sarah, daughter of Samuel Lake and Elizabeth, b. Oct. 14, 1799,
bapt. May 26, 1800. Spon: Sarah Gross.
John, son of Jacob Patter and Catharine, b. April 23, 1800, bapt.
May 26, 1800. Spon: John Becker and Maria.
William, son of Wm. Reiter and Christine, b. March 15, 1800,
bapt. May 26, 1800. Spon: Wm. Baldin and Susanna.
Bernard, son of Henry Westrich and Maria, b. March 31, 1800,
bapt. May 26, 1800. Spon: B. May and Agnes M------.
Elizabeth, daughter of John Gauff and Fanny, b. March 25, 1800,
bapt. May 28, 1800. Spon: M. Seriche.
Rebecca, daughter of David Loyd and Susanna, b. July 22, 1799,
bapt. May 28, 1800. Spon: ----.
Rachel, daughter of John Freyer and wife Eva, b. April 19, 1800,
bapt. May 28, 1800. Spon: ----.
Henry, son of John Riteman and Elizabeth, b. April 27, 1800,
bapt. June --, 1800. Spon: H. Yener and Louisa.
Elizabeth, daughter of Jacob Schreiner and Elizabeth, b. April
17, 1800, bapt. June 8, 1800. Spon: E. Frey (?).
Mary, daughter of John Lees and Elizabeth, b. May 15, 1800, bapt.
June 8, 1800. Spon: ----.
John, son of Jacob Sailor and Elizabeth, b. June 12, 1800, bapt.
June --, 1800. Spon: J.F. Dischong and Margaret.
Henry, son of Godfrey Bockius and Eve, b. Feb. 25, 1800, bapt. --
---- 1800. Spon: ----.
Child of Abraham Hirtulz (?) and Catharine, b. April 29, 1800,
bapt. June 19, 1800. Spon: Henry Laudebach and Elizabeth.
Susanna, daughter of Henry Palm and Maria, b. June 3, 1800, bapt.
June --, 1800. Spon: Anna Mase.
M. Magdalene, daughter of Sebastian Soliday and M. Magdalene, b.
June 2, 1800, bapt. June --, 1800. Spon: ----.

Edward, son of Ludwig Young and Catharine, b. May 28, 1800, bapt. June --, 1800. Spon: ----.

Susan, daughter of John Bleyer and Anna, b. April 24, 1800, bapt. June --, 1800. Spon: ----.

John, son of Moses Decker and wife, b. Oct. 21, 1799, bapt. ----- - 1800. Spon: ----.

John, son of John Brown and Johanna, b. Jan. 23, 1800, bapt. ---- -- 1800. Spon: ----.

Elizabeth, daughter of Fred. Foering, b. Nov. 22, 1799, bapt. --- --- 1800. Spon: ----.

Catharine, daughter of Jacob Bomb and Elizabeth, b. Jan. 18, 1800, bapt. ------ 1800. Spon: John Shettlein and Barbara.

John, son of John Wagner and Elizabeth, b. Dec. 18, 1799, bapt. - ----- 1800. Spon: May Imbele.

George, son of John Snyder and Elizabeth, b. Jan. 11, 1800, bapt. ------ 1800. Spon: ----.

Elizabeth, daughter of George McGrue and Anna, b. Dec. 3, 1799, bapt. ------, 1800. Spon: ---- (?) and Elizabeth.

John, son of Charles McKrevel and Philippina, b. Dec. 7, 1799, bapt. ------ 1800. Spon: Robert Davis and Catharine.

Benjamin, son of Alexander Crawford and Christine, b. Dec. 15, 1799, bapt. ------. Spon: Parents.

Thomas, son of Alexander Crawford and Christine, b. Dec. 1, 1798, bapt. ------. Spon: ----.

John, son of Philip Miller and Sarah, b. Dec. 4, 1800, bapt. ---- --. Spon: John A. Helt and Susanna Peck.

John, son of John Snyder and Maria, b. March 3, 1800, bapt. April 10, 1800. Spon: ----.

John Henry, son of Wm. Breeding and Elizabeth, b. Aug. 8, 1800, bapt. Aug. 31, 1800. Spon: John Henry Weaver and Margaret.

Lamberte, son of John Werf and Susanna, b. Aug. 31, 1800, bapt. Sept. 7, 1800. Spon: Lamberte van Neten Christophe.

Elizabeth, daughter of Solomon Sell and Maria, b. Oct. 14, 1795, bapt. ------. Spon: ----.

William, son of Solomon Sell and Maria, b. Nov. 25, 1797, bapt. - -----. Spon: ----.

Andrew, son of Solomon Sell and Maria, b. Nov. 16, 1799, bapt. -- ----. Spon: ----.

Maria May, daughter of Samuel Schaff and Catharine, b. July 15, 1800, bapt. Sept. 13, 1800. Spon: G. John Weilbech.

George, son of John Michael and Maria, b. Sept. 30, 1800, bapt. Sept. ----. Spon: ----.

Samuel, son of George Swartz and Barbara, b. Sept. 8, 1800, bapt. ------. Spon: ----.

John Daniel, son of Henry Wolf and Catharine, b. Aug. 4, 1800, bapt. Sept. 14, 1800. Spon: John Daniel Jung and Anna Maria.

Maria Eliza, daughter of Daniel Jung and Anna Mary, b. July 16, 1800, bapt. Aug. 10, 1800. Spon: ----.

Daniel, son of Fred Dickes and Catharine, b. June 11, 1800, bapt. Aug. 13, 1800. Spon: Dan. Rush and Susanna.

Maria Christine, daughter of Christian Foebel and Gertrude, b. Sept. 10, 1800, bapt. Sept. 21, 1800. Spon: Anthony Foebel and Maria Christ. Himckel.

James, son of George Wilson and Hannah, b. July 24, 1800, bapt. Sept. 20, 1800. Spon: Wm. Adams and M. Adams.

Francis, son of Francis Plumer and Catharine, b. June --, 1800,
    baptized Sept. 28, 1800. Spon: ----.
Samuel, son of John Stertsebach and Margaret, b. Aug. 23, 1800,
    bapt. Oct. 1, 1800. Spon: ----.
Maria, daughter of Christian Jung and Maria, b. Sept. 2, 1800,
    bapt. Oct. 3, 1800. Spon: ----.
John George, son of Richard Stremel and Catharine, b. Sept. 17,
    1800, bapt. Oct. 3, 1800. Spon: John George Smith, A. Mary
    Freyt and Catharine Stremel.
Maria Elizabeth, daughter of John Huddon and Christine, b. July
    1, 1800, bapt. Oct. 3, 1800. Spon: Francis Sandos, Polly
    Smith and Susan Fisher.
Christine, daughter of Samuel Olowell and Maria, b. July 20,
    1800, bapt. Oct. --, 1800. Spon: Christ. Christel
Elkana, daughter of Samuel Olowell and Maria, 21 wks. old, bapt.
    Oct. --, 1800. Spon: Catharine Kolb.
John, son of Henry Berger and Magdalene, b. Sept. 18, 1800, bapt.
    Oct. 7, 1800. Spon: George Everly and Wilhelmina.
Elizabeth, daughter of John Franck and Catharine, b. Sept. 23,
    1800, bapt. Oct. 7, 1800. Spon: Elizabeth Slow and Anthony
    Foebel.
Eva Margaret, daughter of David Halter and Christine, b. May 8,
    1800, bapt. Oct. 11, 1800. Spon: Mary Souder.
Richard, son of Daniel Clages and Maria, b. Sept. 25, 1800, bapt.
    Oct. 13, 1800. Spon: ----.
John Henry, son of Adam May and Catharine, b. July 29, 1800,
    bapt. Oct. 17, 1800. Spon: Adam May and Barbara Schaetzlein.
Christine, daughter of John Everidge and Hannah, b. Sept. 9,
    1800, bapt. Oct. 19, 1800. Spon: ----.
Elizabeth, daughter of Conrad Baker, Jr. and Susanna, b. Sept. 8,
    1800, bapt. Oct. 19, 1800. Spon: Parents.
Jacob, son of Fred. Ehringer and Elizabeth, b. Sept. 8, 1800,
    bapt. Oct. 22, 1800. Spon: ----.
John Christian, son of John Christ. Vomhoff and Anna Maria, b.
    Oct. 2, 1800, bapt. Oct. 23, 1800. Spon: ----
Michael, son of M. Foest and Elizabeth, b. Oct. 16, 1800, bapt.
    Oct. 23, 1800. Spon: ----.
David, son of Martin Rothore and Maria, b. May 31, 1800, bapt.
    Oct. 24, 1800. Spon: ----.
M. Catharine, daughter of Jacob Smith and Catharine, b. Oct. 23,
    1800, bapt. Oct. 30, 1800. Spon: John Fare and M. Smid.
John Ebert, son of Krafft Snyder and M. Elizabeth, b. Oct. 26,
    1800, bapt. Nov. 1, 1800. Spon: John Ebert Snyder, Christ.
    Baldin and Christ. Garten.
Eliza Harper, daughter of Jacob Harper and Susanna, b. Feb. 10,
    1798, bapt. Nov. 8, 1800. Spon: ----.
Francis Harper, son of Jacob Harper and Susanna, b. March 5,
    1800, bapt. Nov. 8, 1800. Spon: ----.
Henry, son of John Meeke and Catharine, b. Sept. 27, 1800, bapt.
    Nov. 10, 1800. Spon: Parents.
Maria, daughter of Lewis Rush and Maria, b. July 19, 1798, bapt.
    Nov. 10, 1800. Spon: ----.
Nancy, daughter of Lewis Rush and Maria, b. Oct. 1, 1800,
    baptized Nov. 10, 1800. Spon: ----.
Maria Anna, daughter of John Cooper and Elizabeth, b. Oct. 7,

1796, bapt. Nov. 14, 1800. Spon: ----.
Henry, son of John Cooper and Elizabeth, b. Nov. 2, ----, bapt.
Nov. 14, 1800. Spon: ----.
Maria Marg., daughter of Jacob Smidt and Maria Catharine, b. Oct.
16, 1800, bapt. Nov. 14, 1800. Spon: Dan. Hans and Catharine.
Maria, daughter of Henry Bald and A. Maria, b. Oct. 19, 1800,
bapt. Nov. 14, 1800. Spon: Fred. Weisman, Maria Schneder,
wife of Ludw. Henk.
Anna Mary, daughter of Christian Weak and Hannah, b. Sept. 25,
1800, bapt. Nov. 25, 1800. Spon: George Spies and Margaret
Weiten.
Elizabeth, daughter of John Apple and Elizabeth, b. Sept. 20,
1800, bapt. Nov. 27, 1800. Spon: Alexander Scott and Cath.
Bamble.
Catharine, daughter of Christian Fonse and Catharine, b. Nov. 24,
1800, bapt. Nov. 29, 1800. Spon: Parents.
Samuel, son of Fred. Weyly and Barbara, b. Nov. 15, 1800, bapt.
Nov. 29, 1800. Spon: Parents.
Rebecca, daughter of John Hump and Margaret, b. Sept. 5, 1800,
bapt. Nov. 30, 1800. Spon: ----.
Margaret, daughter of Geo. Hains and Maria, b. Aug. 20, 1800,
bapt. Nov. 30, 1800. Spon: ----.
Rebecca, daughter of John Smith and Elizabeth, b. Feb. 4, 1800,
bapt. Nov. 30, 1800. Spon: Nicholas Juvenal and Rebecca
Bishin.
William, son of Christian Funck and Maria, b. March 22, 1800,
bapt. Nov. 30, 1800. Spon: Wm. Hull.
Elizabeth, daughter of John Borns and Elizabeth, b. Nov. 8, 1800,
bapt. Dec. --, 1800. Spon: Benjamin Borns and Elizabeth.
Susanna, daughter of Charles Nelson and Elizabeth, b. Nov. 23,
1800, bapt. Dec. --, 1800. Spon: J. M. Blush and Hannah.
Maria Catharine, daughter of William Arnd and Anna Catharine, b.
Nov. 30, 1800, bapt. Dec. 11, 1800. Spon: Ludw. Soeller,
Phil. Theod. Sedller, Maria Catharine and Maria Helena
Westphal.
Sophia, daughter of George Lutz and Maria, b. Nov. 26, 1800,
bapt. Dec. 15, 1800. Spon: David Aesert and Sophia Conwell.
Antoinetta, daughter of John Rudolph Stang and Maria, b. Dec. 1,
1800, bapt. Dec. 15, 1800. Spon: Gab. Kern and Maria Kann.
Maria, daughter of Philip Justus and Elizabeth, b. Sept. 18,
1800, bapt. Dec. --, 1800. Spon: Parents.
Henry Phillip, son of Jacob Belsterling and M. Magdalene, b. Aug.
12, 1800, bapt. Dec. --, 1800. Spon: P. Wisenbach and M.
Elizabeth.
Maria, daughter of George Kuhn and Margaret, b. April 8, 1799,
bapt. Dec. --, 1800. Spon: Gab. Kern and Margaret.
Maria, daughter of John Johnson and wife, b. Dec. 11, 1800,
baptized Dec. --, 1800. Spon: ----.
Johanna Elizabeth, daughter of John Adam Schlatter and Maria
Catharine, b. Aug. 4, 1800, bapt. Dec. 26, 1800. Spon:
Christian Fetter and Elizabeth Schlatter
M. Anna, daughter of Stephen McGill and Polly, b. Aug. 27, 1800,
bapt. Dec. 26, 1800. Spon: J. Hows and B. Redman.
M. Sophia, daughter of Charles Trout and Barbara, b. Oct. 12,
1800, bapt. Dec. 26, 1800. Spon: ----.

Fanny, daughter of Christian Fonse and Sophia, b. April 7, 1800,
   bapt. Dec. 28, 1800. Spon: Dr. P. Perry and Fanny.
William, son of Jacob Sinck and M. Mary, b. Dec. 11, 1800, bapt.
   Dec. 28, 1800. Spon: ----.
William, son of George Braun and Maria, b. Oct. 16, 1799, bapt.
   Dec. 28, 1800. Spon: ----.
Mary, daughter of Robert Purdy and Hetty, b. Dec. 31, 1789, bapt.
   Dec. 28, 1800. Spon: ----.
Stephen, son of Robert Purdy and Hetty, b. Oct. 29, 1792, bapt.
   Dec. 28, 1800. Spon: ----.
Hester, son of Hugh Robinson and Mary, b. ------ 1798, bapt. Dec.
   28, 1800. Spon: ----.
Sarah, daughter of Hugh Robinson and Mary, b. Oct. 25, 1800,
   bapt. Dec. 28, 1800. Spon: ----.
Peter, son of Henry Brasont and Elizabeth, b. Feb. 1, 1800, bapt.
   Feb. 6, 1801. Spon: Peter Wieder and Hannah.
Cath. Wilhelmina, daughter of George Petri and Louisa, b. Dec.
   19, 1800, bapt. Jan. 13, 1801. Spon: Wm. Snyder and
   Catharine.
Catharine, daughter of J. Ford and Catharine, b. Nov. 30, 1800,
   bapt. Jan. 13, 1801. Spon: ----.
John Jacob, son of Philip Otzler and Catharine, b. Nov. 14, 1800,
   bapt. Jan. 13, 1801. Spon: J. Sagersyler and Susanna.
John, son of Jacob Sybella and Wilhelme, b. Oct. 24, 1800, bapt.
   Jan. 13, 1801. Spon: John Hess and Eleonore.
John, son of Conrad Wigand and Elizabeth, b. Oct. 7, 1800, bapt.
   Jan. 13, 1801. Spon: John Esher and Margaret.
Thomas Jefferson, son of Daniel Vander Slice and Mary, b. Dec.
   15, 1800, bapt. Jan. 19, 1801. Spon: Henry Olsers and Anna
   Genuns.
Mary Nancy, daughter of James Tate and Catharine, b. Dec. 9,
   1800, bapt. Jan. 30, 1801. Spon: John Rusher and Rebecca.
Susanna, daughter of Herman Leck and Anna Mary, b. Dec. 30, 1800,
   bapt. Jan. 31, 1801. Spon: Parents.
Anna Catharine, daughter of Joseph Gally and Anna Catharine, b.
   Jan. 9, 1801, bapt. Feb. --, 1801. Spon: Parents.
Susanna, daughter of George Derfer and Lena, b. Jan. 3, 1801,
   bapt. Feb. 9, 1801. Spon: Parents.
Philip, son of John Mugy and Hannah, b. June 3, 1801, bapt. Feb.
   15, 1801. Spon: ----.
Sarah, daughter of Christian Reinhard and Christine, b. Nov. 8,
   1800, bapt. Feb. 23, 1801. Spon: ---.
Elizabeth, daughter of Daniel Morris and Elizabeth, b. Feb.
   6, 1801, bapt. Feb. 23, 1801. Spon: Conrad Shull and Barbara.
Catharine, daughter of John Rice and Elizabeth, b. Dec. 12, 1800,
   bapt. Feb. 25, 1801. Spon: Martin Trump and Catharine.
Anna Mary, daughter of Abraham Bleyler and Margaret, b. Dec. 16,
   1800, bapt. March 1, 1801. Spon: ----.
John, son of John Reiner and Elizabeth, b. Nov. 12, 1800, bapt.
   March 1, 1801. Spon: ----.
Hannah, daughter of Ludwig Snider and Christine, b. Jan. 26,
   1801, bapt. March 8, 1801. Spon: Bernard Weaver and Hannah.
Benjamin, son of Benjamin Faber and Anna Maria, b. Jan. 29, 1801,
   bapt. March 8, 1801. Spon: ----.

Cath. Elizabeth, daughter of Bernard May and Agnes, b. Feb. 16,
1801, bapt. March 8, 1801. Spon: John Ekert and Catharine
Elizabeth.
John Philip, son of John Rein and Catharine, b. Feb. 13, 1801,
bapt. March 10, 1801. Spon: P. Reypule and B. Dilcart.
M. Elizabeth, daughter of Jacob Snyder and Louisa, b. March 1,
1801, bapt. March 12, 1801. Spon: Ludwig Snyder and W. E.
Smith.
Henrietta, daughter of Henry Sailor and Mary, b. Feb. 18, 1801,
bapt. March 15, 1801. Spon: Parents.
Harriett, daughter of Michael Catz and Margaret, b. Feb. 13,
1801, bapt. March 15, 1801. Spon: ----.
Henry Sailor, Jr., son of Henry Sailor and May, b. Dec. 1, 1800,
bapt. March --, 1801. Spon: ----.
John Matthew, son of Matthew Lemaire and Amsoo, b. Oct. 10, 1800,
bapt. March 23, 1801. Spon: ----.
George, son of Peter Hess and Fanny, b. ------, bapt. April 6,
1801. Spon: Parents.
Anna, daughter of Abraham Winter and Ann Mary, b. Sept. 8, 1800,
bapt. April 6, 1801. Spon: Parents.
Carl, son of Conrad Keller and Catharine, b. March 27, 1801,
bapt. April 7, 1801. Spon: Carl Jung and M. Rubsnider.
John George, son of Jacob Kreider and Elizabeth, b. Feb. 11,
1801, bapt. April 11, 1801. Spon: ----.
Frederick Abraham, son of John Engelhart Bethuske and Anna Maria,
b. July 1, 1800, bapt. April 14, 1801. Spon: John Abraham
Nebis, Carl Fred. Sanda, Fred. Wm. Bartram and Christ. Nebis.
William, son of William Wallace and Margaret, b. Feb. 8, 1801,
bapt. April 14, 1801. Spon: ----.
Conrad, son of Anthony Hinckel and Catharine, b. March 22, 1801,
bapt. April 14, 1801. Spon: Conrad Hinckel and Barbara.
John Jacob, son of John Matthew and Maria, b. Feb. 14, 1801,
bapt. April 17, 1801. Spon: John J. Belsterling and Maria.
Maria Christine, daughter of Jacob Hipp and Maria Susanna, b.
Oct. 28, 1800, bapt. April 19, 1801. Spon: ----
Jacob, son of Henry Sheller and Susanna, b. March 21, 1801, bapt.
April 19, 1801. Spon: J. Haffner and Carl Sink.
John Frederick, son of John H. Strimel and Elizabeth Krate, b.
Jan. 6, 1801, bapt. April 19, 1801. Spon: ----.
John Walter, son of Michael Dubbs and Rachel, b. Oct. 27, 1800,
bapt. April 20, 1801. Spon: ----.
Abraham, son of George Baker and Sophia, b. March 18, 1801, bapt.
April 23, 1801. Spon: ----.
Susanna, daughter of Sen. Watson and Sarah Harriet, b. May 2,
1800, bapt. April 23, 1801. Spon: ----.
Louisa, daughter of Peter Peres and Fanny, b. April 10, 1801,
bapt. April 26, 1801. Spon: ----.
Juliana, daughter of Henry Hains and Phoebe, b. Nov. 13, 1800,
bapt. April 27, 1801. Spon: ----.
Isabella, daughter of Abraham Eberhart and Rebecca, b. April 22,
1798, bapt. May 11, 1801. Spon: ----.
Carl, son of Abraham Eberhart and Rebecca, b. March 29, 1800,
bapt. May 11, 1801. Spon: Baltas Kuhl and wife.
Eliza, daughter of George Opps (?) and A. Maria, b. Feb. 17,
1801, bapt. May 11, 1801. Spon: Cath. Winn.

Catharine, daughter of Nicholas Petit and Susan, b. April 21, 1801, bapt. May 15, 1801. Spon: George Cook and Catharine.

John Jacob, son of Henry Smith and Catharine, b. April 5, 1801, bapt. May 24, 1801. Spon: Parents.

Maria, daughter of Daniel Jefferson and Maria, b. March 30, 1801, bapt. May 24, 1801. Spon: ----.

John George, son of John Frey and M. Magdalene, b. Jan. 30, 1801, bapt. May 24, 1801. Spon: John George Dickel and Johanna Wilhelmina.

Christian, son of Christian Gebert and Marte, b. Oct. 5, 1800, bapt. May 25, 1801. Spon: ----.

Philip, son of Jacob Fouse and Jefferine, b. April 15, 1801, bapt. May --, 1801. Spon: Paul Klein and Frances Paris.

Maria, daughter of ------ Fouse and Frances, b. Sept. 12, 1800, bapt. May --, 1801. Spon: ----.

Henry, son of ------ Fouse and Frances, b. Aug. 30, 1798, bapt. May --, 1801. Spon: ----.

Elizabeth, daughter of ------ Ware and wife, b. Oct. 12, 1788, bapt. May 31, 1801. Spon: ----.

Jacob, son of Jacob Hitaler and Anna, b. Nov. 10, 1799, bapt. May 31, 1801. Spon: Parents.

John, son of Jacob Hitaler and Anna, b. Dec. 13, 1800, bapt. May 31, 1801. Spon: Parents.

John Wessel, son of John Wesel Ensaer and Elizabeth, b. June 11, 1800, bapt. June --, 1801. Spon: ----.

Catharine, daughter of Samuel Garwood and Elizabeth, b. March 14, 1801, bapt. June --, 1801. Spon: Samuel Rutenberger and Catharine.

Catharine, daughter of George Gilbert and Barbara, b. Dec. 30, 1797, bapt. June --, 1801. Spon: ----.

Nanny, daughter of George Cook and Catharine, b. Oct. 5, 1800, bapt. June --, 1801. Spon: ----.

George Henry, son of George Pressler and Catharine, b. March 20, 1801, bapt. June 14, 1801. Spon: ----.

John Christ., son of J. Christ Ostheins and Jane, b. April 27, 1801, bapt. June 14, 1801. Spon: ----.

M. Rachel, daughter of J. Christ Ostheins and Jane, b. Nov. 1, 1798, bapt. June 14, 1801. Spon: ----.

Joseph, son of Henry Meiers and Rebecca, b. June 25, 1800, baptized June 15, 1801. Spon: ----.

Jacob, son of Jacob Deal and Edith, b. April 11, 1801, bapt. June 19, 1801. Spon: Parents.

Elizabeth, daughter of Christian Kirchhoff and Mary Magdalene, b. Sept. 28, 1799, bapt. June 19, 1801. Spon: ----.

Susanna, daughter of Jacob Karr and Elizabeth, b. May 17, 1801, bapt. June 20, 1801. Spon: ----.

Eliza, daughter of Jacob Gardner and Maria, b. June 12, 1800, bapt. July 5, 1801. Spon: Parents.

John, son of Ezekiel Galbet and Susanna, b. Dec. 5, 1800, bapt. July 9, 1801. Spon: ----.

Eliza, daughter of Joseph Gibler and Rachel, b. Feb. 28, 1801, bapt. July 5, 1801. Spon: ----.

Catharine, daughter of Dominic Kimpech and Catharine, b. March 27, 1801, bapt. July 7, 1801. Spon: ----.

Margaret, daughter of George McDere and Anna, b. Oct. 5, 1800,

bapt. July 11, 1801. Spon: ----.
Elizabeth, daughter of Joseph Gibler and Rachel, b. Feb. 28,
1801, bapt. July 5, 1801. Spon: ----.
Elizabeth, daughter of James McKelroy and Dorothy, b. June 30,
1801, bapt. July 12, 1801. Spon: ------.
Henry, son of Peter Weaver and Anna, b. July 2, 1801, bapt. July
12,1801. Spon: ----.
Mary Rever, daughter of Christian Lawyer and Mary Rever, b. June
6, 1801, bapt. July 12, 1801. Spon: ----.
John, son of John Spangenberg and Charlotte, b. July 7, 1801,
bapt. July 14, 1801. Spon: Mary Graff.
M. Margaret, daughter of Ludwig Edris and Margaret, b. July 10,
1801, bapt. July 21, 1801. Spon: ----.
Maria, daughter of Michael Jager and Elizabeth, b. July 8, 1800,
bapt. July 21, 1801. Spon: ----.
Elizabeth, daughter of James Hoffman and Eva, b. Nov. 20, 1800,
bapt. July 25, 1801. Spon: Catharine Poth.
John, son of John Hill and Rebecca, b. March 31, 1801, bapt. July
28, 1801. Spon: ----.
William, son of Jacob Hill and Elizabeth, b. June 28, 1801, bapt.
July 28, 1801. Spon: Anna M. Hill.
Maria, daughter of George Fanse and Susan, b. March 5, 1801,
bapt. July 28, 1801. Spon: Rebecca Fanse.
William, son of George Kucken and Margaret, b. Jan. --, 1800,
bapt. Aug. 2, 1801. Spon: Elizabeth Jones.
Andrew, son of Philip Lowery and Margaret, b. June 30, 1801,
bapt. Aug. 4, 1801. Spon: ----.
Elizabeth, daughter of George Brown and Elizabeth, b. Aug. 19,
1800, bapt. Aug. 4, 1801. Spon: John Statelman and Catharine.
John, son of William Pifer and Esther, b. May 30, 1798, bapt.
Aug. 4, 1801. Spon: ----.
Eliza, daughter of William Pifer and Esther, b. March 28, 1801,
bapt. Aug. 4, 1801. Spon: Fred Lentz and Catharine.
Matilda, daughter of Wm. Wormsider and Ann Mary, b. May 26, 1801,
bapt. Aug. 6, 1801. Spon: ----.
Rebecca, daughter of Daniel Stillwagen and Maria, b. July 19,
1801, bapt. Aug. 11, 1801. Spon: ----.
Mag. Wilhelmina, daughter of Wm. Call and M. Frederica, b. July
27, 1801, bapt. Aug. 15, 1801. Spon: Geo. Wilhelm and M.
Magdalene.
Anna Catharine, daughter of John Sweis and Margaret, b. July 26,
1801, bapt. Aug. 16, 1801. Spon: ----.
Elizabeth, daughter of Jacob Rinedoller and Elizabeth, b. Dec.
24, 1788, bapt. Aug. 16, 1801. Spon: ---
Barbara, daughter of Jacob Rinedoller and Elizabeth, b. March 30,
1791, bapt. Aug. 16, 1801. Spon: ----.
Henry, son of Jacob Rinedoller and Elizabeth, b. June 24, 1793,
bapt. Aug. 16, 1801. Spon: ----.
Margaret, daughter of Jacob Rinedoller and Elizabeth, b. July 16,
1795, bapt. Aug. 16, 1801. Spon: ----.
Samuel, son of Jacob Rinedoller and Elizabeth, b. Dec. 31, 1799,
bapt. Aug. 16, 1801. Spon: ----.
George William, son of John Shuller and Maria, b. June 10, 1801,
bapt. Aug. 17, 1801. Spon: ----.
Balsar (Balthasar), son of Leonard Nagel and Catharine, b. May

17, 1801, bapt. Aug. 17, 1801. Spon: Balsar Nagel.
Samuel, son of Jacob Sigmon and Catharine, b. June 25, 1801,
    bapt. Aug. 19, 1801. Spon: ----.
Anna Maria, daughter of Conrad Bald and Sophia, b. Aug. 13, 1801,
    bapt. Aug. 22, 1801. Spon: Fred Bald and William Dicken.
Henry, son of Matthias Berkenbeil and Catharine, b. July 28,
    1801, bapt. Aug. 23, 1801. Spon: ----.
Catharine, daughter of John Lees and Elizabeth, b. Aug. 1, 1801,
    bapt. Aug. 23, 1801. Spon: Henry Lees and Cath. Davis.
John Bernard, son of John Hains and Maria, b. Aug. 9, 1801, bapt.
    Aug. 29, 1801. Spon: John Hains and Sarah Hains.
Jacob, son of John Sink and Elizabeth, b. Feb. 22, 1801, bapt.
    Aug. 29, 1801. Spon: Peter Field and Rachel.
Courtland Fred, son of Samuel Follwell and Elizabeth, b. Aug. 24,
    1801, bapt. Sept. 5, 1801. Spon: John J. Gubler and Abigail
    Kitts.
Ludwig, son of John Born and A. Mary, b. Aug. 30, 1801, bapt.
    Sept. 5, 1801. Spon: L. Snider and Christine.
Ludwig, son of Henry Dunlap and Sarah, b. Nov. 14, 1800, bapt.
    Sept. 10, 1801. Spon: Jacob Fout and Louisa.
George, son of John Geo. Walter and Hannah, b. Aug. 3, 1800,
    bapt. Aug. 24, 1800. Spon: John Grave and Cath. Streman.
Anna Catharine, daughter of John Carls Peter and wife, b. Sept.
    4, 1801, bapt. Sept. --, 1801. Spon: John Lendeman and
    Catharine.
Henry, son of John German and Elizabeth, 10 wks old, bapt.
    Sept. --, 1801. Spon: ----.
Jost Henry, son of John Jost Young and Catharine, b. Sept. 29,
    1800, bapt. Sept. 26, 1801. Spon: Jost Henry Young and
    Justina Blum.
Samuel Tudor, adult, b. ------ 1778, bapt. Sept. 26, 1801. Spon:
    ----.
Elizabeth, daughter of Samuel Tudor and Catharine, b. Oct. 4,
    1800, bapt. Sept. 26, 1801. Spon: Elizabeth West.
John, son of Jacob Reme(y) and Anna, b. Feb. 16, 1801, bapt.
    Sept. 27, 1801. Spon: ----.
Elizabeth, daughter of Valentine Gardner and M. Magdalene, b.
    Aug. 8, 1801, bapt. Sept. 27, 1801. Spon: Adam Coleman and
    Susanna.
Delisietta(sic), daughter of John Lowery and Dorothea, b. Jan. 8,
    1801, bapt. Sept. 28, 1801. Spon: Peter Lowery and Mary
    Lowery.
Conrad, son of Valentine Barnt and wife, b. Oct. 13, 1800, bapt.
    Sept. 28, 1801. Spon: Conrad Ax.
William, son of Paul Vonagen and Elizabeth, b. Oct. 3, 1799,
    bapt. Sept. 28, 1801. Spon: ----.
Daniel, son of Conrad Ax and Maria, residing at Frankfurt, b.
    Jan. 7, 1798, bapt. Sept. 28, 1801. Spon: ---.
Conrad, son of Conrad Ax and Maria, residing at Frankfurt, b.
    Aug. 10, 1798, bapt. Sept. 28, 1801. Spon: ---.
Margaret, daughter of Conrad Ax and Maria, residing at Frankfurt,
    b. Sept. 26, 1800, bapt. Sept. 28, 1801. Spon: ----.
Jean, daughter of Jonas Porter and Catharine, b. Aug. 30, 1801,
    bapt. Sept. 22, 1801. Spon: Parents.
Philip, son of Philip Miller and Susanna, b. Sept. 1, 1801, bapt.

Sept. 29, 1801. Spon: Catharine Raush.

Rebecca, daughter of Richard Tustin and Hannah, b. Aug. 9, 1801, bapt. Sept. 29, 1801. Spon: ----.

Carl, son of George Abel and Baradea(sic), b. Sept. 12, 1801, bapt. Sept. 30, 1801. Spon: Parents.

Rosina, daughter of John Immel and Maria, b. Sept. 15, 1801, bapt. Oct. --, 1801. Spon: George Rutter and Rosina Immel.

William, son of John Immel and Maria, b. Aug. 18, 1799, bapt. Oct. --, 1801. Spon: Parents.

Maria Catharine, daughter of John Bonn and Mary Catharine, b. Aug. 27, 1801, bapt. Oct. 7, 1801. Spon: Parents.

Susanna, daughter of Fred Zann and Susanna, b. Sept. 4, 1801, bapt. Oct. 8, 1801. Spon: Parents.

John George, son of Jos. Skinner and Gertrude, b. Sept. 26, 1801, bapt. Oct. 11, 1801. Spon: Geo. Hink and Ann and Christ. Badt.

Maria, daughter of Jacob Sellers and Elizabeth, b. Sept. 24, 1801, bapt. Oct. 13, 1801. Spon: ----.

John Henry, son of Henry Lang and Cath. Margaret, b. Oct. 11, 1801, bapt. Oct. 13, 1801. Spon: ----.

Charlotte, daughter of Wm. McSperen and Christine, b. Feb. 21, 1799, bapt. Oct. 13, 1801. Spon: Thomas McSperen and Charlotte Walter.

Maria, daughter of Thos. Jones and Elizabeth, b. July 23, 1801, bapt. Oct. 13, 1801. Spon: Wm. McSperen and Christine.

Sarah Ann, daughter of Henry Raskis and Maria, b. Nov. 19, 1800, bapt. Nov. 4, 1801. Spon: ----.

John, son of John Adolph and Elizabeth, b. July 13, 1801, bapt. Nov. 4, 1801. Spon: ----.

Maria, daughter of Simon Schuckart and Barbara, b. Aug. 5, 1801, bapt. Nov. 4, 1801. Spon: George Hillegas and Maria.

Matthias, son of Matthew Norris and Catharine, b. Nov. 19, 1800, bapt. Nov. 6, 1801. Spon: ----.

Esther, daughter of George Neuden and Margaret, b. Sept. 7, 1801, bapt. Nov. 7, 1801. Spon: ----.

Charles, son of Wilson Haven and Maria, b. Aug. 28, 1801, bapt. Nov. 7, 1801. Spon: ----.

John George, son of John Kapp and Catharine, b. Oct. 21, 1801, bapt. Nov. 7, 1801. Spon: ----.

Ann Mary, daughter of Jacob Krow and Elizabeth, b. Oct. 2, 1798, bapt. Nov. 7, 1801. Spon: ----.

John Oltenbury, son of Henry Wigand and Eleonora, b. Jan. 7, 1801, bapt. Nov. 7, 1801. Spon: John Wigand and Jacob Oltenbury.

John, son of Henry Lang and Cath. Mary, b. Oct. 14, 1801, bapt. Nov. 13, 1801. Spon: John Emerich and Charlotte.

John Michael, son of John Preh and Catharine, b. Oct. 23, 1801, bapt. Nov. 15, 1801. Spon: ----.

Catharine, daughter of Martin Miller and Elizabeth, b. Sept. 24, 1801, bapt. Nov. 15, 1801. Spon: ----.

Hannah, daughter of Henry Kraks and Hannah, b. Nov. 7, 1801, bapt. Dec. 7, 1801. Spon: Bernard Weaver and Hannah.

George, son of Leonard Rothore and Elizabeth, b. Nov. 1, 1801, bapt. Nov. 21, 1801. Spon: Parents.

Elizabeth, daughter of Henry Snider and Elizabeth, b. Oct. 21,

1801, bapt. Dec. 6, 1801. Spon: John Snider and Elizabeth.
Wilhelmina, daughter of Fred Troll and Polly, b. Oct. 12, 1801,
bapt. Dec. 6, 1801. Spon: ----.
Maria Ann, daughter of John Sauder and M. Ann, b. Oct. 22, 1801,
bapt. Dec. 6, 1801. Spon: ----.
Anna Margaret, daughter of Dennis Roloph and A. Margaret, b.
Sept. 21, 1801, bapt. Dec. 7, 1801. Spon: ----.
Ludwig, son of Carl Godfrey Paleske and Hannah Elmslie, b. Jan.
22, 1795, bapt. Dec. 14, 1801. Spon: ----.
Carl Godfrey, son of Carl Godfrey Paleske and Hannah Elmslie, b.
Sept. 16, 1797, bapt. Dec. 14, 1801. Spon: ---.
Maria Wilhelmina, daughter of Carl Godfrey Paleske and Hannah
Elmslie, b. July 28, 1799, bapt. Dec. 14, 1801. Spon: -----.
Elizabeth, daughter of Frederick Gaul and Dorothy, b. Nov. 19,
1801, bapt. Dec. 17, 1801. Spon: ----.
John, son of Dietr. Hartman and wife, b. Nov. 25, 1801, bapt.
Dec. 20, 1801. Spon: Andrew Bodenstein and Hannah.
Anna Catharine, daughter of John Mackensteier and Sally, 10 wks.,
3 days old, bapt. Dec. 27, 1801. Spon: ----.
Sally, daughter of Bost. Hoffman and Elizabeth, b. May 19, 1801,
baptized Dec. 27, 1801. Spon: ----.
Michael, son of Michael Hains and Molly, 9 wks old, bapt. Dec.
27, 1801. Spon: ----.
Susanna, daughter of John Pleyler and Anna, b. Dec. 10, 1801,
bapt. Dec. 27, 1801. Spon: ----.
Anna Isabella, daughter of John Snider and Elizabeth, b. July 29,
1801, bapt. Dec. 27, 1801. Spon: ----.
Maria, daughter of John Lenaman and Elizabeth, b. June 15, 1801,
bapt. Dec. 27, 1801. Spon: Rudolph.
William, son of William Fau and Barbara, b. Nov. 25, 1799, bapt.
Dec. 30, 1801. Spon: ----.
Elizabeth Maria, daughter of John Trangenstein and Maria, b. Aug.
2, 1801, bapt. Jan. 1, 1802. Spon: Eliz. M. Slatter.
Elizabeth, daughter of James Hunt and Maria, b. Oct. 26, 1801,
bapt. Jan. 3, 1802. Spon: ----.
John, son of Daniel Deal and Maria, b. Nov. 25, 1801, bapt. Jan.
5, 1802. Spon: ----.
Geo. Benjamin, son of John P. Maninger and Margaret, b. Nov. 6,
1801, bapt. Jan. 7, 1802. Spon: Geo. Christ. Frank and the
mother.
Rebecca, daughter of John Daudel and Barbara, b. Jan. 3, 1802,
bapt. Jan. 8, 1802. Spon: ----.
Henry Miller, son of Thomas Dungan and Maria, b. Aug. 14, 1800,
bapt. Jan. 13, 1802. Spon: ----.
Maria Ann and John Matthias, son and daughter of John Hangen and
Susanna, b. Dec. 5, 1801, bapt. Jan. 13, 1802. Spon: John
Metzger.
Michael, son of John Snider and Elizabeth, b. Oct. 15, 1801,
bapt. Jan. 14, 1802. Spon: Sophia ------.
Catharine, daughter of John Snider and Elizabeth, b. June 8,
1799, bapt. Jan. 14, 1802. Spon: Sophia ------.
Elizabeth, daughter of John Schreiner and Anna Maria, b. Jan. 6,
1802, bapt. Jan. 16, 1802. Spon: ----.
Elizabeth, daughter of Henry Frey and Barbara, b. Nov. 30, 1801,
bapt. Jan. 17, 1802. Spon: Philip Jung.

Isaac Franciscus, son of Ludwig Schell and Sophia, b. Dec. 15, 1801, bapt. Jan. 18, 1802. Spon: Parents.

Sarah, daughter of Margaret Feilselbach, 4 yrs. old the last of this mo., bapt. Jan. 19, 1802. Spon: ----.

Elizabeth, daughter of Henry Meyer and Rebecca, b. Oct. 25, 1801, bapt. Jan. 20, 1802. Spon: ----.

John, son of Jacob Funterslice and Maria, b. Jan. 12, 1802, bapt. Jan. 23, 1802. Spon: ----.

John Reinhard, son of Henry Haas and Elizabeth, b. Dec. 12, 1801, bapt. Jan. 24, 1802. Spon: ----.

John, son of Nicholas Kayser and Elizabeth, b. Jan. 14, 1798, bapt. Jan. 24, 1802. Spon: Parents.

Catharine, daughter of Nicholas Kayser and Elizabeth, b. June 1, 1801, bapt. Jan. 24, 1802. Spon: M. Haag and Christine.

Michael, son of John Sauerheber and Philippina, b. Dec. 25, 1801, bapt. Jan. 24, 1802. Spon: M. Haag and Christine.

Sarah, daughter of D. Witeman and A. Maria, b. Aug. 10, 1801, bapt. Jan. 24, 1802. Spon: M. Haag and Christine.

M. Eva, daughter of Wm. Ehrman and Elizabeth, b. Jan. 8, 1802, bapt. Jan. 24, 1802. Spon: ----.

M. Anna, daughter of Wm. Cooper and Mary, b. Dec. 18, 1801, bapt. Jan. 24, 1802. Spon: Wm Cooper and Frances Paris.

Emanuel, son of Samuel Helffenstein, Pastor, and wife, b. Oct. 29, 1798, bapt. ----. Spon: ----.

Samuel, son of Samuel Helffenstein, Pastor, and wife, b. Jan. 13, 1800, bapt. ----. Spon: ----.

John Albertus, son of Samuel Helffenstein, Pastor, and wife, b. March 14, 1801. Spon: ----.

Johanna Eva, daughter of John Peter Sann and Hannah Bernadina, b. Jan. 14, 1802, bapt. Jan. 24, 1802. Spon: Johanna Sann.

Hannah, daughter of Jacob Lichtel and Susanna, b. Dec. 16, 1801, bapt. Jan. 31, 1802. Spon: Anna Meyer.

Joseph Cornelius, son of Wm. Cornelius and Margaret, b. Nov. 22, 1801, bapt. Jan. 31, 1802. Spon: Fred. Dice and Elizabeth.

Charles Frederick, son of Matthias Gebler and Anna, b. Dec. 18, 1801, bapt. Jan. 31, 1802. Spon: John F. Gebler and Abigail Gebler.

Maria, daughter of Christian Bosbishel and Elizabeth, b. March 19, 1801, bapt. Feb. --, 1802. Spon: ----.

William, son of Christian Bosbishel and Elizabeth, b. Dec. 16, ----, bapt. Feb. --, 1802. Spon: ----.

John, son of George Reyner and Catharine, b. Jan. 13, 1802, bapt. Feb. 11, 1802. Spon: ----.

George, son of Jacob Heimberger and Elizabeth, b. Aug. 10, 1801, bapt. Feb. 11, 1802. Spon: ----.

Editor's note: From this point on only the births of 1800 and earlier are recorded.

Sarah, daughter of J. Ulrich and wife, b. July 27, 1791, bapt. March 14, 1802. Spon: ----.

Abraham, son of J. Ulrich and wife, b. July 20, 1796, bapt. March 14, 1802. Spon: ----.

Henry, son of J. Ulrich and wife, b. May 6, 1799, bapt. March 14, 1802. Spon: ----.

John George, son of Henry Plane and Christine, b. Aug. 3, 1797,

bapt. March 14, 1802. Spon: ----.
Anna Maria, daughter of Henry Plaine and Christine, b. Feb. 15, 1798, bapt. March 14, 1801.
John, son of John Williams and wife, b. June 28, 1800, bapt. March 28, 1802. Spon: ----.
Sarah, daughter of John Purche and Elizabeth, b. Jan. 19, 1800, bapt. April 3, 1802. Spon: Sam Purche and Christine.
Anna, daughter of Thomas Jones and Elizabeth, b. Nov. 23, 1800, bapt. April 11, 1802. Spon: ----.
John Henry, son of John Geo. Walter and Hannah, b. Aug. 27, 1800, bapt. April 19, 1802. Spon: W. Sahman and Polly Heinman.
Child of Conrad Wial and Elizabeth, b. April 14, 1800, bapt. May 5, 1802. Spon: John Snider and Maria.
Elizabeth, daughter of John Stower and Anna, b. Aug. 22, 1799, bapt. May 16, 1802. Spon: ----.
John, son of John Stower and Anna, b. June 10, 1800, bapt. May 16, 1802. Spon: ----.
Andrew, son of Conrad Fight and Catharine, b. Oct. 17, 1800, bapt. June 19, 1802. Spon: ----.
Elizabeth, daughter of L. Vanderslice and wife, 18 mos and 7 days old, bapt. June 19, 1802. Spon: ----.
John Wagener (Parents unknown, illegitimate child), b. Aug. 29, 1795, bapt. June 6, 1802. Spon: Henry Wagener and Catharine.
Frederick, son of Carl Hendrich and Helena, b. Feb. 25, 1799, bapt. June --, 1802. Spon: ----.
George, son of George Coleman and Susanna, 21 yrs., bapt. Jan. 4, 1803. Spon: ----.
Susanna, daughter of George Coleman and Susanna, 12 yrs., bapt. Jan. 4, 1803. Spon: ----.
Mary, daughter of George Coleman and Susanna, 8 yrs., bapt. January 4, 1803. Spon: ----.
William, son of Henry Fiss and wife, b. Sept. 21, 1797, bapt. March 15, 1803. Spon: ----.
Henry, son of Henry Fiss and wife, b. Oct. 11, 1799, bapt. March 15, 1803. Spon: ----.
Charlotte Catharine, daughter of John Weiberg and Charlotte, b. Oct. 22, 1794, bapt. Nov. 20, 1803. Spon: Catharine Reinhard.
Eveline, daughter of Briton Estial and Salome, b. Nov. 29, 1799, bapt. April 27, 1800. Spon: ----.
Elizabeth, daughter of Daniel Carpon and Maria Elizabeth, b. Jan. 21, 1800, bapt. April 18, 1803. Spon: -----
Andrew, son of Conrad Fight and Catharine, b. Sept. 17, 1800, bapt. July --, 1803. Spon: ----.
Samuel, son of Samuel Follwell and wife, b. March 10, 1764, bapt. July 15, 1803. Spon: ----.
Peter, son of Peter Polk and Maria, b. Aug. 29, 1800, bapt. Aug. 3, 1803. Spon: ----.
Eleonor, daughter of Abraham Sink and wife, b. Dec. 22, 1800, bapt. Sept. 11, 1803. Spon: ----.
Rebecca Maria, daughter Francis Daniel Cash and Margaret, b. Jan. 3, 1797, bapt. Jan. 8, 1804. Spon: -----
Thomas Caleb, son of Francis Daniel Cash and Margaret, b. Feb. 10, 1799, bapt. Jan. 8, 1804. Spon: ----.
Ann Eliza, daughter of Thomas Pastoris and Elizabeth, b. May 28, 1800, bapt. Jan. 8, 1804. Spon: ----.

Juliana, daughter of Jacob Munich and wife, b. Nov. 4, 1798, bapt. Aug. 6, 1804. Spon: ----.

Wm. Monington, son of Carl Wm. Sauder and Susanna, b. Nov. 15, 1798, bapt. Aug. 7, 1804. Spon: Carl Williams and Elizabeth Meyers.
Carl William, son of Carl Wm. Sauder and Susanna, b. Feb. 15, 1801, bapt. Aug. 7, 1804. Spon: Carl Williams and Elizabeth Meyers.
Susanna Sauder, mother, b. May 22, 1775, bapt. Aug. 7, 1804. Spon: Carl Williams and Elizabeth Meyers.
Carl, son of Daniel Sauder and Susanna, b. Dec. 9, 1803, bapt. Aug. 7, 1804. Spon: Carl Williams and Elizabeth Meyers.

Samuel, son of John Owens and Sarah, b. Aug. 24, 1799, bapt. Aug. 7, 1804. Spon: ----.
Carl, son of John Owens and Sarah, b. Oct. 1, 1803, bapt. Aug. 7, 1804. Spon: ----.

John Walter, son of Michael Dubs and Rachel, b. Sept. 27, 1800, bapt. Oct. 4, 1804. Spon: ----.

John, son of John Bouman and Anna, b. Feb. 14, 1784, bapt. Nov. 17, 1804. Spon: Parents.
Daniel, son John Bouman and Anna, b. ------, bapt. Nov. 17, 1804. Spon: Parents.
Anna Maria, daughter of John Bouman and Anna, b. ------, bapt. Nov. 17, 1804. Spon: Parents.
Catharine, daughter of John Bouman and Anna, bapt. Nov. 17, 1804. Spon: Parents.

-A-
ABEL, Anna
  Catharine, 106
  Baradea, 182
  Carl, 182
  Catharine, 167
  Christine, 45,
    64, 115
  Conrad, 106
  George, 79, 94,
    115, 182
  J., 167
  John, 45, 64,
    94, 115, 140
  Joseph, 45
  Margaret, 45,
    106, 167
  Maria, 64, 94,
    115
  Matthias, 1
  Peter, 45, 64,
    115
  Salome, 94
ABKA, Henry, 163
  Sarah, 163
ABRAHAM,
  Magdalene, 23
  Peter, 23
ABT, Hannah, 113
ADAIR, William,
  146
ADAM, Frederick,
  85
  Maria, 165
ADAMS, Catherine,
  35
  John, 11, 35
  M., 174
  Maria, 173
  Maria Esther, 35
  Robert, 173
  William, 174
ADOLPH, Elizabeth,
  182
  John, 182
AESCH, John, 152
AESCHER, John, 157
  Margaret, 157
AESERT, David, 176
AHNER, Jacob, 52
ALBACH, John, 84
ALBERGER, Adam,
  75, 169
  Anna Christine,
  2

Anna Maria, 104
Catharine, 171
Catherine
  Elizabeth, 2
Christian, 11,
  29, 73, 86, 99,
  140
Dolly, 171
Dorothea, 92
Dorothy, 88,
  100, 104, 117
Elizabeth, 100,
  169
George, 169
Henry, 166
John, 88, 100
John Philip, 104
Margaret, 92,
  120, 166, 171
Margaret
  Magdalene, 20
Maria Anna, 86
P., 171
Peter, 142
Philip, 20, 84,
  91, 92, 117,
  120, 171
Sarah, 166
Susan, 92
Susanna, 86, 91,
  99
William, 99
ALBERRY,
  Elizabeth, 84
ALBERT, Casper, 14
  Christine, 27
  Elizabeth, 11
  Maria, 4, 21,
  118, 164
ALBRECHT, Carl,
  119
  Charles, 71
  Maria, 71, 119
ALBURGER, Abraham,
  56
  Dorothea, 56
  Dorothy, 146,
  160
  Elizabeth, 160
  Jacob, 159
  John, 56, 144,
  160
  Margaret, 159
  Mariann, 159
  Philip, 76, 160

ALENTRUE, Francis,
  85
ALEXANDER, George,
  161
ALHAUSEN, John
  Theis, 74
ALLBERGER, John,
  141
ALLBURGER, Henry,
  152
  Jacob, 80
  Philip, 159
ALLENBACH,
  Frederick, 3
ALLIN, Mary, 14
ALLIOTH, Jerem.,
  73
ALMINDEYER,
  Catharine, 119
  Jacob, 119
ALTBERGER, Adam,
  18, 57
  Dorothea, 41
  Elizabeth, 18,
  57
  John, 12, 41
  John Adam, 128
  Margaret, 41
  Philip, 41
  Philip Jacob,
  57, 125
AMSTRONG, Sarah,
  41
ANDERSON,
  Catharine, 138
  John, 138
ANDREA, Anna, 22
  John, 22
  Maria, 22
ANDREAS, Eva, 101
  Philip, 49
  Sophia, 49
ANDRESSEN,
  Elizabeth, 12
ANGEL, Anna Maria,
  119
  Catharine, 119
  John, 119
  Valentine, 119
ANNIS, Anna, 36
  John, 36
  Thomas
    Lawersweiler,
    36

Index

ANNIS, Anna 36
    John 36
    Thomas
    Lawersweiler
    36
ANTHONY,
    Gottlieb 128
    Magdalene 14
APPEL, Anna 114
    Anna
    Elizabeth 75
    Christian 44
    Elizabeth 70
    109 110 120
    157 George
    167 Henry 70
    75 109 110
    114 157 167
    John 70 John
    George 120
    John Henry
    120 John Jost
    150 Margaret
    44 Maria 114
    Philip 44
    Valentine 44
APPLE, Elizabeth
    176 John 176
ARCHER, David 14
    Mary 14
ARCHIBALD,
    Catharine 164
    George 164
    William 164
ARENBOLD, Sarah
    10
ARIS, Anna
    Elizabeth 63
    Cathr. 73
    Catherine 63
    James 63 73
ARMBRISTER,
    Peter 112
ARMBRUSTER,
    Anthony 20
    Maria
    Elizabeth 20
ARMSTRONG, Polly
    81 Sarah 41

ARN, Daniel 15
    127 Dorothy
    15
ARND, Anna
    Catharine 176
    Maria
    Catharine 176
    William 176
ASBERGER,
    Dorothea 121
    John 121
    Peter 121
ASCH, Catharine
    145 Child 145
    Elizabeth 151
    Widow 143
ASH, Catharine
    167 Fred 167
ASHMAN, John
    Peter 165
    Magdalene 165
    Peter 165
ASHTON, Susanna
    80 William 80
ASM---,
    Catharine 172
    John 172
ASSELBACH,
    Margaret 114
    Philip 114
ASSMUS,
    Catherine 21
    John
    Christopher
    21
ATKINS, John 21
AUEL, George 70
    Margaret 70
    Peter 70
AUFFAHRT, Sophia
    79
AUFFORTH,
    Charlotte 77
AUGUST,
    Frederick 158
AULER, Child 130
ANNE, George 128
AUNER, David
    Jouman 93

Elizabeth 43
    Margaret 31
    43 93 Maria
    31 62 Peter
    31 43 62 93
    136 Sarah 136
    William 62
AX, Conrad 181
    Daniel 181
    Margaret 181
    Maria 181
AXS, Conrad 14
AXT, Conrad 93
    Maria 93

-B-
BAAST, Catherine
    37 Michael 37
BACH, Margaret
    158
BACHMAN, Barbara
    105 Catherine
    58 Christine
    105 Conrad 12
    42 58 88 103
    Elizabeth 88
    John Peter 42
    Margaret 103
    Susanna 12 42
    58 88 103
    Sarah 75
    Zacharias 105
BACHMANN, George
    144
BACHOFEN, John
    81 Mara 81
BACHOFF, George
    29 44 58 126
    Jacob 9 44
    John George
    29 Rebecca 58
    Sarah 29 44
    58
BACHOFFEN,
    Elizabeth 75
    George 1
BACHTLE, Daniel
    48 Margaret

48 Mary
Magdalene 48
BACK, Jacob 104
BACKIUS, Hannah
84 John 84
BACKOVEN, Anna
Maria 172
Elizabeth 172
John 172
Maria 153
BADER, Jacob 53
Maria 53
BAECHTLE, Daniel
19 33 61
Elizabeth 33
Margaret 19
33 61 Rebecca
61
BAECHTLEY,
Elizabeth 6
BAER, Elizabeth
81 John 81
BAERDT,
Catherine 63
74 John 4 59
John Michael
63 74 Susanna
4
BAERTH, Madg 77
BAGERT, Adam 65
George 65
Margaret 65
BAKE, Caroline
40 55
Caroline
Henrietta 55
Eva Francisca
40 Eva
Franerina 9
Herman 40 55
BAKER, Abraham
178 Adam 169
Catharine 169
Child 171
Conrad 171
Conrad Jr 175
Elizabeth 21
169 175
George 169 J

169 178 James
167 John 21
P. Conrad 170
Maria 170
Peter Barras
169 Sophia
178 Susanna
170 171 175
BAKES, Mrs 126
BAKOFEN, Anna
Maria 166
John 166
Maria 166
BALD, A.
Catharine 159
163 A. Maria
160 176 Anna
Maria 181
Catharine
Elizabeth 160
Conrad 181
Fred 181
Henry 159 163
176 John Jost
160 Maria 176
Sophia 181
BALDE, Anthony
74 88
Christine 74
88 Elizabeth
88 Maria 142
Maria
Christine 151
BALDI, Anthony
101 118 134
Christine 101
118 Elizabeth
118 134 John
140 Maria 101
BALDIN, Susanna
173 Wm 173
BALT, A.
Catharine 159
A. Christine
159 Frederick
159
BALTIST, John
168 Philippa
168 Wedje 168

BAM, Anna Maria
41 John 41
Maria 41
BAMBERGER,
Catharine
Elizabeth 106
Conrad 135
Elizabeth 130
Mary
Magdalene 4
Margaret 7
Maria 127
Michael 107
130 135
BAMBLE, Cath 176
BANKS, John 84
Maria 84
Sarah 29
William 29
BANTZ, Elizabeth
54 114 George
12 54 114 137
140 Isabella
54 Margaret
138 Maria 114
137 Peter 138
BARD, Sarah 77
BARDT, Magdalene
21 Peter 21
BARE, Elizabeth
85
BARN, Cath 84
BARNET, George
14 Sarah 14
BARNT, Conrad
181 Valentine
181 Wife 181
BARON, Helena 77
Philip 77
BARR, Abigail
101
BARREL, Jeremiah
77 Maria 77
BART, Margaret
81
BARTON, Anthony
81 Charity 81
BARTRAM, Sarah
76

BASELMAN, Sibylla,
  12
BASTIAN, George,
  96
  John George, 22
  Maria, 22
  Maria Eva, 96
BATING, Sarah, 77
BATOW, ---, 125
BATZ, Mr., 4
BAUER, Andrew, 34
  Barbara, 34, 58,
  77
  Elizabeth, 4
  George, 34
  John, 58
  Margaret, 34
  Paul, 77
BAUMAN, Catharine,
  163
  Christian, 163
BAUMER, Catharine,
  142
  Catherine, 64
  Elizabeth, 64
  George, 64, 83
BAUMGARDT, Anna
  Catherine, 63
  Catherine, 66
  Frederick, 66
  Jacob, 63, 66
BAUMGART,
  Catherine, 52
  Frederick, 149
  Jacob, 52
  Magdalene, 81
BAUMGARTEN, Carl
  Ludwig, 139,
  148
  Catharine, 115
  Catherine, 64
  Charles Ludwig,
  90
  George, 115
  Jacob, 64, 115
  John Christ
  Ludwig, 90
  John Christian,
  139
  Ludwig, 134
  Mary Magdalene,
  90
  Philippine
  Frederica, 134
BAUMGARTH,
  Catherine, 57

Gottfried, 57
Jacob, 57, 73
BAUMGARTNER,
  Catharine, 90
  Jacob, 90
BAXTER, Elizabeth,
  79
BAY, Sarah, 142
BAYARD, Adam, 108
  Rebecca, 108
BAYER, Adam, 154,
  157
  Andrew, 154
  Bebs, 77
  Benjamin, 24
  Catherine, 15,
  17
  Dorothea, 75
  Elizabeth, 15,
  24
  Frederick, 15,
  17
  Jacob, 24
  Rebecca, 154,
  157
BAYERLE,
  Diederick, 25
  Joanna, 25
BEAUMIES,
  Bartholomeus,
  75
BECHTLE, David, 74
  Mary Magdalene,
  123
BECK, A. Margaret,
  160
  Adam, 19, 37
  Anna Maria, 9
  Barbara, 80
  Catharine, 110,
  140, 150, 160
  Catherine, 21,
  26, 27, 73
  Conrad, 81
  Elizabeth, 111
  Eva Maria, 57
  George, 83, 110
  Herman, 160
  Jacob, 111
  John, 21, 57,
  73, 160
  John Diehlman,
  26
  John Dielman,
  128
  John Dilman, 110

Magdalene, 160
Margaret, 37
Maria Margaret,
  19
Susanna, 19, 37
BECKE, Elizabeth,
  59
  James, 59
  Susanna, 59
BECKER, A. Maria,
  161
  Abia, 58
  Adam, 107, 156
  Ann Maria, 92
  Anna Elizabeth,
  45, 135
  Anna Margaret,
  27
  Anna Maria, 72,
  44, 55, 62, 72,
  99, 103, 106,
  117, 119, 120,
  137
  Barbara, 157,
  170
  Bernard, 38
  Catharine, 76,
  92, 93, 94, 95,
  112, 133, 161
  Catherine, 9,
  32, 44, 47, 51,
  54, 67, 70
  Christine, 48
  Conead, 117
  Conrad, 72, 18,
  42, 55, 58, 76,
  99, 134, 161
  Elizabeth, 72,
  27, 36, 38, 39,
  45, 55, 59, 71,
  73, 79, 81, 83,
  95, 97, 103,
  107, 113, 118,
  119, 170
  Francis, 63
  Frederick, 162
  George, 93, 103,
  118, 120, 137,
  139, 156, 157
  George William,
  161
  Gertrude, 47,
  59, 94
  Henry, 47, 59,
  70, 94
  Isabella, 63

Jacob, 72, 33,
  51, 58, 59, 67,
  73, 95, 97,
  112, 118
Jana, 47
Jenny, 47
John, 9, 30, 36,
  39, 51, 55, 71,
  78, 103, 109,
  113, 150, 157,
  161, 168, 170,
  173
John David, 65
John Debus, 67
John George, 76,
  106
John Jacob, 2
Julianna, 71
M. Magdalene,
  156
Magdalene, 79
Margaret, 18,
  59, 95, 156
Maria, 18, 39,
  47, 49, 55, 58,
  62, 65, 67, 74,
  81, 109, 125,
  162, 163, 173
Maria Catherine,
  73
Marl., 77
Mary Magdalene,
  20, 42, 55, 58,
  87, 99, 117,
  147
Michael, 47
Mrs., 21
Nancy, 168
Peter, 20, 27,
  42, 45, 55, 58,
  73, 87, 97, 99,
  117, 125
Samuel, 55, 93,
  117, 134
Sarah, 58, 65,
  120, 139
Sophia, 93, 106,
  120, 156, 168
Sophia
  Magdalene, 156
Susanna, 53, 161
Valentine, 58
Wendel, 2
William, 39, 44,
  47, 62, 70, 72,
  92, 93, 103,

119, 120, 123,
  128, 133
BECKLEIN,
  Margaret, 15
BECKLY,
  Christopher,
  111
  Daniel, 111
  Elizabeth, 35
  Margaret, 111
BECKMAN, Barbara,
  39, 53, 68, 93
  Catherine, 39
  Christine, 138
  Christopher, 68
  Daniel, 53
  John Frederick,
  93
  Zacharias, 11,
  39, 68, 93, 138
  Zechariah, 53
BECKMANN, Barbara,
  145
BEDDER, Elizabeth,
  85
  John, 85
BEDELLION,
  Catherine, 10
  Isaac, 10, 75
BEDFORD,
  Catherine, 12
BEERLY, Catharine,
  107
  Henry, 107
  Maria, 107
BEEZLEY, Johnston,
  10
BEGLE, Anna Maria,
  143
BEHLER, Jacob, 118
  Margaret, 118
  Maria, 118
BEHLERT, Jacob,
  145
BEHRNS, John, 77
BEHRT, Margaret,
  79
BEIERT, Catharine,
  80
BELGESTIMEL, John,
  170
  John Jacob, 170
  Mary Catharine,
  170
BELL, Elizabeth,
  168

George, 156
James, 48, 93
Magdalene, 48
Margaret, 37, 64
Rachel, 7
William, 37, 64
BELO, Christine,
  31
  John, 31
  Margaret, 31
BELONI, Judith,
  146
BELSTERLING,
  Catharine, 159
  Henry, 106
  Henry Phillip,
  176
  Jacob, 93, 106,
  123, 159, 176
  John Henry, 143
  John J., 178
  John Jacob, 76
  M. Magdalene,
  159, 176
  Margaret, 123
  Maria, 178
  Maria
  Christianna, 93
  Mary Magdalene,
  93, 106, 123
BELSTERMAN, Lena,
  165
BELTZ, George, 76
  Hannah, 82
BENCIL, Margaret, 84
BENDER, Barbara,
  82
  Catharine, 122
  Henry, 79
  John, 151
  Maria, 122, 163
  Nicholas, 122
  William, 163
BENEDICT,
  Christian, 80
BENER, Rachel, 74
BENET, Catharine,
  160
  Joseph, 160
  Rebecca, 160
BENN, John, 101
  Leona, 101
BENNER, Catharine,
  115
  Catherine, 55
  Christian, 82

Elizabeth, 157
John, 55, 115,
149
Matthew, 157
Sarah, 157
BENNET, Catharine,
95, 98, 113
John, 98
Joseph, 76, 98,
113
Philip, 113
BENSEL, George, 22
Margaret Sarah,
22
BENSER, Catharine,
84
BENSON, Henry, 82
BENTHER, John
George, 125
Nicholas, 125
BERCK, Jacob, 140
BERCKELBACH,
Jacob, 84
BERCKEMEYER,
Daniel, 25
Margaret, 22, 25
BERCKENBEIL, Anna
Margaret, 32
Anna Maria, 32
Barbara, 11
Elizabeth, 130
George, 19
John, 32
Matthew, 130
BERCKENBEUL, Anna
Margaret, 64
Anthony, 23
Barbara, 23, 64
Frederick, 23
John, 64
John Diedrich,
13
John George, 64
BERCKIN,
Catherine, 45
Charles, 2
George, 45
George Henry, 45
BERENSTECHER,
Andrew, 121
BEREY, Jacob, 78
BERG, Widow, 8
BERGENDALLER,
Catherine, 15
BERGER, Barbara,
158

Christopher, 140
Henry, 175
John, 175
Justus, 165
Magdalene, 175
Margaret, 26
BERGHEIMER,
Andrew, 41
Elizabeth, 41
Henry, 41
Isaac, 41
Margaret, 41
William, 41
BERGMAN, John, 75
BERGMAYER, Daniel,
79
BERKENBEIL,
Catharine, 181
Henry, 181
Matthias, 181
BERKENBER,
Catharine, 172
Elizabeth, 172
Margaret, 172
Matthew, 172
BERKINHAUS, Anna
Maria, 165
Elizabeth, 165
Jacob, 165
Susanna, 165
BERLEBACH,
Catharine, 172
J. P., 172
John Philip, 172
BERLY, Elizabeth,
97
Henry, 97
Maria, 97
BERNER, Elizabeth,
15
BERNET, John, 165
BERRY, Alexander,
20, 29
China, 20
Henry, 20, 29
Jane, 29
Nancy, 2, 20
Rachel, 20, 29
BERT, Valentine,
84
BERTZEN, Benjamin,
1
BEST, Henry, 149
BETH, Cornelius,
37
Isabella, 37

Maria Joanna, 37
BETHUSKE, Anna
Maria, 178
Frederick
Abraham, 178
John Engelhart,
178
BETIER, Claudius
Antonius, 76
BETSCH, Dorothy,
76
BETZLER, Casper,
65, 93
Elizabeth, 65,
93
John Henry, 65
John Paul, 93
BEUDEMAN,
Catharine, 69
BEUMER, Anna
Maria, 106
Catharine, 89,
106
George, 55, 74,
89, 106
BEVING, John, 115
Maria, 115
BEYER, Adam, 51
Anna Margaret,
65
Christine, 51
John Henry, 65
Margaret, 51
BICKER, Catharine,
116
BICKMAN,
Frederick, 130
Zacharias, 130
BIEGLE, Christian,
124
Daniel, 31, 85,
94
George, 94
Margaret, 31, 94
BIEL, Susanna, 73
BIER, ---, 6
BIESLE, Susanna,
76
BIGG, Mary, 84
BIGLE, Margaret,
28
BIGONEY,
Catherine, 19
John, 19
BIGONNE, Cath., 51

Catherine, 31,
64
BINDER, Barbara,
14
Hannah, 70
Jacob, 7, 96,
17, 43
Magdalene, 17
Maria, 96
BINGEL, John, 12
BINGEMAN,
Catherine, 15
BIRCKENBEIL, Anna,
97
Anna Margaret,
4, 18, 97
Anthony, 135
Barbara, 38
Catharine, 160
Christian, 108
Elizabeth, 38,
89
George, 13
John, 18, 38, 99
John George, 97
Margaret, 18
Maria, 89, 99,
108, 122, 143,
160
Matthew, 89, 99,
108, 122, 160
Rebecca, 144
William, 122
BIRCKENBEUL, Anna
Margaret, 66
Elizabeth, 66
John George, 66
Sophia, 2
BIRTH, Catherine,
40
Elizabeth, 40
Nicholas, 40
BISCHHOVEN,
Gerhard, 75
BISCHOB,
Elizabeth, 121
BISCHOFFBERGER,
Adam, 5, 24
Anna Catharine,
125
Anna Catherine,
11, 20, 40
Catherine, 24
Christine, 81
Elizabeth, 35,
42, 58, 93

George, 42
Jacob, 11, 24,
35, 40, 42, 58,
75, 93
Sarah, 93
BISCHOFFSBERGER,
Elizabeth, 81
BISCHOT, Maria, 92
Ph. Frederick,
92
Philip
Frederick, 92
BISHIN, Rebecca,
176
BITTING,
Catherine, 25
Elizabeth, 36,
64
John, 64
Joseph, 25
Ludwig, 25, 36
Maria, 25, 85
Mary Magdalene,
64
Sarah, 36
BLACK, Elizabeth,
80
BLAIS, Peter, 84
BLANCKENHAN,
Magdalene, 26
Michael, 26
BLANCKENHORN,
Michael, 5
BLATTEBERGER,
Elizabeth, 79
BLECKER,
Catharine, 80
BLESHE, Jonas, 127
BLETTERMAN,
Elizabeth, 45
Henry, 45
BLEYER, Anna, 174
John, 174
Susan, 174
BLEYLER, Abraham,
177
Anna Mary, 177
Margaret, 177
BLOCHER,
Elizabeth, 83
BLOOM, George, 13,
96
Philippina, 96
BLOYD, David, 154
BLUIS, Barbara,
173

John, 173
Peter, 173
BLUM, Ann
Gertrude, 84
Anna Philippina,
137
Catharine, 87,
116
Catherine, 45,
62, 71
Elizabeth, 13
George, 39, 45,
62, 69, 87,
111, 116, 137
John George, 152
John Harry, 84
Joseph, 62, 116
Justina, 181
Maria, 77
Nicholas, 41
Philippina, 39,
69, 111
Rosina, 87
BLUME, Joseph, 127
BLUSCH, Christine,
70
Jonas, 70
Peter, 70
BLUSH, Hannah, 176
J. M., 176
BLYELER, John, 154
BOB, Emmanuel, 138
BOBSCHEL,
Christian, 84
BOCK, Christine,
57
William, 83
BOCKEMEYER, Philip
Jacob, 1
BOCKENMEYER,
Catherine, 19
Jacob, 19
Maria, 15
Philip Jacob, 15
BOCKIUS, Barbara,
28
Elizabeth, 52
Eva, 18, 30
Eve, 173
Godfrey, 173
Godfried, 148
Gottfried, 18,
30
Hannah, 28, 48,
84
Henry, 173

John, 28, 84
Maria, 30
Mary, 14
Peter, 13, 14,
  48, 52, 73
Philip, 28, 48,
  84
William, 18
BOCKLE,
  Christopher,
  141
BODENSTEIN,
  Andrew, 183
  Hannah, 183
BODT, John, 153
BOEHM, Anna Maria,
  68
  Catharine, 121
  Daniel, 78, 121
  Elizabeth, 128
  John Philip, 130
  Maria, 13, 44
  Philip, 44, 68,
  130
  William, 121
BOEHME, Charles
  Ludwig, 5
  Kitty, 12
BOELER, Catherine,
  49
  Gottfried, 49
  Susanna Louisa,
  49
BOEM, ---, 153
BOGER, Christine,
  61
  Elizabeth, 73
  Frederick, 61
  Susanna, 61
BOHRNHAUS,
  Elizabeth, 108
  George, 108
  Margaret, 108
BOLEBACHER,
  Margaret, 78
BOLENDER, Henry,
  132
  Rhoda, 132
BOLIN, John, 129
BOLLBACH,
  Margaret, 158
BOLLECK, Mary
  Magdalene, 76
BOM, Catherine, 47
  Elizabeth, 2,
  149

George, 47
John, 2, 18, 34,
  47, 149
Margaret, 34
Maria Elizabeth,
  18
Susanna, 18
BOMB, Catharine,
  174
  Elizabeth, 174
  Jacob, 174
BOND, Mary, 73
BONENACKER,
  Elizabeth, 11
BONN, John, 182
  Maria Catharine,
  182
  Mary Catharine,
  182
BONNER, Elizabeth,
  16, 34, 53
  George, 1, 8
  Henry Moser, 16
  Jacob, 6, 16,
  34, 53, 151
  John, 145
  Philip, 53
  Philip Rudolph,
  34
  Rudolph, 8
BONNET, Ann, 76
BOOG, Jacob, 78
BOOM, Catharine,
  86
  Catherine, 58
  Conrad, 58
  Elizabeth, 86
  John, 58, 86
  Susanna, 4
  Theodore, 137
BOOS, Frederick,
  123
BOP, Peter, 56
BORCK, Margaret,
  58
BORCKEN,
  Catherine, 28
  George, 28
  John Frederick,
  28
BORG, Elizabeth,
  29
  Philip, 29
BORN, A. Mary, 181
  John, 80, 181
  Ludwig, 181

BORNHAUS,
  Catharine, 99,
  133
  Christian, 92
  Elizabeth, 47,
  64, 68, 92, 99
  Frederick, 47
  George, 13, 47,
  64, 68, 92, 99,
  133, 138, 141
  Margaret, 138
  Regina, 142
BORNS, Benjamin,
  176
  Elizabeth, 176
  John, 176
BORTZ, Anna Maria,
  141
  Elizabeth, 155
BOSBISHEL,
  Christian, 184
  Elizabeth, 184
  Maria, 184
  William, 184
BOSCH, John, 131
BOSER, Adam, 171
  Catharine, 171
  Rebecca, 171
BOSHARDT, Andrew,
  65
  Catharine, 65
BOSKIS, John, 168
  M. Catharine,
  168
BOSS, Frederick,
  79
BOSSART, Jacob, 17
  Mary Magdalene,
  17
BOSSELS, Catherie,
  18
BOSSERT, Jacob,
  70, 147
  Maria, 70
  Susanna, 70
BOSSERTH, Jacob,
  103
  Maria, 103
  Peter, 103
BOT, Elizabeth, 36
  John, 36
BOTT, Catharine,
  109
  Elizabeth, 101,
  109

John, 101, 109, 132
John Adam, 101, 132
BOTTEM, Catharine, 24
BOTTOM, Catherine, 12
BOTZ, George, 123
Maria, 123
Mary, 12
BOUDEN, Regina, 164
Stephen, 82, 164
BOUMAN, Anna, 186
Anna Maria, 186
Catharine, 186
Daniel, 186
John, 90, 186
Salome, 90
BOUSSIER, Jean, 155
BOUTLER, James, 14
BOUTSCHER, John, 74
BOWEN, John, 73
BOWLE, Elizabeth, 12
BOYER, Adam, 14, 92
Anna Catherine, 34
Catharine, 85, 87
Catherine, 4, 19, 26, 31, 34, 47, 61
Catherine Elizabeth, 38
Christine, 128
Elias, 38
Elizabeth, 38, 92
Fred, 85, 87
Frederick, 19, 26, 31, 34, 47, 61
Jacob, 38
John Fred, 87
Margaret, 92
Martin, 3
Susanna, 47
BOYERT, Hannah, 36
John, 36
BRACKLIN, Christine, 28

BRADENECK, Andrew, 89
Ann Rosina, 89
Clara, 89
BRADERCK, Mr., 127
BRADERICK, Andrew, 15, 33, 46, 70
Elizabeth, 46
John Daniel, 15
Maria, 15, 33, 46, 70
Thomas, 33
BRADLER, Catharine, 154
BRANBY, Elizabeth, 133
John, 133
BRAND, William, 6
BRANDEL, Anna Maria, 37
Christian, 37
Elizabeth, 101
BRANHAM, Ebenezer, 44
BRANHMA, Ebenezer, 44
BRANING, Jacob, 85
Maria, 85
William, 85
BRANSON, Elizabeth, 166
George, 166
Henry, 166
BRASONT, Elizabeth, 177
Henry, 177
Peter, 177
BRATLER, John Jacob, 134
BRAUBERT, Hannah, 106
John, 136
John George, 106
Maria, 136
William, 106
BRAUBET, Catharine, 101
John, 101
Maria, 101
Philippina, 101
BRAUER, Jacob, 79
BRAUHART, Barbara, 115
Elizabeth, 115
John George, 135

William, 115, 135
BRAUN, Abia, 24
Apollonia, 111
Arent, 78
Catharine, 162, 169
Catharine Elizabeth, 156
Elizabeth, 24, 103, 116, 147, 156
Esther, 83
George, 103, 116, 156, 177
George Peter, 103
Henrietta, 152, 162
Henry, 80
Jacob, 101
John, 24, 162
John George, 108
John Peter, 149
John William, 111
Joseph, 101
Leonard, 2
Maria, 101, 108, 145, 177
Mary Magdalene, 145
Peter, 162, 169
William, 83, 111, 177
BRAUNIG, Catherine, 58
Elizabeth, 6, 31, 58
George, 18
Jacob, 18, 31, 39
John, 58
Margaret, 18, 31, 39
Maria, 39
BRAUPERT, John, 159
Philippina, 159
William, 159
BREALSFORD, Morton, 65
BREDA, Henry, 14
BREDE, Anna, 55, 71
David, 55

Henry, 55, 71
BREDING, Margaret,
  75
BREEDING,
  Elizabeth, 174
  John Henry, 174
  Margaret, 158
  Mary, 84
  William, 174
BREESE, Susanna,
  144
BREH, A.
  Elizabeth, 145
BRENNEISEN, John,
  49
BRENNERMAN,
  George, 150
BRENTZ, Catharine,
  107
BRETTER,
  Elizabeth, 72
  John, 72
BRETZ, Anna Maria,
  120
  Elizabeth, 155
  Eva, 105, 120,
  155
  Henry, 77, 105,
  120
  Jacob, 155
  John, 105
BREUNIG,
  Christine, 59
  Frederick, 59
BREUNING,
  Catharine, 101
  Jacob, 101
  Margaret, 101
BREVEN, Barbara,
  169
BREY, Anna Mary,
  173
  Catharine, 170,
  173
  John, 170, 173
BRICKENBEUL,
  Catherine, 3
BRIDGES, Susanna,
  12
BRIMER, Adam, 35
  Maria, 35
BRINGHURST,
  Elizabeth, 84
BRITTEL, Adam, 131
  Barbara, 131

BRITTON, Casper,
  29, 87
  Louisa, 87
  Paul, 154
  Paul Casper, 30,
  39
  Sarah, 80
  Susanna, 39
BROCK, Anna, 15
BRODERICK, Andrew,
  76
BRONNER, Adam, 41,
  56, 128
  Anna Maria, 56
  Catherine, 21,
  66
  Dolly, 49
  George, 49
  Jacob, 86
  John, 21, 66
  John George, 15
  Maria, 41, 56
BRONNERT, Adam, 88
  Maria, 88
  Sarah, 88
BROOKMAN,
  Chressely, 12
BROOMSEN,
  Elizabeth, 60
  John, 60
BROUN, Anna
  Dorothea, 92
  George, 92
  Jacob, 75
  Margaret, 9
  Maria, 13, 92
  Martin, 92
  Rebecca, 76
  Sarah, 12
BROWN, Abia, 40,
  56
  Barbara, 72, 94
  Benage, 80
  Catherine, 66
  Christian, 91
  Elizabeth, 12,
  20, 45, 67, 180
  Frederick, 45,
  67
  George, 13, 54,
  180
  Jacob, 55, 62,
  72
  Johanna, 174

John, 10, 40,
  56, 66, 72, 94,
  174
John George, 54
John Peter, 21
Magdalena, 43
Margaret, 7, 35,
  40, 55
Maria, 54
Nancy, 70
Rebecca, 55
Regina, 21, 35
Valentine, 21,
  35, 125
William, 61
BRUCH, Louisa, 157
BRUCHHOLTZ,
  Bernard, 20, 70
  Catherine, 20,
  70
BRUNNER, Adam, 24,
  112, 142
  Apollonia, 102
  Catharine, 102,
  160
  Elizabeth, 121,
  160
  George, 102, 160
  Jacob, 121
  John, 112
  Maria, 24, 112
BRYEN, Mary, 10
BUCHERT, Agnes,
  143
  Paul, 137
BUCHHAMMER, John,
  80
BUCK, Jacob, 51
BUCKINGHAM,
  Hannah, 84
BUDDY, Elizabeth,
  75
BUETTING,
  Elizabeth, 87,
  112
  John, 87, 112
  John George, 87
BUHN, John, 86
BUMP, Catharine,
  102
  John, 102
  Peter, 102
BUNNER, Anna
  Ursula, 131
BURCH, Maria, 55
  Robert, 55

BURCHHARDT,
Margaret, 11
BURCK, Elizabeth,
10, 25
Ludwig, 15
Mary Catherine,
15
Philip, 25
Robert, 15
Rotbert, 3
BURCKERT, Jacob,
123
Margaret, 123
BURCKHARD, Jacob,
136
John Adam, 136
Martin, 18
BURCKHARDT, Anna
Margaret, 71
Jacob, 60, 71,
100
John Adam, 100
John Jacob, 60
Margaret, 71,
100
BURG, Gottlieb, 61
Maria, 61
BURGETH, Adam, 120
Apollonia, 120
Catharine, 120
BURGHARD, Anna
Maria, 30
Jacob, 30
BURGHART, Anna
Maria, 11
BURTH, Maria, 78
BUSCH, Christian,
10
Christopher, 40
Christopher
Abraham, 19
Elizabeth, 19,
40, 83
Jacob, 40
William, 19
BUSER, A. Maria,
159
Adam, 159
Elizabeth, 144
Margaret, 159
BUSH, Edward, 76
BUTH, Diederich,
79
BUTRET, Catharine,
168
Daniel, 168

BUTTNER, John
Peter, 139
BUTTON, Elizabeth,
12
BYRAM, Mary, 82

-C-
CAEST, Barbara,
120
George, 120
Jacob, 120
CALL, M.
Frederica, 180
Mag. Wilhelmina,
180
William, 180
CAMERON, Anna, 15(
Elizabeth, 158
James, 158
CAMPER, Michael,
25
Susanna, 25
CAMPHER, John
Adam, 165
Maria, 165
CAPP, Anna Maria,
47
Catharine, 111
Catherine, 47
John, 13, 47,
111, 137
Magdalene, 111
Mary Magdalene,
137
CAPPELER, Bernard,
34
David, 34
Elizabeth, 34
CAPTAIN,
Elizabeth, 43
Osman, 43
Thomas, 43
CARBAN, John Carl,
105
John Daniel, 105
Maria Elizabeth,
105
CARBON, Daniel, 16
Elizabeth, 16
CARL, Catharine,
169
Elizabeth, 169
John, 169
CARLSEN, Margaret
Maria, 77

CARPON, Daniel,
185
Elizabeth, 185
Maria Elizabeth,
185
CARRIGAN,
Christine, 83
CARSBACH,
Catherine, 42
Maria, 42
Martin, 42
CARSPACH, Maria,
119
Martin, 98, 119
Mary Magdalene,
98
Susanna, 119
CART, Catharine,
77
CASANDER, Eckhard,
9
CASCHA, Gabriel,
20
Magdalene, 20
Philip, 5, 20
CASCHAH,
Elizabeth, 57
Elizabeth
Louisa, 57
John, 57
CASH, Francis
Daniel, 185
Margaret, 185
Rebecca Maria,
185
Thomas Caleb,
185
CASNER, Catharine,
171
J., 171
CASPER, John, 157
CASSER, Peter, 136
Philip, 136
CASTMER, William,
153
CATZ, Harriett,
178
Margaret, 178
Michael, 178
CAUL, William, 84
CAVE, Thomas, 12
CAX, Margaret, 14
CERISIER, Jean
Baptiste, 79
CERRAL, Dinah, 76

CESH, Catherine, 56
Frederick, 56
CHAMBERLAIN, John, 85
Susanna, 74
CHAMBERLEIN,
Charles, 47, 52, 68
Lydia, 52
Magdalene, 47
Maria, 14, 31, 52, 68
CHAMBERS, John, 8
CHARTER, John, 24
Maria, 24
CHRISTEL,
Christopher, 175
CHRISTIAN, John, 155
CHRISTIE, William, 151
CHYASY, William, 80
CINCH, Anna
Margaret, 96
Catharine, 96
Jacob, 96
CINCK, Elizabeth, 98
John, 98
CIPRIAN, Henry, 75
CLAGES, Daniel, 175
Maria, 175
Richard, 175
CLAMPFER, Adam, 22, 47
Catherine, 32
Elizabeth, 22
John, 47
Maria, 22, 32, 47
Sarah Goodwin, 22
William, 4, 32
CLARCK, Margaret, 76
CLARCKSON, John, 80
CLARMAN,
Elizabeth, 96
John, 96
CLASSEN,
Elizabeth, 111

CLAUDY,
Christopher, 80
CLAWYES, Hannah, 120
John, 120
Rosina, 120
CLEAR, Hannah, 73
CLEMENS,
Catharine, 98
Elizabeth, 116
Joseph, 98
Samuel, 116
Valentine, 98, 116
CLERCK, Elizabeth, 114
Joseph, 114
Rachel, 114
CLETHEN, Anna
Margaret, 18
Margaret, 18
William, 18
CLINNECK,
Catharine, 99
John, 99
John Carl, 99
CLINTON, Maria, 77
CLIVER, Jacob, 23
Maria, 1, 23
CLOEDY, Catharine, 75
CLOUD, Anna Maria, 162
Joseph, 162
CLOYER, Anna, 76
CLUMBER, Anna, 54
John, 54
Philip, 54
Rebecca, 54
Susanna, 54
CLUMBERGER,
Philip, 139
CLUNN, John, 80, 144
COATES, Catharine, 87
Margaret, 87
Stephen, 87
COBER, Charles, 27
Elizabeth, 27
Maria, 27
COFFIN, Jacob, 75
Margaret, 76
COLDFLESH, Henry, 10

COLEMAN, Adam, 93, 181
Catharine, 52
George, 185
Mary, 185
Susanna, 93, 181, 185
COLLER, Anna, 115
Michael, 115
Regula, 115
COLLINS, Aaron, 28
Catharine, 120
Hannah, 28
Maria, 145
Thomas, 28
COLLODAY, Mary, 75
COLP, Catherine, 11
COMELEY, Isaac, 83
CONNELLY, Francis, 82
CONNEN, Nancy, 14
CONRAD, Andrew, 168
Anna, 74
Anna Martha
Catharine, 113
Elizabeth, 81
Eva, 113, 168
Frederick, 141
John, 81, 99
Margaret, 74
William, 75, 113, 168
CONRADT,
Christine, 62
CONRATH, Carl
William, 42
Elizabeth
Catharine, 42
John George, 42
CONSOR, Peggi, 70
CONTERMAN,
Catharine, 171
Catherine, 52
Christian, 63
Elizabeth, 171
John, 52, 63, 171
Susanna, 52, 63
CONTREMAN, Anna
Maria, 98, 135
John, 98, 119
Susanna, 98
CONVER, Anna, 12

Catherine, 42, 46
Peter, 42, 46
Susanna, 42
CONWELL, Sophia, 176
COOCK, John Justus, 136
COOK, Catharine, 179
Charity, 81
George, 179
Nanny, 179
COOLY, Catherine, 20
John, 20
Simon, 20
COOP, Nelly, 14
COOPER, Charles, 34, 41, 131
Daniel, 131
Elizabeth, 175, 176
Henry, 176
John, 175, 176
M. Anna, 184
Maria, 34
Maria Anna, 175
Mary, 184
Mary Magdalene, 41
Matthew, 84
Peter, 139
William, 34, 139, 184
COOTH, Catharine, 132
Stephen, 132
COPE, Anna, 14
COPER, Jacob, 1
CORBY, Elizabeth, 143
CORDIER, Nicholas, 126
COREWELL, Anna Dorothea, 47
Catherine, 40
Dorothea, 40
George, 47
John Adam, 47
Joseph, 47
Michael, 40, 47
CORN, Margaret, 170
William, 170

CORNELIUS, Joseph, 184
Margaret, 184
Maria, 146
William, 78, 184
CORREL, Nancy, 42
CORTIS, John, 76
CORTON, Edward, 91
Susanna, 91
COUERTY, Elizabeth, 43
Paul, 43
COULD, Elizabeth, 126
COWAN, Sarah, 80
Susanna, 82
COX, Albion, 79
Polly, 74
COXE, Henry, 158
CRAIG, Henrietta, 33, 57
Philip De Haas, 33
William, 33, 57
William Joseph Frederick, 57
CRAMES, Maria Christine, 76
CRASS, Elizabeth, 51
James, 51
Robert, 57
CRAWFORD, Alexander, 156, 174
Benjamin, 174
Christine, 174
Elizabeth, 156
Thomas, 174
CREAGHEAD, Job, 81
CREMER, Anna Sophia, 40
Catherine, 40
Henry, 40
CRESS, George, 21
John, 13
CRESSEL, John Andrew, 111
CREUCKER, Jenny, 78
CREUTZ, Elizabeth, 54
James, 54
Mr., 124
CRIPPS, Sarah, 10
CROMBIE, Mary, 13

CRONETFIELD, Elizabeth, 152
CROSS, Hannah, 14
James, 14
Mary Elizabeth, 123
CROUSS, Maria, 132
CRUM, Anna, 110
Gabriel, 110
John, 110
CRYSCOM, ---, 113
Catharine, 113
Esther, 113
CULLMAN, Adam, 12
CUNCKEL, Catherine, 56
John, 56
Michael, 56
CUNNINGHAM, James, 12
CUP, Pale, 21
Polly, 21
CURE, Susan, 169
CURREN, Nancy, 83
CURRY, Jan, 77
CURTIS, Francis, 14

-D-
DADE, Catharine, 166
Charlotte, 166
James, 166
DAG, Andrew, 37, 64
Christine, 37, 64
DAHLMAN, Anna Maria, 154
DALLMAN, John Henry, 112
Margaret, 112
DANECKER, Anna Elizabeth, 75
DANIEL, Sam, 67
DANNEBERG, David, 82
DANNECKER, Anna, 77
Elizabeth, 54, 77
DANZIBECH, Anna Maria, 172
Frederick, 172
Jacob, 172
DARACH, Maria, 46

William, 46
DARNER, Frederick,
7
DARRCH, John
Philip, 39
Magdalene, 39
William, 39
DASHIMER, Anna
Maria, 153
DATZ, Anna Maria,
143
DAUBEL, John, 145
DAUBENDISTEL,
Barbara, 16
Jacob, 16
John, 16
Sarah, 81
DAUBER, Frederick,
15, 127
DAUBERMAN,
Susanna, 84
DAUBERT,
Catharine, 82
Magdalene, 133
Peter, 133
DAUDEL, Barbara,
183
John, 183
Rebecca, 183
DAUM, Elizabeth,
33
John, 33, 57,
139
Magdalene, 57,
128
Maria, 33, 57
Susanna, 139
DAUN, George, 108
Magdalene, 10
Sarah, 108
DAUNS, Maria, 16
William, 16
DAVIDS, Nathaniel,
76
DAVIS, Benjamin,
78
Captain, 54
Catharine, 174,
181
Elizabeth, 10,
13, 54, 148
Nancy, 84
Noah, 79
Robert, 174
DAVISON, John, 160
DAWN, John, 76

DAWSON, Joseph, 12
DAY, Mary, 10
DE FRARAS,
Francisca
Havest, 40
DE GALLATHAN,
Gillome, 42
DE HAAS, Eleonora
Magdalene, 57
Eleonore, 33
John, 57
John Philip, 33,
123
DE ROGUES,
Charlotte
Louise, 41
Jaques Emanuel,
41
William, 41
DEABERGER,
Catherine
Elizabeth, 54
Charlotte, 14
Henry, 54
DEAL, A. Maria,
170
Andrew, 168
Daniel, 170, 183
Edith, 171, 179
Elizabeth, 100,
170
Hannah, 153
Jacob, 171, 179
John, 100, 170,
171, 183
Maria, 183
Peter, 100, 170
DECHEL, George,
173
Hannah, 173
M. Louisa, 173
DECKER, John, 174
Moses, 174
DEFORT, Henry, 158
Jacob, 158
M. Magdalene,
158
Peter Frederick,
147
Werner, 158
DEGENER, Anna
Maria, 65
George, 65
Wilhelmina, 65
DEGENFELD,
Elizabeth, 162

DEGENHARD, George,
93, 152
John Conrad, 93
Wilhelmina, 93
DEGENHARDT, Anna
Catherine, 36
Anna Christina,
112
Christopher, 24
Conrad, 133
George, 10, 24,
36, 112
John, 129, 133
Wilhelmina, 24,
36, 112
DEGENHART, George,
51, 79
John, 51
John George, 149
Wilhelmina, 37,
51
William, 37
DEIS, John Jacob,
125
DEISS, Dorothy,
107
John Jacob, 107
DEIST, Adam, 117
Barbara, 117
Catharine, 117
Christine, 117
John George, 117
DELLICKER,
Frederick, 74
DELLWICH, Casimir,
21, 33
Charles, 21
Elizabeth, 33
Maria, 21, 33
DELLWIG,
Elizabeth, 8
DELWICH, Maria, 14
DELWIG, Casimir, 6
DEMANDS, ---, 7
DEMUT, Ludwig, 141
DEMUTH, Elizabeth,
60
DENCKLE, Christian
Henry, 122
DENDER, Barbara,
86
William, 86
DENICH, Barbara,
18
Henry, 18
John, 18

Maria, 18
DENIG, Anna Maria,
42
Henry, 29, 42,
52, 107
John, 52
John Frederick,
29
John Jacob, 52
Maria, 29, 52,
107
Regina, 52
Susanna, 107
DENIS, Ann Mary,
54
DENN, Maria Clara,
75
DENNE, Christian,
90
DENNIS, Catharine,
169
J., 169
Sally, 76
Sarah, 169
DENTSCH, Henry,
166
DENTZE, Eva
Christine, 40
DENZEL, George,
118
DEPHINES, Anna
Maria, 49
Henry, 49
Sarah, 49
DEREIN, Henry, 6
DERENBERGER,
Maria, 160
DERFER, George,
177
Lena, 177
Susanna, 177
DESCAMPS, Jean, 79
DESCHELER, Mrs.,
128
DESCHLER, Carl,
107
DESNY, Maria, 84
DETRICH,
Sebastian, 171
DETTENWEILER,
John, 79
DETZ, Carl Jacob,
61
Elizabeth, 61
Joseph, 61

DEUBENER, Henry,
124
DEUFFINGER, Henry,
11
DEUSING, Anna
Maria
Christine, 117
Anthony, 77, 117
Elizabeth, 117
DEUSS, Anna
Margaret, 78
DEUSSEN, Thomas,
95
DEVICK, Betsy, 75
DEWALD, Anna
Margaret, 88
Daniel, 7
Elizabeth, 152
Henry, 88, 89,
114
John, 89
Margaret, 89,
114
Philip, 114
DEWALT, Catharine,
135
Henry, 135
DEWEES, Jonathan,
79
DIAMOND, Adam, 128
Anna Margaret,
30
Elizabeth, 19,
30
Jacob, 5, 19, 30
John Adam, 19
DIAMONT,
Elizabeth, 24
Jacob, 24
DIBLERET, George,
158
Magdalene, 158
DICE, Elizabeth,
184
Frederick, 184
DICK, Peter, 91
DICKEL, Johanna
Wilhelmina, 179
John, 84
John George, 179
John Jost, 163
DICKEN, William,
181
DICKES, Catharine,
100, 118, 156,
160, 174

Catherine, 67
Cathrine, 90
Daniel, 174
Elizabeth, 67,
157
Fred, 174
Frederick, 67,
100, 118, 156
John, 145, 156
John Frederick,
74, 90, 160
John Peter, 90
Peter, 157
Sarah, 100
DICKNEY,
Elizabeth, 5
DICKS, Catharine,
169
P., 169
DIEDER, Christine,
54
John Jacob, 54
DIEDERICH, Jacob,
60
susanna, 73
DIEFENDORFER,
Anna, 32
Henry, 32
William, 32
DIEHL, Adolph, 44
Andrew, 106, 113
Anna Catharine,
106
Anna Catherine,
33
Anna Maria, 30,
104
Anna Martha
Catharine, 113
Anna Mary, 54
Carl, 119
Catharine, 83,
85, 89
Catherine, 12,
16, 21, 30, 33,
44, 81
Cathrine, 109
Daniel, 33, 58,
104, 131
David, 38
Dewald, 7, 9
Elizabeth, 31,
33, 34, 38, 40,
71, 82, 86, 98,
119
Elizabeth, 62

George, 21, 109
Henry, 2, 16,
  71, 75
Jacob, 40, 58,
  71, 74, 98, 119
John, 16, 21,
  30, 33, 71, 85,
  89, 109, 121,
  126, 128, 140
Margaret, 12, 79
Maria, 33, 58,
  71, 76, 83,
  104, 131
Mary Magdalene,
  121, 140
Michael, 98
Peter, 31, 33,
  34, 40, 62, 86,
  121
Sarah, 5, 31,
  58, 85
Susanna, 33,
  121, 150
DIEHM, Hannah, 81
DIEK, Catharine,
  74
DIEL, Elizabeth,
  157
Jacob, 157
John, 134
Simon Peter, 157
DIELZ, Ketty, 11
DIEMEL, Anna
  Maria, 27
Elizabeth, 17
Henry, 17, 27
Margaret, 17, 27
DIEMER, Ann
  Margaret, 94
Anna Margaret,
  85
Catherine, 66
Dorothy, 162
Hannah, 93, 157
Henry, 66
John, 93
Louis, 73, 93
Ludwich, 85
Ludwig, 62, 157
Margaret, 41,
  66, 125, 157
Maria, 10
DIES, Anna
  Barbara, 59
Anna Maria, 2
Catherine, 23

Elizabeth, 95
Eva, 23, 38, 59
George, 23, 38,
  59
Ludwig, 135
Maria, 13, 38
Peter, 95
William, 95
DIESS, Elizabeth,
  116
Frederick, 116
John, 116
Margaret, 78
DIETRICH, John,
  83, 160
DIETZ, Anna Mary,
  66
Catharine
  Elizabeth, 106
George, 122
John, 106
John Peter, 66
Maria, 162
William, 78
DIHMER, Dulcine,
  100
Elizabeh, 108
Elizabeth, 100,
  132
Hannah, 108
John, 100
Joseph, 100, 132
Ludwig, 108
DIHNA, Elizabeth,
  115
DILCART, B., 178
DILL, Adam, 53
Catherine, 53
DILWICK, Casimir,
  1
DIMPELER, George,
  25
Henry, 25
DINCKER,
  Elizabeth, 81
DINGES, Catharine,
  119
John, 74, 119
John Jacob, 119
Julia, 76
Juliana, 33
Margaret, 130
Maria, 44
Theis, 52
William, 33

DIPPERLING, Henry,
  159
Margaret, 159
DISCHONG,
  Christian, 43
Elizabeth, 106,
  122, 156
Frederick, 106,
  119
J. F., 173
John Christian,
  43
Margaret, 119,
  173
Matthew, 156
Matthias, 106,
  122
Peter, 43
Susanna, 43
DISHONG, Matthias,
  77
DITHMAR, John, 78
DITTMAN, Conrad,
  156
Gertrude, 156
DITZER, James, 74
DIX, Abraham, 79
DIXON, Elizabeth,
  83
DOER, --- W., 9
Adam, 32, 57
Catherine, 32,
  57
Elizabeth, 32
DOERFFER, George,
  79
DOERINGER,
  Susanna, 78
DOERNBERGER,
  Maria, 83
DOERR, Adam, 51,
  70
Catharine, 155
Catherine, 51,
  70
Conrad Adam, 51
Elizabeth, 82,
  83
William, 70
DOERRN, Elizabeth,
  94
DOERSTEN,
  Elizabeth, 138
John, 138
DOLLMAN, Henry, 94
DOMAN, Ann, 81

DOMINICK, Charles, 112, 169
Frederick, 169
Henry, 6
John, 112, 151, 169
Maria, 112, 169
DONNEL, Gratia, 12
DORFFER,
Catharine, 78
Christine, 11
George, 80
Rachel, 153
DORR, Adam, 159
Catharine, 121, 159
Elizabeth, 80, 132
John, 145
Nicholas, 121
DORSIUS, Cornelia, 10
DORSTEN, Bronner, 15
Regina, 15
Samuel, 15
DOUDER, John
Michael, 123
DOUGHERTY,
Charles, 83
Joseph, 76
DOUGLAS, Sarah, 81
DOUGLISH, Anna, 13
DOWDEL, Anna
Maria, 113
Barbara, 113
John, 113
DOWEL, John, 78
DOWNING, Hannah, 84
DRAGENSTEIN, John, 77
DRANGENSTEIN,
Catharine, 112
John, 112, 122
Magdalene, 112
Maria, 122
Mary Magdalene, 131
Mr., 131
DREEHS, Elizabeth, 102
DREICHSLER, David, 157
Margaret, 157
DRES, Daniel, 20

Maria, 20
DRESS, Maria, 17
Peter, 17
DUBBS, John
Walter, 178
Michael, 178
Rachel, 178
DUBS, Elizabeth, 114
Henry Jones, 152
John, 114
John Walter, 186
Martin, 81, 114, 166
Michael, 186
Rachel, 186
Sarah, 166
William Jones, 166
DUCHE, Maria, 12
DUERR, George, 72, 76
Veronica, 72
Widow, 2
DUEY, Adam, 117
DUFFS, Samuel, 80
DUNGAN, Henry
Miller, 183
Maria, 183
Thomas, 183
DUNLAP, Henry, 181
Ludwig, 181
Sarah, 181
DUPS, Elizabeth, 146
DUPUY, Samuel, 81
DURANGE, John, 52
Margaret, 52
DURANT, Lucia, 3
DURHOR, George, 164
DURR, Adam, 17
Catherine, 17, 25
Christine, 25, 68
George, 25
Jacob, 68
John, 43
Peter, 17
DURSTER, George, 165
Jacob, 165
DUTILL, Gerhard, 84

DUTTIL, Anna
Elizabeth, 122
John, 122
Maria Elizabeth, 122
DUVAL, Louise
Cameron, 164
Seraphim, 164
DUVALL, Maria, 84

-E-

EAKELE, Barbara, 76
EARL, Christian, 10
EBBERTH, Maria
Elizabeth, 124
EBEL, Elizabeth, 155
Jacob, 81, 155
Margaret, 155
Margaret
Elizabeth, 145
EBERHARD, Abraham, 82
Maria, 73
EBERHARDT,
Elizabeth, 97
EBERHART, Abraham, 178
Carl, 178
Isabella, 178
Rebecca, 178
EBERMAN, John, 12
EBERSBACH, Anna, 95
Anna Maria, 95
Martin, 95
EBERT, John, 12
EBERTH, Catherine, 71
Elizabeth, 78
Jost, 71, 128
Maria, 75
ECHENRING, Andrew, 36
Elizabeth, 36
George, 36
ECKEL, Susanna, 43
ECKER, Margaret, 144
Salome, 144
ECKERT, Elizabeth, 133
George, 101, 105
John, 8, 133

Margaret, 101,
105
Michael, 95
ECKHARDT, Maria,
67
William, 67
ECKI, Anthony, 124
John, 100
Lucretia, 100
ECKOFF, Anna
Margaret, 94
Jacob, 94
John David, 94
Maria, 94
Sarah, 94
ECKSTEIN, Anna
Catharine, 126
Anna Catherine,
23, 27
Bernard, 150
Catharine, 97,
115
Elizabeth, 160,
168
Jacob, 79, 97,
115, 160, 168
John, 23, 27
Joseph, 168
Margaret, 115
Maria Elizabeth,
97
Samuel, 160
William, 115
ECKY, Anthony, 64
Catharine, 125
Catherine, 31
Elizabeth, 51,
125
John, 19, 31,
39, 51, 64
Lucretia, 19,
31, 39, 51, 64
Susanna, 9, 39
ECROB, Anna Maria,
98
Jacob, 98
Maria Christine,
98
EDEBOHRN, Jacob,
99
John Philip, 99
Magdalene, 99
EDEBORN, Jacob,
119
Maria, 119

EDEL, Elizabeth,
15
Matthias, 22
EDENBORN,
Catharine, 86
Catherine, 50
Elizabeth, 29,
50, 69, 146
Jacob, 75, 86
John, 29
Margaret, 69
Maria, 86, 148
Peter, 1, 29,
50, 69
Susanna, 169
EDERIS, Elizabeth,
156
EDMAN, Martha, 14
EDRIDGE, Ricloff,
79
EDRIS, Christine,
29
Elizabeth, 29
John, 29
Ludwig, 180
M. Margaret, 180
Margaret, 180
EDWARD, Joseph,
137
Patty, 137
EDWARDS, Margaret,
150
Samuel, 144
William, 144
EGOFF, Jacob, 162
Joseph, 162
Maria, 162
EHRINGER, A.
Maria, 157
Anna, 31
Elizabeth, 175
Elizabeth
Magdalene, 137
Frederick, 175
Hannah, 144
Jacob, 31, 137,
175
Magdalene, 157
Margaret, 31
Philip, 79, 157
Rebecca, 7
EHRLICH, George,
91
Sarah, 91
EHRMAN, Elizabeth,
173, 184

M. Eva, 184
William, 84,
173, 184
EICHBACH,
Margaret, 155
EILAND, Catharine,
91
EIMEL, John, 152
EINWACHTER,
Barbara
Elizabeth, 156
Elizabeth, 156
George, 12, 130
J. George, 156
John Ludwig, 130
EINWAECHTER,
Elizabeth, 40,
48, 65, 113
George, 40, 48,
65
John
Christopher, 48
John George, 113
John Ludwig, 65
John William,
113
Peter, 40
EISENMENGER, Adam,
51
Catherine, 38
Elizabeth, 38,
51
Nicholas, 12,
16, 38, 51
Samuel, 145
EISENMENGR,
Nicholas, 57
EISENRING, Andrew,
21
Anna Maria, 5
Christine
Margaret, 60
Elizabeth, 21,
60, 94, 118
George, 21, 60,
94, 118, 148,
161
John, 161
Lawrence, 118
M. Elizabeth,
161
EKERT, Catharine
Elizabeth, 178
John, 178
ELFEY, Elizabeth,
154

ELFFERIG,
    Elizabeth, 99
    John, 99
ELIOT, Benjamin,
    44
    James, 44
    Sophia, 44
    Thomas Hubsons,
    44
ELLENBERGER, John
    Ewald, 76
ELLIOT, A.
    Catharine, 162
    Henry, 16
    James, 16
    Sophia, 16
    Thomas, 144
ELSTERLY, Jacob,
    100
    Mary Magdalene,
    100
EMERICH,
    Charlotte, 182
    John, 182
EMERIG, Maria, 57
EMERT, Henry, 160
    Magdalene, 160
EMIG, Dorothea,
    24, 32, 48
    Henry, 24, 32,
    48, 63
    Peter, 15, 63
    Susanna, 63
EMMEL, Peter, 8,
    131
EMMERTH, Henry,
    47, 87
    Maria, 47
    Mary Magdalene,
    87
EMMINS, Catherine,
    39
    Elizabeth, 39
    John, 39
ENCK, Anna Maria,
    102
    Catharine, 102,
    105
    Catherine, 18,
    31, 48, 72
    Elizabeth, 105,
    119
    Emilia Margaret,
    119
    Henry, 140

Jacob, 7, 18,
    31, 48, 72,
    102, 125, 140
    Peter, 140
    Philip, 105,
    119, 139
    Sarah, 72
    William, 31
ENGEL, John, 82
    Margaret, 81
    Peter, 140
ENGELHARD, George,
    14
ENGELMANN,
    Abraham, 147
ENGLE, Margaret,
    10
ENSAER, Elizabeth,
    179
    John Wesel, 179
    John Wessel, 179
EPGERT, Anna, 69
    Henry, 69
    Maria, 69
    William, 69
ERB, Margaret, 71
ERCKES, Frederick,
    158
ERHART, Elizabeth,
    99
ERL, Elizabeth, 10
ERNST, Catharine,
    83
    Henry, 82, 167
    John Balsar, 167
ERNSTDORFF,
    Elizabeth, 11
ERRINGER, Hannah,
    6
    Jacob, 14
ERWIN, Catharine,
    139
    Jacob, 75
    Joseph, 36
ESCH, Catharine,
    88
    John, 18, 31
    Margaret, 18, 31
    Maria, 157
    Michael, 148,
    157
    Sarah, 157
ESCHELMAN,
    Albrecht, 26
    Charles, 35
    Christine, 53

Isaiah, 17, 35,
    53, 67, 70
    Jes., 129
    John, 129
    Maria, 53
    Peter, 67
    Sibylla, 17, 35,
    53, 67, 70
ESCHELMANN,
    Albrecht, 6
ESCHER, John
    George, 101
ESCHLER, Henry, 1
    Isaac, 121
    Jacob, 27, 121
    Susanna, 6, 27,
    121
ESCHMAN, Barbara,
    78
    Helena, 82
    Mr., 126
    Peter, 82
ESHER, John, 177
    Margaret, 177
ESHERICH, G., 169
    Margaret, 169
ESHLER, Jacob, 91,
    103
    Rebecca, 103
    Sarah, 91
    Susanna, 91, 103
ESLER, Abraham, 41
    Anna, 41
    Jacob, 41, 59
    Susanna, 59
ESPAY, Maria, 76
ESPY, Eva, 77
ESSLER, Esther, 81
    Jacob, 139
ESSLIN, Margaret,
    121
ESTERLE, George,
    169
ESTIAL, Briton,
    185
    Eveline, 185
    Salome, 185
ESTRISCH,
    Christine, 97
    Daniel, 97
    John, 97
ETLER, Catherine,
    52
ETRIS, ---, 153
    Anna, 67
    Barbara, 78

Christine, 50,
  67, 118
Daniel, 135
John, 50, 67,
  118, 135
Maria, 50
ETTER, Elizabeth,
  14
EULER, Anna
  Gertrude, 117
Anna Maria, 83
Elizabeth, 31
Jacob, 31
Joanna, 31
John, 117
Maria, 145
Philip, 6
William, 78, 117
EVERIDGE,
  Christine, 175
Hannah, 175
John, 175
EVERLY, George,
  175
Wilhelmina, 175
EVERMAN,
  Elizabeth, 10
EXLEY, Anna Maria,
  42
John, 42
EYLER, Jacob, 3,
  15
Jane, 15

-F-
FAANS, Catharine,
  113
Christian, 113
Jacob, 78
Sarah, 113
FABER, Anna Maria,
  177
Benjamin, 177
Catharine, 82,
  87, 98, 114,
  156
Henry, 136
John Casper, 156
John Henry, 98
John Ludwig,
  114, 136, 144,
  156
Louisa, 87
Ludwig, 57, 87,
  98, 133
Maria Eva, 114

Susanna, 133
FACKERT, David,
  139
FACUNDUS, Jacob,
  44
Julianna, 44
FAERING, Margaret,
  11
FAGGOT, Catherine,
  33
David, 33
Elizabeth, 33
FAHL, John
Gabriel, 98
FAHN, Elizabeth,
  166
Jacob, 166
Michael, 166
Rebecca, 166
FAHNS, David, 112
Elizabeth, 105,
  112
Fanny, 11
Henry, 156
Jacob, 81
John, 112
Lawrence, 105
Magdalene, 105
Veronica, 156
FALBIER, John, 80
FALLIER, Matthias,
  137
FALLIERE, David,
  139
Matthew, 139
FALLIES,
  Catherine, 19,
  41, 64
Margaret, 19
Maria Theresia,
  64
Matthew, 41
Matthias, 19, 64
Peter Henry, 41,
  126
FAN, Jacob, 153
FANS, Anna
  Catherine, 37
Catherine, 21,
  52
Christian, 8,
  17, 28, 36, 43,
  52, 68, 91
Christine, 17,
  28, 36, 43, 52,
  68, 91

Christine
  Susanna, 37
Conradt, 36
Elizabeth, 52
George, 1
Henry, 31
Isaac, 68
John, 21, 37,
  52, 126
John Adam, 52
John Christian,
  17
Lawrence, 87
Magdalene, 28,
  87
Margaret, 21, 87
Maria Veronica,
  21, 24
Michael, 9, 43,
  128
Rebecca, 43, 91
Samuel, 21
Sarah, 29, 52
Veronica, 21,
  31, 42
FANSE, George,
  172, 180
Maria, 180
Rebecca, 172,
  180
Susan, 180
Susanna, 172
FANZ, Rebecca, 91
FARE, John, 175
FARMER, Lewis, 73
Ludwig, 30
Margaret, 30
Maria, 6
FARMERET,
  Elizabeth, 95
Lewis, 95
FARNER, Casper,
  103
George, 103
Maria, 103
FARRIS, Catherine,
  61
John, 61
Magdalene, 61
FAU, Barbara, 19,
  183
John, 19
Maria Elizabeth,
  19
William, 19, 183

FAUNCE, George,
153
FAUST, Christian
Bernard, 168
Franciscus, 168
John, 149
FAUT, Hannah, 150
Maria, 81
FAUTH, Catherine,
12
FAX, Anna, 81
George, 70
FEE, John, 4
FEHBRIT, Eleonore,
80
FEHMAN, Anna, 173
Henry, 173
Rebecca, 173
FEHN, Maria, 85
FEHRCLASS, Conrad,
139
FEHRER, John, 102
Maria, 102
FEHRGLASS, Anna
Maria, 97
John Conrad, 97
FEIERING, Anna
Christine, 22
Anna Maria, 22
Matthias, 22
FEIFFERTH, Daniel
Frederick, 78
FEIL, Philip, 48
Susanna, 48
FEILSELBACH,
Margaret, 184
Sarah, 184
FELIN, Anna Maria,
20
Bernard, 20
John, 20
FELKER, Philip,
172
FELTON, William,
152
FELTZNER,
Magdalene, 79
FENEMMEN, Rosina,
24
FENNER, Apollonia,
134
Catharine, 104,
114
Catherine, 52,
66

Elizabeth, 35,
49, 66, 107
Felix, 35, 52,
114
Hannah, 104
Henry, 11, 35,
49, 107, 134
John Felix, 49,
52, 139
John Henry, 66
John Peter, 66
Maria, 35
Maria Eva, 52,
114
Peter, 13, 52,
66, 104, 114
Samuel, 84
FER, George, 169
William, 169
FERIS, John, 88
Maria, 88
William, 88
FERLEY, Elizabeth,
50
William, 50
FERRES, Elizabeth,
121
John, 121
Magdalene, 121
FERRINGER,
Elizabeth, 77
FERRY, Anna Maria,
99
Valentine, 99
FESTINGER, Maria,
79, 152
FETSCHUT, Joseph, 114
Maria Eva, 114
FETTER, Christian,
176
FETTERAL, Stephen,
83
FEYL, Catherine,
34
John, 34
FICHTER, Anna, 23
Catharine, 88
Elizabeth, 88
Helena
Catharine, 110
Henry, 23
John, 88
John Leonard,
110
Magdalene, 23

FIEHMAN, Barbara,
45
Henry, 45
Maria, 45
FIELD, Matthias,
142
Peter, 181
Rachel, 181
FIELS, John, 39
Susanna, 39
FIES, Anna, 62
Anna Maria, 38
Christian, 38
Dorothea, 25,
38, 53, 66
Elizabeth, 169
Frederick, 169
George, 9, 25,
38, 53, 169
Henry, 53
Jacob, 5, 25, 62
John George, 66,
127
John Henry, 53
FIESS, Anna
Dorothea, 120
Catharine, 120
Daniel, 120
Dorothy, 120
George, 120
Jacob, 120
Salome, 120
FIGHT, Andrew, 185
Catharine, 185
Conrad, 185
FILL, Catherine,
21
John, 21
Thomas, 21
FINCK, Catharine,
129
Elizabeth, 62,
125
Eva Margaret, 38
Jacob, 7, 24,
38, 62, 102,
170
John, 107, 126,
135
John George, 24
Margaret, 170
Maria, 102, 148,
170
Maria Margaret,
24, 62, 102
Maria Marget, 38

Rachel, 82, 107
Sophia, 107
FINETON, Charles
Stewart, 165
Elizabeth, 165
John, 165
FISCHBACH,
Elizabeth, 82
FISCHER, A. Maria,
161
Adam, 13, 46
Anna, 52
Catharine, 163
Christine, 81
Elizabeth, 14,
40, 46, 59, 101
George, 40
Henry, 81
John, 46, 101,
161
Maria, 82
Sebastian, 81
Thomas, 59, 101
FISH, Catharine,
93
Dorothy, 90
Elizabeth, 93
George, 90
Henry, 93
John, 90
FISHER, Davd, 84
Esther, 83
Jacob, 169
Maria, 169
Sarah, 14, 169
Susan, 175
Susanna, 169
FISMEIER,
Margaret, 13
FISS, Catharine,
104, 122, 144
Dorothea, 150
George, 10
Henry, 104, 122,
185
Mr., 129
Samuel, 104
William, 185
FISTON, Hannah,
105
Hannah Barbara,
105
Richard, 105
FITLER, Margaret,
55
Maria, 10

FLACHS, John, 11,
32
Magdalene, 32
Margaret, 32
William, 32
FLAUER, Elizabeth,
27
George, 27
FLAUERS, George,
11
FLECK, Elizabeth,
140
George, 136, 169
Jacob, 140, 141
John, 113, 142
John George, 143
Joseph, 136
Lydia, 88, 128
Margaret, 113
Maria, 88, 98
Robert, 169
Sarah, 169
William, 73, 88,
98, 113
FLEECK, George, 86
Jacob, 141
Maria, 86
Sarah, 86
FLEEK, George, 87
Margaret, 87
FLEITZ, John, 60
FLEMING, Michael,
90
FLEMMING, Michael,
115
FLICK, John
Philip, 5
Magdalene, 153
Maria Catherine,
73
FLICKER,
Petronella, 80
FLING, Maria, 75
FLOCK, Justus, 13
FLOCKE, John
George, 43
Justus, 43
Margaret, 43
FLOCKER, Mr., 124
FLOWERS,
Christian, 82
FLUCK, Elizabeth,
167
George, 167
FOEBEL, Anthony,
174, 175

Christian, 174
Frederica, 84
Gertrude, 174
Maria Christine,
174
FOER, Elizabeth,
56
Henry, 56
FOERING,
Elizabeth, 174
Frederick, 174
FOEST, Elizabeth,
175
M., 175
Michael, 175
FOEVER, Sally, 127
FOHR(ER),
Elizabeth, 73
FOHRINGER, Maria,
82
FOLCK, Eva Maria,
25
Maria, 74
FOLCKER, John, 14
FOLLER, Elizabeth,
10
FOLLWELL,
Courtland Fred,
181
Elizabeth, 181
Samuel, 181, 185
Susanna, 153
FOLTZ, John, 141
FOLUK, David, 113
Maria, 113
Peter, 113
FOLWELL, ---, 166
Godfrey, 166
FONDERBECK,
Elizabeth, 170
P., 170
Sarah, 170
FONSE, Catharine,
176
Christian, 176,
177
Elizabeth, 172
Fanny, 172, 177
Jacob, 172
Rebecca, 172
Sophia, 177
FORD, Adam, 155
Catharine, 165,
177
Elizabeth, 144
J., 177

Jacob, 165
FORDEM, A. Maria,
170
Adam, 170
John, 39, 170
Maria, 39
Reichard, 39
FORDHAM, Susan,
128
FORDHEIM, A.
Maria, 163
Anna Maria, 95
John, 95, 163
John Hill, 163
FORDHEN, Anna
Maria, 117
John, 117
Susanna, 117
FORDLAND, John,
126
FOREST, Peter, 76
FORING, John, 81
FORKLAR, Anna
Maria, 108
Conrad, 108
FORNES, Anna
Margaret, 95
FORSTER,
Catherine, 71
Hannah, 11
Johanna
Catharine, 115
Philip, 115
FORTER, Margaret,
58
Sam, 58
FORTH, Christian,
129
Elizabeth, 102
Lawrence, 102,
130
Maria, 111, 130
Zander, 111
FOSTER, A. Maria,
163
Catharine, 115,
163
Conrad, 115
Diana, 75
Frederick, 115,
163
FOT, Catherine, 22
Christopher, 22
FOTH, Catherine,
34, 38
Christoph, 34

Christopher, 38
Elizabeth, 33,
34, 56
John, 34
Lorentz, 11, 33,
34
FOU, Henry, 164
Margaret, 164
Maria, 164
FOUSE, ---, 179
Frances, 179
Henry, 179
Jacob, 179
Jefferine, 179
Maria, 179
Philip, 179
FOUT, Jacob, 181
Louisa, 181
FOX, Abraham, 11
FRAEHLY, Benjamin
Farmer, 143
FRAILY, Catharine,
171
Fred, 171
John, 154
FRALY, Frederick,
161
susanna, 81
FRANCIS, Jacob,
167
John, 167
FRANCK, A. Maria,
162
anna Elizabeth,
103
Catharine, 175
Christian, 84
David, 113
Elizabeth, 175
Henry, 162
Jacob, 147
John, 175
John Christian,
90, 103
John George, 103
FRANK, George
Christopher,
183
FRANKENSTEIN, Anna
Magdalene, 165
John, 165
FRANTZ, Anna, 154
Catharine, 154
John, 154
FRASHER,
Elizabeth, 161

FRAYLEY,
Catharine, 170
Frederick, 170
FREDERIC, Abraham,
168
John, 168
Wilhelmina, 168
FREDERICK, John,
131
Peter Dickes,
131
FREI, Charlotte,
131
Elizabeth, 109
George, 109
Jacob, 109, 131
Margaret, 109
FREIER, John, 79
FREITAG,
Catherine, 44
George, 72
J. George, 97
John George, 44
John Michael,
114
Margaret
Philippina, 44,
72, 97
FRENCH, Catharine,
119
Elizabeth, 119
John, 119
FRESCHER, Ludwig,
77
FREUND, A. Maria,
149
Elizabeth, 80
John, 119
John B., 80
John Henry, 106,
147
Maria, 106, 119
Sophia, 104
William, 119
FREY, Anthony, 39,
65
Barbara, 39, 48,
65, 169, 183
E., 173
Elias, 36
Elizabeth, 71,
183
Henry, 169, 183
Jacob, 14, 71
John, 179
John Anthony, 48

John George, 179
John Henry, 169
M. Magdalene,
179
Margaret, 36
Maria, 126
Sophia, 151
Veronica, 74
FREYER, Eva, 173
John, 173
Rachel, 173
FREYT, A. Mary,
175
FREYTAG, George,
141, 150
Michael, 82
FRICK, Adam, 41,
123
Barbara, 19, 41,
70, 93
Henry, 19, 41,
70, 93, 153
William, 93
FRIEBEL, Barbara,
18
Maria Barbara,
30
Uranus, 30
Urban, 18
FRIEBELE, Maria
Barbara, 25
Urbanus, 25
FRIEBELI, Barbara,
134
Urban, 134
FRIECK, Henry, 136
FRIED, Barbara,
104
Elizabeth, 104
Jacob, 104
FRIEDERICH, Anna, 64
Elizabeth, 75
Jacob William,
64
John Andrew, 73
John Jacob, 64
Margaret, 13
William, 124
FRIEDERIS,
Abraham, 155
Jacobina
Wilhelmina, 155
Wilhelmina, 155
FRIEDRICH, Anna
Catharine, 142
Carl, 144

FRIEND, Catharine,
164
Christian
Frederick, 164
John, 164
FRIES, Anna
Sophia, 30
Catherine, 45
Elizabeth, 27
Jacob, 27
Maria, 74
Philip, 45
Sophia, 88
FRIETZ, John, 118,
140
Nancy, 118
Sarah, 118
FRIOTH, Abraham, 8
Elizabeth, 75
FRISCH, Christine,
95
Jonas, 95
FRISMUTH, Daniel,
101
FRISSELER, Philip,
11
FRITZ, Anna, 70
Carl, 110
Catharine, 112
Catherine, 35
Catherine
Magdalene, 28
Charlotte, 54,
70, 110
Elizabeth, 11,
97
Henry, 54
John, 16, 28,
35, 112
John PHilip, 110
Margaret, 16
Maria, 16
Mary Magdalene,
28
Philip, 14, 16,
54, 70, 97
FROELICH, Benjamin
Farmer, 121
Catharine, 121
Christine, 102
Daniel, 102
Frederick, 100,
121
John, 102
Joseph Whister,
121

Thomas, 100
FROELIG,
Catharine, 85,
87
Catherine, 18,
25, 27, 42, 58
Christian, 43
Christine, 28,
35, 46
Elizabeth, 43,
124
Frederick, 3,
18, 27, 42, 58,
85
Friedrich, 87
George Ros, 58
Hannah, 35
Jacob, 42
John, 13, 28,
35, 46
John Christian,
8
John David, 3
John Frederick,
25
John Jacob, 85
Joseph, 46
Magdalene, 8
Rebecca, 28
FROELING,
Christine, 64
Henoch, 64
John, 64
FROEMMER,
Elizabeth, 39
Franciscus, 39
Gretzelly, 39
FROEMMLER,
Christine, 53
Franciscus, 53
FROH, Catharine,
157
John, 157
Peter, 157
FROLICH, Daniel,
133
John, 133
FROLIG, Christine,
28
Jacob, 127
John, 28
FROMAN, Catherine,
31
Conrad, 31, 52,
68, 95, 131
Elizabeth, 68

Jacob, 125
John, 2
Margaret, 31,
  52, 68, 95
Sarah, 95
FROSCHER,
  Christine, 155
  Ludwig, 155
FROTT, Catherine,
  65
  Frederick, 65
FRUBY, Elizabeth,
  19
  John, 19
FUCHS, Abraham, 17
  Anna Magdalene,
    110
  Christian, 105
  Christine, 144
  Dorothy, 105
  John Fred, 110
  Margaret, 79
  Maria, 110
  Mary Magdalene,
    105
  Peter, 148
  Sophia, 17, 3
FUCKEROLL, George,
  15
FUHR, Elizabeth,
  32, 105
  George, 32
  Henry, 32, 105
  J. Christian,
    153
  William, 3
FULLER, Elizabeth,
  14
  Hannah, 11
FULLERTON, Lydia,
  83
FULMAN, John, 43
FUNCK, Barbara,
  24, 30, 87
  Christian, 176
  Christine, 44
  Dinah, 23
  Henry, 24, 30,
    87
  Hester, 73
  Jacob, 62
  John, 87, 104,
    138
  John Michael, 86

Joseph, 24, 62,
  73, 86, 104,
  138, 141
Maria, 62, 86,
  104, 147, 176
Mary Magdalene,
  30, 128
Mr., 16
William, 176
FUNCKE, Barbara,
  53
Henry, 53
FUNTERSLICE,
  Jacob, 184
  John, 184
  Maria, 184
FURER, Anna Maria,
  55
Hannah, 55
Jacob, 6
John, 55
FURRER, Susanna,
  26
William, 26
FUSELBACH, Anna
  Maria, 97
  Daniel, 49
  Frederick
    William, 71
  Margaret, 49,
    71, 97
  William, 49, 71,
    97
FUSS, Samuel, 4
FUSSELBACH,
  Catharine, 109
  Margaret, 109,
    155
  Sarah, 155
  William, 12,
    109, 155
FUX, Esther, 170
  John, 170
  Margaret, 170
FYNN, Jane, 83

-G-
GABRIEL, Maria, 70
  Peter, 70
GAEFF, Catharine,
  126
GAERTNER,
  Catharine, 161
  Jacob, 97
  John, 112, 140
  M. Magdalene, 161

Mary Magdalene,
  97, 112
Valentine, 97,
  112, 161
GAETZ, Benjamin,
  24
  Joseph, 24
  Maria, 24
GAILLARD,
  Alexander
    Bartholome, 8
GALBET, Ezekiel,
  179
  John, 179
  Susanna, 179
GALLADEIN, Jacob,
  52
  Joseph, 52
  Sarah, 52
GALLADIN, Jacob,
  86
  Sarah, 86
GALLATE, Jacob, 43
  Sarah, 43
GALLE, Sarah, 80
  Sarah Christine,
    147
GALLY, Anna
  Catharine, 164,
    177
  Catharine, 118
  Christian, 118,
    151
  Christine
    Margaret, 164
  Joseph, 78, 118,
    164, 177
  Margaret, 161
  Maria, 118
  Susanna
    Catharine, 164
GAMBER, Catherine,
  14
  Elizabeth, 13,
    100
  George Michael,
    148
  John, 83, 100
  John Henry, 100
  Maria, 2
  Mary Magdalene,
    77, 100
  Philip Jacob, 81
GAMPER, Elizabeth,
  42
  John, 42

Maria, 42
GAMPFER,
　Elizabeth, 116
　John, 116
　Philip Jacob,
　　116
GANITER, Michael,
　147
GARDEN, Edward, 30
　John, 30
　Susanna, 30
GARDNER, Eliza,
　179
　Elizabeth, 181
　Jacob, 166, 179
　John, 84, 170
　M. Christine,
　　170
　M. Magdalene,
　　181
　Maria, 166, 179
　Maria Christine,
　　84
　Valentine, 181
　Wilemin, 170
GARRET, Caharine,
　122
　Elizabeth, 122
　John, 122
GARTEN,
　Christopher,
　　175
GARTNER,
　Catharine, 151
　John, 142
　Rachel, 145
GARWOOD,
　Catharine, 179
　Elizabeth, 179
　Samuel, 179
GASSER, Anna, 42,
　111
　Anna Maria, 60,
　　91
　Jacob, 42
　Maria, 38, 111,
　　121, 160
　Peter, 91
　Philip, 13, 38,
　　42, 60, 91,
　　111, 121, 160
　Salome, 160
GASSMAN, Dorothy,
　80
　M., 159
　Margaret, 80

GASSNER,
　Elizabeth, 43
　Henry, 68
　Margaret, 68
GATE, Anna
　Catherine, 62
　Henry, 62
　Martin, 62
GATES, M., 172
　Margaret, 172
GATHIER, John
　Jacob, 135
　Nicholas, 135
GATTER, Anna
　Maria, 89
　Philip, 89
GAUEL, John
　Abraham, 74
　John Fried, 62
　Margaret, 62
GAUFF, Elizabeth,
　173
　Fanny, 173
　John, 173
GAUL, Adam, 90,
　104, 123, 162
　Adolph, 140
　Anna Catharine,
　　110
　Anna Clara, 105
　Anna Maria, 85
　Catherine, 40,
　　59
　Christian, 50
　Christine, 79
　Clara, 85
　Daniel, 25
　Dorothea, 119
　Dorothy, 101,
　　110, 183
　Elizabeth, 11,
　　67, 90, 104,
　　123, 162, 183
　Fred, 85
　Fred., 50
　Frederick, 75,
　　101, 104, 110,
　　119, 183
　George, 59, 73
　Gottfried, 58,
　　126
　Jacob, 119
　John, 67
　John Adam, 90
　John Bernard, 59

John Frederick,
　12, 40, 85,
　102, 121, 162
　John George, 123
　M. Margaret, 162
　Magdalene, 130
　Margaret, 40,
　　50, 85, 102,
　　121
　Maria, 67, 162
　Maria Elizabeth,
　　121
　Martin, 1, 85
　Sabina, 25, 41,
　　58, 85, 101
　Sigmund
　　Frederick, 101
　Valentine, 25,
　　41, 58, 85,
　　101, 130
　Veronica, 101
　William, 162
　William Henry,
　　85
GEARY, James, 76
GEBBRT, John, 34
　John Michael, 34
　Rachel, 34
GEBEL, George
　William, 161
GEBERT, Christian,
　179
　Marte, 179
GEBHARD, Anna
　Maria, 50
　John, 10, 124
　John Conrad, 50
GEBHARDT, John, 4
GEBLER, Abigail,
　184
　Anna, 184
　Charles
　　Frederick, 184
　Elizabeth, 151
　John F., 184
　Matthew, 81
　Matthias, 184
GECKE, Bernard,
　147
GEIER, Susanna,
　110
　William, 110
GEIGER, Carl, 121
　Dorothea, 121
　Elizabeth, 121
GEIS, Francis, 65

Regina, 65
GEISE, Elizabeth,
    133
    Francis, 133
GEISEL, Christine,
    114
    John George, 114
GEISIN, Elizabeth,
    171
    Philip, 171
GEISS, Anna
    Catharine, 107
    Elizabeth, 95
    Francis, 74, 95,
    107
    Regina, 95, 107
    William, 34
GEISSE, Eva, 69
    Eva Wilhelmina,
    69
    Francis, 69, 144
    Henry William,
    69
    Regina, 69
GEISSEL, Anna
    Christina, 112
    Christian
    George, 77
    Christine, 105
    George, 105, 112
GEIVELL, Anna, 40
    Anna Maria, 40
    Ludwg, 40
GELERS, Mary
    Magdalene, 78
GEMBERLEIN,
    Charles, 35
    Margaret, 35
    Veronica, 35
GEMEINBAUER, Anna
    Maria, 63
    Catherine, 47
    John, 47
    John Wolfgang,
    63
GEMEINBAUERS, Anna
    Maria
    Elizabeth, 12
GENER, A. M., 171
GENNS, Regina, 172
GENTEL, Anna
    Margaret, 172
    Carl, 172
GENTHEMER, Conrad,
    11
    Maria, 11

GENUNS, Anna, 177
GEORG, Anna
    Barbara, 119
    Catharine, 119
    Joseph, 119
    Veronica, 119
GEORGE, John, 157
GERBACH, Anna
    Maria, 76
GERBER, Anna
    Maria, 30
GERBON, Pouilhan,
    146
GERHARD, Conrad,
    10, 28, 46, 87,
    149
    Elizabeth, 28,
    46, 87
    John, 87
    Maria, 46
    Peter, 28
GERHARDT, Jacob,
    78
GERICH, John Adam,
    124
GERIN, Maria
    Oxley, 59
GERLACH,
    Catharine, 102
    Maria, 39, 51,
    62
    Stephen, 51, 76
GERLER, Elizabeth,
    18
    George, 18
    John George, 18
GERMAN, Elizabeth,
    66, 181
    George, 66, 146
    Henry, 181
    James, 81
    John, 66, 181
GERNER, Jacob, 118
GERRET, Catharine,
    110
    John, 68, 110
    Margaret, 68
GERRETH, John, 77
GERRIT, Christine,
    82
    John, 129
GERRITH, Adam, 23,
    24, 36, 51, 91
    Catharine, 124
    Catharine, 51

Christine, 23,
    24, 36, 51
    John, 23, 36,
    51, 91, 127
    Margaret, 23,
    36, 51, 91
    Maria, 36
GERRITT, Margaret,
    3
GERSTENER, Maria,
    75
GERSTER, George,
    74
    John George, 11,
    27
    Margaret, 27, 74
    William, 27
GERTNER, John, 18
GERWIRT, George,
    167
    Sam, 167
GETTER, Catharine,
    116
    Henry, 116
    John Nicholas,
    150
    Maria, 83
GEULER, Barbara,
    18
    John, 18
GEYER, Carl, 155
    Casper, 95, 136
    Elizabeth, 95
    Henry, 149
    Jacob, 58
    Maria, 155
GIBBERT,
    Christian, 98
    Elizabeth, 98
GIBLER, Eliza, 179
    Elizabeth, 180
    Joseph, 179, 180
    Rachel, 179, 180
GIBSON, James, 112
GIDEON, Elizabeth,
    29, 39
    Jacob, 29, 34,
    39, 72
    Paul Casper, 39
    Rebecca, 72
GIEBERT,
    Christian, 75
GILBERT, Anna, 14,
    20, 23, 31, 49,
    55, 115
    Barbara, 179

Catharine, 149, 179
Catherine, 39, 53
Christian, 52, 62, 88, 110
Christine, 22
Conrad, 20
Daniel, 53
David, 23, 31, 34, 36, 39, 55, 80, 115
George, 179
Hannah, 36
Henry, 25
James, 88
Jessed, 20
John, 6, 31
Magdalene, 88, 110
Maria, 20, 52, 123
Martha, 110
Mary Magdalene, 62
Matthew, 22
Michael, 49
Susanna, 75
GILFERT, Anna, 24
George, 24
Maria Veronica, 24
GILHAUER, Adam, 88
Sarah, 88
GILLMAN, Eva, 10
GILMAN, Anna, 18
David, 18
GILMORE, Frances, 75
GILYARD, Eleonore, 11
GINDER, Charlotte, 166
Elizabeth, 51
John, 14, 51, 61
John Henry, 116
Margaret, 51, 61, 116
Sam, 166
GIOHL, Henry, 88
Sophia, 88
GIVIN, David, 83
GLAS, Jacob, 141
GLASER, John Philip, 1
GLEIM, John, 83

GLENTWORTH, Maria, 74
GLOCKENER, Christian, 10
GLOCKNER, George, 122
GLOECKNER, Casper, 132
Christian, 128
GLOTING, Abraham, 15
Catherine, 15
Juliana, 15
GOBELER, Anna Catherine, 65
Anna Margaret, 37
Catharine, 90
Catherine, 25, 37
Gottfried, 25, 37, 65, 90
John William, 90
Maria, 65
Salome, 25
GOBLER, Anna Veronica, 1
Gottfried, 130
Gottfried Joad, 150
Hannah, 2
John William, 130
GOEBEL, Henry, 98
GOEBELER, Catharine, 105
Elizabeth, 15
Gottfried, 102, 105
Henry, 98
GOEBLER, Catharine, 77
Catherine, 17
Elizabeth, 11
Gottfried, 17
Hannah, 17
GOEGER, Barbara, 105
Henry, 105
GOETZ, Anna Brigitta, 137
Brigitta, 99
Carl, 137
Carl Jacob, 99
Eva, 127
Jacob, 136
Susanna, 99, 136

GOFF, c., 172
GOOD, Joseph, 83
GORDEN, Christopher, 68
GORKER, Adam, 144
GORTJUS, ---, 151
GOTTER, John Christopher, 76
GOTTLIEB, Anna, 19
GOTTSCHALCK, Elizabeth, 31
Frederick, 30
Hannah, 11
John, 30
GOTZ, Charles, 129
GRAEBEL, George, 121
John, 137
Margaret, 121
Matthias, 121
GRAF, Elizabeth, 77
GRAFF, Adam, 24
Anna Sabina, 106
Casper, 13, 31
Catherine, 28
Cathrine, 24
Elizabeth, 46
Eva Catherine, 24
Franciscus, 24
George, 26
Gustavianna Frederica, 3
Jacob, 106
John, 24
Mary, 180
Matthias, 46
Mrs., 26
Peter, 28
Sabina, 31
Sam, 127
Susanna, 46
Thomas, 73
GRAFT, John, 76
GRAHAM, Edward, 75
GRAMER, Anna, 173
Catharine, 173
John George, 173
GRAMLICH, Catherine, 37
Christian, 16
Elizabeth, 12, 16, 37, 38, 56, 86, 122
Henry, 38, 56

Margaret, 122
Philip, 16, 37,
  56, 86, 122
GRAMLIG, Anna
  Maria, 63
  Thomas, 63
GRAMLY, Hannah,
  135
  Philip, 135
GRAUEL, Anna
  Cathrine, 107,
  135
  Daniel, 66
  Elizabeth, 66,
  107
  John, 18, 29,
  34, 66, 74,
  107, 135
  John George, 9,
  34
  Mr., 5
  Peter, 131
  Sarah, 18, 29,
  34, 123
GRAUL, Anna Maria,
  121
  Elizabeth, 107,
  121, 172
  George, 108
  John, 107, 121,
  172
  Rosina, 108
  Susanna, 153
GRAVE, Frederick,
  84
  John, 181
GRAY, Richard, 11
GREEN, Catharine,
  158
  Henry, 158
  Jane, 43
  John, 158
  John George, 49
  Maria, 49
  Ned, 49
  Samuel, 75
  Stephen, 76
GREENSTAT, Maria,
  94
GREENWOOD,
  Alexander, 32,
  151
  Catherine, 57
  John, 57
  Maria, 57

GREIM, Elizabeth,
  134
  John, 134
GREINER,
  Catherine, 16
  Elizabeth, 33
  Fred., 33
  John Daniel, 16
GREISS, Anna
  Margaret, 3
  Anna Maria, 33
  Else, 47
  Hannah, 70
  Jacob, 33, 47,
  70
  Margaret, 33,
  47, 70
GRENSDORFFER, Anna
  Maria, 18
  John Michael, 18
  Michael, 18
GRENSTEFFER,
  Maria, 95
  P., 95
GRESSLER, Joseph,
  63, 127
GREY, Catharine,
  115
  Stephen, 115
GRIESSEM, Casper,
  41
  Elizabeth, 41
  Sarah, 41
GRIFFEN, Casper,
  72
  Daniel, 72
  Elizabeth, 72
GRIFFI, Elizabeth,
  107
  Thomas, 107
GRIFFIN, Mary, 80
GRIFFITH, Maria,
  14
  Mary, 12
GRIM, Elizabeth,
  14, 31, 40, 45
  John Peter, 31
  Peter, 40
GRIMES, Elizabeth,
  83
GRIMM, Elizabeth,
  32
  Henry Peter, 20,
  32
  Peter, 32

GRISSEM, Casparus,
  61
  Elizabeth, 61
  Maria, 61
GRISSUM, Casper,
  119, 138
  Elizabeth, 119
  Hannah, 138
  John Adam, 119
GROB, Margaret,
  162
GROFF, Anna
  Elizabeth, 15
  Elizabeth, 15
  Matthias, 15
GROGAN, Patrick,
  10
GROH, Christian,
  76
GRON, Catherine,
  23, 25
  Gabriel, 23, 25
  Maria Margaret,
  23
GRONINGER,
  Catharine, 49
  Francis
  Reinhard, 49
GROS, Elsie, 149
  Jacob, 79
  Maria, 149
  Philip, 82
GROSKOP, Jacob,
  102
  John, 102
  Margaret, 102
GROSMAN, Rachel,
  84
GROSS, Maria, 77
  Sarah, 173
GRUB, Catherine,
  35
  Elizabeth, 74
  Jacob, 35
  Michael, 75
  Sarah Peffer, 73
GRUBB, Catherine,
  13
  Mary, 84
GRUM, Daniel, 66
GRUNINGER,
  Susanna, 78
GRUNSTATT, A.
  Maria, 156
GUBLER, John J.,
  181

GUCKER, Anna
Catherine, 49
Anna Elizabeth,
38
Catharine, 124
Catherine, 49,
68
Christian, 94
Dorothy, 94
Elizabeth, 146,
10
George William,
5, 32
Isabella, 63
Jacob, 13, 68,
81, 161
John Michael,
128
Magdalene, 32,
38, 63, 161
Maria, 68
Martin, 13, 38,
49, 68
Matthias, 32,
38, 63
GUCKES, Catharine,
157
Elizabeth, 157
Martin, 157
GUENTHER, John H.,
140
Margaret, 140
GUIZE, Henry
William, 10
GUL, Anna Maria,
85
Clara, 85
Fred, 85
GULDI, David, 154
GULDIN, Andrew,
173
M. Louisa, 173
GUMMER, Elizabeth,
108
John Adam, 108
Susanna, 108
GUMMY, John, 82
GUNCKEL,
Catharine, 113
Catherine, 24
Christine, 23,
61
John, 23, 30,
61, 63, 93,
164, 36
Jonathan, 113

Joshua, 164
Margaret, 63,
93, 164
Maria, 11
Maria Clara, 30,
36
Michael, 24, 113
Peter, 93
GUNDERMAN, John,
84
GUNTHER,
Catharine, 83
Fredericka, 82
GURTLER, Anna
Maria, 109
Christopher, 109
GUT, Christine, 79
GUTH, Christine,
125
GUWIN, John, 74
GWINN, Elizabeth,
36
John, 36
Joseph, 36
GYNRE, Catherine,
7

-H-
HAAG, Christine,
184
M., 184
Michael, 50
HAALMAN, John, 106
Margaret, 106
HAAS, Anna, 96,
161
Catharine, 81
Conrad, 44
Elizabeth, 14,
173, 184
Frederick, 75,
173
Henry, 184
Jemima, 56, 69
Jemimah, 96, 137
John, 60
John Conrad, 90
John Reinhard,
184
Margaret, 56
Martin, 56, 69,
79, 96, 137,
161
Mary Magdalene,
44
Rachel, 161

HAASS, Martin, 142
HABERSTICH,
George, 66
John, 31
Maria, 31, 43,
56, 66
Michael, 43
Nancy, 56
William, 31, 43,
56, 66
HABERSTICK, Carl,
107
Elizabeth, 23
Maria, 23, 107,
118
William, 23,
107, 118
HABGOOD, Fanny, 9
HACKEDY, Maria, 80
HACKER, A. Maria,
145
HAEFFENER, Anna
Margaret, 90
Philip, 90
HAEFFNER, George,
61
Mary Magdalene,
61
HAEGER, George,
136
HAEHN, Bernard,
142
HAEHNS, George,
158
Magdalene, 158
Michael, 158
HAENS, Anna Maria,
120
Bernard, 133
Margaret, 120
Michael, 120
HAER, Anna Ursula,
92
Christian, 92
Conrad, 92
HAERTH, Mary, 13
HAET, J., 167
HAETTERLEIN,
Gertrude, 67
John, 67
HAFENER,
Catherine, 10
HAFFENER, Ann
Margaret, 93
Anna Margaret,
27

Anna Maria, 74, 86
Catherine, 28
Henry, 17, 56, 86
John Philip, 38
Margaret, 38, 94
Maria, 56
Philip, 27, 28, 64, 93, 94
HAFFNER, Anna Margaret, 102, 104, 108
George, 171
J., 178
M. Magdalene, 171
Philip, 102, 104, 108
HAG, Christine, 170
Michael, 170
HAGEGATZ, Charlotte Catharine, 64
HAGER, Anna Maria, 27, 46
Catherine, 46
George, 7, 27
Gottfried, 27, 46
Maria, 8
HAHL, Anna Maria, 93
Catharine, 93
Stocker, 93
HAHLTER, Catharine, 105
Eva Maria, 105
Jacob, 105
HAHN, Catherine, 34
Christian, 25, 63
Elizabeth, 14, 25
Hannah, 25, 63
John, 4, 63
John William, 127
Margaret, 1, 25
Nicholas, 34
Peter, 5, 34
Susanna, 85
HAHNENGRAD, Elizabeth, 129

HAHNS, Catharine, 159
George, 79
Henry, 159, 162
Jacob, 159
Michael, 152
Veronica, 159, 162
HAHRDT, Elizabeth, 120
Jacob, 120
HAIL, Catharine, 85
HAILER, A. Christine, 162
Frederick, 162
HAIN, Daniel, 165
HAINS, Adam, 172
Catharine, 101, 172
Catherine, 34, 69
Daniel, 34, 101
Elizabeth, 172
George, 168, 176
Henry, 167, 168, 178
Jacob, 75
John, 181
John Bernard, 181
John Peter, 34
Juliana, 178
Margaret, 176
Maria, 101, 168, 176, 181
Michael, 101, 165, 183
Molly, 183
Phoebe, 167, 178
Salome, 128
Sarah, 165, 181
Sophina, 172
William, 167
HAINY, Nicholas, 73
HALBERSTAD, Catherine, 33
John, 33
Solomon, 33
HALBERSTADT, Anna, 51, 70
Catherine, 20, 42, 51, 70
Jacob, 51, 70

John, 8, 20, 42, 51, 70
John Peter, 51
William, 70
HALEY, John, 74
HALL, Catherine, 36
David, 80
Hannah, 42
Philip, 36
Robert, 122
Salome, 80
Thomas, 42
HALLEM, John Jacob, 93
John Peter, 93
Maria, 93
HALLER, Anna, 27
Anna Barbara, 46
Barbara, 13, 54
Christine, 37
Jacob, 14, 37
Joseph, 24
Julianna, 98
Maria, 24, 54, 60, 65, 89, 98, 116
Maria Margaret, 43
Peter, 54, 126
Philip, 13, 43, 54, 60, 65, 89, 98, 116
Regina, 116
Susanna, 24
Susanna Regina, 142
William, 89
HALTER, Anna Margaret, 26, 72
Christine, 26, 72, 175
David, 175
Eva Margaret, 175
Eva Maria, 56
Jacob, 26, 56, 72, 126, 156
Maria, 156
Maria Elizabeth, 56
Sarah, 156
HALVILSON, Philippina, 12
HAM, Christine, 86

Henry, 86
Philip, 86
HAMELER, Barbara,
  85
Godfrey, 85
HAMMER, Ludwig, 12
HAMMERICH,
  Barbara, 145
  Paul, 143
HAMMERLE,
  Catherine, 15
  Fabian, 15
  Regina, 15
HANCOCK, Benjamin,
  14
  Mary, 80
HANDSCHUH, Anna
  Maria, 31
  Christine, 81
  Christopher, 70
  Jacob, 3, 149
  Mary, 76
HANGE, John, 79,
  103, 122
  John George, 122
  Susanna, 122
HANGEN, John, 183
  John George, 149
  John Matthias,
  183
  Maria Ann, 183
  Susanna, 183
HANLEY, Mary, 80
HANLON, John, 78
HANNA, William,
  163
HANNEBACH, George,
  85
  Jacob, 85
  Maria Susanna,
  85
HANS, Catharine,
  176
  Christian, 161
  Daniel, 176
  Henry, 141
  John, 141
  Sophia, 161
  William, 161
HANSAL, Lewis, 73
HANSELL, George,
  74
HANSEN, A. Maria,
  81
  Andrew, 80
HANSMAN, Barbara, 87

Christopher, 49,
  87, 103
  Maria, 49
  Maria Barbara,
  103
HANSON, Matthias,
  8
HANSSEN, Edward,
  50
  Maria, 50
  Matthias, 50
HARDER, David, 93
  Maria, 93
HARFORD, Mary, 81
HARGESHEIMER,
  Jacon, 29
  Maria, 29
HARMER, Elizabeth,
  142
HARMSTADT, Maria
  Anna, 79
HARPER, Eliza, 175
  Franics, 175
  Jacob, 175
  Susanna, 175
HARRER, Joseph,
  147
HARRISON, Anne, 10
HARTMAN, Cath., 63
  Christian, 85
  Dietr., 183
  John, 183
HARTMANN,
  Elizabeth, 152
  Magdalene, 146
HARTNECK,
  Christine, 83
HARTUNG, Anna
  Catharine, 106
  Daniel, 106, 123
  Elizabeth, 106,
  123
HASCHER,
  Frederick, 114
  Philippina, 114
HASELTON, Barbara,
  26
  Isaiah, 26
  Sibylla, 26
HASSELBACH,
  George, 97, 146
  Maria, 97
  Philip, 97
HASSENBACH,
  Philip, 139

HASTER, Elizabeth,
  160
  Frederick, 160
  Jacob Rust, 160
HASTINGS,
  Clarissa, 11
HATKINS, John, 92
  Maria, 92
HATZ, Amelia, 40
  George, 40
  Martin, 40
HAUBT, Elizabeth,
  14
HAUCH, John, 171
  Mary, 171
HAUER, Anthony, 83
HAUGH, John, 116
HAUS, Samuel, 144
HAUSEL, George
  Nicholas, 159
  Hannah, 159
HAUSER, Barbara, 2
  Catharine, 109
  Catherine, 44
  Ernest, 86
  Ernst, 32
  George, 42, 44
  John Adam, 9
  Magdalene, 126
HAUSLER, Jacob, 81
HAUSS, Anna
  Barbara, 108
  Conrad, 108
HAUTZ, Christine,
  160
HAUTZEL,
  Christian, 97,
  122, 133
  Elizabeth, 122
  John Peter, 97
  Margaret, 97,
  122
  Peter, 133
  Samuel, 97
HAUZEL, William,
  140
HAVEMAN,
  Elizabeth, 71
HAVEN, Charles,
  182
  Maria, 182
  Wilson, 182
HAYNS, Catherine,
  67
  Maria, 67
  Michael, 67

HAYS, Addis, 83
HEALY, Edward, 74
HEBENSTREIT, Anna, 117
Anna Elizabeth, 117
John, 117
HECHT, Johanna Christine Henrietta, 78
HECK, Andrew, 101
Anna Margaret, 101
Henrietta Christine, 5
Herman, 101
HECKMAN, Nicholas, 148
HEDER, Carl, 103
George, 103
Susanna, 103
HEEHR, Susanna, 78
HEEWER, Charles, 127
HEFFENER, Maria, 56
HEHER, Catharine, 78
HEHRING, Frederica, 100
HEIBEL, Anna Margaret, 108
Christian, 108
John Philip, 108
HEIBERGER, Anna Maria, 46
Catherine, 33
Elizabeth, 87, 97, 165
George, 23, 33, 46
Jacob, 87, 97, 140, 165
John, 87, 140
John Jacob, 46
Maria, 33
William, 165
HEIDTE, Anna, 11
HEILER, John, 47
Susanna, 47
HEIMBERGER, Anna Margaret, 36
Elizabeth, 184
Fred, 42
Frederick, 12
George, 184

Jacob, 184
Margaret, 35
Maria, 42, 46
Thomas, 35, 36
HEIMER, Anna Maria, 50
Catherine, 35, 55
Catherine Elizabeth, 68
Daniel, 6
Elizabeth, 50, 68, 95, 115, 129
Frederick, 9
Jacob, 4, 55
John, 11, 35, 50, 68, 95, 115, 133
John Jacob, 143
John Peter, 35
Mercy, 55
Peter, 72
Stephen, 115
HEIMS, Frederick, 104
Sarah, 104
HEIN, Catharine, 80
Charlotte, 20
Frederick, 20
John, 20
Philippina, 84, 160
HEINEBERG, Matthias, 80
HEINEMAN, ---, 129
Anna Catharine, 88
Anna Catherine, 67
Catharine, 49
Catherine, 31, 40, 62
Charlotta, 87
Charlotte, 31, 40, 58, 100
Christian, 40
Elizabeth, 58
Fred., 31, 88
Frederick, 29, 40, 67
Fried, 62
George, 78
Hannah, 132

Henry, 31, 40, 58, 87, 100
John, 132
John Frederick, 31
John Philip, 87
Maria, 29, 100
HEINER, Jacob, 9
HEINI, James, 92
HEINIG, Charlotte, 30
Christian, 24
John, 30
Ludwig, 30
Maria Barbara, 24
Mria Barbara, 24
HEINMAN, Polly, 185
HEINS, Catherine, 2
John, 56
Maria, 56
Michael, 56
HEINY, Barbara, 4
Christian, 35
John, 1
John George, 7, 35
Mary Barbara, 35
HEIS, Christian, 29, 58
Janne, 29
Jeane, 29
John, 29
Sarah, 58
William, 58
HEISER, Adam, 74
HEISING, Catherine, 27
HEISS, Anna Catharine, 135
Christian, 69, 112
John, 24, 112
Joseph, 69
Sarah, 69, 112
HEISSLER, Elizabeth, 80
HEIST, Catharine, 83
Christian, 98
Jesse, 98
Sarah, 98
HEITH, Maria, 13
HEKEDY, Louisa, 98

HELBERGER, Anna
  Maria, 22
  George, 22
HELD, Elizabeth,
  69, 91
  John, 83
  John Peter, 91
  John Philip, 69
  Mr., 128
  Peter, 69, 82,
  124
  Rebecca, 12
HELFENSTEIN,
  Samuel, 84,
  153, 164
HELFFENSTEIN,
  Emanuel, 184
  John Albertus,
  184
  Philip, 159
  Samuel, 184
HELL, Jacob, 84
HELLER, Adam, 80
  Catharine, 78
  Joseph, 142
  Miss, 71
  Susanna, 150
HELM, Adam, 109,
  140, 163
  Anna Gertrude,
  109
  Anna Maria, 109
  Gertrude, 163
  John, 140, 163
  Magdalene, 112
HELMIG, Dorothy,
  124
HELT, Carl, 98
  Elizabeth, 75,
  98
  John A., 174
  Peter, 75, 98
HELTZHEIMER, ---,
  154
HELWIG, Jacob, 127
  Margaret, 74
  Maria, 63
HEMBELMAN, Jacob,
  125
HEMER, Richard, 81
HEMERLE,
  Catherine, 23
  Elizabeth, 23
  Fabian, 23
HEMERLIN,
  Catherine, 62

Fabian, 62, 125
HEMERLY,
  Catherine, 45
  Fabian, 45
  Jacob, 45
HEMPELMAN, Eliza,
  39
  Elizabeth, 25,
  163
  Jacob, 25, 39,
  125
  Philip, 39
HEN, Conrad, 130
HENCKEL,
  Cornelius, 77
HENDEL, ---, 123
  Dr., 164
  William, 79, 83,
  122, 141
HENDEN, John
  William, 153
  William, 154
HENDERSON,
  Catherine, 53
  William, 53
HENDRICH, Carl,
  185
  Frederick, 185
  Helena, 185
HENE, Elizabeth,
  69
  John, 69
  Salome, 69
HENEISEN, Jacob,
  103, 120
  Maria, 103, 120
HENEY, Catherine,
  53
  Conrad, 53
  Susanna, 53
HENK, Anna Maria,
  171
  Jost, 171
  Ludwig, 171, 176
HENN, Catharine,
  172
  Catharine
  Elizabeth, 172
  Jacob, 172
HENNEL, Joseph,
  171
HENRICH, Anna, 157
  Casper, 118, 155
  Christine, 164
  Christopher, 157

Elizabeth, 11,
  118, 155
  Henry Martin,
  137
  John, 164
  John Frederick,
  163
  Magdalene, 79
  Martin, 137
  Peter, 118
  Samuel, 155
HENRIEGEL, Jacob,
  162
HENRITZY,
  Catherine, 18
  George, 1
  Henry, 18
HENRY, Catharine,
  76
  Elizabeth, 2
  Maria, 12
HENS, Catherine,
  17
  Daniel, 17
  Elizabeth, 60
  John, 60
  Magdalene, 17
  Salome, 60
HENSEL, Maria, 82
HENSEM, Matthias,
  36
HENSMAN,
  Christopher,
  57, 65
  Maria Barbara,
  57
HENSSEN, Matthew,
  12
HENTZ, Elizabeth,
  82
  Michael, 151
HENVECTER,
  Barbara, 169
  Elizabeth, 169
  G., 169
HENY, Christian,
  60
  John, 60
  Maria Barbara,
  60
  Ottilia H., 129
HEPPLE, Catharine,
  104
HEPPLER, Gertrude,
  59
  Henry, 59

HERA, Charlotte,
32
Christian, 32
HERBERG, John, 128
HERD, Nocholas,
146
HERDERLING,
Elizabeth, 64
HERFORD,
Catharine, 88
George, 14, 56,
88, 109
Maria, 56, 88,
109
HERLEIN,
Catharine, 95
John, 95
HERMAN, Catharine,
79
Charles, 89
John, 157
Lawrence, 157
Maria, 157
HERON, Aime
Blondel, 82
HERR, Catharine,
74
HERTLEIN,
Gertrude, 70
John, 70
HERTZ, Catharine,
171
HERTZOG, John
William, 139
Rachel, 75
Rebecca, 79
Susanna, 10
HESEL, Carl, 159
Catharine, 160
HESS, A.
Catharine, 84
Adam, 36, 56,
102
Anna, 8, 36, 42,
46, 91, 127
Anna Catharine,
106, 164
Anna Elizabeth,
91
Anna Juliana, 92
Carl, 102
Catharine, 166
Catherine, 14,
21
Christian, 133
Eleonore, 177

Elizabeth, 36,
56, 74, 102,
120
Fanny, 178
George, 12, 42,
46, 91, 106,
138, 164, 167,
178
Jesse, 133
Johanna Sophia,
165
John, 138, 177
John L., 166
John Peter, 165
Kisiah, 164
Ludwig, 21, 70,
92
Margaret, 14
Maria, 56
Maria Veronica,
164
Nicholas, 36,
54, 90, 120,
142, 149
Peter, 164, 178
Peter Martin, 80
Rachel, 120
Rosina, 73
Susanna, 164
Wilehelmina, 75
Wilhelmina, 36,
70, 90, 120
William, 46, 164
HESSE, Adam, 90
Anna, 63
Elizabeth, 90
George, 63
John Nicholas,
90
Sarah, 63
HESSHEISEN, A.
Maria, 162
HESTER, Conrad, 24
Eleonora
Catherine, 24
HETTON, George, 75
HETZER, Margaret,
102
William, 102
HEUET, Cathies ,
63
HEUSER, Ernest,
49, 129
Magdalene
Elizabeth, 49

HEUTLINGER, ---,
130
HEY, Rosina, 11
HEYL, Philip, 54
HEYMAN, Catherine,
16
Henry, 16
HEYMER, Elizabeth,
115
HEZENBACH, Carl,
115
Christopher, 115
Eliasi, 115
HIBBS, William, 84
HICK, Carl, 8
HICKERIBADEM,
William, 140
HICKERIBODEM,
Elizabeth, 119
William, 119
HICKHAM, Richard,
84
HICKINBOTTOM,
John, 144
HICKS, Charles, 15
George, 15
Hannah, 15
HIEBEL, Anna
Margaret, 120
Christian, 78,
120
HIGGINS, Comfort,
81
HILDEBRAND, Anna
Margaret, 50
Henry, 13, 50
John, 50
HILL, Anna M., 180
Anna Maria, 42,
86, 118
Daniel, 166
Elizabeth, 40,
52, 53, 76, 86,
96, 117
Hannah, 27
Jacob, 40, 42,
52, 53, 75, 83,
86, 96, 117,
135, 139, 156,
166
John, 117, 124,
180
Lawrence, 156
Maria Elizabeth,
139
Rebecca, 180

Sarah, 96, 150
Susanna, 156
William, 84, 180
HILLEGAS, George,
182
Maria, 182
HILLER, John, 53
Joseph, 53, 71
Susanna, 53, 71
Susanna Miller,
53
HIMBELL,
Christian, 33
Maria Christine,
33
HIMCKEL, Maria
Christine, 174
HIMMEL, Albrecht,
103
Elizabeth, 103
Maria, 103
Nicholas, 103
HIMMELREICH,
Daniel
Bergemeyer, 62
Eva Barbara, 62
William, 62
HIMPEL, Christian,
64
Christine, 26
HIMPELMAN,
Elizabeth, 58
Jacob, 58
HINCKEL, Anthony,
20, 178
Barbara, 20, 33,
52, 70, 104,
178
Catharine, 178
Catherine, 70
Conrad, 20, 33,
70, 178
Daniel, 124
Elizabeth, 132
George, 135, 54,
104
Henry, 124
John, 33, 67
John Conrad, 52
Maria, 50, 67,
141
Marianne, 54
Ruth, 54
HINK, Ann, 182
George, 182

HINKLE, Catharine,
168
Philip, 168
HIPP, Jacob, 178
Maria Christine,
178
Maria Susanna,
178
HIRSCH, Eleonore,
48
HIRSCHHORN,
Catharine, 111
HIRT, Ludwig, 154
HIRTULZ, Abraham,
173
Catharine, 173
HITALER, Anna, 179
Jacob, 179
John, 179
HOCKER, Leonard,
116
Regina, 116
HOEFFLY, Maria, 78
HOF, Philippina,
146
HOFF, Catharine,
79, 104
Christine, 104
Conrad, 45
Elizabeth, 84,
147
George, 147
Jacob, 104
John George
Conrad, 67
Ludwig, 8
Maria Sibylla,
45, 67
HOFFMAN, ---, 153
Adam, 27, 71,
125
Ann Maria, 90
Anna, 158
Anna Maria, 27,
53, 58, 60, 71,
86
Barbara, 68
Bost., 183
Catharine, 64,
76, 154
Charlotte, 74
Christian, 27
Elizabeth, 40,
169, 180, 183
Eva, 59, 67, 180

Francis, 56,
107, 167
George, 24, 27,
40, 58, 90, 96,
131
Henry, 59
Jacob, 134, 154,
158
James, 59, 180
John, 68, 148,
154, 158
John Daniel, 169
John George, 53,
60, 71
Joseph, 134
Lawrence, 74
Magdalene, 143
Margaret, 96,
107, 167
Maria, 40, 68,
96, 131
Sally, 183
Salome, 53
Samuel, 107
Sebastian, 169
Susanna, 16
Valentine, 16,
27
HOFFMANN,
Elizabeth, 145,
156
Eva, 156
Jacob, 156
Maria, 81
Sebastian, 82
HOFFSTAELLER,
John, 41
HOFFSTAETLER,
Henry, 87
Margaret, 87
Maria, 87
HOFFSTAETTEL,
John, 42
HOFFSTAT,
Elizabeth
Catharine, 98
John William, 98
HOFMAN, George,
133
Margaret, 133
HOFSTAEDLER, John,
77
HOHL, Carl, 132
Catharine, 91,
107

Catherine, 24, 40
Charles, 91
Henry Christian, 9
John, 24
Maria, 107, 146
Martin, 41, 92
Mary Magdalene, 41, 92
Peter, 24, 40, 91, 107, 132, 147
HOHMAN, Abrahm, 54
HOHRN, Christine, 108
Henry, 108
John, 108
HOLL, Christine, 108
Elizabeth, 102
John, 108
John Adam, 102
Margaret, 84
Peter, 124
William, 108
HOLLENBRAND, Casper, 155
John Frederick, 155
HOLLER, C., 171
HOLLIDAY, Jacob, 153
HOLTZ, Carl, 103
Christopher, 3
Elizabeth, 2
Margaret, 103
HOLTZBERGER, Carl, 143
HOOD, Thomas, 11
HOOG, William, 42
HOOVER, Catherine, 11
HOPP, Elizabeth, 158
John, 71, 158
Marianna, 71
Nancy, 71
HORN, Abraham, 72
Christine, 37, 55
Henry, 37, 55
Peter, 7
Susanna, 72
William, 37

HORNING, Elizabeth, 10
Jacob, 77
HORTON, Mary, 81
HOTZ, Maria, 67
HOUGH, Isaac, 78
HOUSMAN, Sophia, 11
HOWE, Anna, 152, 162
Margaret, 162
Samuel, 162
HOWER, Jacob, 172
Margaret, 172
Samuel, 172
HOWS, J., 176
HUBER, Anna Maria, 120
Elizabeth, 9, 16, 41, 110, 125
George, 26
Henry, 16, 28, 36, 41, 54, 120
Jacob, 6, 16
John, 74, 84, 110, 142
Joseph, 84
Louisa, 26
Magdalene, 120
Maria, 16, 28, 41, 54, 75
Veronica, 110
William, 16
HUCK, Andrew, 7
Anna Margaret, 75
HUCKES, Christopher, 173
HUCKY, Bessy, 72
Rudolph, 72
HUDDON, Christine, 175
John, 175
Maria Elizabeth, 175
HUETER, Anna Catherine, 65
Anna Maria, 65
Thomas, 65
thomas, 74
HUFF, Jacob Frederick, 110
John George, 110

Margaret Philippine, 110
HUFFARTH, Barbara, 65
George, 65
HUFFNER, M., 172
HUGART, Elizabeth, 172
Elst., 172
Margaret, 172
HUGHES, Caleb, 13, 47, 59
Esther, 127
Garret, 74
Hester, 59
Jane, 10
Maria, 47, 59
Uriah, 13
HUGUEN, Henrietta, 147
HUHN, Barbara, 132
Catharine, 75
Christiana, 158
Christine, 32, 50, 68, 93, 112, 154, 159, 168
Daniel, 32, 158
Dorothy, 168
Elizabeth, 50
Gerard, 76
Gerhard, 158
Jacob, 156
John, 11, 32, 50, 68, 93, 112, 132, 145, 151, 158, 159, 168
Joseph, 159
Magdalene, 128
Maria, 158
Maria Barbara, 93
Maria Magdalena, 68
Susanna, 76
HULL, William, 176
HUMBERGER, Mr., 8
HUMP, John, 176
Margaret, 176
Rebecca, 176
HUMPHREYS, Margaret, 30
HUNER, Margaret, 103
Peter, 103

Sarah, 103
HUNOLTZ, Abraham,
  160
  Catharine, 160
  William, 160
HUNT, Anna Maria,
  166
  Carl, 172
  Elizabeth, 183
  James, 166, 172,
  183
  Maria, 183
  Polly, 172
  Sophia, 166
HUNTER, Charles, 9
HUPFELD,
  Charlotte, 163
  Henry, 163
  John Carl, 163
HUPPEFIELD, Carl,
  171
  Charlotte
  Elizabeth, 171
  Sarah, 171
HUPPFIELD,
  Charles, 171
HURFF, Priscilla,
  74
HUSSELBACH, Sarah,
  150
  William, 149
HUT, Catharine, 81
HUTH, Christopher,
  24, 37, 69, 90,
  129, 136
  Elizabeth, 24,
  37, 50, 69, 90
  Jacob, 50
  John, 24
  John Jacob, 50
  Maria, 113
  Mary Magdalene,
  136
  Peter, 77
  Sarah, 37
  William, 90
HUTTEMAN, Alitta,
  115
  John William,
  115
HUTTEMANN, Thomas
  Lorentz, 82
HUTTER, Alitha
  Jacoba, 163
  Christine, 170
  John, 170

Susan, 170
  William, 163
HUTTERMAN, Alitha
  Jacoba, 163
  Barbara, 163
  Thomas, 163
HUTZ, Catharine,
  97
HUWAR, John, 169
HUYS, Edward, 117
  Gerard, 117
  Susanna, 117
HYETER, Catharine,
  90
  Thomas, 90

-I-
IMBELE, May, 174
IMDORFF,
  Catherine, 5
IMMEL, Elizabeth,
  37
  John, 158, 182
  Joseph, 37
  Margaret, 142
  Maria, 158, 182
  Peter, 37, 76,
  158
  Rosina, 182
  William, 182
INGERTH,
  Elizabeth, 107
  James, 107
  Regina
  Elizabeth, 107
ISTWICK, Charles,
  77

-J-
JACKSON, Rebecca,
  13
JACOB, Christian,
  14, 43, 78
JAEGLI, Magdalene,
  14
JAETE, Martin, 127
JAETTE, Philip,
  125
JAGER, Elizabeth,
  180
  Maria, 180
  Michael, 180
JAHNS, Margaret,
  148
JAHRAUS,
  Elizabeth, 107

George Adam, 107
John Jacob, 107
M. Christine,
  148
JAMESON,
  Elizabeth, 60
  John, 60
JAMISSEN,
  Elizabeth, 75
JANEY, George, 81
JANSSEN,
  Catherine, 32
JANSSON, David, 4
  John, 124
JANTSON, Anna, 20
  Herman, 20
JANUS, Doctor, 39
  George, 11
  Jacob, 127
  Margaret, 39
JARSKY, Joseph, 23
  Magdalene, 23
JAUCH, Elizabeth,
  109
  Eva, 99, 109
  John, 99, 109
  Maria, 149
  William, 99
JAY, Elizabeth, 21
  Francis, 21
JEANIL, Peter, 142
JEBLY, Franklin,
  166
  Jacob, 166
  Miliana, 166
JECKLE, Anna, 156
  Elizabeth, 156
  Henry, 146, 156
JECKLY, Anna
  Maria, 117
  Henry, 117
  John, 117
JEFFERSON, Daniel,
  179
  Maria, 179
JEFFERYS, Mary, 83
JEGLEY, John, 2
JEGLY, Ulrich, 2
JENKINS, David,
  102
  Elizabeth, 102
  Maria, 102
JENNY, John, 117,
  140
  Maria, 117
  Peter, 117

JENSER, Anna
  Catharine, 103
  Barbara, 121
  Catharine, 103,
    107
  Clara, 78
  Elizabeth, 121
  Frederick, 99,
    119, 147
  George, 103,
    107, 143
  Jacob, 121, 136,
    137
  Jacobina, 99,
    119
  John, 136
  John George, 145
  Magdalene, 99
  Maria, 137
  Mary Magdalene,
    107
  Philippina, 119,
    142
JENSOHR, Barbara,
    104
  Jacob, 104
  John, 104
JENTZ, Anna
  Catharine, 78
JENTZER, Anna
  Margaret, 11
  Barbara, 89
  Catherine, 25,
    39, 65
  Christian, 61
  Christine, 72
  Dorothea, 39
  Frederick, 61,
    72, 73
  George, 25, 39,
    65, 72
  Jacob, 25, 58,
    75, 89
  Jacobina, 61
  Maria, 89
  Sarah, 65
  Veronica, 76
JEREMIAS,
  Magdalene, 89
JERGER, Catherine,
    11
JERKIS, Caty, 75
JERYMEY,
  Elizabeth, 85
JETT, Hannah
  Christine, 77

JETTE, Catherine,
    43
  Henry, 43
  Philip, 43
JETTER, Anna
  Catharine, 106
  Anna Margaret,
    106
  Catharine, 162
  Henry, 106, 162
  Peter, 162
JOBST, John, 77
  John Michael, 76
JOCUM, Hannah, 26
  John, 26
  Sarah, 26
JOEST, Carl, 125
  Catharine, 126
  Charles, 60
  Christine, 60
  George, 60
JOETTE, Ann
  Catharine, 89
  Anna Catharine,
    89
  Henry, 89
JOHANNSSON,
  Marlena, 72
JOHNS, Anna Maria,
    110
  Elizabeth, 96,
    110
  Isaac, 96
  John, 110
  William, 96
JOHNSON,
  Alexander, 83
  Anna Maria, 77,
    116
  Catharine, 155
  Elizabeth, 169
  Fanny, 139
  James, 116
  John, 43, 46,
    176
  Margaret, 116
  Maria, 43, 46,
    176
  Martha, 155
  Rebecca, 79
  Richard, 43
  Robert, 13, 46
  William, 155
JOHNSSEN, Maria,
    35

JOHNSTON, Maria,
    140
  Sarah, 74
JOHRAUS,
  Elizabeth, 7
  George, 4
JONAS, Elizabeth,
    35, 71, 136
  George, 35
  John, 71, 136
  William, 71
JONES, A.
  Margaret, 152
  Anna, 71, 185
  Catherine, 10
  David, 167
  Elizabeth, 48,
    71, 92, 162,
    180, 182, 185
  George
    Washington, 36
  Isaac, 10
  Jacob, 85
  John, 13, 48,
    71, 92, 162
  John Philip, 162
  Margaret, 146,
    167
  Maria, 149, 182
  Patty, 167
  Sally, 48
  Sarah, 81, 145
  Thomas, 182, 185
  William, 75, 92
JONSON, J., 169
JONTZER, Jacob, 1
JORAS, Elizabeth,
    51
  George, 51
  John Andrew, 51
JORAUS, Elizabeth,
    72
  George, 7, 72
  John Valentine,
    72
JORDAN, Catharine,
    162
  Frederick, 162
  Maria, 162
JORDEN, Catharine,
    152
JORK, Anna Mary,
    154
JOST, Carl, 42
  Catherine, 42

Charles, 27, 33, 36
Christine, 2, 26, 27, 33, 36, 42, 138
Elizabeth, 27, 85, 124
Peter, 78
JOUCH, Catharine, 76
Christian, 129
Elizabeth, 14
John, 51
JOUSSE, John, 162
JUENGST, Anna Margaret, 94
Henry, 94
John Henry, 109
Margaret, 94
Maria Elizabeth, 109
JUMEN, Sarah, 103
JUNCKER, George, 82, 159
Joseph, 81
Maria, 159
Sarah, 159
JUND, Elizabeth, 84
John, 172
Leonard, 93
Maria, 172
Sarah, 93
JUNDT, Anna, 64
Leonard, 50, 64
Sarah, 50, 64
JUNG, Andrew, 5, 30
Anna Cathrine, 101
Anna Maria, 101, 174
Carl, 178
Caroline, 28, 30, 35
Catharine, 98, 100, 165
Catherine Susanna, 35
Christian, 28, 35, 40, 166, 175
Christian George, 35
Christopher, 158
Cottfried, 165

Elizabeth, 10, 35, 40, 49, 108
George, 158
Godfrey, 165
Henry, 166
Jacob, 35, 52, 61, 82
John, 14, 49
John Christian, 152, 158
John Daniel, 174
John George, 101, 114
John george, 85
Leonard, 40
Ludwig, 30, 100, 165
M. Juliana, 152
Magdalene, 24, 35, 114
Margaret, 74
Maria, 158, 166, 175
Maria Eliza, 174
Mary Magdalene, 61
Peter, 24, 76
Philip, 7, 35, 49, 108, 183
Rebecca, 127
Sarah, 35, 52, 61
Susanna, 52
JUNGELING, Anna Eva, 122
JUNGST, Ann Margaret, 93
Ann Maria, 93
Catherine, d71
Elizabeth, 71, 85
Henry, 74, 85, 93
Henry William, 71
Ludwick Herman, 71
Maria, 85
JUNKER, George, 172
Maria, 172
Regina, 172
JUNT, Anna, 64
JUS, Gerard, 90
Lydia, 90
Susanna, 90

JUSTUS, Anna, 134
Anna Margaret, 4, 16
Anna Maria Magdalena, 16
Elizabeth, 157, 163, 165, 176
George, 16, 51, 65, 134, 144
Maria, 176
Philip, 157, 163, 165, 176
JUTTE, Catherine, 24, 56, 68
Christopher, 24, 56, 68
JUVENAL, Anna Louisa, 166
Elizabeth, 157
Jacob, 101
Maria, 74
Nicholas, 61, 101, 157, 166, 176
Susanna, 61, 101, 157, 166

-K-
KABLER, Rachel, 146
KAERCHER, Anthony, 106
Marianna, 106
Samuel, 106
KAERSBACH, Maria, 129
KAERT, Bernard, 162
Catharine, 162
Elizabeth, 162
Jacob M., 162
Joseph, 162
KAEST, Jacob, 60
KAESTER, Elizabeth, 97
Frederick, 97
KAHMER, Anna, 126
Anna Cathrine, 52
Elizabeth, 52, 66, 67, 89, 112
John Reinhard, 66
Maria, 67
Mr., 52

Reinhard, 66, 67, 129, 143
Reinhardt, 112, 137
William, 14, 24, 52
William Ludwig, 66, 89
KAISER, ---, 137
Adam, 111
Andrew, 111
Anna Elizabeth, 67
Daniel, 96, 111, 117, 138
David, 117, 138
Elizabeth, 63, 116
Hannah, 111
John, 67, 112
John Henry, 112
Maria, 111
Michael, 14, 63
Nicholas, 63, 116
Regina, 96, 111, 117
Sarah, 116
KALBFLEISCH, John, 12
Maria, 11
KALCKBRENNER,
Maria, 100, 107
Philip, 100, 107
KALEY, Hannah, 64
Matthias, 64
Morton Brealsford, 64
KALKBRENNER,
Maria, 87
R., 87
KALTWASSER,
Elizabeth, 162
John Philip, 162
KAMER, Reinhard, 129
KAMMER, Elizabeth, 79
KAMPER, Anna, 40
Anna Barbara, 17
Elizabeth, 63, 65
George Michael, 103
Henry, 63
John, 63, 65

John Henry, 63
Maria, 41
Mary Magdalene, 63
Michael, 17, 19, 40
Rosina, 103
Susanna, 17, 19, 40, 103
KAMPFER,
Catherine, 55
Jacob, 55
Maria, 55
KANN, Maria, 176
KANTZER,
Christopher, 90
KAPP, Catharine, 182
John, 182
John George, 182
KAPPEL, Catherine, 66
Elizabeth, 47
John, 47, 66
Margaret, 10
KAPPES, Jacob, 77
KARCH, Jacob, 62
KARCHER, Laury
Peter, 171
Louisa, 144
Ludwig, 127
Marianne, 150
Norris Philip, 159
Peter Laury, 159
Samuel, 148, 159, 171
Susanna, 159, 171
KARCKER, M., 168
KARGER, Salome, 143
KARPIUM, Samuel, 144
KARPP, Catharine, 95
John, 95
John Casper, 95
KARR, Anna Maria, 171
Elizabeth, 171, 179
Jacob, 171, 179
Susanna, 179
KARSBACH,
Margaret, 1

Maria Elizabeth, 25
Martin, 25, 56
Mary Magdalene, 25, 56
Sarah, 56
KARSCHBACH,
Elizabeth, 142
Susanna, 142
KARSTENS, George, 82
KART, Elizabeth, 76
KARTRIETH, Mary, 76
KASBAN, Anna
Catherine, 67
Daniel, 67
Maria Suess, 67
KASSELMAN,
William, 3
KAST, Bernard, 150
KASTENBACH, John, 83
KATZ, Adam, 106
George, 89
Jacob, 58, 135
Margaret, 58, 89, 106
Michael, 12, 58, 89, 106, 135
KAUCK, Christian, 10, 41, 93, 105
John, 105, 141
Margaret, 41
Maria, 41, 93, 105
KAUFFMAN, Bernard, 158
Henry, 81
Margaret, 158
KAUFMAN, Bernard, 159
Margaret, 159
KAUWERTZ, Conrad, 13
KAY, Barnabas, 126
KAYSER, Catharine, 88, 184
Daniel, 53, 67
Elizabeth, 18, 45, 88, 145, 184
Jacob, 18
John, 13, 184
Margaret, 45

Nicholas, 18,
   45, 88, 184
Regina, 53, 67
Susanna, 67, 127
William, 53, 124
KAYSR, Andrew, 145
KEBLEHAUSER,
   Elizabeth, 12
KEEHLEY,
   Elizabeth, 4
KEELER, Anna, 70
   Michael, 70
   William, 70
KEELY, Elizabeth,
   49, 124
   Hannah, 34, 49
   Matthias, 34, 49
   Samuel, 34
KEESSMAN, Anna
   Margaret, 67
   Frederick
   William, 67
   John, 67
KEFFENER,
   Timotheus, 43
KEHLHEFFR,
   Frederick, 13
KEHM, George
   William, 86
   John, 86
   Maria Elizabeth,
   86
KEHR, Anna, 79
   Anna Elizabeth,
   37, 46
   Daniel, 8, 21,
   38
   Elizabeth, 77
   Gabriel, 22
   John, 22
   John Daniel, 21
   John George, 14
   Mary Magdalene,
   21, 22, 38
   Philip, 37, 46
   William, 38
KEHRN, Father, 87
KEIGER, Martin, 60
KEILER, Barbara,
   14, 29
   John, 81
   Margaret, 11
   Susanna, 80, 120
KEILMAN,
   Catharine, 43
KEISER, Adam, 96

Daniel, 89, 96
Elizabeth, 98
Eva, 66
Jacob, 66
John, 98
John William, 98
Joseph, 89, 140
Maria, 96
Regina, 89
Susanna, 127
KELKER, Margaret,
   149
KELLER, Anna
   Maria, 71
   Carl, 151, 178
   Catharine, 178
   Christ., 43
   Christine, 40,
   82
   Christopher, 9,
   27, 71
   Conrad, 19, 40,
   55, 72, 84, 92,
   99, 108, 120,
   166, 178
   Elizabeth, 19,
   22, 26, 40, 43,
   55, 72, 92, 99,
   108, 120
   George, 80
   Hannah, 160
   Herman, 120
   Jacob, 22
   John, 19, 78
   John Jacob, 26
   Margaret, 12, 55
   Maria, 27, 30,
   128
   Michael, 160
KELLY, Andrew, 158
   Catharine, 158
   Elizabeth, 14,
   59
   John, 59, 82,
   158
   William, 59
KEMP, Jacob, 159
   Mria, 159
   Nicholas, 104
   William, 159
KEMPERT,
   Elizabeth, 12
   John, 12
KEP, Catharine, 76
KEPPERT, Rachel,
   118

KEPPLER, Gertrude,
   120
   Henry, 120
KERBY, Charles, 10
KERCH, Maria, 10
KERLIN, William,
   22
KERN, Andrew, 61
   Charles, 49
   Christine, 22
   Elizabeth, 39
   Gabriel, 61, 96,
   108, 176
   John, 4, 16, 39,
   56
   Margaret, 176
   Maria, 56
   Maria Elizabeth,
   16, 56
   Maria Eva, 96
   Mary Magdalene,
   49, 61, 96,
   108, 123
   Mr., 129
   Peter, 129
KERSCHENER,
   Catherine, 19
   John, 19
KERSMAN, Mr., 124
KERT, Elizabeth,
   79
   Jacob Mitschet,
   79
KERTER, A. Mary,
   171
   L., 171
KESEN, Barbara, 12
KESMAN, Sarah, 91
   William, 91
KESSELMAN,
   Frederick, 40
   John, 40
   Susanna, 40
KESSLER,
   Charlotte, 111
   Conrad, 111
   Margaret, 110
   Nancy, 111
KESSMAN, Mrs., 129
KESTER, A. Maria,
   170
   Ludwig, 170
KETZ, Catherine,
   15
KEULER, Barbara,
   43

KEYSER, Elizabeth,
31, 76, 95
John, 10, 165
John Michael,
165
Nicholas, 31, 95
KHUCK, Christian,
31
George, 31
Maria, 31
KIEBERT, Margaret,
126
KIEGBERT,
Christian, 14
KIEHN, Jacob, 131
John, 131
KIELHOFFER,
Frederick, 138
KIELY, Francis,
147
KIENLY, Henry, 44
KIEPER, Christian,
126
KIEPERT, Anna
Maria, 64
Christian, 64
Margaret, 64
KIESSY, Mr., 129
KIHN, Catharine,
88
Catherine, 63
John, 63, 88
Margaret, 63
KILHOFER, George,
145
KIMP, John, 89
KIMPECH,
Catharine, 179
Dominic, 179
KINDERN,
Charlotte, 91
KING, Catherine,
52
Jacob, 52
John, 52
Robert, 156
KINGSY, Salome
Hains, 125
KINLEY, Henry, 44
KINRY, Anna
Agitae, 74
KINS, Catharine,
91
Catherine, 66
George, 66, 91
James, 91

KINSEL, Daniel
Jacob, 117
Margaret, 117
Michael, 59
Philip, 117
KINSELER, Anna
Elizabeth, 30
John Michael, 30
KINSELY,
Catharine, 88,
114
Catherine, 38
Elizabeth, 38
Henry, 38
Jacob, 38, 88,
114
John George, 114
Mary Magdalene,
88
Sarah, 88
Susanna, 88
KINSEY, Catherine,
19
Jacob, 19
Samuel, 19
KINSI, Anna, 115
Christopher, 115
Susanna, 115
KINSIG, Leonard,
124
Magdalene, 124
KINSINGER, John,
151
Michael, 78
KINSLE,
Christopher, 75
Henry, 163
Maria, 163
KINSLEY, Anna, 135
Catherine, 31
Henry, 135
Jacob, 31
John William, 31
Mr., 6
KINSLY, Anna, 104
Henry, 104, 105
Maria, 104, 105
Rudolph, 104
KINTZINGER,
Catharine, 151
Martha, 163
Michael, 163
KINTZLER,
Margaret, 13
KIRBY, Herriet, 9

KIRCH, John Henry,
30
KIRCHHOF,
Christian, 112
Maria, 112
William, 112
KIRCHHOFF,
Christian, 179
Elizabeth, 179
John Aug., 2
Mary Magdalene,
179
KIRCHNER, John, 25
Magdalene, 25
Maria Elizabeth,
25
KIRCHOFF,
Christian Aug.,
44
Henry, 44
Mary Magdalene,
44
KIRCHOFFF,
Christian Aug.,
26
Christian
August, 26
Maria, 26
KIRSCHENER,
Catherine, 62
John, 62
Joseph, 62
KITH, Charles
Jacob, 71
Margaret, 71
Rebecca, 71
KITHS, M., 167
KITT, Solomon, 41
KITTS, Abigail,
181
Alice, 51
Bridget, 51
Charles, 14, 51
Christine, 83
Jacob, 45
Margaret, 45,
63, 95
Michael, 63, 95
KITZ, Margaret,
116
Maria Margaret,
18
Michael, 18, 116
KLAGES, Anna
Catherine, 69
Carl, 100

Catharine, 144,
147
Daniel, 11, 40,
54, 69, 97,
107, 168
Elizabeth, 40
Hannah, 142
Jacob, 3, 23,
107
John, 23, 34,
48, 54, 59, 87,
100
Maria, 40, 54,
69, 97, 107
Nancy, 168
Polly, 168
Rosian, 54
Rosina, 23, 34,
48, 59, 87, 100
Samuel, 9, 34,
97
Sarah, 48
Thomas, 59
Valentine, 3
William, 87
KLAMPFER, A.
Maria, 147
KLAP, Catharine,
135
John, 14, 53,
135
Maria, 53
KLAPP, Catherine,
71
John, 71, 101,
160
John Henry, 160
Maria, 71, 101, 160
KLARK, Rachel, 10
KLEBER, Maria, 161
KLEDIE, Magdalene,
139
KLEIN, Abraham, 82
Anna Eva, 107
Catharine, 81
Catherine, 13
Elizabeth, 100
George, 12, 25
Hannah, 66
Johanna, 132
John, 66, 132
Maria, 48, 62,
76, 78, 95, 107
Nicholas, 107
Paul, 179
Peter, 95, 107

Sabina, 25
KLEMMER,
Catharine, 144
KLETSCHE, Mrs.,
141
KLEVER, Maria, 104
Philip, 104
KLINE, Elizabeth,
11
Mary, 13
KLION, Anna Maria,
120
John, 120
KLOBER, Catharine,
146
KLOCKENER, Casper,
4
George, 35
KLOCKNER, Casper,
25, 68
Catherine, 35,
68
Christian, 35,
68
John, 35
Susanna, 8, 25
KLOECKNER, Casper,
52
Susanna, 52
KLOETHY,
Catharine, 57
Sam, 57
KLOH, Catherine,
60, 69
Jacob, 69
KLOS, Catherine
Elizabeth, 37
Maria Elizabeth,
37
Peter, 37
KLOSBACH, Maria,
13
KLOTZ, Elizabeth,
173
Elizabeth
Gertrude, 162,
173
John Ludwig,
162, 173
Ludwig, 162
KLUMBERGER,
Catharine, 105
John, 105
Philip, 105
KNAUF, Margaret,
151

Maria, 147
Nicholas, 79,
81, 151
KNAUS, Elizabeth,
25
Henry, 25
Margaet, 5
Margaret, 25
Philippina, 82
KNELL, Christine,
19
Elizabeth, 19
Peter, 19
KNER, Anna, 39
John, 39
KNIES, Christian,
37
Christine, 37
Elizabeth, 58,
74
Hannah, 86
KNOCHEL, John
Bernard, 74
KNORR, Catharine,
81
KOCH, Adam, 52
Anna, 100
Anna Elizabeth,
70
Barbara, 106
Catharine, 83,
102
Daniel, 70
Dorothea, 79
Elizabeth, 3,
19, 33, 38, 155
George, 38, 127,
140
Henry, 100
Jacob, 7, 33,
106, 126
John George, 19,
70
John Jacob, 21
John Justus, 39,
52, 92
Margaret
Elizabeth, 14
Maria, 92
Maria Catherine,
38
Peter, 155
Susan, 39
Susanna, 8, 39,
52, 92

Thomas, 5, 19, 33
KOCHARD, Paul, 78
KOCHENBERGER, Eva, 75
KOCHERSBERGER,
 Anna Maria, 65
 Martin, 90
 Rosina, 90
KOEHL, Elizabeth, 106
 John, 106
KOEHLE, Catharine, 99
KOEHLER, Abraham, 24
 Adam, 51, 98
 Catharine, 98
 Conrad, 4, 24
 Elizabeth, 24
 Gertrude, 51
 Louisa, 98
 Maria, 51
KOERBER, Jacob, 83
KOHL, John, 77
KOHLER, Anna, 31
 Elizabeth, 31
 Michael, 31
KOLB, Catharine, 175
KOLLER, Enoch, 85
KOLLIER, Anna, 98
 Jacob, 98
 Michael, 98
KOMER, Catharine, 97
 Elizabeth, 97
 Reinhard, 97
KOMMER, Elizabeth, 97
 Maria, 97
 Thomas England, 97
 William, 97
KONIG, Christian, 50
KONSER, Margaret, 74
KONTERMAN,
 Catharine, 124
 John, 53
 Susanna, 53
KOOHLMAN, Adam, 109
 Susanna, 109
KOOPER, Charles, 72

Daniel, 72
Maria, 72
Mr., 9
William, 6
KOPIA, Joanna
 Sophia, 24
KOPP, Jacob, 82
 Joachim, 82
KORBI, Charles, 97
KORCK, Anna Maria, 73
KORENTER,
 Frederick, 46
KORNHAUS, George, 130
KORNSTOCK, Maria, 82
KORT, Catharine, 81
KORTERMAN, John, 14
KORTZ, M., 167
 Margaret, 167
 Maria, 167
KOSTER, Margaret, 83
KOTTEN, Elizabeth, 37
 Wilhelmina, 37
 William, 37
KOUCK, Christian, 6, 93
 Maria, 93
KR---, Catharine, 172
 M., 172
KRAEMER, A.
 Sophia, 144
 Anna, 103, 123
 Arnold, 3
 Catharine, 83
 Elizabeth, 134
 George, 123, 134
 John, 107
 John George, 103
 Magdalene, 103
 Matthew, 107
 Susanna, 107
KRAFFT, Charlotte, 82
 Johanna Maria, 82
 Susanna, 79, 110
KRAFT, Christian, 6
KRAKS, Hannah, 182

Henry, 182
KRAMER, Andrew, 150
 Philip, 83
KRAMP, Catharine, 171
 Elizabeth, 171
 Martin, 151, 171
 Susanna, 139
KRAMPF, Catharine, 118
 Dorothy, 1
 John, 118
 Maria Dorothea, 21
 Martin, 118
KRANTZ, Jacob, 13
KRATE, Elizabeth, 178
KRAUEL, Anna, 49
 Ludwig, 49
 Margaret, 49
KRAUER, Daniel, 2
 Ludwig, 22
 Margaret, 22
 Matthew, 5, 22
KRAUFFERTS, Anna, 59
 Conrad, 59
KRAUS, Christina, 82
KRAUSER,
 Catharine, 119
 John, 119
 Maria, 119
KRAUSKOPF, John, 34
 Magdalene, 34
 Maria, 43
 Susanna, 86
KREBEL, Catherine, 2
KREBS, Eva, 98
KREHMER, Anna, 53, 73
 Anna Maria, 53
 Catherine, 65
 Christine, 57, 125
 Elizabeth, 73
 Henry, 65
 John, 73
 John George, 28, 29, 53, 128
 Maria, 91
 Matthew, 21, 72

Matthias, 28, 57
Michael, 91
Nancy, 29
Susanna, 21, 28,
  57, 72
KREIBEL, Catharine
  Margaret, 121
KREIDER, Anthony,
  113
Christian, 77,
  140
Daniel, 75, 87
Elizabeth, 27,
  29, 38, 50, 57,
  59, 72, 103,
  118, 160, 178
Frederick, 15,
  27, 37, 47, 53,
  68, 113, 159
Hannah, 3, 15
Jacob, 12, 38,
  59, 72, 103,
  160, 178
John, 50, 59,
  131
John George, 178
Joseph, 160
Ludwig, 30, 53
Margaret, 87
Maria, 87, 113,
  118, 145
Rebecca, 131
Samuel, 159
Veronica, 15,
  27, 37, 47, 53,
  68, 113, 159
William, 70, 72,
  76, 87, 113,
  118
KREIMES,
  Elizabeth, 47,
  91
John, 47, 91
KREIMS, Anna
  Catherine, 63
Elizabeth, 63
John, 63
KREITER, Samuel,
  153
KREMER, Amalia, 13
Anna Catherine,
  47
Matthias, 47
Michael, 13
Susanna, 47

KREMESS,
  Elizabeth, 100
John, 100
KREPS, John, 2
KRES, Elizabeth, 1
KRESMAN,
  Elizabeth, 63
Jacob, 63
KRESS, Catherine,
  52
George, 52
Henry, 161
Jacob, 100
M., 167
Margaret, 100
Maria, 99, 161
KRESSEL, Andrew,
  120
Sophia, 120
KREUTZ, Maria, 144
KRICHOFF,
  Christian Aug.,
  59
Jacob, 59
Mary Magdalene,
  59
KRIEG, Maria Eva,
  72
Valentine, 72
KRIEGER,
  Catharine, 142
Jacob, 45
KRIESCHER, Maria
  Elizabeth, 1
KRIGER, Barbara,
  77
KRIM, Peter, 11
KROHN, Christine,
  91
KRON, John, 145,
  146
KROOSE, Mary, 13
KROS, Margaret,
  148
KROW, Anna Mary,
  182
Elizabeth, 182
Jacob, 182
KRUG, Catharine,
  107
Eva, 53
Jacob, 107
John, 107
KRUMBACH,
  Christine, 80

KRUSE, Cornelius,
  84
Elizabeth, 80
KUBLER, John, 83
Joseph, 162
Maria, 162
Rachel, 162
KUCHER, Catharine,
  108
Jacob, 82
John, 108
Martin, 108
KUCK, Christian,
  77
Frederick, 106
Jacob, 106
Maria, 106
KUCKEN, George,
  180
Margaret, 180
William, 180
KUCKER, Christian,
  108, 110
Dorothy, 108
George, 114
John, 110
Magdalene, 114
Maria Dorothy,
  110
Matthias, 114
KUEHLY, Francis,
  105, 134
Hannah, 105
Matthias, 105,
  134
KUEHN, Catharine,
  108
George, 108
John, 108
KUEMMEL, Sarah, 14
KUHL, Baltas, 178
Catherine, 12
Margaret, 146
KUHLEY, Simon, 3
KUHLY, Elizabeth,
  77
KUHN, Catharine,
  23
Daniel, 14
Eleonora, 143
Elizabeth, 95
George, 163, 176
George Ludwig,
  163
John, 23, 56,
  77, 95

Margaret, 163,
  176
Maria, 23, 81,
  176
Widow, 2
KUISMAN, Anna
  Margaret, 43
  Christine
  Wilhelmina, 43
  Frederick
  William, 43
KULEY, Esther, 20
  Hannah, 20
  Matthias, 20
KULLENBERG, Isaac,
  150
KUMMEL, Michael,
  132
KUNCKEL, John,
  111, 139
  Margaret, 111
  Sophia, 111, 139
KUPER, Andrew, 143
  Charles, 20
  Elizabeth, 4
  Jacob, 3, 20
  Maria, 20
  Peter, 143
KUPPER, Catherine,
  32, 65
  Charles, 54
  Jacob, 65, 128
  John, 54
  Maria, 54
  Peter, 32, 65
KURRIS, Catharine,
  173
KURTZ, Anna
  Margaret, 36,
  45
  George, 45, 60,
  87, 117
  Henry, 113
  John, 101
  John George, 36,
  101
  John Ludwig, 173
  Margaret, 60,
  101, 117
  Rosina, 113
KURTZROCK,
  Catharine, 124
  Fred, 128
  Frederick, 85
  John, 58, 85

Priscilla, 58,
  85
KUTZROCK,
  Catherine
  Margaret, 50
  John, 50, 51
  Priscilla, 50,
  51

-L-
LACK, Elizabeth,
  44
LADAMUS, John
  SPhilip, 7
LAEMEHR, Anna, 105
  Matthew, 105
  Sarah, 105
LAFARTY, Marl., 75
LAIR, Elizabeth,
  76
LAKE, Catharine,
  172
  Elizabeth, 173
  John, 172
  Joseph, 172
  Samuel, 173
  Sarah, 173
LAMAHR, Anna, 21
  Elizabeth, 21
  Matthias, 21
LAMBACH, Anna
  Maria, 99
  George, 99, 118
  John Philip, 129
  Maria, 118
  Mr., 17
  Sophia, 99
LAMBER, Catharine,
  156
LAMBERT,
  Elizabeth, 164
  George, 81
  Joshua, 164
LAMBERTER,
  Catharine, 83
LAMBETH, Sarah, 11
LAMMERT, Anna, 96
  Matthew, 96
  Rebecca, 96
LAMPATER,
  Catharine, 87
  George, 75, 87
  Maria, 87
  Sophia, 63, 87
LAMPETER,
  Elizabeth, 65

LAMPLY, Hannah,
  151
LAMPSPACH, Anna
  Christine, 108
  Elizabeth, 108
  John, 108
LAMSBACH,
  Charlotte
  Catherine, 64
  Christine, 33,
  48, 64
  George, 144
  John, 26, 33,
  48, 64, 139
  Maria Elizabeth,
  48
LAND, John, 73
LANE, James, 80
  William, 81
LANG, Adam, 116
  Catharine, 116
  Catharine
  Margaret, 182
  Catharine Mary,
  182
  Elizabeth, 116
  Henry, 80, 182
  John, 182
  John Henry, 182
LANGE, A.
  Catharine, 159
  Adam, 20, 32,
  51, 92
  Anna Catherine,
  32
  Catharine, 92
  Catherine, 20,
  32, 51
  Frederick, 5, 20
  George, 159
  Henry, 92, 159
  John, 51
LANGEBACH,
  Elizabeth, 103
  George, 103
  Maria, 103
LANGENBACH,
  Elizabeth, 155
  George, 155
LANGKOF, Eberhard,
  57
LANGKOPF,
  Catharine, 149
  Magdalene, 161
LANGPATER,
  Elizabeth, 18

LANGSTRAAK, Anna, 145
LANTZ, Anna
Elizabeth, 39
Juliana, 39
Martin, 39
LAP, Andrew, 31
Anna Catharine, 29
Christine, 31
John Adam, 29
LAPITI, James, 91
LAPOSTOLAIT,
Ursula, 79
LAPP, Adam, 10
Ann Dorothea, 92
Elizabeth, 1
Lawrence, 92
LARTSCH,
Catherine, 10
LATCH, Jacob, 11
LATOUR, Francis, 81
LATSCH, Catherine, 66
Christine, 25, 29, 68
Elizabeth, 9, 47
Jacob, 25, 29
Johannes John, 10
John, 29, 35, 47, 56, 66
John Jacob, 29
Margaret, 29, 35
Maria, 47
Maria Christine, 25
LAUB, Peter, 1, 10
LAUBACH, Maria, 12
LAUDEBACH,
Elizabeth, 173
Henry, 173
LAUDENBACH, John
Frederick, 28
LAUDER, Elizabeth, 87
John, 87
LAUER, Philip, 107
Susanna, 107
LAURI, Eleonora, 104
John, 77, 104
Maria, 104
LAURS, George, 74
LAURY, Jane, 93

Jean, 171
Johanna, 159
John, 80
P., 171
Peter, 93, 159
Philip, 82
Susanna, 149
LAUTEN, Elizabeth, 138
Isaac, 26
John, 26
LAUTH, Anthony, 133
William, 133
LAWERSWEIL, ---
Thomas, 9
LAWERSWEILER,
Abigail, 35, 69
Bernard, 35, 69
Elizabeth, 19, 21, 41
Frances
Elizabeth, 41
Jacob, 21, 41
Jacob Weiny, 21
Maria, 35
Maria Frances, 69
Mary, 36
Thomas, 35, 36
Thomas Charles, 35
LAWYER, Christian, 10, 43, 60, 68, 106, 180
Elizabeth, 60
John, 106
Margaret, 60, 68
Maria, 43
Maria Margaret, 43
Mary Rever, 180
Polly, 106
William, 68
LAYER, Elizabeth, 126
Maria, 143
LAYSLE, Elizabeth
Louise, 114
Philip, 114
LE FEBRE, Isaac, 41
Magdalene, 41
LE TELIER, John, 73
LEAP, Peter, 10

LEARIGHT,
Elizabeth, 152
LEBER, Adam, 110
Anna Susanna, 110
Charlotte, 146
M. Magdalene, 145
Mary Magdalene, 110
Sophia
Magdalena, 146
William, 110
LEBLER, Esther, 94
LECHEREN, John, 16
Maria Catherine, 16
LECK, A. Margaret, 157
Adam, 114
Anna Margaret, 114
Anna Margart, 37
Anna Mary, 177
Elizabeth, 151
Henry, 78, 88
Herman, 37, 53, 88, 114, 157, 177
Jacob, 53
John, 82
Margaret, 53, 88
Paul, 140
Susanna, 177
William, 37
LEE, Fanny, 83
Lydia, 85
LEER, Elizabeth, 168
Henry, 168
William, 168
LEES, Catharine, 181
Christopher
Hansman, 130
Elizabeth, 173, 181
George, 130
Henry, 181
John, 173, 181
Mary, 173
LEFEBER,
Catherine, 52
John, 52
William, 52
LEFERBER, Mr., 124

LEFEVERE,
Magdalene, 124
LEHER, Catharine,
158
David, 158
John, 158
LEHM, Anna Maria,
106
Joseph, 106
LEHMAN, Anna, 11
Elizabeth, 30,
75, 155
Hannah, 13
John, 155
William, 55, 86,
155
LEHMANN, John, 79
Sarah, 83
LEHMER, Anna, 39
John George, 39
Matthias, 39
LEHN, Jacob, 74
LEHNHARD, Anna
Catherine, 22
Michael, 22
Susanna, 22
LEHR, Abigail, 126
Adam, 11, 31,
45, 65, 106
Catharine, 94,
106, 173
Catherine, 20,
26, 38, 51, 68
Elizabeth, 96,
114
George, 26, 31
Henry, 38, 73,
96, 114
Isaac, 68
Jacob, 51
John, 20, 26,
38, 51, 65, 68,
94, 106, 173
John Adam, 19
John Peter, 96
Joseph, 106
Margaret, 5, 26
Maria, 19, 94
Rebecca, 31, 45,
65, 106
Susanna, 106
William, 173
LEIBERGER, Anna
Catherine, 59
Anna Magdalene,
59

John, 59
LEIBINGER, Adam, 6
Anna Catherine,
38
Anna Magdalene,
126
Catharine, 108
Catherine, 15,
18, 26, 69
Elizabeth, 69
George Peter,
108
John, 15, 69,
108, 129
John Adam, 26
John Henry, 38
John Jost, 18,
26, 38
Martin, 18
LEICHBRANDT,
Conrad, 107
Hannah, 107
LEIM, Maria, 10
LEISH, John, 77
LEMAIR, Anna, 69
Maria, 69
Matthias, 69
LEMAIRE, Amsoo,
178
John Matthew,
178
Matthew, 178
LENAMAN,
Elizabeth, 183
John, 183
Maria, 183
LENDEMAN,
Catharine, 181
John, 181
LENHARDT, Anna
Catharine, 109
Michael, 109
LENIMAN,
Elizabeth, 171
John, 171
LENNINSCHID, Anna
Margaret, 96
John Carl, 96
LENON, Hannah, 84
LENSBACH, Hannah
Christine, 132
John, 132
LENTZ, Catharine,
180
Fred, 180
John, 74

Juliana, 39
Maria Margaret,
39
Martin, 39
LEOKEROM, Maria
Catharine, 75
LEONARD,
Catherine, 49
Hannah, 84
John Jost, 49
Magdalene, 49
LEONHARD, Anna, 36
Anna Catherine,
53
Anna Maria, 37
Catharine, 116
Catherine, 71
Eleonora, 37
James, 75
John, 10, 36,
116
M. Magdalene,
152
Michael, 36, 53,
126
Rothar, 37
Susan, 4
LEONHARDT, Anna
Elizabeth, 66
Catherine, 66
John Jost, 66
LESCH, Louisa, 151
Margaret, 103,
143
Peter, 146
Philip, 103
Valentine, 131
LESCHER, ---, 152
Anna, 113, 167
George, 113, 167
Henry, 113
Jacob, 155
John, 155
Joseph, 167
Maria, 155
LESH, Margaret,
172
Martin, 172
Philip, 172
LESHER, George, 10
Jacob, 170
Maria, 170
LESKY, Anna Maria,
118
LETTLE, George, 8

LEVILL, Zacharias, 84
LEVY, Andrew, 154
   Magdalene, 154
LEWER, Adam, 89
   Charlotte, 89
   John, 5
   Maria, 89
LEWIS, Daniel, 167
   David, 105
   Edward, 105
   Elizabeth, 167, 168
   H., 168
   Henry, 168
   Jonas, 14
   Polly, 105
LEWYER, Christian, 29
   John Adam, 29
   Maria, 29
LEX, Andrew, 21, 36, 44, 49, 51, 61
   Anna Maria, 36
   Elizabeth, 51
   George, 89
   Maria, 21, 44
   Mary, 49
   Mary Magdalene, 61
LEY, Anna Margaret, 165
   Herman, 165
   Maria, 142
   Samuel, 165
LEYER, Valentine, 153
LIBER, George, 1
LICHTEL, Hannah, 184
   Jacob, 184
   Susanna, 184
LIEBECK, Anthony, 20
   Elizabeth, 20
   Maria Elizabeth, 20
LIEBER, Mr., 3
LIES, Anna Elizabeth, 48, 65, 127
   Anna Margaret, 19, 23, 49, 67, 103, 131
   Catharine, 79

Christine, 61
Christopher Hansman, 87
Conrad, 61
Elizabeth, 34, 38, 67, 70, 105, 123
George, 19, 23, 36, 49, 65, 87, 103
Henry, 20, 34, 38, 48, 67, 92, 105, 123, 131
John, 20
John Conrad, 61
John George, 103, 105
John Henry, 67
John Peter, 23
John William, 36
Magdalene, 123
Margaet, 87
Margaret, 36, 65
Maria Catherine, 49
Maria Elizabeth, 20, 34, 67, 92
Susanna, 48
LIEST, Elizabeth, 85
   Martin, 11
LIGHT, John, 148
LIMEBURNER, Philip, 12
LINCK, John, 76
   Rosina, 83
LINDEMAN, Catharine, 169
   John, 69, 169
   Margaret, 69
LINDLEY, Rebecca, 13
LINDSAY, Richard, 83
LINN, John, 70
LINNEN, Ann Margaret, 91
LISCH, Elizabeth, 155
   Henry, 155
   Maria, 155
LIST, Catharine, 119, 151
   Elizabeth, 79, 119, 121
   Ludwig, 119, 150

LITSCH, John, 158
   Maria, 158
   Maximilian, 158
LITTLE, George, 8
   Robert, 8
LOB, Andrew, 169
   Elizabeth, 169
LOCK, Maria, 81
LOCKIN, Adam, 106
   Maria, 106
LODGE, John, 171
   Mary, 171
   Murger, 171
LOEFLER, Elizabeth, 113
   John, 113
LOEHR, Catherine, 61
   Elizabeth, 61
   Gottfried, 111
   Henry, 61
LOERA, Charlotte Louisa, 60
   Dorothea Elizabeth, 60
   Henry, 60
LOESCH, John, 149
   Philip, 13
LOESCHER, Anna, 30, 38, 51, 138
   Catharine, 78
   Elizabeth, 30, 104
   George, 30, 38, 51, 104, 138
   Jacob, 107
   Maria, 38, 51, 107
   Mary Magdalene, 104
LOFFBERRY, Elizabeth, 58
   John, 58
LOFSBERRY, Conrad, 55
   Elizabeth, 32, 55
   John, 32, 55
   Samuel, 32
LOGAN, Adam, 165
   John Adam, 55
   Maria, 55, 165
LOGIN, Adam, 26
LOHIT, Adam, 70
LOHMAN, Adam, 24
   Elizabeth, 31

Veronica, 24, 99
William, 24, 99
LOHRMAN, Anna
    Justina, 9
LOMBARD, Maria
    Frances, 75
LOMBRANDT, Sophia,
    111
LONG, Mary, 76
LONO, Christman,
    84
LORA, Maria, 54
LORAH, Ann Mary,
    73
LORENTZ,
    Catherine, 21,
    72
    Elizabeth, 94
    George, 72, 94
    Joachim, 78
    John, 21
    Maria, 12, 117
    Susanna, 72, 94
LORJE, Anna
    Catherine, 29
    Christine, 29
    Mr., 4
    Peter, 29
LORY, Margaret, 61
    Peter, 74
LOSCH, John Jacob,
    126
    Magdalene, 14
    Margaret, 62,
    64, 87
    Maria Elizabeth,
    47
    Mary Magdalene,
    62
    Philip, 47, 62,
    64, 87, 124
    William, 87
LOSCHER, Anna, 63,
    72
    Barbara, 72
    Charles, 63
    George, 11, 30,
    33, 38, 51, 63,
    72, 149
    Jacob, 10, 33,
    55
    John, 72
    Margaret, 55
    Maria, 9, 33,
    38, 51, 124
    William, 33

LOSTON, Anna Mary,
    13
LOTSCH, George, 98
    John, 98
    Margaret, 98
LOTZ, Adam, 20,
    79, 90
    Anna Maria, 20
    Christine, 30
    Elizabeth, 74
    Jacob, 71
    Maria, 67, 71,
    77, 90
    Rosina, 71
LOUDEN, Stephen,
    67
LOUISA, Elizabeth,
    145
LOURY, Peter, 61
    Philip, 61
    Susanna, 61
LOVEBERRY, Andrew,
    118
    Elizabeth, 118
    John, 118
LOVEBURRY,
    Elizabeth, 95
    John, 95
LOWDAN, Anthony,
    42
    Elizabeth, 42
    John, 42
LOWDEN, Anthony, 8
LOWERY, Andrew,
    180
    Delisietta, 181
    Dorothea, 181
    John, 181
    John George, 165
    Margaret, 85,
    180
    Mary, 181
    Peter, 181
    Philip, 165,
    173, 180
    Rebecca, 165,
    173
    William, 173
LOXLEY, Benjamin,
    10
LOYD, David, 173
    Elizabeth, 153
    Rebecca, 173
    Susanna, 173
LUBRIAN, Barbara,
    68

Maria, 13
LUCAS, Eva, 39
    George, 39
    James, 163
    John, 39
LUCHARD,
    Christian, 73
LUCKHART, Anna
    Maria, 97
    Christopher, 97
    Elizabeth, 97
LUDWICH,
    Christopher
    Abraham, 19
LUDWIG,
    Christopher, 90
LUGHARD,
    Christopher, 58
    Elizabeth, 58
LUKAS, Elizabeth,
    7
LUKES, James, 169
    Margaret, 169
    Sarah, 169
LUPRIAN, Barbara,
    135
LURO, John, 44
    Maria, 44, 54
    Philip, 54
LUTSCH, John, 115
    Margaret, 115
    Michael, 115
LUTTS, John, 84
LUTY, Mark, 73
LUTZ, Adam, 153
    Carolina, 16
    Catherine, 8
    Catherine
    Elizabeth, 35
    Christian, 16
    Christine, 46,
    54, 56
    Conrad, 68
    Elizabeth
    Catharine, 96
    George, 158, 176
    Goerge, 81
    Jacob, 11, 35,
    54, 96, 112
    John Jacob, 96
    Magdalene, 145
    Margaret, 112,
    150
    Maria, 68, 158,
    176

Rosina, 35, 54, 112
Sophia, 176
Susanna, 68, 119
LYCH, George, 111
John, 111
Maria, 111
LYNN, Francis, 76
LYON, Polly, 84
LYONS, John, 83
Susanna, 82

-M-
M----, A., 172
Agnes, 173
MAAG, Barbara, 126
Elizabeth, 45, 49, 63
Henry, 5, 12, 49, 125
Jacob, 41
John, 9, 11, 45
Maria, 41
Sarah, 41
William, 75
MCALROY, Anne, 51
MCCANNISTER, Francisca, 59
MCCAULEY, James, 80
MCCHARTI, Abigail, 98
Thomas, 98
MCCHILDON, Catharine, 143
MCCLAIN, Mary, 75
MACCLATSCHI, William, 133
MCCLATSCHIE, Alexander, 121
Andrew, 121, 141
Anna, 121, 141
John, 121
Maria, 121
Susanna, 121, 141
Widow, 141
William, 121
MCCLUER, John, 13
MCCORD, Catherine, 12
MCCORMICK, Anna, 2
MCCOSH, Peter, 147
MCCOY, Daniel, 14
MCCULLY, Hugh, 80
MCDERE, Anna, 179

George, 179
Margaret, 179
MCDONNEL, Anna, 107
Daniel, 107
Elizabeth, 107
MCDOUGAL, ---, 143
MCGILL, M. Anna, 176
Polly, 176
Stephen, 176
MCGOUEN, Elizabeth, 73
MCGRUE, Anna, 174
Elizabeth, 174
George, 174
MACK, Anna, 84
Anna Margaret, 58
Catharine, 173
M. Magdalene, 173
Magdalene, 58, 87
Maria, 87
Mary Magdalene, 51, 107
Nicholas, 51, 58, 87, 107, 173
Rosina, 51
MCKAY, Edward, 126
MACKEL, Anna
Catharine, 108
MCKELROY, Catharine, 157
Dorothy, 180
Elizabeth, 180
James, 180
John, 157
Sarah Anna, 157
MACKENSTEIER, Anna
Catharine, 183
John, 183
Sally, 183
MACKENTIER, ---, 154
MACKNAIR, John, 139
MCKREVEL, Charles, 174
John, 174
Philippina, 174
MACKS, Elizabeth, 157

M. Magdalene, 157
Nicholas, 157
MCMEEKEN, Margaret, 60
MCNACHTANE, John, 10
MCNAIR, Jacob, 128
MACNAIR, Mr., 128
MCNAIR, Thomas, 123
MCNEHR, Elizabeth, 25, 35
John, 25, 35
Margaret, 35
William, 4, 25
MACNORTEN, Elias, 112
Maria, 112
Susanna, 112
MACNORTHEN, Elias, 136
Susanna, 136
MCPHARRIN, Maria, 26
MACPHY, Nacy, 118
MACSHERRY, Catharine, 118
Thomas, 118
William, 118
MCSPARREN, Christine, 35, 52, 59
John, 35, 124
Maria, 59
Peter, 52
William, 35, 52, 59
MCSPEREN, Charlotte, 182
Christine, 182
Thomas, 182
William, 182
MCSPORREN, Peter, 124
MACSPURNAER, Mr., 134
Ruth, 134
M'STARREN, Christine, 85
Ruth, 85
William, 85
MADERY, Anna, 163
Christopher, 20, 34

Elizabeth, 20,
34
Esther, 34
George, 163
Jacob, 2, 163
Samuel, 20
MAENCHEN,
Margaret, 146
MAGOLD, Elizabeth,
1
MAILLARD, Victory,
81
MAN, Elizabeth,
171
Jacob, 171
John, 170, 171
MANGOLD, Anna, 3,
17, 32, 103
Barbara, 17, 32,
38, 59, 88, 103
Elizabeth, 59
Frederick, 17,
32, 38, 59, 88,
103
Jacob, 38
Maria, 88
MANINGER, George
Benjamin, 183
John P., 183
Margaret, 183
MANLE, Catherine,
22
James, 22
Robert, 22
MANN, John, 8
MAR---, A., 172
MARCKEL, Maria,
126
MARERS, John, 77
MARK, Sarah, 165
MARKLE, Susan, 85
MARKS, Daniel, 32
John, 32
Margaret, 32, 82
MARSCHAL, David,
99
Maria Barbara,
99
Maria Catharine,
99
MARSCHALL, David,
120
Maria Barbara,
120
MARSH, Gottlieb,
78

MARSHALL, Barbara,
53
David, 53, 151
Francis, 42
Francis Paul, 53
James, 42
John, 80
Margaret, 42
MARTERY, Anna, 168
Catharine, 168
George, 168
MARTIN, Daniel, 14
John, 37, 74
Martha, 126
MARTY, Sophia M.,
156
MARTZLE,
Catharine, 79
MASE, Anna, 173
MASON, Maria, 22,
79
MAST, Anna, 88
Christopher, 88
Conrad, 125
John, 88
Maria, 88
MAT, Frederick,
149
MATCHIO, Isaac,
129
MATERAN, Andrew,
39
Anna Maria, 39
MATHEAS, Mary, 74
MATLACK, Anna, 74
MATTHEW, John, 178
John Jacob, 178
Maria, 178
MATTHIAS, Barbara,
6
Jacob, 65
Maria, 55
MATZENER, Anna
Magdalene, 86
Elizabeth, 86
John Michael, 86
MATZINGER,
Catherine, 38,
40
Elizabeth, 27,
38, 50, 62
Jacob, 27
John, 38, 40, 50
John Michael, 27
John Philip, 50
Michael, 62

MAUER, Jacob, 94
Rudolph, 94
MAUGER, Catharine,
82
MAURER, Catharine,
162
Dorothy, 162
Esther, 111
Jacob, 111, 162
MAUS, ---, 95
Anna, 22
Elizabeth, 22,
38, 56
Frances Heap, 95
Francis Clawsin,
55
Frederick, 8,
22, 38, 56, 123
Jacob Wevr, 22
Mary Magdalene,
55
Philip, 14, 22,
55
Susanna, 134
Veronica, 22
William, 56
MAUSS, Elizabeth,
99
Frederick, 99
Joseph Herman,
99
Maria, 97
Samuel, 97
MAXFIELD, Robert,
150
MAXINGER,
Elizabeth, 110
John George, 110
John Michael,
110
MAY, ---, 163
A. Maria, 155
Adam, 12, 38,
50, 65, 88, 95,
122, 155, 161,
173, 175
Agnes, 165, 178
Amelia, 161
Anna Maria, 143
B., 173
Bernard, 165,
178
Catharine, 88,
95, 122, 155,
161, 173, 175

Catharine
  Elizabeth, 178
Catherine, 38,
  65
Elizabeth, 38,
  165
Henrietta, 147
John Bernard,
  157
John Henry, 175
Maria Catherine,
  50, 65
Sarah, 88
William, 173
MAYER, A.
  Margaret, 143,
  156
Adam, 95, 151,
  162
Barbara, 31
Catharine, 99
Christine, 163
Elizabeth, 77,
  78, 111, 143,
  155
George, 156, 158
George Lucas,
  163
Gottfried, 155
Hannah, 83, 95,
  162
Henry, 95, 111
Jacob, 142, 162
John, 31, 99,
  136, 163
John George, 99,
  116, 136
John Philip, 80
Margaret, 111
Mary Magdalene,
  145
Nicholas, 84
Philip, 99, 163
Sarah, 156
Susanna, 116,
  158
Wilhelmina, 163
MAYLAND, Margaret,
  59, 60
Samuel, 59
Sarah, 59
Simeon, 59, 60
William, 60
MECKY, John, 168
MECMOLLEN,
  Isabella, 12

MEDER, Charles, 84
MEEKE, Catharine,
  175
Henry, 175
John, 175
MEETER, George,
  130
Maria, 130
MEGERT, Margaret,
  85
Samuel Berge, 85
MEIBER, Ann
  Elizabeth, 88
James, 88
John, 88
MEIBERT, Anna
  Elizabeth, 115
Catherine, 55
Elizabeth, 55,
  115, 121
John, 15, 55,
  115, 121, 149
MEICHLY,
  Catharine, 108
John, 108
Sarah, 108
MEIERS, Henry, 179
Joseph, 179
Rebecca, 179
MEILAND, Elizabeth
  Margaret, 125
MEILE, A. Maria,
  148, 156
Anna Maria, 29,
  143
Barbara, 51, 64,
  94, 156
Catharine, 89
Catherine, 29,
  60
Elizabeth, 60,
  64
Fred, 94
Frederick, 51,
  64, 156
Jacob, 68, 95
John, 29, 60, 89
John George, 94
Julianna, 89
Margaret, 68, 95
Maria Barbara,
  95
Sarah, 46, 68,
  76
William, 68

MEILI, Anna
  Catharine, 132
Anna Maria, 132
Catharine, 112
Jacob, 116
John, 132
Margaret, 116
Samuel, 116
MEILICH, Barbara,
  114
Catharine, 114
Frederick, 114
John, 114
Maria, 113
MEILY, Catherine,
  43
Frederick, 43
John, 43
MEINIGER, Anna
  Margaret, 29
Christopher, 29
MEININGER, Anna
  Catharine, 124
Anna Catherine,
  40
Anna Mary, 53
Christopher, 36,
  40, 53, 68
Jacob, 68
Margaret, 36,
  40, 68
William, 53, 124
MEINUNG,
  Christopher, 27
Margaret, 27
Peter, 27
MEISNER, A. Maria,
  158
John, 158
MEISTERSHEIM,
  Margaret, 82
MELCHER, John, 82
MENCHE, Anna, 103
John, 103
MENCHER,
  Catharine, 99
MENES, A.
  Elizabeth, 159
Jost, 159
Maria, 159
MENG, Anna
  Catharine, 97
Catherine, 69
Melchior, 75
Susanna, 73

MENGEL, George,
103
MENN, Anna M., 153
MENSCH, Peter, 13
MERCKEL, Ann
Catharine, 94
Anna Catharine,
131
Anna Catherine,
30
Francis, 83
Margaret, 83
Maria Clara, 30
Peter, 6, 30,
94, 98, 131
MERCKER, Andrew,
27, 37, 45, 53,
60
Andrew
Christian, 110
Anna Catharine,
125
Anna Maria, 71,
110
Catherine, 27,
37, 45, 53, 60
Christina, 45
Christine, 103,
115
Elizabeth, 5,
27, 71, 99,
113, 143
George, 23, 35,
115, 139, 149
Godfrey, 83
Henry, 113
Jacob, 103, 115,
139, 142
John, 37, 71,
99, 113
John Andrew, 23
John George, 99
Margaret, 23,
35, 115
Maria, 103
Maria Margaret,
71
Sebastian, 53
Veronica, 73
MERCKLE, Anna
Catherine, 66
Catherine, 17,
36
Jacob, 17
Maria Catherine,
66

Maria Clara, 5,
36
Maria Sarah, 66
Peter, 17, 36,
66
MERIAN, Samuel,
139
MERKEL, Dolly, 84
MERKER, Elizabeth,
166
J., 166
Jacob, 166
MERRETH, Mary
Magdalene, 98
MERTZ, Elizabeth,
66
Simon, 66
MESEMER,
Catherine, 34,
35
Jacob, 34
John, 34
MESSEMER, John,
17, 61, 81, 90,
147
Maria, 2
Maria Catharine,
90
Maria Catherine,
2, 17, 61
Mary Magdalene,
17, 90
Sarah, 2
MESSERSCHMIDT,
Catherine, 24,
33
John Andrew, 24,
33
MESSNER,
Catharine, 160
John, 160
Maria, 160
METHER, George,
133
METZ, James, 91
Philippina, 91
METZER, Francis
Anthony, 74
METZGER, Anna, 92
Anna Elizabeth,
66, 127
Elizabeth, 107,
143
Francis, 92
Francis Anthony,
66, 119

Frederick
Anthony, 71
Hannah, 66, 71,
119
Helena, 65, 107,
142
John, 65, 80,
107, 183
Maria Margaret,
143
William, 92
William Henry,
119
METZINGER,
Elizabeth, 114
Margaret, 12
MEY, Adam, 51
Catherine, 51
Sarah, 78
MEYER, Adam, 71
Andrew, 77
Anna, 18, 184
Anna Elizabeth,
127
Anna Margaret,
20
Anna Margr., 20
Anna Maria, 118
Barbara, 126
Bernard, 87,
108, 139
Catharine, 87,
108, 118
Catherine, 12,
23, 33, 41, 57
Charlotte, 30
Christine, 71
Christopher, 77
Daniel, 15
Edward, 32
Eleonora, 15
Elizabeth, 5,
32, 57, 69, 87,
96, 109, 138,
184
Frederick, 14,
19
George, 35, 51,
112, 148
Hannah, 34
Henry, 15, 23,
30, 33, 41, 184
Jacob, 32, 57,
69, 74, 87, 96,
97

John, 18, 20,
30, 34, 41, 57,
76, 99, 124,
138, 139
John Adam, 34
John George, 32,
41, 112
John Godfrey,
103
John Michael,
108
Magdalene, 33,
71
Marg., 36
Margaret, 77, 97
Maria, 99, 103
Maria Elizabeth,
97
Maria Margaret,
19
Mary, 12
Mrs., 60
Nicholas, 14,
109
Philippina, 112
Rebecca, 184
Rosina, 20
Sarah, 32, 41,
112
Susanna, 35, 51
Werni, 57
Wernig, 33
William, 99
MEYERS, Catherine,
12, 56
Elizabeth, 186
George, 56
Henry, 167
Joseph, 167
Margaret, 167
Sarah, 56
MEYLAND, William,
126
MEYLE, Anna
Catharine, 30
Catharine, 136
Elizabeth, 30
Frederick, 30
Jacob, 30, 136
MEYLY, Frederick,
165
M. Barbara, 165
MICHAEL,
Elizabeth, 165
George, 174

Johanna Maria,
159
John, 159, 165,
174
Maria, 174
MICHAELIS, John,
82
MICHAELSEN, Maria
Elizabeth, 78
MICKLE, Catherine,
10
MIDDLETON, James,
76
MIEBERT, Anna
Elizabeth, 70
John, 70
MIEDERMOTT,
Eleonora, 84
MIELE, Jacob, 46
Margaret, 46
Sarah, 46
MIELEFELD,
Elizabeth, 73
MIESER, Maria, 96
Philip, 76, 96
MIKZER, Elizabeth,
64
Isaac, 64
John George, 64
MILEFELD, Sophia,
76
MILEY, Frederick,
14
Jacob, 11
MILHAUS, Anna, 100
Casper, 100
Catharine, 100
MILL, A. Margaret,
172
Anna, 109, 120,
142, 171
Catharine, 155
Christine, 146
George, 79, 155,
172
James, 171
John George, 77,
109, 120
John Henry, 109
Margaret, 155,
172
Sarah, 171
MILLEN, Mary
Magdalene, 142
MILLER, ---, 36

Alexander
William, 3
Andrew, 45
Barbara, 89
Benjamin, 13
Catharine, 82,
157, 182
Catherine, 23,
46, 56, 68
Catherine
Magdalene, 7
Charlotte, 39
Daniel, 79, 144
David, 5, 56
Elizabeth, 49,
94, 141, 147,
165, 182
Eva, 75, 145
Frederick, 22
George, 23, 68,
125, 145
Hannah, 91
Henrietta, 161
Henry, 128
Henry William,
157
Jacob, 81
James, 89
Jane, 94
John, 6, 23, 49,
75, 122, 125,
131, 137, 161,
165, 174
John George, 39
John Henry, 92
John Peter, 46
Jonathan, 78,
157
Joseph, 32
Lorentz, 23, 46,
56
Margaret, 11,
22, 36, 157,
161, 165
Margart, 35
Maria, 13, 91,
164
Martha, 150
Martin, 94, 182
Mary Elizabeth,
37
Peter, 37
Philip, 39, 80,
164, 174, 181
Philippina, 36
Phoebe, 13

Sarah, 122, 131,
152, 164, 174
Susanna, 32, 45,
181
Weygand, 82
William, 8, 10,
22, 32, 35, 36,
39, 45, 91,
126, 134, 161
MILLES, John, 11
MILLS, Christine,
11
MILTENBERGER,
Elizabeth, 25
Henry, 25
Margaret, 127
Michael, 25
MINCK, John, 75
MINICH, Anna
Margaret, 118
Barbara, 118
Godfrid, 118
Gottfried, 101
Jacob, 118
John, 118
Veronica, 101,
118
MIRRETH, John, 25
Mary Magdalene,
25
MISCHODT, Philip
Frederick, 75
MISCHOT, Jacob,
106
Maria Clara, 106
Philip
Frederick, 106
MISCHOTT, Clara,
136
Frederick, 136
Jacob, 136
John Frederick,
136
MITMANN, Philip,
79
MITSCHET,
Catharine, 73
MIXER, Elizabeth,
31
Isaac, 31
William, 31
MIXTER, William, 7
MOGY, Elizabeth,
77
MOHR, Maria, 84

MOLCHON,
Charlotte, 29
Harriet, 29
William, 29
MOLITOR, Maria, 82
MOLL, Elizabeth,
27
Simon, 27, 80
MOLLOHON, William,
10
MONSCHEHR, Agnes,
83
MONSERS,
Catharine, 83
MONTGOMERY, John,
80
Maria, 58
Sarah, 122
MOOG, Elizabeth,
112
Jacob, 146
MOOR, George, 118
John George, 108
Margaret, 108
Philippina
Elizabeth, 115
Rebecca, 118
MOORE, Catharine,
84
George, 33
Sarah, 63
Susanna, 32, 53,
67
William, 32, 53,
67
MORALT, Casper, 9
MORDOCH,
Elizabeth, 112
Maria Christine,
112
Robert, 112
MORE, James, 80
Margaret, 82
MORGAN, Elizabeth,
13
MORRAY, Mr., 129
MORRIS, Catherine,
73
Daniel, 177
Elizabeth, 18,
177
Mary, 84
Robert, 18
MORRISON,
Catharine, 103

MOSCH, Catherine,
42
MOSELL, Catharine,
124
MOSER, Carl, 115
Charlotte, 10
Cornelia, 115
Henry, 96
Margaret, 115
Maria, 115
Philip, 5, 16
Philippina, 53
Samuel, 115, 149
Susan, 93
Susanna, 16, 96,
158
MOSES, Philippina,
4
MOTZFELD, Anna
Christine, 3
MOUCKTY,
Elizabeth, 21
George, 21
MOUNTY, Eva
Margaret, 24,
38
George, 38
John George, 24
MOUTY, George, 33
MOYER, John, 89
MOYERLEY,
Fredeick, 12
MUCKELRAY, Detty
Arethe, 167
James, 167
John, 167
MUELLER, Andrew,
28, 63
Anna, 27, 103
Anna Elizabeth,
104
Anna Maria, 98
Apollonia, 28
Barbara, 17
Catharine, 105,
151
Catherine
Magdalene, 27
Christine, 50,
63
Christopher, 77
Conrad, 63
David, 4
Dorothy, 77
Elizabeth, 61,
105

Eva, 98
George, 61, 73
George Michael,
  108
Henry, 104
Jacob, 14, 17
John, 21, 98,
  103
John Adam, 4
John Henry, 27
Magdalene, 78
Margaret, 50, 63
Maria, 21
Martin, 61, 105
Michael, 63, 105
Peter, 58
Philip, 119
Philippina
  Margaret, 21
Philp, 83
Rebecca, 28
Susanna, 75
William, 50
MUENCH, Jacob, 78
MUENICH, Simon,
  144
MUENIG, Anna, 27
  Conrad, 27, 47
  Eva Margaret,
    27, 47
  Gottfried, 58
  John, 47, 124
  Veronica, 58
MUENNICH,
  Catherine, 25
  Gottfried, 25
  Veronica, 25
MUENTZ, Charles
  Victor, 48
  William, 48, 123
MUGY, Hannah, 177
  John, 177
  Philip, 177
MULLER, Andrew, 92
  Anna, 43, 58,
    86, 112
  Anna Catharine,
    139
  Barbara, 116
  Catharine, 152
  Charlotte, 27
  Christian, 27
  Christine, 13,
    18, 45
  Christopher, 64,
    74

Conrad, 43
Daneil, 159
Daniel, 15
David, 11, 18
Elizabeth, 64,
  160
George, 13, 27,
  61, 127
Henry, 116
Jacob, 116, 164
Jacobus, 58
John, 43, 58,
  86, 112, 139
John Henry, 18
Joseph, 86, 152
M. Magdalene,
  159
M. Susanna, 152
Margaret, 43
Maria, 64, 160
Martin, 73, 160
Michael, 45
Peter, 83
Salome, 164
Susanna, 80
William, 83
MUM, Catharine, 84
MUNCH, A.
  Margaret, 148
  Conrad, 153
  Godfried, 147
  John, 149
MUNGER, Anna Maria
  Christine, 117
  John Philip, 117
MUNICH, Jacob, 186
  Juliana, 186
  Susanna, 80
MUNIG, Gottfried,
  5, 57, 67, 95
  Veronica, 57,
    67, 95
  Veronica
    Barbara, 67
MUNNIG, Elizabeth,
  45
  Gottfried, 45
  Veronica, 45
MUNTZ, ---, 9
  Eckhard
    Casander, 40
  Elizabeth, 27,
    40
  John
    Christopher, 27

William, 2, 27,
  40
MUNTZER,
  Engelbert, 53
  Joseph, 82
  Maria, 53
  Sarah Elizabeth,
    87
MUNY, Margaret, 34
  Michael, 34
MURALT, Anna, 154
MURDOCK,
  Christine, 151
  James, 151
  M. Christine,
    156
  Margaret, 156
  Robert, 156
MURRAY, Jemima, 43
MUSCH, Anna, 81
MUSCHEL,
  Catherine, 45
  Charles, 127
  Elizabeth, 45
  Samuel, 45
MUSCHELL, Samuel,
  13
MUSSEL, Charles,
  67
  Elizabeth, 67
  Samuel, 67
MUTH, Anna
  Elizabeth, 21
  Anthony, 14
  Bernard, 16, 21,
    130
  Catharine, 151
  Dolly, 69
  Dorothea, 80
  Elizabeth, 16,
    130
  John, 69
  John Peter, 69
  Maria Dorothea,
    21
  Martha, 7
  Peter, 69

-N-
NAEFF, Anna, 20
  Esther, 34
  Jacob, 20
  Melchior, 4
NAFTY, Cunigunda,
  109
  Isaac, 109

Thomas, 109
NAGEL, Balsar,
 180, 181
 Balthasar, 180
 Catharine, 180
 John, 163
 Leonard, 180
 Magdalene
 Elizabeth, 163
NAGELSCHMIDT,
 Barbara, 59
NANECKER,
 Catharine, 170
 Jacob, 170
NANEKER, Jacob,
 168
NANNEKER,
 Magdalene, 168
NANNETTER, Anna
 Catharine, 98
 Anna Catherine,
 67
 Anna Cathrine,
 22
 Anna Elizabeth,
 15, 28
 Catherine, 31,
 44, 61
 Elizabeth, 16,
 22, 67, 73
 Jacob, 22, 31,
 44, 61, 67, 98
 John, 22
 John Charles, 44
 John Peter, 96
 Magdalene, 97
 Mr., 129
 Peter, 15, 16,
 22, 28, 77, 97,
 124
 Stephanus, 98
NAOKS, Maria
 Elizabeth, 9
NAY, Bernard, 83
NEADN(ER--),
 Engelbert, 172
NEAFF, Margaret,
 37
NEBEL, Maria, 60
NEBIS,
 Christopher,
 178
 John Abraham,
 178
NEEFIS, Sarah, 80
NEESS, Adam, 107

NEHS, Elizabeth,
 82
 Henry, 82
NEIDLINGER, John
 Adam, 92
 Samuel, 92
 Susanna, 12, 92
NEILER, Bernard,
 83
NEIS, George, 49
 John, 49
 Veronica, 49
NEISS, George, 62,
 104, 140
 John, 104
 John Fried, 62
 Veronica, 62,
 104
NEITLINGER,
 Elizabeth, 109
 Samuel, 109
 Susanna, 109
NELSON, A. Maria,
 157
 Andrew, 158
 Charles, 163,
 176
 Elizabeth, 163,
 176
 John George, 157
 Lucy, 158
 Matthias, 157
 Susanna, 176
 William, 163
NEU, Anna
 Elizabeth, 66
 Catharine, 76
 Christine, 81
 Elizabeth, 76
 John, 66
NEUDEN, Esther,
 182
 George, 182
 Margaret, 182
NEUMAN, Elizabeth,
 71
 Frederick
 William, 71
 Rebecca, 14
NEUSCHWANGER,
 Peter, 6
NEVELING, Maria,
 91
 Minister, 121
NEWMAN, A.
 Margaret, 155

John, 155
NEWTON, Anna, 155
 Elizabeth, 155
 Forbes, 155
 George, 163
 Margaret, 163
 Sarah, 152, 163
NICHOLAS,
 Catherine, 59
 Hannah, 59
 William, 59
NICHOLS, Joanna,
 69
 John, 69
 Maria Christine,
 7
 William, 69
NICHOLSON, Sarah,
 79
NICK, Margaret, 12
NICKE, Catherine
 Louisa, 31
 Ludwig, 31
 Maria, 31
NICKELS, George,
 43
 Hannah, 155
 Joanna, 29, 43
 Maria Christine,
 29
 William, 29, 43,
 155
NICKLER, Carl, 132
 William, 132
NIEDERHAUS,
 Daniel, 14
NIEMAND, John, 11
NIES, Catherine,
 58
 David, 26
 Flora, 26
 George, 58
 Margaret, 50
 Mr., 50
NILFORTH, Barbara,
 78
NOBEL, Phoebe, 73
NOCK, James, 88
NOELSEL, Anna
 Maria, 109
 Matthew, 109
NOHW, Elizabeth,
 77
NONNETTER,
 Magdalene, 122
 Peter, 122

NORD, Daniel, 45
  Elizabeth, 143
NORDIOCK,
  Frederick, 80
NORRIS, Catharine,
  182
  Matthew, 182
  Matthias, 182
NORTH, Daniel, 138
  Nancy, 77
NOSSER,
  Wilhelmina, 25
NOTTENIUS, Willy,
  80
NOTZ, Leonard, 109
  Margaret, 109
NOVICK,
  Christiana, 161
  Frederick, 161
  Sarah, 161
NUCH, Krants, 170
NUNNEMACHER,
  Elizabeth, 148
NUSAG, Carl
  William, 121
  Charles William,
  104
  Maria Catharine,
  104
NUSHAG, Barbara,
  61
  Charles William,
  89
  Maria Catharine,
  89

-O-
OBERDORFF, Andrew,
  26
  Catherine, 11
OBERMAN, Anna
  Elizabeth, 37
  Catherine, 51
  Elizabeth, 9
  Gratia, 37, 51,
  67
  Henry, 12, 37,
  51, 67
  Lawrence, 149
  Sam, 129
  Samuel, 67
OBERMANN, Maria,
  152
OBISCHUE, Regina,
  105
OCHS, Barbara, 49

Conrad, 14
  Jacob, 49
OCKEL, Elizabeth,
  157
ODENHEIMER,
  Catharine, 141
  Catherine, 21,
  36, 57
  Christine, 140
  Daniel, 6, 21
  Peter, 113, 138
  Philip, 21, 36,
  57, 72, 81,
  128, 141
  Thomas, 113, 138
  Veronica, 113
  Wilhelmina, 57
OELLER, Jacob, 171
  Leah, 171
  M. Theresa, 171
OEMIG, Anna
  Dorothea, 120
  Peter, 120
  Susanna, 120
OGELBIE, William,
  10
OHL, Christine, 74
OHLE, Elizabeth,
  88
OHLER, Anna
  Catharine, 83,
  117
  Catharine, 162
  Catherine, 57
  Philip, 4, 162
  Philip Jacob,
  57, 132
OHLWEIN, Abraham,
  161
  Anthony Wayne,
  161
  Elizabeth, 161
  Rebecca, 161
OHMAN, John, 81
OHMENSETTER, Mary
  Magdalene, 79
OLIVER, Maria, 15
  William, 15
OLOWELL,
  Christine, 175
  Elkana, 175
  Maria, 175
  Samuel, 175
OLSERS, Henry, 177
OLTENBURY, Jacob,
  182

OMEN, Christian,
  87
  Nancy, 87
OMENSELTER,
  Elizabeth, 13
OMENSETTER,
  Christan
  Catherine, 40
  Elizabeth, 40
  Jacob, 40
OPMAN, Anna
  Margaret, 92
  Anna Mary, 92
  John, 64, 115,
  131
  Lawrence, 92,
  131
  Lorentz, 64
  Margaret, 64
  Maria, 115
OPPS, A. Maria,
  178
  Eliza, 178
  George, 178
ORD, Barbara, 10
  Catherine, 23
  Conrad, 23
OREFFGEN, Ann
  Maria, 123
OREFGEN, Anna
  Barbara, 27
  Catherine, 49,
  69
  Catherine
  Magdalene, 27
  Elizabeth, 49,
  69
  John, 12, 27,
  49, 69
  John Philip, 49
  Mary Magdalene,
  49
OREFGON, Samuel,
  65
  Susanna, 65
  William, 65
ORLOB, Adam, 124
  Elizabeth, 60
  Maria, 10
ORNER, Jacob, 63,
  74, 88, 118
  John, 88
  Margaret, 11,
  125
  Maria, 118

Sarah, 63, 88, 118
ORPHY, Catharine, 110
John, 110
ORTH, Anna Margaret, 120
Barbara, 51
Elizabeth, 51
Ludiwg, 51
Ludwig, 73, 120
OSMAN, Anna, 161
Carolus, 97
Elizabeth, 27, 58, 71, 97, 161
Esther, 27
John, 27, 58, 71, 97, 161
Sarah, 58
OSMANN, Captain, 151
OSMON, John, 154
OSTHEIM, Jacob, 156
Johanna, 156
John, 156
OSTHEINS, J.
Christ, 179
Jane, 179
John Christopher, 179
M. Rachel, 179
OTH, Elizabeth, 111
Jacob Francis, 111
John, 111
OTHSNERNI, Maria Barbara, 25
OTTENHEIMER, Magdalene, 133
Peter, 133
OTTINGER, Christopher, 84
Maria, 82
OTTO, Catherine, 44
Elizabeth, 38
Lawrence, 150
Philip, 5
Regina, 155
OTZLER, Catharine, 177
John Jacob, 177
Philip, 177

OVERMAN, Gratia, 114
Henry, 114
OVERSTAKE, Jacob, 74
OWEN, Griffith, 10
Ruth, 13
OWENS, Carl, 186
Elizabeth, 79
John, 186
Samuel, 186
Sarah, 186
OXEMER, Barbara, 40
Peter, 40
OXLEY, Edward, 6
Margaret, 46
OZEAS, Amelia, 158
Elizabeth, 94
George, 57, 67, 94, 158
John, 130
Margaret, 57
Maria, 67, 94, 144, 158
Peter, 57, 148
OZIAS, George, 111
John, 111
Maria, 111

-P-
PAINE, Eleonora, 145
PAINTER, Henry, 170
John, 13
Magdalene, 170
Maria Margaret, 137
Maria Martha, 101
Mary, 170
Mary Magdalene, 101
Murger, 170
Nicholas, 101, 137
PALESKE, Carl Godfrey, 183
Hannah Elmslie, 183
Ludwig, 183
Maria Wilhelmina, 183
PALM, Henry, 173
Maria, 173

Susanna, 173
PALMER, Phineas, 6
PAMPINIOR, Barbara, 8
PANEKUCHEN, John George, 85
PANTZ, Daniel, 9, 44
George, 44
Isabella, 44
PARCKER, Charles, 125
PARIS, Frances, 179, 184
Henry, 31
Maria, 64
Mary Magdalene, 49
Peter, 4, 11, 31, 42, 49, 64, 73
Sarah, 49
Veronica, 31, 42, 64, 73
PARISH, Catharine, 111
John, 111
Maria, 111, 126
PARK, Samuel, 81
PASTORIS, Ann Eliza, 185
Elizabeth, 185
Thomas, 185
PATISSEN, Sarah, 75
PATTER, Catharine, 173
Jacob, 173
John, 173
PATTERSON, Elizabeth, 124
PATTISON, Elizabeth, 48
Robert, 48
Sarah, 48
PATTON, Elizabeth, 115
James, 115
Joseph, 115
PAUKS, Esther, 80
PAUL, Agnes, 93
Benjamin, 154
Hannah, 154
John, 93
Susanna, 154

PAULI, Catherine, 42
Elizabeth, 42, 55
Ludwig, 55
Philip, 55
Philip Reinhold, 42
PAUSEN, Anna Margaret, 30
John Adam, 30
PAWLING, Rachel, 12
PEARSON, Sally, 82
PECK, Susanna, 174
PEDDLE, George, 12
PEFFER, Catharine, 78
PEIFFER, Christine, 77
Jane, 18
John, 18
Mr., 129
Samuel, 18
William, 129
PEILER, Mary, 170
PEISCH, Magdalene, 18
Martin, 18
PELLO, John, 11
PELSTERLING, Jacob, 117
Mary Magdalene, 117
PELTZ, Catharine, 78, 125
Catherine, 6
Daniel, 78
Elizabeth, 44
John, 91, 134
Maria, 44, 64, 170
P., 170
Philip, 76, 91, 102, 113, 129, 138, 159
Rebecca, 91, 102, 113, 159, 170
William, 13, 44, 64, 113
PENNER, Catherine, 17
Daniel, 17
Henry, 31
John Peter, 17

Margaret, 31
PENTER, Catherine, 22
Christopher, 22
John, 22
Peter, 22
PENTHER, Anna Maria, 30
Catherine, 30, 60
Christopher, 30, 60
Daniel, 60, 125
Dorothy, 10
Elizabeth, 5, 14
George, 95
Gottfried, 19
Jacob, 65, 75
John, 48, 62, 95
John Peter, 114
Margaret, 26, 56
Maria, 42, 48, 62, 75, 89, 95, 114
Maria Barbara, 7
Nicholas, 42, 45, 48, 76, 89
Sarah, 114, 128
PENTLER, George Adam, 2
PEPPER, Benjamin, 32
Elizabeth, 32
Rebecca, 32, 75
PEPPERLEY, Mary, 10
PERES, Fanny, 104, 178
Joseph, 104
Louisa, 178
Maria, 146, 149, 156
Peter, 104, 156, 162, 178
Veronica, 156, 162
William, 162
PERJEH, Maria, 101
PERKINS, George, 5
PERROT, Samuel, 83
PERRY, Fanny, 177
Henry, 4
Nancy, 89
P., 177

PETER, Abraham, 6, 14, 27, 41, 56, 141
Anna Catharine, 181
Anna Maria, 63
George, 63
Henry, 6
John Carls, 181
Magdalene, 27
Maria Barbara, 56
Peter, 63
PETERMAN, George, 83
PETERS, Margaret, 75
Rosina, 75
PETERSON, J., 165
Martha, 11
Susanna, 165
PETH, Matthew, 73
Veronica, 73
PETIT, Catharine, 179
Nicholas, 179
Susan, 179
PETR, Henry, 6
PETRI, Ann Elizabeth, 75
Catharine Wilhelmina, 177
Elizabeth, 91
Elizabeth Margaret, 69
George, 177
John Philip, 91
Louisa, 177
Philip, 69
PETRY, John Philip, 75
PETZLER, Casper, 73
PFAFF, Anna, 42, 60, 90, 108, 122, 140
Anna Barbara, 108
Burckhardt, 42
Conrad, 90
George, 80, 90, 108, 122
Henry, 60
John, 42, 60

John George, 9,
42, 60, 122,
140
PFAFFHAUSEN,
Conrad, 76, 78,
137
Maria Christine,
137
PFAFFHAUSER,
Catharine, 80
PFANKUCHEN,
Magdalene, 29
Philip, 29
PFANNENKUCHEN,
Catherine, 51
Philip, 51
PFAU, ---, 30
Barbara, 30, 65,
100, 164
Elizabeth, 30
Henry, 106, 122,
147
Jacob, 65, 122
John, 30, 81,
106, 149, 156
M. Elizabeth, 156
M. Magdalene,
164
Maria, 106, 122
Maria Elizabeth,
65, 106
William, 65,
100, 126, 132,
164
William Henrich,
132
William Henry,
100
PFEIFER, Mary
Magdalene, 78
PFEIFFER, Anna, 37
Anna Maria, 46,
143
Christine, 20,
32, 49, 52, 80,
86, 117, 135
David, 33
George, 46, 148
Henry, 20, 32,
86, 117, 135,
144
Jacob, 32, 58
Jane, 33, 46, 65
Jeane, 83
Jenny, 131

John, 33, 46,
65, 131, 139,
147
John Henry, 49
John Peter, 46,
57
Joseph, 65, 128
Kitty, 74
Magdalene
Elizabeth, 49
Margaret, 58,
71, 80
Maria, 3, 20,
23, 71, 147
Maria Margaret,
57
Peter, 23, 57,
117, 147
William, 58, 71
PFEIHL, Philip,
101
Susanna, 101
PFEILL, Philip, 33
Susanna, 33
William, 33
PFIFER, Michael,
15
PFIFS, Stephen,
110
Susanna
Elizabeth, 110
PFISTER, Anna
Maria, 33
Joanna Maria
Sophia, 33
John, 33
PHARLOCK,
Albertus, 154
PHEIL, Maria, 102,
137
Philip, 102, 137
Susanna, 102
PHEISSER,
Christine, 92
Henry, 92
PHILE, William,
170
PHILIP, Ann Maria,
76
PHILIPS, Barbara,
54
John, 54, 165
Maria, 54
PHOENIX, ---, 117
Salome, 117
PICARD, George, 79

PICK, Charlotte,
169
Edward, 169
Sarah, 169
PIDGEON, William,
13
PIEHLER, Andrew,
30
Elizabeth, 30
PIERE, Francois
Reti, 131
PIETER, Catharine,
80
PIFER, Eliza, 180
Esther, 180
John, 180
William, 180
PIGLER, Anna
Elizabeth, 77
PIPER, Sally, 85
PISTER, Barbara,
25
Elizabeth, 25
John, 25
John George, 25
Rebecca, 25
PISTOR, John, 4,
154
PITT, John, 82
PLAINE, Anna
Maria, 185
Christine, 185
Henry, 185
PLANE, Christine,
184
Henry, 184
John George, 184
PLENN, Henry, 77
PLESCH, Adam, 57
Christine, 20,
57
Jacob, 20
Jonas, 20, 57
PLESCHE, Jonas,
129
PLESH, Andrew, 45
Christine, 45
Jonas, 45
PLETTERMAN, Aug.
Henry, 46
PLEYLER, Anna, 183
John, 183
Susanna, 183
PLUMER, Catharine,
175
Conrad, 169

Francis, 169, 175
Gertrude, 169
PLUNCKET, Sarah, 79
PLUSCH, Christine, 122
Jonas, 122
Jonathan, 149
POHL, Adam, 38
Catherine, 38
Elizabeth, 16
POHT, Matthias, 159
Veronica, 156, 159
POINT, Sarah, 14
POLK, Maria, 185
Peter, 185
POLLARD, John, 12
POLLMAN, Henry, 123
POMP, Catharine, 109
John, 109
Maria, 109, 148
POOTH, Dorothy, 111
Henry, 111
POP, Elizabeth, 113
Margaret, 113
POPE, John, 75
PORKENPINE, Mr., 154
PORKEPINE, Hetty, 168
John, 168
Sarah, 168
PORTER, Catharine, 97, 156, 163, 181
Catherine, 41, 56, 70
Eliza, 163
Elizabeth, 56
Henry, 156
Jean, 181
John, 12, 41, 56, 70, 97, 156, 163
Jonas, 181
Thomas, 70, 156
William, 97
POSSER, Jacob, 61
John, 61

Mary Magdalene, 61
POT, Daniel, 167
Maria, 167
Peter, 167
POTEY, Elizabeth, 78
POTH, Catharine, 180
Catherine Elizabeth, 68
Elizabeth, 31
Henry, 31, 68
Matthias, 25
Veronica, 25
POTT, Elizabeth, 56
John, 56
POTTS, Margaret, 12
POVERT, John Henry, 52
Magdalene, 52
Margaret, 52
POWEL, Hannah, 14
PRAETLER, Catherine, 27
Jacob, 27
PRAHL, Catherine, 29
John, 29
Ludwig, 5
PRATLER, Peggy, 92
PRATTLER, Catherine, 16
Jacob, 16
PRAUPERT, Anna, 10
Barbara, 73
Catharine, 75
John, 68
Margaret, 68
Philippina, 68
William, 11, 73
PREH, Catharine, 182
John, 79, 182
John Michael, 182
PREIS, Carl, 160
Elizabeth, 160
John Carl, 82
John Frederick, 160
Maria, 160
Rebecca, 150

PRESSLER, Catharine, 179
George, 38, 179
George Henry, 179
Maria, 38
PREST, Eva, 170
Jacob, 170
Philip, 170
Philip Henry, 170
PRETE, Adam, 111
Anna, 111
Henry, 111
PRETHAST, William, 76
PREUSS, John Frederick, 152
PRICE, Lewis, 11
Margaret, 13
Mr., 148
Pamelia, 13
PRIESSE, James, 42
Magdalene, 42
PROBERT, Hannah, 168
Maria, 168
William, 168
PROCTER, Anna, 160
Sarah, 74
PROTZMAN, Maria, 78
PROUPERT, Barbara, 31, 51
Catharine, 51
Catherine, 51
William, 31, 51
PRUN, Leonhard, 71
PUND, Jacob, 9
PURCHE, Christine, 185
Elizabeth, 185
John, 185
Sam, 185
Sarah, 185
PURDY, Hetty, 177
Mary, 177
Robert, 177
Stephen, 177
PUS, Anna, 22
Benjamin, 22
John, 22
PYERON, Sarah
Riet, 98
Stephen, 98

-Q-
QUANDEL, Elizabeth
Maria, 16
John Jacob, 16
QUAST, Henry, 127
John, 65
Susanna, 65
QUIGLEY, Hugh, 81

-R-
RABANUS,
Elizabeth, 156
RABEL, Sarah, 155
RACE, Molly, 84
RAESMAN, John, 127
RAFFERTY, James,
88
RAMBO, John, 148
Maria, 27
RANCK, Christian,
73
Maria, 73
Sarah, 73
RANDON, Paul, 82
RAPP, Elizabeth,
31
Frederick Jacob,
31
RARAH,
Christopher, 77
RASBER, Elizabeth,
76
Eva, 162
John, 98, 162
M. Magdalene,
152
RASH, Nicholas, 13
RASKIS, Henry, 182
Maria, 182
Sarah Ann, 182
RASPER, Elizabeth,
119
Philip, 119
RASTER, Catharine,
122
RAUCH, Carl, 166
Charles, 164
Christian, 164,
166
Christopher, 16,
51
Conrad, 51
Maria, 51, 64
Rosina, 16, 51
Samuel, 51

RAUCHBART, Anna
Barbara, 59
Charles, 59
RAUCK, Christian,
62
Ludwig, 62
Maria, 62
RAUH, Bernard, 107
Dorothy, 77
RAUL, William, 153
RAUS, Elijah, 154
RAUSCH, ---, 142
Anna, 107
Anna Maria, 19
Elizabeth, 141
John Adam, 19
RAUSH, Catharine,
182
RAVANS, Maria, 14
RAWLE, Eleonore,
62
Samuel, 62
RAY, Meckle, 65
READER, Michael,
77
REB, Catherine, 17
Frederick, 17
John, 17
REBALT, Anna, 168
Peter, 168
REBLE, Clara, 76
REBSEL, William,
154
RECHERN, George,
84
RECKSTEIN,
Catharine, 91
Jacob, 91
Maria, 91
REDER, Elliam, 13
REDICKER,
Catharine, 103
David, 103
Sarah, 103
REDISSEN, Anthony,
76
REDMAN, B., 176
REED, A. Margaret,
167
Anna Margaret, 8
C., 167
Catharine, 148
Elizabeth, 153,
167
REEGERSTEIN,
Henry, 106

REES, Hannah, 14
REHBEIN, John
Adam, 156
REHBOHL, Philip,
39
REICHARD,
Elizabeth, 156
Richard, 6
Sarah, 156
William, 156
REICHEL, Augustus,
85
REICHERT, John,
152
REIDE, Casper, 161
Elizabeth, 4
Henry, 160
John, 11, 160
Margaret, 160
Maria, 75, 144
Samuel, 102
Sarah, 102, 161
William, 102,
161
REIDER, John, 113
Margaret, 113
REIDLE, Jacob, 144
REIF, George, 12
REIFF,
Christopher,
154
REIFFSCHNEIDER,
Anna Maria, 45
John, 3, 45
REIFSCHNEIDER,
Adam, 7
REIFSCHNYDER, Anna
Maria, 29
Elizabeth, 29
John, 29
REIGER, John, 113
REIL, John, 79
REIMER, Eva, 82
Maria, 126
Maria Tauen, 76
REIN, Anna, 168
Anna Eva, 168
Anna Maria, 111
Catharine, 111,
178
Jacob, 168
John, 111, 178
John Philip, 178
REINCKE, Godfrey,
95
Gottfried, 95

Ludwig, 95
REINDAHLER, Anna
　Maria, 44
　Elizabeth, 44
　Jacob, 44
REINDY, William,
　150
REINECK, A. Maria,
　158
　Anna Margaret,
　55
　Godfrey, 130
　Jacob, 158
　Ludwig, 15, 55,
　130
　Maria Elizabeth,
　55
　Mary Elizabeth,
　15
　Peter, 15
　William, 158
REINECKE, Ludwig,
　152
REINER, Elizabeth,
　177
　John, 177
REINERT,
　Catherine, 23
REINHARD,
　Catharine, 185
　Christian, 177
　Christine, 160,
　177
　Elisabeth, 89
　Elizabeth, 164
　John, 57, 102,
　126, 160
　Maria, 81
　Maria Sarah, 7
　Peter, 57
　Sarah, 57, 74,
　150, 177
　William, 160,
　164
REINHARDT,
　Catherine, 1
　Christian, 78
　Elizabeth, 118
　John, 118
　Peter, 124
　William, 118
REINHART,
　Elizabeth, 172
　William, 172
REINHOLD,
　Elizabeth, 14

REINHOLDT,
　Susanna, 79,
　103
REIS, Adam, 95
　Catherine, 37, 54
　Elizabeth, 95,
　96
　George, 27
　John Philip, 4,
　76, 96
　Margaret, 7
　Peter, 9, 96
　Susanna, 146
　Veronica, 80
REISCHEL,
　Catharine, 79
REISER, Eva, 94
　Jacob, 94
REISNER, Anna
　Maria
　Frederica, 90
　Catharine, 90
　John Herman, 90
REISS, Elizabeth,
　117, 118
　John, 117, 118
REITER, Christine,
　173
　William, 173
REITLINGER,
　Elizabeth, 43
　Jacob, 13, 43,
　44
　John, 43
REME, Anna, 181
　Jacob, 181
　John, 181
REMEL, Anna
　Catharine, 128
REN, Jacob, 129
RENCK, Jacob, 59
　Margaret, 59
RENNARD, Phoebe,
　13
RENNO, Susanna, 60
RENNOH, John, 135
REPART, Daniel, 69
　Dorothea, 69
RESTEIN, J., 170
REUBOLD,
　Elizabeth, 53
　Philip, 53
REUDE, Elizabeth,
　64
　John, 36, 70
　Margaret, 36, 70

William, 36, 76
REUDI, John, 139
REUDY, Catharine,
　94
　Elizabeth, 94
　John, 94
　Margaret, 94
REUS, Jacob, 80
REUSS, Elizabeth,
　163
　John, 163
　William, 163
REUTER, John, 74
REUTLINGER,
　Elizabeth, 87
　Jacob, 87
　William, 87
REVANS, Maria
　Elizabeth, 70
REYBOLD,
　Elizabeth, 81
REYDE, Elizabeth,
　4
　Sarah, 88, 172
　William, 68, 88,
　172
REYER, M.
　Catharine, 156
REYLI, Maria, 78
REYNER, Catharine,
　184
　George, 184
　John, 184
REYPULE, P., 178
REYSER, Eva, 112
　Jacob, 112
RHEILY, Barbara,
　78
RHINHARDT, Sophia,
　12
RHOADS, Susanna,
　83
RHODT, Dorothy, 11
RIBBEL, Nicholas,
　123
RIBLET, Abraham, 2
RICE, Catharine,
　177
　Elizabeth, 171,
　177
　J., 171
　John, 177
RICHARD, Anna, 100
　Elizabeth, 100
　Joachim, 100

RICHARDSON, Meine, 74
RICHARDT,
  Elizabeth, 116
  Henry, 116
  Joachim, 116
RICHERTON, Robert, 14
RICHESTEIN,
  Balthasar, 6
RICHSTEIN,
  Balthasar, 34, 51
  Catharine, 82
  Catherine, 51
  Charles, 34, 51
  Christine, 34
  Hannah, 51
  John, 51
  Maria, 34
RICK, Anna
  Christine, 139
RICKELS, Catharine
  Dorothy, 166
  Henry, 166
RICKER, John, 52
RICKETS, Joseph, 79
RIDGE, Catherine, 49
  Mary, 10
RIEBEL, Henry, 47
  John Peter, 31
  Nicholas, 31
  Nicolas, 47
  Salome, 31, 47
RIEBER, Barbara, 49
RIED, Anna
  Margaret, 17
  Anna Maria, 69
  Anna Susanna, 36
  Elizabeth, 17, 69, 150, 152, 155
  John, 22, 155, 36
  John Leonard, 69
  Leonard, 17, 69, 149
  Sarah, 69
  Susanna, 22
  Thomas, 76
RIEDLINGER,
  Elizabeth, 53
  Jacob, 53

RIEDLINGR, Maria, 7
RIEDT, Elizabeth, 112
  Henry, 112
  Leonardt, 112
RIEGEL, David, 118
  Elizabeth, 131
  Henry, 131
RIEGELER,
  Catherine, 51, 70
  Elizabeth, 23, 70
  Henry, 51, 70
  John, 51
  Mr., 8
  Stephen, 23
RIEGENER,
  Catharine, 89
  Elizabeth, 63
  George, 49, 63, 86, 87, 89
  Henry, 49
  Sarah, 49, 63, 86, 87, 89
RIEGER, John
  George, 77
RIEGLER,
  Elizabeth, 62
  Eva, 45
  Stephen, 62
RIEGNER, Anna, 112
  George, 100, 112
  Sarah, 100, 112
RIEHLE, Jacob, 80
RIEHM, Elizabeth, 83
RIEHMER, George, 12
RIES, Andrew, 23, 54
  Anna Maria, 73
  Catherine, 73
  Christopher, 155
  Daniel, 73
  Elizabeth, 17, 21, 38, 48, 50, 59, 62, 88, 137, 32
  Francis, 80
  George, 21, 50
  Henry, 17, 21, 38, 50, 59, 88
  Jacob, 49, 54, 65

  John, 48
  John George, 13, 54
  Lawrence, 137
  Lorentz, 48, 62
  M. Dunsula, 155
  Magdalene, 49, 54
  Margaret, 23, 54
  Maria, 23, 50, 65
  Nicholas, 155
RIESE, George, 129
RIESELER, Henry, 12
RIESER, Frederick, 78
RIESS, Elizabeth, 115
  Lawrence, 115, 138
  Lawrence Ford, 115
  Sarah, 115
RIESTER, Rebecca, 78
RIETH, Maria, 98
  Regula, 98
  Thomas, 98
RIFFERT,
  Catharine, 75
  Griffith, 33, 34
  Joseph, 33
  Philip, 87
  Rebecca, 87
  Robert, 34
  Sarah, 33, 34
  Ursula, 87
RIFFERTH, Breide, 69
  John, 69
  Peter, 74
RIFFET, John, 54
  William, 54
RIFFIT, John, 42
  Matthias, 42
RIGERLER,
  Elizabeth, 15
  Stephen, 15
RIGG, Charlotte, 156
  Edward, 156
  William, 156
RINEDOLLER,
  Barbara, 180
  Elizabeth, 180
  Henry, 180

Jacob, 180
Margaret, 180
Samuel, 180
RIONTEAU,
Elizabeth
Helena, 37
RIPPETTE, Daniel,
18
Dorothea, 18
Maria Margaret,
18
RISCHONG,
Catherine, 15,
24, 43
David, 15, 24,
43
Joanna Sophia,
24
Mary Magdalene,
43
RISTEIN,
Balthasar, 47
Catherine, 47
Charles, 11, 30,
47
Elizabeth, 30
Hannah, 30, 47
J., 170
Joseph, 47
Maria, 6
RITCH, Catherine,
41
John, 41
Morgan, 41
RITEMAN,
Elizabeth, 173
Henry, 173
John, 173
RITSCH, Catharine,
92
Maria Magdalene,
92
Morgan, 92
RITTENHOUSE,
Hannah, 80
RITTER, Anna, 23,
34, 48, 63, 116
Anna Maria, 23
Catherine, 12
Dorothea, 50
Elizabeth, 2,
58, 59, 63
Henry, 23, 34,
48, 63, 96, 116
Jacob, 50
Maria, 96

Sarah, 34
William, 59, 116
RITTR, Henry, 10
RITZ, Friederica
Philippina, 3
ROBERT, Elizabeth,
166
ROBERTS,
Catherine, 59
Jemimah, 78
Magdalene, 60
William, 59
ROBINSON, Hatty,
167
Hester, 177
Hugh, 177
Joseph, 82
Louis, 167
Luy, 167
Maria, 167
Mary, 177
Sarah, 177
ROCH, George
Henry, 25
John Justus, 25
Susanna, 25
RODEN, Charlotte,
58
ROEBSAMEN, George,
78
ROEHRMAN, Anna
Margaret, 49,
66
David, 49, 66
Francis
Reinhard, 49
Simon, 66
ROEMER, Juliana,
128
ROESCH, Julianna,
7
ROGERS, John
Peter, 145
ROH, Adam, 71
Catherine
Friderica, 71
Maria, 71
ROHD, Adam, 43
Maria, 43
Sally, 43
ROHE, Ursula, 75
ROHR, Elizabeth,
80
ROHRMAN, Adam, 95
Anna Margaret,
95, 116

Conrad, 32, 40,
51, 69
David, 95, 116
Dorothy, 116
Elizabeth, 32,
40, 51
Maria, 11
ROLOPH, A.
Margaret, 183
Anna Margaret,
183
Dennis, 183
ROMER, Margaret,
73
ROMP, John, 135
ROODT, A.
Margaret, 169
Conrad, 169
Dennis, 169
ROOS, Elizabeth,
14
Peter, 21
Sarah Elizabeth,
21
ROOTHAAR, Anna
Maria, 110
Leonard, 134
Martin, 110
Sarah, 110, 134
ROOTHAR, Eleonora,
108
Leonard, 108
Sarah, 108
ROS, Peter, 17, 32
Sarah, 32
Sarah Elizabeth,
17
ROSCH, A. Maria,
167
Andrew, 44
Anna, 50
Barbara, 167
Conrad, 30, 44
Elizabeth, 128
Leonard, 50
Ludwig, 30
Margaret, 30, 44
Maria, 34, 50
Nicholas, 127
William, 50
ROSE, Jane, 11
Peter, 21
ROSENBERGER,
Abraham, 84
Maria, 84

ROSENBUSCH,
  Sophia, 77
ROSK, Anthony, 70
  Charles, 41
  Christine, 41,
  70
  Samuel, 41, 70
ROSKER, Henry,
  113, 136
  Maria, 113
  Maria Catharine,
  136
ROSKES, Cathrine,
  90
  Frederick, 36
  Hendericus, 90
  Henricus, 36
  Henry, 21, 158
  Jacobus, 21
  M., 158
  Maria, 21, 36,
  90
  Rachel, 158
ROSS, Christine,
  81
  John George, 112
  Peter, 112
  Sarah, 112
  Sophia, 112
ROSSEL, Philip, 80
ROSSET, Elizabeth,
  172
  Ferdinand, 143
  Jacob, 172
  Maria, 172
ROSSIN, Catherine,
  16, 59
  Christian, 16,
  59
  Paul, 59
ROSSY, Catherine,
  36
  Christian, 36
  Maria, 36
ROST, Matthias,
  149
ROTH, Adam, 11,
  55, 104, 122
  Andrew, 79
  Anna Elizabeth,
  104
  Anna Maria, 122
  Dorothy, 116
  Elizabeth, 54
  George, 55, 127
  John Adam, 147

Lorentz, 54
Maria, 31, 55,
  102, 104, 122
Peter, 116
Philip, 102
Sally, 9
Samuel, 54
ROTHAR, Elizabeth,
  50
  Fred., 39
  Frederick, 50
  John, 50
  Leonard, 50
  Margaret, 164
  Maria, 164
  Martin, 164
  Nelly, 50
ROTHARE, Leonard,
  11
ROTHENBECK,
  Christopher, 49
  George, 49
  Maria, 49
ROTHENWALDER,
  Elizabeth, 161
  Nicholas, 161
ROTHHAAR, Anna
  Maria, 110
  Bernard, 148
  Henry, 144, 145
  Leonard, 83
  Martin, 77, 110
ROTHORE, David,
  175
  Elizabeth, 182
  George, 182
  Leonard, 182
  Maria, 175
  Martin, 175
ROTHSHULL,
  Elizabeth, 172
  Leonard, 172
ROTZELL, Charles,
  79
ROUN, Polly, 77
ROUSH, Charles, 58
  John, 58
ROUW, Conrad, 14
RU---, Jacob, 156
  Margaret, 156
RUAULT, Catharine,
  83
RUB, Henry, 142
RUBEL, Catharine,
  163
  John, 83

RUBERT, John, 77
RUBSAM, Jacob, 165
  Susanna, 80
RUBSAMEN, Anna, 13
  Hannah, 41
  Rachel, 79
RUBSNIDER, M., 178
RUCKER, Catherine,
  38
  Christian, 38
  Dorothea, 38
RUDI, Elizabeth,
  98
RUDOLPH, 183
  Anna Christine,
  59
  John, 34, 55
  John Jacob, 106
  Magdalene, 59,
  106
  Peter, 83
  Sarah, 34, 55
  William, 13, 59,
  106, 146
RUDY, Fanny, 83
  John, 13
  Rachel, 46
RUDYBACH,
  Margaret, 12
RUEB, Catharine,
  95, 131
  Leonard, 95,
  131, 132
  Magdalene, 132
RUEBER, Barbara,
  73
  Jacob, 73
RUEBSAM, Anna
  Kleopha, 141
RUEGNER, George,
  133
  Sarah, 133
RUEHL, Catherine,
  6
RUMBO, Peter, 84
RUMEL, Charlotte,
  57
  Jacob, 6
  John Philip, 57
  Maria, 7
  Nicholas, 22
  Rebecca, 57
RUMMEL, Anna
  Barbara, 46
  Anna Margaret,
  46

Barbara, 60
Catharine, 119,
  143
Christine, 35
Frederick, 39,
  148
George, 48, 99
Jacob, 27, 35,
  99, 114
John, 77
John George,
  110, 114, 157
John Michael, 62
Magdalene, 22,
  62, 86, 99,
  110, 114, 138,
  146, 157
Maria, 35, 119
Maria Elizabeth,
  48
Mary Magdalene,
  22
Michael, 11, 19,
  22, 119
Mr., 141
Nicholas, 13,
  30, 46, 60
Philip, 12, 39,
  60, 127, 150
Rebecca, 39
RUMMER, Anna
  Maria, 13
RUMOF, Jacob, 45
RUMPF, Anna
  Elizabeth, 103
Anna Margaret,
  85
Elizabeth, 54,
  85
Jacob, 54, 85
Jacob Henry, 103
John Henry, 14,
  103
Peter, 54
RUNNER, Elizabeth,
  169
George, 169
Maria, 169
Martin, 11
RUP, Anna Barbara,
  136
Catharine, 133
Catherine, 19,
  42
Elizabeth, 23,
  39

Kilian, 19, 42
Susanna, 19
William, 15
RUPERT, Anna
  Gertrude, 78
RUPP, Maria, 79
RUPPEL, Conrad, 79
RUPPERT, Dorothy,
  107
John, 107
RUSCH, Elizabeth,
  39
Jacob, 39
RUSH, Conrad, 11,
  64
Daniel, 174
Elizabeth, 64
Lewis, 175
Margaret, 64
Maria, 175
Nancy, 175
Susanna, 174
RUSHER, John, 177
Rebecca, 177
RUSK, ---, 84
RUSS, Christine,
  25
George, 25
Samuel, 25
Susanna, 25
RUSTEIN,
  Elizabeth, 168
Jacob, 168
Maria Eliza, 168
RUTENBERGER,
  Catharine, 179
Samuel, 179
RUTTER, George,
  182
RYAN, Catharine,
  157, 160
Elizabeth, 145
Jeane, 82
John, 82, 157,
  160

-S-
SACKMAN, Christine
  Margaret, 60
Elizabeth, 47
Martin, 47
SACKREUTER,
  Catharine, 79
SAEHLER, Matthias,
  139
SAFFRAN, Mr., 126

SAGERSYLER, J.,
  177
Susanna, 177
SAHMAN, W., 185
SAHNER, Anna
  Catharine, 118
Elizabeth, 118
John George, 118
SAILER, Henry, 169
Mary, 169
Samuel, 169
SAILOR, Elizabeth,
  173
Henrietta, 178
Henry, 178
Jacob, 173
John, 173
Mary, 178
May, 178
SALADE, Sebastian,
  79
SALDER, Jacob, 85
SALLEDE,
  Frederick, 158
M. Magdalene,
  158
Sebastian, 158
SAMSON, Paul, 148
SANDA, Carl
  Frederick, 178
SANDER, Herman, 82
Maria Catherine,
  32
Peter, 32
SANDERS,
  Elizabeth, 83
John, 65
Maria, 39
Mary Margaret,
  65
William, 9, 39,
  65
SANDMAN, Lorentz,
  11
SANDOS, Francis,
  175
SANN, Hannah
  Bernadina, 184
Johanna, 184
Johanna Eva, 184
John Peter, 184
SASSEMANSCHAUSEN,
  George Henry,
  146
SATTLER, John, 74

SAUBER, Catharine,
  111
  Jacob Frederick,
  111
SAUDER, Carl, 186
  Carl William,
  186
  Catherine, 29,
  38
  Daniel, 186
  John, 29, 183
  John George, 29
  M. Ann, 183
  Margaret, 6
  Maria Ann, 183
  Susanna, 186
  William
  Monington, 186
SAUER, Henry, 158
SAUERHEBER,
  George, 82
  John, 184
  Michael, 184
  Philippina, 184
SAUERHOFFER,
  Catharine, 159
  George, 159
  Jacob, 159
  M. Catharine,
  159
  Philippina, 159
SAUERMAN,
  Elizabeth, 108
  Philip, 108
SAUERS, David, 154
SAUNDERS, George
  Washington, 23
  Maria, 23
  William, 23
SAUTER, John, 149
SAVOY, Pierre, 81
SCHA, Ezechial, 68
  Jemima, 68
  Phoebe, 68
  Viba, 68
SCHAAF, George, 41
  Maria, 41, 82
  Samuel, 83
SCHAAFF, Anna
  Maria, 67
  Catherine, 12,
  26
  George, 9
  M. Eva, 162
  Maria, 88
  Peter, 162

SCHABERER,
  Margaret, 79
SCHACKA, Carl,
  107, 136
  Christine, 101
  John George, 101
  Margaret, 107
SCHACKY, Janna, 61
SCHAD, George, 81,
  148
SCHAE, Elizabeth,
  130
  Francis, 130
SCHAED, George,
  83, 92
  Maria, 92
SCHAEFF, Anna
  Elizabeth, 28
  Catharine, 73
  Catherine, 53
  Elizabeth, 16,
  28, 53, 71
  George, 53, 126
  John George, 28,
  42
  John Jacob, 16
  John Peter, 28,
  53
  Peter, 16, 71
SCHAEFFER, Adam,
  19, 41
  Anna Catherine,
  72
  Bernard, 141
  Catharine, 74,
  130
  Catherine, 58
  Christian, 67,
  75
  Dorothea, 19, 41
  Elizabeth, 12
  Jacob, 100
  John, 67, 92,
  109, 128, 129,
  137
  John Adam, 140
  Juliana, 100
  Margaret, 67
  Maria, 109, 137
  Melchior, 72,
  74, 130
  Philip, 58
  Sophia, 141
  Susanna, 92, 109
SCHAETZLEIN,
  Barbara, 175

SCHAFE, Christine,
  45
  Elizabeth, 45
  John George, 45
SCHAFF, Anna
  Maria, 90
  Catharine, 174
  Elizabeth, 90
  John Jacob, 1
  John Peter, 90
  Maria, 140
  Maria May, 174
  Samuel, 174
SCHAFFER, Carl, 80
  Catharine, 152
  Christian, 81
  John, 168
  Maria, 79
  Sarah, 168
  Susanna, 168
SCHAFFERY,
  Catherine, 13
SCHAFFNER, Anna
  Magdalene, 153
SCHAKA, Charles,
  131
  William, 131
SCHAKAHR, Charles,
  86
  Margaret, 86
  William, 86
SCHAKAR, Anna
  Maria Sophia,
  63
  Carl, 40
  Catherine, 49
  Charles, 12, 57
  Christine, 49,
  62
  Frederick David,
  62
  George, 49, 62
  John Charles, 57
  Margaret, 40, 57
  Matthias, 62
SCHAKE, Charles,
  130
SCHAKER, Anna
  Maria, 37
  Christine, 37
  George, 37
SCHAKOR, Matthias,
  139
SCHALLUS,
  Elizabeth, 61,
  79

Francis Casper
  Hasenclever, 61
Jacob, 61, 135,
  147
Julia, 135
Julianna, 61
Louisa, 61
SCHAMBERLAINE,
  Catherine, 13
SCHARP, Henry, 92
Maria Eva, 92
SCHAUB, Elizabeth,
  18, 32, 66
John, 18, 32, 66
SCHAUMENKESSEL,
  Elizabeth, 94
Elizabeth
  Barbara, 46, 93
Frederick, 46
George, 94
George
  Frederick, 93
SCHAUP, Anna
  Elizabeth, 97
Barbara, 81
John, 97
SCHAWE, David
  Israel, 36
Ezechiel, 36
Jemima, 36
SCHAWES, Bernard,
  142
SCHEAF, Maria, 73
SCHEARER, Henry,
  13
SCHEDERER,
  Catharine, 99
Catharine
  Christine, 99
Frederick, 99
SCHEE, Jacob, 18
SCHEH, John, 90
Philippina, 90
SCHEIBELE,
  Christopher,
  146
Maria, 37
SCHEIBELER,
  George, 26
SCHEIBLE,
  Frederick, 148
Henry, 37
Joseph, 37
Maria, 37
SCHEIBLIN, Anna,
  155

Frederick, 155
SCHEIT, George,
  110
John, 110
Maria, 110
SCHEIVE,
  Catherine, 60
Dina, 59
John, 59, 60
Maria Christine,
  60
SCHEIVELIN, Anna,
  112
Anna Rosina, 112
Frederick, 112
SCHEIW, Anna
  Margaret, 1
Christine, 18
John, 18
SCHEIWE, Anna
  Maria, 39
Christine, 23,
  39
John, 23, 39
SCHELL, Hannah,
  160
Henry, 81, 160
Isaac
  Franciscus, 184
John Ludwig, 147
Ludwig, 184
Margaret, 160
Sophia, 143, 184
SCHELLENBERGER,
  Dorothea, 20
Simon, 5, 20
SCHELLER, Barbara,
  120
Christine, 78
Fred, 124
Frederick, 137
Ludwig, 120
Sophia, 120
SCHEMO, Bernard,
  98
Juliana, 98
SCHENCKEL,
  Frederick, 59
Susanna, 59
SCHEPPY, Anthony,
  5
SCHERADIN, Jacob,
  7
SCHERER, Anna
  Maria, 63
Barbara, 13

Catharine, 74,
  80
Catherine, 59
Conrad, 75, 153,
  161
Elizabeth, 50,
  75, 89, 101,
  112
George, 63
Henry, 50, 89,
  112, 139
James, 89
Leonard, 112
Magdalene, 107
Margaret, 89
Mary Magdalene,
  161
Peter, 6, 63
Philip, 101, 132
Robert, 101,
  128, 132
Sarah, 127
Susanna, 50
William, 89
SCHERIDAN,
  Abraham, 87
Anna Barbara, 87
Elizabeth, 87
SCHERMAYER,
  Benjamin, 162
Catharine, 162
John, 162
SCHERMER,
  Elizabeth, 164
Hannah, 164
Jacob, 137, 164
Maria, 150
SCHERREDEN,
  Dorothy, 12
SCHERRIDAN,
  Abraham, 42
Barbara, 42
Thomas, 42
SCHESTERSTEIN, A.
  Margaret, 157
Jacob, 157
SCHET, George, 76,
  99
Jacob, 99
Maria, 99
SCHEWER, John, 4
SCHIBELE, Jacob,
  144
SCHIBLE, Adam, 46
Elizabeth, 16,
  46

Jacob, 16, 46
Susanna, 16
SCHICK, ---, 91
SCHIEBLE,
Elizabeth, 33
Jacob, 33
SCHIEFFER, Adam,
116
Hannah, 116
Jacob, 116
Julianna, 116
Sarah, 116
SCHIELLE,
Elizabeth, 24
Jacob, 24
SCHIFFERER, Adam,
55, 86, 98
Catherine, 30
Dorothy, 86, 98
Jacob, 18
John Jacob, 30
Joseph, 18
Juliana, 30
Maria Juliana,
18
Philip, 86, 123
Sarah, 98
SCHILL, Ludwig, 77
SCHILLACH,
Albertus, 18
Maria, 18
SCHILLACK, Albert,
92
Alberti, 62
Albertus, 30,
68, 96, 109,
114
Maria, 30, 62,
68, 92, 109,
114
SCHILLER, Conrad,
132
Sarah, 132
SCHILLINGSWORTH,
Margaret, 61
Rosina, 61
Thomas, 61
SCHINCKEL,
Frederick, 80
Susanna, 123
SCHINGEL,
Frederick, 134
Susanna, 134
SCHIRMER, Hannah,
123
Jacob, 123

John Jacob, 123
SCHIRSLER, Clara,
107
Lawrence, 107
SCHITTEL, Anna
Maria, 168
Daniel, 35, 59,
155, 168
Elizabeth, 35,
59, 155, 168
Samuel, 59
Simon, 35, 123
SCHLACK, Maria,
147
SCHLACTER, Anna
Magdalene, 110
John, 110
SCHLAECHTER,
Elizabeth, 77
SCHLAGMUELLER,
Carolina
Mariann, 83
SCHLATER, Anna
Magdalene, 122
John, 122
SCHLATTER, Adam,
114
Anna Catharine,
88
Anna Maria, 54
Elizabeth, 88,
176
Gottlieb, 88
Henry, 54
Johanna
Elizabeth, 176
John Adam, 176
John Jacob, 54
Joseph, 54
Maria, 77
Maria Catharine,
114, 176
Michael, 130
SCHLAUCH, Eva
Elizabeth, 115
John, 117
John Peter, 115
Sophia
Catharine, 115
SCHLECHTER, Anna
Elizabeth, 47
Elizabeth, 12
John, 47
SCHLEMER, Jacob,
11, 124

SCHLEMMER, ---,
153
Anna, 93
Catherine, 35
Conrad, 29, 35,
37, 124
Elizabeth, 93
Hannah, 29, 37,
48, 61, 158
Hannah Eleonore,
29
Jacob, 29, 37,
48, 61, 93, 158
M. Catharine,
158
Mary Magdalene,
48
Rosina, 11
SCHLER, Anna
Maria, 117
Henry, 117
Jacob, 117
SCHLIMER, Jacob,
132
SCHLIMMER, Adam, 106
Hannah, 106
Jacob, 106
SCHLING, Margaret,
92
Maria, 74
SCHLOESMAN,
Michael, 96
Philippina, 96
SCHLOESSMAN,
Michael, 113
Philippina, 113
SCHLOPFER, Anna,
149
SCHLOTMAN, Adam,
26
George, 41
Maria, 26, 41
Paul, 26, 41
SCHLOTTER,
Elizabeth, 108,
144
Gottlieb, 108
Hannah, 144
SCHLOTTERER,
Elizabeth, 67
Gottlieb, 67
John Frederick,
67, 128
SCHLOTTMAN, Anna
Barbara, 4
George, 129

SCHLY, Barbara, 16
SCHMALTZ,
Catherine, 50
Elizabeth, 30,
116
Henry, 17, 30,
50, 72, 78
John Henry, 116
Margaret, 17,
30, 50, 72
Margaret
Philippina, 72
Maria Margaret,
130
Maria Sophia,
17, 127
Sarah, 147
Widow, 1
SCHMALWOD,
Catherine, 27
Peter, 27
Sarah, 27
SCHMALWOOD,
Catherine, 67
Magdalene, 67
Peter, 67
SCHMEILE, Maria,
23
William, 23
SCHMELTZ,
Reinhard, 74
SCHMID, Adam, 80
Barbara, 159
Catharine, 142,
150
Charlotte, 158
Christopher, 157
Elizabeth, 157,
158
Elizabeth
Charlotte, 141
Frederick, 145,
160
George, 80, 83,
151
Gottfr. Ernst,
74
Henry, 157, 158,
160
John, 159
John Henry, 83
Joseph, 159
Joshua, 157
M. Gertrude, 163
Margaret, 143,
157, 160, 163

Maria, 83, 148,
157
Martha, 151
Michael, 153
Philp, 146
Salome, 145
William, 142
SCHMIDT, Abraham,
12
Ann Catherine,
45
Anna, 45
Anna Catharine,
102
Anna Dorothy, 90
Anna Margaret,
50
Anna Maria, 26,
30, 45, 46, 87,
97
Barbara, 26, 48,
90
Catharine, 76,
101, 102, 111
Catherine, 5,
34, 48
Charlotte, 91
Christine, 8,
46, 48
Christine
Margaret, 91
Christopher, 45,
52, 64, 91,
121, 122
Conrad, 3, 26,
30, 46, 125,
139
David, 102
Eleonore, 48
Elizabeth, 10,
18, 35, 38, 45,
48, 60, 85, 90,
91, 93, 102,
130, 133
Elizabeth
Catherine, 21
Elizabeth
Charlotte, 117
Fanny Bower, 43
Fred., 48
Frederick, 48,
49, 102, 111
George, 6, 35,
45, 60, 102,
126, 132
George Henry, 46

Hannah, 26, 102,
136
Henry, 2, 11,
18, 75, 91, 111
Jacob, 50, 75,
87, 97, 106,
119, 130
John, 7, 21, 26,
30, 46, 48, 74,
111, 136, 162
John Conrad, 30
John George, 85,
101
John Henry, 38,
45
John Jacob, 34
Joseph, 90, 105
M. Magdalene,
162
Magdalene, 106
Marcus, 9
Margaret, 18,
21, 30, 43, 46,
90, 101, 117
Maria, 91, 121
Maria Barbara,
30, 105
Maria Catherine,
60
Mary, 13
Mary Magdalene,
105
Peggy, 91
Peter, 69, 93
Philip, 121
Samuel, 111
Sarah, 74, 122
Valentine, 23,
102
William, 28, 31,
36, 48, 62, 75,
76, 90, 101,
117
SCHMIT, Elizabeth,
2, 89
James, 89
Janne, 89
SCHMITH, Anna
Maria, 17, 22,
23, 56
Catherine, 41
Conrad, 17, 23,
56
Henry, 41
James, 15

John Conrad, 23,
56
SCHMITT, Ann, 89
Anna Maria, 75
Elizabeth, 2
Margaret, 73
SCHMOLTZ,
Catharine, 101
Reinhardt, 101
SCHNACK, Albertus,
81
SCHNDIDER,
Catherine, 66
SCHNECK,
Elizabeth, 12
SCHNEDER, Maria,
176
SCHNEIDER, A.
Maria, 163
Agnes, 158
Anna, 49, 63, 78
Barbara, 11, 17,
23, 49, 140
Benedict, 116
Catharine, 87,
101, 106, 163
Catherine, 13,
37, 54, 71
Christian, 19,
32
Daniel, 27
Dorothy, 156
Elizabeth, 32,
64, 86, 105,
116, 122, 159
Frederick, 17,
23, 49, 140
Frederick A.,
152
Frederick
August, 158
George, 5, 54,
71, 83
Hannah, 27, 104
Henry, 82, 140,
159
Herman, 99, 120
Jacob, 7, 27,
63, 86, 105,
122, 130, 150,
158
John, 23, 78,
94, 106, 108,
116, 129, 138,
147, 158, 159

John Frederick,
163
John George,
106, 116, 138
John Jost, 163
John Just, 101
John Michael, 9
Joseph, 158
Krafft, 163
Ludwig, 159
M. Elizabeth,
163
M. Magdalene,
158
Magdalene, 31,
105
Margaret, 71,
94, 106, 108,
122, 159
Margaret Salome,
99
Maria, 4, 82, 116
Maria Elizabeth,
32
Maria Sophia, 17
Mary, 73
Mary Magdalene,
87
Michael, 17, 37
Peter, 66, 82,
87
Prudence, 99
Rosina, 90
Salome, 120
Sophia, 37, 159
Valentine, 90
William, 79, 99,
163
SCHNELL, Maria, 78
SCHNEYDER,
Archibald, 8
Christine, 98,
135
John, 135
SCHNIFF, Maria, 27
SCHNYDER, Agnes,
48
Anna Magdalene,
32
Catharine, 44
Catherine, 14,
17, 21, 26, 28,
35, 51
Christian, 6
Elizabeth, 23,
35

Eva, 34
George, 17, 26,
28, 35, 44
George Henry, 23
Jacob, 9, 10,
32, 35
John, 21, 34,
48, 51, 77
John Henry, 48
John Michael, 20
Magdalene, 11
Margaret, 4, 28,
37
Maria Elizabeth,
32
Michael, 6, 20,
26
Peter, 21, 44
Sophia, 20, 86
Susan, 26
Susanna, 91
SCHOBER, Barbara,
11
SCHOCH, Elizabeth,
164
George, 164
Jacob, 98
Margaret, 98
SCHOCK, Frederick,
145
SCHOEFF,
Elizabeth, 106,
121
Peter, 106, 121
SCHOELLER,
Christian, 24
Conrad, 24
Maria, 128
Maria Catherine,
24
Maria Elizabeth,
7, 24
Peter, 6
SCHOEN, Anna
Margaret, 95
Casper, 15, 45,
95
Christian, 118
George, 121
Margaret, 15,
45, 118, 150
Maria, 121
Martha, 12
Susanna, 118
SCHOF, Elizabeth,
142

SCHOHWALTER,
  Andrew, 68
  Dorothea, 68
  Jacob, 68
SCHOLL, Andrew, 11
  Anna, 68, 81,
    114
  Catharine, 74
  Conrad, 10, 68,
    114
  John
    Christopher, 68
  John George, 114
  Reinhardt, 79
SCHOLLE, Anna, 97
  Anna Maria, 30
  Conrad, 97
  Jacob, 97
  John Conrad, 30
  John Henry, 30
SCHOLLER,
  Christian, 5
  Christopher, 17
  Elizabeth, 17
  Frederick, 17
SCHOMO, Bernard,
    46
  Julianna, 46
SCHOPP, Helena, 77
SCHOUT, Christian,
    63
SCHREIBER, Anna
  Margaret, 3, 19
  Barbara, 81
  Jacob, 1
  John, 139
  John George, 158
  John Peter, 5,
    28, 115
  John William,
    57, 125
  Magdalene, 21
  Maria, 65, 75
  Mary Magdalene,
    19, 23, 28, 70
  Peter, 19, 21,
    23, 28, 57, 70,
    77, 158
  Sarah, 115, 158
SCHREIER, Anna
  Maria, 8
  George, 77
SCHREINER, A.
  Maria, 161
  Anna Catharine,
    97

Anna Maria, 113,
  170, 183
Catherine, 1
Charles William,
  86
Charlotte, 3
Chrisopher, 66
Christopher, 53,
  58, 69, 73, 79,
  83, 86, 97,
  114; 135, 141,
  161
Dorothea, 66
Elizabeth, 39,
  52, 53, 58, 66,
  67, 69, 86, 97,
  101, 107, 108,
  114, 118, 141,
  144, 166, 173,
  183
Frederick, 57,
  166
George, 114, 170
Henry, 52
Jacob, 12, 39,
  52, 66, 67, 76,
  96, 101, 107,
  108, 118, 140,
  161, 173
John, 77, 113,
  161, 183
John William,
  113
Joseph, 108
Ludwig, 53
Maria, 43, 125
Maria Elizabeth,
  135
Mary, 76
Nicholas, 43,
  69, 127
Philip, 8
Rebecca, 96
Sarah, 39
Susanna, 161,
  166
William, 43, 58,
  67, 96, 126,
  128, 147
SCHREIT,
  Elizabeth, 61,
    131
  Ludwig, 61
  Philip, 61, 131
SCHROEPEL,
  Catherine, 64

George, 64
SCHRUB, Eva, 31
  Frederick Jacob,
    31
  Henry, 31
SCHUBART, Maria,
    76
SCHUBBARTH, Jacob,
    25
SCHUBERT,
  Christine, 17
  Christopher, 17,
    126
  David, 17
  Elizabeth, 17
  George, 167
  John, 167
  Maria, 17
SCHUCHART, Anna
  Barbara, 105
  Barbara, 167
  Louisa, 105
  P., 167
  Simon, 105, 167
SCHUCHERT,
  Barbara, 20
  Elizabeth, 20
  Simon, 20
SCHUCHHARD,
  Barbara, 86
  Simon, 86
SCHUCK, Anna
  Maria, 90
  Catharine, 78,
    96
  Catherine, 72
  George, 147
  Henry, 7, 90
  John, 127
  John George, 4
  John Jacob, 4
  John Peter, 96,
    134
  Peter, 72, 96,
    134
  Philip, 12
  Susanna, 72
SCHUCKARD,
  Catherine, 59
  John, 59
  Maria, 59
SCHUCKARDT, Simon,
    133
SCHUCKART,
  Barbara, 182
  Maria, 182

Simon, 182
SCHUCKER, John,
149
SCHUCKHARD,
Barbara, 36
John, 41
John George, 36
Maria, 41
Simon, 36
SCHUESSLER,
Lorentz, 78
SCHUETTEL, Daniel,
109
Elizabeth, 109
John, 109
SCHUETZ, Barbara,
115
Christian, 105
John, 129
Juliana, 115
Mary Magdalene,
105
Matthew, 115
SCHUF, Maria, 76
SCHUG, Catherine,
3, 55
John, 55
Peter, 55
SCHUH, Anna
Margaret, 29
Catherine, 29
Jacob, 29
Margaret, 7
SCHUHL, Widow, 2
SCHUHLER,
Elizabeth, 37,
58
Jacob, 37, 58
William, 6
SCHUHLIN,
Margaret, 1
SCHULER,
Catherine, 5
Elizabeth, 107,
167
Jacob, 107
SCHULTE, George, 7
SCHULTES, Martin,
7
SCHULTZ, Anna
Catherine, 61
Caroline, 64
Catharine, 98
Catherine, 41,
55, 67
Charlotte, 45

Christian
William, 6
Christiana
Dorothea, 45
Elizabeth, 27,
55, 60, 125
George, 16, 26,
35, 60, 98
Henry, 98
Jacob, 35, 45
John, 37
John
Christopher, 27
John Gabriel, 98
John George, 8,
41
Julianna, 67
Martin, 26
Nicholas, 12,
16, 41, 55, 61,
64, 67, 98
Susanna, 16, 26,
35, 60
SCHUMACHER,
Elizabeth, 29,
75
Margaret, 14, 32
Michael, 29
Philip, 7, 29
SCHURSLER,
Christine, 137
Godfrey, 137
SCHUSSLER, Regina,
74
SCHUSTER, Andrew,
11
Casper, 8
Catharine, 95
Catherine, 50,
66
Daniel, 138
Frederick, 50,
132
Gottfried, 8
Jacob, 168
Leonard, 14
Margaret, 37
Maria, 95, 132,
138
Maria Elizabeth,
6
Martin, 13, 50,
66, 95, 129,
132
Mary, 168
Paul, 37

SCHUTEIS, John,
159
M. Magdalene,
159
Margaret, 159
SCHUTTEL, John,
141
William, 141
SCHUTZ, Barbara,
58
Daniel, 22
Elizabeth, 70
George, 58
John, 58, 70, 73
Maria, 14, 58,
70, 81
SCHWAB, Catharine,
122
Jacob, 5
Lorentz, 36
Margaret, 76,
101
Maria, 36
SCHWAM, Elizabeth,
13
SCHWARTZ, Abigail,
31
Anna, 70, 150
Barbara, 24, 33,
50, 66, 94, 112
Eva, 112
Frederick, 31,
125
George, 40, 50,
78, 94, 112
Jacob, 66
John, 33, 66
John George, 24,
33
Joseph, 94
Maria, 80
Maria Catherine,
24
Mrs., 46
Rebecca, 11
SCHWEFEL, Anna
Margaret, 28
Jacob, 19, 28,
36, 55, 68
Maria Margaret,
19, 36, 55, 68
SCHWEFFEL,
Elizabeth, 123
Jacob, 123, 143
SCHWEICK,
Catharine, 80

SCHWEIGHAUSER,
John Jacob, 5
Margaret, 4
SCHWEITZER, John,
124
Valentine, 81
SCHWENCK, Bernard,
28, 43, 93, 113
Brnard, 60
Elizabeth, 93
John, 43
John Adam, 28
Magdalene, 60
Margaret, 28,
43, 60, 93, 113
Sarah, 113, 142
SCHWOB, Elizabeth,
78
Maria, 50, 123
Mr., 129
SCHWOP, Lawrence,
141
SCOTT, Alexander,
176
SEBOLD, Ann
Catherine, 50
Elizabeth, 50
Leonard, 50
SECKEL, Henry, 115
Sophia
Catharine, 115
SEDIBERT, Adam, 76
SEDLLER, Philip
Theod., 176
SEERIGHT, James,
80
SEFFERENG, Peter,
127
SEFFRAN, George,
127
SEHLER, Amelia, 28
Anna Margaret,
45
Anna Maria, 45
Catherine, 28,
63
Elizabeth, 63,
140
Frederick, 56,
126
George, 60
Jacob, 28, 42,
45, 60, 63
John, 28, 56, 63
Margaret, 42, 63

Maria, 1, 60,
63, 128
Susanna, 56
Thomas, 42
SEHNN, Henry, 78
SEIBER, John
George, 122
SEIBERHOLT,
George, 48
Maria, 48
SEIBERT, Conrad,
109
Henry, 80
Maria Christine,
106, 109
Sarah, 74
SEIDEL, Anna, 112
Catherine, 35
John, 49
Julianna, 49
Michael, 35, 51
SEIFFER, Eliza,
167
Fred, 167
SEIFFERT,
Catherine, 57
Maria, 94
Michael, 57
Sam, 128
SEIFFERTH, John
Adam, 28
SEILER, Ammi, 111
Anna, 98
Anna Maria, 101
Henry, 80
Jacob, 87, 101
John, 73
Lydia, 98, 132
Margaret, 111
Mary Magdalene,
87
Matthew, 98
Matthias, 111,
132
Sarah Elizabeth,
87
SEIPERT, Conrad,
93
Maria, 93
SEITZ, Adam, 131
Anna, 131
Charles, 21, 28,
40, 58, 95
Charlotte, 28,
40, 58, 95, 123

Elizabeth, 40,
123
George, 123
Sibylla, 28, 150
SEIVERT,
Christine, 136
SELL, Andrew, 174
Elizabeth, 62,
174
Henry, 62, 73
Maria, 62, 174
Solomon, 174
William, 174
SELLER, Anna
Catharine, 167
Jacob, 167
Maria, 167
SELLERS,
Elizabeth, 85,
182
Hannah, 10
Jacob, 182
Maria, 182
Sarah, 14
SELTENREICH,
David, 12
SENDERIK,
Christine, 75
SENFT, Elizabeth,
10
SENN, Henry, 148
John Jacob, 5
SENS, Joseph, 52
Maria, 52
SERICHE, M., 173
SETHEN, Catharine,
111
Edward, 111
SEYFERHELD,
Christine
Elizabeth, 25
John George, 25
SHAFLEY, Joseph,
75
SHALLUS,
Elizabeth, 109
Harriet, 109
Henrietta, 109
Jacob, 109
William August,
109
SHAMBOUGH, Joseph,
12
SHARD, Christian
E., 91

SHARKY, Elizabeth,
73
SHARP, Mary, 82
SHAUGH, Richard,
73
SHAW, Albertus, 96
Ezekiel, 96
Jemimah, 96
SHEA, Daniel, 10
SHEIBLE, George,
32
SHELLER, George
Conrad, 171
Henry, 171, 178
Jacob, 178
Susanna, 171,
178
SHEPARD,
Catherine, 12
SHEPPARD, James,
148
SHERIDAN, Abraham,
61, 100, 127,
133
Barbara, 61, 100
Elizabeth, 133
Paul, 10
Thomas, 61
SHERRER, Barbara,
84
SHERRIDAN,
Abraham, 56
Barbara, 56
SHETTLEIN,
Barbara, 174
John, 174
SHILLINGFORD,
Jacob, 156
Rosina, 156
Thomas, 156
SHIMER, Elizabeth,
171
Jacob, 171
Molly, 171
SHIMPELMAN, Jacob,
10
SHLOTTERY,
William, 74
SHMALLWOOD,
Catherine, 47
John, 47
Peter, 47
SHMALWOOD, Maria,
127
SHONE, John, 74

SHRUNK, Bernard,
166
Elizabeth, 166
Eloisa, 166
SHULL, Barbara,
177
Conrad, 177
SHULLER, George
William, 180
John, 180
Maria, 180
SHUMACHER,
Catherine, 51
Elizabeth, 51
Henry, 84
Michael, 51
SICKMAN, Michael,
138
SIEBERICK, Anna
Maria, 80
SIEBLE, Anna, 70
Jacob, 70
Wilhelmina, 70
SIEGMUND,
Catharine, 122,
123
Jacob, 76, 122,
123
Michael, 122,
123
SIGMAN, Carolina,
108
Jacob, 108
SIGMON, Catharine,
181
Jacob, 181
Samuel, 181
SIGMUND,
Catharine, 159,
169
Jacob, 159, 169
John, 169
Margaret, 148,
151
Maria, 159
SILVIUS, Casper,
140
SIMON, A. Maria,
152
Anna Maria, 3,
18, 121
Bernard, 22, 31
Casper, 134
Catharine, 121
Catherine, 70

Christine, 15,
22, 31, 53, 69,
108
Daniel, 121
David, 53
Elizabeth, 15,
18, 25, 91
George, 25, 152
John, 2, 3, 22,
53, 69, 70, 91,
134
John Bernard,
15, 108
Maria, 108
Philip, 67
Samuel, 69
Walrab, 15, 18
William, 7, 31
Wilrab, 25
SIMONS, Henrietta,
82
SIMPSON,
elizabeth, 80
John, 160
Margaret, 160
Susanna, 160
SINCER, Anna
Margaret, 24
SINCK, Catharine,
122, 150, 162
Christian, 152
Christine, 83
Jacob, 83, 162,
177
John, 122
M. Mary, 177
Susanna, 80
William, 177
SING, Andrew, 69
Catharine, 91
Catherine, 54,
69
Elizabeth, 91
Jacob, 54, 69
John, 91
John
Christopher, 54
SINK, Abraham, 185
Carl, 178
Eleonor, 185
Elizabeth, 181
Jacob, 181
John, 181
SINNIFF,
Elizabeth, 84
SINSFELD, John, 79

SIXKEL, Henry, 85
  Sophia, 85
SKINNER,
  Elizabeth, 60,
  88, 118, 159
  Gertrude, 182
  John, 118
  John George, 182
  Joseph, 182
  Margaret, 60
  Mary, 74
  Reinhardt, 101
  William, 60, 73,
  88, 101, 118,
  153, 159
SKREIMES, John, 12
SLATTER, Elizabeth
  M., 183
SLEMER, Hannah,
  171
  Jacob, 171
  Susanna, 171
SLEMMER, Hannah,
  123
  Jacob, 123
  Matthew, 123
SLESMAN, Peter, 82
SLICE, Daniel
  Vander, 177
  Mary, 177
  Thomas
  Jefferson, 177
SLIDE, William, 15
SLIZE, Daniel, 166
  Daniel Vonder,
  166
  Elizabeth, 166
  George, 166
  George Vonder,
  166
  Margaret, 166
SLOW, Elizabeth,
  175
SMALLWOOD, Isac,
  14
  Joseph, 13
  Manly, 14
SMID, M., 175
SMIDT, Jacob, 176
  Maria Catharine,
  176
  Maria Margaret,
  176
SMITH, ---, 84
  Catharine, 168,
  175, 179

Christine, 170,
  171
Christopher, 170
Eleonora, 162
Elizabeth, 109,
  162, 165, 167,
  176
George, 109, 167
H., 168
Henry, 179
J. William, 170
Jacob, 165, 175
John, 84, 176
John George, 175
John Jacob, 179
John Ludwig,
  170, 171
John William,
  171
M. Catharine,
  175
Margaret, 81,
  84, 109, 172
Maria, 109, 165,
  170
Matthias, 172
Melia, 84
Patrick, 162
Peter, 170
Polly, 175
Rebecca, 176
Sarah, 165
W. E., 178
Wilheme, 84
William, 172
SNEIDER, Jacob,
  167
  John, 167
SNIDER, Anna
  Isabella, 183
  Catharine, 85,
  183
  Christine, 168,
  177, 181
  Elizabeth, 182,
  183
  Ernst, 84
  Hannah, 177
  Henry, 182
  John, 153, 172,
  173, 183, 185
  L., 181
  Ludwig, 168, 177
  M. Margaret, 172
  Margaret, 168
  Maria, 185

Michael, 183
  Rebecca, 173
SNYDER, Catharine,
  177
  Dolly, 84
  Elizabeth, 174
  George, 174
  Jacob, 178
  John, 165, 174
  John Ebert, 175
  Krafft, 175
  Louisa, 178
  Ludwig, 178
  M. Elizabeth,
  175, 178
  Magdalene, 168
  Maria, 174
  Sarah, 165
  William, 168,
  177
SOCKEL, Elizabeth,
  19
  Joseph, 19
  Susanna, 19
SOELLER, Ludwig,
  176
SOEST, Catharine,
  54
  Elizabeth, 54
  Henry, 54
  John Henry, 6
  Philip, 54
SOLCHER,
  Christian, 64
SOLIDAY, M.
  Magdalene, 173
  Sebastian, 173
SOLOMON, Henry, 72
SOMINI, Magdalene,
  133
SOMMERKAMP,
  Philip, 86
SOMMERS, Henry, 84
SONLEDER, Maria,
  70
  Peter, 70
SOPHIA, 28
SORCK, Jacob, 77
SORECK, Maria, 19
SORG, Ann Maria,
  76
  Anna Maria, 117
  Barbara, 167
  Elizabeth, 167
  G., 167
  Maria, 160

Simon, 81
Valentine, 117
SOUDER, Anna
Margaret, 95
Casper, 10, 15,
16
Catharine, 95,
114
Catherine, 6,
13, 15, 44, 45,
63
Charles, 44
Eleonora, 44
Elizabeth, 63
Elizabeth
Louisa, 114
Gottfried, 15
Jacob, 74
John, 9, 15, 45,
63, 95, 114
John Jacob, 17
John Michael, 45
Joseph, 44
Margaret, 15,
17, 37, 44
Mary, 175
Peter, 17, 37
Philip, 62
Sarah Anna, 44
Wilhelmina, 15,
16
William, 44
SOUDERN, Casper,
46
John, 46
Wilhelmina, 46
SOUER, Catherine,
62
SOUERMAN, Martin, 75
SOUTER, Catherine,
72
Edward, 72
Maria, 72
SOUTHAM,
Catherine, 10
SOYER, Abraham, 37
Apollonia, 115
Eva Elizabeth,
115
Gottfried, 115
SPADE, William, 14
SPAET, John, 55,
66
Philippina, 66
Sarah, 55, 88
Susanna, 88

Wilhelmina, 146
William, 55, 66,
88, 128
SPAETH, Hannah,
105
Henry, 134
John, 105, 134
Philippina, 105
Samuel, 144
Susanna, 131
William, 131
SPALTER, Catharine
Barbara, 93,
94, 137
Charles Ludwig,
6
Elizabeth, 41,
46, 64, 68, 93,
94
George, 68
John, 41, 46,
64, 68, 93, 94,
137
SPANGENBER,
Charlotte, 162
John, 162
Michael, 162
SPANGENBERG, ---,
125
Barbara, 92, 114
Catharine, 114
Charlotte, 180
Conrad, 9, 21,
38, 92, 114,
131, 137
Elizabeth, 1,
21, 38
Frederick, 92,
131, 137
John, 180
John George, 21
John Michael,
152
Mr., 9
SPANGENBERGER,
Barbara, 104
Conrad, 104
George
Frederick, 104
John, 82
SPANNENBERG,
George, 84
SPATH, Sarah, 99
Susanna, 99
William, 99

SPATZ, Elizabeth,
78
SPECHT, Ann
Margaret, 71
John George, 71
SPENGLER,
Catharine, 80
Peter, 57
SPETH, Anna Maria,
109
Henry, 109
Philip Jacob,
109
SPETZROLER, A. M.,
163
SPIELHOFFER,
Maria, 87
Rudolph, 87
SPIES, Elizabeth,
153
George, 176
SPILLENBERG,
Cath., 51
SPORN, Johanna
Catharine, 82
SPRINGER,
Catharine
Barbara, 126
SPROHL, Andrew,
162
Elizabeth, 162
Hannah, 162
SPROSON, John, 15
SQUARE, Alexander,
75
SSPROHL, Andrew,
83
STAAD, ---, 138
Nicholas, 138
STAADT, Barbara,
121
Esther, 121
Nicholas, 121
William, 121
STAATS, Jacob, 30
Jacobus, 68
Maria, 68
Martha, 30
Peter, 68
Rachel, 68
Rchel, 30
Sarah, 68
STADEMAN, Susanna,
63
STADT, Barbara,
121

Esther, 121
Nicholas, 121
William, 121
STAER, Charles, 68
Garret Hawes, 68
Susanna, 68
STAERINGER, Anna
Maria, 70
Justus, 70
STAGGART, Sarah,
13
STAHL, Catharine,
96
Christian, 73,
96, 131, 133
Elizabeth, 65
John, 65
John Michael,
96, 131
STAMM, Elizabeth,
77
John Rudolph,
81, 163
Louisa
Elizabeth, 163
Maria, 163
STANG, Antoinetta,
176
John Rudolph,
176
Maria, 176
STANLEY, John,
143, 145
STANLY, Maria, 111
STANTON, Jemima,
81
STARCK, Andrew, 73
STAT---, John, 165
STATELMAN,
Catharine, 180
John, 180
Susanna, 77
STATH, Esther, 149
STATS, Abraham,
18, 109
Demar, 18
Isaac, 18
Jacob, 109, 114
James, 10, 92
Jemimah, 92
John George, 43
Rachel, 92, 109,
114
STATTLER,
Catharine, 79

STAUD, Anna Maria,
118
John, 118
STAUFFER, Esther,
83
STAUT, Anna Maria,
110
George Peter,
110
John Leonard,
110
Margaret, 147
STAYGER, Hannah,
15
STECKER, Bernard,
16
David, 16
STEEL, Catherine,
55
Elizabeth, 146
George, 119
Henrietta, 55
James, 12, 55
John, 11, 119
Maria, 119
STEEMEL,
Elizabeth, 154
STEFFEN,
Catherine, 48
Christine
Barbara, 48
George, 48
STEIBER,
Catherine, 15
Magdalene, 28,
48
Michael, 28, 48
William, 28
STEIGER,
Catherine, 17,
36
Conrad, 10, 36
John Conrad, 17
Mary, 13
STEIN, Adam, 136,
172
Catharine, 172
Eleonora, 93
Gratia, 93
John, 89, 93
Magdalene, 89
Maria, 87, 172
William, 87, 140
STEINBACH, Anna,
41
John, 41

STEINBRECHER, John
Gottlieb, 116
Maria Catharine,
116
STEINER, Andrew, 170
Catharine, 170
Elizabeth, 27,
71
Frederick, 42,
94, 111
Jacob, 111
John, 27, 71
John Adam, 10,
27
John Conrad, 93
Malchior, 93
Maria, 42, 94,
111
Mary Magdalene,
71
Melchior, 42, 76
Philippina, 99
Sam, 124
Samuel, 42
Susanna, 76
Wilhelmina, 80
STEINFURTH, Maria,
30
STEINHAUER,
Barbara, 26
Elizabeth, 44,
62, 86, 128
Francis Rowles,
86
George, 44
George William,
44, 62, 79, 86
Michael, 26
STEINHEISER,
Christine, 111
Peter, 111
STEINMETZ, Anna,
161
Anna Maria, 128
Elizabeth, 28
J. Conrad, 161
Jacob, 18, 28,
50, 93, 130
Jane, 147
John, 112, 149
Margaret, 64
Maria, 50, 112,
130, 161
Mrs., 37
Priscilla, 112

Rachel, 18, 28,
  50, 93, 130
William, 18
STELEKOM, Anna
  Maria, 40
Simon, 40
STELLWAGEN, Carl,
  101
Daniel, 82
John, 101, 115,
  140
Margaret, 101,
  115
Maria Anna, 115
STELTZ, Anna
  Julianna, 90
Catherine, 35
Elizabeth, 35,
  46, 57, 90
John, 35, 46,
  57, 90
Margaret, 46, 74
STENTLY, Anna
  Maria, 102
John, 102
Susanna, 102
STEPFEN, Mary
  Elizabeth, 88
Sophia, 88
William, 88
STEPHAN, Catherine
  Barbara, 33
Christine
  Margaret, 33
John George, 33
STEPHEN,
  Catherine, 66
George, 66
John, 66
STERDIGER, Justus,
  49
Maria, 49
Sophia, 49
STERN, Catharine,
  85, 91
Catherine, 19,
  22, 54, 56
Elizabeth, 56
Johanna
  Solomome, 91
Margaret, 38
Maria Cathrine,
  22
Martin, 8
Samuel, 22, 38,
  56, 91

Sarah Catherine,
  38
Thomasina Maria,
  91
STERTSEBACH, John,
  175
Margaret, 175
Samuel, 175
STETZEBACH,
  Margaret, 161
STETZENBACH, John,
  162
Margaret, 143,
  162
STETZER,
  Catherine, 44
Catherine
  Frederica, 28
Catherine
  Friderica, 46
David, 28, 46,
  47
Elizabeth, 5,
  28, 34, 46, 47
Henry, 28, 44
John, 21, 28, 34
John William, 14
Margaret
  Elizabeth, 21
Maria, 28, 34,
  44
Maria Elizabeth,
  8, 21, 28
Martha, 56
Peter, 56
William, 56
STEUERWALD, Anna,
  25
Margaret, 75
Maria, 53
Mary, 10
Susanna, 15
STEWARD, Robert,
  13
STEWART, Charles,
  82
James, 120
Johanna, 83
John, 83
STEY, Elizabeth,
  135
Peter, 135
STEZENBACH,
  Elizabeth, 80
STICKJES, Anna, 80

STIEFFERS,
  Catherine, 26
John, 26
Susanna, 26
STIEL, Catharine,
  93
James, 93
Joseph, 3
Louise, 3
STILES, Priscilla,
  14
STILLWAGEN, Anna,
  1, 16
Daniel, 180
Elizabeth, 12,
  16, 27, 28, 76
John, 9, 66, 85
Margaret, 66, 85
Maria, 3, 180
Rebecca, 180
Sophia Maria, 85
Valentine, 1,
  16, 66
STIMEL, Catharine,
  129
J., 170
Sophia, 125
STIMMEL, Anna, 16,
  28, 34, 42, 58
Catherine
  Elizabeth, 42
Christine, 58
Elizabeth, 16,
  28, 86, 132
Hannah, 13, 86
Henry, 16
Letitia, 16
Margaret, 12
Matthias, 6
Nicholas, 16,
  28, 139, 142
Philip, 16, 28,
  34, 42, 58, 86,
  132
Sophia, 58
STOCKY, Elizabeth,
  39
Jacob, 16
STOERGER, Anna
  Maria, 111
Justus, 111, 133
Sophia, 133
STOEZER, William,
  136
STOFFER, Pliges, 9

STOLL, Adam, 10,
37, 119, 134,
155
Anna Elizabeth,
37
Anna Margaret,
94
Anna Maria, 54,
125
Christine, 33,
52, 54, 85
Christine
Elizabeth, 18
Elizabeth, 52,
94, 119, 155
Jacob, 78, 117
Jenny, 117
Johanna, 151
John, 94, 119
John Adam, 52
John William, 85
Juliana, 33
Ludwig, 155
Margaret, 134
Maria Elizabeth,
37
Maria Margaret,
18
William, 7, 18,
33, 54, 85
STOLTZ, Catherine,
16
Charles, 19, 51,
91
Christopher, 16
Conrad, 16, 151
Margaret, 19,
51, 91
Maria, 77
William, 79
STOO---, Justus,
157
Maria, 157
STORGER, Anna
Maria, 133
Justus, 133, 134
Margaret, 134
STORY, Anna, 32
Elizabeth, 32
Peter, 32
STOTTENWORK, Peter
Angel, 81
STOUD, Anna Maria,
90
George, 89, 90,
168

George Peter,
73, 90
Margaret, 168
Philip, 168
STOUDT, Barbara,
63
Elizabeth, 50,
74
John Peter, 63
STOWER, Anna, 185
Elizabeth, 185
John, 185
STOY, Daniel, 32
Elizabeth, 32
Mrs., 123
STOZELBACH, John,
109
Margaret, 109
Michael, 109
STRAUCH, Maria
Barbara, 86
STRAUSS, Barbara,
55
STREEPER, Dorothy,
15
STREETON, George,
10
STREHLEY, Maria,
25
STREIT, John, 125
STREITH,
Catherine, 52
John, 52
John George, 12
Mary Magdalene,
52
STREMAN,
Catharine, 181
STREMBECK, Jacob,
88
Maria, 88
STREMEL,
Catharine, 84,
175
John George, 175
Richard, 175
STRIBE, Christine,
45
Jacob, 45
STRIBEL, Casper,
105
Catharine, 105
STRIBY, Adam, 41
Christine, 63
Dorothy, 41
Jacob, 63

John Adam, 52
STRICKER, Adam,
22, 33, 65, 89,
107
Anna, 150
Anna Cathrine,
89
Barbara, 22, 33,
65, 89, 107
Daniel, 22
Elizabeth, 33,
98, 161
George, 55
Hannah, 1
John, 14, 55,
58, 66, 104,
133, 161
Maria, 104
Peter, 98
Rudolph, 65, 127
Sarah, 55, 58,
66, 104, 153,
161
Veronica, 66
STRIEKER, George,
126
STRIMEL, John
Frederick, 178
John H., 178
STROHAUER, George,
116
Margaret, 116
Maria, 116
STROHHAUER,
George, 100,
152
Jacob, 100
Margaret, 100
STROHMANN,
Elizabeth, 80
STROHOUER, George,
165
Maria, 165
STROUD, Henry, 12
STRUB, Carl, 156
Catharine, 43
Henry, 43, 156
John, 39
Maria, 43
Susanna, 43, 156
STRUBLY, Margaret,
72
STRUMBECK, Anna
Maria, 34
Jacob, 34

STRUP, Elizabeth,
1
Henry, 22, 65,
101
John, 1, 101
Susanna, 22, 65,
101
STRUPP, Henry, 154
John George, 154
Susanna, 154
STRUPT, Catharine,
77
STUART, Elizabeth,
113
George, 86
John William,
113
Peter Nella, 86
Petronella, 86
William, 113
STUBER, Adam, 113
Elizabeth, 162
Henry, 113
John, 70, 92,
127
John Jacob, 92
Maria, 113
Veronica, 70, 92
STUBERT,
Elizabeth, 82,
148
John, 151
Mary, 11
STUCKI, Jacob, 128
Maria, 14, 143
STUCKY, Catharine,
89
Elizabeth, 73
Jacob, 58
Margaret, 58,
146
Maria, 145
STUERTZ, Margaret,
13
STUMB, Magdalene,
151
STUMPF, John, 160,
168
Magdalene, 160,
168
William, 168
STURMFELDT,
Margaret, 104
Paul, 104
Sarah, 104

STURMFELS, Anna
Margaret, 29,
89
George, 61
John Geo., 29
John George, 34,
127
Margaret, 34,
61, 121
Maria, 121
Maria Cathrine,
89
Paul, 61, 89,
121
STURTZEBACH,
Elizabeth, 65
John, 39, 65, 74
Margaret, 65
STUTERE,
Elizabeth, 164
Gottlieb, 164
Samuel, 164
SULLIVAN, Maria,
15
SULTZBACH,
Elizabeth, 46
Joseph, 46
SUMMERS,
Catherine, 13
SUMNEY, Isaac, 1
SUNEBER, George,
170
Maria, 170
Philippina, 170
SUPPER, Sarah, 11
SURZEBACH, John,
91
Margaret, 91
Maria, 91
SUTER, John, 11
Maria, 143
SUTHER, Abba
Catharine, 137
Anna, 101
Daniel, 137
Henry, 101
SUTTEN, Catherine,
49
Edward, 49
Robert, 49
Susanna, 14
SUTTER, Anna, 22,
43
Anna Catharine,
85, 89, 104

Anna Catherine,
27, 34, 43, 50,
63, 67
Charles John, 85
Daniel, 22, 27,
34, 43, 50, 58,
63, 67, 80, 85,
89, 104, 117,
123, 105
Eva Catherine,
58
Joseph William,
104
Samuel, 58
William, 27
SWARTZ, Barbara,
174
George, 174
Samuel, 174
SWEIS, Anna
Catharine, 180
John, 180
Margaret, 180
SWENCK, B., 169
J. Bernard, 169
SWOOP, Maria, 73
SYBELLA, Jacob,
177
John, 177
Wilhelme, 177
SYSERHELT,
Christine
Elizabeth, 33
John George, 33

-T-
TABER, John
Ludwig, 75
TAG, Jacob, 81
TAGGART,
Catherine, 57
David, 57
Robert, 57
TARDY, Adeline,
162
Alexander, 162
Catharine, 162
TARTER, Margaret,
63
Maria Margaret,
63
Samuel, 63
TATE, Catharine,
177
James, 83, 177
Mary Nancy, 177

TAUBERMAN,
  Elizabeth, 163
  Jacob, 163
  Susanna, 163
TAUBSTRICH,
  Balthasar, 65
TAUENHEIM,
  Catharine, 83
  John, 19, 37,
    100, 124
  John Jacob, 5
  John Philip, 8
  Mary Magdalene,
    19, 37, 100
TAUER, John
  George, 81
TAUPE, Dorothy,
  169
  J., 169
TAUSCHEMER,
  Andrew, 83
TAXES, Catharine,
  114
  Frederick, 92,
    114
TAYLOR, Henry, 169
  Mary, 77, 169
TEDDERS, SHannah,
  10
TEHNER, John
  Felix, 125
TEILOTZ, John
  Casper, 13
TEISS, Henry, 138
  Jacob, 138
TEMPER, William, 3
TENNER, Catharine,
  91
  Elizabeth, 92
  Felix, 49
  Henry, 92
  John Peter, 91
  Magdalene, 92
  Maria Eva, 49
  Peter, 91
TEPES, Henry, 75
TEPPENBORTH,
  Catharine, 105
  Nicholas, 105
TERLE, Elizabeth,
  93
  William, 93
TESSLE, Catharine,
  82
TESTON, A. Maria,
  162

Hannah, 162
Richard, 162
TETHERS, Jacobus,
  76
TEUERING,
  Matthias, 5
THEIS, Andrew, 5
  Dorothea, 25, 39
  Elizabeth, 89
  Fred, 89
  Jacob, 25, 39
  Maria, 89
  Theresa, 15
THEISS, Anna
  Dorothy, 90
  Catherine, 70
  Elizabeth, 148
  George, 1
  Henry, 70
  Jacob, 70, 90
THEOBALD, Henry,
  166
  Margaret, 166
THERRY, Elizabeth,
  26
  Magdalene, 1
THETZER, Thomas,
  128
THEYERS,
  Catherine, 34
  Margaret, 34
THIEL, Anna
  Catherine, 72
  Catherine, 54
  Frederick, 142
  Henry, 94
  Jacob, 54
  Jeremiah, 127
  John, 54, 72
  Maria, 94, 148,
    151
THIELEMAN, Anna,
  59
THIELMAN, Anna, 164
  Henry, 164
THIELMANN, Henry,
  151
THIES, Bernard,
  158
  Elizabeth, 158
  Frederick, 158
THOMAS, Ann, 76
  Deborah, 74
  Elizabeth, 163
  Ludwig, 80
  Marsey, 13

Peter, 82, 163
Peter May, 163
THOMSON, ---, 111
  Nancy, 111, 136
  Nelly, 111
  Rebecca, 14
  William, 136
THRESCHER,
  Catherine, 73
THRESHER, Anna
  Elizabeth, 63
THREYER, Maria, 13
  Peter, 54
THUYE, Catherine,
  14
TIESS, Daniel, 100
  Elizabeth, 100
  Frederick, 100
TILLIER, Rudolph,
  37
TIPPERT,
  Elizabeth, 125
TISCHONG, Anna
  Margaret, 37
  Anne Elizabeth,
    29
  Christian, 15,
    29, 49, 88
  Frederick, 23,
    37
  John Frederick,
    93
  Margaret, 23, 93
  Peter, 7, 15, 29
  Susa Louisa, 15
  Susanna, 29, 49
TISE, Anna Maria,
  84
TISS, Henry, 76
TITMAN, Catharine,
  169
TOER, Anna
  Catharine, 89
  Elizabeth, 89
  Henry, 89
TOMBLENSON,
  Phoebe, 78
TOPLIFT, Sarah, 10
TORTER, Samuel, 74
TOTH, Elizabeth,
  85
  Lawrence, 85
  Maria Catharine,
    85
TOTHAM, John, 72
  Maria, 72

Susanna, 72
TOY, Elias, 83
TRANGENSTEIN,
    Elizabeth
    Maria, 183
    John, 183
    Maria, 183
TRAUB, Margaret, 151
TRAUT, Catharine,
    77
    John, 80
TRAUTMAN, Mr., 7
TREMMER,
    Christine, 101
    Francis, 101
    Maria, 101
    Susanna, 101
TREMPER,
    Elizabeth, 170
    Henry, 170
    William, 170
TRIMBER,
    Elizabeth, 155
    Henry, 155
    M. Margaret, 155
TRIMBLE, James, 11
TRIMMER, Anna
    Catherine, 61
    Chresella, 61
    Francis, 61
TRIMMLER, Griseli,
    145
TRIMPER,
    Elizabeth, 118
    Henry, 77, 118
    John, 118
TRIPOLET,
    Charlotte, 146
TRIPPEL, Eva, 81
TROEMNER, Francis
    William, 12
TROLL, Fred, 183
    Frederick, 84
    Polly, 183
    Wilhelmina, 183
TROLLINGER, Eva,
    79
TRONNER,
    Chressaly, 33
    Francis William,
    33
TROUT, Barbara,
    176
    Charles, 176
    M. Sophia, 176

TROUTMAN,
    Christian, 15
    George
    Christian, 15
TROUTWEIN, Maria,
    56
    William, 56
TRUBER, Elizabeth,
    84
TRUBILLY, Henry,
    55
    Margaret, 55
TRUM, A. Maria,
    145
TRUMP, Catharine,
    177
    George, 81
    Martin, 177
TSCHUDI, Sirach,
    13
TSCHUDY, Barbara,
    58, 75
    Elizabeth, 11
    Frederick, 12,
    64
    Nancy, 14
TUDOR, Catharine,
    181
    Elizabeth, 181
    Samuel, 181
TUES, Elizabeth,
    109
    Maria, 109
    Peter, 109
TUNIS, Benjamin,
    12
TURNER, Conrad,
    110
    David, 10
    George, 52
    John, 110
    Margaret, 52
TUSTIN, Hannah,
    182
    Rebecca, 182
    Richard, 182
TUSTON, John, 80
TUTTEL, John, 78
    Susanna, 135
TYL, Margaret, 112

-U-
UHLER, Andrew, 45
    Regina, 45
ULLER, George, 142

ULRICH, Abraham,
    184
    Henry, 184
    J., 184
    Margaret, 94
    Philip, 9
    Sarah, 184
    Valentine, 20,
    78, 81, 129
ULRICK, Fredeica,
    153
UMBACH, Elizabeth,
    21, 33, 45
    John George, 21
UMBACK, George, 4
UMBRISTER, John
    Mather, 114
    Maria, 114
UMRICHHAUS, Carl,
    155
    Maria, 155
    Peter, 155
UNBEREIT, Anthony,
    20
    Louisa, 20
UNGAR, Elizabeth,
    90
    John, 90
    Salome, 90
URLOB, Elizabeth
    Catharine, 142
URWEILER, Susanna,
    83
USS, Francis
    Joseph, 12
UTTRE, Catherine,
    57
    Jacob, 21, 28,
    57
    Maria, 28
    Mary Magdalene,
    21
    Veronica, 9

-V-
VAERNER, Maria,
    15, 19
    Michael, 15, 19
VALENTIN, Maria,
    80
    Rosina, 79
VAN CLEVE, Anna,
    150
VAN DER LOCHT,
    William, 41

VAN DER SCHLEUSS,
  Abigail, 101
  Anthony, 96
  Daniel, 101
  Elizabeth, 96
  Isaac, 96
  Phoebe, 101
VAN DER VOORDT,
  Sarah, 76
VAN DEREN, Esther,
  125
VAN DILGE,
  Elizabeth, 117
  John, 117
  Maria Catharine,
  117
VAN DILJE,
  Elizabeth, 100
  John, 100
  Maria Elizabeth,
  100
VAN ERDTEN,
  Christian, 2
VAN NETEN
  CHRISTOPHE,
  Lamberte, 174
VAN PHUL, Anna
  Catharine, 106
  Catharine, 96
  Graff, 96
  William, 96, 106
VAN SANT, Anna,
  148
VAN SCIVER,
  Susanna, 81
VAN VEEN, Aart, 81
VANDERSLICE,
  Elizabeth, 185
  George, 84
  L., 185
VEH, Elizabeth, 1
VEIT, Maria
  Magdalene, 82
VELBACH, Margaret
  Henrietta, 11
VELLBACH, Ernst,
  29
  Maria Elizabeth,
  29
VELTEN, A. Maria,
  159
VERFLAS, Anna
  Maria, 37
  Conrad, 37
VERGOUDEREN,
  Elizabeth, 73

VERLE, Elizabeth,
  68
VETTER, Ann
  Barbara, 54
  Anna Barbara,
  41, 96
  Catharine, 113
  Christian, 112
  Christopher, 96,
  154
  Hannah Barbara,
  105
  John, 105
  John
  Christopher, 41
VIAL, Annanias,
  135
  Daniel, 135
VIELMALTER,
  Catharine, 104
  Catherine, 64
  Jeremiah, 14,
  64, 104, 135
  Ludwig, 104, 135
VIELMATTER,
  Catherine, 46
  Jeremiah, 46
  Julianna, 46
VIELWALTER, Adam,
  117
  Catharine, 117
  Jeremiah, 117
VIRGIN, Maria, 10
VITALIS,
  Catharine, 166
  Elizabeth, 166
  P., 166
  Peter, 166
VOGEL, Barbara,
  103
  Dorothy, 103
  Elizabeth, 47,
  161
  George, 15
  Johanna Maria,
  161
  John, 47, 103
  Joseph, 161
  Maria, 15
VOLBACH, Maria, 18
VOLCK, A.
  Catharine, 155
  Andrew
  Christian, 110
  Anna, 153

Anna Catherine,
  59
  Catharine, 110
  Cordilla, 160
  Henry, 59, 110,
  155
  Jacob, 150
  John, 150
VOLCKRATH, John
  Philip, 75
VOLK, Peter, 138
  William David,
  138
VOLLBACK,
  Christine, 159
  Jacob, 159
  Solomon, 159
VOLWEILER,
  Barbara, 153
VOMHOFF, Anna
  Maria, 175
  John Christian,
  175
VON DER HALD,
  Oswald, 3
VON DER HALT,
  Elizabeth, 5,
  11, 76
VON DER LIND,
  John, 92
VON DER SCHLEIS,
  Adam, 89
  Andrew, 31
  Anthony, 1, 27,
  89, 154
  Catherine, 57
  Catherine
  Elizabeth, 27
  Daniel, 12, 41,
  57
  Elizabeth, 27,
  89, 154
  George, 154
  Henry, 17
  Jacob, 17, 31
  James, 41
  John, 154
  Maria, 17, 31
  Philippina, 41,
  57
  Samuel, 89
VON DER SCHLEISS,
  Anthony, 16
  Daniel, 85
  Elizabeth, 16
  John, 151

Joseph Henry, 85
Phoebe, 85
VON DER SCHLEUS,
Catharine, 146
VON DER SCHLEUSS,
Daniel, 78, 137
Philippina, 137
VON ERDEN, ---,
151
VON HOFF, John
Matthew, 147
VON OBSTRAND,
Wilhelma, 10
VON PHOST, Sarah,
105
William, 105
VON PHUL, A.
Catharine, 156
Catharine, 113
Catherine, 26,
39, 53, 73
Elizabeth, 113
George, 26
Henry, 39
Maria, 53
Philip, 73
Sarah, 26
William, 26, 39,
53, 73, 113,
156
VON RIED, Jacob,
25
Margaret, 25
VON WEH, Jonathan,
128
VON WEHT,
Elizabeth, 125
VON WEILER,
Andrew, 79
VON WILLER,
Andrew, 44
Catherine, 44
VONAGEN,
Elizabeth, 181
Paul, 181
William, 181
VULMAN, John, 109
Maria, 109

-W-

WAACKER,
Catharine, 134
John, 134
WAAS, Adam, 139
John Peter, 139

WAASEM,
Christopher,
115
Maria, 115
William, 115
WAASS, Adam, 140
Elizabeth, 140
WACK, Elizabeth,
31, 41, 51, 61
George, 41, 51,
61
Margaret, 14
Maria, 19
WACKER, Anna
Margaret, 45
John, 40, 45,
154
John William, 45
Margaret, 40
Mr., 154
Richard, 99
Susanna, 99
WACKEREN, Peggy,
126
WADLOW, Moses, 83
WAGENER, Adam, 25,
28, 44, 47, 65,
71
Catharine, 171,
185
Catharine
Friderica, 47
Catherine, 28,
44, 65
Catherine
Friderica, 71
Christine, 19
Cyriacus, 19,
33, 47
Elizabeth, 19,
33, 47
Frederick, 33
Henry, 171, 185
John, 128, 185
John Christian,
43
Magdalene, 43
Margaret, 25
Philippina, 43
WAGENHORST, ---,
143
WAGNER, Adam, 122
Anthony, 145
Catharine, 122,
154
Caty, 84

Cyriacus, 59
Elizabeth, 59,
92, 154, 174
Henry, 154
John, 92, 151,
174
John Henry, 59
Ludwig, 132
Magdalene, 144
Margaret, 150
Sarah, 132
Susan, 92
WAGONER, John, 12
WAHL, Christine,
16, 53, 62, 70,
89
Maria, 16
Martin, 16, 53,
62, 70, 89, 129
Sarah, 70
WAIDE, Elizabeth,
41
Hannah, 41
Jonathan, 41
WAITH, Nancy, 141
WALER, John, 118
WALK, Anna Maria,
126
WALKER, ---, 147
A. Margaret, 159
Catharine, 84,
154
John, 13, 151,
154, 159
M. Margaret, 159
Samuel, 75, 150,
154
WALL, Christine,
39
John, 39
Martin, 39
WALLACE, Margaret,
178
William, 178
WALLAS, Margaret,
170
Milcah, 170
William, 170
WALLAUER, Peter,
82
WALLIS, Catharine,
100
Elizabeth, 83
Matthew, 100
WALPERT, Thomas,
77

WALTEN, Clara, 75
WALTER, Anna
  Maria, 96
  Barbara, 120
  Cath., 52
  Catharine, 131
  Catherine, 9, 44
  Charlotte, 16,
    29, 44, 59, 89,
    182
  Daniel, 76, 96,
    133
  Elizabeth, 52,
    122
  Eva Maria, 70
  George, 52, 73,
    122, 181
  Hannah, 181, 185
  Henry, 73
  Jacob, 70, 86
  John, 13, 134
  John George, 84,
    181, 185
  John Henry, 185
  John Lawrence,
    96
  Lawrence, 126,
    133
  Margaret, 86,
    136
  Maria, 52
  Maria Catharine,
    125
  Peter, 16, 29,
    44, 52, 59, 86,
    89, 131, 134,
    136, 154
  Sarah, 29, 122
  Susanna, 89
  William, 59, 125
WALTHER, Daniel,
    150
  Elizabeth, 157
WALTON, Harietta,
    82
  Margaret, 82
WALTUWER, A.
  Maria, 172
  Margaret, 172
  P., 172
WARDT, Anna, 2
WARE, ---, 179
  Elizabeth, 179
WARNER, Elizabeth,
    119
  Jacobina, 12

John, 10
  Martin, 5
  Peter, 146
  Regina, 10
WARNOUER, John
  Frederick, 83
WAS, Adam, 72
  Elizabeth, 34,
    72
  John, 34
  John Adam, 34
WASKAN, John
  Henry, 153
WASSEM,
  Christopher,
    46, 99, 138
  Elizabeth, 46
  John, 99, 138
  Maria, 46, 99
  William, 138
WASSER, Jeremiah,
    64
  Margaret, 64
WASSUM, Christine,
    62
  Christopher, 62
  Maria, 62
WATER, Conrad, 93
  Elizabeth, 93
WATERS, Martin, 82
WATSON, Carl, 121
  Elizabeth, 121
  John, 84
  Matthew, 84
  Sarah Harriet,
    178
  Sen., 178
  Susanna, 178
  Thomas, 77
  William, 121
WATTLES, Henry, 78
WEAK, Anna Mary,
    176
  Christian, 176
  Hannah, 176
WEAVER, Ann
  Catharine, 94
  Anna, 180
  Anna M., 171
  Bernard, 177,
    182
  Catharine, 169
  Elizabeth, 77
  Frederica, 171
  Frederick, 171
  Hannah, 177, 182

Henry, 180
  John, 169
  John George, 94
  John Henry, 174
  Margaret, 174
  Mary Anna, 169
  Peter, 180
WEBB, Simon, 121
WEBER, A.
  Catharine, 162
  A. Elizabeth,
    155
  A. Maria, 81
  Adam, 138
  Alexander, 74
  Andrew, 35
  Anna, 16, 28,
    158
  Anna Christine,
    30, 50
  Anna Margaret,
    50
  Anna Maria, 16
  Anna Maria
    Catharine, 142
  Catharine, 161
  Elizabeth, 16,
    52
  Eva, 35
  Frederica, 161
  Frederick, 82,
    161
  George, 28
  Hannah, 80, 154
  Henry Peter, 144
  John, 4, 5, 16,
    28, 30, 50,
    133, 158, 162, 166
  John Jacob, 30
  John Jost, 161,
    162
  John Krafft, 82
  John Theobald,
    166
  Jost, 129
  Lora, 141
  Margaret, 28,
    122, 129, 158,
    166
  Michael, 35
  Philip, 154
  Regina, 16
  Wilhelmina, 79
  William, 52,
    122, 138

WECKERLE, John
  Ulrich, 150
  Ulrich, 82
WECKERLY,
  Catharine, 43
  George, 43
WEED, Bright, 42
  George, 9
WEGMAN, Margaret,
  15
  Mr., 15
WEHAHER,
  Elizabeth, 166
  P., 166
WEIAND, Christine,
  31, 97
  Christopher, 47
  Elizabeth, 47
  Graft, 31
  John, 52, 111,
  133
  John George, 52
  John Henry, 31
  John Jost, 32,
  99
  John Krafft, 97
  Joseph, 111
  Magdalene, 32,
  99, 111, 133
  Maria, 52, 99
  Maria Elizabeth,
  97
  Sarah, 32
WEIBERG,
  Charlotte, 143,
  185
  Charlotte
  Catharine, 185
  Isabella, 37
  John, 154, 185
WEID, Catharine,
  79
WEIDEMAN, Casper,
  158
  David, 158
  Maria, 158
WEIDMAN, Maria,
  149
  Sarah, 149
WEIDMANN, David,
  148
WEIDNER, Anna
  Margaret, 173
  Catharine, 157
  Peter, 157

WEIEL, Anna
  Margaret, 55
  Catherine, 36
  Conrad, 76
  Elizabeth, 55,
  68, 93
  Jacob, 68
  John, 93
  John Jacob, 36
  Peter, 14, 36,
  55, 68, 93, 128
WEIERICH,
  Catherine, 42
  Christian, 42
  John Christian,
  42
  Nicholas, 73
WEIERMAN,
  Elizabeth, 11
  Johnston, 11
WEIGAND, Conrad,
  83
  John, 69
  Magdalene, 69
  Peter, 69
WEIHLER,
  Catharine, 103
  Frederick, 103
WEIL, A. Maria,
  146
  Catherine, 17
  Conrad, 161
  Daniel, 60, 123,
  149
  Elizabeth, 60,
  140, 161
  Joseph
  Frederick, 123,
  141
  Maria Margaret,
  3
  Peter, 7, 17
  Rebecca, 123,
  148
WEILAND, Margaret,
  49
  Martin, 49
WEILBECH, G. John,
  174
WEILER, Catharine,
  73, 144
  Catherine, 63,
  64, 66
  Frederick, 63,
  64, 66, 134
  Jacob, 63, 126

WEILI, Charlotte,
  103
  George, 103
WEILSON, George,
  165
  William, 165
WEINDEL,
  Charlotte, 92
  George, 92
  John Henry, 92
WEINEMAN, Barbara,
  166
  Catharine, 166
  John, 166
WEINEMAR, Andrew,
  117
  Regina, 117
WEINERT, Andrew,
  44
  Jacob, 7, 44
  Susanna, 44
WEINGAERTNER,
  Elizabeth, 77
WEINY, Jacob, 143
WEIRICH,
  Elizabeth, 119
  Jacob, 140
  Nicholas, 119
  Susanna, 119
WEIS, Adam, 58,
  163
  Anna, 129
  Anthony, 155
  Catherine, 33
  Elizabeth, 58,
  155, 163
  George, 156
  Magdalene, 58
  William, 155,
  163
WEISBACH, John, 52
  John Frederick,
  52
  Sophia, 52
WEISBROD, Henry,
  76
WEISER, George, 78
  Jeremiah, 54
  Margaret, 54
  Samuel, 54
WEISERT,
  Elizabeth, 127
WEISMAN,
  Frederick, 176
WEISNOHR, Andrew,
  111

Rosina, 111
WEISS, Adam, 26,
 72, 117
Anna, 72
Anthony, 14
Catharine, 117
Elizabeth, 26,
 72, 78, 117
George, 117
Jeremiah, 117
Jesse, 117
Joseph, 26
Margaret, 117
Susanna, 117
WEISSBROD, John,
 100
John Henry, 100
Maria, 100
WEISSER, Jacob, 50
Jeremiah, 86
Margaret, 86
Sarah, 86
Susanna, 50
WEISSLER, Sarah, 8
WEISSMAN, Anna
 Maria, 77
Catherine, 31
David, 110
Johannetta, 110
John, 87
Philip, 31
Sarah, 110
Susan, 87
WEIT, Susanna, 156
WEITEN, Margaret,
 176
WEITENER, Michael,
 76
WEITH, Julianna, 6
Mary, 73
WEITHMAN, Andrew,
 22, 40
Catharine, 23
Catherine, 40
Elizabeth, 13,
 22
Jacob, 22, 23,
 40
Joseph, 40
Sarah, 23
Thomas, 23
Veronica, 40
WEITMAN, Jacob,
 127
WELCH, Biddy, 14

WELLER, Elizabeth,
 82
John, 57
Maria, 57
Mary Magdalene,
 57
WELSH, Maria, 154
WELT, Anna, 164
WENGEN, Jacobine,
 73
WENKLE, A. Maria,
 167
Catharine, 167
Elizabeth, 167
J., 167
Ludwig, 167
WENTZ, Frederick,
 66, 70
George Jacob,
 118
Jacob, 76
Margaret, 83
Maria, 51, 70,
 118
Philip, 51, 70,
 118
Philippina, 82
Susanna, 51
WENTZEL, Mary
 Magdalene, 13
WENZEL, Anna
 Margaret, 99
Elizabeth
 Catherine, 20
George, 20
Joanna
 Charlotte, 20
WERCKERLE,
 Elizabeth, 123
George, 123
WERF, John, 174
Lamberte, 174
Susanna, 174
WERNER, Maria, 1
WERNT, Lydia, 72
WERNTZ, Anna
 Elizabeth, 4
Henrietta, 2
Jacob, 2
Lawrence, 127
Lorentz, 2, 11
Margaret, 125
Philip, 137
Rebecca, 76
WERTH, Elias, 8
Philip, 10

WESEM,
 Christopher, 86
Maria, 86
Peter Nella, 86
Petronella, 86
WEST, Catharine,
 164
Elizabeth, 100,
 158, 164, 181
George, 80
John, 146
John Adam, 100
Joseph, 156
Maria, 156
Thomas, 146,
 153, 157, 164
WESTENBERGER,
 George, 76
WESTER, ---, 148
Anna Margaret,
 105
Catharine, 147
Elizabeth, 105
Henry, 56, 124,
 143
John, 14, 45,
 56, 67, 105,
 159
M. Margaret, 159
Margaret, 45, 56
Maria Margaret,
 67
WESTPHAL, Maria
 Catharine, 176
Maria Helena,
 176
WESTRICH, Bernard,
 173
Henry, 173
Maria, 173
WETHMAN, Jacob,
 137
WETSTEIN, Anna
 Margaret, 34
Henry, 34
Isaac, 34
Sarah, 34
WETTERSTEIN, John,
 141
WETZLER, Adam, 130
Anna, 130
Catherine, 7, 62
Henry, 13, 62
Philipina, 62
WETZSTEIN, Sarah,
 123

WEVER, Adam, 11,
  57, 63, 116,
  140
Andrew, 20
Anna, 17, 66,
  117
Anna Catharine,
  109
Anna Maria
  Catharine, 109
Catharine, 116
Catherine, 57,
  63, 66, 69
David, 57
Elizabeth, 18,
  60, 94, 104
Eva, 20
George, 49, 69
Hannah, 20, 24,
  57
Henry, 17, 24,
  57, 75, 109,
  135
Henry Peter, 60
Hohn, 132
Jacob, 18, 46,
  60
John, 5, 18, 66,
  117
John Jost, 109
Ludwig Henry,
  109
Margaret, 49,
  69, 104, 109
Maria, 24
Michael, 57,
  124, 135
Mr., 49
Sally, 69
Samuel, 116
Sarah, 17, 63
William, 13, 49,
  69, 94, 104,
  116
WEYAND, Christine,
  38, 62
Elizabeth, 62
Graft, 38, 62
Jacob, 158
John, 15, 38
John Jost, 15,
  95
John Peter, 95
Magdalene, 15,
  158
Maria, 95

Salome, 158
WEYBEL, George, 74
WEYBERG, Casper,
  1, 10, 15, 73,
  93, 123
John, 91
Rev., 95
Salome, 93
Samuel, 91
Solomomeh, 91
WEYEBERG, Casper,
  85
WEYEL, Catherine,
  19, 27
Elizabeth, 27
Jacob, 7
Maria Margaret
  19
Peter, 19, 27
WEYERICH, Anna
  Catherine, 16,
  34
Christian, 16,
  34
Henry, 86
Jacob, 60
John Jacob, 34
John Philip, 16
Nicholas, 60, 86
Susanna, 60, 86
WEYL, Christina,
  141
WEYLY, Barbara,
  176
Frederick, 176
Samuel, 176
WEYRICH, George,
  158
Nicholas, 158
Susanna, 158
WHEELER, Conrad,
  107
Elizabeth, 107
William Conrad,
  107
WHEIL, Daniel, 107
Elizabeth, 107
WHEITMAN, ---, 53
Maria, 53
Nancy, 53
WHILES, Daniiel,
  75
WHITE, James, 84
Mary, 75, 79
WHITMAN, Jacob, 74
William, 77

WHITMER, Abia, 10
WHITMORE, Maria,
  134
WHITTAKER,
  Margaret, 150
WIAL, Conrad, 185
Elizabeth, 185
WIAND, ---, 150
Maria Christine,
  156
Thomas, 145
William, 145,
  156
WICHARD, Anna, 20
John, 20
WICHMAN,
  Frederick, 35
Margaret, 35
WICHOR, John
  Gottlieb, 78
WICKHARD, Hannah,
  15
John, 15
WICKHERT, Hannah,
  51
John, 51
Michael, 51
WIDDERSTEIN, Adam,
  118
Sophia, 118
WIDERSTEIN, Adam,
  77
Elizabeth, 23,
  82, 117
John, 23
Salome, 23
WIEDBECK, Anna, 53
John, 53
Susanna, 53
WIEDER, Hannah,
  177
Peter, 177
WIEDERSTEIN,
  Maria, 163
WIEGAND,
  Christian, 146
WIEGMAN, George,
  45
Sophia, 45
WIEHLER, Elizabeth
  Catherine, 72
John, 72
Maria, 72
WIELER, Catharine,
  128
WIENEY, John, 99

Magdalene, 99
WIENG, Christine,
   22
   Frederick, 22
WIERMAN,
   Catharine, 74
WIGAND, A. M.
   Elizabeth, 165
   Adam, 25
   Catherine, 44
   Christian, 25,
   44
   Conrad, 165, 177
   Eleonora, 182
   Elizabeth, 25,
   44, 177
   Henry, 182
   John, 177, 182
   John Oltenbury,
   182
   Sarah, 165
WILBANK,
   Catharine, 163
WILCKY, Barbara,
   45, 55
   Elizabeth, 45
   John, 45, 55
   Margaret, 55
WILD, Abraham, 104
   Anna Barbara, 17
   John, 17
WILDFANG, Anna, 96
   Elizabeth, 116
   John, 96, 116
WILEY, Ann, 158
WILHELM, Anna
   Margaret, 9
   Catherine, 13
   George, 38, 180
   M. Magdalene,
   180
   Susanna Maria,
   38
WILKESON, Daniel,
   83
WILKINS, George,
   165
WILKY, Ann
   Barbara, 36
   Catharine, 74
   John, 36
   John George, 36
WILL, Anna, 19,
   20, 32, 66, 71
   Anna Charlotte,
   19

Anna Maria, 22,
   47
   Charlotte, 19
   Elizabeth, 19,
   29, 36
   George, 56
   Hannah, 74
   Henrietta, 71,
   130
   John, 33
   Maria, 47, 56
   Philip, 19, 125
   Susanna, 36
   William, 19, 20,
   22, 29, 32, 36,
   47, 56, 66, 71,
   92, 119, 151
WILLE, John, 85
WILLET, Abraham,
   75
   Hannah, 75
WILLIAMS, Carl,
   186
   Elizabeth, 73
   Hannah, 81
   Jane, 74
   Jenny, 153
   John, 26, 35,
   39, 57, 185
   Maria, 26, 35,
   39, 57, 146
   Marl., 75
   Moses, 79
   Peter, 129
   Robert, 57
   Susanna, 26
   William, 43
WILLMER, John
   Nicholas, 52
   Maria Dorothea,
   52
WILLNER, Margaret,
   152
WILLOW, Catharine,
   84
WILLS, Sarah, 10
WILMAN, John
   Christoph, 33
WILPERT,
   Christopher, 29
   Margaret, 29
   Sarah, 29
WILSON, A. Maria,
   157
   Carl, 166
   David, 111

Elizabeth, 2
   George, 111,
   157, 166, 174
   Hannah, 111,
   157, 174
   James, 174
   Maria, 166
   Rachel, 73
WILT, Maria, 80
WILTFANG, Anna, 67
   Elizabeth, 117
   John, 67, 74
   Maria, 67
   Maria Barbara,
   77
   William, 67
WILTI, Anna Maria,
   60
   John Adam, 60
   Opethy, 60
WINCKELER,
   Catherine, 61
WINCKHAUS, Anna
   Catharine, 106,
   139
   Catharine, 106
   Frederick, 134
   H., 79
   Herman, 77, 95,
   130
   John Herman, 14,
   106, 139
   Rev., 122, 134,
   141
WINCKLER,
   Catharine, 111
   Catherine, 49
   Elizabeth, 118
   Jacob, 111, 118
WIND, Ann
   Margaret, 91
   Ann Maria, 91
   Hannah, 21, 112
   John, 21
   Maria, 113
   Opidien, 91
   Rebecca, 151
   Thomas, 21, 112,
   113, 149, 152
   William, 113
WINE, Elizabeth,
   14
WING, Christine,
   19, 33, 50, 61
   Christine
   Wilhelmina, 43

Fred, 19
Frederick, 33,
   43, 50
Philippina, 119
WINN, Cath., 178
WINTER, Abraham,
   178
Ann Mary, 178
Anna, 178
Frederick, 20
WINTHEBEL,
   Abraham, 166
Albert, 166
WIRICK, Nicholas,
   13
WIRTH, Clara, 43
Dorothea, 16,
   19, 29, 43, 48,
   65
Dorothy, 124,
   168
Elizabeth, 29
Eva, 74
George, 24
Jacob, 43
Maria, 65, 126,
   135
Maria Clara, 65
P., 168
Philip, 16, 19,
   29, 43, 48, 65,
   135
Salome, 24
Sarah, 19
WIRTZ, Maria, 149
WISAR, Anna
   Esther, 20
Anna Maria, 36
Anne Maria, 85
David, 20, 36,
   52, 85
Frederick, 85
Hannah, 36
Maria, 20, 52
WISAUER, Anna
   Maria, 140
David, 140
WISENBACH,
   Elizabeth, 165
Henry, 165
M. Elizabeth,
   176
P., 176
WISER, Anna
   Esther, 4
John, 85

WISHART, Clara, 26
Hannah, 26
John, 26
WISOR, Anna Maria,
   98
David, 98
Emmanuel, 98
WISPEN, Elizabeth,
   28, 36
WISPER, Margaret,
   11
WISSAUER, David,
   81
Elizabeth, 82
WISSELER, Jacob,
   10
WISTON, Elizabeth,
   94
WITEMAN, A. Maria,
   184
Charles, 170
D., 184
David, 171
Hendel, 165
John, 170, 171
Maria, 170
Michael, 172
Nancy, 171
Peter, 165
Rebecca, 171
Sarah, 184
Susanna, 165,
   172
Tester, 165
Wendel, 165
William, 172
WITHPAIN, Sarah,
   73
WITMAN, Margaret,
   1
WITNER, william,
   123
WITTMANN, Jacob,
   151
WITZEL, Anna
   Margaret, 43
Margaret, 30
Philip, 43, 50
Rebecca, 50
WITZELL, Anna
   Margaret, 106
Philip, 106
WITZER, Margaret,
   114
Philip, 114

WIVEL, Elizabeth,
   108
John George, 108
Peter, 108
WOELPPER, John
   David, 15
WOHL, John, 124
WOHLFAHRT, Sarha,
   145
WOLF, Barbara, 146
Catharine, 174
Frederick, 80
Henry, 174
John Daniel, 174
Maria Catharine,
   129
WOLFF, Elizabeth
   Margaret, 53
Mary Magdalene,
   135
Michael, 53
WOLFFKUEHL,
   William, 77
WOLFINGER,
   Elizabeth
   Catharine, 96
Sebastian, 96
WOLFURT, M., 166
WOLLENSCHLEGER,
   Jacob, 8
WOOD, Anna Maria,
   131
James, 120
Joseph, 120, 161
Margaret, 120,
   161
WOODLEIN, M., 171
Maria, 171
WOODMAN, William,
   82
WOODS, John, 157
Joseph, 157
Margaret, 157
Mary, 84
WOODWARD, Jacob,
   10
WOOLLEY,
   Christine, 53
Sebastian, 53
WORCK, Elizabeth,
   39, 66
Philip, 39
WORL, Sarah, 84
WORLE, Christine,
   54
Sebastian, 54

WORM, Catharine,
    104
John, 104
Michael, 104
WORMSIDER, Ann
    Mary, 180
    Matilda, 180
    William, 180
WORN, Anna Maria,
    129
Catherine, 28,
    38
Elizabeth, 83
John Philip, 38
Maria, 27, 54,
    113
Martin, 2, 7,
    11, 14, 128
Michael, 10, 28,
    38, 148
Philip, 6, 27,
    28, 54
Phuilip, 113
Samuel Henry,
    113
Thomas, 27
William, 54
WORRALL, Abigail,
    74
WORTH, John, 72
Maria, 72
WRIGHT, Elizabeth,
    146
Jane, 83
Joseph, 76
WUCHERER,
    Elizabeth, 17,
    90
John, 17, 20, 90
WUERTZLER,
    Catharine, 140
Henry, 113, 140
John Henry, 139
Michael, 113
Philippina, 113
WUEST, Catherine,
    44
Elizabeth, 44
Ludwig, 44
WULLE, Christine,
    45
Sebastian, 45
WULLY, Elizabeth
    Catherine, 72
    Sebastian, 72

WULPERT,
    Catherine, 39
    Charles, 39
WUNDERT, Maria, 80
WURGES, Juliana,
    80
WURTZLER, Henry,
    46
    Maria, 46, 124
    Philippina, 46

-Y-
YEAGER, Elizabeth,
    154
YENER, H., 173
    Louisa, 173
YOUNG, Anna Maria,
    117
Catharine, 114,
    174, 181
Edward, 174
Henry William,
    115
Jacob, 138
John George, 117
John Jost, 181
Jost Henry, 181
Lewis, 114
Ludwig, 174
Maria, 115
Maria Elizabeth,
    78
Sarah, 138
William, 114

-Z-
ZACHERI, Anna
    Catharine, 74
ZAHN, Ann
    Catherine, 35
Elizabeth, 35
Frederick, 82,
    160
John George, 35
Magdalene, 82
Maria, 160
Susanna, 160
ZAHNER, Anthony,
    161
Barbara, 50,
    101, 113, 120
Catharine, 76,
    89, 108, 150,
    161
Catherine, 19,
    55

Catherine
    Elizabeth, 50
Daniel, 82
George, 55, 153
John, 12, 50,
    55, 101, 113,
    120
John Adam, 19
John George, 19,
    89, 108, 135
Maria, 89
Maria Elizabeth,
    101
ZANN, Fred, 182
    Susanna, 182
ZEBLY, Jacob, 100
    Wilhelmina, 100
ZEBOLD, Catherine,
    40
    Leonard, 40
ZEES, Andrew, 168
    John, 168
    Mary, 168
ZEIL, Apollonia,
    72
Gottlieb, 72
Peter, 72
ZEINER, Elizabeth,
    155
Jacob, 155
John, 67
Maria, 67
Thomas, 67, 155
ZEISINGER, Anna
    Catherine, 2
Anna Maria, 32
Charlotte
    Elizabeth, 60
George, 60
George
    Christian, 32
John George, 32
Maria Margaret,
    60
ZEISSIGER, George,
    30
Maria, 30
ZELLER, Anna
    Maria, 90
Daniel, 78, 122
Elizabeth, 122
Jacob, 83, 166
John, 110, 130
John Philip, 51
John William, 22
Magdalene, 122

Margaret, 22, 51
Maria, 110
Philip, 22, 51
William, 166
ZENCK, Barbara, 91
George, 91
ZENS, Anna, 171
Francis, 171
ZEPLE, Jacob, 142
Ludwig, 142
ZEPPERNICK,
Gottfried, 21,
46
Maria, 46
ZERBAN, Catherine,
21, 71
Cathrine, 48
Eleonora, 48
Henrietta Maria,
71
Mr., 129
Philippina, 78
Wendel, 21, 48,
71, 78
William Wendel,
3, 21
ZERBEHN,
Catharine, 78
ZERBUR,
Philippina, 116
Rosina
Philippina
Elizabeth, 116
Wendel, 116
ZESSINGER, Anna
Catherine, 20
Anna Maria, 20
Margaret, 29
Maria Elizabeth,
29
Nicholas, 11,
20, 29
ZEUNER, Catharine,
74
ZEYHER, Elizabeth,
142
ZIBLE, Jacob, 75
ZIBOLD, Barbara,
87
John George, 87
Martin, 87
ZIBOLT, Barbara,
41
John Adam, 41

Martin
Sigismund, 11,
41
ZIEBBLE, Jacob, 92
John Ludwig, 92
Wilhelmina, 92
ZIEGELER,
Catherine, 22
Ernst, 22
John Christian,
74
ZIEGLER, Abraham,
77
Christopher, 137
Elizabeth, 137
ZIGLER, Elizabeth,
78
ZILLENDER, Jacob,
114
Wilhelmina, 114
ZIMMERMAN, Anna
Margaret, 90
Christian, 120
Christina, 76
Elizabeth, 90,
102, 120, 136
Henry, 136
Henry William,
90, 102, 120
Jacob, 136
Johanna
Catharine, 136
Maria, 155
ZINCK, Anna
Margaret, 41,
124
Catherine, 41
Elizabeth, 13
Jacob, 41
ZING, Catherine,
28
Christian, 28
Jacob, 28
ZINSE, Franciscus,
31
ZIPOLT, Anna
Barbara, 102
Barbara, 102
Martin, 102
ZOBKE, John, 149
ZOBLE, Rudolph,
148
ZOEBLE, Esther,
111
Jacob, 111
Rachel, 111

Rudolph, 111
ZOLLINGER, Casper,
84
Elizabeth, 152
Maria, 144
ZOLLNER, Carl, 80
ZOMSTER,
Catharine, 169
Maria, 169
William, 169
ZOTTEN, Catharine,
88
Edward, 88
ZUR HORST,
Frederick
William, 4
ZWEIFEL, Eliza, 21
ZYBOLD, Barbara,
56
John Samuel, 56
Martin, 56

Heritage Books by F. Edward Wright:

*18th Century Records of the German Lutheran Church at Philadelphia, Pennsylvania
(St. Michael's and Zion): Volume 1, Baptisms, 1745–1769*
Robert L. Hess and F. Edward Wright

*18th Century Records of the German Lutheran Church at Philadelphia, Pennsylvania
(St. Michael's and Zion): Volume 2, Baptisms, 1770–1786*
Translated by Robert L. Hess, Ph.D. Edited by F. Edward Wright

*18th Century Records of the German Lutheran Church of Philadelphia, Pennsylvania
(St. Michael's and Zion): Volume 3, Baptisms, 1787–1800*
Translated by Robert L. Hess, Ph.D. Edited by F. Edward Wright

*18th Century Records of the German Lutheran Church at Philadelphia, Pennsylvania
(St. Michael's and Zion): Volume 4, Marriages and Confirmations*
Robert L. Hess and F. Edward Wright

*18th Century Records of the German Lutheran Church at Philadelphia, Pennsylvania
(St. Michael's and Zion): Volume 5, Burials*
Robert L. Hess and F. Edward Wright

Abstracts of Bucks County, Pennsylvania, Wills, 1685–1785

Abstracts of Cumberland County, Pennsylvania, Wills, 1750–1785

Abstracts of Cumberland County, Pennsylvania, Wills, 1785–1825

*Abstracts of Philadelphia County, Pennsylvania, Wills:
Volumes: 1682–1726; 1726–1747; 1748–1763; 1763–1784; 1777–1790;
1790–1802; 1802–1809; 1810–1815; 1815–1819; and 1820–1825*

Abstracts of South Central Pennsylvania, Newspapers, Volume 1, 1785–1790

Abstracts of South Central Pennsylvania, Newspapers, Volume 3, 1796–1800

Abstracts of the Newspapers of Georgetown and the Federal City, 1789–99

Abstracts of York County, Pennsylvania, Wills, 1749–1819

Adams County [Pennsylvania] Church Records of the 18th Century

Baltimore Directory of 1807

Berks County, Pennsylvania, Church Records of the 18th Century, Volumes 1–4

Bible Records of Washington County, Maryland

*Bucks County, Pennsylvania, Church Records of the 17th and 18th Centuries,
Volume 1: German Church Records*

*Bucks County, Pennsylvania, Church Records of the 17th and 18th Centuries,
Volume 2: Quaker Records: Falls and Middletown Monthly Meetings*
Anna Miller Watring and F. Edward Wright

*Bucks County, Pennsylvania, Church Records of the 17th and 18th Centuries,
Volume 4*

Caroline County, Maryland, Marriages, Births and Deaths, 1850–1880

Citizens of the Eastern Shore of Maryland, 1659–1750

Colonial Families of Cape May County, New Jersey, Revised 2nd Edition

*Colonial Families of Delaware:
Volumes: Volume 1; Volume 2: Kent and Sussex Counties;
Volume 3 (2nd Edition): Kent and Sussex Counties;
Volume 4: Sussex County; Volume 5: New Castle; Volume 6: Kent*

Heritage Books by F. Edward Wright:

*18th Century Records of the German Lutheran Church at Philadelphia, Pennsylvania
(St. Michael's and Zion): Volume 1, Baptisms, 1745–1769*
Robert L. Hess and F. Edward Wright

*18th Century Records of the German Lutheran Church at Philadelphia, Pennsylvania
(St. Michael's and Zion): Volume 2, Baptisms, 1770–1786*
Translated by Robert L. Hess, Ph.D. Edited by F. Edward Wright

*18th Century Records of the German Lutheran Church of Philadelphia, Pennsylvania
(St. Michael's and Zion): Volume 3, Baptisms, 1787–1800*
Translated by Robert L. Hess, Ph.D. Edited by F. Edward Wright

*18th Century Records of the German Lutheran Church at Philadelphia, Pennsylvania
(St. Michael's and Zion): Volume 4, Marriages and Confirmations*
Robert L. Hess and F. Edward Wright

*18th Century Records of the German Lutheran Church at Philadelphia, Pennsylvania
(St. Michael's and Zion): Volume 5, Burials*
Robert L. Hess and F. Edward Wright

Abstracts of Bucks County, Pennsylvania, Wills, 1685–1785

Abstracts of Cumberland County, Pennsylvania, Wills, 1750–1785

Abstracts of Cumberland County, Pennsylvania, Wills, 1785–1825

*Abstracts of Philadelphia County, Pennsylvania, Wills:
Volumes: 1682–1726; 1726–1747; 1748–1763; 1763–1784; 1777–1790;
1790–1802; 1802–1809; 1810–1815; 1815–1819; and 1820–1825*

Abstracts of South Central Pennsylvania, Newspapers, Volume 1, 1785–1790

Abstracts of South Central Pennsylvania, Newspapers, Volume 3, 1796–1800

Abstracts of the Newspapers of Georgetown and the Federal City, 1789–99

Abstracts of York County, Pennsylvania, Wills, 1749–1819

Adams County [Pennsylvania] Church Records of the 18th Century

Baltimore Directory of 1807

Berks County, Pennsylvania, Church Records of the 18th Century, Volumes 1–4

Bible Records of Washington County, Maryland

*Bucks County, Pennsylvania, Church Records of the 17th and 18th Centuries,
Volume 1: German Church Records*

*Bucks County, Pennsylvania, Church Records of the 17th and 18th Centuries,
Volume 2: Quaker Records: Falls and Middletown Monthly Meetings*
Anna Miller Watring and F. Edward Wright

*Bucks County, Pennsylvania, Church Records of the 17th and 18th Centuries,
Volume 4*

Caroline County, Maryland, Marriages, Births and Deaths, 1850–1880

Citizens of the Eastern Shore of Maryland, 1659–1750

Colonial Families of Cape May County, New Jersey, Revised 2nd Edition

*Colonial Families of Delaware:
Volumes: Volume 1; Volume 2: Kent and Sussex Counties;
Volume 3 (2nd Edition): Kent and Sussex Counties;
Volume 4: Sussex County; Volume 5: New Castle; Volume 6: Kent*

Colonial Families of New Jersey, Volume 1: Middlesex and Somerset Counties

Colonial Families of Northern Neck, Virginia, Volume 1 and Volume 2
Holly G. Wright and F. Edward Wright

Colonial Families of the Eastern Shore of Maryland: Volumes 1 and 2
Robert W. Barnes and F. Edward Wright

Colonial Families of the Eastern Shore of Maryland: Volume 4
Christos Christou and F. Edward Wright

Colonial Families of the Eastern Shore of Maryland:
Volumes 5, 6, 7, 8, 9, 11, 12, 13, 14, 16, and 19
Henry C. Peden, Jr. and F. Edward Wright

Colonial Families of the Eastern Shore of Maryland: Volumes 15 and 17
Ralph A. Riggin and F. Edward Wright

Colonial Families of the Eastern Shore of Maryland: Volumes 10, 18, 20, and 22
Vernon L. Skinner, Jr. and F. Edward Wright

Colonial Families of the United States of America, Volume II
Holly G. Wright and F. Edward Wright

Cumberland County, Pennsylvania, Church Records of the 18th Century

Delaware Newspaper Abstracts, Volume 1: 1786–1795

Early Charles County, Maryland, Settlers, 1658–1745
Marlene Strawser Bates, F. Edward Wright

Early Church Records of Alexandria City and Fairfax County, Virginia
F. Edward Wright and Wesley E. Pippenger

Early Church Records of Bergen County, New Jersey, 1740–1800

Early Church Records of Dauphin County, Pennsylvania

Early Church Records of Lebanon County, Pennsylvania

Early Church Records of New Castle County, Delaware, Volume 1: 1701–1800

Early Church Records of Rockingham County, Virginia

Early Lists of Frederick County, Maryland, 1765–1775

Early Records of the First Reformed Church of Philadelphia, Volume 1, 1748–1780

Early Records of the First Reformed Church of Philadelphia, Volume 2, 1781–1800

Frederick County, Maryland, Militia in the War of 1812
Sallie A. Mallick and F. Edward Wright

Henrico County, Virginia, Marriage References and Family Relationships, 1654–1800

Inhabitants of Baltimore County, Maryland, 1692–1763

Judgment Records of Dorchester, Queen Anne's, and Talbot Counties [Maryland]

Kent County, Delaware, Marriage References and Family Relationships

King George County, Virginia, Marriage References
and Family Relationships, 1721–1800
Anne M. Watring and F. Edward Wright

Lancaster County Church Records of the 18th Century, Volumes 1–4

Lancaster County, Pennsylvania, Church Records of the 18th Century, Volume 1
F. Edward Wright and Robert L. Hess

Lancaster County, Pennsylvania, Church Records of the 18th Century, Volume 3

Lancaster County, Pennsylvania, Church Records of the 18th Century, Volume 5

Lancaster County, Pennsylvania, Church Records of the 18th Century: Volume 6
Robert L. Hess and F. Edward Wright

Lancaster County, Virginia, Marriage References
and Family Relationships, 1650–1800

Land Records of Sussex County, Delaware, 1769–1782

Land Records of Sussex County, Delaware, 1782–1789: Deed Book N No. 13
Elaine Hastings Mason and F. Edward Wright

Marriage Licenses of Washington, District of Columbia, 1811–1830

Marriage References and Family Relationships of Charles City,
Prince George, and Dinwiddie Counties, Virginia, 1634–1800

Marriages and Deaths from Eastern Shore Newspapers, 1790–1835

Marriages and Deaths from the Newspapers of Allegany
and Washington Counties, Maryland, 1820–1830

Marriages and Deaths from the York Recorder, 1821–1830

Marriages and Deaths in the Newspapers of Frederick
and Montgomery Counties, Maryland, 1820–1830

Marriages and Deaths in the Newspapers of
Lancaster County, Pennsylvania, 1821–1830

Marriages and Deaths in the Newspapers of
Lancaster County, Pennsylvania, 1831–1840

Marriages and Deaths of Cumberland County, [Pennsylvania], 1821–1830

Marriages, Births, Deaths and Removals of New Castle County, Delaware

Maryland Calendar of Wills:
Volume 9: 1744–1749; Volume 10: 1748–1753; Volume 11: 1753–1760;
Volume 12: 1759–1764; Volume 13: 1764–1767; Volume 14: 1767–1772;
Volume 15: 1772–1774; and Volume 16: 1774–1777

Maryland Eastern Shore Newspaper Abstracts
Volume 1: 1790–1805; Volume 2: 1806–1812;
Volume 3: 1813–1818; Volume 4: 1819–1824;
Volume 5: Northern Counties, 1825–1829
F. Edward Wright and Irma Harper;
Volume 6: Southern Counties, 1825–1829;
Volume 7: Northern Counties, 1830–1834
Irma Harper and F. Edward Wright;
Volume 8: Southern Counties, 1830–1834

Maryland Eastern Shore Vital Records:
Book 1: 1648–1725, Second Edition; Book 2: 1726–1750; Book 3: 1751–1775;
Book 4: 1776–1800; and Book 5: 1801–1825

Maryland Militia in the War of 1812:
Volume 1: Eastern Shore; Volume 2: Baltimore City and County;
Volume 3: Cecil and Harford Counties; Volume 4: Anne Arundel and Calvert Counties;
Volume 5: St. Mary's and Charles Counties; Volume 6: Prince George's County;
and Volume 7: Montgomery County

Maryland Militia in the Revolutionary War
S. Eugene Clements and F. Edward Wright

www.ingramcontent.com/pod-product-compliance
Lightning Source LLC
Chambersburg PA
CBHW071331280526
45787CB00001B/63